IN THE KITCHEN WITH

Favorite Brand Name

LIGHT
COOKING
RECIPES

Publications International, Ltd.

ISBN: 0-7853-1533-0

Cover photography by Sacco Productions Limited, Chicago, IL.

Photography on pages 237, 243, 251, 255, 260, 266, 268, 275, 291, and 299 by Shanoor Studio, Chicago, IL.

Pictured on the front cover, clockwise from top: Mocha Fudge Marble Delight (page 242), Italian Pasta Salad (page 184) and Ginger Spicy Chicken (page 131).

Pictured on the back cover, clockwise from top: Beef Kabobs over Lemon Rice (page 102), Mediterranean Tuna Salad (page 166), Individual Strawberry Shortcakes (page 250) and Ground Turkey Chinese Spring Rolls (page 24).

8 7 6 5 4 3 2 1

Manufactured in U.S.A.

Microwave ovens vary in wattage and power output; cooking times given with microwave directions in this book may need to be adjusted. Consult manufacturer's instructions for suitable microwave-safe cooking dishes.

CONTENTS

INTRODUCTION

The New Way to Cook Light

America has entered a new age of eating that is revolutionizing the way we think about food. Remember the once-popular high-protein diet, grapefruit diet and all-liquid diet? These dieting fads have been replaced by a healthier, more balanced approach toward food. Study after study indicates that the best way to stay trim is to develop better eating habits by following a low-fat, high-carbohydrate diet. Besides keeping hunger pangs at bay, following this approach toward eating can also help lower your blood cholesterol levels and reduce your risk of heart disease. So whether you are looking to lose a few pounds or would just like to shape up your eating habits, this marvelous recipe collection can help you achieve your goal with hundreds of recipes "fit" for any meal or occasion.

Everyone is concerned with calories, fat, cholesterol and sodium. Because of this concern, there seems to be an abundance of advice, often conflicting, pertaining to food and diets. There is no question, though, that when it comes to fat, health professionals agree—we need to decrease our fat intake. More specifically, we need to limit our total fat intake to no more than 30 percent of our daily calories, instead of our typical 40 percent. This recommendation applies to healthy adults and children over the age of two, whether or not they have a high blood cholesterol level.

Why has fat become such a villain in our diet? Why is this usually flavorless substance, which adds such richness and creaminess to so many of our favorite foods, something we should cut back on? The reason is that consuming excess saturated fat, the type found in meat and whole-milk dairy products, suppresses the body's natural mechanism for pulling cholesterol out of the bloodstream. Instead, cholesterol may be deposited on the inner walls of arteries. Over time, this buildup can constrict the blood flow to the heart. The latest research also links a high-fat diet with an increased risk for certain types of cancers. A high-fat diet also contributes to weight gain, further increasing health risks. For these reasons, experts recommend decreasing our daily fat intake.

The good news is that substituting complex carbohydrates (grains, beans, fruits and vegetables) for high-fat foods (fatty meats, cheese and butter) is an easy way to modify your diet and still enjoy nourishing meals. And, since a gram of fat contains nine calories while a gram of carbohydrate or protein contains only four, you can actually add more complex carbohydrates to your dinner plate in place of those calorie-dense fat grams. Of course, if you wish to lose weight you still have to take in fewer calories than you expend in energy. But consider that for the same number of calories, you can substitute a plain 12-ounce baked potato for a 1.5-ounce bag of potato chips and feel full and satisfied. Substituting complex carbohydrates for fats allows you to eat larger quantities of food without gaining weight. Choosing lean meats, substituting skim milk for whole and substituting low-fat or nonfat yogurt for ice cream are other ways to reduce your fat consumption.

Guidelines for Healthy Eating

We've made it easy to carry out your stay-slim and stay-healthy strategies by providing a nutritional chart with every recipe that tells you the number of calories, the grams (g) of fat, the milligrams (mg) of cholesterol and the milligrams of sodium for each serving.

Each recipe in this book contains no more than 300 calories and no more than 10 grams of fat per serving. If you do choose higher-fat items for a meal, try to choose other foods that day that are low in fat. By mixing and matching your selection of recipes and foods, your weekly diet will follow the guidelines for healthy eating. Many of the recipes are low-cholesterol and low-sodium as well. Most recipes contain less than 50 mg of cholesterol and less than 300 mg of sodium. These values were chosen after careful consideration of a number of factors.

The Food and Nutrition Board of the National Academy of Sciences proposes the Recommended Dietary Allowances (RDAs) for essential nutrients including calories, carbohydrates, fat, protein, amino acids, vitamins and minerals. The RDAs were most recently revised in 1989. The RDA for calories is broken down according to age groups and sex. For healthy men between the ages of 19 and 50, for example, the RDA for total calorie intake is 2,900 calories per day. For healthy women between the ages of 19 and 50 (who are neither pregnant nor lactating), it is 2,200 calories per day. Thus, the 300 calories or less per serving for the recipes in this book represents only about 10 percent of the RDA for most men and about 14 percent of the RDA for most women.

The American Heart Association has recommended that total fat intake should be no more than 30 percent of calories. For most men, that amounts to about 870 calories from fat (or about 97 grams of fat) per day; for most women, about 660 calories from fat (or about 73 grams of fat) per day. Thus, the 10 grams of fat or less per serving for each recipe in this book is well within recommended guidelines. The American Heart Association also recommends that cholesterol intake be less than 300 mg a day and sodium intake not exceed 3,000 mg a day.

About the Nutritional Information
The analysis for each recipe includes all the ingredients that are listed, except ingredients labeled "optional" or "for garnish." If a range is given in the yield of a recipe ("Makes 6 to 8 servings," for example), the *higher* yield was used to calculate the per serving information. If a range is offered for an ingredient (¼ to ⅛ teaspoon, for example) the *first* amount given was used to calculate the nutrition information. If an ingredient is presented with an option ("2 tablespoons margarine or butter") the *first* amount given was used to calculate the nutrition information. Foods shown in photographs on the same serving plate and offered as "serve with" suggestions at the end of a recipe are also *not* included in the recipe analysis unless it is stated in the per serving line.

The nutrition information that appears with each recipe was submitted in part by the participating companies and associations. **Every effort has been made to check the accuracy of these numbers. However, because numerous variables account for a wide range of values for certain foods, all nutritive analyses that appear in this book should be considered approximate.**

This cookbook offers you a wide variety of recipes that are, on a per serving basis, low in calories, fat and cholesterol. **The recipes in this book are NOT intended as a medically therapeutic program, nor as a substitute for medically approved diet plans for people on fat-, cholesterol- or sodium-restricted diets. You should consult your physician before beginning any diet plan.** The recipes offered here can be part of a healthy lifestyle that meets recognized dietary guidelines. A healthy lifestyle includes not only eating a balanced diet, but engaging in proper exercise as well.

Delicious recipes that follow today's nutritional guidelines, combined with easy-to-follow instructions and beautiful color photographs will inspire you to learn this healthy new approach to eating. Take that first step on the road to better living as you balance good health with pleasurable eating.

Hold off those hunger pangs with these tasty recipes perfect for guilt-free munching and crunching. Spicy salsa and guacamole, stuffed mushrooms and mini-pizzas are just a few predinner (or late-night) possibilities. Whip up a frothy milk shake, a refreshing fruit slush or a crowd-pleasing punch for powerful thirst quenching any time of day.

Shrimp Toast

Makes 2 dozen appetizers

½ pound raw shrimp, peeled, deveined
2 tablespoons chopped green onion
2 tablespoons finely chopped water chestnuts
2 tablespoons low-sodium soy sauce
1 teaspoon Oriental sesame oil
1 egg white, slightly beaten
6 slices white sandwich bread, crusts removed
  Red and yellow bell peppers and green onions for garnish

Finely chop shrimp. If using food processor, process with on/off pulses, about 10 times or until shrimp are finely chopped.

Combine shrimp, onion, water chestnuts, soy sauce and sesame oil in medium bowl; mix well. Stir in egg white; mix well.*

Toast bread lightly on both sides. Cut toast diagonally into quarters. Spread shrimp mixture evenly over toast to edges.

Place toast on foil-lined baking sheet or broiler pan. Broil, 6 inches from heat, 4 minutes or until lightly browned. Garnish with peppers and green onions.

The filling may be made ahead to this point; cover and refrigerate filling up to 24 hours. Proceed as directed for toasting and broiling.

Nutrients per serving (1 appetizer):

Calories	30	Cholesterol	18 mg
Fat	1 g	Sodium	102 mg

Garden Vegetable Dip

Makes 5½ cups dip

1 pound DOLE® Carrots
1 bunch DOLE® Broccoli
1 head DOLE® Cauliflower
½ cup minced onion
2 packages (8 ounces *each*) cream cheese, softened
1 teaspoon dill weed
½ teaspoon ground cumin
¼ teaspoon chili powder
⅛ teaspoon salt
10 drops hot pepper sauce
  Vegetable dippers: reserved carrot slices and broccoli and cauliflower florettes; celery and cucumber slices; bell pepper strips; mushroom slices; cherry tomatoes

Mince 1 cup of carrots; slice remaining for dippers. Break broccoli and cauliflower into florettes. Mince 1 cup of each; reserve remaining florettes for vegetable dippers. In food processor fitted with metal blade, combine minced carrots, broccoli, cauliflower, onion, cream cheese and seasonings; process until smooth. Refrigerate dip 1 hour or overnight in covered serving bowl. Serve with vegetable dippers and crackers.

Nutrients per serving (1 tablespoon dip):

Calories	19	Cholesterol	6 mg
Fat	2 g	Sodium	19 mg

Shrimp Toast

Top to bottom: Spicy Zucchini and Bacon Canapé, Party Ham Sandwich

Party Ham Sandwiches

Makes 24 appetizer sandwiches

¾ cup plain nonfat yogurt
1 tablespoon chopped fresh chives
1 teaspoon dill mustard
1 loaf party rye or pumpernickel bread
    Leaf lettuce, washed, torn and well drained
1 ARMOUR® Lower Salt Ham Nugget (about
    1¾ pounds), shaved
1 small cucumber, thinly sliced
12 cherry tomatoes, cut in half *or* 24 slices tomato

Combine yogurt, chives and mustard in small bowl. Arrange bread slices on serving tray; spread evenly with yogurt mixture. Layer lettuce, ham, cucumber slice and tomato half on top of each bread slice. Garnish as desired.

Nutrients per serving (1 sandwich):

Calories	101	Cholesterol	16 mg
Fat	3 g	Sodium	413 mg

Spicy Zucchini and Bacon Canapés

Makes 22 to 24 canapés

1 (4-ounce) carton low-fat cottage cheese, well
    drained
2 green onions, finely chopped
½ tablespoon finely chopped jalapeño peppers
½ teaspoon MRS. DASH®, Original Blend
2 medium zucchini, cut into ¼-inch slices
8 slices ARMOUR® Lower Salt Bacon, cooked
    crisp and crumbled
2 tablespoons finely chopped red pepper *or*
    6 cherry tomatoes, quartered

Combine cottage cheese, green onions, jalapeño peppers and seasoning in small bowl. Mound cottage cheese mixture evenly on top of zucchini slices; sprinkle with bacon. Top with sprinkle of red pepper or cherry tomato quarter. Garnish with fresh chives or small sprig of parsley, if desired.

Nutrients per serving (1 canapé):

Calories	17	Cholesterol	2 mg
Fat	1 g	Sodium	66 mg

Grilled Mushrooms with Lamb and Herbs

Makes 6 appetizer servings

¼ cup olive oil
¼ cup fresh lime juice
1 small green onion, minced
½ teaspoon grated fresh ginger
¼ teaspoon salt
¼ teaspoon black pepper
1 bunch parsley
36 medium mushroom caps
6 ounces cooked American lamb,* cut in
    ½-inch cubes or to fit mushroom caps

Combine all ingredients except mushrooms and lamb in blender and process until finely minced. Brush each mushroom generously with mixture and arrange on baking sheet. Place a lamb cube in each mushroom cap. Broil, about 4 inches from heat source, until hot. Garnish with parsley, if desired.

*Leftover leg of lamb may be used.

Nutrients per serving:

Calories	62	Cholesterol	20 mg
Fat	4 g	Sodium	14 mg

Favorite recipe from **American Lamb Council**

Black Bean Dip

Makes 2¼ cups

1 can (15 ounces) black beans, rinsed, drained
½ cup MIRACLE WHIP® FREE® Nonfat
   Dressing
½ cup reduced-calorie sour cream
1 can (4 ounces) chopped green chilies, drained
2 tablespoons chopped cilantro
1 teaspoon chili powder
½ teaspoon garlic powder
   Few drops hot pepper sauce

Mash beans with fork. Stir in remaining ingredients until well blended; refrigerate. Serve with tortilla chips.

Prep time: 10 minutes plus refrigerating

Nutrients per serving (2 tablespoons dip):			
Calories	70	Cholesterol	0 mg
Fat	1 g	Sodium	119 mg

Eggplant Caviar

Makes 1½ cups

1 large eggplant, unpeeled
¼ cup chopped onion
2 tablespoons lemon juice
1 tablespoon olive or vegetable oil
1 small clove garlic
½ teaspoon salt
¼ teaspoon TABASCO® pepper sauce
   Cooked egg white, sieved (optional)
   Lemon slice (optional)
   Toast points (optional)

Preheat oven to 350°F. Pierce eggplant with fork. Place eggplant in shallow baking dish. Bake 1 hour or until soft, turning once. Trim off ends; slice eggplant in half lengthwise. Place cut sides down in colander and let drain 10 minutes. Scoop out pulp; set aside pulp and peel. In blender or food processor, combine eggplant peel, onion, lemon juice, oil, garlic, salt and TABASCO sauce. Cover; process until peel is finely chopped. Add eggplant pulp. Cover; process just until chopped. Place in serving dish. Garnish with egg white and lemon slice, if desired. Serve with toast points, if desired.

Nutrients per serving (1 tablespoon caviar):			
Calories	10	Cholesterol	0 mg
Fat	1 g	Sodium	45 mg

Ginger Shrimp

Makes about 2 dozen appetizers

1 cup (8 ounces) WISH-BONE® Lite Italian
   Dressing
½ cup sherry
4 medium shallots, peeled and halved*
3 medium green onions, cut into pieces
1 (2-inch) piece fresh ginger, peeled and cut
   into pieces**
1 teaspoon soy sauce
1 teaspoon lemon juice
1 pound uncooked large shrimp, cleaned
   (keep tails on)

Place all ingredients except shrimp in food processor or blender; process until smooth. In large shallow baking dish, combine dressing mixture with shrimp. Cover and marinate in refrigerator, stirring occasionally, at least 3 hours.

Remove shrimp and marinade to large shallow baking pan or aluminum-foil-lined broiler rack. Broil shrimp with marinade, turning once, 10 minutes or until shrimp are opaque. Serve remaining marinade with shrimp. Garnish as desired.

***Substitution:** Use ⅓ medium onion, cut into pieces.*
****Substitution:** Use 1 teaspoon ground ginger.*

Nutrients per serving (1 appetizer):			
Calories	24	Cholesterol	23 mg
Fat	0 g	Sodium	178 mg

Black Bean Dip

Shanghai Party Pleasers

Shanghai Party Pleasers

Makes 2 dozen appetizers

1 can (20 ounces) crushed pineapple in juice, undrained
¼ cup firmly packed brown sugar
2 tablespoons cornstarch
   Dash of ground ginger
1 cup water
2 tablespoons margarine
1 pound finely chopped, cooked, skinned turkey or chicken
¾ cup QUAKER® Oat Bran hot cereal, uncooked
⅓ cup plain low-fat yogurt
⅓ cup finely chopped water chestnuts, drained
⅓ cup sliced green onions
2 tablespoons lite soy sauce
1 egg white, slightly beaten
1 teaspoon ground ginger
½ teaspoon salt (optional)
   Red and green bell pepper pieces, fresh pineapple wedges and whole water chestnuts (optional)

Drain crushed pineapple, reserving juice. In medium saucepan, combine brown sugar, cornstarch and dash of ginger; mix well. Add combined pineapple juice, water, ¼ cup crushed pineapple and margarine; mix well. Bring to a boil over medium-high heat; reduce heat to low. Simmer about 1 minute, stirring frequently or until sauce is thickened and clear. Set aside.

Heat oven to 400°F. Lightly spray 13×9-inch baking pan with nonstick cooking spray, or oil lightly. Combine turkey, oat bran, yogurt, water chestnuts, onions, soy sauce, egg white, 1 teaspoon ginger, salt and remaining crushed pineapple; mix well. Shape into 1-inch balls. Place in prepared pan. Bake 20 to 25 minutes or until light golden brown. If desired, alternately thread meatballs, pepper pieces, pineapple wedges and water chestnuts onto skewers to serve. Serve with pineapple sauce.

Nutrients per serving (⅛th of recipe):			
Calories	240	Cholesterol	45 mg
Fat	6 g	Sodium	240 mg

Pineapple Shrimp Appetizers

Makes 30 appetizers

1 can (8 ounces) DOLE® Crushed Pineapple in Juice, drained
1 can (4¼ ounces) Pacific shrimp, drained
¼ cup reduced-calorie mayonnaise
1 tablespoon minced DOLE® Green Onion
2 teaspoons Dijon-style mustard
½ teaspoon dill weed
2 cucumbers

Combine all ingredients except cucumbers in medium bowl. Cut cucumbers in ⅛- to ¼-inch-thick slices. Spoon heaping teaspoon of pineapple mixture on top of each slice. Garnish with additional dill or minced green onion, if desired.

Nutrients per serving (1 appetizer):			
Calories	15	Cholesterol	6 mg
Fat	trace	Sodium	15 mg

Garden Vegetable Platter

Makes 1½ cups

1 cup torn spinach
½ cup fresh parsley, stemmed
¼ cup cold water
3 tablespoons sliced green onions
½ teaspoon dried tarragon leaves, crushed
1 package (8 ounces) Light PHILADELPHIA BRAND® Neufchatel Cheese, softened
¾ cup chopped cucumber
½ teaspoon lemon juice
3 drops hot pepper sauce
¼ teaspoon salt

Bring to boil spinach, parsley, water, onions and tarragon in small saucepan. Reduce heat. Cover; simmer 1 minute. Drain.

Place spinach mixture and all remaining ingredients in blender or food processor container; cover. Blend until smooth. Cover. Refrigerate. Serve with assorted vegetable dippers.

Prep time: 30 minutes plus refrigerating

Nutrients per serving (about 1 tablespoon dip):			
Calories	25	Cholesterol	5 mg
Fat	2 g	Sodium	60 mg

Clockwise from top right: Colorful Corn Bread Squares, Buttermilk Herb Dip, Sour Cream Gouda Spread

Colorful Corn Bread Squares

Makes 64 squares

Corn Bread
- 1 egg
- 1 (16-ounce) carton LAND O LAKES® Light Sour Cream (2 cups), divided
- ¾ cup skim milk
- 1 cup all-purpose flour
- 1 cup yellow cornmeal
- 3 tablespoons sugar
- 2 teaspoons baking powder
- ½ teaspoon salt
- ½ teaspoon chili powder

Topping
- ½ teaspoon chili powder
- 1 cup finely chopped lettuce
- 1 cup chopped tomato
- ½ cup (2 ounces) finely shredded Cheddar cheese
- Salsa

For Corn Bread, heat oven to 400°F. In large bowl, slightly beat egg; stir in ¾ cup Light Sour Cream and milk. In medium bowl, combine remaining Corn Bread ingredients. Stir flour mixture into Light Sour Cream mixture just until moistened. Spread into greased 15×10×1-inch jelly-roll pan. Bake for 10 to 15 minutes or until wooden pick inserted in center comes out clean. Cool completely.

For Topping, just before serving spread remaining Light Sour Cream over corn bread. Sprinkle with ½ teaspoon chili powder, lettuce, tomato and cheese. Cut into 64 squares; top each square with ½ teaspoon salsa.

Nutrients per serving (1 square):			
Calories	33	Cholesterol	7 mg
Fat	1 g	Sodium	62 mg

Sour Cream Gouda Spread

Makes 2¼ cups

1 (7-ounce) Gouda cheese round
1 (8-ounce) carton LAND O LAKES® Light
    Sour Cream (1 cup)
1 tablespoon Dijon-style mustard
1 teaspoon Worcestershire sauce
¼ teaspoon garlic powder
¼ cup shredded carrot
¼ cup finely chopped celery
2 tablespoons finely chopped red bell pepper
    Crackers

Cut thin slice of wax from top of Gouda. Carefully scoop out cheese, leaving wax shell intact. Chop cheese into small (about ¼-inch) pieces; set aside. In medium bowl stir together Light Sour Cream, mustard, Worcestershire sauce and garlic powder. Stir in cheese, carrot, celery and red pepper. Cover; refrigerate until flavors are well blended (about 2 hours). To serve, fill wax shell with spread; refill as necessary. Garnish as desired. Serve with crackers.

Nutrients per serving (1 tablespoon dip):			
Calories	29	Cholesterol	75 mg
Fat	2 g	Sodium	67 mg

Buttermilk Herb Dip

Makes 1¼ cups

1 (8-ounce) carton LAND O LAKES® Light
    Sour Cream (1 cup)
¼ cup buttermilk*
2 tablespoons chopped fresh parsley
½ teaspoon dill weed
¼ teaspoon salt
¼ teaspoon minced fresh garlic
⅛ teaspoon black pepper
    Fresh vegetable sticks

In medium bowl stir together all ingredients except vegetable sticks. Cover; refrigerate until flavors are well blended (about 2 hours). Garnish as desired. Serve with vegetable sticks.

¾ teaspoon vinegar plus enough milk to equal ¼ cup can be substituted for ¼ cup buttermilk.

Tip: *Dip can also be used as a salad dressing or potato topper.*

Nutrients per serving (1 tablespoon dip):			
Calories	16	Cholesterol	2 mg
Fat	1 g	Sodium	42 mg

Turkey Antipasto Tray

Makes 20 appetizer servings

1 package (8 ounces) Oven-Roasted Turkey
    Breast Slices
1 can (5¾ ounces) jumbo pitted black olives,
    drained
1 package (8 ounces) Turkey Salami Slices
1 package (6 ounces) Provolone cheese slices
1 package (8 ounces) Turkey Ham Slices
1 jar (16 ounces) sweet gherkins, drained
1 pound Smoked Turkey, cut into ½-inch cubes
1 jar (6 ounces) pimiento-stuffed green olives,
    drained
1 package (8 ounces) Turkey Pastrami Slices
1 package (3½ ounces) sesame breadsticks
1 jar (7 ounces) baby corn cobs, drained
1 large green bell pepper, cut in half and seeds
    removed
1 jar (6 ounces) marinated artichoke hearts,
    drained
4 ounces jalapeño Monterey Jack cheese, cut
    into ½-inch cubes
1 large yellow bell pepper, cut in half and seeds
    removed
1 can (7½ ounces) capanato*

Cut oven-roasted turkey breast slices into 3×½-inch strips; fold strips crosswise in half and stuff into holes of black olives.

Layer 3 slices turkey salami alternately with 2 slices Provolone cheese. Cut stack into 8 wedges. Repeat with remaining slices. Spear each wedge with frilled toothpick.

Cut turkey ham slices in half; roll each half into cornucopia-style horn. Place gherkin in center of each horn. Secure turkey ham and gherkin with toothpick.

Spear smoked turkey cubes and green olives alternately onto frilled toothpicks.

Cut turkey pastrami slices into ½-inch-wide strips. Wrap strips around breadsticks. (If desired, spread breadsticks with mustard before wrapping with pastrami.)

Place corn cobs on serving tray. Fill 1 green pepper half with marinated artichokes. Fill remaining green pepper half with jalapeño Monterey Jack cheese cubes. Fill each yellow pepper half with capanato.

Capanato is an eggplant relish and can be found in the Italian section of most supermarkets or specialty food stores.

Nutrients per serving:			
Calories	219	Cholesterol	44 mg
Fat	10 g	Sodium	1102 mg

Favorite recipe from **National Turkey Federation**

Cheddar-Rice Patties

Cheddar-Rice Patties

Makes 4 servings, about 1 dozen

2 cups cooked rice
1 cup (4 ounces) shredded low-fat Cheddar
  cheese
½ cup minced onion
3 tablespoons all-purpose flour
½ teaspoon salt
¼ teaspoon ground black pepper
3 egg whites
⅛ teaspoon cream of tartar
  Nonstick cooking spray
  Apple wedges (optional)
  Low-fat sour cream (optional)

Combine rice, cheese, onion, flour, salt, and pepper in medium bowl. Beat egg whites with cream of tartar in small bowl until stiff but not dry. Fold beaten egg whites into rice mixture. Coat large skillet with nonstick cooking spray and place over medium heat until hot. Spoon 2 to 3 tablespoons batter into skillet for each patty; push batter into diamond shape using spatula. Cook patties, turning once, until golden brown on both sides. Garnish as desired. Serve warm with apple wedges and sour cream.

Nutrients per serving (3 patties):

| Calories | 233 | Cholesterol | 18 mg |
| Fat | 6 g | Sodium | 550 mg |

Favorite recipe from **USA Rice Council**

Guacamole with Tortilla Chips

Makes 12 appetizer servings

1 package (4-serving size) JELL-O® Brand Lemon Flavor Sugar Free Gelatin
1 cup boiling water
1 container (16 ounces) 1% low-fat cottage cheese
1 cup chopped ripe avocado
¾ cup chopped green onions, divided
¼ cup drained pickled jalapeño pepper slices
¼ cup lemon juice
2 cloves garlic
1 to 2 teaspoons chili powder
¼ cup chopped tomato
4 pitted ripe olives, sliced
Chili Tortilla Chips (recipe follows)

Completely dissolve gelatin in boiling water; pour into blender container. Add cottage cheese, avocado, ½ cup green onions, jalapeño peppers, lemon juice, garlic and chili powder; cover. Blend on low speed, scraping down sides occasionally, about 2 minutes or until mixture is smooth. Pour into shallow 5-cup serving dish; smooth top. Chill until set, about 4 hours.

When ready to serve, top guacamole with remaining ¼ cup chopped green onions, tomato and olives. Serve as a dip with fresh vegetables or Chili Tortilla Chips.

Nutrients per serving:			
Calories	60	Cholesterol	0 mg
Fat	3 g	Sodium	230 mg

Chili Tortilla Chips

6 flour tortillas (7 inches diameter)
Nonstick cooking spray
Chili powder

Heat oven to 350°F. Lightly spray tortillas with nonstick cooking spray; sprinkle with chili powder. Turn tortillas over; repeat process. Cut each tortilla into 8 wedges; place on cookie sheet. Bake 8 to 10 minutes until crisp and lightly browned. Makes 12 servings, 48 chips.

Nutrients per serving (4 chips):			
Calories	60	Cholesterol	0 mg
Fat	1 g	Sodium	90 mg

Antipasto Mini Pizzas

Makes 16 appetizer servings

1¾ cups (14.5-ounce can) CONTADINA® Pasta Ready Tomatoes
¾ cup (4-ounce can) water-packed artichoke hearts, drained and coarsely chopped
½ cup (2-ounce can) sliced ripe olives, drained
½ cup chopped green bell pepper
2 tablespoons grated Parmesan cheese
8 plain bagels, lightly toasted, each half cut crosswise into 2 pieces
1 cup (4 ounces) grated mozzarella cheese

In medium bowl, combine tomatoes, artichoke hearts, olives, bell pepper and Parmesan cheese. Place bagel pieces, cut-side up, on cookie sheets. Spoon about 4 teaspoons vegetable mixture onto each bagel piece. Sprinkle mozzarella cheese evenly over vegetable mixture. Bake in preheated 400°F oven for 6 to 8 minutes or until heated through.

Nutrients per serving:			
Calories	140	Cholesterol	3 mg
Fat	3 g	Sodium	320 mg

Guacamole with Tortilla Chips

Scandinavian Smörgåsbord

Makes 36 appetizers

36 slices party bread, crackers or flat bread
   Reduced-calorie mayonnaise or salad dressing
   Mustard
36 small lettuce leaves *or* Belgian endive leaves
 1 can (6⅛ ounces) STARKIST® Tuna, drained
   and flaked or broken into chunks
 2 hard-cooked eggs, sliced
¼ pound frozen cooked bay shrimp, thawed
½ medium cucumber, thinly sliced
36 pieces steamed asparagus tips *or* pea pods
   Capers, plain yogurt, dill sprigs, pimento
   strips, red or black caviar, sliced green
   onion for garnish (optional)

Arrange party bread on a tray; spread each slice with
1 teaspoon mayonnaise and/or mustard. Top with a
small lettuce leaf. Top with tuna, egg slices, shrimp,
cucumber or steamed vegetables. Garnish as desired.

Nutrients per serving (1 appetizer):

Calories	47	Cholesterol	24 mg
Fat	1 g	Sodium	103 mg

Bruschetta

Makes 8 appetizer servings

 2 Italian rolls (each 5 inches long)
1¾ cups (14.5-ounce can) CONTADINA®
   Italian-Style Pear-Shaped Tomatoes
 2 tablespoons chopped fresh basil
 1 tablespoon finely chopped onion
 1 tablespoon olive oil
 1 small clove garlic, crushed
¼ teaspoon dried oregano leaves, crushed
¼ teaspoon salt
⅛ teaspoon black pepper

Cut rolls lengthwise in half. Cut each half crosswise
into 2 pieces. Toast cut sides. Drain tomatoes
thoroughly; chop tomatoes. Combine tomatoes with
remaining ingredients. Spoon tomato mixture onto
toasted rolls. Broil, 5 inches from heat source, until
tomato mixture is hot, about 2 minutes.

Nutrients per serving:

Calories	100	Cholesterol	17 mg
Fat	3 g	Sodium	280 mg

Steamed Mussels in White Wine

Makes 6 appetizer servings

⅓ cup WISH-BONE® Lite Italian Dressing
½ cup chopped shallots or onions
 3 pounds mussels, well scrubbed
⅔ cup dry white wine
½ cup chopped fresh parsley
¼ cup water
   Generous dash crushed red pepper

In large saucepan or stockpot, heat Italian dressing
and cook shallots over medium heat, stirring
occasionally, 2 minutes or until tender. Add
remaining ingredients. Bring to a boil. Reduce heat to
low and simmer, covered, 4 minutes or until mussel
shells open. *(Discard any unopened shells.)* Serve
with Italian or French bread, if desired.

Nutrients per serving:

Calories	74	Cholesterol	18 mg
Fat	1 g	Sodium	378 mg

Artichoke Puffs

Makes 16 puffs

16 to 20 slices small party rye bread
 2 tablespoons CRISCO® Shortening, melted
 1 can (14 ounces) artichoke hearts, drained
 2 egg whites
⅓ teaspoon salt
¼ cup grated Parmesan cheese
 2 tablespoons shredded sharp Cheddar cheese
   Dash ground red pepper
   Paprika

Preheat oven to 400°F. Brush 1 side of each bread
slice with melted Crisco®. Place brushed side up on
ungreased cookie sheet.

Cut artichoke hearts in half; drain on paper towels.
Place an artichoke piece, cut side down, on each
bread slice.

Beat egg whites and salt in large bowl with electric
mixer at high speed until stiff, not dry, peaks form.
Fold in cheeses and ground red pepper.

Spoon about 1 measuring teaspoonful of egg white
mixture over each artichoke piece; sprinkle with
paprika.

Bake at 400°F for 10 to 12 minutes or until golden
brown. Serve hot. Garnish with celery leaves and
carrot curls, if desired.

Nutrients per serving (1 puff):

Calories	52	Cholesterol	2 mg
Fat	2 g	Sodium	113 mg

Scandanavian Smörgåsbord

Clams Diablo

Makes 6 appetizer servings

½ cup chopped onion
¼ cup chopped celery
1 crushed garlic clove
2 tablespoons olive oil
1¾ cups (14½-ounce can) CONTADINA®
  Whole Peeled Tomatoes, cut up, with juice
¼ cup red wine
½ teaspoon dried thyme leaves, crushed
¼ teaspoon salt
¼ teaspoon crushed red pepper
24 (about 4½ pounds total) scrubbed, fresh
  littleneck clams
2 tablespoons chopped fresh parsley or thyme
  leaves

Cook and stir onion, celery and garlic in oil in
medium saucepan until onion and celery are tender.
Stir in tomatoes with juice, wine, dried thyme leaves,
salt and crushed red pepper. Heat to a boil. Reduce
heat to low; simmer 10 minutes, stirring occasionally.
Add clams. Cover; boil gently just until clams open,
about 10 minutes. (Discard any clams that do not
open.) Sprinkle with parsley and serve.

Nutrients per serving:

Calories	130	Cholesterol	55 mg
Fat	6 g	Sodium	440 mg

Twelve Carat Black-Eyed Pea Relish

Twelve Carat Black-Eyed Pea Relish

Makes 2 to 3 pints

1 cup vinegar
¼ cup vegetable oil
2 cans (15 ounces each) black-eyed peas, drained
12 small carrots, steamed until crisp-tender,
  coarsely chopped
1 sweet onion, finely chopped
1 green bell pepper, finely chopped
1 cup sugar
¼ cup Worcestershire sauce
2 teaspoons black pepper
2 teaspoons salt (optional)
2 dashes ground red pepper

Combine vinegar and oil in small saucepan. Bring to
a boil over high heat. Meanwhile, combine black-
eyed peas, carrots, onion, green pepper, sugar,
Worcestershire sauce, black pepper, salt and ground
red pepper in large bowl. Pour oil mixture over
vegetable mixture. Cover and refrigerate at least
24 hours to allow flavors to blend. Store, covered, in
glass container in refrigerator. Serve cold; garnish as
desired.

Nutrients per serving (⅓ cup):

Calories	112	Cholesterol	0 mg
Fat	3 g	Sodium	45 mg

Favorite recipe from the **Black-Eyed Pea Jamboree–Athens, Texas**

Pan-Roasted Herbed Almonds

Makes 2 cups

1 teaspoon *each* dried thyme, oregano and basil
  leaves, crushed
½ teaspoon *each* garlic salt and onion powder
¼ teaspoon ground black pepper
2 tablespoons HOLLYWOOD® Peanut Oil
¾ pound (about 2 cups) whole blanched almonds

In small bowl, combine seasonings. In large skillet,
heat oil over low heat; add almonds and seasonings
and cook slowly, stirring, until almonds are lightly
browned, approximately 10 minutes. Place mixture
on paper towels to absorb excess oil. Can be served
immediately or at room temperature.

Note: *As almonds cool, seasonings will not adhere;
however, herb flavor will remain.*

Nutrients per serving (2 tablespoons):

Calories	122	Cholesterol	0 mg
Fat	6 g	Sodium	135 mg

Mediterranean Appetizer

Mediterranean Appetizer

Makes 8 appetizer servings

1 container (8 ounces) Light PHILADELPHIA
    BRAND® Pasteurized Process Cream
    Cheese Product, softened
2 teaspoons red wine vinegar
1 clove garlic, minced
½ teaspoon dried oregano leaves, crushed
½ teaspoon lemon pepper seasoning
24 lahvosh crackers (3 inches in diameter) *or*
    4 pita bread rounds, split
1½ cups finely torn spinach
1 tomato, chopped
4 ounces CHURNY® ATHENOS® Feta Cheese,
    crumbled
½ cup Greek ripe olives, pitted, chopped

Stir cream cheese product, vinegar, garlic and
seasonings in small bowl until well blended.

Spread crackers with cream cheese mixture. Top with
remaining ingredients.

Prep time: 20 minutes

Nutrients per serving:

Calories	180	Cholesterol	30 mg
Fat	10 g	Sodium	620 mg

Spinach Rice Balls

Makes about 3 dozen rice balls

2 cups cooked rice
1 package (10 ounces) frozen chopped spinach,
    thawed and squeezed dry*
⅔ cup dry Italian-style bread crumbs, divided
½ cup grated Parmesan cheese
⅓ cup minced onion
3 egg whites, beaten
¼ cup skim milk
1 tablespoon Dijon-style mustard
    Nonstick cooking spray

Combine rice, spinach, ⅓ cup bread crumbs, cheese,
onion, egg whites, milk, and mustard in large bowl.
Shape into 1-inch balls. Roll each ball in remaining
⅓ cup bread crumbs. Place on baking sheet coated
with nonstick cooking spray. Bake at 375°F for 10 to
15 minutes. Serve warm.

*Substitute 1 package (10 ounces) frozen chopped broccoli,
thawed and well drained, for the spinach, if desired.*

Nutrients per serving (1 rice ball):

Calories	32	Cholesterol	1 mg
Fat	1 g	Sodium	102 mg

Favorite recipe from **USA Rice Council**

Crab Curry Dip

Crab Curry Dip

Makes 2 cups

½ cup *undiluted* **CARNATION®** Lite Evaporated
    Skimmed Milk
1 package (8 ounces) light Neufchâtel cream
    cheese, softened
4 ounces (¾ cup) imitation crabmeat, shredded
2 tablespoons finely sliced green onion
2 tablespoons finely chopped red bell pepper
½ teaspoon curry powder
¼ teaspoon garlic salt
    Assorted raw vegetables

In small mixer bowl, beat evaporated skimmed milk
and cream cheese. Stir in crab, onion, red pepper,
curry powder and garlic salt. Cover and refrigerate.
Serve with assorted raw vegetables.

Variation: *For Crab Horseradish Dip, substitute 1 to
2 teaspoons prepared horseradish for curry powder.*

Nutrients per serving (¼ cup dip):

Calories	108	Cholesterol	28 mg
Fat	7 g	Sodium	320 mg

Italian Bread Pizza

Makes 12 appetizer servings

1 large loaf Italian bread
1½ cups (6 ounces) shredded lower salt Monterey
    Jack cheese, divided
1 (16-ounce) jar prepared no salt added, no
    sugar, no fat pasta sauce
1½ tablespoons dried Italian seasoning
12 ounces **ARMOUR®** Lower Salt Ham, thinly
    sliced
1 (20-ounce) can pineapple rings, well drained
8 thin green bell pepper rings
8 thin red bell pepper rings

Slice bread lengthwise in half. Toast cut sides under
broiler until lightly browned. Sprinkle ¼ cup cheese
on each half; broil again about 1 to 2 minutes or until
cheese is melted. Combine pasta sauce and seasoning
in small saucepan; cook over medium heat until hot.
Spoon sauce evenly over bread halves; top evenly with
ham and pineapple rings. Place green and red pepper
rings alternately on top. Sprinkle each half with
½ cup of remaining cheese; place on baking sheet.
Broil, 4 to 5 inches from heat source, about 4 to
6 minutes or until cheese is melted. Cut each half
into 6 pieces. Garnish with parsley, if desired.

Nutrients per serving:

Calories	253	Cholesterol	29 mg
Fat	6 g	Sodium	482 mg

Sweet & Spicy Salsa

Makes 8 appetizer servings

¾ cup fresh pineapple, peeled, cored and cut
    into ¼-inch cubes
½ cup (¼-inch) red bell pepper pieces
½ cup (¼-inch) yellow bell pepper pieces
½ cup finely chopped red onion
½ cup finely chopped cilantro
1 jalapeño pepper, seeded and minced
2 tablespoons fresh lime juice
1½ teaspoons firmly packed brown sugar
    Dash salt
    Dash black pepper

In medium bowl, combine pineapple, red and yellow
peppers, onion, cilantro, jalapeño pepper, lime juice,
brown sugar, salt and black pepper. Cover and
refrigerate 30 minutes before serving.

Nutrients per serving:

Calories	19	Cholesterol	0 mg
Fat	0 g	Sodium	18 mg

Favorite recipe from **National Turkey Federation**

Tuna-Stuffed Artichokes

Makes 8 appetizer servings

4 medium artichokes
  Lemon juice
1½ cups chopped fresh mushrooms
  1 cup diced yellow squash or zucchini
  ⅓ cup chopped green onions
  1 clove garlic, minced
  2 tablespoons vegetable oil
  1 can (12½ ounces) STARKIST® Tuna, drained
    and flaked
  ½ cup (2 ounces) shredded low-fat Cheddar,
    mozzarella or Monterey Jack cheese
  ¼ cup seasoned bread crumbs
  2 tablespoons diced drained pimento

With kitchen shears trim sharp points from artichoke leaves. Trim stems; remove loose outer leaves. Cut off 1 inch from tops. Brush cut edges with lemon juice. In a large covered saucepan or Dutch oven, bring artichokes and salted water to a boil; reduce heat to low. Simmer until a leaf pulls out easily, 20 to 30 minutes. Drain upside down.

Preheat oven to 450°F. Cut cooled artichokes lengthwise into halves. Remove fuzzy chokes and hearts. Finely chop hearts; discard chokes. In a medium skillet cook mushrooms, artichoke hearts, squash, onions and garlic in oil for 3 minutes, stirring frequently. Stir in tuna. Place artichoke halves, cut sides up, in a lightly oiled baking dish. Mound tuna mixture in centers of artichokes. In a small bowl stir together remaining ingredients; sprinkle over tuna mixture. Bake 5 to 8 minutes or until cheese is melted and topping is golden.

Nutrients per serving:

Calories	136	Choiesterol	47 mg
Fat	10 g	Sodium	522 mg

Spinach Ricotta Pie

Makes 10 to 12 appetizer servings

4 cups chopped spinach
  ½ cup chopped onion
  1 package (8 ounces) Light PHILADELPHIA
    BRAND® Neufchatel Cheese, softened
  ¾ cup low-fat ricotta cheese
  ½ teaspoon dried basil leaves, crushed
  ½ teaspoon dried oregano leaves, crushed
  ¼ teaspoon salt
  ⅛ teaspoon garlic powder
  ⅛ teaspoon pepper
  ¾ cup chopped tomato
  2 tablespoons KRAFT® 100% Grated
    Parmesan Cheese

Heat oven to 350°F. Place spinach and onion in small saucepan. Cover; cook 5 minutes or until tender. Beat cheeses and seasonings in small mixing bowl at medium speed with electric mixer until well blended. Stir in spinach mixture; spread into 9-inch pie plate. Bake 15 to 20 minutes or until thoroughly heated. Top with remaining ingredients. Serve with crisp rye crackers or bagel chips.

Prep time: 15 minutes
Cook time: 20 minutes

Nutrients per serving:

Calories	90	Cholesterol	20 mg
Fat	6 g	Sodium	190 mg

Tuna-Stuffed Artichokes

Indonesian Satay

Indonesian Satay

Makes 15 appetizer servings

- ¼ cup lime juice
- 2 cloves garlic, minced
- 1 teaspoon grated lime peel
- ½ teaspoon ground ginger
- ½ teaspoon ground red pepper
- 4 boneless skinless chicken breasts (about 2 pounds), cut into strips
  Spicy Peanut Sauce (recipe follows)

Mix together lime juice, garlic, lime peel, ginger and pepper; pour over chicken. Cover. Refrigerate 1 hour. Drain.

Prepare coals for grilling.

Thread chicken on individual skewers; place on greased grill over hot coals (coals will be glowing).

Grill, uncovered, 3 to 5 minutes on each side or until tender. Serve with Spicy Peanut Sauce.

Spicy Peanut Sauce

- 1 package (8 ounces) PHILADELPHIA BRAND® Cream Cheese, cubed
- ½ cup milk
- 3 tablespoons peanut butter
- 2 tablespoons firmly packed brown sugar
- ½ teaspoon ground cardamom
- ⅛ teaspoon ground red pepper

Stir ingredients in small saucepan over low heat until smooth.

Prep time: 20 minutes plus marinating
Cooking time: 10 minutes

Nutrients per serving:			
Calories	130	Cholesterol	35 mg
Fat	8 g	Sodium	85 mg

Slim-Trim Cheese Dip

Makes about 2½ cups

- 2 cups (16 ounces) low-fat cottage cheese
- ¼ cup skim milk
- 1 tomato, chopped
- ½ cup (2 ounces) crumbled blue cheese
- 1 tablespoon chopped chives
- 1 teaspoon salt
  Red cabbage (for serving container)
  Additional crumbled blue cheese, chopped tomato and chives for garnish
  Assorted fresh vegetable dippers

Combine cottage cheese and milk in food processor or blender container. Cover; process until smooth. Spoon into medium bowl. Stir in 1 chopped tomato, ½ cup blue cheese, 1 tablespoon chopped chives and salt. Refrigerate until serving time.

Just before serving, discard any damaged outer leaves from cabbage. Slice small portion from bottom so cabbage will sit flat. Carefully cut out and remove inside portion of cabbage, leaving a 1-inch-thick shell. Spoon dip into cabbage or into small bowl and place bowl in cabbage. Garnish with additional blue cheese, tomato and chives. Serve with vegetable dippers.

Nutrients per serving (¼ cup dip):			
Calories	65	Cholesterol	8 mg
Fat	3 g	Sodium	480 mg

Sherried Turkey Cocktail Meatballs

Makes 80 meatballs

- 2 pounds Turkey Sausage
- ⅔ cup seasoned bread crumbs
- 1 bottle (9 ounces) mango chutney
- 1 cup low-fat plain yogurt
- ⅓ cup dry sherry

Preheat oven to 375°F. In medium bowl combine sausage and bread crumbs. Form mixture into 1-inch balls. Arrange meatballs in two (15×10-inch) baking pans. Bake 25 to 30 minutes or until meatballs are no longer pink in center. In blender or food processor, blend chutney until smooth. In small saucepan over low heat, combine chutney, yogurt and sherry; cook until mixture is slightly thickened. *Do not allow mixture to boil.* To serve, combine meatballs and sauce in chafing dish.

Nutrients per serving (1 meatball):			
Calories	33	Cholesterol	7 mg
Fat	1 g	Sodium	95 mg

Favorite recipe from **National Turkey Federation**

Ground Turkey Chinese Spring Rolls

Makes 16 spring rolls

     1 pound Ground Turkey
     1 large clove garlic, minced
1½ teaspoons minced fresh ginger
     2 cups thinly sliced bok choy
     ½ cup thinly sliced green onions
     2 tablespoons reduced-sodium soy sauce
     1 teaspoon dry sherry or rice wine
     1 teaspoon sesame oil
     8 sheets phyllo pastry
        Nonstick cooking spray

Preheat oven to 400°F. In medium nonstick skillet, over medium-high heat, cook and stir turkey, garlic and ginger 4 to 5 minutes or until turkey is no longer pink. Drain thoroughly.

In medium bowl combine turkey mixture, bok choy, onions, soy sauce, sherry and oil.

On clean, dry counter, layer phyllo sheets into a stack and cut into 2 (18×7-inch) rectangles. Work with one rectangle of phyllo at a time. (Keep remaining phyllo covered with a damp cloth following package instructions.)

Coat rectangle of phyllo with nonstick cooking spray. On counter, arrange phyllo sheet so 7-inch side is parallel to counter edge. Place ¼ cup of turkey mixture in 5-inch strip, 1 inch away from bottom and side edges of phyllo. Fold 1-inch bottom edge of phyllo over filling and fold longer edges of phyllo toward center; roll up, jelly-roll style. Phyllo may break during rolling, but will hold filling once the roll is completed.

Repeat process with remaining rectangles of phyllo and filling to make remaining spring rolls. Place rolls, seam-side-down, on 2 (10×15-inch) cookie sheets coated with nonstick cooking spray. Coat tops of rolls with nonstick cooking spray. Bake 14 to 16 minutes or until all surfaces of rolls are golden brown.

Serve immediately with Chinese mustard, hoisin sauce and additional soy sauce, if desired.

Nutrients per serving (1 spring roll):

Calories	86	Cholesterol	1 mg
Fat	3 g	Sodium	140 mg

Favorite recipe from **National Turkey Federation**

Ground Turkey Chinese Spring Rolls

Two-Tone Ricotta Loaf

Makes 8 appetizer servings

2 envelopes unflavored gelatin
1 cup cold skim milk

Pepper Layer
    1 container (15 ounces) POLLY-O FREE®
        Natural Nonfat Ricotta Cheese or
        POLLY-O LITE® Reduced-Fat Ricotta
        Cheese
    1 jar (7 ounces) roasted red peppers, undrained
    ¼ teaspoon salt
    Pinch ground black pepper

Basil Layer
    1 container (15 ounces) POLLY-O FREE®
        Natural Nonfat Ricotta Cheese or
        POLLY-O LITE® Reduced-Fat Ricotta
        Cheese
    1 cup fresh basil leaves
    ⅓ cup fresh parsley leaves
    ¾ teaspoon salt
    1 small garlic clove, crushed
    Pinch ground black pepper
    ½ cup skim milk
    Additional basil leaves for garnish (optional)

In small saucepan, sprinkle gelatin over 1 cup cold milk; let stand 5 minutes. Stir over low heat until gelatin is completely dissolved.

For Pepper Layer, in food processor combine ricotta, roasted red peppers and their juice, salt and black pepper. Process until smooth. Add ½ cup dissolved gelatin mixture and process until combined. Pour into 8×4-inch loaf pan; refrigerate until partially set, about 20 minutes.

For Basil Layer, in food processor combine ricotta, 1 cup basil, parsley, salt, garlic and black pepper. Process until herbs are finely chopped. Add remaining gelatin mixture and ½ cup skim milk. Pour into large bowl and chill, stirring occasionally, until mixture is the consistency of unbeaten egg whites. Spoon over partially set pepper layer; smooth top. Cover and refrigerate until set, at least 4 hours or overnight. To serve, unmold onto serving dish. Garnish with fresh additional basil leaves, if desired.

Nutrients per serving:

Calories	167	Cholesterol	20 mg
Fat	4 g	Sodium	382 mg

Stuffed Mushrooms

Stuffed Mushrooms

Makes 4 appetizer servings

    1 pound medium mushrooms, washed
    2 tablespoons olive oil, divided
    ½ cup finely chopped red bell pepper
    ¼ cup finely chopped onion
    ¼ cup FRENCH'S® Creamy Spread™ Mustard
    ¼ teaspoon *each* garlic powder and dried
        oregano leaves, crushed
    1 tablespoon grated Parmesan cheese
    Chopped fresh parsley for garnish (optional)

Remove and finely chop mushroom stems. Place mushroom caps right sides up on foil-lined broiler pan. Brush tops of caps with 1 tablespoon oil. Broil 5 to 10 minutes until tender; drain and set aside. Heat remaining 1 tablespoon oil in medium skillet. Over high heat, cook and stir mushroom stems, red pepper and onion for 5 minutes or until almost dry. Add French's® Creamy Spread™ Mustard and seasonings. Spoon about 1 teaspoon vegetable mixture into each mushroom cap. Sprinkle Parmesan cheese evenly over caps. Broil for 5 minutes until lightly browned. Garnish with parsley, if desired.

Nutrients per serving:

Calories	124	Cholesterol	1 mg
Fat	9 g	Sodium	229 mg

Sour Cream Clam Dip

Makes 1¼ cups

1 (8-ounce) carton LAND O LAKES® Light
    Sour Cream (1 cup)
1 (6¼-ounce) can minced clams, drained
2 tablespoons chopped green onions
2 teaspoons Worcestershire sauce
⅛ teaspoon black pepper
2 tablespoons cocktail sauce
    Green onion strips
    Crackers, cocktail bread or potato chips

In medium bowl stir together Light Sour Cream,
clams, 2 tablespoons chopped green onions,
Worcestershire sauce and pepper. Cover; refrigerate
until flavors are well blended (about 2 hours). Spoon
into shallow serving dish or plate; swirl cocktail sauce
over top. If desired, garnish with green onion strips.
Serve with crackers, cocktail bread or potato chips.

Nutrients per serving (1 tablespoon dip):			
Calories	30	Cholesterol	8 mg
Fat	1 g	Sodium	48 mg

Artichoke Dip

Makes 2½ cups

½ cup *each* light sour cream and processed light
    cream cheese
¼ cup FRENCH'S® Creamy Spread™ Mustard
1 package (9 ounces) frozen artichoke hearts,
    thawed and finely chopped
½ cup *each* finely chopped red and green bell
    peppers
1 teaspoon chili powder
2 tablespoons sliced green onions

To Microwave: In 1-quart microwavable bowl, combine
sour cream, cream cheese and French's® Creamy Spread™
Mustard. Stir in artichokes, peppers and chili powder.
Cover with waxed paper. Microwave at HIGH (100%
power) for 5 minutes or until hot, stirring halfway through
cooking. Garnish with green onions. Serve with vegetable
crudites or low-salt tortilla or potato chips.

Nutrients per serving (¼ cup dip):			
Calories	81	Cholesterol	16 mg
Fat	5 g	Sodium	158 mg

Greek Isles Appetizers

Makes 70 meatballs

1 pound ground beef
1 pound ground lamb
2 eggs
½ cup finely chopped onion
2 garlic cloves, minced
2 teaspoons dry mustard
1 teaspoon dried thyme leaves, crushed
1 teaspoon ground coriander
½ teaspoon salt
½ teaspoon pepper
    Cucumber Sauce (recipe follows)

Heat oven to 350°F. Mix meat, eggs, onion, garlic
and seasonings in large bowl until well blended.
Shape into 1-inch balls. Place meatballs on rack in
15×10×1-inch jelly-roll pan. Bake 15 to 20 minutes
or until lightly browned. Serve with Cucumber Sauce.

Cucumber Sauce

1 container (8 ounces) PHILADELPHIA
    BRAND® Soft Cream Cheese with Herb &
    Garlic
½ cup plain yogurt
1 tablespoon lemon juice
½ cup shredded cucumber, well drained

Stir together cream cheese, yogurt and lemon juice in
small bowl until well blended. Stir in cucumber.

Prep time: 35 minutes
Cook time: 20 minutes

Nutrients per serving (3 meatballs plus 2 tablespoons sauce):			
Calories	128	Cholesterol	55 mg
Fat	9 g	Sodium	161 mg

Sour Cream Clam Dip

Black Bean Tortilla Pinwheels

Black Bean Tortilla Pinwheels

Makes 12 to 16 appetizer servings

1 (8-ounce) package cream cheese, softened
1 cup dairy sour cream
1 cup (4 ounces) shredded Wisconsin Monterey
    Jack cheese
¼ cup chopped, well drained pimento-stuffed
    green olives
¼ cup chopped red onion
½ teaspoon seasoned salt
⅛ teaspoon garlic powder
1 (15-ounce) can black beans, drained
5 (10-inch) flour tortillas
    Salsa

Beat cream cheese and sour cream in medium bowl
until well blended. Stir in Monterey Jack cheese,
olives, onion, salt and garlic powder. Cover;
refrigerate 2 hours. Place beans in food processor or
blender; process until smooth. Spread each tortilla
with thin layer of beans. Spread thin layer of cream
cheese mixture over beans. Roll up tortillas tightly.
Wrap in plastic wrap; refrigerate until chilled. Cut
tortillas into ¾-inch slices. Serve with salsa. Garnish
as desired.

Nutrients per serving (includes 1 teaspoon salsa):

Calories	159	Cholesterol	13 mg
Fat	9 g	Sodium	175 mg

Favorite recipe from **Wisconsin Milk Marketing Board** © 1994

Toasted Sesame Seed Wafers

Makes 4 to 4½ dozen wafers

¼ cup sesame seeds
1½ cups all-purpose flour
¾ teaspoon salt
⅛ teaspoon paprika
    Dash garlic powder
½ cup BUTTER FLAVOR CRISCO®
3 to 4 drops hot pepper sauce
4 tablespoons cold water
1 tablespoon 2% milk

Preheat oven to 375°F. Spread sesame seeds in
8×8×2-inch baking pan. Bake for 6 to 10 minutes,
stirring occasionally, until golden brown. Transfer to
small dish; set aside.

In medium bowl, combine flour, salt, paprika and
garlic powder. Cut in Butter Flavor Crisco® until
coarse crumbs form. Stir in 3 tablespoons toasted
sesame seeds.

Combine hot pepper sauce and 4 tablespoons water.
Sprinkle over flour mixture, 1 tablespoon at a time,
mixing with fork until particles are moistened and
cling together. Form dough into ball.

Roll dough ⅛ inch thick on lightly floured board. Cut
with 2- or 2½-inch cookie cutter. Transfer cutouts to
ungreased baking sheet. Brush with milk. Sprinkle
lightly with remaining sesame seeds. Bake for 12 to
15 minutes, or until light golden brown. Cool. Store in
covered container.

Nutrients per serving (1 wafer):

Calories	31	Cholesterol	trace
Fat	2 g	Sodium	30 mg

Pickle Roll-Em-Ups

Makes 48 appetizers

1 package (6 ounces) sliced ham
1 container (8 ounces) soft cream cheese
8 medium CLAUSSEN® Whole Kosher Dill
    Pickles

Spread 1 side of each ham slice with 1 tablespoon
cream cheese. Place 1 pickle on edge of each ham
slice. Roll ham slice around pickle; press edges to
seal. Repeat with remaining ham slices. Cover and
refrigerate 1 hour. To serve, cut each pickle into
6 slices.

Nutrients per serving (1 appetizer):

Calories	20	Cholesterol	5 mg
Fat	2 g	Sodium	215 mg

Southwest Barbecue Kabobs

Makes 6 appetizer servings

   1 cup beer
   ¾ cup A.1.® Steak Sauce
   2 cloves garlic, crushed
   2 teaspoons chili powder
   1 teaspoon ground cumin
1½ pounds round steak, cut into ½-inch strips
   3 small red or green bell peppers, cut into
      1-inch pieces
   1 teaspoon cornstarch

In small bowl, combine beer, steak sauce, garlic, chili powder and cumin. Pour marinade over sliced steak in nonmetal dish. Cover; refrigerate 2 hours, stirring occasionally.

Remove steak from marinade; reserve marinade. Thread steak and pepper pieces alternately onto 6 skewers. In small saucepan, heat reserved marinade and cornstarch to a boil. Grill or broil kabobs, 4 inches from heat source, for 15 minutes or until done, turning and brushing often with marinade. Heat remaining marinade to a boil; serve with kabobs.

Nutrients per serving:

Calories	198	Cholesterol	71 mg
Fat	4 g	Sodium	624 mg

Two Cheese Pesto Dip

Makes 2 cups dip

   1 cup light sour cream
   ½ cup light mayonnaise
   ½ cup finely chopped fresh parsley
   ¼ cup finely chopped walnuts
   1 clove garlic, minced
1½ teaspoons dried basil leaves, crushed *or*
   3 tablespoons fresh minced basil
   ½ cup (2 ounces) SARGENTO® Preferred Light
      Fancy Supreme Shredded Mozzarella
      Cheese
   2 tablespoons SARGENTO® Grated Parmesan
      Cheese

Combine all ingredients in medium bowl. Cover and refrigerate several hours or overnight. Garnish with whole walnuts, if desired. Serve with assorted fresh vegetables.

Nutrients per serving (1 tablespoon dip):

Calories	35	Cholesterol	5 mg
Fat	3 g	Sodium	36 mg

Tuna-Stuffed Endive

Makes about 24 appetizers

4 ounces soft-spread herb cheese
4 ounces reduced-calorie cream cheese,
   softened
1 teaspoon lemon or lime juice
2 heads Belgian endive *or* small lettuce leaves *or*
   crackers
1 can (3¼ ounces) STARKIST® Tuna, drained
   and finely flaked
   Watercress sprigs *or* pimento strips for garnish

In blender container or food processor bowl, place cheeses and lemon juice. Cover and process until mixture is well blended. Trim ½ inch from bottom stems of endive; separate heads into leaves. Sprinkle 1 to 2 teaspoons tuna into each endive leaf; spoon or pipe 2 teaspoons cheese filling into each endive leaf. Garnish each with a sprig of watercress.

Nutrients per serving (1 appetizer):

Calories	29	Cholesterol	7 mg
Fat	2 g	Sodium	65 mg

Southwest Barbecue Kabobs

White Sangria

White Sangria

Makes 20 servings

1 carton (64 ounces) DOLE® Pine-Orange-
   Guava Juice
2 cups fruity white wine
¼ cup orange-flavored liqueur
¼ cup sugar
1 DOLE® Orange, thinly sliced
1 lime, thinly sliced
2 cups sliced DOLE® Fresh Strawberries
   Ice cubes
   Mint sprigs for garnish

Combine all ingredients except ice and mint in
2 large pitchers; cover and refrigerate for 2 hours to
blend flavors. Serve over ice. Garnish with mint sprig.

Nutrients per serving (4 ounces):

Calories	93	Cholesterol	0 mg
Fat	trace	Sodium	7 mg

Mulled Cider

Makes about 2 quarts

2 quarts apple cider
¾ to 1 cup REALEMON® Lemon Juice from
   Concentrate
1 cup firmly packed light brown sugar
8 whole cloves
2 cinnamon sticks
¾ cup rum (optional)

In large saucepan, combine all ingredients except
rum; bring to a boil. Reduce heat; simmer, uncovered,
10 minutes to blend flavors. Remove spices; add rum
just before serving, if desired. Serve hot. Garnish with
additional cinnamon sticks, if desired.

Tip: *Can be served cold.*

Nutrients per serving (¾ cup):

Calories	135	Cholesterol	0 mg
Fat	trace	Sodium	7 mg

Strawberry Fizz

Makes 4 servings

1 can (5 fluid ounces) PET® Evaporated Milk *or*
   PET® Light Evaporated Skimmed Milk
⅔ cup lemon-lime or orange soda, regular or
   diet
1½ cups fresh or frozen strawberries
4 teaspoons sugar *or* 1 teaspoon artificial
   sweetener

Combine all ingredients in blender until smooth.
Serve immediately.

Note: *Frozen fruit makes this beverage icy cold; if using
fresh fruit, we suggest serving over crushed ice.*

*Nutrients per serving (with PET® Evaporated Milk,
regular soda and sugar):*

Calories	99	Cholesterol	10 mg
Fat	3 g	Sodium	44 mg

*Nutrients per serving (with PET® Light Evaporated
Skimmed Milk, diet soda and artificial sweetener):*

Calories	51	Cholesterol	1 mg
Fat	trace	Sodium	46 mg

Easy Chocolate Pudding
Milk Shake

Makes 5 servings

3 cups cold skim milk
1 package (4-serving size) JELL-O® Chocolate
   Flavor Sugar Free Instant Pudding and Pie
   Filling
1½ cups vanilla ice milk

Pour milk into blender container. Add remaining
ingredients; cover. Blend at high speed 15 seconds or
until smooth. Serve at once. (Mixture thickens as it
stands. Thin with additional milk, if desired.)

Note: *For double chocolate impact, use chocolate ice milk
instead of vanilla ice milk.*

Nutrients per serving:

Calories	150	Cholesterol	10 mg
Fat	2 g	Sodium	370 mg

Double Strawberry Coconut Punch

Makes 25 servings

2 cans (12 ounces each) frozen DOLE®
    Pine-Orange Banana Juice concentrate,
    thawed
4 cups DOLE® Fresh Strawberries, divided
1 can (15 ounces) real cream of coconut
4 ripe, medium DOLE® Bananas,
    peeled
1 pint vanilla ice cream, softened
1 cup flaked coconut (optional)

Reconstitute juice in large punch bowl according to directions. Place 2 cups strawberries, cream of coconut and bananas in blender. Process until smooth; stir into juice in punch bowl. Process remaining 2 cups strawberries in blender until smooth. Swirl into punch along with ice cream. Top with coconut, if desired.

Nutrients per serving (6 ounces):

Calories	130	Cholesterol	5 mg
Fat	5 g	Sodium	23 mg

Hot Orchard Peach Cup

Berry Power Drink

Makes 2 servings

1 cup cranberry juice
1 cup fresh or frozen strawberries
1 (8-ounce) carton vanilla low-fat yogurt
⅔ cup QUAKER® Oats (quick or old fashioned,
    uncooked)*
    Sugar to taste (optional)
1 cup ice cubes

Place all ingredients except ice in blender container. Cover; blend on high speed about 2 minutes or until smooth. Gradually add ice; blend on high speed an additional minute or until smooth. Serve immediately.

*Or substitute ⅔ cup QUAKER® Oat Bran hot cereal, uncooked, for oats.

Nutrients per serving (about 1½ cups):

Calories	300	Cholesterol	5 mg
Fat	4 g	Sodium	80 mg

Hot Orchard Peach Cup

Makes 6 servings

1 bottle (40 ounces) DOLE® Pure & Light
    Orchard Peach Juice
¼ cup packed brown sugar
2 cinnamon sticks
2 tablespoons margarine
½ cup peach schnapps (optional)
    Additional cinnamon sticks for garnish
    (optional)

Combine juice, brown sugar, 2 cinnamon sticks and margarine in Dutch oven. Heat to a boil. Remove from heat; discard cinnamon sticks. Add schnapps, if desired. Garnish with additional cinnamon sticks, if desired.

Nutrients per serving (7 ounces):

Calories	181	Cholesterol	0 mg
Fat	4 g	Sodium	70 mg

Peaches and Cream Punch

Makes 24 (4 ounce) servings

4 cups boiling water
6 LIPTON® Flo-Thru Regular or Decaffeinated Tea Bags
4 cans (12 ounces each) peach nectar, chilled
2 cups champagne or seltzer water, chilled
2 cups (1 pint) frozen low-fat vanilla yogurt

In teapot, pour boiling water over tea bags; cover and brew 5 minutes. Cool.

In chilled 4-quart punch bowl, blend peach nectar with tea. Add champagne. Top with scoops of yogurt and garnish, if desired, with fresh peach slices. Serve immediately.

Nutrients per serving:

Calories	77	Cholesterol	1 mg
Fat	0 g	Sodium	20 mg

Kokomo Quencher

Makes 47 servings

1 carton (64 ounces) DOLE® Pine-Orange-Guava Juice
2 bottles (32 ounces each) lemon-lime soda, chilled
1 can (46 ounces) DOLE® Pineapple Juice, chilled
1 package (16 ounces) frozen blackberries
1 can (15 ounces) real cream of coconut
1 lime, thinly sliced

Combine all ingredients in large punch bowl.

Nutrients per serving (4 ounces):

Calories	82	Cholesterol	0 mg
Fat	2 g	Sodium	13 mg

Lemony Light Cooler

Lemony Light Cooler

Makes 7 servings, about 7 cups

3 cups white grape juice *or* 1 bottle (750 ml) dry white wine, chilled
½ to ¾ cup sugar
½ cup REALEMON® Lemon Juice from Concentrate
1 bottle (1 liter) club soda, chilled
Strawberries *or* plum, peach or orange slices *or* other fresh fruit
Ice

In large pitcher, combine grape juice, sugar and ReaLemon® brand; stir until sugar dissolves. Cover; chill. Just before serving, add club soda and fruit. Serve over ice.

***Tip:** Recipe may be doubled.*

Nutrients per serving (without fruit):

Calories	110	Cholesterol	0 mg
Fat	trace	Sodium	31 mg

Strawberry Watermelon Slush

Strawberry Watermelon Slush

Makes about 1 quart

1 pint (about ¾ pound) fresh strawberries,
    cleaned and hulled
2 cups seeded and cubed watermelon
⅓ cup sugar
⅓ cup vodka (optional)
¼ cup REALEMON® Lemon Juice from
    Concentrate
2 cups ice cubes

In blender container, combine all ingredients except
ice; blend well. Gradually add ice, blending until
smooth. Serve immediately. Garnish as desired.

Nutrients per serving (1 cup):

Calories	110	Cholesterol	0 mg
Fat	1 g	Sodium	6 mg

Piña Colada Mocktail

Makes 4 servings

1½ cups DOLE® Pineapple Juice, chilled
⅓ cup canned real cream of coconut
1½ teaspoons rum extract
    Crushed ice

Place all ingredients in blender. Process until smooth.

Nutrients per serving:

Calories	100	Cholesterol	0 mg
Fat	4 g	Sodium	13 mg

Cherry Punch

Makes 16 servings

1 can (6 ounces) frozen lemonade concentrate,
    thawed
5 cups DOLE® Pure & Light Mountain Cherry
    Juice, chilled
1 bottle (28 ounces) mineral water, chilled
    DOLE® Lemon slices for garnish
    Mint sprigs for garnish

Reconstitute lemonade according to directions in
large punch bowl. Stir in remaining ingredients. Serve
immediately.

Nutrients per serving:

Calories	61	Cholesterol	0 mg
Fat	trace	Sodium	4 mg

Hot Spiced Lemonade

Makes 4 servings, about 4 cups

3 cups water
⅔ cup firmly packed light brown sugar
½ cup REALEMON® Lemon Juice from
    Concentrate
8 whole cloves
2 cinnamon sticks
    Additional cinnamon sticks for garnish
    (optional)

In medium saucepan, combine all ingredients except
garnish. Simmer, uncovered, 20 minutes to blend
flavors; remove spices. Serve hot in mugs with
cinnamon sticks, if desired.

To Microwave: In 1-quart glass measure, combine
ingredients as directed. Heat on HIGH (100% power) 4 to
5 minutes or until hot. Serve as directed.

Nutrients per serving:

Calories	112	Cholesterol	0 mg
Fat	trace	Sodium	17 mg

ReaLemonade

Makes about 1 quart

½ cup sugar
½ cup REALEMON® Lemon Juice from
    Concentrate
3¼ cups cold water
    Ice

In pitcher, dissolve sugar in ReaLemon® brand; add
water. Cover; chill. Serve over ice.

Variations

Sparkling: *Substitute club soda for cold water.*

Slushy: *Reduce water to ½ cup. In blender container,
combine sugar, ReaLemon® brand and ½ cup water.
Gradually add 4 cups ice cubes, blending until smooth.
Serve immediately.*

Pink: *Stir in 1 to 2 teaspoons grenadine syrup or 1 to
2 drops red food coloring.*

Minted: *Stir in 2 to 3 drops peppermint extract.*

Low Calorie: *Omit sugar. Add 4 to 8 envelopes sugar
substitute or 1½ teaspoons liquid sugar substitute.*

Strawberry: *Increase sugar to ¾ cup. In blender or food
processor, purée 1 quart fresh strawberries, cleaned and
hulled (about 1½ pounds); add to lemonade.*

Grape: *Stir in 1 (6-ounce) can frozen grape juice
concentrate, thawed.*

Nutrients per serving (1 cup):			
Calories	97	Cholesterol	0 mg
Fat	trace	Sodium	6 mg

Frosty Fruit Shake

Makes 1 serving

1 can (6 ounces) *or* ¾ cup DOLE® Pineapple
    Juice, chilled
1 cup DOLE® Fresh Strawberries
1 ripe, medium DOLE® Banana, peeled
    Ice cubes

Place all ingredients in blender. Process until smooth.
Pour into tall glass.

Nutrients per serving:			
Calories	253	Cholesterol	0 mg
Fat	1 g	Sodium	5 mg

Orange Milk Shake

Makes 4 servings

2 cups skim milk
1 package (4-serving size) JELL-O® Brand
    Orange Flavor Sugar Free Gelatin
1 cup vanilla ice milk

Pour milk into blender container. Add remaining
ingredients; cover. Blend at high speed 30 seconds or
until smooth. Serve at once.

Note: *For a thicker shake, pour over crushed ice or add
1 cup crushed ice to ingredients in blender.*

Nutrients per serving:			
Calories	100	Cholesterol	10 mg
Fat	2 g	Sodium	150 mg

Sparkling Raspberry Mint Cooler

Makes 32 servings

1 to 2 cups fresh mint leaves
1 can (46 ounces) DOLE® Pineapple Juice,
    chilled
1 bottle (40 ounces) DOLE® Pure & Light
    Country Raspberry Juice
1 bottle (32 ounces) lemon-lime soda, chilled
1 package (12 ounces) frozen raspberries
1 DOLE® Lemon, thinly sliced

Rub mint leaves around sides of punch bowl, then
drop the bruised leaves in bottom of bowl. Combine
remaining ingredients in punch bowl.

Nutrients per serving (4 ounces):			
Calories	66	Cholesterol	0 mg
Fat	trace	Sodium	7 mg

Strawberry Banana Yogurt Shake

Makes 6 servings

2 cups cold skim milk
1 package (4-serving size) JELL-O® Brand
   Strawberry Flavor Sugar Free Gelatin
1 container (8 ounces) plain low-fat yogurt
1 cup crushed ice
1 large banana, cut into chunks

Pour milk into blender container. Add remaining ingredients; cover. Blend at high speed 30 seconds or until smooth. Serve at once.

Nutrients per serving:			
Calories	80	Cholesterol	5 mg
Fat	1 g	Sodium	115 mg

Birthday Punch

Makes 18 servings

2 quarts DOLE® Pineapple Juice
1 bottle (32 ounces) lemon-lime soda
1 can (12 ounces) frozen DOLE® Pine-Orange
   Banana Juice concentrate, thawed
   DOLE® citrus slices for garnish
   DOLE® Fresh Strawberries, halved (optional)

Combine all ingredients in large punch bowl.

Nutrients per serving (6 ounces):			
Calories	89	Cholesterol	0 mg
Fat	trace	Sodium	7 mg

Birthday Punch

Skim Milk Hot Cocoa

Makes two (7-ounce) servings

3 tablespoons sugar
2 tablespoons HERSHEY'S Cocoa
¼ cup hot water
1½ cups skim milk
⅛ teaspoon vanilla extract

Blend sugar and cocoa in small saucepan; gradually add hot water. Cook over medium heat, stirring constantly, until mixture boils; boil and stir for 2 minutes. Add milk; heat thoroughly. Stir occasionally; *do not boil.* Remove from heat; add vanilla. Serve hot.

Nutrients per serving:			
Calories	160	Cholesterol	5 mg
Fat	1 g	Sodium	100 mg

Gone Bananas Shake

Makes 4 servings

1½ cups skim milk
½ cup Light PHILADELPHIA BRAND®
   Pasteurized Process Cream Cheese Product
1 large banana, cut into chunks
3 tablespoons chocolate syrup
6 ice cubes

Gradually add milk to cream cheese product in blender or food processor container; cover. Blend until smooth. Add banana and syrup; blend until smooth. Add ice; blend 1 minute.

Prep time: 10 minutes

Nutrients per serving:			
Calories	160	Cholesterol	15 mg
Fat	5 g	Sodium	220 mg

Sunlight Sipper

Makes 1 serving

¾ cup DOLE® Pine-Passion-Banana Juice,
   chilled
1 tablespoon puréed peaches
1 tablespoon orange-flavored liqueur (optional)
1 teaspoon rum extract
   Cracked ice

Combine all ingredients in glass.

Nutrients per serving:			
Calories	106	Cholesterol	0 mg
Fat	trace	Sodium	9 mg

Hawaiian Tea

Makes 3 servings

3 cups DOLE® Pineapple Orange Juice
1 cinnamon stick
2 tablespoons chopped crystallized ginger
¼ teaspoon anise seeds
¼ teaspoon whole cloves
1 orange tea bag
1 peppermint tea bag
    Brown sugar (optional)
    Additional cinnamon sticks for garnish
       (optional)

Combine juice and spices in saucepan. Bring to a boil. Reduce heat to low; simmer 1 minute. Add tea bags. Cover and steep 5 to 7 minutes. Remove tea bags and spices. Sweeten with brown sugar, if desired. Garnish with additional cinnamon sticks, if desired.

Nutrients per serving:

Calories	170	Cholesterol	0 mg
Fat	trace	Sodium	17 mg

Orange Tea Punch

Makes about 16 servings, 4 quarts

4 cups brewed tea
2 cups orange juice, chilled
1 cup REALEMON® Lemon Juice from
       Concentrate
1 cup sugar
1 (1-liter) bottle ginger ale, chilled
1 quart BORDEN® or MEADOW GOLD®
       Orange Sherbet

In large pitcher, combine tea, orange juice, ReaLemon® brand and sugar; stir until sugar dissolves. Chill. Just before serving, pour tea mixture into large punch bowl; add ginger ale and scoops of sherbet.

Nutrients per serving:

Calories	82	Cholesterol	0 mg
Fat	trace	Sodium	9 mg

Banana-Raspberry Smoothie

Banana-Raspberry Smoothie

Makes 2 to 3 servings

2 ripe, medium DOLE® Bananas, peeled
1½ cups DOLE® Pure & Light Country
       Raspberry Juice, chilled
1 cup frozen vanilla yogurt, softened
1 cup DOLE® Fresh Raspberries

Place all ingredients in blender. Process until smooth.

Nutrients per serving:

Calories	196	Cholesterol	7 mg
Fat	2 g	Sodium	64 mg

Why oversleep when a bevy of breakfast delights awaits? Quick-to-fix muffins, fluffy pancakes and hearty cereals will provide the necessary energy and stamina to meet the morning's challenges. Enjoy a leisurely brunch this weekend with slimmed-down versions of your favorite egg entrées.

Blintzes with Raspberry Sauce

Makes 10 servings

Raspberry Sauce (recipe follows)
1 (16-ounce) container low-fat cottage cheese (1% milkfat)
3 tablespoons EGG BEATERS® 99% Real Egg Product
½ teaspoon sugar
10 prepared Crêpes (recipe follows)

Prepare Raspberry Sauce. Set aside. In small bowl, combine cottage cheese, Egg Beaters® and sugar; spread about 2 tablespoonfuls mixture down center of each crêpe. Fold crêpes into thirds; fold top and bottom of each crêpe to meet in center, forming blintzes. In lightly greased nonstick skillet, over medium heat, place blintzes seam-side down; cook 4 minutes or until golden brown. Turn over; cook 4 more minutes or until golden brown. Top with Raspberry Sauce and garnish as desired.

Raspberry Sauce: In blender or food processor, purée 1 (16-ounce) package thawed frozen raspberries; strain. Stir in 2 tablespoons sugar.

Crêpes

1 cup all-purpose flour
1 cup skim milk
½ cup EGG BEATERS® 99% Real Egg Product
1 tablespoon FLEISCHMANN'S® Margarine, melted

In medium bowl, blend flour, milk, Egg Beaters® and margarine; let stand 30 minutes.

Heat lightly greased 8-inch nonstick skillet or crêpe pan over medium-high heat. Pour in scant ¼ cup batter, tilting pan to cover bottom. Cook 1 to 2 minutes; turn crêpe over and cook 30 seconds to 1 minute more. Place on waxed paper. Stir batter and repeat to make a total of 10 crêpes.

Nutrients per serving:			
Calories	161	Cholesterol	2 mg
Fat	2 g	Sodium	231 mg

Latkes (Potato Pancakes)

Makes 12 pancakes

⅔ cup EGG BEATERS® 99% Real Egg Product
⅓ cup all-purpose flour
¼ cup grated onion
¼ teaspoon ground black pepper
4 large potatoes, peeled and shredded (about 4 cups)
3 tablespoons FLEISCHMANN'S® Margarine, divided
1½ cups sweetened applesauce

In medium bowl, combine Egg Beaters®, flour, onion and pepper; set aside.

Pat shredded potatoes dry with paper towel. Stir into Egg Beaters® mixture. In skillet, over medium-high heat, melt 1½ tablespoons margarine. For each pancake, spoon ⅓ cup potato mixture into skillet, spreading into 4-inch circle. Cook for 5 to 6 minutes, turning over once to brown both sides. Remove and keep warm. Repeat to make a total of 12 pancakes, using remaining margarine as needed. Garnish as desired and serve topped with applesauce.

Nutrients per serving (1 pancake plus 2 tablespoons applesauce):			
Calories	115	Cholesterol	0 mg
Fat	3 g	Sodium	52 mg

Clockwise from top right: Jam French Toast Triangles (page 40),
Blintzes with Raspberry Sauce, Latkes (Potato Pancakes)

Rainbow Trout Breakfast Fillet

Rainbow Trout Breakfast Fillets

Makes 4 servings

½ cup all-purpose flour
1½ teaspoons paprika
1 teaspoon ground thyme
¼ teaspoon salt
   Dash black pepper
4 CLEAR SPRINGS® Brand Idaho Rainbow
   Trout fillets (4 ounces *each*)
1 egg, beaten
1 tablespoon olive oil

Combine flour, paprika, thyme, salt and pepper on waxed paper; set aside. Dip each trout fillet in egg; coat with seasoned flour mixture. Cook trout in hot oil in large skillet over medium-high heat 1 to 2 minutes per side or until fish flakes easily with fork. Serve with fruit and potatoes, if desired. Garnish as desired.

Nutrients per serving:

Calories	240	Cholesterol	115 mg
Fat	9 g	Sodium	179 mg

Banana Bran Loaf

Makes 1 loaf, 16 servings

1 cup mashed ripe bananas (about 2 large)
½ cup granulated sugar
⅓ cup liquid vegetable oil margarine
⅓ cup skim milk
2 egg whites, slightly beaten
1¼ cups all-purpose flour
1 cup QUAKER® Oat Bran hot cereal, uncooked
2 teaspoons baking powder
½ teaspoon baking soda

Heat oven to 350°F. Lightly spray 8×4-inch or 9×5-inch loaf pan with nonstick cooking spray, or oil lightly. Combine bananas, sugar, margarine, milk and egg whites; mix well. Add combined flour, oat bran, baking powder and baking soda, mixing just until moistened. Pour into prepared pan. Bake 55 to 60 minutes or until wooden toothpick inserted in center comes out clean. Cool 10 minutes; remove from pan. Cool completely on wire rack.

Tips: To freeze bread slices, layer waxed paper between each slice of bread. Wrap securely in foil or place in freezer bag. Seal, label and freeze.

To reheat bread slices, unwrap frozen bread slices and wrap in paper towels. Microwave at HIGH (100% power) about 30 seconds for each slice, or until warm.

Nutrients per serving (1 slice):

Calories	130	Cholesterol	0 mg
Fat	4 g	Sodium	110 mg

Jam French Toast Triangles

Makes 6 pieces

¼ cup preserves, any flavor
6 slices whole wheat bread, divided
6 tablespoons EGG BEATERS®
   99% Real Egg Product
¼ cup skim milk
2 tablespoons FLEISCHMANN'S® Margarine
1 tablespoon sugar
¼ teaspoon ground cinnamon

Evenly divide and spread preserves on 3 bread slices; top with remaining bread slices to make 3 sandwiches, pressing to seal. Cut each sandwich diagonally in half. In shallow bowl, combine Egg Beaters® and skim milk. Dip each sandwich in egg mixture to coat.

In skillet or on griddle, over medium-high heat, brown sandwiches in margarine until golden brown on both sides. Combine sugar and cinnamon; sprinkle over sandwiches. Garnish as desired and serve warm.

Nutrients per serving (1 piece):

Calories	175	Cholesterol	1 mg
Fat	5 g	Sodium	224 mg

Rice Bran Granola Cereal

Makes 10 servings, 5 cups

2 cups uncooked old-fashioned rolled oats
1 cup crisp rice cereal
¾ cup rice bran
¾ cup raisins
⅓ cup slivered almonds
1 tablespoon ground cinnamon
⅓ cup honey
1 tablespoon margarine, melted
Nonstick cooking spray

Combine oats, cereal, bran, raisins, almonds, and cinnamon in large bowl; stir in honey and margarine. Spread mixture on baking sheet coated with nonstick cooking spray. Bake in preheated 350°F oven for 8 to 10 minutes. Let cool. Serve as a topping for yogurt and/or fresh fruit. Store in a tightly covered container.

Tip: Can be served as a cereal (with milk) or as a snack.

Nutrients per serving (½ cup cereal only):			
Calories	199	Cholesterol	0 mg
Fat	7 g	Sodium	57 mg

Favorite recipe from **USA Rice Council**

Banana-Orange Muffins

Makes 12 muffins

2 cups all-purpose flour
1 tablespoon baking powder
¼ teaspoon salt
2 egg whites
½ cup *undiluted* CARNATION® Lite Evaporated Skimmed Milk
½ cup mashed very ripe banana
⅓ cup honey
¼ cup vegetable oil
1 teaspoon grated orange zest
1 tablespoon granulated sugar

In large bowl, combine flour, baking powder and salt; set aside. In small mixer bowl, slightly beat egg whites. Add evaporated skimmed milk, banana, honey, oil and orange zest; beat until blended. Add liquid ingredients to dry ingredients; stir *just* until moistened. Mixture will be lumpy. Spoon batter into 12 greased or paper-lined 2½-inch muffin cups. Sprinkle tops with sugar. Bake in preheated 400°F oven 13 to 15 minutes or until wooden pick inserted in center comes out clean. Remove from pan; cool on wire rack.

Nutrients per serving (1 muffin):			
Calories	169	Cholesterol	0 mg
Fat	5 g	Sodium	175 mg

Lemon Blueberry Poppy Seed Bread

Makes 1 loaf, 12 servings

Bread
1 package DUNCAN HINES® Bakery Style Blueberry Muffin Mix
2 tablespoons poppy seeds
1 egg
¾ cup water
1 tablespoon grated lemon peel

Drizzle
½ cup confectioners sugar
1 tablespoon lemon juice

1. Preheat oven to 350°F. Grease and flour 8×4-inch loaf pan.

2. Rinse blueberries with cold water and drain.

3. For Bread, combine muffin mix and poppy seeds in medium bowl. Break up any lumps. Add egg and water. Stir until moistened, about 50 strokes. Fold in blueberries and lemon peel. Pour into pan. Sprinkle with contents of topping packet from mix.

4. Bake at 350°F for 57 to 62 minutes or until wooden toothpick inserted in center comes out clean. Cool in pan 10 minutes. Loosen loaf from pan. Invert onto cooling rack. Turn right side up. Cool completely.

5. For Drizzle, combine confectioners sugar and lemon juice in small bowl. Stir until smooth. Drizzle over loaf.

Tip: To help keep topping intact when removing loaf from pan, place aluminum foil over top.

Nutrients per serving (1 slice):			
Calories	133	Cholesterol	18 mg
Fat	2 g	Sodium	186 mg

Lemon Blueberry Poppy Seed Bread

Cinnamon Spiced Muffins

Makes 36 miniature or 12 regular-size muffins

1½ cups all-purpose flour
½ cup sugar
2 teaspoons baking powder
½ teaspoon salt
½ teaspoon ground nutmeg
½ teaspoon ground coriander
½ teaspoon ground allspice
½ cup low-fat milk
⅓ cup margarine, melted
1 egg
¼ cup sugar
1 teaspoon ground cinnamon
¼ cup margarine, melted

Preheat oven to 400°F. Grease 36 miniature muffin cups. In large bowl, combine flour, ½ cup sugar, baking powder, salt, nutmeg, coriander and allspice. In small bowl, combine milk, ⅓ cup margarine and egg. Stir into flour mixture just until moistened.

Spoon into muffin cups. Bake 10 to 13 minutes or until edges are lightly browned and wooden toothpick inserted in centers comes out clean. Remove from pan.

Meanwhile, combine ¼ cup sugar and cinnamon in a shallow dish. Roll warm muffin tops in ¼ cup margarine, then sugar-cinnamon mixture. Serve warm.

Cinnamon Spiced Muffins

To Microwave: Line 6 (2½-inch) microwavable muffin-pan cups with double paper liners. Prepare batter as directed. Spoon batter into each cup, filling ½ full. Microwave at HIGH (100% power) 2½ to 4½ minutes or until wooden toothpick inserted in centers comes out clean. Rotate dish ½ turn halfway through cooking. Let stand 5 minutes. Remove from pan. Repeat procedure with remaining batter.

Meanwhile, combine ¼ cup sugar and cinnamon in a shallow dish. Roll warm muffin tops in ¼ cup margarine, then sugar-cinnamon mixture. Serve warm.

Nutrients per serving (1 miniature muffin):			
Calories	64	Cholesterol	6 mg
Fat	3 g	Sodium	86 mg

Nutrients per serving (1 regular-size muffin):			
Calories	193	Cholesterol	18 mg
Fat	9 g	Sodium	257 mg

Pineapple-Almond Date Bread

Makes 28 servings

1 cup DOLE® Sliced Almonds, divided
¾ cup sugar
½ cup margarine, softened
1 egg
1 can (8¼ ounces) DOLE® Crushed Pineapple
  in Syrup or Juice
1 tablespoon grated orange peel
2 cups all-purpose flour
1 teaspoon baking powder
1 teaspoon baking soda
¼ teaspoon ground nutmeg
1 cup DOLE® Chopped Dates

Toast ¾ cup almonds; reserve remaining ¼ cup for topping. Beat sugar and margarine in large bowl until light and fluffy. Beat in egg until blended. Stir in undrained pineapple and orange peel. Combine flour, baking powder, baking soda and nutmeg in medium bowl. Beat into pineapple mixture until blended. Stir in ¾ cup toasted almonds and dates. Pour batter into well-greased 9×5-inch loaf pan. Sprinkle remaining ¼ cup untoasted almonds on top. Bake in 350°F oven 55 to 60 minutes or until cake tester inserted in center comes out clean. Cool in pan on wire rack 10 minutes. Remove from pan. Cool completely on wire rack before slicing. To serve, cut loaf into 14 slices, then cut each slice lengthwise in half.

Prep time: 15 minutes
Bake time: 60 minutes

Nutrients per serving:			
Calories	147	Cholesterol	10 mg
Fat	7 g	Sodium	83 mg

Brunch Quesadillas with Fruit Salsa

Brunch Quesadillas with Fruit Salsa

Makes 4 servings

1 pint fresh strawberries, hulled and diced
1 fresh ripe Anjou pear, cored and diced
1 tablespoon chopped fresh cilantro
1 tablespoon honey
1 cup (4 ounces) SARGENTO® Preferred Light Fancy Supreme Shredded Mozzarella Cheese
4 flour tortillas (8 inches in diameter)
2 teaspoons light margarine, melted
2 tablespoons light sour cream

To make Fruit Salsa, combine strawberries, pear, cilantro and honey in medium bowl; set aside.

Sprinkle 2 tablespoons cheese on one half of each tortilla. Top with ⅓ cup Fruit Salsa (drain and discard any liquid from fruit) and another 2 tablespoons cheese. Fold tortillas in half. Brush top of each folded tortilla with some of the melted margarine.

Grill folded tortillas, greased sides down, in dry preheated skillet until light golden brown and crisp, about 2 minutes. Brush tops with remaining melted margarine; turn and brown other sides. Remove to serving plate or platter. Cut each tortilla in half. Serve with remaining Fruit Salsa. Garnish with sour cream. Serve immediately.

Nutrients per serving:

Calories	278	Cholesterol	14 mg
Fat	9 g	Sodium	264 mg

Rice Bran Buttermilk Pancakes

Rice Bran Buttermilk Pancakes

Makes about 10 (4-inch) pancakes

1 cup rice flour or all-purpose flour
¾ cup rice bran
1 tablespoon sugar
1 teaspoon baking powder
½ teaspoon baking soda
1¼ cups low-fat buttermilk
3 egg whites, beaten
Nonstick cooking spray
Fresh fruit or reduced-calorie syrup (optional)

Sift together flour, bran, sugar, baking powder, and baking soda into large bowl. Combine buttermilk and egg whites in small bowl; add to flour mixture. Stir until smooth. Pour ¼ cup batter onto hot griddle coated with nonstick cooking spray. Cook over medium heat until bubbles form on top and underside is lightly browned. Turn to brown other side. Serve with fresh fruit or syrup.

Variation: For Cinnamon Pancakes, add 1 teaspoon ground cinnamon to dry ingredients.

Nutrients per serving (1 pancake):			
Calories	99	Cholesterol	1 mg
Fat	2 g	Sodium	119 mg

Favorite recipe from **USA Rice Council**

Alpine Fruited Oatmeal

Makes 6 servings

2 cups QUAKER® Oats (quick or old fashioned, uncooked)*
1 cup apple juice
1 cup water
¾ cup diced, dried mixed fruit or raisins
¼ teaspoon ground cinnamon
¼ teaspoon salt (optional)

Combine all ingredients; mix well. Cover; refrigerate at least 8 hours or overnight. Stir well before serving. Serve cold or hot with milk or yogurt, if desired. Store tightly covered in refrigerator for up to 1 week.

*Or, substitute 1 cup QUAKER® Oat Bran hot cereal, uncooked, for 1 cup of the oats.

Note: To heat, place ½ cup cereal in microwavable bowl. Microwave at HIGH (100% power) about 1½ minutes; stir.

Nutrients per serving (½ cup):			
Calories	175	Cholesterol	0 mg
Fat	2 g	Sodium	5 mg

Aloha Muffins

Makes 12 muffins

1½ cups whole wheat flour
¾ cup sugar
¼ cup oat bran
1½ teaspoons baking powder
¾ teaspoon baking soda
1 teaspoon ground cinnamon
¼ teaspoon ground nutmeg
2 cans (8 ounces *each*) DOLE® Crushed Pineapple, drained, ¼ cup juice reserved
½ cup DOLE® Raisins
3 egg whites
¼ cup *plus* 1 tablespoon vegetable oil
½ teaspoon almond extract
¼ cup DOLE® Sliced Almonds

Preheat oven to 350°F. Combine flour, sugar, oat bran, baking powder, baking soda, cinnamon and nutmeg in small bowl. Combine drained pineapple, reserved ¼ cup juice, raisins, egg whites, oil and almond extract in large bowl. Stir dry ingredients into pineapple mixture until just moistened. Spoon into 12 greased 2½-inch muffin cups. Top with almonds. Bake 25 minutes. Remove from pan; cool on wire rack.

Nutrients per serving (1 muffin):			
Calories	226	Cholesterol	0 mg
Fat	8 g	Sodium	112 mg

Cheese 'n' Apple Spread

Makes 1⅔ cups

1 package (8 ounces) Light PHILADELPHIA BRAND® Neufchatel Cheese, softened
½ cup KRAFT® FREE® Nonfat Mayonnaise Dressing
½ cup (2 ounces) KRAFT® Light Naturals Shredded Mild Reduced Fat Cheddar Cheese
½ cup finely chopped apple

Blend together neufchatel cheese and dressing. Stir in Cheddar cheese and apple; refrigerate. Serve on toasted bagelette halves.

Prep time: 10 minutes plus refrigerating

Nutrients per serving (2 tablespoons):			
Calories	82	Cholesterol	5 mg
Fat	3 g	Sodium	420 mg

Country Breakfast Cereal

Makes 6 servings

3 cups cooked brown rice
2 cups skim milk
½ cup raisins or chopped prunes
1 tablespoon margarine (optional)
1 teaspoon ground cinnamon
⅛ teaspoon salt
    Honey or brown sugar (optional)
    Fresh fruit (optional)

Combine rice, milk, raisins, margarine, cinnamon, and salt in 2- to 3-quart saucepan. Bring to a boil; stir once or twice. Reduce heat to medium-low; cover and simmer 8 to 10 minutes or until thickened. Serve with honey and fresh fruit.

Nutrients per serving:

Calories	174	Cholesterol	2 mg
Fat	1 g	Sodium	98 mg

Favorite recipe from **USA Rice Council**

Pineapple-Orange Sauce

Makes 8 servings, about 2 cups

1 can (20 ounces) DOLE® Pineapple Chunks in Juice, undrained
    Juice and grated peel from 1 DOLE® Orange
1 tablespoon cornstarch
1 tablespoon sugar
1 teaspoon ground ginger

Combine pineapple with juice, ½ cup orange juice and 1 teaspoon orange peel with remaining ingredients in saucepan. Cook and stir until sauce boils and thickens. Cool to room temperature.

Use sauce over frozen yogurt, pancakes or waffles.

Nutrients per serving (about ¼ cup sauce):

Calories	64	Cholesterol	0 mg
Fat	trace	Sodium	1 mg

Pineapple-Orange Sauce

Lemon-Glazed Peach Muffins

Makes 8 muffins

1 cup all-purpose flour
3 tablespoons sugar
2 teaspoons baking powder
½ teaspoon salt
½ teaspoon pumpkin pie spice
1 can (16 ounces) sliced cling peaches in light syrup
1 cup KELLOGG'S® ALL-BRAN® Cereal
½ cup skim milk
1 egg white
2 tablespoons vegetable oil
    Lemon Sauce (recipe follows)

Stir together flour, sugar, baking powder, salt and pumpkin pie spice. Set aside. Drain peaches, reserving ⅓ cup syrup. Set aside 8 peach slices; chop remaining peach slices.

Measure Kellogg's® All-Bran® cereal, milk and ⅓ cup reserved syrup into large mixing bowl. Stir to combine. Let stand 2 minutes or until cereal is softened. Add egg white and oil. Beat well. Stir in chopped peaches.

Add flour mixture, stirring only until dry ingredients are moistened. Portion batter evenly into 8 lightly greased 2½-inch muffin pan cups. Place 1 peach slice over top of each muffin.

Bake at 400°F for 25 minutes or until golden brown. Serve warm with Lemon Sauce.

Lemon Sauce

⅓ cup sugar
2 tablespoons cornstarch
1½ cups cold water
1 teaspoon grated lemon peel
1 tablespoon lemon juice

Combine sugar and cornstarch in 2-quart saucepan. Add water, stirring until smooth. Cook over medium heat, stirring constantly, until mixture boils. Continue cooking and stirring 3 minutes longer. Remove from heat; stir in lemon peel and juice. Serve hot over warm peach muffins.

Nutrients per serving (1 muffin plus 3 tablespoons sauce):

Calories	210	Cholesterol	1 mg
Fat	4 g	Sodium	355 mg

Bacon Morning Muffins

Makes 12 muffins

**12 slices LOUIS RICH® Turkey Bacon, cut into
 ¼-inch pieces**
1¼ cups all-purpose flour
 1 cup quick-cooking oats, uncooked
 2 teaspoons baking powder
 ½ cup skim milk
 ⅓ cup honey
 ¼ cup corn oil
 2 large egg whites

Combine Turkey Bacon, flour, oats and baking
powder in large mixing bowl. Combine remaining
ingredients; add to bacon mixture. Stir just until
moistened (batter will be lumpy). Spray 12 (2½-inch)
muffin cups with nonstick cooking spray or line with
paper bake cups. Spoon batter into muffin cups.
Bake in 400°F oven 15 minutes. Refrigerate or freeze
leftover muffins.

Nutrients per serving (1 muffin):

Calories	185	Cholesterol	10 mg
Fat	8 g	Sodium	260 mg

Breakfast in a Cup

Italian Baked Frittata

Makes 6 servings

 1 cup broccoli flowerettes
 ½ cup sliced mushrooms
 ½ small red bell pepper, cut into rings
 2 green onions, cut into 1-inch pieces
 2 teaspoons FLEISCHMANN'S® Margarine
 **2 (8-ounce) containers EGG BEATERS®
 99% Real Egg Product**
 **½ cup low-sodium low-fat cottage cheese
 (1% milkfat)**
 2 tablespoons GREY POUPON® Dijon Mustard
 ½ teaspoon Italian seasoning

In 10-inch nonstick ovenproof skillet, over medium-
high heat, cook and stir broccoli, mushrooms, red
pepper and green onions in margarine until tender-
crisp, about 3 minutes. Remove from heat.

In large bowl, with electric mixer at medium speed,
beat Egg Beaters®, cottage cheese, mustard and
Italian seasoning until foamy, about 3 minutes. Pour
into skillet over vegetables. Bake at 375°F for 20 to
25 minutes or until set. Serve immediately.

Nutrients per serving:

Calories	68	Cholesterol	1 mg
Fat	2 g	Sodium	270 mg

Breakfast in a Cup

Makes 12 servings

 3 cups cooked rice
 **1 cup (4 ounces) shredded Cheddar cheese,
 divided**
 1 can (4 ounces) diced green chilies, drained
 1 jar (2 ounces) diced pimientos, drained
 ⅓ cup skim milk
 2 eggs, beaten
 ½ teaspoon ground cumin
 ½ teaspoon salt
 ½ teaspoon ground black pepper
 Nonstick cooking spray

Combine rice, ½ cup cheese, chilies, pimientos,
milk, eggs, cumin, salt, and pepper in large bowl.
Divide mixture evenly into 12 muffin cups coated
with nonstick cooking spray. Sprinkle with remaining
½ cup cheese. Bake at 400°F for 15 minutes or
until set.

Tip: *Breakfast in a Cup may be stored in the freezer in
freezer bags or tightly sealed containers. To reheat,
microwave each frozen cup on HIGH (100% power)
1 minute.*

Nutrients per serving (1 cup):

Calories	123	Cholesterol	45 mg
Fat	4 g	Sodium	368 mg

Favorite recipe from **USA Rice Council**

Peachy Cinnamon Coffee Cake

Brunch Sandwiches

Makes 4 servings

- 1 carton (8 ounces) HEALTHY CHOICE® Cholesterol Free Egg Product
- ¼ cup nonfat mayonnaise
- ½ teaspoon Dijon-style mustard
  Dash black pepper
- 4 whole wheat English muffins, toasted
- 4 lettuce leaves
- 4 slices tomato

In 8-inch skillet sprayed with nonstick cooking spray, cook egg product, covered, over very low heat 10 minutes or until just set. Cut egg product into 4 wedges.

In small bowl, combine mayonnaise, mustard and pepper. To make sandwiches, spread 4 bottom muffin halves evenly with mayonnaise mixture. Top with egg product, tomato, and lettuce. Top with remaining muffin halves.

Nutrients per serving:

Calories	190	Cholesterol	0 mg
Fat	2 g	Sodium	560 mg

Peachy Cinnamon Coffee Cake

Makes 9 servings

- 1 can (8¼ ounces) juice pack sliced yellow cling peaches
  Water
- 1 package DUNCAN HINES® Bakery Style Cinnamon Swirl with Crumb Topping Muffin Mix
- 1 egg

1. Preheat oven to 400°F. Grease 8-inch square or 9-inch round pan.

2. Drain peaches, reserving juice. Add water to reserved juice to equal ¾ cup liquid. Chop peaches.

3. Combine muffin mix, egg and ¾ cup peach liquid in medium bowl; fold in peaches. Pour batter into pan. Knead swirl packet 10 seconds before opening. Squeeze contents on top of batter and swirl with knife. Sprinkle topping over batter.

4. Bake at 400°F for 28 to 33 minutes for 8-inch pan (or for 20 to 25 minutes for 9-inch pan) or until golden. Serve warm.

Nutrients per serving:

Calories	205	Cholesterol	0 mg
Fat	7 g	Sodium	248 mg

Orange Chocolate Chip Bread

Makes 16 servings

- 1 cup skim milk
- ¼ cup orange juice
- ⅓ cup sugar
- 1 egg, slightly beaten
- 1 tablespoon grated fresh orange peel
- 3 cups all-purpose biscuit baking mix
- ½ cup HERSHEY₂S MINI CHIPS® Semi-Sweet Chocolate

Combine milk, orange juice, sugar, egg and orange peel in small bowl. Place baking mix in medium mixing bowl. Stir milk mixture into baking mix, beating until well combined, about 1 minute. Stir in Mini Chips®. Pour into greased 9×5×3-inch loaf pan. Bake at 350°F for 45 to 50 minutes or until cake tester inserted in center comes out clean. Cool in pan on wire rack 10 minutes; remove from pan. Cool completely. Slice and serve. To store leftovers, wrap in foil or plastic wrap.

Nutrients per serving (1 slice):

Calories	161	Cholesterol	17 mg
Fat	5 g	Sodium	274 mg

Banana-Cinnamon Rolls

Makes 12 servings

¼ cup granulated sugar
1 teaspoon ground cinnamon
2 cups KELLOGG'S® RAISIN BRAN® Cereal
½ cup mashed ripe banana
½ cup milk
1 egg
1 teaspoon vanilla
1¾ cups all-purpose flour
4 teaspoons baking powder
½ teaspoon salt
½ cup cold margarine

Frosting
1½ cups confectioners' sugar
2 tablespoons hot water
1 tablespoon lemon juice
¼ cup sliced almonds (optional)

Combine granulated sugar and cinnamon; set aside.

Measure Kellogg's® Raisin Bran® cereal, banana and milk into large mixing bowl. Stir to combine. Let stand 2 minutes or until cereal softens. Add egg and vanilla; beat well.

In large mixing bowl, combine flour, baking powder and salt. Using pastry blender, cut in margarine until mixture resembles coarse crumbs. Add cereal mixture, stirring only until combined.

On lightly floured surface, gently knead dough 10 times. Roll out dough to measure 12×10-inch rectangle. Sprinkle dough with sugar mixture. Starting with long side, roll up dough jelly-roll style. Cut roll into twelve 1-inch pieces. Place, cut-side-down, in greased 13×9-inch pan.

Bake in 400°F oven about 25 minutes or until lightly browned. Invert onto serving plate.

For frosting, stir together confectioners' sugar, water and lemon juice until smooth. Spread over hot rolls and sprinkle with almonds. Serve warm.

Nutrients per serving (1 roll):			
Calories	260	Cholesterol	19 mg
Fat	9 g	Sodium	360 mg

Fruit & Ham Kabobs

Makes 8 to 10 kabobs

¾ cup pineapple juice
¼ cup packed brown sugar
2 tablespoons unsalted margarine or butter
1 ARMOUR® Lower Salt Ham Nugget (about 1¾ pounds), cut into 1¼-inch cubes
2 large red apples, cored and cut into sixths
2 large green apples, cored and cut into sixths
1 fresh pineapple, peeled, cored and cut into 1-inch chunks
3 kiwifruit, peeled and cut into ½-inch slices

Preheat oven to 350°F. Place pineapple juice, brown sugar and margarine in bottom of large casserole dish. Heat in oven until margarine is melted. Thread ham, apples, pineapple and kiwifruit onto 8 to 10 (10-inch) metal or wooden skewers, alternating ingredients. Place kabobs in warm sauce; turn to coat all sides with sauce. Bake 20 to 25 minutes, or until heated through. Turn kabobs twice during cooking, basting with sauce mixture. Serve over rice and garnish with red grapes, if desired.

Nutrients per serving (1 kabob):			
Calories	277	Cholesterol	39 mg
Fat	7 g	Sodium	676 mg

Fruit & Ham Kabobs

Fresh Strawberry Banana Omelets

Makes 2 servings

1 cup fresh strawberries, hulled and sliced
1 banana, sliced
1½ tablespoons sugar
¼ teaspoon grated lemon peel
1 tablespoon fresh lemon juice
1 cup egg substitute *or* 4 eggs, beaten
¼ teaspoon salt
2 tablespoons margarine, divided

Combine strawberries, banana, sugar, lemon peel and juice in medium bowl; mix lightly. Cover; let stand 15 minutes. Meanwhile, mix egg substitute and salt with fork in small bowl.

Heat 1 tablespoon margarine in 8-inch omelet pan or skillet over medium-high heat until just hot enough to sizzle a drop of water. Pour in half of egg mixture (about ½ cup). Mixture should set at edges at once. With back of pancake turner, carefully push cooked portions of edges toward center so that uncooked portions flow underneath. Slide pan rapidly back and forth over heat to keep mixture in motion. While top is still moist and creamy-looking, spoon ½ cup fruit mixture over half of omelet. With pancake turner, fold in half; turn onto heated platter. Keep warm. Repeat with remaining margarine, egg mixture and ½ cup fruit mixture. Top omelets with remaining fruit mixture.

Nutrients per serving:			
Calories	267	Cholesterol	1 mg
Fat	10 g	Sodium	556 mg

Irish Soda Bacon Bread

Makes 12 to 15 servings

4 cups all-purpose flour
3 tablespoons sugar
1½ tablespoons low-sodium baking powder
1 teaspoon baking soda
6 tablespoons unsalted margarine or butter, cold
1 cup golden raisins
6 slices ARMOUR® Lower Salt Bacon, cooked crisp and crumbled
2 eggs
1½ cups buttermilk

Preheat oven to 375°F. Combine flour, sugar, baking powder and baking soda in large bowl; cut in cold margarine until mixture resembles coarse crumbs.

Stir in raisins and bacon. Beat eggs slightly in small bowl; reserve 1 tablespoon egg. Add buttermilk and remaining eggs to flour mixture; stir to make soft dough.

Turn out onto lightly floured surface; knead 1 to 2 minutes or until smooth. Shape dough into round loaf. Spray round 2-quart casserole dish with nonstick cooking spray; place dough in dish. With floured knife, cut a 4-inch cross about ¼ inch deep on top of loaf. Brush loaf with reserved egg.

Bake 55 to 65 minutes or until wooden toothpick inserted in center comes out clean. (Cover loaf with foil during last 30 minutes of baking to prevent overbrowning.) Cool on wire rack 10 minutes; remove from dish. Serve with light cream cheese or honey butter, if desired.

Nutrients per serving:			
Calories	231	Cholesterol	40 mg
Fat	7 g	Sodium	130 mg

Fiber-Rich Muffins

Makes 12 muffins

1 inner-pack KAVLI® Rye-Bran Crispbread (½ package)
1 cup skim milk
½ cup unsweetened applesauce
1 egg, lightly beaten
2 tablespoons firmly packed brown sugar
2 tablespoons vegetable oil
1 tablespoon molasses
½ teaspoon ground cinnamon
¼ teaspoon ground cloves
¼ teaspoon ground nutmeg
¼ teaspoon salt
1¼ cups all-purpose flour
1 tablespoon baking powder

Preheat oven to 400°F. Break crispbread into chunks; process in food processor or blender until finely crushed. Place in mixing bowl. Heat milk to almost boiling. Pour over bread crumbs. Stir to mix. Let stand 5 minutes. Stir applesauce and egg into crumb mixture. Break up large lumps, if present. Add sugar, oil, molasses, spices and salt. Combine flour and baking powder. Add to crumb mixture, stirring just until flour is moistened. Fill 12 greased 2½-inch muffin cups half full. Bake 20 to 25 minutes or until browned. Remove from pans and cool slightly on wire rack before serving.

Nutrients per serving (1 muffin):			
Calories	124	Cholesterol	22 mg
Fat	3 g	Sodium	152 mg

Fresh Strawberry Banana Omelet

Bran-Cherry Bread

Makes 1 loaf, 15 slices

2 cups all-purpose flour
¾ cup sugar, divided
1 tablespoon baking powder
1 teaspoon salt
½ teaspoon ground nutmeg
1½ cups KELLOGG'S® CRACKLIN' OAT BRAN®
    Cereal
1¼ cups skim milk
1 egg
2 tablespoons vegetable oil
1 jar (10 ounces) maraschino cherries, drained
    and finely chopped
1 cup chopped walnuts, divided
1 tablespoon margarine

Combine flour, ½ cup sugar, baking powder, salt and nutmeg. Set aside.

Measure Kellogg's® Cracklin' Oat Bran® cereal and milk into large mixing bowl. Let stand 10 minutes or until cereal is softened. Add egg and oil. Beat well. Stir in flour mixture. Set aside 2 tablespoons chopped cherries. Fold remaining cherries and ¾ cup nuts into batter. Spread in 9×5×3-inch loaf pan coated with nonstick cooking spray.

Melt margarine in small skillet until bubbly. Remove from heat. Stir in remaining ¼ cup sugar, remaining ¼ cup nuts and reserved cherries. Sprinkle over batter.

Bake at 350°F about 1 hour. Cool in pan on wire rack 10 minutes. Remove from pan.

Nutrients per serving (1 slice):

Calories	240	Cholesterol	20 mg
Fat	9 g	Sodium	260 mg

Bran-Cherry Bread

Double Bran-Lemon Muffins

Makes 12 muffins

1 cup 100% wheat bran cereal
½ cup oat bran
    Grated peel of 1 SUNKIST® Lemon
½ cup fresh squeezed lemon juice (3 SUNKIST®
    Lemons)
½ cup nonfat milk
1¼ cups all-purpose flour
2 teaspoons baking powder
½ teaspoon baking soda
¼ cup firmly packed brown sugar
2 egg whites
¼ cup honey
¼ cup vegetable oil

In medium bowl, combine wheat bran cereal, oat bran, lemon peel, lemon juice and milk; let stand 10 minutes. In large bowl, sift together flour, baking powder and baking soda; stir in brown sugar. In small bowl, beat egg whites until foamy; add honey and oil. Stir egg mixture into bran mixture; mix well. Add to dry ingredients all at once; stir just until dry ingredients are moistened. Quickly spoon into 12 paper-lined 2½-inch muffin cups; fill about ⅞ full. (Or, spray muffin pan with nonstick cooking spray.) Bake at 400°F for 20 to 23 minutes.

Nutrients per serving (1 muffin):

Calories	153	Cholesterol	0 mg
Fat	5 g	Sodium	138 mg

Weekend Skillet Breakfast

Makes 4 servings

12 slices LOUIS RICH® Turkey Bacon, cut into
    ½-inch pieces
1 medium potato, peeled and cut into small
    cubes
2 green onions with tops, thinly sliced
½ teaspoon chili powder
1 carton (8 ounces) cholesterol-free egg
    substitute or 4 eggs, beaten

Place Turkey Bacon and potato in nonstick skillet. Cook over medium heat about 12 minutes, stirring frequently until potatoes are fork-tender. Stir in onions and chili powder; pour egg substitute evenly over mixture. Cover; reduce heat to low. Cook 5 minutes more or until mixture is set. Cut into wedges.

Nutrients per serving:

Calories	155	Cholesterol	30 mg
Fat	7 g	Sodium	650 mg

Breakfast Burrito

Breakfast Burritos

Makes 2 burritos

4 slices LOUIS RICH® Turkey Bacon
2 flour tortillas (7 inches in diameter)
2 tablespoons shredded sharp Cheddar cheese
2 large egg whites
1 tablespoon chopped mild chilies
   Salsa or taco sauce (optional)
   Additional shredded sharp Cheddar cheese
   (optional)

Cook and stir Turkey Bacon in nonstick skillet over medium-high heat 8 to 10 minutes or until lightly browned.

Place 2 turkey bacon slices on each tortilla; sprinkle each tortilla with 1 tablespoon cheese.

Beat egg whites and chilies; add to hot skillet. Cook and stir about 2 minutes or until set.

Divide egg mixture between tortillas. Fold tortillas over filling. Top with salsa and additional cheese, if desired.

To keep burritos warm: *Wrap filled burritos in foil and place in warm oven up to 30 minutes.*

Nutrients per serving (1 burrito):

Calories	220	Cholesterol	25 mg
Fat	9 g	Sodium	470 mg

Bran Sticky Buns

Makes 9 buns

1 cup NABISCO® 100% Bran, divided
⅓ cup firmly packed light brown sugar
¼ cup FLEISCHMANN'S® Margarine, melted
1 apple, cored and sliced
2 cups buttermilk baking mix
½ cup water
¼ cup EGG BEATERS® 99% Real Egg Product
   or 2 egg whites

In small bowl, combine ¼ cup bran, brown sugar and margarine; spread in 8×8×2-inch pan. Top with apple slices; set aside. In medium bowl, combine baking mix, remaining ¾ cup bran, water and Egg Beaters® until soft dough forms. Drop dough by ¼ cupfuls over apple slices. Bake at 450°F for 13 to 15 minutes or until done. Invert onto heat-proof plate, leaving pan over buns for 2 to 3 minutes. Cool slightly; serve warm.

Nutrients per serving (1 bun):

Calories	225	Cholesterol	0 mg
Fat	6 g	Sodium	435 mg

Apricot Date Mini-Loaves

Apricot Date Mini-Loaves

Makes 16 servings, 4 mini-loaves

**1 package DUNCAN HINES® Bakery Style
   Cinnamon Swirl Muffin Mix**
½ teaspoon baking powder
2 egg whites
⅔ cup water
½ cup chopped dried apricots
½ cup chopped dates

1. Preheat oven to 350°F. Grease four 5⅜×2⅝×1⅞-inch pans.

2. Combine muffin mix and baking powder in large bowl. Break up any lumps. Add egg whites, water, apricots and dates. Stir until well blended, about 50 strokes.

3. Knead swirl packet for 10 seconds before opening. Cut off one end of swirl packet. Squeeze contents onto batter. Swirl into batter with knife or spatula, folding from bottom of bowl to get an even swirl. Do not completely mix into batter. Divide evenly into pans. Sprinkle with contents of topping packet from mix.

4. Bake at 350°F for 30 to 35 minutes or until wooden toothpick inserted in centers comes out clean. Cool in pans 15 minutes. Loosen loaves from pans. Lift out with knife. Place on cooling racks. Cool completely.

Tip: Recipe may also be baked in 1 greased 8½×4½×2½-inch pan at 350°F for 55 to 60 minutes or until wooden toothpick inserted in center comes out clean. Cool 10 minutes before removing from pan.

Nutrients per serving (1 slice):

Calories	167	Cholesterol	0 mg
Fat	5 g	Sodium	198 mg

Brown Rice, Mushroom, and Ham Hash

Makes 8 servings

1 tablespoon olive oil
2 cups (about 8 ounces) sliced fresh mushrooms
1 small onion, minced
1 clove garlic, minced
3 cups cooked brown rice
1 cup (6 ounces) diced turkey ham
½ cup chopped walnuts (optional)
¼ cup snipped fresh parsley
1 tablespoon white wine vinegar
1 tablespoon Dijon-style mustard
¼ teaspoon ground black pepper

Heat oil in Dutch oven or large saucepan over medium-low heat until hot. Add mushrooms, onion, and garlic; cook and stir until tender. Stir in rice, ham, walnuts, parsley, vinegar, mustard, and pepper; cook, stirring until thoroughly heated.

To Microwave: Combine oil, mushrooms, onion, and garlic in 2- to 3-quart microproof baking dish. Cook on HIGH (100% power) 3 to 4 minutes. Stir in rice, ham, walnuts, parsley, vinegar, mustard, and pepper. Cook on HIGH 3 to 4 minutes, stirring after 2 minutes, or until thoroughly heated.

Nutrients per serving:

Calories	133	Cholesterol	10 mg
Fat	4 g	Sodium	184 mg

Favorite recipe from **USA Rice Council**

Gingerbread Pancakes

Makes 12 pancakes

1½ cups all-purpose flour
½ cup SPOON SIZE® Shredded Wheat, finely
  rolled (about ⅓ cup crumbs)
1 tablespoon DAVIS® Baking Powder
1 teaspoon pumpkin pie spice
1¼ cups skim milk
½ cup EGG BEATERS® 99% Real Egg Product
3 tablespoons BRER RABBIT® Light Molasses
2 tablespoons FLEISCHMANN'S® Margarine,
  melted

In large bowl, mix flour, cereal, baking powder and
pumpkin pie spice. In small bowl, blend milk, Egg
Beaters®, molasses and margarine; stir into dry
ingredients just until moistened.

On lightly greased preheated griddle or skillet, pour
¼ cup batter for each pancake. Cook over medium
heat until surface is bubbly and bottom is lightly
browned. Turn carefully and cook until done. Remove
and keep warm.

Nutrients per serving (1 pancake):

Calories	110	Cholesterol	1 mg
Fat	2 g	Sodium	128 mg

Mixed Fruit Soufflé

Makes 8 servings

1 cup skim milk
¼ cup cornstarch
1½ cups chopped fresh fruit*
⅓ cup sugar
1 teaspoon vanilla extract
1 (8-ounce) container EGG BEATERS®
  99% Real Egg Product

In small saucepan, gradually blend milk into
cornstarch; cook over medium heat until mixture
thickens and begins to boil, stirring constantly.
Remove from heat; stir in fruit, sugar and vanilla.
Set aside.

In medium bowl, with electric mixer at high speed,
beat Egg Beaters® until foamy, about 3 minutes; fold
into fruit mixture. Spoon into greased 1½-quart
soufflé or casserole dish. Bake at 375°F for 45 to
50 minutes or until set. Serve immediately.

*Thawed and well-drained frozen or canned fruit may be
substituted.*

Nutrients per serving:

Calories	86	Cholesterol	1 mg
Fat	0 g	Sodium	54 mg

Brunch Potato Cassoulet

Makes 4 to 6 servings

2 tablespoons unsalted margarine or butter
2 cups (8 ounces) ARMOUR® Lower Salt Ham,
  cut into ½-inch cubes
2 cups frozen natural potato wedges
1 cup sliced mushrooms
½ cup chopped red onion
½ cup chopped green bell pepper
1 cup frozen speckled butter beans, cooked and
  drained according to package directions
  (omit salt)
Low-salt cheese (optional)

Preheat oven to 350°F. Melt margarine in large skillet
over medium heat. Add ham, potatoes, mushrooms,
onion and green pepper; cook and stir over medium
heat 5 to 6 minutes or until onion is soft. Stir in
cooked beans. Transfer to medium earthenware pot
or ovenproof Dutch oven. Bake, covered, 10 to 12
minutes or until heated through. Sprinkle with low-
salt cheese, if desired. Broil, 4 to 6 inches from heat
source, 2 to 3 minutes or until cheese is melted and
slightly browned.

Nutrients per serving:

Calories	161	Cholesterol	19 mg
Fat	7 g	Sodium	391 mg

Brunch Potato Cassoulet

Cheese "Danish"

Makes 20 servings

1 tablespoon sugar
1 teaspoon ground cinnamon
5 flour tortillas (6 or 7 inches in diameter)
  Nonstick cooking spray
1 cup cold skim milk
1 package (4-serving size) JELL-O® Vanilla
  Flavor Sugar Free Instant Pudding and Pie
  Filling
1 container (8 ounces) light pasteurized process
  cream cheese product
2 cups thawed COOL WHIP® LITE® Whipped
  Topping
1 square BAKER'S® Semi-Sweet Chocolate

Heat oven to 350°F.

Mix sugar and cinnamon. Spray tortillas with
nonstick cooking spray. Sprinkle each tortilla with
scant ½ teaspoon sugar-cinnamon mixture. Turn
tortillas over; repeat process. Cut each tortilla into
4 wedges. Stand rounded edge of each tortilla wedge
in bottom of muffin cup by curling in sides. Bake
10 minutes or until lightly browned and crispy. Cool
in pan.

Pour milk into large mixing bowl. Add pudding mix.
Beat at low speed with electric mixer until well
blended, 1 to 2 minutes. Beat in cream cheese
product at medium speed until smooth. Gently stir in
whipped topping. Refrigerate at least 1 hour.

To serve, fill each tortilla shell with scant 3
tablespoons topping mixture using pastry bag or
spoon. Place chocolate in small plastic sandwich bag

or self-closing bag. Microwave on HIGH (100%)
about 1 minute or until chocolate is melted. Fold over
top of bag tightly; snip off one corner (about ⅛ inch).
Holding bag tightly at top, drizzle chocolate through
opening over prepared desserts. Refrigerate until
chocolate sets, about 5 minutes.

*Note: Freeze any leftover "Danish." Thaw in refrigerator as
needed.*

Nutrients per serving (1 "Danish"):

Calories	90	Cholesterol	5 mg
Fat	4 g	Sodium	180 mg

Belgian Waffle Dessert

Makes 10 waffles

2¼ cups cold 2% low-fat milk
1 package (4-serving size) JELL-O® Vanilla
  Flavor Sugar Free Instant Pudding and Pie
  Filling
2 tablespoons lemon juice
1 teaspoon grated lemon peel
1 cup thawed COOL WHIP® LITE® Whipped
  Topping
1 pint (about 2 cups) strawberries, sliced
½ pint (about 1 cup) raspberries
½ pint (about 1 cup) blueberries or blackberries
10 small frozen Belgian or regular waffles,
  toasted

Pour milk into large mixing bowl. Add pudding mix,
lemon juice and peel. Beat with wire whisk until well
blended, 1 to 2 minutes. Gently stir in whipped
topping. Refrigerate.

Mix fruit in bowl; refrigerate.

To serve, spoon about 3 tablespoons pudding mixture
on each dessert plate. Top each with waffle,
additional 2 tablespoons pudding mixture and scant
½ cup fruit. Garnish if desired. Repeat for remaining
desserts as needed. Store leftover pudding mixture
and fruit in refrigerator.

Nutrients per serving (1 waffle):

Calories	170	Cholesterol	5 mg
Fat	5 g	Sodium	310 mg

Top to bottom: Cheese "Danish",
Belgian Waffle Dessert

Honey Peanut Muffins

Makes 12 muffins

¾ cup whole wheat flour
¾ cup all-purpose flour
¼ cup sugar
1 teaspoon baking soda
¼ teaspoon salt (optional)
1¼ cups KELLOGG'S® ALL-BRAN® Cereal
1¼ cups low-fat buttermilk
¼ cup honey
2 egg whites
3 tablespoons vegetable oil
¼ cup chopped dry roasted peanuts
    Nonstick cooking spray

Stir together flours, sugar, baking soda and salt. Set aside.

Measure Kellogg's® All-Bran® cereal and buttermilk into large mixing bowl. Stir to combine. Let stand 3 minutes or until cereal is softened. Add honey, egg whites, oil and peanuts. Beat well.

Add flour mixture, stirring only until combined. Portion batter evenly into 12 (2½-inch) muffin pan cups coated with nonstick cooking spray.

Bake at 400°F about 22 minutes or until golden brown. Serve warm.

Nutrients per serving (1 muffin):

Calories	180	Cholesterol	45 mg
Fat	6 g	Sodium	230 mg

Ham & Fruit Pancake Rolls

Makes 8 rolled pancakes

2 cups complete pancake mix
8 ounces ARMOUR® Lower Salt Ham, thinly sliced
8 tablespoons bottled fruit-flavored applesauce *or* canned lite cherry fruit filling

Prepare pancake mix according to package directions. Spray griddle or large skillet with nonstick cooking spray. Using ⅓ cup measure, pour batter onto hot griddle. Cook as directed on package, making eight 5-inch pancakes. Place 1 ounce of ham on each cooked pancake; top with 1 tablespoon applesauce. Roll up pancake around ham; secure with toothpicks, if needed. Repeat with remaining pancakes. Serve with additional applesauce, if desired.

Nutrients per serving (1 pancake):

Calories	145	Cholesterol	14 mg
Fat	2 g	Sodium	596 mg

Cranberry Oat Bran Muffins

Cranberry Oat Bran Muffins

Makes 12 muffins

2 cups flour
1 cup oat bran
½ cup packed brown sugar
2 teaspoons baking powder
½ teaspoon baking soda
½ teaspoon salt (optional)
½ cup MIRACLE WHIP® LIGHT Reduced Calorie Salad Dressing
3 egg whites, slightly beaten
½ cup skim milk
⅓ cup orange juice
1 teaspoon grated orange peel
1 cup coarsely chopped cranberries

Preheat oven to 375°F. Line 12 medium muffin cups with paper baking cups or spray with nonstick cooking spray. Mix together dry ingredients. Add combined dressing, egg whites, milk, juice and peel; mix just until moistened. Fold in cranberries. Fill prepared muffin cups almost full. Bake 15 to 17 minutes or until golden brown.

Nutrients per serving (1 muffin):

Calories	183	Cholesterol	4 mg
Fat	4 g	Sodium	191 mg

Rice Crêpe

Rice Crêpes

Makes 10 crêpes

1 carton (8 ounces) egg substitute*
⅔ cup evaporated skim milk
1 tablespoon margarine, melted
½ cup all-purpose flour
1 tablespoon granulated sugar
1 cup cooked rice
  Nonstick cooking spray
2½ cups fresh fruit (strawberries, raspberries, blueberries, or other favorite fruit)
  Low-sugar fruit spread (optional)
  Light sour cream (optional)
1 tablespoon confectioners' sugar for garnish (optional)

Combine egg substitute, milk, and margarine in large bowl. Stir in flour and granulated sugar until smooth and well blended. Stir in rice; let stand 5 minutes.

Heat 8-inch nonstick skillet or crêpe pan; coat with nonstick cooking spray. Spoon ¼ cup batter into pan. Lift pan off heat; quickly tilt pan in rotating motion so that bottom of pan is completely covered with batter. Place pan back on heat and continue cooking until surface is dry, about 45 seconds. Turn crêpe over and cook 15 to 20 seconds; set aside. Continue with remaining crêpe batter. Place waxed paper between crêpes. Spread each crêpe with your favorite filling: strawberries, raspberries, blueberries, fruit spread, or sour cream.

Roll up and sprinkle with confectioners' sugar for garnish.

Substitute 8 egg whites or 4 eggs for 8 ounces egg substitute, if desired.

Nutrients per serving (1 crêpe):			
Calories	111	Cholesterol	1 mg
Fat	2 g	Sodium	152 mg

Favorite recipe from **USA Rice Council**

Mini Sausage Biscuit Sandwiches

Makes 20 mini-sandwiches

1 package (1 pound) LOUIS RICH®, fully cooked, Turkey Smoked Sausage
2 cans (10 ounces each) refrigerated buttermilk flaky biscuits
  Honey, barbecue sauce or ketchup (optional)

Preheat oven to 400°F. Cut sausage lengthwise into quarters; cut each quarter into 5 pieces.

Remove biscuits from can; separate. Using fingers, flatten each biscuit to about 4 inches. Place small amount of honey, barbecue sauce or ketchup, if desired, in center of each biscuit; top each with 1 piece of sausage.

Bring up edges of biscuit and pinch together to seal over top of sausage. Place on baking sheet. Bake about 10 minutes or until lightly browned.

Nutrients per serving (1 mini-sandwich):			
Calories	125	Cholesterol	15 mg
Fat	6 g	Sodium	500 mg

Blueberry Bran Muffins

Makes 12 muffins

1½ cups all-purpose flour
¼ cup sugar
1 tablespoon baking powder
¼ teaspoon salt
1½ cups KELLOGG'S® COMPLETE® BRAN FLAKES Cereal
1 cup skim milk
1 egg
¼ cup vegetable oil
1½ cup fresh or frozen blueberries
  Nonstick cooking spray

Stir together flour, sugar, baking powder and salt. Set aside.

Measure Kellogg's® Complete® Bran Flakes cereal and milk into large mixing bowl. Stir to combine. Let stand about 3 minutes or until cereal is softened. Add egg and oil, mixing well.

Add flour mixture, stirring only until combined. Stir in blueberries. Portion batter evenly into 12 (2½-inch) muffin pan cups coated with nonstick cooking spray.

Bake at 400°F about 20 minutes or until golden brown. Serve warm.

Nutrients per serving (1 muffin):			
Calories	140	Cholesterol	25 mg
Fat	5 g	Sodium	170 mg

Ham Breakfast Sandwich

Almond Cocoa Muffins

Makes 12 muffins

¾ cup whole wheat flour
¾ cup all-purpose flour
½ cup sugar
1 tablespoon baking powder
1 tablespoon unsweetened cocoa powder
1 teaspoon ground cinnamon
¼ teaspoon salt (optional)
1½ cups KELLOGG'S® ALL-BRAN® Cereal
1½ cups skim milk
2 egg whites
2 tablespoons vegetable oil
¼ cup chopped almonds
Nonstick cooking spray

Stir together flours, sugar, baking powder, cocoa, cinnamon and salt. Set aside.

Measure Kellogg's® All-Bran® cereal and milk into large mixing bowl. Stir to combine. Let stand 3 minutes or until cereal is softened. Add egg whites, oil and almonds. Beat well.

Add flour mixture, stirring only until well combined. Portion batter evenly into 12 (2½-inch) muffin pan cups coated with nonstick cooking spray.

Bake at 400°F about 22 minutes or until lightly browned. Serve warm.

Nutrients per serving (1 muffin):			
Calories	160	Cholesterol	45 mg
Fat	6 g	Sodium	250 mg

Ham Breakfast Sandwiches

Makes 3 sandwiches

1 ounce Neufchâtel or light cream cheese, softened
2 teaspoons apricot spreadable fruit
2 teaspoons plain nonfat yogurt
6 slices raisin bread
Lettuce leaves
1 package (6 ounces) ECKRICH® Lite Lower Salt Ham
3 Granny Smith apple rings

Combine cheese, spreadable fruit and yogurt in small bowl. Spread on bread. To make each sandwich: Place lettuce on 1 slice bread. Top with 2 slices ham, 1 apple ring and another slice of bread.

Nutrients per serving (1 sandwich):			
Calories	223	Cholesterol	5 mg
Fat	5 g	Sodium	963 mg

Five-Minute Fruit Dip

Makes 1¼ cups

½ cup MIRACLE WHIP® FREE® Nonfat Dressing
1 container (8 ounces) lemon-flavored low-fat yogurt

Mix ingredients until well blended; refrigerate. Serve with assorted fruit kabobs.

Prep time: 5 minutes plus refrigerating

Nutrients per serving (2 tablespoons):			
Calories	60	Cholesterol	0 mg
Fat	1 g	Sodium	230 mg

Northern California Banana Bread

Makes 28 servings

3 extra-ripe, medium DOLE® Bananas, peeled
½ cup margarine, softened
½ cup firmly packed brown sugar
½ cup granulated sugar
1 egg
1 teaspoon vanilla extract
1¼ cups all-purpose flour
⅔ cup oat bran
½ cup whole wheat flour
2 teaspoons baking powder
1 teaspoon ground cinnamon
½ teaspoon salt
1 cup DOLE® Chopped Dates
1 cup DOLE® Chopped Almonds, toasted

Place bananas in blender. Process until puréed; use 1½ cups for recipe. Beat margarine and sugars in large bowl until light and fluffy. Beat in 1½ cups puréed bananas, egg and vanilla. Combine all-purpose flour, oat bran, whole wheat flour, baking powder, cinnamon and salt in medium bowl. Beat into banana mixture until blended. Stir in dates and almonds. Pour batter into greased 9×5-inch loaf pan. Bake in 350°F oven 65 minutes or until cake tester inserted in center comes out clean. Cool in pan on wire rack 10 minutes. Remove from pan. Cool completely on wire rack before slicing. To serve, cut loaf into 14 slices, then cut each slice lengthwise in half.

Prep time: 15 minutes
Bake time: 65 minutes

Nutrients per serving:

Calories	163	Cholesterol	10 mg
Fat	7 g	Sodium	96 mg

Brunch Rice

Makes 6 servings

1 teaspoon margarine
¾ cup shredded carrots
¾ cup diced green bell pepper
¾ cup (about 3 ounces) sliced fresh mushrooms
6 egg whites, beaten
2 eggs, beaten
½ cup skim milk
½ teaspoon salt
¼ teaspoon ground black pepper
3 cups cooked brown rice
½ cup (2 ounces) shredded Cheddar cheese
6 corn tortillas, warmed (optional)

Heat margarine in large skillet over medium-high heat until hot. Add carrots, green pepper, and mushrooms; cook and stir 2 minutes. Combine egg whites, eggs, milk, salt, and black pepper in small bowl. Reduce heat to medium and pour egg mixture over vegetables. Continue stirring 1½ to 2 minutes. Add rice and cheese; stir to gently separate grains. Heat 2 minutes. Serve immediately or spoon mixture into warmed corn tortillas.

To Microwave: Heat margarine in 2- to 3-quart microproof baking dish. Add carrots, green pepper, and mushrooms; cover and cook on HIGH (100% power) 4 minutes. Combine egg whites, eggs, milk, salt, and black pepper in small bowl; pour over vegetables. Cook on HIGH 4 minutes, stirring with fork after each minute to cut cooked eggs into small pieces. Stir in rice and cheese; cook on HIGH about 1 minute or until thoroughly heated. Serve immediately or spoon mixture into warmed corn tortillas.

Nutrients per serving:

Calories	212	Cholesterol	79 mg
Fat	7 g	Sodium	353 mg

Favorite recipe from **USA Rice Council**

Brunch Rice

Double Oat Muffins

Makes 12 muffins

- 2 cups QUAKER® Oat Bran hot cereal, uncooked
- ⅓ cup firmly packed brown sugar
- ¼ cup all-purpose flour
- 2 teaspoons baking powder
- ¼ teaspoon salt (optional)
- ¼ teaspoon ground nutmeg (optional)
- 1 cup skim milk
- 2 egg whites, slightly beaten
- 3 tablespoons vegetable oil
- 1½ teaspoons vanilla
- ¼ cup QUAKER® Oats (quick or old fashioned, uncooked)
- 1 tablespoon firmly packed brown sugar

Heat oven to 400°F. Line 12 medium muffin cups with paper baking cups or grease lightly. Combine oat bran, ⅓ cup brown sugar, flour, baking powder, salt and nutmeg. Add combined milk, egg whites, oil and vanilla, mixing just until moistened. Fill muffin cups almost full. Combine oats and 1 tablespoon brown sugar; sprinkle evenly over muffin tops. Bake 20 to 22 minutes or until golden brown. Remove to wire rack. Cool completely.

To Microwave: Line 6 microwavable muffin cups with double paper baking cups. Combine oat bran, ⅓ cup brown sugar, flour, baking powder, salt and nutmeg. Add combined milk, egg whites, oil and vanilla, mixing just until moistened. Fill muffin cups almost full. Combine oats and 1 tablespoon brown sugar; sprinkle evenly over muffin tops. Microwave at HIGH (100% power) 2½ to 3 minutes or until wooden toothpick inserted in centers comes out

clean. Remove from pan; cool 5 minutes before serving. Line muffin cups with additional double paper baking cups. Repeat procedure with remaining batter.

Tips: *To freeze muffins, wrap securely in foil or place in freezer bag. Seal, label and freeze.*

To reheat muffins, unwrap frozen muffins. Microwave at HIGH (100% power) about 30 seconds per muffin.

Nutrients per serving (1 muffin):

Calories	140	Cholesterol	0 mg
Fat	5 g	Sodium	90 mg

Carrot Spice Loaf

Makes 1 loaf, 12 servings

- 2¼ cups all-purpose flour
- 1¼ cups plus 3 tablespoons QUAKER® Oats (quick or old fashioned, uncooked), divided
- ¾ cup firmly packed brown sugar
- 4 teaspoons baking powder
- ½ teaspoon baking soda
- ½ teaspoon ground cinnamon
- ¼ teaspoon salt (optional)
- ¼ teaspoon ground ginger (optional)
- ⅛ teaspoon ground cloves (optional)
- ½ cup frozen apple juice concentrate, thawed
- ⅓ cup vegetable oil
- ¼ cup water
- 4 egg whites
- 1 cup shredded carrots (about 2 medium)
- ½ cup chopped dates or raisins

Heat oven to 350°F. Lightly oil 8×4- or 9×5-inch loaf pan. Combine dry ingredients except for 3 tablespoons oats; mix well. Add combined juice concentrate, oil, water and egg whites, mixing just until moistened. Fold in carrots and dates. Spread evenly into prepared pan. Sprinkle top with remaining 3 tablespoons oats. Bake 1 hour and 10 minutes or until wooden toothpick inserted in center comes out clean. Cool 10 minutes; remove from pan. Cool completely on wire rack. Store tightly covered.

Nutrients per serving (1 slice):

Calories	265	Cholesterol	0 mg
Fat	7 g	Sodium	200 mg

Double Oat Muffins

Apple Streusel Coffee Cake

Makes 9 servings

Cake
- ¼ cup CRISCO® Shortening
- ½ cup sugar
- 2 egg whites
- 1 teaspoon vanilla
- ¾ cup dry oat bran high fiber hot cereal
- 1 cup chunky applesauce
- 1¼ cups all-purpose flour
- 1½ teaspoons ground cinnamon
- 1 teaspoon baking powder
- ¾ teaspoon baking soda
- ¼ teaspoon salt (optional)
- ¼ teaspoon ground nutmeg

Filling and Topping
- 1 cup chunky applesauce, divided
- ¼ cup sugar
- ¼ teaspoon ground cinnamon

Heat oven to 375°F. Grease 8-inch square pan.

For Cake, combine Crisco® and ½ cup sugar in medium bowl with fork until blended and crumbly. Add egg whites and vanilla. Beat until fairly smooth. Stir in oat bran, then 1 cup applesauce. Let stand 5 minutes. Combine flour, 1½ teaspoons cinnamon, baking powder, baking soda, salt and nutmeg in small bowl. Stir into oat bran mixture. Spread half of batter in pan.

For Filling and Topping, spread ¾ cup applesauce over batter. Combine ¼ cup sugar and ¼ teaspoon cinnamon. Sprinkle half over applesauce. Add remaining batter; spread gently and evenly. Top with remaining ¼ cup applesauce; spread thinly and evenly. Sprinkle with remaining sugar-cinnamon mixture. Bake at 375°F for 30 to 35 minutes or until top is golden brown and center springs back when touched lightly. Cut into squares. Serve warm.

Nutrients per serving:

Calories	242	Cholesterol	0 mg
Fat	6 g	Sodium	120 mg

Mexican Egg Muffin

Mexican Egg Muffin

Makes 1 serving

- 1 large egg
- 2 teaspoons water
- 1 teaspoon chopped green onion
- 1 teaspoon diet margarine
- ½ English muffin, toasted
- 4 teaspoons prepared salsa
- 1 slice BORDEN® Lite-line® Process Cheese Product, any flavor, cut into triangles*

In small bowl, beat egg, water and green onion. In small skillet, melt margarine; add egg mixture. Cook and stir until egg is set. Spoon egg mixture onto muffin; top with salsa, then cheese product slice. Place on baking sheet; broil until cheese product slice begins to melt. Garnish as desired.

**"½ the calories"– 8% milkfat product*

Nutrients per serving:

Calories	220	Cholesterol	226 mg
Fat	10 g	Sodium	614 mg

Papaya Muffin

Papaya Muffins

Makes 12 muffins

1½ cups whole wheat flour
1 tablespoon baking powder
½ teaspoon salt
1½ cups KELLOGG'S® ALL-BRAN® Cereal
1¼ cups skim milk
¼ cup honey
¼ cup vegetable oil
1 tablespoon dark molasses
1 egg
¾ cup chopped fresh papaya
2 teaspoons finely chopped crystallized ginger

Stir together flour, baking powder and salt. Set aside. Measure Kellogg's® All-Bran® cereal and milk into large mixing bowl. Stir to combine. Let stand 2 minutes or until cereal is softened. Add honey, oil, molasses and egg. Beat well. Stir in papaya and ginger.

Add flour mixture, stirring only until combined. Portion batter evenly into 12 greased 2½-inch muffin pan cups.

Bake at 400°F about 25 minutes or until muffins are golden brown. Serve warm.

Nutrients per serving (1 muffin):

Calories	160	Cholesterol	19 mg
Fat	6 g	Sodium	314 mg

Honey-Bran Muffins

Makes 12 servings

¾ cup 100% bran cereal
¼ cup nonfat milk
1 cup all-purpose flour
1 teaspoon baking soda
¼ teaspoon salt
2 extra-ripe, medium DOLE® Bananas, peeled
1 egg *or* 3 egg whites
¼ cup honey
¼ cup vegetable oil
¾ cup DOLE® Raisins

Combine cereal and milk in small bowl; let stand 10 minutes to soften. Stir in flour, baking soda and salt. Meanwhile, place bananas in blender. Process until puréed; use 1 cup for recipe. Combine 1 cup banana purée, egg, honey and oil in large bowl. Add cereal mixture to banana mixture, stirring until just moistened. Fold in raisins. Spoon batter into 12 greased 2½-inch muffin cups. Bake in 375°F oven 20 minutes. Cool in pan on wire rack 3 minutes. Remove from pan.

Prep time: 20 minutes
Bake time: 20 minutes

Nutrients per serving (1 muffin):

Calories	169	Cholesterol	23 mg
Fat	5 g	Sodium	165 mg

Breakfast Sausage Bake

Makes 12 servings

2 tablespoons margarine
1 pound fresh mushrooms, finely chopped
1 cup dry fine bread crumbs
1 package (1 pound) LOUIS RICH® Turkey Breakfast Sausage, thawed
1 red or green bell pepper, chopped
3 tablespoons chopped fresh parsley *or* 1 tablespoon dried parsley flakes
¼ teaspoon ground red pepper
2 cartons (8 ounces each) cholesterol-free egg substitute *or* 8 eggs, beaten

Preheat oven to 350°F. Melt margarine in large nonstick skillet over medium-high heat. Add mushrooms. Cook and stir about 10 minutes or until mixture boils and moisture evaporates. Remove from heat; stir in bread crumbs. Spray 13×9-inch baking dish with nonstick cooking spray. Press mushroom mixture onto bottom of prepared baking dish to form crust.

In same nonstick skillet, cook sausage over medium heat about 12 minutes, breaking sausage apart into small pieces and stirring frequently until lightly browned. Remove from heat.

Stir in chopped bell pepper, parsley and ground red pepper. Spread sausage mixture over crust; pour egg substitute evenly over mixture. Bake 25 to 30 minutes or until mixture is set.

Note: For 6 servings, use half of the ingredients; prepare and bake as above in 9-inch pie plate.

Nutrients per serving:

Calories	140	Cholesterol	20 mg
Fat	6 g	Sodium	370 mg

Frittata Primavera

Makes 4 servings

- 1 medium onion, chopped
- 1 medium red or green bell pepper, cut into strips
- 1 medium potato, peeled and grated (about 1 cup)
- 1 cup coarsely chopped broccoli
- 1 teaspoon dried oregano leaves, crushed
- ⅛ teaspoon ground black pepper
- 1 tablespoon FLEISCHMANN'S® Margarine
- 1 (8-ounce) container EGG BEATERS® 99% Real Egg Product

In 10-inch nonstick skillet or omelet pan, cook and stir onion, bell pepper, potato, broccoli, oregano and black pepper in margarine until vegetables are tender-crisp.

In small bowl, with electric mixer at high speed, beat Egg Beaters® for 2 minutes until light and fluffy; pour over vegetables. Cover and cook over medium heat for 5 to 7 minutes until eggs are set. Serve from pan or carefully invert onto warm serving plate. Serve immediately.

Nutrients per serving:

Calories	97	Cholesterol	0 mg
Fat	3 g	Sodium	109 mg

Praline Pancakes

Makes 6 servings

- 1½ cups skim milk
- 2 tablespoons margarine, melted
- 2 teaspoons brandy
- 1 teaspoon vanilla extract
- 1 cup all-purpose flour
- 2 tablespoons sugar
- 1 teaspoon baking powder
- ¼ teaspoon salt
- ⅛ teaspoon ground cinnamon
- 1 cup cooked rice, cooled
- ⅓ cup pecans, coarsely chopped
- 4 egg whites, stiffly beaten
- Nonstick cooking spray
- Low-calorie syrup (optional)

Combine milk, margarine, brandy, vanilla, flour, sugar, baking powder, salt, and cinnamon in large bowl; stir until smooth. Stir in rice and pecans. Fold in beaten egg whites. Pour scant ¼ cup batter onto hot griddle coated with nonstick cooking spray. Cook over medium heat until bubbles form on top and underside is lightly browned. Turn to brown other side. Serve warm drizzled with syrup.

Nutrients per serving:

Calories	252	Cholesterol	1 mg
Fat	9 g	Sodium	387 mg

Favorite recipe from **USA Rice Council**

Apple Cinnamon Muffins

Makes 18 muffins

- 2¼ cups oat bran cereal
- ¼ cup firmly packed brown sugar
- 1 tablespoon baking powder
- 1¼ teaspoons ground cinnamon
- ¾ cup apple juice or cider
- ½ cup skim milk
- 2 egg whites
- 2 tablespoons vegetable oil
- 1 medium apple, peeled and chopped
- ¼ cup chopped walnuts
- ¼ cup raisins

Preheat oven to 400°F. In large bowl, combine cereal, brown sugar, baking powder and cinnamon. In small bowl, combine apple juice, milk, egg whites and oil. Stir into flour mixture just until moistened. Add chopped apple, walnuts and raisins. Fill 18 greased medium muffin cups ¾ full with batter. Bake 15 to 17 minutes or until golden.

Nutrients per serving (1 muffin):

Calories	89	Cholesterol	trace
Fat	3 g	Sodium	68 mg

Favorite recipe from **Western New York Apple Growers Association**

Apple Cinnamon Muffins

A steaming bowlful of hearty soup coupled with a square of tender cornbread is perfect for a lightweight lunch or supper. Create your own tempting combination, such as Beef Stew à la Italia teeming with chunky vegetables and paired with a wedge of hearty Cheesy Onion Flatbread.

Southwest Chili

Makes 4 servings

1 tablespoon olive oil
1 large onion, chopped
2 large tomatoes, chopped
1 can (4 ounces) chopped green chilies, undrained
1 tablespoon chili powder
1 teaspoon ground cumin
1 can (15 ounces) red kidney beans, undrained
1 can (15 ounces) great Northern beans, undrained
¼ cup cilantro leaves, chopped (optional)

Heat oil in large saucepan over medium heat. Add onion; cook until tender, stirring occasionally.

Stir in tomatoes, chilies with liquid, chili powder and cumin. Bring to a boil. Add beans with liquid.

Reduce heat to low; cover. Simmer 15 minutes, stirring occasionally. Sprinkle individual servings with cilantro, if desired.

Nutrients per serving:

Calories	285	Cholesterol	0 mg
Fat	5 g	Sodium	459 mg

Dijon Lamb Stew

Makes 4 servings

½ pound boneless lamb, cut into small pieces
½ medium onion, chopped
½ teaspoon dried rosemary leaves, crushed
1 tablespoon olive oil
 Salt and pepper (optional)
1 can (14½ ounces) DEL MONTE® Italian Recipe Stewed Tomatoes
1 carrot, julienne cut
1 tablespoon Dijon-style mustard
1 can (15 ounces) white beans or pinto beans, drained
 Sliced ripe olives (optional)
 Chopped fresh parsley (optional)

In large skillet, brown lamb, onion and rosemary in oil over medium-high heat, stirring occasionally. Season with salt and pepper, if desired. Add tomatoes with juice, carrot and mustard. Cover and cook over medium heat 10 minutes; add beans. Cook, uncovered, over medium heat 5 minutes, stirring occasionally until lamb is tender. Garnish with sliced ripe olives and chopped parsley, if desired.

Variation: Top sirloin steak may be substituted for lamb.

Prep time: 10 minutes
Cook time: 20 minutes

Nutrients per serving:

Calories	209	Cholesterol	29 mg
Fat	7 g	Sodium	753 mg

Top to bottom: Southwest Chili, Cheesy Corn Sticks (page 99)

Calico Chicken Soup

Navy Bean Soup

Makes 4 servings

2 tablespoons vegetable oil
1 cup chopped leeks
1½ cups (6 ounces) ARMOUR® Lower Salt Ham
 cut into ½-inch cubes
1 cup uncooked navy beans, soaked overnight
 and drained
1 tablespoon chopped jalapeño peppers

Heat oil in 3-quart saucepan over medium heat. Add leeks; cook and stir 3 to 5 minutes or until tender. Stir in ham, beans and peppers; add enough water to just cover beans. Bring to a boil over high heat. Reduce heat to low. Cover; simmer 1 to 1½ hours or until beans are tender.

Nutrients per serving:

Calories	282	Cholesterol	21 mg
Fat	10 g	Sodium	420 mg

Calico Chicken Soup

Makes 8 servings, 2 quarts

1 pound skinned boneless chicken breasts, cut
 into chunks
1 tablespoon vegetable oil
6 cups water
2 tablespoons WYLER'S® or STEERO® Chicken-
 Flavor Instant Bouillon *or* 6 Chicken-
 Flavor Bouillon Cubes
2 cups broccoli flowerets
2 cups pared, sliced carrots
¾ cup chopped red bell pepper
¼ teaspoon black pepper

In large kettle or Dutch oven, brown chicken in oil. Add remaining ingredients. Bring to a boil; reduce heat. Simmer uncovered 45 minutes, stirring occasionally. Refrigerate leftovers.

Nutrients per serving (1 cup):

Calories	86	Cholesterol	23 mg
Fat	3 g	Sodium	716 mg

Vegetable Bean Soup

Makes about 6 servings, 6 cups

1 cup sliced leeks
1 clove garlic, minced
1 tablespoon vegetable or olive oil
3 cups water
1 can (16 ounces) HEINZ® Vegetarian Beans in
 Tomato Sauce
1 can (8 ounces) whole kernel corn, drained
1 cup cubed (½-inch) potatoes
½ cup sliced celery
½ cup sliced carrots
2 teaspoons HEINZ® Worcestershire Sauce
1 bay leaf
¼ teaspoon dried thyme leaves, crushed
¼ teaspoon salt
⅛ teaspoon black pepper

In 3-quart saucepan, cook and stir leeks and garlic in oil until tender. Add water and remaining ingredients; bring to a boil. Reduce heat to low; cover and simmer 30 minutes or until vegetables are tender. Remove bay leaf before serving.

Nutrients per serving:

Calories	197	Cholesterol	0 mg
Fat	3 g	Sodium	542 mg

Beef Noodle Soup

Makes 10 servings

- 2 tablespoons CRISCO® PURITAN® Oil
- ½ pound boneless beef sirloin, cut into thin strips
- ¼ cup chopped green onions
- 1 tablespoon all-purpose flour
- 3 cans (10½ ounces each) condensed chicken broth
- 3 cups water
- 2 cups cooked vermicelli or very fine egg noodles

Heat Crisco® Oil in 3-quart saucepan. Add beef. Cook and stir over medium-high heat until beef is browned.

Add onions. Cook, stirring occasionally, about 2 minutes or until onions are tender. Stir in flour. Add chicken broth and water.

Heat to boiling, stirring occasionally. Reduce heat to low. Simmer about 5 minutes. Stir in noodles. Simmer until soup is heated through.

Nutrients per serving:

Calories	144	Cholesterol	28 mg
Fat	6 g	Sodium	579 mg

Souper Surprise Barley Soup

Makes about 8 servings, 8 cups

- 3 cups water
- ½ cup medium pearled barley
- 3 beef bouillon cubes
- 2 cups cut asparagus or broccoli pieces (fresh or frozen), cooked and drained
- 4 cups low-fat milk
- 5 slices American cheese
- ¼ teaspoon ground nutmeg
- ¼ teaspoon black pepper
- 4 slices bacon (optional), cooked crisp and crumbled

In large saucepan, combine water, barley and bouillon. Bring to a boil over medium-high heat. Reduce heat to low and simmer, 50 to 60 minutes, stirring often, until barley is tender and nearly all of the liquid is absorbed.

Stir in asparagus, milk, cheese, nutmeg and pepper. Add bacon, if desired. Increase heat to medium-high and cook, stirring constantly, until cheese melts.

Nutrients per serving:

Calories	169	Cholesterol	20 mg
Fat	6 g	Sodium	618 mg

Favorite recipe from **North Dakota Barley Council**

Zesty Tomato Turkey Soup

Makes 4 servings

- 2 slices bacon
- ¼ cup chopped onion
- 1 small clove garlic, minced
- 2 cans (12 ounces each) cocktail vegetable juice
- 1 can (8 ounces) stewed tomatoes, cut up
- 1 cup (5 ounces) diced cooked BUTTERBALL® Turkey
- ⅓ cup chopped seeded cucumber
- ¼ cup chopped green bell pepper
- 1 teaspoon chicken bouillon granules
- 1 teaspoon Worcestershire sauce
- ½ teaspoon sugar

Cook bacon in large saucepan over medium-high heat until crisp; crumble into small pieces and set aside. In drippings, cook and stir onion and garlic until tender. Add remaining ingredients, including reserved bacon. Bring to a boil over high heat. Reduce heat to low; simmer 5 minutes or until hot.

To Microwave: Cut bacon into 1-inch pieces. Cook bacon in 2-quart microwave-safe casserole on HIGH (100% power) 2½ to 3 minutes, stirring once. Remove bacon and set aside. In drippings, cook onion and garlic on HIGH 2 minutes, stirring once. Add remaining ingredients, including reserved bacon. Cook on HIGH 7 to 8 minutes or until hot, stirring twice.

Nutrients per serving:

Calories	127	Cholesterol	27 mg
Fat	3 g	Sodium	912 mg

Zesty Tomato Turkey Soup

Seafood Corn Chowder

Makes 6 servings

1 tablespoon margarine
1 cup chopped onions
½ cup chopped green bell pepper
½ cup chopped red bell pepper
⅓ cup chopped celery
1 tablespoon all-purpose flour
1 can (10½ ounces) low-sodium chicken broth
2 cups skim milk
1 can (12 ounces) evaporated skim milk
8 to 12 ounces crab-flavored SURIMI Seafood chunks
2 cups fresh or frozen whole kernel corn
½ teaspoon black pepper
½ teaspoon paprika

Melt margarine in large saucepan over medium heat. Add onions, bell peppers and celery. Cook and stir, uncovered, over medium heat 4 to 5 minutes or until vegetables are tender. Add flour to vegetable mixture; cook and stir constantly 2 minutes. Gradually add chicken broth and bring to a boil. Stir in milk, evaporated milk, Surimi Seafood, corn, black pepper and paprika. Heat, stirring occasionally, 5 minutes or until chowder is hot. Serve.

Nutrients per serving:

Calories	217	Cholesterol	17 mg
Fat	3 g	Sodium	630 mg

Favorite recipe from **Surimi Seafood Education Center**

Asparagus and Surimi Seafood Soup

Makes 4 servings

3 cans (10½ ounces *each*) low-sodium chicken broth (about 4 cups)
2 thin slices fresh ginger
2 cups (about ¾ pound) diagonally sliced asparagus pieces (*each* ½ inch long)
¼ cup sliced green onions, including part of green tops
3 tablespoons rice vinegar or white wine vinegar
¼ teaspoon crushed red pepper
8 to 12 ounces crab-flavored SURIMI Seafood legs or chunks, cut diagonally

Bring chicken broth and ginger to a boil in large saucepan. Add asparagus, green onions, vinegar and crushed red pepper. Simmer 5 minutes or until asparagus is crisp-tender. Add Surimi Seafood and simmer 5 minutes longer or until seafood is hot. Remove and discard ginger. Serve hot.

Nutrients per serving:

Calories	136	Cholesterol	18 mg
Fat	3 g	Sodium	784 mg

Favorite recipe from **Surimi Seafood Education Center**

Left to right: Seafood Corn Chowder, Asparagus and Surimi Seafood Soup

Quick Deli Turkey Soup

Makes 4 servings

1 can (13¾ ounces) ready-to-serve chicken
    broth
1 can (14½ ounces) stewed tomatoes
1 small zucchini, cut up (about 1 cup)
¼ teaspoon dried basil leaves, crushed
½ pound BUTTERBALL® Deli Turkey Breast,
    cubed
½ cup cooked chili-mac pasta or macaroni

Combine broth, tomatoes with juice, zucchini and
basil in large saucepan. Bring to a boil over high heat.
Reduce heat to low; simmer 10 minutes or until
zucchini is tender. Stir in turkey and pasta. Continue
heating until turkey is hot.

Nutrients per serving:

Calories	152	Cholesterol	40 mg
Fat	3 g	Sodium	537 mg

Savory Lentil Soup

Makes 6 servings

1 cup uncooked lentils
3 cups (12 ounces) small cubes ARMOUR®
    Lower Salt Ham
1 (14½-ounce) can no salt added stewed
    tomatoes
1 small onion, chopped
½ cup chopped celery
1 teaspoon hot pepper sauce
1 teaspoon MRS. DASH®, Original Blend

Wash lentils; remove any grit or broken shells.
Combine all ingredients in large covered kettle; stir in
4 cups water. Bring to a boil over medium-high heat,
stirring often. Reduce heat to low. Simmer, covered,
for 1 hour or until lentils are tender and soup is thick.
Garnish with celery leaves, if desired.

Nutrients per serving:

Calories	220	Cholesterol	28 mg
Fat	3 g	Sodium	537 mg

Savory Seafood Soup

Savory Seafood Soup

Makes 4 servings

2½ cups water or chicken broth
1½ cups dry white wine
1 small onion, chopped
½ red bell pepper, chopped
½ green bell pepper, chopped
1 small clove garlic, minced
½ pound halibut, cut into 1-inch chunks
½ pound sea scallops, halved crosswise
1 teaspoon dried thyme leaves, crushed
    Juice of ½ lime
    Dash of hot pepper sauce
    Salt and black pepper (optional)

Combine water, wine, onion, red and green peppers
and garlic in large saucepan. Bring to a boil. Reduce
heat to medium; cover. Cook 15 minutes or until
vegetables are tender, stirring occasionally.

Add halibut, scallops and thyme. Continue cooking
2 minutes or until fish and scallops turn opaque. Stir
in lime juice and hot pepper sauce. Season with salt
and black pepper, if desired.

Nutrients per serving:

Calories	187	Cholesterol	37 mg
Fat	2 g	Sodium	178 mg

Picante Onion Soup

Picante Onion Soup

Makes 6 servings

3 cups thinly sliced onions
1 clove garlic, minced
¼ cup butter or margarine
2 cups tomato juice
1 can (10½ ounces) condensed beef broth
1 soup can water
½ cup PACE® Picante Sauce
1 cup unseasoned croutons (optional)
1 cup (4 ounces) shredded Monterey Jack
    cheese (optional)
    Additional PACE® Picante Sauce

Cook onions and garlic in butter in 3-quart saucepan over medium-low heat about 20 minutes, stirring frequently, until onions are tender and golden brown. Stir in tomato juice, broth, water and ½ cup picante sauce; bring to a boil over high heat. Reduce heat to low. Simmer, uncovered, 20 minutes. Ladle soup into bowls and sprinkle with croutons and cheese. Serve with additional Pace® picante sauce, if desired.

Nutrients per serving:

Calories	119	Cholesterol	42 mg
Fat	8 g	Sodium	1051 mg

Chilled Carrot Soup

Makes 8 servings

2 tablespoons vegetable oil
1 large onion, chopped
1½ teaspoons curry powder
3½ cups chicken broth
1 pound carrots, sliced
2 stalks celery, sliced
1 bay leaf
½ teaspoon ground cumin
½ teaspoon TABASCO® pepper sauce
1 cup low-fat milk
1 cup low-fat cottage cheese

In large saucepan heat oil; cook and stir onion and curry 3 to 5 minutes. Add broth, carrots, celery, bay leaf, cumin and TABASCO sauce; mix well. Cover; simmer 25 minutes or until vegetables are tender. Remove bay leaf. Spoon about ⅓ each carrot mixture, milk and cottage cheese into blender container or food processor. Cover; process until smooth. Pour into serving bowl. Repeat with remaining carrot mixture, milk and cottage cheese. Cover; refrigerate until chilled. Serve with additional TABASCO sauce, if desired.

Nutrients per serving:

Calories	120	Cholesterol	5 mg
Fat	5 g	Sodium	508 mg

Hearty Vegetable Stew

Makes 4 servings

1 tablespoon HOLLYWOOD® Safflower Oil
½ pound small mushrooms, sliced
½ cup chopped onion
2½ cups water
1 bay leaf
1 teaspoon dried thyme leaves, crushed
1 teaspoon low-sodium instant beef bouillon
    granules
¾ teaspoon garlic powder
½ teaspoon salt (optional)
¼ teaspoon ground black pepper
3 medium baking potatoes, cut into 2-inch
    chunks
3 large carrots, cut into 2-inch strips
2 cups coarsely chopped celery
1 pound tofu, cut into small cubes

In large saucepan, heat oil until hot. Add mushrooms and onion; cook and stir 5 minutes. Add water, bay leaf, thyme, bouillon, garlic powder, salt (if used), pepper, potatoes and carrots. Bring to a boil; reduce heat to low. Cover and simmer 20 minutes. Add celery; cover and simmer an additional 10 minutes or until vegetables are tender. Add tofu and heat through, about 5 minutes. Remove bay leaf before serving.

Nutrients per serving:

Calories	273	Cholesterol	0 mg
Fat	8 g	Sodium	88 mg

Meatball & Vegetable Soup

Makes 10 servings, about 2½ quarts

1 pound lean ground beef
½ cup fresh bread crumbs (1 slice)
⅓ cup chopped onion
1 egg, slightly beaten
4 teaspoons WYLER'S® or STEERO® Beef-
   Flavor Instant Bouillon
⅛ teaspoon garlic powder
6 cups water
1 (28-ounce) can whole tomatoes, undrained
   and broken up
½ teaspoon black pepper
2 cups frozen hash brown potatoes
1 cup frozen peas and carrots

In large bowl, combine meat, crumbs, onion, egg,
1 teaspoon bouillon and garlic powder; mix well.
Shape into 1-inch meatballs. In Dutch oven, brown
meatballs; pour off fat. Add water, tomatoes, pepper
and remaining *3 teaspoons* bouillon. Bring to a boil;
reduce heat. Simmer, uncovered, 20 minutes. Stir in
vegetables; cook 15 minutes or until tender, stirring
occasionally. Refrigerate leftovers.

Nutrients per serving:

Calories	201	Cholesterol	49 mg
Fat	10 g	Sodium	378 mg

Meatball & Vegetable Soup

Chicken & Rice Gumbo

Makes 10 servings

1 (46-fluid ounce) can COLLEGE INN®
   Chicken Broth
1 pound boneless chicken, cut into bite-size
   pieces
1 (17-ounce) can whole kernel sweet corn,
   drained
1 (14½-ounce) can stewed tomatoes, chopped
1 (10-ounce) package frozen okra, thawed and
   chopped
½ cup uncooked rice
1 teaspoon ground black pepper

In large saucepan, over medium-high heat, heat
chicken broth, chicken, corn, tomatoes with juice,
okra, rice and pepper until mixture comes to a boil.
Reduce heat; simmer, uncovered, 20 minutes or until
chicken and rice are cooked.

Nutrients per serving:

Calories	150	Cholesterol	19 mg
Fat	2 g	Sodium	699 mg

French Onion Soup

Makes 4 to 6 servings

1 extra-large onion (1 pound)
3 tablespoons BUTTER FLAVOR CRISCO®
1 clove garlic, minced
1 tablespoon all-purpose flour
5 cups water
¼ cup white wine (optional)
3 tablespoons instant beef bouillon granules
1 tablespoon instant chicken bouillon granules
1 teaspoon Worcestershire sauce
   Seasoned croutons
   Grated Parmesan cheese

Peel onion. Cut in half lengthwise, then crosswise into
thin slices.

Melt Butter Flavor Crisco® in 3-quart saucepan over
medium heat. Add onion and garlic; cook about
20 minutes or until onion is soft and transparent,
stirring occasionally. Stir in flour. Add water, wine,
beef and chicken bouillon granules and
Worcestershire sauce. Heat to boiling. Reduce heat to
low; cover and simmer for 15 minutes.

Ladle soup into individual serving bowls. Top with
seasoned croutons and sprinkle with Parmesan
cheese.

Nutrients per serving:

Calories	95	Cholesterol	trace
Fat	6 g	Sodium	602 mg

Potato-Cheese Calico Soup

Makes 6 servings, 6 cups

1 pound potatoes, peeled and thinly sliced
1 cup sliced onion
2½ cups chicken broth
½ cup low-fat milk
1 cup sliced mushrooms
½ cup diced red bell pepper
½ cup sliced green onions
1 cup (4 ounces) finely shredded Wisconsin
    Asiago Cheese
    Salt and black pepper (optional)
2 tablespoons chopped fresh parsley

In 3-quart saucepan, combine potatoes, 1 cup onion and broth. Bring to a boil. Reduce heat to low. Cover; cook until potatoes are tender, about 10 minutes. Transfer to blender container; blend until smooth. Return to saucepan. Stir in milk, mushrooms, bell pepper and green onions. Bring to simmer over medium-low heat. Add cheese, a few tablespoons at a time, stirring to melt. Season with salt and black pepper. Sprinkle with parsley.

Nutrients per serving (1 cup):			
Calories	151	Cholesterol	9 mg
Fat	4 g	Sodium	526 mg

Favorite recipe from **Wisconsin Milk Marketing Board** © 1993

Easy Chili Con Carne

Makes 4 servings

½ medium onion, chopped
1 stalk celery, sliced
1 teaspoon chili powder
1 can (15¼ ounces) kidney beans, drained
1 can (14½ ounces) DEL MONTE® Chili Style
    Chunky Tomatoes
1 cup cooked cubed beef

To Microwave: In 2-quart microwavable dish, combine onion, celery and chili powder. Add 1 tablespoon water. Cover and microwave on HIGH (100% power) 3 to 4 minutes. Add remaining ingredients. Cover and cook on HIGH 6 to 8 minutes or until heated through, stirring halfway through. For a spicier chili, serve with hot pepper sauce.

Prep time: 8 minutes
Microwave cook time: 12 minutes

Nutrients per serving:			
Calories	193	Cholesterol	28 mg
Fat	3 g	Sodium	612 mg

Beef Stew à la Italia

Beef Stew à la Italia

Makes 8 servings, about 8 cups

1½ pounds lean beef chuck, cut into 1-inch cubes
2 teaspoons olive or vegetable oil
1 large onion, cut into thin wedges
2 garlic cloves, minced
1 can (28 ounces) plum tomatoes, undrained,
    coarsely chopped
1 large baking potato, peeled and cut into
    ¾-inch chunks (2 cups)
⅔ cup PACE® Picante Sauce
1 teaspoon dried basil leaves, crushed
½ teaspoon dried oregano leaves, crushed
½ teaspoon salt (optional)
1 large green bell pepper, cut into 1-inch pieces
1 large zucchini, sliced ½-inch thick (2 cups)
¼ cup (1 ounce) grated Parmesan cheese
    Additional Pace® Picante Sauce (optional)

Place meat on rack of broiler pan. Broil, 4 inches from heat, until lightly browned on all sides. Heat oil in large saucepan or Dutch oven over medium heat. Add onion and garlic; cook and stir 3 minutes. Add meat, tomatoes with juice, potato, ⅔ cup Pace® Picante Sauce, basil, oregano and, if desired, salt. Bring to a boil. Reduce heat to low; cover and simmer until meat is tender, about 1 hour. Stir in green pepper and zucchini; continue to simmer until vegetables are crisp-tender, about 10 minutes. Ladle into bowls; sprinkle with cheese. Serve with additional Pace® Picante Sauce, if desired.

Nutrients per serving:			
Calories	222	Cholesterol	56 mg
Fat	10g	Sodium	466 mg

Beef Soup with Noodles

Beef Soup with Noodles

Makes 4 servings, 6 cups

2 tablespoons low-sodium soy sauce
1 teaspoon minced fresh ginger
¼ teaspoon crushed red pepper
**1 boneless beef top sirloin steak, cut 1 inch
    thick (about ¾ pound)**
1 tablespoon peanut or vegetable oil
2 cups sliced fresh mushrooms
**2 cans (about 14 ounces each) low-sodium beef
    broth**
**3 ounces (1 cup) fresh snow peas, cut diagonally
    into 1-inch pieces**
**1½ cups hot cooked fine egg noodles (2 ounces
    uncooked)**
1 green onion, cut diagonally into thin slices
**1 teaspoon Oriental sesame oil (optional)
    Red bell pepper strips for garnish**

Combine soy sauce, ginger and crushed red pepper
in small bowl. Spread mixture evenly over both sides
of steak. Marinate at room temperature 15 minutes.

Heat deep skillet over medium-high heat. Add peanut
oil; heat until hot. Drain steak; set aside soy sauce
mixture (there will only be a small amount of
mixture). Add steak to skillet; cook 4 to 5 minutes
per side for medium-rare. (Adjust time for desired
doneness.) Remove steak from skillet; let stand on
cutting board 10 minutes.

Add mushrooms to skillet; stir-fry 2 minutes. Add
broth, snow peas and soy sauce mixture; bring to a
boil, scraping up browned meat bits. Reduce heat to
medium-low. Stir in noodles.

Cut steak across the grain into ⅛-inch slices; cut
each slice into 1-inch pieces. Stir into soup; heat
through. Stir in onion and sesame oil. Ladle into
soup bowls. Garnish with red pepper strips.

Nutrients per serving:

Calories	245	Cholesterol	62 mg
Fat	10 g	Sodium	1004 mg

Hearty Pork Soup

Makes 12 servings

2 tablespoons olive or vegetable oil
**1 pound pork tenderloin, trimmed and cut into
    ¾-inch cubes**
1 medium onion, chopped
2 cloves garlic, minced
10 cups water
2 cups fresh broccoli flowerets
2 cups sliced fresh mushrooms
1 cup sliced celery
4 medium carrots, sliced
2 tablespoons chicken-flavor instant bouillon
2 teaspoons dried thyme leaves, crushed
½ teaspoon black pepper
**½ teaspoon salt-free herb seasoning *or*
    marjoram leaves**
**½ of a (1-pound) package CREAMETTE®
    Rotelle, uncooked**

In large Dutch oven, heat oil. Add pork, onion and
garlic; cook and stir until meat is cooked through.
Add remaining ingredients except pasta. Bring to a
boil. Reduce heat to low; simmer 20 minutes.
Prepare Creamette® Rotelle according to package
directions; drain. Stir into soup. Heat through.
Refrigerate leftovers.

Note: *To reduce sodium, substitute low-sodium bouillon.*

Nutrients per serving:

Calories	179	Cholesterol	35 mg
Fat	5 g	Sodium	480 mg

Black Bean Rice Soup

Makes 7 servings, 7 cups

½ cup chopped onion
1 clove garlic, minced
2 teaspoons vegetable oil
1½ cups water
1 can (about 14 ounces) beef broth
1 can (15 ounces) black beans or pinto beans, rinsed and drained
1 can (14½ ounces) no-salt-added stewed tomatoes
¾ cup uncooked UNCLE BEN'S® Brand Rice In An Instant
⅓ cup medium picante sauce or salsa
1 teaspoon ground cumin
¼ teaspoon dried oregano leaves, crushed
2 tablespoons chopped fresh cilantro (optional)

Cook and stir onion and garlic in hot oil in large saucepan or Dutch oven until onion is tender. Add water, broth, beans, tomatoes with juice, rice, picante sauce, cumin and oregano; bring to a boil. Cover; reduce heat to low and simmer until rice is tender, about 5 minutes. Sprinkle with cilantro before serving, if desired.

Nutrients per serving:

Calories	113	Cholesterol	trace
Fat	2 g	Sodium	405 mg

Creole-Flavored Beef Soup

Makes 8 servings

3 to 4 pounds beef shank cross cuts
4 cups water
1 can (28 ounces) crushed tomatoes
1 cup sliced celery
1 large onion, chopped
2 cloves garlic, minced
2 beef bouillon cubes
½ teaspoon salt
¼ teaspoon *each* ground black pepper and ground red pepper
2 cups chopped cabbage
1 green bell pepper, chopped
¼ cup fresh lemon juice
2 cups cooked rice

Place beef shank cross cuts, water, tomatoes with juice, celery, onion, garlic, bouillon cubes, salt and black and red pepper in Dutch oven. Bring to a boil; reduce heat to low and simmer, covered, 2 hours, stirring occasionally. Remove shanks; cool slightly. Cut meat from bones into small pieces. Skim fat from broth. Return meat to Dutch oven; add cabbage and green pepper. Continue to simmer, covered, 30 minutes or until meat and vegetables are tender. Stir in lemon juice. To serve, spoon about ¼ cup cooked rice into each serving.

Prep time: 30 minutes
Cook time: 2 hours and 45 minutes

Nutrients per serving:

Calories	241	Cholesterol	44 mg
Fat	5 g	Sodium	582 mg

Favorite recipe from **National Live Stock and Meat Board**

Chunky Ham Stew

Makes 4 to 6 servings

1 medium onion, chopped
2 stalks celery, sliced
2 carrots, sliced
4 cups low-sodium chicken broth
2 cups (8 ounces) ARMOUR® Lower Salt Ham cut into ½-inch cubes
1 tablespoon MRS. DASH®, Original Blend
1 cup frozen peas
2 tablespoons cornstarch

Combine onion, celery, carrots, broth, ham and seasoning in Dutch oven. Cover and cook over medium-high heat for 20 minutes or until carrots are almost tender. Stir in peas. Mix ¼ cup water and cornstarch in small bowl; add to stew. Stir constantly until stew comes to a boil and thickens. Garnish with celery leaves, if desired.

To Microwave: Combine ingredients as directed above in 10-inch microwave-safe tube pan. Cover with vented plastic wrap. Cook on HIGH (100%) power for 10 minutes. Stir; rotate pan. Continue cooking, covered, on HIGH power about 10 to 15 minutes, or until carrots are almost tender. Stir in peas. Mix ¼ cup water and cornstarch; stir into stew. Cook, covered, on HIGH power about 2 to 3 minutes or until stew comes to a boil and thickens, stirring 3 times during cooking. Garnish as above.

Nutrients per serving:

Calories	131	Cholesterol	19 mg
Fat	3 g	Sodium	410 mg

Chunky Ham Stew

Gazpacho

Makes 4 to 5 servings

6 ripe tomatoes, divided
2 cucumbers, divided
1 small onion, quartered
1 clove garlic, peeled and minced
2 cups chicken broth
3 tablespoons red wine vinegar
2 tablespoons olive oil
¼ teaspoon hot pepper sauce
1 large green pepper, seeded and finely chopped
1 small bunch green onions, trimmed and finely chopped

Cut 5 tomatoes into quarters; remove and discard cores. Cut 1 cucumber into quarters; remove and discard seeds. Place quartered tomatoes, quartered cucumber and small onion in food processor or blender container. Cover; process until coarsely chopped. Spoon vegetable mixture into large bowl. Stir in garlic, broth, vinegar, olive oil and hot pepper sauce; cover. Chill. Just before serving, finely chop remaining tomato and cucumber. Ladle soup into chilled bowls or cups. Top with tomato, cucumber, green pepper and green onions.

Nutrients per serving:

Calories	170	Cholesterol	1 mg
Fat	9 g	Sodium	24 mg

Country Japanese Noodle Soup

Makes 4 servings, 5 cups

1 can (14½ ounces) DEL MONTE® Original Recipe Stewed Tomatoes
1 can (14 ounces) low-salt chicken broth
3 ounces uncooked linguine
2 teaspoons low-sodium soy sauce
1 to 1½ teaspoons minced ginger root *or* ¼ teaspoon ground ginger
¼ pound sirloin steak, cut crosswise into thin strips
5 green onions, cut into thin 1-inch slivers
4 ounces firm tofu, cut into small cubes
Ground black pepper (optional)
Additional soy sauce (optional)

In large saucepan, combine tomatoes with juice, broth, pasta, 2 teaspoons soy sauce and ginger with 1¾ cups water; bring to a boil. Cook, uncovered, over medium-high heat 5 minutes. Add meat, green onions and tofu; cook 4 minutes or until pasta is tender. Season to taste with pepper and additional soy sauce, if desired.

Prep time: 10 minutes
Cook time: 15 minutes

Nutrients per serving:

Calories	220	Cholesterol	40 mg
Fat	7 g	Sodium	535 mg

Pizza Soup

Makes 7 servings, 3½ cups

1 medium onion, chopped
2 ounces pepperoni or salami, cut into small pieces*
½ teaspoon LAWRY'S® Garlic Powder with Parsley
½ teaspoon dried oregano leaves, crushed
1 envelope LIPTON® Noodle Soup Mix with Real Chicken Broth
3 cups water
2 tablespoons tomato paste
½ cup (2 ounces) shredded mozzarella cheese

In medium saucepan, cook onion, pepperoni, garlic powder and oregano over medium-high heat, stirring frequently, 3 minutes or until onion is tender. Stir in remaining ingredients except cheese. Bring to a boil. Reduce heat to low and simmer, stirring occasionally, 5 minutes. Sprinkle with cheese before serving.

To Microwave: In 2-quart microwave-safe casserole, microwave onion, pepperoni, garlic powder and oregano at HIGH (100% Power) 2 minutes. Stir in remaining ingredients except cheese. Microwave, uncovered, for 10 minutes, stirring once. Sprinkle with cheese before serving.

Variation: *Omit pepperoni or salami. Add 1 tablespoon oil.*

Nutrients per serving (½ cup):

Calories	99	Cholesterol	11 mg
Fat	6 g	Sodium	604 mg

Gazpacho

Chicken Cilantro Bisque

Makes 4 servings, about 4 cups

6 ounces (2 medium) boneless skinless chicken breast halves, cut into chunks
2½ cups low-sodium chicken broth
½ cup cilantro leaves
½ cup sliced green onions
¼ cup sliced celery
1 large clove garlic, minced
½ teaspoon ground cumin
⅓ cup all-purpose flour
1½ cups (12-ounce can) *undiluted* CARNATION® Lite Evaporated Skimmed Milk
Freshly ground black pepper, to taste

In large saucepan, combine chicken, broth, cilantro, green onions, celery, garlic and cumin. Bring to a boil. Reduce heat to low; cover and simmer for 15 minutes or until chicken is tender. Pour into blender container; add flour. Cover and blend, starting at low speed, until smooth. Pour mixture back into saucepan. Cook over medium heat, stirring constantly, until mixture comes to a boil and thickens. Remove from heat. Gradually stir in evaporated skimmed milk. Reheat just to serving temperature. *Do not boil.* Season with pepper to taste. Garnish as desired.

Nutrients per serving:			
Calories	178	Cholesterol	30 mg
Fat	2 g	Sodium	610 mg

Chicken Cilantro Bisque

Spicy Garden Gazpacho

Makes 7 servings, 7 cups

1 small cucumber, peeled, seeded and coarsely chopped (1¼ cups)
1 medium red bell pepper, coarsely chopped
1 stalk celery, coarsely chopped
2 medium tomatoes, coarsely chopped
¼ cup coarsely chopped onion
¼ cup cilantro leaves
1 clove garlic
3 cups chilled tomato juice, divided
½ cup PACE® Picante Sauce
½ teaspoon salt
Chopped cucumber (optional)
Additional Pace® Picante Sauce (optional)

Place 1 small cucumber, red pepper and celery in food processor or blender container; process just until vegetables are finely chopped. Transfer to large bowl. Place tomatoes, onion, cilantro and garlic in food processor or blender container; process until smooth, about 1 minute. Add to vegetables in large bowl. Stir in 1 cup tomato juice, ½ cup Pace® Picante Sauce and salt. Cover and refrigerate at least 3 hours. Stir in remaining 2 cups tomato juice. Ladle into soup bowls; garnish with chopped cucumber, if desired. Serve with additional Pace® Picante Sauce, if desired.

Nutrients per serving:			
Calories	45	Cholesterol	0 mg
Fat	0 g	Sodium	564 mg

Wild Rice Soup

Makes 4 servings, about 4 cups

⅓ cup chopped carrot
⅓ cup chopped celery
⅓ cup chopped onion
2 teaspoons margarine or butter
1⅓ cups cooked wild rice
1 jar (12 ounces) HEINZ® HomeStyle Turkey Gravy
1½ cups skim milk
2 tablespoons dry sherry

Cook and stir vegetables in margarine in 2-quart saucepan over medium-high heat until tender. Stir in rice, gravy and milk. Reduce heat to low. Simmer 5 minutes. Stir in sherry.

Nutrients per serving (about 1 cup):			
Calories	164	Cholesterol	7 mg
Fat	4 g	Sodium	645 mg

Southwestern Beef Stew

Southwestern Beef Stew

Makes 4 servings

- 1 tablespoon vegetable oil
- 1¼ pounds well-trimmed beef tip roast, cut into 1-inch pieces
- ½ cup coarsely chopped onion
- 1 large clove garlic, minced
- 1½ teaspoons dried oregano leaves, crushed
- 1 teaspoon ground cumin
- ½ teaspoon *each* crushed red pepper and salt
- 4 medium tomatoes, chopped, divided (about 4 cups)
- ½ cup water
- 1 can (4 ounces) whole green chilies
- 1 tablespoon cornstarch
- ¼ cup sliced green onion tops

Heat oil in Dutch oven over medium-high heat. Add beef pieces, onion and garlic; cook and stir until beef is browned. Pour off drippings. Combine oregano, cumin, red pepper and salt; sprinkle over beef. Add 3 cups tomatoes and water, stirring to combine. Reduce heat to low; cover tightly and simmer 1 hour and 55 minutes or until beef is tender, stirring occasionally. Drain green chilies; set aside liquid. Cut chilies into ½-inch pieces; add to beef mixture. Combine cornstarch and liquid; gradually stir into stew and cook, uncovered, until stew comes to a boil and thickens. Stir in remaining tomatoes; garnish with green onion tops.

Nutrients per serving:

Calories	250	Cholesterol	85 mg
Fat	8 g	Sodium	546 mg

Favorite recipe from **National Live Stock and Meat Board**

Cuban Black Bean & Ham Soup

Cuban Black Bean & Ham Soup

Makes 4 servings

1 cup uncooked black beans, soaked overnight and drained
1 slice (2 ounces) ARMOUR® Lower Salt Ham
½ cup chopped green bell pepper
1 medium onion, finely chopped
2 teaspoons MRS. DASH®, Original Blend
1 teaspoon garlic powder
1 teaspoon ground cumin
¼ teaspoon black pepper
1½ cups (6 ounces) ARMOUR® Lower Salt Ham cut into ¾-inch cubes

Combine beans, ham slice, green pepper, onion and seasonings in medium saucepan; add enough water to just cover beans. Bring to a boil; reduce heat to low, cover and simmer about 1½ to 2 hours or until beans are tender and most of liquid is absorbed. Add ham cubes. Cook 10 minutes or until ham cubes are heated through. Remove ham slice before serving. Serve over rice, if desired.

Nutrients per serving:			
Calories	244	Cholesterol	28 mg
Fat	4 g	Sodium	489 mg

Clam Chowder

Makes 12 servings, 3 quarts

3 tablespoons CRISCO® Shortening
6 medium potatoes (about 2 pounds), pared and thinly sliced
2 large yellow onions, peeled and thinly sliced
1½ cups water
2 cans (10 ounces each) shelled whole baby clams *or* 3 cans (6½ ounces each) minced clams, undrained
1 quart low-fat milk
1 teaspoon salt
¼ teaspoon ground white pepper

Melt Crisco® in large, heavy saucepan. Cook and stir potatoes and onions for about 5 minutes until golden brown. Add water; heat to boiling. Reduce heat to low; simmer, covered, 10 to 15 minutes or until potatoes are tender. Stir in clams and their liquid. Heat 2 to 3 minutes. Remove from heat. Add milk, salt and pepper.

Cool chowder, uncovered, 30 minutes. Place chowder, uncovered, in refrigerator. Prior to serving, heat chowder over medium-low heat just until steam rises from top (about 20 minutes); *do not boil.*

Nutrients per serving (1 cup):			
Calories	180	Cholesterol	23 mg
Fat	5 g	Sodium	295 mg

Three-Bean Chili

Makes 6 servings, about 6½ cups

1 can (16 ounces) tomatoes, cut into bite-size pieces
1 jar (12 ounces) HEINZ® HomeStyle Brown Gravy
1 tablespoon chili powder
1 can (15 ounces) chili beans in chili gravy
1 can (15 ounces) garbanzo beans, drained
1 can (15 ounces) pinto or kidney beans, drained
1 can (4 ounces) chopped green chilies, drained
Plain nonfat yogurt or light dairy sour cream, sliced green onions and/or shredded low-fat Cheddar cheese (optional)

Combine tomatoes, gravy and chili powder in 3-quart saucepan. Bring to a boil over high heat. Stir in beans and chilies. Reduce heat to low. Cover; simmer 15 minutes, stirring occasionally. Serve with desired toppings.

Nutrients per serving (about 1 cup):			
Calories	281	Cholesterol	0 mg
Fat	4 g	Sodium	1135 mg

Mushroom and Rice Soup

Makes 10 servings

2 cups (about 8 ounces) sliced fresh mushrooms
1 cup (about 4 ounces) chopped fresh
    mushrooms
1 cup sliced green onions
2 tablespoons olive oil
6 cups chicken broth
2 jars (7 ounces each) whole straw mushrooms,
    undrained
1 cup water
¾ teaspoon cracked black pepper
¾ teaspoon dried thyme leaves, crushed
3 cups cooked rice
1 tablespoon dry sherry

Cook sliced and chopped mushrooms and onions in oil in Dutch oven over medium-high heat until tender crisp. Add broth, straw mushrooms, water, pepper, and thyme. Reduce heat to low; simmer, uncovered, 5 to 7 minutes. Stir in rice and sherry; simmer 1 to 2 minutes.

Nutrients per serving:

Calories	142	Cholesterol	0 mg
Fat	4 g	Sodium	861 mg

Favorite recipe from **USA Rice Council**

Carrot-Rice Soup

Makes 6 servings

1 pound carrots, peeled and chopped
1 medium onion, chopped
1 tablespoon margarine
4 cups chicken broth, divided
¼ teaspoon dried tarragon leaves, crushed
¼ teaspoon ground white pepper
2¼ cups cooked rice
¼ cup light sour cream
    Snipped fresh parsley or mint leaves for
    garnish

Cook and stir carrots and onion in margarine in large saucepan or Dutch oven over medium-high heat 2 to 3 minutes or until onion is tender. Add 2 cups broth, tarragon and pepper. Reduce heat to low; simmer 10 minutes. Combine vegetables and broth in food processor or blender; process until smooth. Return to saucepan. Add remaining 2 cups broth and rice; thoroughly heat. Dollop sour cream on each serving of soup. Garnish with parsley.

Nutrients per serving:

Calories	183	Cholesterol	0 mg
Fat	3 g	Sodium	860 mg

Favorite recipe from **USA Rice Council**

West Coast Bouillabaisse

Makes 6 servings

1 cup sliced onions
2 stalks celery, cut diagonally into slices
2 cloves garlic, minced
1 tablespoon vegetable oil
4 cups chicken broth
1 can (28 ounces) tomatoes with juice, cut up
1 can (6½ ounces) minced clams with juice
½ cup dry white wine
1 teaspoon Worcestershire sauce
½ teaspoon dried thyme leaves, crushed
¼ teaspoon bottled hot pepper sauce
1 bay leaf
1 cup frozen cooked bay shrimp, thawed
1 can (6½ ounces) STARKIST® Tuna, drained
    and broken into chunks
    Salt and black pepper (optional)
6 slices lemon
6 slices French bread

In a Dutch oven, cook and stir onions, celery and garlic in oil for 3 minutes. Stir in broth, tomatoes with juice, clams with juice, wine, Worcestershire, thyme, hot pepper sauce and bay leaf. Bring to a boil; reduce heat to low. Simmer for 15 minutes. Stir in shrimp and tuna; cook for 2 minutes to heat. Remove bay leaf. Season with salt and pepper. Garnish with lemon slices and serve with bread.

Nutrients per serving:

Calories	212	Cholesterol	70 mg
Fat	6 g	Sodium	1146 mg

West Coast Bouillabaisse

Golden Tomato Soup

Makes 8 servings

4 teaspoons reduced-calorie margarine
1 cup chopped onion
2 cloves garlic, coarsely chopped
½ cup chopped carrots
¼ cup chopped celery
8 medium tomatoes, blanched, peeled, seeded, chopped
6 cups chicken broth
¼ cup uncooked rice
2 tablespoons tomato paste
1 tablespoon Worcestershire sauce
¼ to ½ teaspoon black pepper
½ teaspoon dried thyme leaves, crushed
5 drops hot pepper sauce

Melt margarine in large Dutch oven over medium-high heat. Add onion and garlic; cook and stir 1 to 2 minutes or until onion is tender. Add carrots and celery; cook and stir 7 to 9 minutes or until tender, stirring frequently. Stir in tomatoes, broth, rice, tomato paste, Worcestershire sauce, black pepper, thyme and hot pepper sauce. Reduce heat to low; cook about 30 minutes, stirring frequently.

Remove from heat. Let cool about 10 minutes. In food processor or blender, process soup in small batches until smooth. Return soup to Dutch oven; simmer 3 to 5 minutes or until heated through. Garnish as desired.

Nutrients per serving:

Calories	91	Cholesterol	1 mg
Fat	2 g	Sodium	641 mg

Favorite recipe from **Florida Tomato Committee**

Chicken Noodle Soup

Makes 8 servings

1 (46-fluid ounce) can COLLEGE INN® Chicken Broth
½ pound boneless chicken, cut into bite-size pieces
1½ cups uncooked medium egg noodles
1 cup sliced carrots
½ cup chopped onion
⅓ cup sliced celery
1 teaspoon dill weed
¼ teaspoon ground black pepper

In large saucepan, over medium-high heat, heat chicken broth, chicken, noodles, carrots, onion, celery, dill and pepper until mixture comes to a boil. Reduce heat to low; simmer, uncovered, 20 minutes or until chicken and noodles are cooked.

Nutrients per serving:

Calories	88	Cholesterol	19 mg
Fat	2 g	Sodium	579 mg

Split Pea Soup

Makes 6 servings

¼ cup FILIPPO BERIO® 100% Pure Olive Oil
2 medium onions, chopped
2 cloves garlic *or* 1 shallot *or* 2 green onions, chopped
6 cups water
1 cup dried split peas, sorted and rinsed
½ cup sliced carrots
1 stalk celery, chopped
1 bay leaf
¼ teaspoon black pepper

Heat olive oil in Dutch oven over medium heat. Add 2 medium onions and garlic; cook and stir 5 minutes or until onions are tender.

Stir in water, split peas, carrots, celery, bay leaf and black pepper. Bring to a boil over medium-high heat.

Reduce heat to low and simmer for 2 hours, stirring occasionally, until peas are tender. Remove bay leaf before serving.

Nutrients per serving:

Calories	173	Cholesterol	0 mg
Fat	10 g	Sodium	21 mg

Golden Tomato Soup

Basil-Vegetable Soup

Makes 10 to 12 servings

1 package (9 ounces) frozen cut green beans
1 can (15 ounces) cooked cannellini beans, undrained
3 medium carrots, cut into thin slices
3 medium zucchini or yellow squash, cut into thin slices
2 quarts beef broth
2 cloves garlic, minced
  Salt and pepper (optional)
2 to 3 ounces uncooked vermicelli or spaghetti
½ cup tightly packed fresh basil leaves, finely chopped
  Grated Romano cheese

Combine beans, carrots, zucchini, broth and garlic in Dutch oven. Bring to a boil over high heat. Reduce heat to low. Cover; simmer until carrots are tender. Season to taste with salt and pepper. Add vermicelli; bring to a boil over high heat. Reduce heat to low. Simmer until pasta is tender, yet firm. (If desired, pasta may be cooked separately, then added to soup just before serving.) Add basil; continue to simmer until basil is completely tender. Sprinkle with cheese.

Nutrients per serving:

Calories	110	Cholesterol	trace
Fat	1 g	Sodium	585 mg

Basil-Vegetable Soup

Italian Wedding Soup

Makes about 8 servings, 8 cups

½ pound lean ground beef
½ cup fresh bread crumbs (1 slice)
1 egg, slightly beaten
1 tablespoon finely chopped onion
5 teaspoons WYLER'S® or STEERO® Chicken-Flavor Instant Bouillon
8 cups water
½ cup uncooked CREAMETTE® Rosamarina or Acini de Pepe
1½ cups cut-up fresh spinach leaves
  Grated Parmesan cheese (optional)

In small bowl, mix meat, crumbs, egg, onion and *1 teaspoon* bouillon. Shape into 40 small meatballs. In large kettle or Dutch oven, bring water and remaining *4 teaspoons* bouillon to a boil. Add meatballs and pasta; cook 10 minutes. Add spinach; reduce heat to low and simmer 3 to 5 minutes or until tender. Serve with cheese if desired. Refrigerate leftovers.

Nutrients per serving:

Calories	109	Cholesterol	44 mg
Fat	5 g	Sodium	226 mg

Speedy Turkey Sausage Soup

Makes 10 servings

8 cups water
1 can (14½ ounces) stewed tomatoes
1 package (10 ounces) frozen chopped spinach
2 carrots, sliced
1 medium onion, chopped
2 teaspoons instant beef bouillon *or* 2 bouillon cubes
¼ teaspoon black pepper
1 package (1 pound) LOUIS RICH® Turkey Breakfast Sausage, thawed
1 cup uncooked elbow macaroni *or* other small-size pasta
  Grated Parmesan cheese (optional)

Bring water, tomatoes with juice, spinach, carrots, onion, bouillon and pepper to a full boil in large saucepan. Drop bite-size pieces of uncooked sausage into boiling soup mixture to form "dumplings," stirring occasionally. Stir in macaroni. Simmer 10 minutes or until macaroni is tender. Ladle into serving bowls and sprinkle with Parmesan cheese, if desired. Refrigerate or freeze unused portions.

Nutrients per serving:

Calories	145	Cholesterol	35 mg
Fat	3 g	Sodium	670 mg

Hearty Minestrone Gratiné

Makes 4 servings

1 cup diced zucchini
1 cup diced celery
1 can (28 ounces) tomatoes, chopped, juice
    reserved
2 cups water
2 teaspoons sugar
1 teaspoon Italian seasoning
1 can (15 ounces) garbanzo beans, drained
4 (½-inch-thick) slices French bread, toasted
1 cup (4 ounces) SARGENTO® Preferred Light
    Fancy Supreme Shredded Mozzarella
    Cheese
2 tablespoons SARGENTO® Grated Parmesan
    Cheese
    Chopped fresh parsley

Spray large saucepan or Dutch oven with nonstick cooking spray. Over medium heat, cook and stir zucchini and celery until tender. Add tomatoes with juice, water, sugar and seasoning. Simmer, uncovered, 15 to 20 minutes. Add garbanzo beans; simmer 10 minutes.

Meanwhile, heat broiler. Place toasted bread on broiler pan. Divide mozzarella evenly over bread slices. Broil until cheese melts. Ladle soup into bowls and top with cheese-topped bread slices. Sprinkle Parmesan cheese over bread slices and garnish with parsley. Serve immediately.

Nutrients per serving:			
Calories	273	Cholesterol	15 mg
Fat	5 g	Sodium	999 mg

Canton Pork Stew

Makes 6 servings

1 pound lean pork shoulder or pork loin roast,
    cut into 1-inch pieces
1 teaspoon ground ginger
¼ teaspoon ground cinnamon
¼ teaspoon ground red pepper
1 tablespoon peanut or vegetable oil
1 large onion, coarsely chopped
3 cloves garlic, minced
1 can (about 14 ounces) chicken broth
¼ cup dry sherry
1 package (about 10 ounces) frozen baby
    carrots, thawed
1 large green bell pepper, cut into 1-inch pieces
3 tablespoons low-sodium soy sauce
1½ tablespoons cornstarch
    Cilantro for garnish

Canton Pork Stew

Sprinkle pork with ginger, cinnamon and ground red pepper; toss well. Heat large saucepan or Dutch oven over medium-high heat. Add oil; heat until hot.

Add pork to saucepan; brown on all sides. Add onion and garlic; cook 2 minutes, stirring frequently. Add broth and sherry. Bring to a boil over high heat. Reduce heat to medium-low. Cover and simmer 40 minutes.

Stir in carrots and green pepper; cover and simmer 10 minutes or until pork is fork tender. Blend soy sauce into cornstarch in cup until smooth. Stir into stew. Cook and stir 1 minute or until stew boils and thickens. Ladle into soup bowls. Garnish with cilantro.

Nutrients per serving:			
Calories	208	Cholesterol	50 mg
Fat	10 g	Sodium	573 mg

Hearty Chicken and Rice Soup

Hearty Chicken and Rice Soup

Makes 8 servings

10 cups chicken broth
 1 medium onion, chopped
 1 cup sliced celery
 1 cup sliced carrots
 ¼ cup snipped fresh parsley
 ½ teaspoon cracked black pepper
 ½ teaspoon dried thyme leaves, crushed
 1 bay leaf
1½ cups chicken cubes (about ¾ pound)
 2 cups cooked rice
 2 tablespoons lime juice
   Lime slices for garnish

Combine broth, onion, celery, carrots, parsley, pepper, thyme, and bay leaf in Dutch oven. Bring to a boil over high heat. Stir once or twice. Reduce heat to low. Simmer, uncovered, 10 to 15 minutes. Add chicken; simmer, uncovered, 5 to 10 minutes or until chicken is cooked. Remove and discard bay leaf. Stir in rice and lime juice just before serving. Garnish with lime slices.

Nutrients per serving:

Calories	184	Cholesterol	23 mg
Fat	4 g	Sodium	1209 mg

Favorite recipe from **USA Rice Council**

Quick 'n Easy Corn and Pepper Chowder

Makes 6 servings, 6 cups

 1 tablespoon margarine
 1 cup coarsely chopped green or red bell pepper
 1 cup chopped onion
3½ cups (16-ounce package) frozen whole-kernel corn
 1 cup chicken broth
 4 ounces (¾ cup) cooked, lean ham (95% fat free), cubed
 ½ teaspoon ground cumin
 ¼ teaspoon ground white pepper
 3 cups (two 12-ounce cans) *undiluted* CARNATION® Evaporated Lowfat Milk, divided
 ⅓ cup plus 1 tablespoon all-purpose flour

In large saucepan, melt margarine; cook and stir bell pepper and onion over medium heat for 5 minutes or until tender. Stir in corn, broth, ham, cumin and white pepper. Cook for an additional 5 minutes, stirring occasionally, until corn is cooked. Pour *½ cup* evaporated lowfat milk into medium bowl; whisk in flour until well blended. Add *remaining 2½ cups* evaporated lowfat milk; mix well. Slowly pour into saucepan. Increase heat to medium-high; cook, stirring constantly, for 5 minutes until mixture comes to a boil and thickens slightly. Boil for 1 minute. (If a thinner chowder is desired, add additional chicken broth.) Garnish as desired.

Nutrients per serving:

Calories	213	Cholesterol	15 mg
Fat	6 g	Sodium	355 mg

Chilled Pear Helene Soup

Makes 4 to 6 servings

4 pears, peeled, cored, cubed
1 can (12 ounces) pear nectar
1 container (8 ounces) Light PHILADELPHIA
    BRAND® Pasteurized Process Cream
    Cheese Product
½ cup champagne
½ pint raspberries

Place pears in blender or food processor container; cover. Blend until smooth. Add nectar, cream cheese product and champagne; blend until smooth. Pour into medium bowl; cover. Refrigerate.

When ready to serve, place raspberries in blender or food processor container; cover. Blend until smooth. Strain.

Spoon soup into individual serving bowls. Spoon approximately 2 tablespoons raspberry purée at intervals onto each serving. Pull wooden pick through purée making decorative design as desired. Garnish with additional raspberries and fresh mint leaves, if desired.

Prep time: 10 minutes plus refrigerating

Nutrients per serving:			
Calories	200	Cholesterol	20 mg
Fat	7 g	Sodium	220 mg

Creole Fish Soup

Makes 8 servings, 2 quarts

4 slices bacon
½ cup chopped celery
½ cup chopped green bell pepper
½ cup chopped onion
1 clove garlic, finely chopped
1 (28-ounce) can whole tomatoes, undrained
    and broken up
4 cups water
1 tablespoon WYLER'S® or STEERO® Chicken-
    Flavor Instant Bouillon *or* 3 Chicken-
    Flavor Bouillon Cubes
1 bay leaf
1 teaspoon oregano leaves
¼ teaspoon black pepper
1 pound fish fillets, fresh or frozen, thawed, cut
    into 1-inch pieces

In large kettle or Dutch oven, cook bacon until crisp; remove and crumble. In drippings, cook and stir celery, green pepper, onion and garlic until tender. Add tomatoes with juice, water, bouillon, bay leaf, oregano and black pepper; bring to a boil. Reduce heat; simmer uncovered 30 minutes, stirring occasionally. Add fish; simmer 5 to 8 minutes or until fish flakes with fork. Remove bay leaf. Garnish with bacon. Refrigerate leftovers.

Nutrients per serving (1 cup):			
Calories	114	Cholesterol	41 mg
Fat	3 g	Sodium	619 mg

Apple-Squash Soup

Makes 6 servings

1 tablespoon corn oil
1 apple, peeled and chopped
½ onion, chopped
1 cup (8 ounces) low-fat ricotta cheese
1 can (13¾ ounces) low-sodium chicken broth,
    divided
2 packages (11 ounces each) frozen butternut
    squash, thawed
½ cup FRENCH'S® Creamy Spread™ Mustard
¼ teaspoon dried tarragon leaves, crushed

Heat oil in large saucepan. Cook and stir apple and onion in hot oil until tender; remove from heat. Place ricotta cheese in blender container; process until very smooth. Add 1 cup broth and apple mixture to blender. Cover; process until very smooth. Return to saucepan. Add remaining broth, squash, French's® Creamy Spread™ Mustard and tarragon; whisk until smooth. Cook over low heat, stirring occasionally, until heated through, 5 to 10 minutes. *(Do not boil.)* Garnish as desired.

Nutrients per serving:			
Calories	159	Cholesterol	7 mg
Fat	6 g	Sodium	446 mg

Apple-Squash Soup

Freezer Buttermilk Biscuits

Freezer Buttermilk Biscuits

Makes 16 biscuits

  3 cups all-purpose flour
  1 tablespoon baking powder
  1 tablespoon sugar
  1 teaspoon baking soda
  ½ teaspoon salt
  ⅔ cup shortening
  1 cup buttermilk

Combine flour, baking powder, sugar, baking soda and salt in large bowl. Cut in shortening with pastry blender until mixture resembles fine crumbs.

Stir buttermilk into flour mixture until mixture forms a soft dough that leaves sides of bowl.

Turn dough out onto well-floured surface. Knead dough 10 times. (To knead dough, fold dough in half toward you; press dough away from you with heels of hands. Give dough a quarter turn and continue folding, pushing and turning.) Roll dough out into 8-inch square. Cut dough into 16 (2-inch) squares.*

Line baking sheet with plastic wrap. Place squares on lined sheet. Freeze about 3 hours or until firm. Remove frozen squares from sheet and place in freezer container. Freeze up to 1 month.

Preheat oven to 400°F. Place frozen squares, 1½ inches apart, on ungreased baking sheets.

Bake 20 to 25 minutes until golden brown. Serve warm.

*To bake biscuits immediately, preheat oven to 450°F. Prepare dough as directed, but do not freeze. Place squares, 1½ inches apart, on ungreased baking sheets. Bake 10 to 12 minutes until golden brown. Serve warm.

Note: *If desired, biscuits can be split and filled with turkey ham.*

Nutrients per serving (1 biscuit):			
Calories	141	Cholesterol	2 mg
Fat	9 g	Sodium	196 mg

Whole Wheat Herb Muffins

Makes 12 muffins

  1 cup all-purpose flour
  1 cup whole wheat flour
  ⅓ cup sugar
  2 teaspoons baking powder
  ½ teaspoon baking soda
  ½ teaspoon salt
  ½ teaspoon dried basil leaves, crushed
  ¼ teaspoon dried marjoram leaves, crushed
  ¼ teaspoon dried oregano leaves, crushed
  ⅛ teaspoon dried thyme leaves, crushed
  ¾ cup raisins
  1 cup buttermilk
  2 tablespoons margarine or butter, melted
  1 egg, beaten
  2 tablespoons wheat germ

Preheat oven to 400°F. Grease 12 (2½-inch) muffin cups. In large bowl, combine flours, sugar, baking powder, baking soda, salt, herbs and raisins. In small bowl, combine buttermilk, margarine and egg. Stir into flour mixture just until moistened. Spoon into muffin cups. Sprinkle wheat germ over tops. Bake 15 to 20 minutes or until lightly browned and wooden toothpick inserted in centers comes out clean. Remove from pan.

Nutrients per serving (1 muffin):			
Calories	152	Cholesterol	19 mg
Fat	3 g	Sodium	230 mg

Spicy Onion Bread

Makes 8 servings

  2 tablespoons instant minced onion
  ⅓ cup water
  1½ cups biscuit baking mix
  1 egg, slightly beaten
  ½ cup milk
  ½ teaspoon TABASCO® pepper sauce
  2 tablespoons butter, melted
  ½ teaspoon caraway seeds (optional)

Preheat oven to 400°F. Soak instant minced onion in water 5 minutes. Combine biscuit mix, egg, milk and TABASCO sauce in large bowl and stir until blended. Stir in onion. Turn into greased 8-inch pie plate. Brush with melted butter. Sprinkle with caraway seeds. Bake 20 to 25 minutes or until golden brown.

Nutrients per serving:			
Calories	139	Cholesterol	43 mg
Fat	7 g	Sodium	310 mg

Touch of Honey Bread

Cheesy Hot Pepper Bread

Makes 4 loaves, 12 slices per loaf

**3 cups KELLOGG'S® NUTRI-GRAIN®
    Wheat Cereal, crushed to fine crumbs**
5 to 6 cups all-purpose flour, divided
2 packages active dry yeast
2 teaspoons salt
1½ cups low-fat milk
¼ cup salad oil
2 eggs
**1½ cups (6 ounces) shredded Monterey Jack
    cheese with jalapeño peppers**
½ cup finely chopped onions
2 tablespoons margarine, melted (optional)

In large electric mixer bowl, stir together crushed
Kellogg's® Nutri-Grain® cereal, 2 cups flour, yeast
and salt. Set aside.

Heat milk and oil until very warm (120° to 130°F).
Gradually add to cereal mixture and beat until well
combined. Add eggs. Beat on medium speed for
2 minutes. Stir in cheese and onions.

By hand, stir in enough remaining flour to make a
stiff dough. On well-floured surface, knead dough
about 5 minutes or until smooth and elastic. Place
dough in lightly greased bowl, turning once to grease
top. Cover loosely. Let rise in warm place (80° to
85°F) until double in volume (about 1 hour).

Punch dough down. Divide into 4 pieces. On lightly
floured surface, roll each into a 7×10-inch rectangle.
Roll up loaves from long sides. Place, seam-side-
down, on greased baking sheets. Let rise in warm
place until double in volume. Make diagonal slits
across top of loaves.

Bake at 400°F about 15 minutes or until golden
brown. Brush baked loaves with margarine, if desired.
Serve warm or cool.

Nutrients per serving (1 slice):			
Calories	100	Cholesterol	10 mg
Fat	3 g	Sodium	129 mg

Touch of Honey Bread

Makes 1 loaf, 16 slices

2½ to 3 cups all-purpose flour, divided
1 cup QUAKER® Oat Bran hot cereal, uncooked
1 package quick-rise yeast
½ teaspoon salt
1¼ cups water
2 tablespoons honey
2 tablespoons margarine

In large mixer bowl, combine 1 cup flour, oat bran,
yeast and salt. Heat water, honey and margarine until
very warm (120° to 130°F). Add to dry ingredients;
beat at low speed of electric mixer until moistened.
Increase speed to medium; continue beating 3
minutes. Stir in enough remaining flour to form a stiff
dough.

Lightly spray another large bowl with nonstick
cooking spray, or oil lightly. Turn dough out onto
lightly floured surface. Knead 8 to 10 minutes or
until dough is smooth and elastic. Place in prepared
bowl, turning once to coat surface of dough. Cover; let
rise in warm place (80° to 85°F) 30 minutes or until
doubled in size.

Lightly spray 8×4-inch loaf pan with nonstick
cooking spray, or oil lightly. Punch down dough. Roll
into 15×7-inch rectangle. Starting at narrow end, roll
up dough tightly. Pinch ends and seam to seal; place,
seam-side-down, in prepared pan. Cover; let rise in
warm place 30 minutes or until doubled in size.

Heat oven to 375°F. Bake 35 to 40 minutes or until
golden brown. Remove from pan; cool on wire rack at
least 1 hour before slicing.

Nutrients per serving (1 slice):			
Calories	120	Cholesterol	0 mg
Fat	2 g	Sodium	85 mg

Scones with Herbs and Parmesan

Makes 16 scones

2½ cups unbleached all-purpose flour
  1 tablespoon baking powder
  ¼ teaspoon salt (optional)
  ¼ teaspoon black or white pepper
  ¼ cup grated Parmesan cheese
  ½ cup low-fat buttermilk *or* plain nonfat yogurt
  ⅓ cup FILIPPO BERIO® Extra-Virgin Flavorful
    Olive Oil
  2 egg whites
  2 teaspoons lemon juice
  1 clove garlic, minced
  2 tablespoons finely minced fresh chives or
    green onions
  1 tablespoon minced fresh basil *or* 1 teaspoon
    dried basil leaves, crushed
  1 teaspoon minced fresh thyme or oregano
    leaves *or* ½ teaspoon dried thyme or
    oregano leaves, crushed

Preheat oven to 375°F. In large bowl, sift together flour, baking powder, salt and pepper. Stir in cheese until well blended.

In medium bowl, whisk together buttermilk, olive oil, egg whites, lemon juice, garlic, chives and herbs. (Mixture will look slightly curdled).

Add herb mixture to flour mixture; beat with wooden spoon until dough forms a soft ball. (Add additional flour, 1 tablespoon at a time, if necessary.)

Turn dough out onto lightly floured surface; knead 10 to 12 times. Divide dough in half; roll each half into a ball. Place each ball on ungreased baking sheet; press each ball into an 8-inch circle. Cut each circle into 8 wedges.

Bake for 15 to 20 minutes until lightly browned. Cool on wire racks 20 minutes; serve.

Nutrients per serving (1 scone):

Calories	119	Cholesterol	1 mg
Fat	5 g	Sodium	104 mg

Crusty Oval Rolls

Makes 10 rolls

  1 package active dry yeast
1⅓ cups warm water (105° to 115°F)
  1 tablespoon honey
  1 tablespoon shortening, melted, cooled
  1 teaspoon salt
3¼ to 4 cups bread flour, divided
  ¼ cup cold water
  1 teaspoon cornstarch

In large bowl, combine yeast and warm water; stir to dissolve yeast. Stir in honey, shortening, salt and 2½ cups flour; beat until very elastic. Stir in enough of the remaining flour to make dough easy to handle.

Turn dough out onto floured surface. Knead 15 minutes or until dough is smooth and elastic, adding as much remaining flour as needed to prevent sticking. Shape dough into ball. Place in large, greased bowl; turn dough once to grease surface. Cover with towel; let rise in warm place (85°F) until doubled, about 1 hour.

Punch dough down; knead briefly on floured surface. Cover; let rest 10 minutes. Divide dough into 10 equal pieces; shape each piece into ball. Starting at center and working toward opposite ends, roll each ball on floured surface with palms of hands into tapered oval. Place, evenly spaced, on 2 greased baking sheets. Cover; let rise in warm place until almost doubled, about 25 minutes.

In small saucepan, combine cold water and cornstarch. Bring to a boil over high heat, stirring constantly. Boil until thickened and clear, about 2 minutes; cool slightly. Brush risen rolls with warm cornstarch mixture. Slash each roll lengthwise with sharp knife about ½ inch deep and to about ½ inch from each end.

Preheat oven to 375°F. Bake 30 to 35 minutes or until rolls are golden brown and sound hollow when tapped. Remove to wire racks to cool.

Nutrients per serving (1 roll):

Calories	180	Cholesterol	0 mg
Fat	2 g	Sodium	214 mg

Crusty Oval Rolls

Dill-Sour Cream Scones

Makes 1 dozen scones

  2 cups all-purpose flour
  2 teaspoons baking powder
  ½ teaspoon baking soda
  ½ teaspoon salt
  ¼ cup margarine, softened
  2 eggs
  ½ cup sour cream
  1 tablespoon chopped dill *or* 1 teaspoon dill
     weed

Preheat oven to 425°F. Combine flour, baking powder, baking soda and salt in large bowl. Cut in margarine with pastry blender until mixture resembles fine crumbs.

Beat eggs with fork in small bowl. Add sour cream and dill; beat until well combined. Stir into flour mixture until mixture forms soft dough that leaves sides of bowl.

Turn dough out onto well-floured surface. Knead dough 10 times. Roll dough out, using floured rolling pin, into 9×6-inch rectangle.

Cut dough, using floured knife, into 6 (3-inch) squares. Cut each square diagonally in half, making 12 triangles. Place triangles, 2 inches apart, on ungreased baking sheets.

Bake 10 to 12 minutes or until golden brown. Cool on wire racks for 10 minutes. Serve warm.

Nutrients per serving (1 scone):

Calories	137	Cholesterol	40 mg
Fat	7 g	Sodium	238 mg

Dill-Sour Cream Scones

Jalapeño-Bacon Corn Bread

Makes 9 to 12 servings

  4 slices bacon
  ¼ cup minced green onions with tops
  2 jalapeño peppers, stemmed, seeded and
     minced
  1 cup yellow cornmeal
  1 cup all-purpose flour
  2½ teaspoons baking powder
  ½ teaspoon baking soda
  ½ teaspoon salt
  1 egg
  ¾ cup plain yogurt
  ¾ cup milk
  ¼ cup butter or margarine, melted
  ½ cup (2 ounces) shredded Cheddar cheese

Preheat oven to 400°F. Cook bacon in skillet until crisp; drain on paper towels. Pour 2 tablespoons bacon drippings into 9-inch cast-iron skillet or 9-inch square baking pan. Crumble bacon into small bowl; add green onions and peppers.

Combine cornmeal, flour, baking powder, baking soda and salt in large bowl. Beat egg slightly in medium bowl; add yogurt and whisk until smooth. Whisk in milk and butter. Pour liquid mixture into dry ingredients; stir just until moistened. Stir in bacon mixture. Pour into skillet; sprinkle with cheese. Bake 20 to 25 minutes or until wooden toothpick inserted in center comes out clean. Cut into wedges or squares; serve hot.

Nutrients per serving:

Calories	165	Cholesterol	27 mg
Fat	8 g	Sodium	335 mg

Garlic Mustard Loaf

Makes 10 servings

  1 loaf (about 15 inches) Italian bread
  2 tablespoons *each* FRENCH'S® Creamy
     Spread™ Mustard and olive oil
  1¼ teaspoon *each* garlic powder and dried basil
     leaves, crushed

Partially cut loaf into 10 slices, cutting down to, but not through, bottom of loaf. Combine remaining ingredients in small bowl. Brush mixture evenly onto each cut bread slice. Wrap loaf in aluminum foil. Bake at 400°F for 20 minutes or until heated through.

Nutrients per serving (1 slice):

Calories	110	Cholesterol	0 mg
Fat	3 g	Sodium	214 mg

Savory French Bread

Makes 6 to 8 servings

1 large loaf French bread
¼ cup butter or margarine, softened
½ teaspoon dried basil leaves
½ teaspoon dill weed
½ teaspoon chopped dried chives
¼ teaspoon garlic powder
¼ teaspoon paprika
¼ teaspoon TABASCO® pepper sauce

Preheat oven to 400°F. Slice bread diagonally, but do not cut through bottom crust of loaf. In small bowl mix remaining ingredients. Spread between bread slices; wrap bread in aluminum foil and heat in oven 15 to 20 minutes. Serve warm.

Nutrients per serving:			
Calories	216	Cholesterol	17 mg
Fat	7 g	Sodium	390 mg

Sun-Dried Tomato Muffins

Makes 12 muffins

1 cup all-purpose flour
½ cup whole wheat flour
2 teaspoons baking powder
2 teaspoons sugar
½ teaspoon black pepper
¼ teaspoon salt
1 cup low-fat milk
¼ cup vegetable oil
1 egg
4 to 6 tablespoons chopped green olives
2 tablespoons chopped oil-packed sun-dried tomatoes, drained*

Preheat oven to 425°F. Grease or paper-line 12 (2½-inch) muffin cups. Combine dry ingredients in medium bowl. Whisk together milk, oil and egg. Add to dry ingredients, mixing just until moistened. Gently stir in olives and tomatoes.

Spoon batter into prepared muffin cups. Bake 15 minutes or until lightly browned.

*If using sun-dried tomatoes not packed in oil, hydrate according to package directions before chopping.

Nutrients per serving (1 muffin):			
Calories	59	Cholesterol	10 mg
Fat	3 g	Sodium	79 mg

Pepperoni 'n' Chive Mini Muffins

Pepperoni 'n' Chive Mini Muffins

Makes 24 muffins

1½ cups buttermilk baking mix
1 (8-ounce) carton LAND O LAKES® Light Sour Cream (1 cup)
¼ cup chopped fresh chives *or* 4 teaspoons dried chives
¼ cup skim milk
1 egg, slightly beaten
¼ teaspoon garlic powder
⅓ cup chopped pepperoni

Heat oven to 400°F. In medium bowl combine all ingredients except pepperoni. Stir just until moistened. Fold in pepperoni. Spoon into greased mini-muffin pans. Bake for 18 to 20 minutes or until lightly browned. Cool 5 minutes; remove from pans.

Nutrients per serving (1 muffin):			
Calories	58	Cholesterol	15 mg
Fat	3 g	Sodium	146 mg

Spanish Olive-Cheddar Muffins

Makes 12 muffins

2 cups all-purpose flour
1 tablespoon sugar
2 teaspoons baking powder
1 teaspoon dry mustard
½ teaspoon baking soda
½ teaspoon salt
⅛ teaspoon ground red pepper
¼ cup margarine, softened
1 cup (4 ounces) shredded Cheddar cheese
½ cup chopped pimento-stuffed green olives
1 cup buttermilk
1 egg

Preheat oven to 375°F. Grease or paper-line 12 (2½-inch) muffin cups.

Combine flour, sugar, baking powder, mustard, baking soda, salt and red pepper in large bowl. Cut in margarine with pastry blender until mixture resembles fine crumbs. Stir in cheese and olives.

Combine buttermilk and egg in small bowl until blended. Stir into flour-cheese mixture just until moistened. Spoon evenly into prepared muffin cups.

Bake 25 to 30 minutes or until golden brown and wooden toothpick inserted in centers comes out clean. Immediately remove from pan. Cool on wire rack. Serve warm or cool completely.

Nutrients per serving (1 muffin):

Calories	171	Cholesterol	28 mg
Fat	8 g	Sodium	379 mg

Easy Country Biscuits

Makes about 1½ dozen biscuits

4 cups buttermilk baking mix
⅔ cup wheat germ
1½ cups (12-ounce can) *undiluted* CARNATION®
    Evaporated Lowfat Milk
1 to 2 tablespoons all-purpose flour

In medium bowl, combine baking mix and wheat germ. Stir in evaporated lowfat milk to make a soft dough. Turn dough out onto floured surface; knead 10 times, adding additional flour as necessary to keep dough from sticking. Roll to ½-inch thickness. Cut with floured 2½-inch round biscuit cutter; place on ungreased baking sheet. Bake in preheated 450°F oven for 8 to 10 minutes. Serve warm.

Nutrients per serving: (1 biscuit):

Calories	148	Cholesterol	2 mg
Fat	4 g	Sodium	370 mg

Common Sense® Oat Bran Bread

Makes 1 loaf, 14 slices

1¾ cups bread flour
1 cup whole wheat flour
1½ cups KELLOGG'S® COMMON SENSE®
    Oat Bran Cereal, any variety
½ teaspoon salt (optional)
1 package active dry yeast
2 tablespoons firmly packed brown sugar
1 cup skim milk
¼ cup margarine
3 egg whites

Stir together flours. In large electric mixer bowl, combine ½ cup flour mixture, Kellogg's® Common Sense® Oat Bran cereal, salt, yeast and sugar.

Heat milk and margarine until very warm (120° to 130°F). Gradually add to cereal mixture and beat 2 minutes on medium speed, scraping bowl occasionally. Add egg whites and 1 cup flour mixture. Beat 2 minutes on high speed.

Using dough hook on electric mixer or by hand, stir in remaining flour mixture. Knead on low speed or by hand for 5 minutes or until dough is smooth and elastic.

Place dough in lightly greased bowl, turning once to grease top. Cover and let rise in warm place (80° to 85°F) until double in volume. Punch down dough and let rest 10 minutes.

Roll dough on lightly floured surface into 14×8½-inch rectangle. Starting with short side, roll up dough lengthwise. Place, seam-side-down, in lightly greased 9×5×3-inch loaf pan. Let rise until double in volume, about 1½ hours.

Bake in 375°F oven about 30 minutes or until golden brown. Remove from pan and cool on wire rack.

Nutrients per serving (1 slice):

Calories	160	Cholesterol	0 mg
Fat	4 g	Sodium	110 mg

Spanish Olive-Cheddar Muffins

Cheesy Onion Flatbread

Cheesy Onion Flatbread

Makes 2 flatbreads, 8 wedges each

½ cup plus 3 tablespoons honey, divided
2⅓ cups warm water (105° to 115°F), divided
1½ packages active dry yeast
6 tablespoons olive oil, divided
3 cups whole wheat flour
⅓ cup cornmeal
1½ tablespoons coarse salt
3 to 4 cups all-purpose flour, divided
1 large red onion, thinly sliced
1 cup red wine vinegar
Additional cornmeal
1 cup grated Parmesan cheese
½ teaspoon onion salt
Freshly ground black pepper to taste

Place 3 tablespoons honey in large bowl. Pour ⅓ cup water over honey. *Do not stir.* Sprinkle yeast over water. Let stand about 15 minutes until bubbly. Add remaining 2 cups water, 3 tablespoons olive oil, whole wheat flour and cornmeal. Mix until well blended. Stir in salt and 2 cups all-purpose flour. Gradually stir in enough remaining flour until mixture clings to sides of bowl.

Turn dough out onto lightly floured surface. Knead in enough remaining flour to make a smooth and satiny dough, about 10 minutes. Divide dough in half. Place each half in large, lightly greased bowl; turn over to grease surface. Cover; let rise in warm place (80° to 85°F) until doubled.

Meanwhile, combine onion, vinegar and remaining ½ cup honey. Marinate at room temperature at least 1 hour.

Grease two 12-inch pizza pans; sprinkle each with additional cornmeal. Stretch dough and pat into pans; create valleys with fingertips. Cover; let rise in warm place until doubled, about 1 hour.

Preheat oven to 400°F. Drain onions; scatter over dough. Sprinkle with remaining 3 tablespoons olive oil, cheese and onion salt. Season with pepper.

Bake 25 to 30 minutes or until flatbread is crusty and golden. Cut each flatbread into 8 wedges. Serve warm.

Nutrients per serving (1 wedge):

Calories	296	Cholesterol	5 mg
Fat	8 g	Sodium	916 mg

Touchdown Cheese Scones

Makes 8 scones

2 cups all-purpose flour
2½ teaspoons baking powder
½ teaspoon baking soda
¼ teaspoon salt
2 tablespoons cold butter or margarine, cut into pieces
1 cup (4 ounces) shredded mild Cheddar cheese
⅔ cup buttermilk
2 large eggs, divided
¼ teaspoon TABASCO® pepper sauce

Preheat oven to 350°F. In a large bowl, sift together flour, baking powder, baking soda and salt. Cut in butter until mixture resembles cornmeal. Stir in cheese. In small bowl, blend together buttermilk, 1 egg and TABASCO sauce. Make a well in center of dry ingredients; add buttermilk mixture. Stir quickly and lightly with fork to form sticky dough. Turn dough out on lightly floured board. Knead gently 10 times. Divide dough in half; pat each half into circle about ½ inch thick. Cut each circle into 4 wedges. Combine remaining egg and 1 tablespoon water. Brush each wedge with egg mixture. Arrange on greased baking sheet. Bake 13 to 15 minutes or until golden.

Nutrients per serving (1 scone):

Calories	225	Cholesterol	92 mg
Fat	9 g	Sodium	385 mg

Cheddar-Onion Casserole Bread

Makes 1 loaf, 12 wedges

2½ cups flour
1 tablespoon baking powder
½ teaspoon salt
½ cup HELLMANN'S® or BEST FOODS®
   Light Reduced Calorie Mayonnaise
2 cups (8 ounces) shredded Cheddar cheese
½ cup minced green onions
¾ cup milk
1 egg

Preheat oven to 425°F. Grease 1½-quart casserole dish. In large bowl, combine flour, baking powder and salt. Stir in mayonnaise until mixture resembles coarse crumbs. Add cheese and green onions; toss. In small bowl, beat milk and egg. Stir into cheese mixture just until moistened. Spoon into prepared casserole dish.

Bake 35 to 45 minutes or until wooden toothpick inserted into center comes out clean. Cut into wedges; serve immediately.

Nutrients per serving (1 wedge):			
Calories	214	Cholesterol	43 mg
Fat	10 g	Sodium	301 mg

Cheesy Corn Sticks

Makes 7 to 9 corn sticks

½ cup all-purpose flour
½ cup cornmeal
2 teaspoons baking powder
¼ teaspoon salt
½ cup low-fat milk
1 egg, beaten
3 tablespoons vegetable oil
½ cup (2 ounces) shredded Cheddar cheese

Preheat oven to 425°F. Heat cast-iron corn stick pan in oven while preparing batter.

Combine flour, cornmeal, baking powder and salt in medium bowl; set aside. Combine milk, egg and oil. Add to dry ingredients, stirring just until moistened.

Carefully brush hot pan with additional oil. Spoon batter into prepared pan. Sprinkle batter with cheese. Bake 10 minutes or until lightly browned.

Nutrients per serving (1 corn stick):			
Calories	148	Cholesterol	35 mg
Fat	9 g	Sodium	211 mg

Garden Herb Muffins

Makes 12 muffins

2 cups all-purpose flour
2 tablespoons sugar
1 tablespoon baking powder
¼ teaspoon salt
1 package (3 ounces) cream cheese
¾ cup milk
½ cup finely shredded or grated carrots
¼ cup chopped green onions
¼ cup vegetable oil
1 egg

Preheat oven to 400°F. Grease or paper-line 12 (2½-inch) muffin cups.

Combine flour, sugar, baking powder and salt in large bowl. Cut in cream cheese with pastry blender until mixture resembles fine crumbs.

Combine milk, carrots, green onions, oil and egg in small bowl until blended. Stir into flour mixture just until moistened. Spoon evenly into prepared muffin cups.

Bake 25 to 30 minutes or until golden brown and wooden toothpick inserted in centers comes out clean. Immediately remove from pan. Cool on wire rack for 10 minutes. Serve warm.

Nutrients per serving (1 muffin):			
Calories	166	Cholesterol	27 mg
Fat	8 g	Sodium	163 mg

Garden Herb Muffins

Cottage Herb Rolls

Makes 1½ to 2 dozen rolls

 1 package active dry yeast
 ¼ cup warm water (105° to 115°F)
2½ cups unsifted flour
 ¼ cup sugar
 1 teaspoon oregano leaves
 1 teaspoon salt
 ½ cup cold margarine or butter
 1 cup **BORDEN®** or **MEADOW GOLD®**
  Cottage Cheese
 1 egg, beaten
  Melted margarine or butter

Dissolve yeast in warm water. In large bowl, combine flour, sugar, oregano and salt; mix well. Cut in cold margarine until mixture resembles coarse cornmeal. Blend in cheese, egg and yeast mixture. Turn onto well-floured surface; knead. Shape into ball; place in well-greased bowl. Brush top with melted margarine. Cover; let rise until doubled. Punch down; shape as desired. Brush with melted margarine; cover. Let rise again until nearly doubled. Bake in preheated 375°F oven 12 to 15 minutes. Serve warm.

Nutrients per serving (1 roll):			
Calories	102	Cholesterol	10 mg
Fat	5 g	Sodium	174 mg

Cottage Herb Rolls

Vegetable Dinner Rolls

Makes 1 dozen rolls

1½ cups all-purpose flour
1½ cups whole wheat flour
 1 cup **KELLOGG'S® ALL-BRAN®** Cereal
 2 tablespoons sugar
 1 package active dry yeast
 1 teaspoon dried basil leaves, crushed
 ½ teaspoon salt
 1 cup water
 2 tablespoons margarine
 2 egg whites
 1 cup shredded zucchini
 ½ cup shredded carrots
 ¼ cup sliced green onions
  Nonstick cooking spray
 2 teaspoons sesame seeds (optional)

Stir together flours. Set aside.

In large mixing bowl, combine Kellogg's® All-Bran® cereal, 1 cup flour mixture, sugar, yeast, basil and salt. Set aside.

Heat water and margarine until very warm (115° to 120°F). Add water mixture and egg whites to cereal mixture. Beat on low speed with electric mixer 30 seconds or until thoroughly combined. Increase speed to high and beat 3 minutes longer, scraping bowl frequently. Mix in vegetables.

By hand, stir in enough remaining flour to make sticky dough. Cover loosely. Let rise in warm place (80° to 85°F) until doubled in volume. Stir down batter. Portion evenly into 12 (2½-inch) muffin pan cups coated with nonstick cooking spray. Sprinkle with sesame seeds, if desired. Let rise in warm place until doubled in volume.

Bake at 400°F about 17 minutes or until golden brown. Serve warm.

Nutrients per serving (1 roll):			
Calories	160	Cholesterol	0 mg
Fat	3 g	Sodium	190 mg

Easy Poppy Seed Yeast Bread

Makes 2 loaves

2 packages (¼ ounce *each*) active dry yeast
1 cup warm water (105° to 110°F)
1½ cups (12-ounce can) *undiluted* CARNATION®
   Evaporated Lowfat Milk
3 tablespoons margarine, softened
3 tablespoons granulated sugar
2 teaspoons salt
¼ cup poppy seeds, divided
5 to 5½ cups all-purpose flour, divided
1 egg white
1 tablespoon water

In large mixer bowl, dissolve yeast in warm water.
Add evaporated lowfat milk, margarine, sugar, salt
and *3 tablespoons* poppy seeds. Gradually add *3 cups*
flour, beating on medium speed until almost smooth
(about 1 minute). Add remaining *2 to 2½ cups* flour
to form a stiff dough. Use spatula to push dough
down off beater stems. (Dough will be sticky.) Cover
bowl; let rise in warm, draft-free place (80° to 85°F)
for 30 minutes. Stir for 2 minutes. Divide dough
equally into 2 greased 8½×4½×2½-inch loaf pans.
(Flour hands for easier handling.) Push dough into
corners and pat tops until smooth. In small bowl,
combine egg white and water; brush tops of loaves.
Sprinkle with remaining *1 tablespoon* poppy seeds.
Let dough rise for 25 minutes. Bake at 375°F for
20 to 30 minutes or until loaves are brown and sound
hollow when tapped. Remove from pans; cool
completely on wire rack.

Nutrients per serving (½-inch slice):

Calories	195	Cholesterol	2 mg
Fat	3 g	Sodium	330 mg

Bran Pita Bread

Bran Pita Bread

Makes 12 servings

1 package active dry yeast
1¼ cups warm water (110° to 115°F)
1½ cups KELLOGG'S® ALL-BRAN® Cereal
1½ cups all-purpose flour, divided
½ teaspoon salt
¼ cup vegetable oil
1 cup whole wheat flour

In large bowl of electric mixer, dissolve yeast in warm
water, about 5 minutes. Add Kellogg's® All-Bran®
cereal, mixing until combined. On low speed, beat in
1 cup all-purpose flour, salt and oil. Beat on high
speed 3 minutes, scraping sides of bowl.

Using dough hook on electric mixer or by hand, stir in
whole wheat flour. Continue kneading with mixer on
low speed or by hand 5 minutes longer or until dough
is smooth and elastic. Add remaining ½ cup all-
purpose flour, if needed, to make soft dough.

Divide dough into 12 portions. Roll each portion
between floured hands into a very smooth ball. Cover
with plastic wrap or a damp cloth; let rest 10 minutes.

On a well-floured surface, lightly roll one piece of
dough at a time into 6-inch round, turning dough over
once. Do not stretch, puncture or crease dough. Keep
unrolled dough covered while rolling each dough
piece. Place 2 rounds of dough at a time on
ungreased baking sheet.

Bake in 450°F oven about 4 minutes or until dough
is puffed and slightly firm. Turn with a spatula;
continue baking about 2 minutes or until lightly
browned; cool. Repeat with remaining dough. Cut in
half and fill with a vegetable or meat filling.

Nutrients per serving (2 pita bread halves):

Calories	160	Cholesterol	0 mg
Fat	5 g	Sodium	210 mg

For guaranteed dinnertime delights, turn low-fat cuts of beef, pork and lamb into exciting new entrées. Quick stir-fries are perfect for short-notice meals on hectic weeknights while a succulent roast or tenderloin will turn your dinner parties into memorable, yet health-minded, occasions.

Beef Kabobs over Lemon Rice

Makes 2 servings

6 ounces boneless beef sirloin steak, cut into 1-inch cubes
1 small zucchini, sliced
1 small yellow squash, sliced
1 small red bell pepper, cut into squares
1 small onion, cut into chunks
¼ cup low-calorie Italian dressing
1 cup hot cooked rice
2 teaspoons fresh lemon juice
1 tablespoon snipped fresh parsley
¼ teaspoon seasoned salt

Combine beef and vegetables in large plastic food bag with zippered closing. Add dressing and marinate 4 to 6 hours in refrigerator. Remove beef and vegetables from marinade; heat reserved marinade to a boil. Alternately thread beef and vegetables onto 4 skewers. Grill or broil kabobs, turning and basting with marinade, 5 to 7 minutes or to desired doneness. Combine rice and remaining ingredients. Serve kabobs over rice mixture. Garnish as desired.

Nutrients per serving:

Calories	273	Cholesterol	50 mg
Fat	9 g	Sodium	545 mg

Favorite recipe from **USA Rice Council**

Saucy Stuffed Peppers

Makes 12 servings

6 medium green bell peppers
1¼ cups water
2 cups low-sodium tomato juice, divided
1 can (6 ounces) tomato paste
1 teaspoon dried oregano leaves, crushed, divided
½ teaspoon dried basil leaves, crushed
½ teaspoon garlic powder, divided
1 pound lean ground beef
1½ cups QUAKER® Oats (quick or old fashioned, uncooked)
1 medium tomato, chopped
¼ cup chopped carrot
¼ cup chopped onion

Heat oven to 350°F. Cut peppers lengthwise in half. Remove membranes and seeds; set peppers aside. In large saucepan, combine water, 1 cup tomato juice, tomato paste, ½ teaspoon oregano, basil and ¼ teaspoon garlic powder. Simmer 10 to 15 minutes.

Combine beef, oats, remaining 1 cup tomato juice, ½ teaspoon oregano and ¼ teaspoon garlic powder with tomato, carrot and onion; mix well. Fill each pepper half with about ⅓ cup meat mixture. Place in 13×9-inch glass baking dish; pour sauce evenly over peppers. Bake 45 to 50 minutes.

Nutrients per serving:

Calories	174	Cholesterol	28 mg
Fat	9 g	Sodium	145 mg

Beef Kabobs over Lemon Rice

Beef 'n Broccoli

Beef 'n Broccoli

Makes 4 servings

½ cup A.1.® Steak Sauce
¼ cup soy sauce
2 cloves garlic, crushed
1 pound top round steak, thinly sliced
1 (16-ounce) bag frozen broccoli, red bell
    peppers, bamboo shoots and mushrooms,
    thawed*
   Hot cooked rice (optional)

In small bowl, combine steak sauce, soy sauce and garlic. Pour marinade over steak in nonmetal dish. Cover; refrigerate 1 hour, stirring occasionally.

Remove steak from marinade; reserve marinade. In large lightly oiled skillet, over medium-high heat, stir-fry beef 3 to 4 minutes or until meat is no longer pink. Remove steak with slotted spoon; keep warm.

In same skillet, heat vegetables and reserved marinade to a boil; reduce heat to low. Cover; simmer for 2 to 3 minutes. Stir in beef. Serve over rice, if desired.

*1 (16-ounce) package frozen broccoli cuts, thawed, can be substituted.

Nutrients per serving:

Calories	209	Cholesterol	65 mg
Fat	4 g	Sodium	1669 mg

Barbecued Pork Chops

Makes 6 servings

2 tablespoons CRISCO® PURITAN® Oil
6 loin pork chops, trimmed of excess fat
1 medium onion, chopped
3 cloves garlic, minced
1 can (6 ounces) no-salt-added tomato paste
½ cup cider vinegar
¼ cup plus 2 tablespoons firmly packed brown
    sugar
¼ cup water
3 tablespoons Worcestershire sauce
1 teaspoon dry mustard
1 teaspoon chili powder
¼ teaspoon black pepper
¼ teaspoon salt

Heat oven to 350°F. Heat Crisco® Puritan® Oil in large skillet over medium-high heat. Cook pork chops until lightly browned on both sides. Remove chops from skillet. Place in 11×7-inch baking dish in single layer. Set aside. Add onion and garlic to skillet. Cook and stir over medium heat until soft. Stir in remaining ingredients. Simmer 5 minutes. Pour sauce over chops. Turn to coat. Cover. Bake at 350°F for 45 to 60 minutes or until chops are tender.

To Microwave: Combine Crisco® Puritan® Oil, onion and garlic in 11×7-inch microwave-safe dish. Cover with plastic wrap. Microwave on HIGH (100% power) 3 minutes, stirring after 1½ minutes. Add remaining ingredients, except for chops. Stir well. Place uncooked chops in sauce. Turn to coat. Cover. Microwave on HIGH 16 minutes, turning dish after every 4 minutes. Rearrange chops after 8 minutes. Let stand 5 minutes, covered, before serving.

Nutrients per serving:

Calories	200	Cholesterol	70 mg
Fat	10 g	Sodium	90 mg

Oriental Beef and Broccoli Stir-Fry

Makes 4 servings

- ½ cup PACE® Picante Sauce
- 2 tablespoons light or regular soy sauce (optional)
- 1 tablespoon water
- 1 tablespoon cornstarch
- ¾ pound boneless beef top sirloin steak, cut into 2×¼-inch strips
- 1 tablespoon finely shredded fresh ginger
- 2 garlic cloves, minced
- 1 tablespoon peanut or vegetable oil, divided
- 1 teaspoon Oriental sesame oil (optional)
- 1½ cups quartered mushrooms
- 1½ cups (1-inch) broccoli florets
- 1 red bell pepper, cut into 1-inch pieces
- 4 green onions with tops, cut into 1-inch pieces
  Hot cooked rice (optional)
  Additional PACE® Picante Sauce (optional)

Combine ½ cup Pace® Picante Sauce, soy sauce, water and cornstarch in small bowl; mix well and set aside. Toss beef with ginger and garlic. Heat 2 teaspoons peanut oil and, if desired, sesame oil, in 10-inch skillet over medium-high heat. Add beef mixture and stir-fry 3 minutes or until no longer pink. Remove beef mixture with slotted spoon; set aside. Add remaining 1 teaspoon oil to skillet. Add mushrooms, broccoli and red pepper; stir-fry 3 minutes or until vegetables are crisp-tender. Add Pace® Picante Sauce mixture, beef mixture and green onions; cook and stir 1 minute or until sauce boils and thickens. Serve over rice, if desired. Serve with additional Pace® Picante Sauce, if desired.

Nutrients per serving:

Calories	201	Cholesterol	51 mg
Fat	8 g	Sodium	398 mg

Fiesta Meat Loaf

Makes 6 servings

- 1 pound HEALTHY CHOICE® Extra Lean Ground Beef
- ¾ cup quick oats, uncooked
- ½ cup HEALTHY CHOICE® Cholesterol Free Egg Product
- ½ cup salsa, divided
- ½ cup diced green bell pepper
- ¼ cup diced onion
- 1 tablespoon chili powder
- ½ teaspoon salt

In medium bowl, combine beef, oats, egg product, ¼ cup salsa, green pepper, onion, chili powder and salt. Form meat mixture into loaf shape and place in 8×4×3-inch loaf pan sprayed with nonstick cooking spray. Top with remaining ¼ cup salsa. Bake in 350°F oven for 55 minutes.

Nutrients per serving:

Calories	150	Cholesterol	35 mg
Fat	4 g	Sodium	400 mg

Pork Tenderloin Waldorf

Makes 4 to 6 servings

- 2 pork tenderloins (about 1½ pounds)
- ¾ cup apple jelly
- ¼ cup REALEMON® Lemon Juice from Concentrate
- ¼ cup soy sauce
- ¼ cup vegetable oil
- 1 tablespoon finely chopped fresh ginger root
- 1 cup chopped apple
- 1 cup fresh bread crumbs (2 slices bread)
- ¼ cup finely chopped celery
- ¼ cup chopped pecans

Partially slice tenderloins lengthwise, being careful not to cut all the way through; arrange in shallow dish. In small saucepan, combine jelly, ReaLemon® brand, soy sauce, oil and ginger; cook and stir until jelly melts. Reserving *3 tablespoons* jelly mixture, pour remainder over meat. Cover; refrigerate 4 hours or overnight. Place meat in shallow baking pan. Combine apple, crumbs, celery, nuts and reserved jelly mixture. Spread slits open; fill with apple mixture. Bake 30 minutes in preheated 375°F oven. Loosely cover meat; bake 10 minutes longer or until meat thermometer reaches 160°F. Refrigerate leftovers.

Nutrients per serving:

Calories	273	Cholesterol	81 mg
Fat	10 g	Sodium	448 mg

Pork Tenderloin Waldorf

Saucy Pork and Peppers

Makes 4 servings

2 fresh limes
¼ cup 62%-less-sodium soy sauce
4 cloves garlic, crushed
1 teaspoon dried oregano leaves, crushed
½ teaspoon dried thyme leaves, crushed
   Dash ground red pepper
2 to 3 fresh parsley sprigs
1 bay leaf
1 pound pork tenderloin, cut into 1-inch cubes
1 tablespoon olive oil
1 teaspoon firmly packed brown sugar
2 medium onions, each cut into 8 pieces
2 medium tomatoes, each cut into 8 pieces and
   seeded
2 large bell peppers, each cut into 8 pieces

Remove peel from limes using vegetable peeler.
Squeeze juice from limes. In small bowl, combine
lime juice and peel, soy sauce, garlic, oregano leaves,
thyme leaves, ground red pepper, parsley and bay
leaf; blend well. Place pork cubes in plastic bag or
nonmetal bowl. Pour marinade mixture over pork,
turning to coat. Seal bag or cover bowl; marinate at
least 2 hours or overnight in refrigerator, turning pork
several times.

Remove lime peel, parsley sprigs and bay leaf from
marinade; discard. Remove pork from marinade,
reserving marinade. Drain pork well. Heat oil in large
skillet over high heat. Add brown sugar; stir until
sugar is brown and bubbly. Add pork cubes; cook and
stir about 5 minutes or until pork is browned. Reduce
heat to low. Add onions, tomatoes, bell peppers and
reserved marinade; simmer 10 to 15 minutes or until
pork is tender.

Nutrients per serving:

Calories	243	Cholesterol	79 mg
Fat	8 g	Sodium	547 mg

Favorite recipe from **National Pork Producers Council**

Saucy Pork and Peppers

Pork Curry

Makes 4 servings

1 tablespoon vegetable oil
1 pound pork tenderloin, cut into ½-inch cubes
¾ cup coarsely chopped onion
⅓ cup chopped celery
1½ cups chopped apple, unpared
1 medium tomato, seeded and chopped
1 cup water
¼ cup golden raisins
1 to 3 tablespoons curry powder
1 teaspoon instant chicken bouillon granules
⅛ teaspoon garlic powder
  Hot cooked rice (optional)
  Plain yogurt (optional)
¼ cup chopped peanuts (optional)

In large frying pan, heat oil to medium hot. Add pork cubes, onion and celery. Cook, stirring occasionally, until pork is brown and vegetables are tender. Stir in apple, tomato, water, raisins, curry powder, bouillon granules and garlic powder; mix well. Reduce heat to low. Cover and cook, stirring occasionally, 10 minutes. Remove cover and continue cooking, stirring occasionally, 5 to 10 minutes, until of desired consistency. Serve on bed of hot cooked rice and top each serving with plain yogurt and chopped peanuts, if desired.

Nutrients per serving:			
Calories	243	Cholesterol	73 mg
Fat	7 g	Sodium	311 mg

Favorite recipe from **National Pork Producers Council**

Fast Beef Roast with Mushroom Sauce

Makes 6 to 8 servings

1 boneless beef rib-eye roast (about 2 pounds)
2 tablespoons vegetable oil
4 cups water
1 can (10¾ ounces) condensed beef broth
1 cup dry red wine
2 cloves garlic, minced
1 teaspoon dried marjoram leaves, crushed
4 black peppercorns
3 whole cloves
  Mushroom Sauce (recipe follows)

Tie roast with heavy string at 2-inch intervals. Heat oil in Dutch oven over medium-high heat. Cook roast until evenly browned. Pour off drippings. Add water, broth, wine, garlic, marjoram, peppercorns and cloves; bring to a boil. Reduce heat to medium-low.

Fast Beef Roast with Mushroom Sauce

Cover; simmer 15 minutes per pound. Check temperature with instant-read thermometer; temperature should be 130°F for rare. *Do not overcook.* Remove roast to serving platter; reserve cooking liquid. Cover roast tightly with plastic wrap or foil; allow to stand 10 minutes before carving (temperature will continue to rise about 10°F to 140°F for rare). Prepare Mushroom Sauce. Remove strings from roast. Carve into thin slices and top with Mushroom Sauce. Serve with assorted vegetables, if desired.

Note: A boneless beef rib-eye roast will yield 3 to 4 (3-ounce) cooked servings per pound.

Mushroom Sauce

1 tablespoon butter
1 cup sliced fresh mushrooms
1 cup reserved beef cooking liquid, strained
1½ teaspoons cornstarch
¼ teaspoon salt
2 dashes black pepper
1 tablespoon thinly sliced green onion tops

Melt butter in medium saucepan over medium-high heat. Add mushrooms; cook and stir 5 minutes. Remove and reserve. Add cooking liquid, cornstarch, salt and pepper to pan. Bring to a boil; cook and stir until thickened, 1 to 2 minutes. Remove from heat. Stir in reserved mushrooms and green onion.

Nutrients per serving (includes 3 tablespoons sauce):			
Calories	188	Cholesterol	59 mg
Fat	8 g	Sodium	327 mg

Favorite recipe from **National Live Stock and Meat Board**

Sweet and Spicy Pork Tenderloin

Sweet and Spicy Pork Tenderloin

Makes 4 servings

2 teaspoons dried tarragon leaves, crushed
½ teaspoon dried thyme leaves, crushed
⅛ to ½ teaspoon black pepper
¼ teaspoon ground red pepper
    Dash salt
1 pound pork tenderloin, trimmed and cut
    crosswise into ½-inch pieces
2 tablespoons margarine, melted
1½ tablespoons honey

In small bowl, combine tarragon, thyme, peppers and salt; blend well. Brush both sides of each pork tenderloin piece with margarine; sprinkle both sides with seasoning mixture. Arrange tenderloin pieces on broiler pan. Broil, 5 to 6 inches from heat source, for 2 minutes per side. Remove from broiler. Brush top side of each piece with honey. Broil for an additional minute. Place pork pieces on serving plate.

Nutrients per serving:

Calories	219	Cholesterol	79 mg
Fat	10 g	Sodium	158 mg

Favorite recipe from **National Pork Producers Council**

Spaghetti Pizza Deluxe

Makes 8 servings

1 package (7 ounces) CREAMETTE® Spaghetti,
    uncooked
½ cup skim milk
1 egg, beaten
    Nonstick cooking spray
½ pound lean ground beef
1 medium onion, chopped
1 medium green bell pepper, chopped
2 cloves garlic, minced
1 can (15 ounces) tomato sauce
1 teaspoon Italian seasoning
1 teaspoon salt-free herb seasoning
¼ teaspoon black pepper
2 cups sliced fresh mushrooms
2 cups shredded part-skim mozzarella cheese

Prepare Creamette® Spaghetti according to package directions. In medium bowl, blend milk and egg; add spaghetti and toss to coat. Spray 15×10-inch jelly-roll pan with nonstick cooking spray. Spread spaghetti mixture evenly in prepared pan. In large skillet, cook and stir beef, onion, green pepper and garlic until beef is no longer pink; drain. Add tomato sauce and seasonings; simmer 5 minutes. Spoon beef mixture evenly over spaghetti. Top with mushrooms and cheese. Bake in 350°F oven for 20 minutes. Let stand 5 minutes before cutting. Refrigerate leftovers.

Note: *To reduce sodium, substitute no salt added tomato sauce.*

Nutrients per serving:

Calories	267	Cholesterol	76 mg
Fat	9 g	Sodium	499 mg

Stuffed Cabbage Rolls

Makes 6 servings

¾ pound lean ground beef
½ cup chopped onion
1 cup cooked long grain white rice
¼ teaspoon ground cinnamon
1 egg white
6 large cabbage leaves
1 can (14½ ounces) DEL MONTE® Original
    Style Stewed Tomatoes (No Salt Added)
1 can (15 ounces) DEL MONTE® Tomato Sauce
    (No Salt Added)

In medium skillet, brown meat and onion over medium-high heat; drain. Add rice and cinnamon. Season with salt-free herb seasoning, if desired. Remove from heat; stir in egg white. Pre-cook cabbage leaves 3 minutes in small amount of boiling water; drain. Divide meat mixture among cabbage leaves. Roll cabbage leaves loosely around meat mixture, allowing room for rice to swell. Secure with toothpicks. In 4-quart saucepan, combine tomatoes and tomato sauce; bring to boil. Reduce heat; add cabbage rolls. Simmer, uncovered, 30 minutes.

Prep time: 15 minutes
Cook time: 30 minutes

Nutrients per serving:

Calories	238	Cholesterol	42 mg
Fat	8 g	Sodium	86 mg

Herb-Marinated Chuck Steak

Herb-Marinated Chuck Steak

Makes 4 servings

¼ cup chopped onion
2 tablespoons *each* chopped fresh parsley and
  white vinegar
1 tablespoon vegetable oil
2 teaspoons Dijon-style mustard
1 clove garlic, minced
½ teaspoon dried thyme leaves, crushed
1 pound boneless beef chuck shoulder steak, cut
  1 inch thick

Combine onion, parsley, vinegar, oil, mustard, garlic
and thyme. Place beef chuck shoulder steak in plastic
bag; add onion mixture, spreading evenly over both
sides. Close bag securely; marinate in refrigerator
6 to 8 hours (or overnight, if desired), turning at least
once. Pour off marinade; discard. Place steak on rack
in broiler pan so surface of meat is 3 to 5 inches from
heat source. Broil, about 16 minutes for rare and
about 18 minutes for medium, turning once. Carve
steak diagonally across the grain into thin slices.
Garnish as desired.

Nutrients per serving:

Calories	216	Cholesterol	85 mg
Fat	10 g	Sodium	94 mg

Favorite recipe from **National Live Stock and Meat Board**

Linguine Primavera

Makes 8 servings

2 tablespoons olive or vegetable oil
2 tablespoons lemon juice
1 medium red bell pepper, cut into strips
1 large onion, chopped
1 package (8 ounces) fresh mushrooms, sliced
½ pound lean fully cooked ham, cut into
  julienne strips
1 package (10 ounces) frozen peas, thawed
1 package (6 ounces) frozen snow peas, thawed
1 can (5 ounces) evaporated skimmed milk
½ cup shredded Provolone cheese, divided
½ of (1-pound) package CREAMETTE®
  Linguine
Freshly ground black pepper

In large skillet, heat olive oil and lemon juice. Add
bell pepper, onion and mushrooms; cook and stir
until tender-crisp. Add ham, peas, milk and ¼ cup
cheese; heat through, stirring frequently. Keep warm.
Prepare Creamette® Linguine according to package
directions; drain. Combine hot cooked linguine and
vegetable mixture in large bowl; toss to coat. Top with
remaining ¼ cup cheese. Serve immediately with
freshly ground black pepper. Refrigerate leftovers.

Nutrients per serving:

Calories	273	Cholesterol	22 mg
Fat	8 g	Sodium	493 mg

Polynesian Kabobs

Makes 8 kabobs

3 cups (12 ounces) ARMOUR® Lower Salt Ham
  cut into 1-inch cubes
1 fresh pineapple, peeled and cut into 1-inch
  cubes
1 green, red and yellow bell pepper, each cut
  into 1-inch pieces
8 medium mushrooms
¼ cup bottled low-calorie, low-sodium red wine
  vinegar salad dressing

Preheat oven to 350°F. Thread ham, pineapple,
peppers and mushrooms onto 8 (10-inch) metal or
wooden skewers, alternating ingredients. Place in
baking dish. Brush all sides with dressing. Bake for
8 minutes. Turn kabobs and baste all sides with
dressing. Cook about 6 to 8 minutes or until ham
is heated through. Serve over rice, if desired.

Nutrients per serving (1 kabob):

Calories	133	Cholesterol	21 mg
Fat	2 g	Sodium	368 mg

Lasagna

Makes 12 servings

- 1 cup chopped onions
- 3 cloves garlic, minced
- 2 tablespoons CRISCO® PURITAN® Oil
- 1 pound extra lean ground beef
- 2 cans (14½ ounces *each*) no-salt-added stewed tomatoes
- 1 can (6 ounces) no-salt-added tomato paste
- 2 teaspoons dried basil leaves, crushed
- 1 teaspoon dried oregano leaves, crushed
- ½ teaspoon sugar
- ¼ teaspoon black pepper
- 2 cups low-fat cottage cheese
- ½ cup grated Parmesan cheese, divided
- ¼ cup chopped fresh parsley
- 8 ounces wide lasagna noodles
- 1 cup (4 ounces) shredded low-moisture part-skim mozzarella cheese, divided

Cook and stir onions and garlic in Crisco® Puritan® Oil in large skillet over medium heat until soft. Push to one side of skillet. Add ground beef. Cook, stirring well, to crumble beef. Drain, if necessary. Add tomatoes with juice. Break tomatoes into smaller pieces. Add tomato paste, basil, oregano, sugar and pepper. Stir until well blended. Simmer 30 minutes. Combine cottage cheese, ¼ cup Parmesan cheese and parsley. Set aside.

Cook lasagna noodles 7 minutes in unsalted boiling water. Drain well. Heat oven to 350°F. Place thin layer of meat sauce in 13×9×2-inch pan. Add, in layers, half the noodles, half the cottage cheese mixture, 2 tablespoons Parmesan cheese, ⅓ cup mozzarella and thin layer of sauce. Repeat noodle and cheese layers. Top with remaining sauce and remaining ⅓ cup mozzarella. Bake at 350°F for 45 minutes. Let stand 15 minutes before serving. Cut into 12 rectangles.

Nutrients per serving:

Calories	270	Cholesterol	55 mg
Fat	10 g	Sodium	300 mg

Glazed Ham with Sweet Potatoes

Makes 4 servings

- 1 (1¼-pound) slice ham steak
- 1 (16-ounce) can sliced peaches, drained
- 1 (16-ounce) can sweet potatoes, drained
- 2 tablespoons maple syrup, divided
- 2 tablespoons apricot jam or preserves
- 1 teaspoon Dijon-style mustard
- Hot cooked Brussels sprouts (optional)

Preheat broiler. Position oven rack about 4 inches from heat source. Place ham in shallow pan. Surround with peaches and sweet potatoes; drizzle peaches and sweet potatoes with 1 tablespoon maple syrup. Broil 5 minutes or until lightly browned.

Meanwhile, heat combined jam and mustard in microwave or in saucepan on rangetop until jam is melted; stir until well blended. Turn ham, peaches and sweet potatoes over; brush ham with jam mixture. Drizzle peaches and sweet potatoes with remaining 1 tablespoon maple syrup. Continue broiling 5 minutes or until thoroughly heated. Serve with Brussels sprouts, if desired.

Nutrients per serving:

Calories	300	Cholesterol	60 mg
Fat	7 g	Sodium	1462 mg

Glazed Ham with Sweet Potatoes

Pork Loin Roulade

Makes 4 servings

    4 boneless center pork loin slices, about 1 pound
 ½ red bell pepper, cut into strips
 ½ green bell pepper, cut into strips
    1 tablespoon vegetable oil
 ⅔ cup orange juice
 ⅔ cup bottled barbecue sauce
    1 tablespoon prepared Dijon-style mustard

Place pork slices between 2 pieces of plastic wrap. Pound with a mallet to about ¼-inch thickness. Place several red and green pepper strips crosswise on each pork slice; roll up jelly-roll style. Secure rolls with wooden toothpicks.

In large heavy skillet, brown pork rolls in hot oil. Drain fat from pan. Combine remaining ingredients and add to skillet. Bring mixture to a boil; reduce heat to low. Cover and simmer 10 to 12 minutes or until pork is tender. Remove toothpicks and serve.

Nutrients per serving:

Calories	255	Cholesterol	72 mg
Fat	10 g	Sodium	530 mg

Favorite recipe from **National Pork Producers Council**

Pork Loin Roulade

Spaghetti and Bacon Toss

Makes 4 to 6 servings

    1 small zucchini, sliced
    4 green onions, chopped
    1 (8-ounce) carton plain nonfat yogurt
 ½ cup canned white sauce
 ¼ cup skim milk
    8 ounces uncooked spaghetti, cooked and drained according to package directions (omit salt)
    1 (12-ounce) package ARMOUR® Lower Salt Bacon slices, cooked crisp and crumbled
    1 large fresh tomato, seeded and chopped

Spray medium saucepan with nonstick cooking spray; place over medium heat. Add zucchini and green onions; cook and stir until tender. Combine yogurt, white sauce and milk in small bowl; add to vegetables. Cook until heated through and mixture steams. Toss warm spaghetti with bacon; top with sauce. Garnish each serving with chopped tomato.

Nutrients per serving:

Calories	289	Cholesterol	19 mg
Fat	10 g	Sodium	485 mg

Swiss and Beef Grilled Sandwiches

Makes 4 servings

    8 slices French bread (each 5 × ½-inch), divided
    4 slices (3 ounces) SARGENTO® Preferred Light Sliced Swiss Cheese, halved, divided
    1 medium tomato, cut into 8 thin slices
    4 ounces thinly sliced lean deli roast beef
    2 tablespoons light mayonnaise
    1 tablespoon Dijon-style mustard
    1 teaspoon snipped chives *or* finely chopped green onion tops

Top 4 bread slices with half the cheese and all the tomato and beef slices. Top beef with remaining cheese and bread slices. Combine mayonnaise, mustard and chives in small bowl. Spread mayonnaise mixture on outside of sandwiches. Grill over medium heat in a dry preheated skillet 2 to 3 minutes or until light golden brown. Turn and grill other side 2 to 3 minutes. Serve immediately.

Nutrients per serving:

Calories	256	Cholesterol	23 mg
Fat	9 g	Sodium	824 mg

Tabbouli Lamb Sandwiches

Makes 6 half-pocket sandwiches

1 can (14½ ounces) DEL MONTE® Original
    Style Stewed Tomatoes
½ cup bulgur wheat, uncooked
1½ cups cooked diced lamb or beef
¾ cup diced cucumber
3 tablespoons minced fresh mint or parsley
1 tablespoon fresh lemon juice
1 tablespoon olive oil
3 pita breads, cut into halves

Drain tomatoes reserving liquid; pour liquid into measuring cup. Add water, if needed, to measure ¾ cup. In small saucepan, bring liquid to a boil; add bulgur. Cover and simmer over low heat 20 minutes or until tender. Cool. Chop tomatoes. In medium bowl, combine tomatoes, meat, cucumber, mint, lemon juice and oil. Stir in cooled bulgur. Season with salt and pepper, if desired. Spoon about ½ cup tabbouli into each pita bread half.

Prep & Cook time: 25 minutes
Chill time: 30 minutes

Nutrients per serving (1 half-pocket sandwich):

Calories	239	Cholesterol	35 mg
Fat	7 g	Sodium	343 mg

Pork Tenderloin Diane

Makes 5 servings

1 pound pork tenderloin, cut crosswise into
    10 pieces
2 teaspoons lemon pepper seasoning
2 tablespoons butter
2 tablespoons lemon juice
1 tablespoon Worcestershire sauce
1 teaspoon Dijon-style mustard
1 tablespoon finely chopped chives or parsley
    Whole chives for garnish

Press each tenderloin piece into 1-inch-thick medallion; sprinkle surfaces with lemon pepper. Melt butter in large heavy skillet over medium heat. Add medallions; cook 3 to 4 minutes on each side. Remove pork to serving platter; keep warm. Stir lemon juice, Worcestershire sauce and mustard into pan juices in skillet. Cook, stirring, until heated through. Pour sauce over medallions; sprinkle with chopped chives. Garnish with whole chives.

Nutrients per serving:

Calories	198	Cholesterol	84 mg
Fat	9 g	Sodium	157 mg

Favorite recipe from **National Pork Producers Council**

Beef Cubed Steak Provençale

Beef Cubed Steaks Provençale

Makes 4 servings

2 cloves garlic, minced
½ teaspoon dried basil leaves, crushed
¼ teaspoon black pepper
4 lean beef cubed steaks (about 4 ounces *each*)
1½ teaspoons olive oil
2 small zucchini, thinly sliced
6 cherry tomatoes, cut in half
1½ teaspoons grated Parmesan cheese
    Salt (optional)

Combine garlic, basil and pepper; divide mixture in half. Press ½ of seasoning mixture evenly into both sides of beef cubed steaks; set aside. Heat oil and remaining seasoning mixture in large nonstick skillet over medium heat. Add zucchini; cook and stir 3 minutes. Add tomatoes; continue cooking 1 minute, stirring frequently. Remove zucchini mixture to platter; sprinkle with cheese and keep warm. Increase heat to medium-high. Add 2 steaks to same skillet; cook to desired doneness, 3 to 4 minutes, turning once. Repeat with remaining 2 steaks. Season steaks with salt, if desired. Serve with zucchini mixture; garnish as desired.

Nutrients per serving:

Calories	223	Cholesterol	81 mg
Fat	10 g	Sodium	60 mg

Favorite recipe from **National Live Stock and Meat Board**

Steak & Snow Peas Stir-Fry

Steak & Snow Peas Stir-Fry

Makes 6 servings

- ¾ pound lean, well-trimmed boneless beef top round steak
- 2 tablespoons cornstarch, divided
- 2 tablespoons soy sauce
- 1 tablespoon dry sherry
- ½ teaspoon sugar
- ½ teaspoon salt
- 1 cup uncooked UNCLE BEN'S® CONVERTED® Brand Rice
- 2 tablespoons thinly sliced green onions with tops
- 2 tablespoons diced red bell pepper
- 1 tablespoon vegetable oil
- ¾ cup water
- 1 can (8 ounces) water chestnuts, drained and sliced
- 1 package (6 ounces) frozen pea pods, thawed

Freeze meat until slightly firm. Cut meat diagonally across grain into very thin slices; place in shallow baking dish. Combine 1 tablespoon cornstarch, soy sauce, sherry, sugar and salt; pour over meat. Marinate at room temperature 30 minutes.

Prepare rice according to package directions, omitting butter. Stir green onions and bell pepper into rice; set aside. Drain meat, reserving marinade. Heat oil in large nonstick skillet until hot but not smoking. Add meat; cook and stir until lightly browned, 3 to 4 minutes. Combine remaining 1 tablespoon cornstarch and water with meat marinade; mix well. Add to skillet with water chestnuts and pea pods. Cook and stir until sauce boils and is thickened and clear. Serve meat mixture over rice mixture.

Nutrients per serving:			
Calories	255	Cholesterol	40 mg
Fat	4 g	Sodium	560 mg

Greek Lamb Sauté with Mostaccioli

Makes 8 servings

- ½ of (1-pound) package CREAMETTE® Mostaccioli, uncooked
- 1 tablespoon olive or vegetable oil
- 1 medium green bell pepper, chopped
- 1 medium onion, chopped
- 1 medium eggplant, peeled, seeded and cut into 1-inch cubes
- 2 cloves garlic, minced
- ½ pound lean boneless lamb, cut into ¾-inch cubes
- 2 tomatoes, peeled, seeded and chopped
- ¼ teaspoon ground nutmeg
- ¼ cup grated Parmesan cheese

Prepare Creamette® Mostaccioli according to package directions; drain. In large skillet, heat oil. Add green pepper, onion, eggplant and garlic; cook and stir until tender-crisp. Add lamb; cook until tender. Stir in tomatoes and nutmeg; cook until heated through. Toss meat mixture with hot cooked mostaccioli and Parmesan cheese. Serve immediately. Refrigerate leftovers.

Nutrients per serving:			
Calories	205	Cholesterol	29 mg
Fat	5 g	Sodium	82 mg

Marinated Flank Steak

Makes 4 to 6 servings

- ½ cup REALEMON® Lemon Juice from Concentrate
- ¼ cup vegetable oil
- 2 teaspoons WYLER'S® or STEERO® Beef-Flavor Instant Bouillon
- 2 cloves garlic, finely chopped
- 1 teaspoon ground ginger
- 1 (1- to 1½-pound) flank steak

In large shallow dish or plastic bag, combine ReaLemon® brand, oil, bouillon, garlic and ginger; add steak. Cover; marinate in refrigerator 4 to 6 hours, turning occasionally. Remove steak from marinade; heat marinade thoroughly. Grill or broil steak 5 to 7 minutes on each side or until steak is cooked to desired doneness, basting frequently with marinade. Serve immediately. Refrigerate leftovers.

Nutrients per serving:			
Calories	156	Cholesterol	48 mg
Fat	8 g	Sodium	345 mg

Sunday Super Stuffed Shells

Makes 9 to 12 servings

    3 cloves fresh garlic
    2 tablespoons olive oil
    ¾ pound ground veal
    ¾ pound ground pork
    1 package (10 ounces) frozen chopped spinach,
        cooked, drained and squeezed dry
    1 cup finely chopped fresh parsley
    1 cup bread crumbs
    2 eggs, beaten
    3 cloves fresh garlic, minced
    3 tablespoons grated Parmesan cheese
      Salt (optional)
    1 package (12 ounces) uncooked jumbo pasta
        shells, cooked, rinsed and drained
    3 cups spaghetti sauce
      Sautéed zucchini slices (optional)

Cook and stir 3 whole garlic cloves in hot oil in large skillet over medium heat until garlic is browned. Discard garlic. Add veal and pork. Cook until lightly browned, stirring to separate meat; drain fat. Set aside.

Combine spinach, parsley, bread crumbs, eggs, minced garlic and cheese in large bowl; blend well. Season to taste with salt. Add cooled meat mixture; blend well. Fill shells with meat mixture.

Spread about 1 cup spaghetti sauce over bottom of greased 12×8-inch pan. Arrange shells in pan. Pour remaining sauce over shells. Cover with foil. Bake in preheated 375°F oven 35 to 45 minutes or until bubbly. Serve with zucchini. Garnish as desired.

Nutrients per serving:

Calories	290	Cholesterol	81 mg
Fat	10 g	Sodium	428 mg

Favorite recipe from **Fresh Garlic Association**

Sunday Super Stuffed Shells

Applesauce-Stuffed Tenderloin

Makes 8 servings

  2 pork tenderloins (about 1 pound *each*), trimmed
¼ cup dry vermouth *or* apple juice
    Nonstick cooking spray
⅔ cup chunky applesauce
¼ cup finely chopped dry-roasted peanuts
¼ teaspoon salt
¼ teaspoon finely crushed fennel seed
⅛ teaspoon black pepper

Using sharp knife, form a "pocket" in each pork tenderloin by cutting a lengthwise slit down center of each almost to, but not through, bottom of each tenderloin. Place in nonmetal baking dish. Pour vermouth in pockets and over tenderloins; cover dish. Marinate about 1 hour at room temperature.

Heat oven to 375°F. Spray 15×10-inch jelly-roll pan or shallow baking pan with nonstick cooking spray. In small bowl, combine applesauce, peanuts, salt, fennel seed and pepper; blend well. Spoon mixture into pocket in each tenderloin. Secure stuffed pockets with wooden toothpicks. Place stuffed tenderloins in prepared pan. Roast at 375°F for about 30 minutes or until meat thermometer registers 155°F. Let stand 5 to 10 minutes. Remove toothpicks and slice. Garnish as desired.

Nutrients per serving:

Calories	179	Cholesterol	79 mg
Fat	6 g	Sodium	131 mg

Favorite recipe from **National Pork Producers Council**

North Beach Skillet Dinner

Makes 6 to 8 servings

½ pound bulk sausage
½ pound ground turkey
1 onion, chopped
1 clove garlic, pressed
1 teaspoon ground cumin
1 teaspoon dried oregano leaves, crumbled
⅛ to ¼ teaspoon ground red pepper
2 cups water
1 package (10 ounces) frozen chopped spinach, thawed
1 package (6.5 ounces) 5-minute long-grain and wild rice mix
1 cup DOLE® Chopped Dates

In 12-inch nonstick skillet, cook and stir sausage, turkey, onion and garlic over medium-high heat until onion is soft. Add cumin, oregano and red pepper. Stir in water, spinach and rice mix with its seasoning packet. Heat to a boil. Reduce heat to low. Cover; simmer 5 minutes. Stir in dates. Heat through.

Prep time: 5 minutes
Cook time: 10 minutes

Nutrients per serving:

Calories	260	Cholesterol	26 mg
Fat	9 g	Sodium	587 mg

Curried Black Beans and Rice with Sausage

Makes 10 servings

1 tablespoon olive oil
1 medium onion, minced
1 tablespoon curry powder
½ pound smoked turkey sausage, thinly sliced
¾ cup chicken broth
2 cans (16 ounces *each*) black beans, drained
1 tablespoon white wine vinegar (optional)
3 cups cooked rice

Heat oil in large heavy skillet over medium heat. Cook onion and curry powder, stirring well, until onion is tender. Stir in turkey sausage and broth; simmer 5 minutes. Stir in beans; cook until hot, stirring constantly. Remove from heat and stir in vinegar. Spoon over rice.

To Microwave: Combine oil, onion and curry powder in 2- to 3-quart microproof baking dish. Cook on HIGH (100% power) 2 minutes or until onion is tender. Add turkey sausage, broth and beans; cover with vented plastic wrap and cook on HIGH 5 to 6 minutes, stirring after 3 minutes, or until thoroughly heated. Continue as directed above.

Nutrients per serving:

Calories	267	Cholesterol	16 mg
Fat	5 g	Sodium	481 mg

Favorite recipe from **USA Rice Council**

Applesauce-Stuffed Tenderloin

Beef Fajitas

Makes 10 fajitas

½ cup REALEMON® Lemon Juice from
   Concentrate
¼ cup vegetable oil
2 teaspoons WYLER'S® or STEERO® Beef-
   Flavor Instant Bouillon
2 cloves garlic, finely chopped
1 (1- to 1½-pound) top round steak
10 (6-inch) flour tortillas, warmed as package
   directs
   Garnishes: Picante sauce, shredded lettuce,
      shredded Cheddar cheese and sliced green
      onions (optional)

In large shallow dish or plastic bag, combine
ReaLemon® brand, oil, bouillon and garlic; add
steak. Cover; marinate in refrigerator 6 hours or
overnight. Remove steak from marinade; heat
marinade thoroughly. Grill or broil steak 8 to
10 minutes on each side or until steak is cooked to
desired doneness, basting frequently with marinade.
Slice steak diagonally into thin strips; place on
tortillas. Top with one or more garnishes; fold
tortillas. Serve immediately. Refrigerate leftovers.

Nutrients per serving (1 fajita):

Calories	187	Cholesterol	29 mg
Fat	7 g	Sodium	115 mg

Beef Fajitas

Southwestern Stir-Fry

Makes 5 servings

1 pound pork tenderloin
2 tablespoons dry sherry
2 tablespoons cornstarch
1 teaspoon ground cumin
1 clove garlic, finely chopped
½ teaspoon seasoned salt
1 tablespoon vegetable oil
1 medium onion, thinly sliced
1 medium green bell pepper, cut into strips
12 cherry tomatoes, halved
   Warm flour tortillas and green chili salsa for
      serving

Cut pork tenderloin lengthwise into quarters. Cut
each quarter into ¼-inch thick slices. Combine
sherry, cornstarch, cumin, garlic and seasoned salt
in medium bowl. Add pork slices; stir to coat.

Heat oil in large, heavy skillet over medium-high
heat. Add pork mixture; stir-fry 3 to 4 minutes. Stir
in onion, bell pepper and tomatoes. Reduce heat to
low; cover and simmer 3 to 4 minutes. Serve hot with
tortillas and salsa.

Nutrients per serving:

Calories	180	Cholesterol	41 mg
Fat	9 g	Sodium	255 mg

Favorite recipe from **National Pork Producers Council**

Eckrich® Lite Hoagie Sandwiches

Makes 8 servings

3 tablespoons low-calorie mayonnaise
1 tablespoon thinly sliced green onion
¼ teaspoon chili powder
1 loaf French bread (about 14 inches)
   Spinach leaves
1 package (6 ounces) ECKRICH® Lite Lower
   Salt Ham
2 ounces sliced Swiss cheese
1 package (6 ounces) ECKRICH® Lite Oven
   Roasted Turkey Breast
1 medium tomato, sliced

Combine mayonnaise, onion and chili powder in
small bowl. Cut bread into halves lengthwise. Spread
mayonnaise mixture on bread. Top bottom half of
bread with spinach leaves, ham, cheese, turkey and
tomato. Complete sandwich by adding top half of
bread. Cut into portions about 1½ inches wide.

Nutrients per serving:

Calories	173	Cholesterol	28 mg
Fat	6 g	Sodium	654 mg

Oriental Stuffed Peppers

Makes 6 servings

½ pound extra-lean ground beef
2 cups frozen Oriental vegetable combination
1 cup cooked white rice
1 jar (12 ounces) HEINZ® HomeStyle Brown Gravy
2 tablespoons low-sodium soy sauce
½ teaspoon ground ginger
⅛ teaspoon black pepper
3 medium green, red or yellow bell peppers, split lengthwise and seeded

Brown beef in large skillet; drain, if necessary. Stir in vegetables and rice. Combine gravy, soy sauce, ginger and black pepper in small bowl; reserve ½ cup. Stir remaining gravy mixture into beef mixture. Place bell peppers in lightly greased 2-quart oblong baking dish. Fill bell peppers with beef mixture. Spoon reserved gravy mixture over bell peppers. Bake in 350°F oven 35 to 45 minutes or until hot.

To Microwave: Crumble beef into 2-quart microwave-safe casserole. Cover with lid or vented plastic wrap. Microwave at HIGH (100% power) 2½ to 3½ minutes or until meat is no longer pink, stirring once to break up meat. Drain. Stir in vegetables and rice. Combine gravy, soy sauce, ginger and pepper in small bowl; reserve ½ cup. Stir remaining gravy mixture into beef mixture. Place bell peppers in 2-quart microwave-safe oblong baking dish. Fill bell peppers with beef mixture. Spoon reserved gravy mixture over bell peppers. Cover with vented plastic wrap. Microwave at HIGH 10 to 11 minutes or until bell peppers are tender-crisp and beef mixture is hot.

Nutrients per serving:			
Calories	217	Cholesterol	33 mg
Fat	8 g	Sodium	575 mg

Pork with Three Onions

Makes 4 servings

⅓ cup teriyaki sauce
2 cloves garlic, minced
¾ pound pork tenderloin
2 tablespoons peanut or vegetable oil, divided
1 small red onion, cut into thin wedges
1 small yellow onion, cut into thin wedges
1 teaspoon sugar
1 teaspoon cornstarch
2 green onions, cut into 1-inch pieces
Fried bean threads* (optional)

Pork with Three Onions

Combine teriyaki sauce and garlic in shallow bowl. Cut pork across the grain into ¼-inch slices; cut each slice in half. Toss pork with teriyaki mixture. Marinate at room temperature 10 minutes.

Heat large skillet over medium-high heat. Add 1 tablespoon oil; heat until hot. Drain pork; reserve marinade. Stir-fry pork 3 minutes or until no longer pink. Remove and set aside.

Heat remaining 1 tablespoon oil in skillet; add red and yellow onions. Reduce heat to medium. Cook 4 to 5 minutes until onions are softened, stirring occasionally. Sprinkle with sugar; cook 1 minute more.

Blend reserved marinade into cornstarch in cup until smooth. Stir into skillet. Stir-fry 1 minute or until sauce boils and thickens.

Return pork along with any accumulated juices to skillet; heat through. Stir in green onions. Serve over bean threads.

**To fry bean threads, follow package directions.*

Nutrients per serving:			
Calories	217	Cholesterol	61 mg
Fat	10 g	Sodium	958 mg

Naturally lean chicken and turkey have always been popular and delicious mealtime choices, and this chapter is overflowing with healthy new twists on old favorites. Let savory Chicken Cordon Bleu or down-home Turkey Stuffed Green Peppers take center stage on your dinner plate tonight.

Chicken Olé

Makes 6 servings

- ½ cup medium-hot chunky taco sauce
- ¼ cup Dijon-style mustard
- 2 tablespoons fresh lime juice
- 3 whole chicken breasts, split, skinned and boned
- 2 tablespoons margarine
  Chopped fresh parsley for garnish
  Reduced fat sour cream (optional)

Combine taco sauce, mustard and lime juice in large bowl. Add chicken, turning to coat. Cover; marinate in refrigerator at least 30 minutes.

Melt margarine in large skillet over medium heat until foamy. Remove chicken from marinade; reserve marinade. Add chicken to skillet; cook about 10 minutes or until brown on both sides. Add marinade; cook about 5 minutes or until chicken is tender and marinade glazes chicken. Remove chicken to serving platter. Boil marinade over high heat 1 minute; pour over chicken. Garnish with parsley. Serve with sour cream.

Nutrients per serving:

Calories	194	Cholesterol	73 mg
Fat	8 g	Sodium	329 mg

Chicken Cordon Bleu

Makes 4 servings

- 4 large chicken breast halves, boned and skinned (1 pound)
- 1 tablespoon Dijon-style mustard
- ½ teaspoon dried thyme leaves, crushed
- 4 slices (4 ounces) lean cooked ham
- 2 slices (1½ ounces) SARGENTO® Preferred Light Sliced Swiss Cheese
- ¼ cup seasoned bread crumbs
- 1 tablespoon SARGENTO® Grated Parmesan Cheese
- 4 teaspoons melted light margarine

Place chicken between 2 pieces wax paper. Pound to ¼-inch thickness. Spread mustard evenly down center of each breast. Sprinkle with thyme. Top with slice of ham and half slice cheese. Roll up, jelly-roll style, tucking in sides of ham and chicken to seal. Secure with skewers or large wooden toothpicks. Combine bread crumbs and Parmesan cheese in shallow dish. Brush each chicken breast with melted margarine and roll in crumb mixture. Place in 9×9-inch baking pan. Bake at 400°F for 10 minutes. *Reduce oven temperature to 350°F* and continue baking 20 to 25 minutes or until chicken is tender. Remove skewers. Serve immediately.

Nutrients per serving:

Calories	262	Cholesterol	86 mg
Fat	10 g	Sodium	692 mg

Chicken Olé

Pineapple & Citrus Sauced Turkey Slices

Pineapple & Citrus Sauced Turkey Slices

Makes 4 servings

2 cans (8 ounces each) DOLE® Pineapple Slices in Juice
2 tablespoons flour
¼ teaspoon ground dried sage
¼ teaspoon dried thyme leaves, crushed
¼ teaspoon salt
¼ teaspoon paprika
⅛ teaspoon black pepper
8 fresh turkey breast slices (1 pound)
1 teaspoon margarine
1 teaspoon vegetable oil
  Grated peel and juice of ½ DOLE® Orange
  Grated peel and juice of ½ DOLE® Lemon
1 chicken bouillon cube
1 large clove garlic, pressed
2 tablespoons chopped fresh parsley

Drain pineapple; reserve juice. Combine flour and seasonings in shallow dish. Coat turkey with flour mixture.

In large nonstick skillet, brown half the turkey in ½ teaspoon margarine and ½ teaspoon oil. Remove and set aside. Repeat procedure with remaining turkey,

margarine and oil. In same skillet, combine browned turkey slices, reserved pineapple juice, orange peel and juice, lemon peel and juice, bouillon and garlic. Bring to a boil. Add pineapple. Reduce heat to low; simmer 1 to 2 minutes. Remove turkey and pineapple to serving platter. Bring sauce to a boil; boil until reduced by half. Stir in parsley. Spoon sauce over turkey and pineapple; serve immediately.

Nutrients per serving:

Calories	155	Cholesterol	22 mg
Fat	3 g	Sodium	403 mg

Herb-Marinated Chicken Kabobs

Makes 4 servings

4 skinless boneless chicken breast halves
2 small zucchini, cut into ½-inch slices
1 large red bell pepper, cut into 1-inch squares
½ cup HEINZ® Gourmet Wine Vinegar
½ cup tomato juice
2 tablespoons vegetable oil
1 tablespoon chopped sweet onion
1 tablespoon firmly packed brown sugar
2 cloves garlic, minced
½ teaspoon dried oregano leaves, crushed
½ teaspoon black pepper

Lightly flatten chicken breasts; cut each breast lengthwise into 3 strips. Place chicken in bowl with zucchini and bell pepper. For marinade, combine vinegar and remaining ingredients in jar. Cover; shake vigorously. Pour marinade over chicken and vegetables. Cover; marinate in refrigerator about 1 hour.

Drain marinade into small saucepan; boil marinade. Alternately thread chicken and vegetables onto skewers; brush with marinade. Broil, 3 to 5 inches from heat source, until chicken is cooked, about 8 to 10 minutes; turn and brush occasionally with marinade. Serve with rice, if desired.

Nutrients per serving:

Calories	224	Cholesterol	66 mg
Fat	8 g	Sodium	189 mg

Oriental Barbecued Chicken

Makes 2 servings

¾ cup DOLE® Pineapple Juice
1 tablespoon light soy sauce
1 clove garlic, pressed
¼ teaspoon Chinese five-spice powder*
2 boneless skinless chicken breast halves
      (½ pound)
¾ teaspoon cornstarch

In small bowl, combine pineapple juice, soy sauce, garlic and five-spice powder. Place chicken in plastic bag or nonmetal bowl. Add juice mixture; marinate, covered, in refrigerator 15 minutes or overnight.

Drain marinade into small saucepan. Stir in cornstarch; cook and stir until marinade boils and thickens. Place chicken on greased broiler pan. Broil, 4 inches from heat source, 10 to 15 minutes on each side or until chicken is tender and no longer pink. Baste chicken with marinade frequently during broiling.

Chinese five-spice powder is a combination of fennel, anise, ginger, cinnamon and cloves.

Prep time: 5 minutes
Cook time: 30 minutes

Nutrients per serving:

Calories	190	Cholesterol	68 mg
Fat	2 g	Sodium	377 mg

Honey Mustard Turkey Loaf

Makes 4 to 6 servings

1½ pounds ground fresh turkey
1 cup fresh bread crumbs (2 slices)
½ cup BORDEN® or MEADOW GOLD® Milk
¼ cup chopped onion
1 egg, beaten
2 teaspoons WYLER'S® or STEERO® Chicken-
      Flavor Instant Bouillon
2½ teaspoons prepared mustard
1 teaspoon poultry seasoning
2 tablespoons honey
1 tablespoon firmly packed brown sugar

Preheat oven to 350°F. Combine turkey, crumbs, milk, onion, egg, bouillon, *1 teaspoon* mustard and poultry seasoning; mix well. In shallow baking dish, shape into loaf. Bake 40 minutes. Combine remaining *1½ teaspoons* mustard, honey and brown sugar. Spoon over loaf; bake 10 minutes longer. Refrigerate leftovers.

Nutrients per serving:

Calories	235	Cholesterol	112 mg
Fat	9 g	Sodium	469 mg

Chicken Fajitas

Makes 4 servings

1 tablespoon vegetable oil
1 large green bell pepper, thinly sliced
1 large red bell pepper, thinly sliced
1 large onion, thinly sliced
1 clove garlic, minced
4 boneless skinless chicken breast halves
      (about 1 pound), cut into ½-inch strips
½ teaspoon dried oregano leaves, crushed
2 tablespoons dry white wine or water
      Salt and black pepper (optional)
12 (8-inch) flour tortillas
      Guacamole (optional)

Heat oil in large skillet over medium-high heat. Add green and red pepper, onion and garlic. Cook 3 to 4 minutes or until crisp-tender, stirring occasionally. Remove vegetables with slotted spoon; set aside.

Add chicken and oregano to skillet. Cook 4 minutes or until chicken is no longer pink in center, stirring occasionally.

Return vegetables to skillet. Add wine. Season with salt and black pepper, if desired; cover. Continue cooking 2 minutes or until thoroughly heated.

Meanwhile, warm tortillas following package directions. Fill tortillas with chicken mixture; serve with guacamole, if desired.

Nutrients per serving:

Calories	286	Cholesterol	30 mg
Fat	7 g	Sodium	31 mg

Chicken Fajitas

Chicken Parmesan

Makes 4 servings

- **4 half boneless chicken breasts, skinned (about 1 pound)**
- **2 cans (14½ ounces each) DEL MONTE® Italian Style Stewed Tomatoes**
- **2 tablespoons cornstarch**
- **½ teaspoon dried oregano or basil leaves, crushed**
- **¼ teaspoon hot pepper sauce (optional)**
- **¼ cup grated Parmesan cheese**
  Chopped fresh parsley, for garnish

Preheat oven to 425°F. Slightly flatten each chicken breast; place in 11×7-inch baking dish. Cover with foil; bake 20 minutes or until chicken is no longer pink. Remove foil; drain. Meanwhile, in large saucepan, combine tomatoes with juice, cornstarch, oregano and pepper sauce. Stir until cornstarch dissolves. Cook, stirring constantly, until mixture boils and thickens. Pour over chicken; top with cheese. Return to oven; bake, uncovered, 5 minutes or until cheese is melted. Garnish with chopped parsley. Serve with hot cooked rice or pasta, if desired.

Prep & Cook time: 30 minutes

Nutrients per serving:

Calories	228	Cholesterol	73 mg
Fat	4 g	Sodium	716 mg

Chicken Parmesan

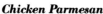

Turkey with Orange Sauce

Makes 4 servings

- **2 Turkey Thighs or Turkey Drumsticks (2 to 3 pounds)***
- **½ teaspoon paprika**
- **1 medium onion, sliced**
- **½ cup thawed orange juice concentrate, undiluted**
- **⅓ cup water**
- **2 tablespoons firmly packed brown sugar**
- **2 tablespoons chopped fresh parsley**
- **2 teaspoons soy sauce**
- **½ teaspoon ground ginger**

Rinse turkey and pat dry; place on rack of broiler pan. (If using only thighs, remove skin.) Broil, 4 inches from heat source, until turkey is brown. Remove to Dutch oven or roasting pan and sprinkle with paprika. Arrange onion slices over turkey. In small bowl, combine juice concentrate, water, brown sugar, parsley, soy sauce and ginger. Pour over turkey and onions.

Cover and bake approximately 1 hour in preheated 400°F oven until turkey is tender, basting once or twice. Slice turkey; coat with sauce and garnish with orange twists. Serve with rice or pasta.

*Thighs may be boned before cooking.

Nutrients per serving:

Calories	152	Cholesterol	56 mg
Fat	5 g	Sodium	210 mg

Favorite recipe from **National Turkey Federation**

Mini Turkey Loaves

Makes 4 servings

- **1 pound ground turkey**
- **1 small apple, chopped**
- **½ small onion, chopped**
- **½ cup uncooked rolled oats**
- **2 teaspoons Dijon-style mustard**
- **1 teaspoon dried rosemary leaves, crushed**
- **1 teaspoon salt**
  Dash black pepper

Preheat oven to 425°F. Grease 12 medium muffin cups. Combine all ingredients in large bowl. Press evenly into prepared muffin cups.

Bake 20 minutes or until lightly browned and no longer pink in center. Serve with cranberry sauce and garnish, if desired.

Nutrients per serving:

Calories	210	Cholesterol	42 mg
Fat	9 g	Sodium	619 mg

Baked Tomatoes Florentine

Makes 4 servings

1 cup sliced fresh mushrooms (optional)
1 tablespoon finely chopped onion
¼ cup water
1 cup BORDEN® Lite-line® or Viva® Protein Fortified Skim Milk
3 tablespoons flour
2 teaspoons WYLER'S® or STEERO® Chicken-Flavor Instant Bouillon
6 slices BORDEN® Lite-line® Process Cheese Product,* any flavor, cut into small pieces
2 cups cubed cooked chicken (breast meat)
1 (10-ounce) package frozen chopped spinach or broccoli, thawed and well drained
4 large tomatoes, tops cut off and insides scooped out

Preheat oven to 350°F. In small saucepan, cook mushrooms, if desired, and onion in water until tender; drain. In another small saucepan, combine milk, flour and bouillon; over low heat, cook and stir until thickened. Add cheese product pieces; cook and stir until melted. In medium bowl, combine mushroom mixture, chicken, spinach and ¾ cup sauce; stuff tomatoes. Arrange in baking dish; cover and bake 15 to 20 minutes or until hot. Over low heat, heat remaining sauce with 1 to 2 tablespoons water. Spoon over tomatoes before serving. Garnish as desired. Refrigerate leftovers.

*"½ the calories"– 8% milkfat product

Nutrients per serving:

Calories	290	Cholesterol	71 mg
Fat	6 g	Sodium	1053 mg

Dad's Favorite Turkey Kabobs

Dad's Favorite Turkey Kabobs

Makes 4 servings, 8 kabobs

3 ears corn, cut into 1-inch pieces
2 medium zucchini, cut into ¾-inch pieces
2 red bell peppers, cut into 1-inch cubes
2 Turkey Tenderloins (about 1 pound), cut into 1-inch cubes
⅓ cup reduced-calorie Italian salad dressing
Additional reduced-calorie Italian salad dressing

In medium saucepan over high heat, blanch corn in boiling water about 1 to 2 minutes. Remove corn from saucepan and plunge into cold water.

In large glass bowl, place corn, zucchini, peppers, turkey and ⅓ cup dressing; cover and refrigerate 1 to 2 hours.

Drain turkey and vegetables, discarding marinade. Alternately thread turkey cubes and vegetables on skewers, leaving ½-inch space between turkey and vegetables.

On outdoor charcoal grill, cook kabobs 18 to 20 minutes or until turkey is tender, brushing with additional dressing. Turn skewers after first 10 minutes of grilling.

Nutrients per serving (2 kabobs):

Calories	218	Cholesterol	70 mg
Fat	4 g	Sodium	381 mg

Favorite recipe from **National Turkey Federation**

Turkey and Rice Quiche

Turkey and Rice Quiche

Makes 8 servings, 16 triangles

3 cups cooked rice, cooled to room temperature
1½ cups chopped cooked turkey
1 medium tomato, seeded and finely diced
¼ cup sliced green onions
¼ cup finely diced green bell pepper
1 tablespoon chopped fresh basil *or* 1 teaspoon dried basil leaves, crushed
½ teaspoon seasoned salt
⅛ to ¼ teaspoon ground red pepper
½ cup skim milk
3 eggs, beaten
   Nonstick cooking spray
½ cup (2 ounces) shredded Cheddar cheese
½ cup (2 ounces) shredded mozzarella cheese

Combine rice, turkey, tomato, onions, green pepper, basil, salt, ground red pepper, milk, and eggs in 13×9-inch pan coated with nonstick cooking spray. Top with cheeses. Bake at 375°F for 20 minutes or until knife inserted near center comes out clean. To serve, cut quiche into 8 squares; cut each square diagonally into 2 triangles. Garnish as desired.

Nutrients per serving (2 triangles):

Calories	231	Cholesterol	111 mg
Fat	7 g	Sodium	527 mg

Favorite recipe from **USA Rice Council**

Oven-Crisped Chicken Breasts

Makes 8 servings

8 boneless skinless chicken breast halves (about 2 pounds)
2 egg whites
½ cup skim milk
½ cup all-purpose flour
1 tablespoon paprika
1 teaspoon dried basil leaves, crushed
½ teaspoon salt
¼ teaspoon black pepper
1 cup fine dry bread crumbs
¼ cup CRISCO® Oil or CRISCO® PURITAN® Oil

Heat oven to 425°F. Rinse chicken breast halves. Pat dry with paper towels.

Beat egg whites in small bowl until frothy. Beat in milk. Combine flour, paprika, basil, salt and pepper in large plastic food bag. Place bread crumbs in another large plastic food bag. Dip breast halves, 1 or 2 at a time, in flour mixture, then in egg whites, then in crumbs.

Place Crisco® Oil in 15¼×10¼×¾-inch jelly-roll pan or other shallow pan. Place in 425°F oven for 3 or 4 minutes or until oil is hot, but not smoking. Add chicken breasts in single layer.

Bake at 425°F for 10 minutes. Turn chicken over. Bake for an additional 5 minutes or until chicken is tender.

Nutrients per serving:

Calories	240	Cholesterol	65 mg
Fat	8 g	Sodium	220 mg

Turkey Tostados

Makes 4 servings

2 cups cubed cooked Turkey
1 package (1½ ounces) taco seasoning mix
   Water
4 corn tortillas
¼ cup canned refried beans
¼ cup (1 ounce) shredded reduced-calorie Cheddar cheese
½ cup chopped tomatoes
½ cup shredded lettuce
2 tablespoons chopped onions
½ cup taco sauce
   Plain low-fat yogurt (optional)
   Guacamole (optional)

Preheat oven to 375°F. In large skillet, over medium heat, combine turkey and taco seasoning mix. Add water according to package directions. Bring mixture to a boil; reduce heat to low and simmer 5 minutes, stirring occasionally.

Place tortillas on large cookie sheet. Bake 5 to 7 minutes or until tortillas are crispy and lightly browned.

Spread each tortilla with 1 tablespoon beans. Top evenly with meat mixture and cheese. Return to oven 2 to 3 minutes or until cheese is melted.

To serve, top with tomatoes, lettuce, onions and taco sauce. Garnish with yogurt and guacamole, if desired.

Nutrients per serving:

Calories	277	Cholesterol	59 mg
Fat	6 g	Sodium	1102 mg

Favorite recipe from **National Turkey Federation**

Tex-Mex Ground Turkey Potato Boat

Tex-Mex Ground Turkey Potato Boats

Makes 4 servings

 2 potatoes, baked and cooled
½ pound Ground Turkey
½ cup chopped onion
 1 clove garlic, minced
 1 can (8 ounces) stewed tomatoes
 1 teaspoon chili powder
¼ teaspoon dried oregano leaves, crushed
¼ teaspoon ground cumin
¼ teaspoon crushed red pepper
¼ teaspoon salt
½ cup (2 ounces) shredded reduced-fat Cheddar
   cheese

Slice potatoes lengthwise in half. Scoop out center of each potato to within ¼ inch of potato skin. Reserve potato for other use.

In medium skillet, over medium-high heat, combine turkey, onion and garlic. Cook and stir 5 minutes or until turkey is no longer pink; drain if necessary. Add tomatoes with juice, chili powder, oregano, cumin, crushed red pepper and salt. Simmer 15 minutes or until most of liquid has evaporated.

Spoon turkey mixture evenly into potato shells and sprinkle with cheese. Place shells in 13×9×2-inch pan; bake in 375°F oven 15 minutes or until cheese melts.

Nutrients per serving:

| Calories | 209 | Cholesterol | 51 mg |
| Fat | 7 g | Sodium | 446 mg |

Favorite recipe from **National Turkey Federation**

Turkey-Apple Bake

Makes 6 to 8 servings

1½ pounds ground turkey
1½ cups dry bread crumbs
  1 cup unsweetened applesauce
  2 egg whites
  ¼ cup minced onion
  ¼ cup finely chopped celery
  1 tablespoon prepared mustard
  1 tablespoon Worcestershire sauce
  1 teaspoon salt
  ¾ teaspoon poultry seasoning
  ⅛ teaspoon black pepper
  ⅔ cup chili sauce

In large bowl, combine all ingredients except chili sauce; mix lightly. Press into 9×5×3-inch loaf pan. Top with chili sauce. Bake at 350°F for 1 hour or until meat is cooked through. Let stand 10 minutes before slicing.

Nutrients per serving:

Calories	223	Cholesterol	32 mg
Fat	7 g	Sodium	768 mg

Favorite recipe from **Western New York Apple Growers Association**

Chicken & Vegetable Medley

Makes 4 servings

  4 skinned boneless chicken breast halves
      (about 1 pound)
  1 tablespoon vegetable oil
  ½ cup water
  2 teaspoons WYLER'S® or STEERO® Chicken-
      Flavor Instant Bouillon *or* 2 Chicken-
      Flavor Bouillon Cubes
  ½ teaspoon thyme leaves
  ¼ teaspoon onion powder
  1 cup *each* thin strips carrots, red bell pepper,
      summer squash and zucchini

In large skillet, brown chicken in oil. Add water, bouillon, thyme, onion powder and carrots. Cover; simmer 10 minutes. Add remaining vegetables; cover and cook 5 to 10 minutes longer or until tender. Garnish as desired. Refrigerate leftovers.

Nutrients per serving:

Calories	216	Cholesterol	80 mg
Fat	7 g	Sodium	513 mg

Chicken Rosemary

Makes 2 servings

  2 boneless skinless chicken breast halves
      (½ pound)
  1 teaspoon margarine
  1 teaspoon olive oil
    Salt and black pepper (optional)
  ½ small onion, sliced
  1 large clove garlic, minced
  ½ teaspoon dried rosemary, crumbled
  ⅛ teaspoon ground cinnamon
  ½ cup DOLE® Pine-Orange-Guava Juice
  1 tablespoon orange marmalade
  2 cups sliced DOLE® Carrots

Pound chicken to ½-inch thickness. In medium skillet, over medium heat, brown chicken on both sides in margarine and oil. Sprinkle with salt and pepper.

Stir in onion, garlic, rosemary and cinnamon. Cook and stir until onion is soft.

Blend in juice and marmalade. Spoon over chicken. Cover; bring to a boil. Reduce heat to low; simmer 10 minutes. Stir in carrots. Cover; simmer 5 minutes or until carrots are tender-crisp and chicken is tender. Serve with pasta, if desired, and garnish with rosemary sprig.

Prep time: 10 minutes
Cook time: 20 minutes

Nutrients per serving:

Calories	241	Cholesterol	46 mg
Fat	6 g	Sodium	102 mg

Chicken Rosemary

Turkey Medallions Piccata

Makes 4 servings

1 pound Turkey Tenderloins, cut into ¾-inch medallions
Salt and black pepper (optional)
1 teaspoon olive oil
1 teaspoon margarine
1 large clove garlic, crushed
1 tablespoon lemon juice
4 teaspoons drained capers

Lightly sprinkle one side of each medallion with salt and pepper, if desired.

In large non-stick skillet, over medium-high heat, heat oil and margarine. Add medallions and garlic; cook turkey for approximately 1½ minutes per side, turning each medallion over when edges have turned from pink to white. Stir garlic occasionally and continue cooking until medallions are no longer pink in centers and register 170°F on meat thermometer.

Remove skillet from heat. Pour lemon juice over turkey medallions and sprinkle with capers; serve immediately.

Nutrients per serving:

Calories	150	Cholesterol	70 mg
Fat	4 g	Sodium	162 mg

Favorite recipe from **National Turkey Federation**

Turkey Medallions Piccata

Chicken Curry Bombay

Makes 4 servings

1 medium onion, cut into wedges
2 cloves garlic, minced
2 teaspoons curry powder
1 tablespoon olive oil
2 boneless chicken breast halves, skinned and sliced ¼-inch thick (about ½ pound)
1 can (14½ ounces) DEL MONTE® Original Style Stewed Tomatoes
⅓ cup DEL MONTE® Seedless Raisins
1 can (16 ounces) DEL MONTE® Whole New Potatoes, drained and cut into chunks
1 can (16 ounces) DEL MONTE® Blue Lake Cut Green Beans, drained

In large skillet, cook onion, garlic and curry in oil over medium-high heat until onion is tender, stirring occasionally. Stir in chicken, tomatoes with juice and raisins; bring to a boil. Reduce heat to low. Cover and simmer over medium heat 8 minutes. Add potatoes and green beans. Cook, uncovered, 5 minutes, stirring occasionally. Season to taste with salt and pepper, if desired.

Prep time: 10 minutes
Cook time: 18 minutes

Nutrients per serving:

Calories	233	Cholesterol	34 mg
Fat	5 g	Sodium	643 mg

Turkey Vegetable Medley

Makes 4 servings

4 fresh turkey breast slices *or* 4 skinned boneless chicken breast halves (about 1 pound)
1 tablespoon vegetable oil
½ cup water
2 teaspoons WYLER'S® or STEERO® Chicken-Flavor Instant Bouillon *or* 2 Chicken-Flavor Bouillon Cubes
½ teaspoon thyme leaves or tarragon
¼ teaspoon onion powder
1 cup thin carrot strips
1 cup *each* thin red and green bell pepper strips

In large skillet, brown turkey in oil. Add water, bouillon, thyme, onion powder and carrots. Cover; simmer 10 minutes. Add peppers; cover and cook 5 minutes longer or until tender. Refrigerate leftovers.

Nutrients per serving:

Calories	145	Cholesterol	30 mg
Fat	6 g	Sodium	501 mg

Sagebrush Turkey Steaks

Makes 4 servings

1 package (about 1 pound) LOUIS RICH®
   Fresh Turkey Breast Steaks

Marinade
   ½ cup dry white wine
   ¼ cup olive oil
   1 tablespoon finely chopped onion
   1 teaspoon dried parsley flakes
   ½ teaspoon dried sage
   ½ teaspoon salt
   ⅛ teaspoon black pepper

Pierce turkey steaks well with fork. Combine
marinade ingredients in glass baking dish. Add
turkey to marinade; cover. Refrigerate at least 1 hour
or up to 24 hours. Broil, 5 inches from heat, or cook
in covered grill 8 to 10 minutes or until juices run
clear, turning turkey over halfway through cooking.

Prep time: 5 minutes
Cook time: 10 minutes

Nutrients per serving:

| Calories | 200 | Cholesterol | 60 mg |
| Fat | 9 g | Sodium | 225 mg |

Sweet Sour Chicken Sauté

Makes 4 servings

1 can (8 ounces) pineapple chunks in juice
1 tablespoon cornstarch
⅓ cup HEINZ® Apple Cider Vinegar
¼ cup firmly packed brown sugar
⅛ teaspoon black pepper
1 small red bell pepper, cut into thin strips
1 small green bell pepper, cut into thin strips
1 medium onion, thinly sliced
1 pound skinless boneless chicken breasts, cut
   into ½-inch strips

Drain pineapple; reserve juice. Combine juice,
cornstarch, vinegar, sugar and black pepper in small
bowl; set aside. Spray large skillet with nonstick
cooking spray. Cook and stir bell peppers and onion
until tender-crisp; remove. Spray skillet again; cook
and stir chicken 2 to 3 minutes or until chicken
browns. Stir in reserved juice mixture; cook 2 to
3 minutes or until chicken is cooked and sauce boils
and thickens. Add vegetables and pineapple; heat,
stirring occasionally. Serve with rice if desired.

Nutrients per serving:

| Calories | 235 | Cholesterol | 66 mg |
| Fat | 2 g | Sodium | 80 mg |

Ginger Spicy Chicken

Ginger Spicy Chicken

Makes 4 servings

   Salt
2 whole chicken breasts, split, skinned and
   boned (1 pound)
2 tablespoons vegetable oil
1 medium red bell pepper, cut into 2×¼-inch
   strips
1 medium green bell pepper, cut into 2×¼-inch
   strips
1 can (8 ounces) pineapple chunks in juice,
   undrained
½ cup PACE® Picante Sauce
2 tablespoons chopped cilantro *or* fresh parsley
2 to 3 teaspoons grated fresh ginger *or* ¾ to
   1 teaspoon ground ginger

Lightly salt chicken breasts. Heat oil in large skillet
over medium heat. Add chicken; cook about
5 minutes on each side or until light brown and
tender. Remove chicken; keep warm. Add pepper
strips, pineapple with juice, Pace® Picante Sauce,
cilantro and ginger to skillet. Cook, stirring
frequently, 5 to 7 minutes or until peppers are tender
and sauce is thickened. Return chicken to skillet and
heat through.

Nutrients per serving:

| Calories | 256 | Cholesterol | 73 mg |
| Fat | 10 g | Sodium | 284 mg |

Herb Marinated Chicken Breasts

Herb Marinated Chicken Breasts

Makes 6 servings

¾ cup MIRACLE WHIP® Salad Dressing
¼ cup dry white wine
2 garlic cloves, minced
2 tablespoons finely chopped green onion
2 teaspoons dried basil leaves, crushed
1 teaspoon dried thyme leaves, crushed
6 boneless skinless chicken breast halves (about 1¾ pounds)

Stir together salad dressing, wine and seasonings. Pour dressing mixture over chicken. Cover; refrigerate several hours or overnight. Drain, reserving dressing mixture. Place chicken on greased rack of broiler pan. Broil 4 to 6 minutes on each side or until tender, brushing frequently with dressing mixture.

Prep time: 15 minutes plus refrigerating
Cook time: 12 minutes

Nutrients per serving:

Calories	170	Cholesterol	55 mg
Fat	7 g	Sodium	110 mg

Chicken with Cherries

Makes 6 servings

1 package (1½ pounds) PERDUE® Fit 'n Easy fresh skinless and boneless Oven Stuffer Roaster breasts
Salt and ground black pepper to taste (optional)
2 teaspoons vegetable oil
2 cups canned pitted tart cherries, undrained, divided
2 teaspoons cornstarch
1 tablespoon Worcestershire sauce
1 tablespoon dry sherry
1 teaspoon firmly packed brown sugar
1 small clove garlic, peeled
½ cup finely chopped onion
¼ cup raisins
1 tablespoon minced fresh parsley
2 cups hot cooked wild rice

Preheat oven to 350°F. Sprinkle chicken lightly with salt and generously with pepper. In nonstick skillet over medium-high heat, heat oil. Add chicken and cook 6 to 8 minutes until lightly browned on both sides. Remove chicken to baking dish; set aside. Drain cherries, reserving ¼ cup juice. Add cherry juice to skillet; stir in cornstarch.

In food processor or blender container, combine 1 cup cherries, Worcestershire sauce, sherry, sugar and garlic. Process or blend until smooth; add to skillet. Stir in remaining cherries, onion and raisins; cook over medium-high heat 2 to 3 minutes until sauce boils and thickens, stirring constantly. Spoon sauce over chicken; bake 25 to 35 minutes until chicken is cooked through. To serve, sprinkle chicken with parsley. Serve with rice.

Nutrients per serving:

Calories	290	Cholesterol	66 mg
Fat	3 g	Sodium	111 mg

Pollo Empanizado

Makes 4 servings

½ cup **WISH-BONE® Olive Oil Classics Italian Dressing**
½ teaspoon grated lime peel
2 tablespoons lime juice
4 boneless skinless chicken breast halves (about 1 pound), pounded ¼ inch thick
½ cup yellow cornmeal
½ teaspoon **LAWRY'S® Garlic Powder with Parsley**
¼ teaspoon salt
1 medium red onion, chopped
Chopped fresh cilantro or parsley

In large shallow baking dish, blend Olive Oil Classics Italian Dressing, lime peel and juice. Add chicken; turn to coat. Cover and marinate in refrigerator at least 2 hours, turning occasionally. Meanwhile, in shallow dish, combine cornmeal, garlic powder and salt.

Remove chicken, reserving marinade. Dip chicken in cornmeal mixture, coating well. Place on aluminum-foil-lined broiler rack or in greased shallow baking pan. Arrange onion around chicken. Drizzle chicken and onion with reserved marinade. Broil, 4 inches from heat source, 7 minutes or until chicken is tender. Sprinkle with cilantro and serve, if desired, with freshly ground black pepper.

Note: *Also terrific with WISH-BONE® Olive Oil Classics Red Wine Vinaigrette Dressing.*

Nutrients per serving:

Calories	261	Cholesterol	66 mg
Fat	8 g	Sodium	591 mg

Brown Rice Chicken Bake

Makes 6 servings

3 cups cooked brown rice
1 package (10 ounces) frozen green peas
2 cups cooked chicken breast cubes
½ cup cholesterol-free, reduced-calorie mayonnaise
⅓ cup slivered almonds, toasted (optional)
2 teaspoons soy sauce
¼ teaspoon ground black pepper
¼ teaspoon garlic powder
¼ teaspoon dried tarragon leaves, crushed
Nonstick cooking spray

Combine rice, peas, chicken, mayonnaise, almonds, soy sauce, and seasonings in large bowl. Transfer to 3-quart baking dish coated with nonstick cooking spray. Cover and bake at 350°F for 15 to 20 minutes.

Nutrients per serving:

Calories	270	Cholesterol	44 mg
Fat	7 g	Sodium	272 mg

Favorite recipe from **USA Rice Council**

Turkey Sloppy Joes

Makes 8 servings

1 pound Ground Turkey
1 cup thinly sliced onion
½ cup chopped green bell pepper
1 cup low-calorie, low-sodium ketchup
¼ cup sweet pickle relish
1½ teaspoons chili powder
1 teaspoon Worcestershire sauce
½ teaspoon seasoned salt
½ teaspoon garlic powder
¼ teaspoon celery seed
8 hard rolls (about 1 pound)

In large skillet over medium-high heat, cook and stir turkey, onion and bell pepper 5 minutes or until turkey is no longer pink. Drain if necessary. Add ketchup, relish, chili powder, Worcestershire sauce, seasoned salt, garlic powder and celery seed. Bring to a boil. Reduce heat to low; cover and simmer 30 minutes.

Slice rolls in half and toast under broiler 1 to 2 minutes or until lightly browned.

To serve, spoon turkey mixture onto bottom halves of rolls. Place top halves of rolls over turkey mixture.

Nutrients per serving:

Calories	294	Cholesterol	40 mg
Fat	8 g	Sodium	745 mg

Favorite recipe from **National Turkey Federation**

Turkey Sloppy Joe

Citrus Chicken

Makes 4 servings

1 tablespoon vegetable oil
4 boneless skinless chicken breast halves
   (about 1 pound)
1 cup orange juice
4 teaspoons sugar
1 clove garlic, minced
1 teaspoon dried rosemary leaves, crushed
2 teaspoons cornstarch
¼ cup dry white wine
   Salt and black pepper (optional)
2 pink grapefruits, sectioned and peeled

Heat oil in large skillet over medium heat. Add chicken; cook 8 minutes or until browned on both sides and no longer pink in center, turning after 4 minutes. Remove chicken from skillet; keep warm.

Add orange juice, sugar, garlic and rosemary to skillet; bring to a boil.

Combine cornstarch and wine. Add to skillet; cook, stirring constantly, until sauce boils and thickens. Season with salt and pepper, if desired.

Add grapefruit; heat thoroughly, stirring occasionally. Serve over chicken.

Nutrients per serving:			
Calories	216	Cholesterol	46 mg
Fat	6 g	Sodium	49 mg

Savory Apple Topped Turkey Medallions

Makes 4 servings

1 pound Turkey Tenderloins, cut into ¾-inch
   medallions
   Salt and pepper (optional)
1 teaspoon olive oil
1 teaspoon margarine
1 large clove garlic, crushed
⅔ cup peeled, diced apples
⅓ cup orange juice
3 tablespoons jellied cranberry sauce
4 teaspoons orange marmalade

Lightly sprinkle one side of each medallion with salt and pepper, if desired.

In large nonstick skillet over medium-high heat, heat oil and margarine. Add medallions and garlic; cook turkey approximately 1½ minutes per side, turning each medallion over when edges have turned from

pink to white. Stir garlic occasionally and continue cooking until medallions are no longer pink in centers and register 170°F on meat thermometer. Remove from skillet.

In same skillet over medium heat, combine apples, orange juice, cranberry sauce and marmalade. Cook and stir until sauce is hot and apples are tender but hold their shape. Spoon sauce over medallions.

Nutrients per serving:			
Calories	206	Cholesterol	70 mg
Fat	4 g	Sodium	92 mg

Favorite recipe from **National Turkey Federation**

Chicken Curry

Makes 4 servings

½ cup all-purpose flour
¼ teaspoon black pepper
2 whole chicken breasts, split, skinned and
   boned
3 tablespoons FILIPPO BERIO® Extra-Virgin
   Olive Oil
1 cup chopped onion
½ cup chopped green bell pepper
1 clove garlic, chopped
1½ teaspoons curry powder
½ teaspoon dried thyme leaves, crushed
2 cups diced fresh or canned tomatoes
   Hot cooked rice (optional)

Preheat oven to 350°F. Combine flour and pepper; sprinkle over both sides of chicken breasts.

Heat olive oil in large skillet over medium heat. Cook chicken 15 minutes or until lightly browned on both sides. Remove from skillet; place in large ovenproof casserole.

In same skillet, cook and stir onion, green pepper, garlic, curry powder and thyme 5 minutes or until onions are lightly browned. Add tomatoes. Stir until heated through.

Pour tomato mixture over chicken in casserole. Bake, uncovered, for 30 minutes or until chicken is tender. Serve over hot cooked rice, if desired.

Nutrients per serving:			
Calories	294	Cholesterol	94 mg
Fat	7 g	Sodium	47 mg

Citrus Chicken, Poppy Seed Noodles (page 207)

Picante Chicken Skillet

Makes 4 servings

- 1 pound boneless skinless chicken or turkey breasts
- 1 tablespoon olive or vegetable oil
- 1 clove garlic, minced
- 1 can (14½ or 16 ounces) whole tomatoes, chopped, with juice
- ⅓ cup PACE® Picante Sauce
- 1 medium yellow or green bell pepper, cut into ¾-inch chunks
- 1 medium onion, cut into ¼-inch wedges
- ¾ teaspoon ground cumin
- ½ teaspoon salt (optional)
- 1 tablespoon cornstarch
- 1 tablespoon water
- 2 cups hot cooked rice
- 1 to 2 tablespoons chopped cilantro
  Additional PACE® Picante Sauce (optional)

Cut chicken into 1½×½×½-inch strips. Sprinkle with salt and black pepper to taste, if desired. Heat oil in 10-inch skillet. Add chicken and garlic; cook and stir until chicken is almost cooked through, about 5 minutes. Combine tomatoes with juice, ⅓ cup Pace® Picante Sauce, bell pepper, onion, cumin and salt; mix well. Stir into skillet. Simmer 5 minutes, stirring occasionally. Dissolve cornstarch in water; stir into skillet. Simmer about 1 minute or until sauce is thickened, stirring constantly. Serve over rice with cilantro and additional Pace® Picante Sauce, if desired.

Nutrients per serving:

Calories	298	Cholesterol	65 mg
Fat	5 g	Sodium	674 mg

Picante Chicken Skillet

Turkey Stuffed Green Peppers

Makes 4 servings

- 1 pound Ground Turkey
- ½ cup instant rice, uncooked
- ½ cup grated carrot
- ¼ cup chopped onion
- 3 tablespoons chopped fresh parsley
- 1 to 2 cloves minced garlic
- ½ teaspoon salt
- ½ teaspoon black pepper
- 1 can (12 ounces) tomato sauce, divided
- 4 small green bell peppers

To Microwave: In medium bowl, combine turkey, rice, carrot, onion, parsley, garlic, salt, black pepper and 1 cup tomato sauce. Mix well. Cut tops off green peppers. Remove and discard seeds and membranes. Spoon turkey mixture evenly into peppers. Place in 8-inch square baking dish. Cover with vented plastic wrap. Microwave at HIGH (100% power) 8 to 10 minutes, rotating halfway through cooking time, until peppers and rice are tender. Spoon remaining ½ cup tomato sauce over peppers. Microwave at HIGH (100% power) 1 minute. Let stand, covered, 3 minutes.

Nutrients per serving:

Calories	265	Cholesterol	72 mg
Fat	10 g	Sodium	885 mg

Favorite recipe from **National Turkey Federation**

Barbecue Bacon Meatloaf

Makes 10 servings

- 2 packages (1 pound *each*) LOUIS RICH® Ground Turkey
- 12 slices LOUIS RICH® Turkey Bacon, diced
- 1 cup quick-cooking oats, uncooked
- 1 medium onion, finely chopped
- ½ cup barbecue sauce
- 2 large egg whites
- 1 tablespoon Worcestershire sauce

Mix all ingredients in large bowl. Press mixture into ungreased 9×5-inch loaf pan. Top with additional barbecue sauce, if desired. Bake at 375°F for 1 hour 15 minutes. Allow to stand 10 minutes before slicing.

Note: Meatloaf ingredients may be combined a day ahead and refrigerated. Bake at 375°F for 1½ hours.

Nutrients per serving:

Calories	215	Cholesterol	70 mg
Fat	9 g	Sodium	525 mg

Herbed Chicken and Broccoli

Makes 4 servings

10 ounces boneless skinless chicken breasts, cut into ½-inch strips
1 teaspoon Italian seasoning
1 cup *undiluted* CARNATION® Evaporated Skimmed Milk
2 tablespoons all-purpose flour
1 clove garlic, crushed
¼ teaspoon salt (optional)
⅛ teaspoon white pepper
½ cup (2 ounces) shredded reduced-fat Swiss cheese
1 package (10 ounces) frozen broccoli spears, thawed, drained and cut into bite-size pieces
Paprika

Sprinkle chicken with Italian seasoning. Pound between sheets of waxed paper. Remove paper. Spray nonstick skillet with nonstick cooking spray. Cook and stir chicken strips just until no longer pink. Set aside; keep warm. In small saucepan, whisk *small amount* of evaporated skimmed milk into flour. Stir in *remaining* milk with garlic, salt and pepper. Cook over medium heat, stirring constantly, until mixture just comes to a boil and thickens. Add cheese; stir until melted.

Spray 10×6×2-inch baking dish with nonstick cooking spray. Spread about ¼ cup sauce on bottom of dish. Arrange broccoli over sauce, then chicken pieces over broccoli. Pour *remaining* sauce over top. Sprinkle with paprika. Cover. Bake in preheated 350°F oven for 20 to 25 minutes or until heated through.

Nutrients per serving:

Calories	197	Cholesterol	49 mg
Fat	3 g	Sodium	315 mg

Creamy Turkey Fajitas

Creamy Turkey Fajitas

Makes 6 servings

⅓ cup *each* FRENCH'S® Creamy Spread™ Mustard and light sour cream
½ teaspoon *each* garlic powder and ground cumin
½ teaspoon dried oregano leaves, crushed
1 tablespoon corn oil
2 cups sliced red or yellow bell peppers
½ cup sliced red onion
2 cups (12 ounces) thin strips cooked turkey
6 (7-inch) flour tortillas

In small bowl, combine French's® Creamy Spread™ Mustard, sour cream, garlic powder, cumin and oregano; set aside. Heat oil in large skillet; cook and stir peppers and onion until tender. Stir in mustard mixture and turkey. Cook over medium-low heat, stirring, until heated through. Spoon about ½ cup mixture into center of each tortilla; fold sides over. Serve hot.

Nutrients per serving:

Calories	176	Cholesterol	4 mg
Fat	8 g	Sodium	304 mg

Teriyaki Kabobs

Teriyaki Kabobs

Makes 4 servings

 2 whole chicken breasts, split, boned and
    skinned (about 1 pound)
16 (2-inch) broccoli florets, cooked crisp-tender,
    or 1 large green bell pepper, cut into 1-inch
    squares
16 large mushrooms, stems trimmed
 ½ cup PACE® Picante Sauce
 ¼ cup reduced-calorie Italian dressing
 2 tablespoons light soy sauce
1½ teaspoons finely shredded fresh ginger
 ½ teaspoon sugar
 8 cherry tomatoes

Pound chicken to ½-inch thickness; cut lengthwise
into 1-inch-wide strips. Place chicken, broccoli and
mushrooms in large plastic food storage bag.
Combine Pace® Picante Sauce, Italian dressing, soy
sauce, ginger and sugar in small bowl; mix well. Add
Pace® Picante Sauce mixture to chicken mixture in
bag; press out air and fasten securely. Refrigerate
1 hour, turning bag frequently. Drain chicken and
vegetables, reserving marinade. Alternately thread
chicken accordion-style with broccoli and mushrooms
onto skewers. Heat reserved marinade to a boil. Place
kabobs on grill over hot coals or on rack of broiler
pan. Brush with marinade. Grill or broil 9 to
12 minutes or until chicken is cooked through,
turning and basting once with marinade. Add
tomatoes to skewers during last minute of cooking.

Nutrients per serving:

Calories	254	Cholesterol	67 mg
Fat	6 g	Sodium	850 mg

Chicken Breasts Florentine

Makes 6 servings

6 boneless skinless chicken breast halves (about
    1½ pounds)
1 package (10 ounces) frozen chopped spinach,
    thawed, squeezed dry
1 jar (2½ ounces) sliced mushrooms, drained
½ cup chopped onion
½ cup (2 ounces) shredded low-fat mozzarella
    cheese
½ cup low-fat ricotta cheese
⅛ teaspoon black pepper
1 jar (12 ounces) HEINZ® HomeStyle Chicken
    Gravy
½ teaspoon dried thyme leaves, crushed

Place chicken breasts in lightly greased 13×9-inch
baking pan. Combine spinach, mushrooms, onion,
cheeses and pepper in medium bowl. Spoon spinach
mixture on top of chicken breasts. Combine gravy and
thyme; spoon over spinach mixture and chicken.
Cover; bake in 375°F oven 40 to 45 minutes or until
chicken is no longer pink in center.

To Microwave: Place chicken breasts in 13×9-inch
microwave-safe baking dish. Combine spinach,
mushrooms, onion, cheeses and pepper in medium bowl.
Spoon spinach mixture on top of chicken breasts. Combine
gravy and thyme; spoon over spinach mixture and chicken.
Cover dish with waxed paper. Microwave at HIGH (100%)
18 to 20 minutes or until chicken is no longer pink in
center, rearranging halfway through cooking.

Nutrients per serving:

Calories	227	Cholesterol	77 mg
Fat	7 g	Sodium	573 mg

Orange Glazed Chicken

Makes 4 servings

¼ cup HEINZ® Chili Sauce
¼ cup orange marmalade
1½ teaspoons prepared mustard
4 boneless skinless chicken breast halves
    (about 1 pound)
1 tablespoon margarine

For glaze, combine chili sauce, marmalade and
mustard in small bowl. Lightly flatten chicken breasts
to uniform thickness. In large skillet, melt margarine.
Add chicken; cook until brown on both sides. Pour
glaze over chicken. Simmer, uncovered, 8 minutes,
basting occasionally or until chicken is tender and no
longer pink in center.

Nutrients per serving:

Calories	219	Cholesterol	66 mg
Fat	4 g	Sodium	361 mg

Mesquite Grilled Turkey Tenderloins

Makes 8 servings

1 cup mesquite chips
2 pounds Turkey Breast Tenderloins
Black pepper to taste
Caribbean Salsa (recipe follows)

In small bowl cover mesquite chips with water; soak for 2 hours. Preheat charcoal grill for direct-heat cooking. Drain water from mesquite chips; add chips to hot coals. Sprinkle tenderloins with black pepper; grill 8 to 10 minutes on each side until tenderloins are no longer pink in centers and register 170°F on meat thermometer. Allow to stand 10 minutes before serving.

To serve, slice tenderloins into ½-inch medallions and arrange on serving plate. Top with Caribbean Salsa.

Caribbean Salsa

2 cups (¼-inch) mango cubes
½ cup peeled, seeded (¼-inch) cucumber cubes
¼ cup chopped fresh cilantro or parsley
2 tablespoons finely chopped green onion
½ jalapeño pepper, seeded and finely chopped
3 tablespoons fresh lime juice
1½ teaspoons firmly packed brown sugar
1 teaspoon minced fresh ginger
Dash black pepper

In medium bowl combine mango, cucumber, cilantro, green onion, jalapeño pepper, lime juice, brown sugar, ginger and black pepper. Cover and refrigerate at least 1 hour to allow flavors to blend.

Nutrients per serving:

Calories	163	Cholesterol	70 mg
Fat	2 g	Sodium	79 mg

Favorite recipe from **National Turkey Federation**

Mesquite Grilled Turkey Tenderloins

Top to bottom: Fiesta Turkey Pie, Black Pepper Patty

Fiesta Turkey Pie

Makes 6 to 8 servings

1 package (about 1 pound) LOUIS RICH®
    Fresh Ground Turkey
1 cup salsa
1 can (8 ounces) refrigerated crescent dinner
    rolls
¼ cup (1 ounce) shredded sharp Cheddar cheese

Preheat oven to 450°F. Cook turkey in nonstick skillet over medium heat about 10 minutes or until turkey is no longer pink, stirring to break turkey into small pieces. Stir in salsa.

Press crescent roll dough onto bottom, up side and on rim of 9-inch pie plate to form crust. Spread turkey mixture evenly over crust; sprinkle with cheese. Bake 18 to 20 minutes or until crust is browned.

Nutrients per serving:			
Calories	196	Cholesterol	35 mg
Fat	10 g	Sodium	413 mg

Black Pepper Patties

Makes 4 servings

1 package (about 1 pound) LOUIS RICH®
    Fresh Ground Turkey
1 teaspoon instant chicken bouillon
¼ teaspoon dried thyme leaves, crushed
1 teaspoon coarsely ground black pepper

Sauce
  1 large tomato, chopped
  ½ cup plain nonfat yogurt
  1 tablespoon chopped fresh parsley

Mix turkey, bouillon and thyme in large bowl. Shape into four 4-inch patties. Sprinkle pepper on patties (about ⅛ teaspoon per side), lightly pressing pepper into turkey. Cook turkey in nonstick skillet over medium heat about 12 minutes or until no longer pink, turning occasionally.

Meanwhile, mix sauce ingredients in small bowl. Serve cold sauce over turkey patties.

Nutrients per serving (1 patty):			
Calories	190	Cholesterol	75 mg
Fat	8 g	Sodium	315 mg

Summer Turkey and Vegetable Bake

Makes 8 servings

1½ pounds zucchini squash, cut into ¼-inch-thick
    slices
1 pound Ground Turkey
1 cup chopped onion
2 cloves garlic, minced
1 cup uncooked instant rice
2½ teaspoons Italian seasoning, crushed, divided
1 teaspoon salt
½ teaspoon pepper
2 cups low-fat cottage cheese
1 cup (4 ounces) shredded low-fat mozzarella
    cheese
2 tablespoons finely chopped fresh parsley
2½ pounds tomatoes, peeled and cut into ½-inch
    slices*
1 teaspoon sugar
3 tablespoons grated Parmesan cheese

To Microwave: Arrange zucchini in 13×9-inch microwave-safe dish; cover with vented plastic wrap. Microwave at HIGH (100% power) 8 minutes or until tender, rotating dish halfway through cooking. Drain zucchini slices on paper towels; cover with additional paper towels to absorb all liquid.

In large nonstick skillet over medium-high heat, cook and stir turkey, onion and garlic 5 to 6 minutes or until turkey is no longer pink. Drain if necessary. Add rice, 2 teaspoons Italian seasoning, salt and pepper. In medium bowl combine cottage cheese, mozzarella cheese and parsley.

In bottom of same microwave-safe dish, layer half the zucchini slices; top with turkey mixture, half the tomato slices, ¼ teaspoon Italian seasoning, ½ teaspoon sugar and cheese mixture. Layer remaining zucchini and tomato slices over cheese; sprinkle with remaining ¼ teaspoon Italian seasoning and ½ teaspoon sugar. Cover dish with vented plastic wrap.

Microwave at HIGH (100% power) 5 minutes. Rotate dish one-half turn. Microwave at MEDIUM (50% power) 10 minutes. Remove plastic wrap and sprinkle with Parmesan cheese. Cover with foil and let stand 10 minutes. Cut into 8 portions.

***Note:** To peel a tomato, cut a skin-deep "X" in the blossom end. Drop into boiling water and blanch for 15 seconds. Lift out with slotted spoon; drop into a bowl of ice water. Skin will slip off easily.*

Nutrients per serving:			
Calories	260	Cholesterol	53 mg
Fat	8 g	Sodium	679 mg

Favorite recipe from **National Turkey Federation**

Turkey Burgers

Makes 4 servings

1 pound ground fresh turkey
¼ cup BENNETT'S® Chili Sauce
1 teaspoon WYLER'S® or STEERO®
**   Chicken-Flavor Instant Bouillon**

Combine ingredients; shape into 4 patties. Grill, broil or pan-fry as desired. Refrigerate leftovers.

Nutrients per serving:

Calories	172	Cholesterol	75 mg
Fat	7 g	Sodium	510 mg

Pineapple-Mustard Glazed Turkey Breast

Makes 6 servings

1 bone-in Turkey Breast Half (2½ pounds)
⅓ cup pineapple preserves
2 teaspoons Dijon-style mustard
1 teaspoon lemon juice

Prepare grill for indirect heat cooking by pushing hot coals up sides of grill around drip pan. Place turkey, breast side up, on rack over drip pan. Cover grill; cook 1 to 1¼ hours or until meat thermometer inserted in thickest portion of breast registers 170°F.

Meanwhile, in small bowl combine preserves, mustard and lemon juice. Brush glaze on breast during last 30 minutes of cooking. Remove turkey breast from grill; let stand 15 minutes. To serve, slice breast and arrange on platter. Garnish as desired.

Nutrients per serving:

Calories	295	Cholesterol	96 mg
Fat	10 g	Sodium	134 mg

Favorite recipe from **National Turkey Federation**

Pineapple-Mustard Glazed Turkey Breast

Stuffed Chicken Breasts

Makes 4 servings

4 boneless, skinless chicken breast halves (about
**   1 pound), pounded to ¼-inch thickness**
½ teaspoon ground black pepper, divided
¼ teaspoon salt
1 cup cooked brown rice (cooked in chicken
**   broth)**
¼ cup minced tomato
¼ cup (1 ounce) finely shredded mozzarella
**   cheese**
3 tablespoons toasted rice bran* (optional)
1 tablespoon chopped fresh basil
**   Nonstick cooking spray**

Season insides of chicken breasts with ¼ teaspoon pepper and salt. Combine rice, tomato, cheese, bran, basil, and remaining ¼ teaspoon pepper. Spoon rice mixture on top of chicken breasts; fold over and secure sides with wooden toothpicks soaked in water. Wipe off outsides of chicken breasts with paper towel.

Coat a large skillet with nonstick cooking spray and place over medium-high heat until hot. Cook stuffed chicken breasts 1 minute on each side or just until golden brown. Transfer chicken to shallow baking pan. Bake at 350°F for 8 to 10 minutes or until chicken is tender.

*To toast rice bran, spread on baking sheet and bake at 325°F for 7 to 8 minutes.

Nutrients per serving:

Calories	223	Cholesterol	79 mg
Fat	5 g	Sodium	337 mg

Favorite recipe from **USA Rice Council**

Turkey Bacon Club Sandwiches

Makes 2 sandwiches

4 slices LOUIS RICH® Turkey Bacon, cut in half
4 teaspoons reduced-calorie mayonnaise
4 slices whole wheat bread, toasted
2 lettuce leaves
4 thin slices tomato
4 slices LOUIS RICH® Oven Roasted Deli-Thin
**   Turkey Breast**

Cook and stir Turkey Bacon in nonstick skillet over medium heat 8 to 10 minutes or until lightly browned. For each sandwich, spread 2 teaspoons mayonnaise on one toast slice; top with half the Turkey Bacon, lettuce, tomato, Turkey Breast and another toast slice. Repeat for remaining sandwich.

Nutrients per serving (1 sandwich):

Calories	255	Cholesterol	30 mg
Fat	10 g	Sodium	845 mg

Rotini Stir-Fry

Makes 8 servings

½ of a (1-pound) package CREAMETTE®
    Rotini, cooked according to package
    directions and drained
2 tablespoons olive or vegetable oil
2 whole boneless skinless chicken breasts, cut
    into strips
1 cup fresh broccoli flowerets
1 cup carrot curls
½ cup sliced red onion
¼ cup water
½ teaspoon WYLER'S® or STEERO® Chicken-
    Flavor Instant Bouillon*
½ teaspoon dried tarragon leaves, crushed
2 tablespoons grated Parmesan cheese

In large skillet, heat oil; add chicken, broccoli, carrots and onion. Cook and stir over medium heat until broccoli is tender-crisp. Add water, bouillon and tarragon; cook and stir until chicken is cooked through. Add hot cooked rotini and Parmesan cheese; toss to coat. Serve immediately. Refrigerate leftovers.

*To reduce sodium, substitute low-sodium bouillon.

Nutrients per serving:			
Calories	225	Cholesterol	37 mg
Fat	6 g	Sodium	123 mg

Crunchy Ranch Chicken Fingers

Makes 4 servings

1 cup cornflake crumbs
1 tablespoon chopped fresh parsley
⅓ cup WISH-BONE® Healthy Sensation! Ranch
    Dressing
1 teaspoon water
1 pound boneless skinless chicken breasts, cut
    into thin strips

Preheat oven to 425°F. In small bowl, combine cornflake crumbs and parsley. In separate small bowl, combine ranch dressing and water. Dip chicken in dressing mixture, then cornflake mixture, coating well.

On baking pan lightly sprayed with nonstick cooking spray, arrange chicken. Bake 8 minutes or until chicken is tender.

Nutrients per serving:			
Calories	258	Cholesterol	66 mg
Fat	2 g	Sodium	609 mg

Chicken with Pineapple Salsa

Chicken with Pineapple Salsa

Makes 4 servings

1 can (20 ounces) DOLE® Crushed Pineapple
    in Juice
4 boneless skinless chicken breast halves
    (1 pound)
1 large clove garlic, pressed
1 teaspoon ground cumin
    Salt and black pepper (optional)
1 tablespoon vegetable oil
½ cup minced DOLE® Red Bell Pepper
¼ cup minced DOLE® Green Bell Pepper
1 tablespoon minced DOLE® Green Onion
2 teaspoons minced cilantro
2 teaspoons minced fresh or drained canned
    jalapeño chilies
1 teaspoon grated lime peel

Drain pineapple; reserve juice.

Rub chicken with garlic; sprinkle with cumin, salt and black pepper. In 12-inch skillet, cook chicken in hot oil over medium-high heat until browned; turn once. Add ½ cup reserved pineapple juice to chicken. Reduce heat to low. Cover; simmer 7 to 10 minutes.

For salsa, in medium bowl, combine pineapple, remaining reserved juice and remaining ingredients.

Cut each breast into slices. Serve chicken with salsa. Garnish as desired.

Prep time: 5 minutes
Cook time: 15 minutes

Nutrients per serving:			
Calories	262	Cholesterol	68 mg
Fat	5 g	Sodium	81 mg

Chicken Crimini

Chicken Crimini

Makes 6 servings

 1 package (1½ pounds) PERDUE® Fit 'n Easy
    fresh skinless and boneless pick of the chick
 ½ teaspoon ground thyme leaves, crushed
    Salt and ground black pepper (optional)
 1½ tablespoons olive oil
 ¼ pound wild mushrooms, such as crimini,
    shiitake or oyster, thinly sliced
 ¼ cup reduced-sodium beef broth
 3 tablespoons Marsala wine
 1 tablespoon grated Parmesan cheese
 2 tablespoons minced fresh parsley
 1 lemon, thinly sliced (optional)

Place chicken pieces between sheets of plastic wrap. Pound chicken with meat mallet until slightly flattened. Season with thyme, salt and pepper and set aside. In large, nonstick skillet over medium heat, heat oil. Add mushrooms; cook and stir 1 to 2 minutes. With slotted spoon, remove mushrooms and set aside. Add chicken to skillet and cook about 5 minutes on each side or until lightly browned. Remove chicken and keep warm.

With wooden spatula or spoon, stir beef broth and wine into skillet, scraping bottom to incorporate browned bits into pan juices. Return chicken to skillet; top with mushrooms. Sprinkle with Parmesan and spoon pan juices over all. Reduce heat to low; cover skillet and simmer 5 to 10 minutes until chicken is cooked through. To serve, sprinkle with parsley and garnish with lemon slices, if desired.

Nutrients per serving:

| Calories | 181 | Cholesterol | 81 mg |
| Fat | 7 g | Sodium | 103 mg |

Turkey Kabobs with Gingered Mustard Sauce

Makes 5 servings

 ½ cup FRENCH'S® Creamy Spread™ Mustard
 1 can (8 ounces) pineapple chunks, drained,
    juice reserved
 1 to 2 tablespoons firmly packed brown sugar
 ½ teaspoon ground ginger
 1 pound fresh boneless turkey cutlets, cut into
    1-inch strips
 1 medium green bell pepper, cut into bite-size
    pieces
 10 cherry tomatoes
 5 skewers
    Hot cooked rice (optional)

In small bowl, combine French's® Creamy Spread™ Mustard, reserved pineapple juice, brown sugar and ginger. Alternately thread pineapple chunks, turkey strips, pepper pieces and tomatoes onto skewers. Reserve half of mustard mixture. Grill or broil kabobs, basting with remaining mustard mixture, 15 to 20 minutes or until turkey is tender. Serve warm over rice with reserved mustard mixture.

Nutrients per serving:

| Calories | 169 | Cholesterol | 54 mg |
| Fat | 3 g | Sodium | 357 mg |

Pepper-Chicken Fettucini Toss

Makes 12 servings

 1 package (1 pound) CREAMETTE® Fettucini,
    uncooked
 ¼ cup olive or vegetable oil
 3 whole boneless skinless chicken breasts, cut
    into strips (about 18 ounces)
 2 large red bell peppers, cut into strips
 2 large yellow bell peppers, cut into strips
 1 medium green bell pepper, cut into strips
 1 medium onion, cut into chunks
 2 cups sliced fresh mushrooms
 1 teaspoon salt-free herb seasoning
 2 tablespoons grated Parmesan cheese

Prepare Creamette® Fettucini according to package directions; drain. In large skillet, heat oil; add chicken, peppers, onion, mushrooms and seasoning. Cook and stir over medium heat until chicken is cooked through, 8 to 10 minutes. Add hot cooked fettucini and Parmesan cheese; toss to coat. Serve immediately. Refrigerate leftovers.

Nutrients per serving:

| Calories | 264 | Cholesterol | 36 mg |
| Fat | 7 g | Sodium | 33 mg |

Rosemary Chicken Stir-Fry

Makes 4 servings

1 Family Size bag UNCLE BEN'S® Brand
    Boil-in-Bag Rice
1½ tablespoons vegetable oil
  1 cup short thin carrot strips
  ½ cup sliced celery
  ¼ teaspoon dried rosemary leaves, crushed
  ½ pound boneless skinless chicken breasts, cut
    into thin strips
  1 cup sliced mushrooms
  ¼ cup sliced green onions with tops
  1 can (10¾ ounces) condensed chicken broth
  4 teaspoons cornstarch

Cook rice according to package directions; set aside.
Meanwhile, heat oil in large skillet over medium-high
heat. Add carrots, celery and rosemary; stir-fry until
vegetables are crisp-tender. Push vegetables to one
side of skillet; add chicken. Stir-fry 3 minutes or until
chicken is tender and no longer pink. Add mushrooms
and green onions; stir-fry 3 minutes. Stir broth into
cornstarch in small bowl until smooth; add to skillet.
Cook and stir over medium heat until mixture boils
and thickens, stirring frequently. Serve chicken
mixture over rice.

Nutrients per serving:			
Calories	250	Cholesterol	23 mg
Fat	7 g	Sodium	550 mg

Turkey Parmesan

Makes 1 serving

1 teaspoon diet margarine
1 (2-ounce) fresh turkey breast slice
3 tablespoons CLASSICO® Pasta Sauce, any
    flavor
1 teaspoon grated Parmesan cheese
1 slice BORDEN® Lite-line® Process Cheese
    Product,* any flavor

In small skillet, over medium heat, melt margarine.
Add turkey breast slice. Cook 2 minutes; turn.
Reduce heat to low; top turkey with remaining
ingredients. Cover; cook 2 to 3 minutes longer or
until turkey is no longer pink. Garnish as desired.
Refrigerate leftovers.

* "½ the calories"– 8% milkfat product

Nutrients per serving:			
Calories	198	Cholesterol	54 mg
Fat	7 g	Sodium	646 mg

Monterey Chicken Sandwiches

Makes 4 sandwiches

½ tablespoon vegetable oil
½ tablespoon margarine
4 boneless skinless chicken breast halves
    (about 1 pound)
1 teaspoon dried thyme leaves, crushed
    Salt and black pepper (optional)
1 large red onion, thinly sliced
4 Kaiser rolls, split
    Radicchio or lettuce leaves

Heat oil and margarine in large skillet over medium
heat. Add chicken; sprinkle with thyme. Cook
8 minutes or until browned on both sides and no
longer pink in center, turning after 4 minutes. Season
with salt and pepper, if desired. Remove from skillet;
keep warm. Add onion to skillet; cook and stir until
tender.

Fill rolls with radicchio leaves, chicken and onion.
Serve with mango chutney and olives, if desired.

Nutrients per serving (1 sandwich):			
Calories	283	Cholesterol	46 mg
Fat	7 g	Sodium	369 mg

***Monterey Chicken Sandwiches,
Corn-on-the-Cob with Chili Spread (page 221)***

Turn the heads of even the most die-hard meat lovers with these enticing and nutritious seafood recipes. Flavorful marinades and sauces enhance the delicate flavors of shrimp, scallops and your favorite fish fillets. Try preparing seafood on the grill for an especially tantalizing taste treat.

Poached Salmon with Basil Mayonnaise

Makes 4 servings

    Basil Mayonnaise (recipe follows)
 1 bay leaf
 4 peppercorns
 4 salmon steaks, 1 to 1½ inches thick (1 pound)

Prepare Basil Mayonnaise; cover. Set aside.

Add bay leaf, peppercorns and enough water to medium skillet to fill to 1-inch depth. Bring to a boil. Add salmon. Reduce heat to low; cover. Simmer 5 minutes or until salmon flakes easily when tested with fork.

Remove salmon from poaching liquid; serve with Basil Mayonnaise.

Basil Mayonnaise
 ¼ cup light mayonnaise
 ¼ cup plain low-fat yogurt
 1 green onion, cut into 1-inch pieces
 1 tablespoon fresh parsley sprigs
 1 tablespoon fresh basil
    Salt and black pepper (optional)

Combine mayonnaise, yogurt, onion, parsley and basil in food processor or blender container; process until well blended. Season with salt and pepper, if desired.

Nutrients per serving (includes 2 tablespoons Basil Mayonnaise):

Calories	211	Cholesterol	69 mg
Fat	10 g	Sodium	60 mg

West Coast Tuna Pitas

Makes 8 servings

 ½ cup HEALTHY CHOICE® Cholesterol Free
    Egg Product
 1 can (6⅛ ounces) tuna packed in water, drained
 ¼ cup nonfat mayonnaise
 ¼ cup reduced-calorie cream cheese spread
 ¼ cup chopped water chestnuts
 1 tablespoon sliced green onion
 1 teaspoon lemon juice
 1 teaspoon Dijon-style mustard
 ¼ teaspoon dill weed
 4 pita bread rounds, cut in half
 1 cucumber, thinly sliced
 1 tomato, thinly sliced
    Alfalfa sprouts

Lightly coat 8-inch skillet with nonstick cooking spray. Cook egg product, covered, over very low heat 5 minutes or until just set. Let egg product cool; coarsely chop. In medium bowl, combine egg product, tuna, mayonnaise, cream cheese spread, water chestnuts, onion, lemon juice, mustard and dill; refrigerate. To serve, fill pita halves with cucumber and tomato slices, sprouts and ¼ cup tuna mixture.

Nutrients per serving:

Calories	150	Cholesterol	10 mg
Fat	1 g	Sodium	395 mg

Poached Salmon with Basil Mayonnaise, Pea-Pod Medley (page 213)

Broiled Orange Roughy with
Green Peppercorn Sauce

Broiled Orange Roughy with Green Peppercorn Sauce

Makes 4 servings

Green Peppercorn Sauce (recipe follows)
4 orange roughy fillets (about 6 ounces each)

Preheat broiler. Position oven rack about 4 inches from heat source. Prepare Green Peppercorn Sauce; set aside.

Place fish in shallow baking pan; top with sauce. Broil 10 minutes or until fish flakes easily when tested with fork.

Green Peppercorn Sauce
  1 cup loosely packed cilantro leaves
  2 tablespoons country-style Dijon mustard*
  2 tablespoons dry white wine
  ½ teaspoon green peppercorns, rinsed, drained

Combine all ingredients in food processor or blender container; process until well blended.

*Substitute your favorite herbed mustard for the country-style Dijon mustard.

Nutrients per serving:

Calories	195	Cholesterol	28 mg
Fat	10 g	Sodium	203 mg

Citrus Marinated Fish Steaks

Makes 4 servings

  ¼ cup frozen orange juice concentrate, thawed
  ¼ cup REALEMON® Lemon Juice from Concentrate
  1 tablespoon vegetable oil
  ½ teaspoon dill weed
  4 (1-inch-thick) salmon, halibut or swordfish steaks (about 1½ pounds)

In large shallow dish or plastic bag, combine juices, oil and dill weed; mix well. Add fish. Cover; marinate in refrigerator 2 hours, turning occasionally. Remove fish from marinade; heat marinade thoroughly. Grill or broil until fish flakes with fork, basting frequently with marinade. Garnish as desired. Refrigerate leftovers.

Nutrients per serving:

Calories	211	Cholesterol	30 mg
Fat	9 g	Sodium	1039 mg

Sautéed Rainbow Trout with Wild Mushrooms

Makes 4 servings

  1 tablespoon olive oil
  1 cup chopped shallots
  1 cup sliced button mushrooms
  1 cup small whole oyster mushrooms
  ¼ cup light soy sauce
  ¼ cup dry sherry
  ¼ cup water
  Ground black pepper to taste
  4 CLEAR SPRINGS® Brand Idaho Rainbow Trout fillets, butterflied (4 ounces *each*)

In large nonstick skillet, combine olive oil and shallots; cook, covered, over medium heat until shallots are translucent. Add mushrooms; continue cooking, covered, until mushrooms are soft. Stir in soy sauce, sherry and water; simmer 1 minute. Remove from heat; season with pepper. Transfer mixture to medium bowl; cover to keep warm. Coat same skillet lightly with oil. Cook trout, flesh side down, over high heat 2 minutes. Gently turn trout; cook 2 minutes more or until trout flakes with fork. Serve immediately with mushroom mixture.

Nutrients per serving:

Calories	233	Cholesterol	65 mg
Fat	7 g	Sodium	592 mg

Broiled Oriental Fish

Makes 4 servings

¼ cup CRISCO® PURITAN® Oil
¼ cup reduced-sodium soy sauce
¼ cup dry white wine
1½ teaspoons sesame seeds
1 teaspoon sugar
½ teaspoon ground ginger
1 pound Dover sole fillets
12 green onions
½ teaspoon black pepper (optional)

Heat broiler. Combine Crisco® Puritan® Oil, soy sauce, wine, sesame seeds, sugar and ginger in shallow baking dish. Stir until blended.

Place fillets in marinade. Turn to coat. Marinate 20 minutes; turn fillets occasionally.

Wash green onions. Trim tops so onions are 5 to 6 inches in length. Make 3-inch lengthwise slices in onion tops to give onions feathered look.

Place onions in marinade for last 10 minutes of marinating time.

Remove fish and onions from marinade. Place on broiler pan. Sprinkle with pepper, if desired. Place pan in oven 4 to 5 inches from heat.

Broil 3 minutes. Turn fish and onions carefully using pancake turner and broil 3 minutes more or until fish flakes easily when tested with fork.

To Microwave: Prepare and marinate fish and green onions as above. Remove fish and onions from marinade. Place in 12×8-inch microwave-safe dish. Sprinkle with pepper, if desired. Cover with vented plastic wrap. Microwave on HIGH (100% power) 2 minutes. Rotate dish. Microwave on HIGH 1½ minutes or until fish flakes easily when tested with fork. Let stand, covered, 1 minute.

Nutrients per serving:

Calories	190	Cholesterol	75 mg
Fat	9 g	Sodium	180 mg

Festival Shrimp and Saffron Rice

Makes 2 servings

⅓ cup diced red bell pepper
¼ cup sliced green onion with tops
1 clove garlic, minced
1 teaspoon margarine
½ pound peeled and deveined medium shrimp
½ teaspoon seafood seasoning blend
1½ cups cooked rice (cooked with 1/16 teaspoon ground saffron or turmeric)
1 tablespoon grated Parmesan cheese

Cook and stir bell pepper, onions, and garlic in margarine in medium skillet over medium heat 1 to 2 minutes. Add shrimp and seasoning blend; cook, stirring, 3 to 4 minutes or until shrimp are opaque. Stir in rice and cheese; cook and stir until thoroughly heated, about 2 to 3 minutes. Garnish as desired.

To Microwave: Combine bell pepper, onions, garlic, and margarine in 1-quart microproof baking dish. Cover and cook on HIGH (100% power) 2 minutes. Add shrimp and seasoning blend. Reduce setting to MEDIUM-HIGH (70% power); cover and cook 3 to 4 minutes or until shrimp are opaque. Stir in rice and cheese; cover and cook on MEDIUM-HIGH 1 to 2 minutes or until thoroughly heated. Let stand 2 minutes. Garnish as desired.

Nutrients per serving:

Calories	247	Cholesterol	176 mg
Fat	4 g	Sodium	817 mg

Favorite recipe from **USA Rice Council**

Festival Shrimp and Saffron Rice

Scallop Kabobs

Makes 8 kabobs

¼ cup REALEMON® Lemon Juice from
  Concentrate
2 tablespoons vegetable oil
1 teaspoon oregano leaves
½ teaspoon basil leaves
1 clove garlic, finely chopped
⅛ teaspoon salt
1 pound sea scallops
8 ounces fresh mushrooms
2 small zucchini, cut into chunks
2 small onions, cut into wedges
½ red, yellow or green bell pepper, cut into bite-
  size pieces
  Additional REALEMON® Brand

In shallow dish, combine ¼ cup ReaLemon® brand,
oil and seasonings; add scallops. Cover; marinate in
refrigerator 2 hours, stirring occasionally. Remove
scallops from marinade; discard marinade. Divide
scallops and vegetables equally among 8 skewers.
Grill or broil as desired, until scallops are opaque,
basting frequently with additional ReaLemon® brand.
Refrigerate leftovers.

Nutrients per serving (2 kabobs):			
Calories	213	Cholesterol	37 mg
Fat	8 g	Sodium	255 mg

Scallop Kabobs

Fish Vera Cruz

Makes 4 servings

1¼ pounds fish fillets or fish steaks (about ½ inch
  thick)
1 tablespoon lime juice
1 medium onion, sliced
1 medium green bell pepper, cut into ¾-inch
  chunks
1 clove garlic, minced
1 tablespoon vegetable oil
2 medium tomatoes, cut into chunks
½ cup HEINZ® Chili Sauce
¼ cup sliced pimiento-stuffed olives
  Dash ground red pepper

Sprinkle fish with lime juice; set aside. In large
skillet, cook and stir onion, green pepper and garlic
in oil until tender-crisp. Add tomatoes and remaining
ingredients. Simmer, uncovered, 3 to 5 minutes or
until most of liquid evaporates. Place fish in skillet,
spooning sauce over. Cover; simmer 6 to 8 minutes
or until fish turns opaque and begins to flake when
tested with fork. Remove fish; simmer sauce to
thicken, if necessary. Serve sauce over fish.

Nutrients per serving:			
Calories	222	Cholesterol	68 mg
Fat	6 g	Sodium	754 mg

Italian-Style Microwaved Halibut Steaks

Makes 4 servings

4 (1-inch-thick) halibut steaks (about 1 pound)
⅓ cup low-calorie Italian dressing
1 tablespoon lemon juice
¼ teaspoon black pepper
¼ teaspoon paprika

To Microwave: Place fish in microwave-safe dish.
Combine remaining ingredients; pour over fish. Cover dish
with plastic wrap and refrigerate 30 minutes, turning fish
over once. Turn back one corner of plastic wrap to vent.
Cook 4 to 5 minutes on HIGH (100% power), rotating dish
¼ turn after 2 minutes. Fish is done when it flakes with
fork. Let stand 2 to 3 minutes before serving.

Nutrients per serving:			
Calories	128	Cholesterol	34 mg
Fat	5 g	Sodium	216 mg

Favorite recipe from **National Fisheries Institute**

Oriental Seafood Stir-Fry

Oriental Seafood Stir-Fry

Makes 4 servings

½ cup water
3 tablespoons REALEMON® Lemon Juice from
   Concentrate
3 tablespoons soy sauce
1 tablespoon firmly packed brown sugar
1 tablespoon cornstarch
2 ounces fresh pea pods
¾ cup sliced fresh mushrooms
¾ cup diced red bell pepper
1 medium onion, cut into wedges
1 tablespoon vegetable oil
½ pound imitation crab blend, flaked
   Shredded napa (Chinese cabbage), angel hair
   pasta or rice noodles (optional)

Combine water, ReaLemon® brand, soy sauce, sugar
and cornstarch in small bowl. In large skillet or wok,
over medium-high heat, cook and stir vegetables in oil
until tender-crisp; remove. Add soy mixture; over
medium heat, cook and stir until slightly thickened.
Add vegetables and crab blend; heat through. Serve
with napa, pasta or rice noodles. Refrigerate leftovers.

Nutrients per serving:

Calories	151	Cholesterol	11 mg
Fat	4 g	Sodium	1266 mg

Dieter's Fish and Spinach

Makes 2 servings

2 (4-ounce) frozen sole fillets, thawed
1 tablespoon REALEMON® Lemon Juice from
   Concentrate
   Salt and pepper
1 (10-ounce) package frozen chopped spinach,
   cooked and well drained
¼ cup BORDEN® Lite-line® or Viva® Protein
   Fortified Skim Milk
2 slices BORDEN® Lite-line® Process Cheese
   Product,* any flavor, cut into small pieces
   Paprika

Preheat oven to 400°F. Brush fillets with ReaLemon®
brand; sprinkle lightly with salt and pepper. Spread
spinach over bottom of 8-inch baking dish. Pour milk
over spinach; top with cheese product pieces, then
fillets. Cover; bake 20 minutes or until fish flakes
with fork. Sprinkle with paprika. Refrigerate leftovers.

"½ the calories"– 8% milkfat product

Nutrients per serving:

Calories	182	Cholesterol	65 mg
Fat	4 g	Sodium	716 mg

Garlic Skewered Shrimp

Garlic Skewered Shrimp

Makes 4 servings

1 pound large raw shrimp, peeled, deveined
2 tablespoons light soy sauce
1 tablespoon peanut or vegetable oil
3 cloves garlic, minced
¼ teaspoon crushed red pepper flakes (optional)
3 green onions, cut into 1-inch pieces

Soak 4 (12-inch) bamboo skewers in water 20 minutes.

Place shrimp in large plastic food bag. Combine soy sauce, oil, garlic and crushed red pepper in cup; mix well. Pour over shrimp. Close bag securely; turn to coat. Marinate at room temperature 10 to 15 minutes.

Drain shrimp; reserve marinade. Alternately thread shrimp and onions onto skewers. Place on rack of broiler pan. Brush with reserved marinade; discard remaining marinade.

Broil shrimp, 5 to 6 inches from heat, 5 minutes. Turn shrimp over; broil an additional 5 minutes or until shrimp are opaque.

Nutrients per serving:

Calories	127	Cholesterol	174 mg
Fat	4 g	Sodium	478 mg

Sole in Ratatouille

Makes 6 servings

½ cup thinly sliced onion
1 crushed garlic clove
2 tablespoons olive oil
2 cups (½ pound) peeled cubed eggplant
1¾ cups (14.5-ounce can) CONTADINA® Whole Peeled Tomatoes, cut up, with juice
1½ cups sliced fresh mushrooms
1 cup coarsely chopped green bell pepper
1 cup water
⅔ cup (6-ounce can) CONTADINA® Tomato Paste
⅓ cup finely chopped fresh parsley
1 tablespoon finely chopped fresh basil
½ teaspoon salt
¼ teaspoon black pepper
1½ pounds sole fillets
1½ cups (3 medium) sliced zucchini or yellow squash

Cook and stir onion and garlic in oil in 12-inch skillet. Add eggplant, tomatoes with juice, mushrooms, bell pepper, water, tomato paste, parsley, basil, salt and black pepper. Cover and simmer 10 minutes, stirring occasionally. Roll up sole fillets; place in skillet, pushing down into tomato mixture. Cover; simmer 20 minutes. Add zucchini to skillet. Simmer 10 to 15 minutes or until sole flakes when tested with fork and zucchini is tender. Serve with cooked pasta, if desired.

Nutrients per serving:

Calories	300	Cholesterol	0 mg
Fat	7 g	Sodium	500 mg

Tangy Baked Fish Fillets

Makes 6 to 8 servings

¼ cup CRISCO® PURITAN® Oil
2 medium onions, thinly sliced and separated into rings
1½ to 2 pounds fish fillets, ½ inch thick, cut into serving-size pieces
½ teaspoon salt
¼ teaspoon black pepper
3 medium tomatoes, seeded and chopped
2 lemons, thinly sliced
1 bay leaf
1 tablespoon white vinegar
1 tablespoon sugar

Preheat oven to 325°F. Heat Crisco® Puritan® Oil in deep skillet with ovenproof handle. Add onions. Cook and stir over moderate heat until tender. Remove from heat.

Arrange fish over onions. Sprinkle with salt and pepper. Top with tomatoes and lemons. Add bay leaf. Sprinkle with vinegar and sugar. Cover.

Bake at 325°F for 45 minutes to 1 hour or until fish flakes easily with fork. Remove and discard bay leaf.

Nutrients per serving:

Calories	190	Cholesterol	49 mg
Fat	8 g	Sodium	200 mg

Fish Françoise

Fish Françoise

Makes 4 servings

1 can (14½ ounces) DEL MONTE® Original
    Style Stewed Tomatoes
1 tablespoon lemon juice
2 cloves garlic, minced
½ teaspoon dried tarragon leaves, crushed
⅛ teaspoon black pepper
3 tablespoons whipping cream
    Vegetable oil
1½ pounds firm white fish (such as halibut or cod)
    Lemon wedges

Preheat broiler; position rack 4 inches from heat. In large saucepan, combine tomatoes with liquid, lemon juice, garlic, tarragon and pepper. Cook, uncovered, over medium-high heat about 10 minutes or until liquid has evaporated. Add cream. Cook over low heat 5 minutes or until very thick; set aside. Brush broiler pan with oil. Arrange fish on pan; season with salt and pepper, if desired. Broil fish 3 to 4 minutes per side or until fish flakes easily with fork. Spread tomato mixture over top of fish. Broil 1 minute. Serve immediately with lemon wedges.

Prep time: 5 minutes
Cook time: 19 minutes

Nutrients per serving:

Calories	240	Cholesterol	78 mg
Fat	7 g	Sodium	341 mg

Oven Steamed Rainbow Trout in Parchment

Makes 4 servings

4 tablespoons chopped fresh parsley
2 teaspoons minced garlic
2 teaspoons grated orange peel
¼ teaspoon salt
⅛ teaspoon ground black pepper
    Parchment paper
4 CLEAR SPRINGS® Brand Idaho Rainbow
    Trout fillets (4 ounces *each*)
4 teaspoons olive oil

Preheat oven to 375°F. In small bowl, combine parsley, garlic, orange peel, salt and pepper; set aside. Cut four 15×12-inch pieces of parchment; fold each piece in half and trim to form semicircle. Unfold parchment; place trout fillets, skin sides down, on parchment near fold. Sprinkle each fillet with 1 tablespoon parsley mixture and 1 teaspoon oil. Fold top half of parchment over trout; fold and seal edges tightly. Place parchment bundles on baking sheet; bake 10 minutes until parchment is browned and puffed. Serve immediately.

Nutrients per serving:

Calories	178	Cholesterol	65 mg
Fat	8 g	Sodium	166 mg

Tuna Casserole with a Twist

Makes 4 servings

1 can (5 ounces) PET® Evaporated Skimmed
    Milk
1½ teaspoons all-purpose flour
1 cup (4 ounces) shredded low-fat Cheddar
    cheese
2 cups (8 ounces) broccoli flowerets, cooked
1 can (about 6½ ounces) tuna packed in spring
    water, drained
4 ounces corkscrew noodles, cooked according
    to package directions and drained
⅓ cup chopped onion

In large saucepan, whisk together evaporated milk and flour; cook over medium heat until thick and bubbly, stirring occasionally. Add cheese; stir until cheese melts.

Stir in remaining ingredients. Cook until heated through.

Nutrients per serving:

Calories	220	Cholesterol	38 mg
Fat	6 g	Sodium	412 mg

Singing Shrimp with Pineapple

Makes 4 servings

1 medium DOLE® Fresh Pineapple

Singing Spice
¼ teaspoon *each* ground allspice, ground anise
    seed (optional), ground cinnamon, ground
    cloves, ground ginger and crushed red
    pepper flakes

1 pound large shrimp, peeled and deveined
½ teaspoon salt
1 onion, cut into wedges
1 large DOLE® Red Bell Pepper, seeded and
    sliced
1 clove garlic, pressed
1 teaspoon vegetable oil
¾ cup water
1½ teaspoons cornstarch
2 tablespoons chopped cilantro, divided
2 tablespoons chopped fresh mint leaves,
    divided

Twist crown from pineapple. Cut pineapple in half
lengthwise. Refrigerate half for another use, such as
salads. Cut fruit from shell with knife. Cut fruit
crosswise into thin slices.

Combine spices in cup. Sprinkle half the spice
mixture over shrimp. Sprinkle shrimp with salt.

In 10-inch nonstick skillet, cook and stir onion, bell
pepper and garlic in oil over medium-high heat until
tender.

Blend water and cornstarch in cup. Stir cornstarch
mixture and remaining spice mixture into skillet.

Arrange shrimp on top of onion mixture. Reduce heat
to low. Cover; simmer 5 to 7 minutes or until shrimp
are opaque, stirring occasionally. Remove shrimp to
serving plate with slotted spoon.

Add pineapple to onion mixture in skillet with
1 tablespoon *each* cilantro and mint. Stir until heated
through. Serve over shrimp. Sprinkle with remaining
cilantro and mint.

Nutrients per serving:

Calories	270	Cholesterol	157 mg
Fat	3 g	Sodium	270 mg

"Grilled" Tuna with Vegetables in Herb Butter

Makes 4 servings

4 pieces heavy-duty aluminum foil, *each*
    12×18 inches
1 can (12½ ounces) STARKIST® Tuna, drained
    and broken into chunks
1 cup slivered red or green bell pepper
1 cup slivered yellow squash or zucchini
1 cup pea pods, cut crosswise into halves
1 cup slivered carrots
4 green onions, cut into 2-inch slices
    Salt and black pepper to taste (optional)

Herb Butter
3 tablespoons butter or margarine, melted
1 tablespoon lemon or lime juice
1 clove garlic, minced
2 teaspoons dried tarragon leaves, crushed
1 teaspoon dried dill weed

On each piece of foil, mound tuna, bell pepper,
squash, pea pods, carrots and onions. Sprinkle with
salt and black pepper.

For Herb Butter, in small bowl stir together butter,
lemon juice, garlic, tarragon and dill weed. Drizzle
over tuna and vegetables. Fold edges of each foil
square together to make packets.

To grill: Place foil packets about 4 inches above hot coals.
Grill for 10 to 12 minutes or until heated through, turning
packets over halfway through grill time.

To bake: Place foil packets on baking sheet. Bake in
preheated 450°F oven for 15 to 20 minutes, or until heated
through.

To serve: Cut an "X" on top of each packet; peel back
foil.

Nutrients per serving:

Calories	235	Cholesterol	70 mg
Fat	9 g	Sodium	519 mg

"Grilled" Tuna with Vegetables in Herb Butter

Baja Fish and Rice Bake

Baja Fish and Rice Bake

Makes 6 servings

¾ cup chopped onion
½ cup chopped celery
1 clove garlic, minced
3 tablespoons vegetable oil
½ cup uncooked rice
3½ cups (two 14½-ounce cans) **CONTADINA®** Stewed Tomatoes, cut up, with juice
1 teaspoon lemon pepper seasoning
½ teaspoon salt
⅛ teaspoon ground red pepper
1 pound fish fillets (any firm white fish)
¼ cup finely chopped fresh parsley
Lemon slices (optional)

Cook and stir onion, celery and garlic in hot oil in large skillet over medium heat until vegetables are tender. Add rice; cook and stir about 5 minutes or until rice browns slightly. Add tomatoes with juice, lemon pepper, salt and ground red pepper. Place fish fillets on bottom of 12×7½×2-inch baking dish. Spoon rice mixture over fish. Cover with foil; bake in preheated 400°F oven for 45 to 50 minutes or until rice is tender and fish flakes with fork. Allow to stand 5 minutes before serving. Sprinkle with parsley. Garnish with lemon slices, if desired.

To Microwave: Combine onion, celery and garlic in microwave-safe bowl. Microwave at HIGH (100% power) for 3 minutes. Stir in rice, tomatoes with juice, lemon pepper, salt and ground red pepper. Microwave at HIGH power for an additional 5 minutes. Place fish fillets in 12×7½×2-inch microwave-safe baking dish. Spoon rice mixture over fish. Cover tightly with plastic wrap, turning up corner to vent. Microwave at HIGH power for 20 to 25 minutes or until rice is tender and fish flakes when tested with fork. Allow to stand 5 minutes before serving. Serve as above.

Nutrients per serving (conventional method):			
Calories	241	Cholesterol	38 mg
Fat	8 g	Sodium	580 mg

Nutrients per serving (microwave method):			
Calories	181	Cholesterol	38 mg
Fat	2 g	Sodium	580 mg

Grilled Summer Fish

Makes 4 servings

1¼ pounds fish fillets (such as cod, bluefish, haddock, sole)
1 medium green bell pepper, seeded and chopped
1 medium tomato, cored and chopped
¼ cup chopped green onions
1 tablespoon chopped dill
½ teaspoon salt
2 tablespoons lemon juice
1 cup (4 ounces) shredded Jarlsberg cheese

Grease 12×18-inch piece of heavy-duty aluminum foil. Place fish fillets in center of foil. Combine vegetables and place over fish. Sprinkle with dill and salt; drizzle with lemon juice. Top with Jarlsberg cheese. Fold up sides of foil, crimping to make a tight seal on top and ends. Place foil packet on top of hot barbecue grill. Grill for 25 minutes. Carefully open packet; if fish is still translucent in the middle, reseal and grill for an additional 5 to 10 minutes.

To Microwave: Assemble ingredients as above (omitting foil) in microwave-safe baking dish. Cover; microwave at HIGH (100% power) for 7 minutes. Fish is done when it flakes easily when tested with fork near center. If necessary, continue cooking on HIGH for an additional minute. Let stand, covered, for 5 minutes.

To Bake: Assemble ingredients as above (omitting foil) in large baking dish. Bake, uncovered, in 375°F oven for 20 minutes, or until fish flakes with fork and cheese is browned.

Nutrients per serving:

Calories	230	Cholesterol	92 mg
Fat	8 g	Sodium	429 mg

Favorite recipe from **Norseland Foods, Inc.**

Vegetable-Shrimp Stir-Fry

Makes 4 servings

1 tablespoon olive oil
6 ounces snow peas, trimmed
6 green onions, cut into 1-inch pieces
1 red bell pepper, cut into ½-inch strips
1 pound peeled, deveined medium shrimp
¼ pound large mushrooms, quartered
2 tablespoons soy sauce
1 tablespoon seasoned rice vinegar
1 teaspoon sesame oil
Hot cooked rice (optional)

Heat olive oil in large skillet or wok over medium-high heat. Add snow peas, onions and red pepper; stir-fry 2 minutes.

Add shrimp; stir-fry 2 minutes or until shrimp are opaque. Add mushrooms; stir-fry until tender and most of liquid evaporates.

Add soy sauce, vinegar and sesame oil; heat thoroughly, stirring constantly. Serve over rice, if desired.

Nutrients per serving:

Calories	198	Cholesterol	175 mg
Fat	7 g	Sodium	688 mg

Vegetable-Shrimp Stir-Fry

Paella

Makes 6 servings

1 tablespoon olive oil
½ pound chicken breast cubes
1 cup uncooked long-grain white rice*
1 medium onion, chopped
1 clove garlic, minced
1½ cups chicken broth*
1 can (8 ounces) stewed tomatoes, chopped,
      reserving liquid
½ teaspoon paprika
⅛ to ¼ teaspoon ground red pepper
⅛ teaspoon ground saffron
½ pound medium shrimp, peeled and deveined
1 small red pepper, cut into strips
1 small green pepper, cut into strips
½ cup frozen green peas

Heat oil in Dutch oven over medium-high heat until hot. Add chicken and stir until browned. Add rice, onion, and garlic. Cook, stirring, until onion is tender and rice is lightly browned. Add broth, tomatoes, tomato liquid, paprika, ground red pepper, and saffron. Bring to a boil over high heat; stir. Reduce heat to low; cover and simmer 10 minutes. Add shrimp, pepper strips, and peas. Cover and simmer 10 minutes or until rice is tender, liquid is absorbed and shrimp are opaque.

If using medium grain rice, use 1¼ cups broth; if using parboiled rice, use 1¾ cups broth.

Nutrients per serving:			
Calories	253	Cholesterol	82 mg
Fat	4 g	Sodium	392 mg

Favorite recipe from **USA Rice Council**

Shrimp Linguine

Makes 8 servings

1 pound medium shrimp, shelled and deveined
½ cup dry white wine
1 tablespoon lemon juice
1 tablespoon lime juice
¼ pound fresh snow peas
6 green onions, thinly sliced
1 tablespoon chopped fresh parsley
¾ teaspoon dried basil leaves, crushed
½ teaspoon lemon pepper seasoning
2 cloves garlic, minced
1 bay leaf
½ of a (1-pound) package CREAMETTE®
      Linguine, uncooked

In large skillet, combine shrimp, wine, lemon juice and lime juice. Bring to a boil. Reduce heat to low; simmer, covered, 3 minutes. Add remaining ingredients, *except* linguine. Cook, stirring constantly, just until snow peas are tender and shrimp are opaque, about 5 minutes. Prepare Creamette® Linguine according to package directions; drain. Remove bay leaf from shrimp mixture. Combine shrimp mixture and hot cooked linguine; toss to coat. Refrigerate leftovers.

Nutrients per serving:			
Calories	191	Cholesterol	86 mg
Fat	1 g	Sodium	73 mg

No-Fuss Tuna Quiche

Makes 8 servings

1 unbaked 9-inch deep-dish pastry shell
1½ cups low-fat milk
3 extra large eggs
⅓ cup chopped green onions
1 tablespoon chopped drained pimiento
1 teaspoon dried basil leaves, crushed
½ teaspoon salt
1 can (6⅛ ounces) STARKIST® Tuna, drained
      and flaked
½ cup (2 ounces) shredded low-fat Cheddar
      cheese
8 spears (4 inches *each*) broccoli

Preheat oven to 450°F. Bake pastry shell for 5 minutes; remove to rack to cool. *Reduce oven temperature to 325°F.* For filling, in large bowl whisk together milk and eggs. Stir in onions, pimiento, basil and salt. Fold in tuna and cheese. Pour into prebaked pastry shell. Bake at 325°F for 30 minutes.

Meanwhile, in a saucepan steam broccoli spears over simmering water for 5 minutes. Drain; set aside. After 30 minutes baking time, arrange broccoli spears, spoke-fashion, over quiche. Bake 25 to 35 minutes more or until a knife inserted 2 inches from center comes out clean. Let stand for 5 minutes. Cut into 8 wedges, centering a broccoli spear in each wedge.

Note: *If desired, 1 cup chopped broccoli may be added to the filling before baking.*

Nutrients per serving:			
Calories	226	Cholesterol	95 mg
Fat	10 g	Sodium	461 mg

No-Fuss Tuna Quiche

Southwest Snapper

Makes 4 servings

1 pound red snapper, scrod or halibut fillets
Salt and black pepper (optional)
½ cup PACE® Picante Sauce
1 medium tomato, chopped
¼ cup sliced green onions with tops
¼ cup chopped cilantro or fresh parsley
¼ cup sliced ripe olives (optional)
Additional PACE® Picante Sauce (optional)

Place fish in shallow baking dish. Sprinkle with salt and pepper to taste. Cover; bake at 400°F or until fish just flakes when tested with fork (about 10 minutes per inch of thickness). Pour off juices. Spoon ½ cup Pace® Picante Sauce evenly over fish; top with tomato and green onions. Bake, uncovered, until heated through, about 5 minutes. Sprinkle with cilantro and olives. Serve with additional Pace® Picante Sauce, if desired. Garnish as desired.

Nutrients per serving:

Calories	130	Cholesterol	56 mg
Fat	1 g	Sodium	545 mg

Southwest Snapper

Microwaved Lemon-Apple Fish Rolls

Makes 4 servings

4 sole, cod or red snapper fillets (1 pound)
Grated peel of 1 SUNKIST® Lemon, divided
1 teaspoon dill weed, divided
¾ cup *plus* 2 tablespoons apple juice, divided
Juice of ½ SUNKIST® Lemon
2 tablespoons finely minced onion
1 tablespoon unsalted margarine
1 tablespoon all-purpose flour
1 tablespoon chopped fresh parsley

To Microwave: Sprinkle fish with half the lemon peel and half the dill. Roll up each fillet; place seam sides down in 8-inch round microwave-safe dish. Combine ¾ cup apple juice, lemon juice, onion, remaining lemon peel and dill; pour over fish. Dot with margarine. Cover dish loosely with vented plastic wrap. Microwave at HIGH (100% power) for 3 minutes. Uncover; spoon cooking liquid over fish. Cook, covered, 3 to 4 minutes longer, until fish flakes easily with fork. Remove fish to serving dish; let stand, covered, while preparing sauce.

Pour cooking liquid from fish into small microwave-safe bowl. Gradually blend remaining 2 tablespoons apple juice into flour; stir into cooking liquid. Microwave at HIGH, uncovered, 3 to 4 minutes (stirring twice), until sauce boils and thickens slightly. Add parsley; spoon over fish.

Nutrients per serving:

Calories	164	Cholesterol	55 mg
Fat	4 g	Sodium	94 mg

Tuna Bruschetta

Makes 4 servings

1 cup (4 ounces) SARGENTO® Preferred Light
   Fancy Shredded Supreme Mozzarella
   Cheese
1 can (3½ ounces) tuna packed in water, well
   drained and flaked
4 plum tomatoes, seeded and chopped
2 tablespoons minced onion
2 teaspoons minced fresh parsley
½ teaspoon dried oregano leaves, crushed
4 slices Italian bread (*each* 6×½ *inches*)
2 tablespoons olive oil
2 cloves garlic, halved

In medium bowl, combine cheese, tuna, tomatoes,
onion, parsley and oregano. Set aside. Brush both
sides of bread slices with olive oil and rub surfaces
with cut sides of garlic. In dry preheated skillet, grill
bread until light golden brown. Turn and top each
toasted surface with ¼ of cheese mixture. Continue
to grill until cheese melts and bread is golden brown
on bottom. Serve immediately.

Nutrients per serving:			
Calories	249	Cholesterol	29 mg
Fat	10 g	Sodium	420 mg

Oven Camp-Out Fish with BBQ Sauce

Makes 4 servings

¼ cup minced onion
1 clove garlic, minced
1 teaspoon margarine
1 can (8 ounces) DOLE® Pineapple Tidbits in
   Juice
½ cup bottled barbecue sauce
1 tablespoon packed brown sugar *or* honey
4 cod or red snapper fillets (1 pound)
1 tablespoon vegetable oil
   Juice from 1 DOLE® Lemon

In large skillet, cook and stir onion and garlic in
margarine until onion is soft. Add pineapple with
juice, barbecue sauce and brown sugar. Cook over
medium heat, stirring, until thickened and slightly
reduced. Brush fish with oil. Sprinkle with lemon
juice. Broil, 4 to 6 inches from heat, 5 minutes. Turn
fish and continue cooking 5 to 7 minutes longer until
fish flakes when tested with fork. Serve fish with
barbecue sauce.

Nutrients per serving:			
Calories	238	Cholesterol	63 mg
Fat	6 g	Sodium	356 mg

Grilled Prawns with Salsa Vera Cruz

Grilled Prawns with Salsa Vera Cruz

Makes 4 servings

1 can (14½ ounces) DEL MONTE® Mexican
   Recipe Stewed Tomatoes
1 orange, peeled and chopped
¼ cup sliced green onion
¼ cup chopped cilantro or fresh parsley
1 tablespoon olive oil
1 to 2 teaspoons minced jalapeño pepper
1 small clove garlic, crushed
1 pound medium shrimp, peeled and deveined

Drain tomatoes, reserving liquid; chop tomatoes. For
salsa, in medium bowl combine tomatoes, reserved
liquid, orange, green onion, cilantro, oil, jalapeño
pepper and garlic. Season to taste with salt and black
pepper, if desired. Thread shrimp onto skewers;
season with salt and black pepper, if desired. Brush
grill lightly with olive oil. Cook shrimp over hot coals
about 3 minutes per side or until shrimp just turn
opaque. Top with salsa. Serve over rice, if desired.

Prep time: 27 minutes
Cook time: 6 minutes

Nutrients per serving:			
Calories	166	Cholesterol	166 mg
Fat	5 g	Sodium	463 mg

Scallop Stir-Fry

Makes 4 servings

6 ounces uncooked ramen noodles or vermicelli
1 tablespoon olive oil
1 pound asparagus, cut into 1-inch pieces
1 red bell pepper, cut into thin rings
3 green onions, chopped
1 large clove garlic, minced
1 pound sea scallops, halved crosswise
2 tablespoons soy sauce
1 teaspoon hot pepper sauce
1 teaspoon sesame oil
Juice of ½ lime

Cook noodles in lightly salted boiling water according to package directions.

Meanwhile, heat olive oil in wok or large skillet over high heat. Add asparagus, red pepper, onions and garlic. Stir-fry 2 minutes.

Add scallops; stir-fry until scallops turn opaque.

Stir in soy sauce, hot pepper sauce, sesame oil and lime juice. Add noodles; heat thoroughly, stirring occasionally.

Nutrients per serving:

Calories	220	Cholesterol	37 mg
Fat	7 g	Sodium	864 mg

Sweet and Sour Prawns

Makes 6 servings

1 can (8¼ ounces) DOLE® Pineapple Chunks in Syrup*
2 tablespoons vegetable oil
¾ pound medium shrimp, peeled and deveined
1 DOLE® Carrot, cut diagonally in thin slices
1 small DOLE® Green Bell Pepper, seeded and chunked
1 can (11 ounces) lychee fruit, drained (optional)
2 tablespoons white vinegar
2 tablespoons catsup
1½ tablespoons soy sauce
1 tablespoon chopped crystallized ginger
1 tablespoon cornstarch
2 tablespoons water
3 cups hot cooked rice

Drain pineapple; reserve syrup.

Heat wok or skillet until hot. Add oil, swirling to coat sides. Add shrimp; stir-fry 1 to 2 minutes until shrimp are opaque. Add carrot, bell pepper, lychee and pineapple. Stir-fry for about 2 minutes.

Add reserved pineapple syrup, vinegar, catsup, soy sauce and ginger. Cook, stirring, for 1 minute.

Blend cornstarch with water in cup. Add to wok. Cook, stirring, until sauce boils and thickens. Serve over rice.

*Use pineapple packed in juice, if desired.

Nutrients per serving:

Calories	260	Cholesterol	78 mg
Fat	5 g	Sodium	316 mg

Easy Tuna Melt

Makes 2 servings

1 (3½-ounce) can solid white water-pack tuna, drained
2 teaspoons reduced-calorie salad dressing
1 teaspoon dill pickle relish
1 English muffin, split and toasted
2 tomato slices
2 slices BORDEN® Lite-line® Process Cheese Product,* any flavor

Combine tuna, salad dressing and relish. Top each muffin half with tomato slice, then half the tuna mixture and cheese product slice. Broil or heat in microwave oven until cheese product begins to melt. Refrigerate leftovers.

*"½ the calories"– 8% milkfat product

Nutrients per serving:

Calories	193	Cholesterol	34 mg
Fat	7 g	Sodium	833 mg

Scallop Stir-Fry

Orange Roughy with Cucumber Relish

Orange Roughy with Cucumber Relish

Makes 4 servings

   1 can (11 ounces) mandarin oranges, drained
   1 small cucumber, peeled, seeded and finely
      chopped
 ⅓ cup HEINZ® Distilled White Vinegar
   1 green onion, minced
   1 tablespoon snipped fresh dill *or* 1 teaspoon
      dill weed
      Nonstick cooking spray
   4 orange roughy fillets (about 5 ounces *each*)
      Dill sprigs

Reserve 8 orange sections for garnish; coarsely chop remaining sections and combine with cucumber, vinegar, onion and dill in small bowl. Spray broiler pan with nonstick cooking spray; place fish on pan. Spoon 1 tablespoon liquid from cucumber mixture over each fillet. Broil, 3 to 4 inches from heat source, 8 to 10 minutes or until fish flakes with fork. To serve, spoon cucumber relish on top of fish. Garnish with reserved orange sections and dill sprigs.

Nutrients per serving:

Calories	229	Cholesterol	28 mg
Fat	10 g	Sodium	95 mg

Garlic Shrimp & Vegetables

Makes 4 servings

   2 tablespoons margarine
   1 tablespoon olive oil
   1 bunch green onions, chopped
   1 red bell pepper, chopped
   1 pound peeled, deveined large shrimp
   2 cloves garlic, minced
      Juice of 1 lime
      Salt and black pepper (optional)
   1 (9-ounce) package fresh spinach fettuccine,
      cooked and drained

Heat margarine and oil in medium skillet or wok over medium heat. Add onions and red pepper. Stir-fry 2 minutes or until vegetables are crisp-tender.

Add shrimp and garlic; stir-fry 2 minutes or until shrimp are opaque.

Stir in lime juice. Season with salt and black pepper, if desired. Serve over hot fettuccine. Garnish as desired.

Nutrients per serving:

Calories	269	Cholesterol	196 mg
Fat	9 g	Sodium	412 mg

Peppercorn-Crusted Rainbow Trout with Corn-Yogurt Sauce

Makes 4 servings

   1 can (8 ounces) corn, undrained
 ¾ cup nonfat plain yogurt
 ¾ teaspoon curry powder, divided
   2 tablespoons mixed whole peppercorns (pink,
      green and white), coarsely ground
 ½ teaspoon ground nutmeg
   4 CLEAR SPRINGS® Brand Idaho Rainbow
      Trout fillets (4 ounces *each*)

Preheat broiler. In blender or food processor, blend corn with liquid, yogurt and ¼ teaspoon curry powder until smooth. Transfer to small saucepan; heat over low heat. Meanwhile, in shallow dish, combine peppercorns with remaining ½ teaspoon curry and nutmeg. Press flesh sides of fillets into pepper mixture; arrange, skin sides down, in shallow baking dish. Broil, 4 inches from heat, for 3 minutes or until trout turns opaque. To serve, spoon hot corn sauce on each plate and top with trout. Serve immediately.

Nutrients per serving:

Calories	221	Cholesterol	86 mg
Fat	8 g	Sodium	75 mg

Catfish Parmesan

Makes 4 servings

½ cup dry bread crumbs
¼ cup grated Parmesan cheese
2 tablespoons chopped fresh parsley
½ teaspoon paprika
¼ teaspoon dried oregano leaves, crushed
¼ teaspoon dried basil leaves, crushed
¼ teaspoon black pepper
1 pound skinless catfish fillets
⅓ cup low-fat milk
2 teaspoons vegetable oil

In small bowl, combine bread crumbs, Parmesan cheese and seasonings. Dip fillets in milk; roll in crumb mixture. Spray baking pan with nonstick cooking spray. Arrange fish in pan; drizzle with oil. Bake at 450°F for 8 to 10 minutes or just until fish flakes easily when tested with fork.

Nutrients per serving:			
Calories	231	Cholesterol	73 mg
Fat	10 g	Sodium	213 mg

Favorite recipe from **National Fisheries Institute**

Oven-Crisped Fish

Makes 4 servings

½ cup unseasoned bread crumbs
2 tablespoons grated Parmesan cheese
2 teaspoons grated lemon peel
¾ teaspoon dried marjoram leaves, crushed
½ teaspoon paprika
¼ teaspoon dried thyme leaves, crushed
⅛ teaspoon garlic powder
1 pound cod fillets
3 tablespoons lemon juice
2 tablespoons white wine
2 tablespoons CRISCO® PURITAN® Oil

Heat oven to 425°F. Oil 13×9×2-inch pan. Combine bread crumbs, Parmesan cheese, lemon peel, marjoram, paprika, thyme and garlic powder in shallow bowl. Set aside.

Rinse fillets. Pat dry. Combine lemon juice and wine in another shallow bowl. Dip each fillet in lemon mixture, then in seasoned crumbs, coating well. Place fish in pan. Drizzle evenly with Crisco® Puritan® Oil.

Bake at 425°F for 20 to 25 minutes or until fish flakes easily when tested with fork. Cut into serving size pieces, if desired.

Nutrients per serving:			
Calories	223	Cholesterol	51 mg
Fat	9 g	Sodium	201 mg

Wisconsin Tuna Cakes with Lemon-Dill Sauce

Makes 4 servings

1 can (12½ ounces) STARKIST® Tuna, drained and finely flaked
¾ cup seasoned bread crumbs
¼ cup minced green onions
2 tablespoons chopped drained pimentos
1 egg
½ cup low-fat milk
½ teaspoon grated lemon peel
2 tablespoons margarine or butter

Lemon-Dill Sauce
¼ cup chicken broth
1 tablespoon lemon juice
¼ teaspoon dried dill weed

Hot steamed shredded zucchini and carrots
Lemon slices

In large bowl, toss together tuna, bread crumbs, onions and pimentos. In small bowl, beat together egg and milk; stir in lemon peel. Stir into tuna mixture; toss until moistened. With lightly floured hands, shape into eight 4-inch patties.

In large nonstick skillet, melt margarine. Fry patties, a few at a time, until golden brown on both sides, about 3 minutes per side. Place on ovenproof platter in 300°F oven until ready to serve.

For Lemon-Dill Sauce, in small saucepan, heat broth, lemon juice and dill. Serve tuna cakes with zucchini and carrots; spoon sauce over cakes. Garnish with lemon slices.

Nutrients per serving (2 patties plus 1 tablespoon sauce):			
Calories	278	Cholesterol	85 mg
Fat	10 g	Sodium	576 mg

Wisconsin Tuna Cakes with Lemon-Dill Sauce

Whether main dishes or side dishes, salads have become a way of life. Expand your horizons with these creative and taste-tempting recipes designed to wake up your salad bowl. Chicken, seafood, pasta and fruit are just a few of the light and refreshing possibilities. Which salad to choose? It's a toss-up!

Mediterranean Tuna Salad

Makes 4 servings

¼ pound fresh green beans
1 can (12 ounces) tuna, drained, separated into chunks
2 tablespoons drained capers (optional)
1 can (15 ounces) great Northern beans, drained, rinsed
1 large tomato, chopped
12 ripe Greek olives
Snipped fresh chives (optional)
¼ cup bottled low-calorie Italian salad dressing

Cook green beans in lightly salted boiling water 5 minutes or until crisp-tender; drain. Rinse with cold water; drain again.

Place tuna in center of serving platter; sprinkle with capers. Arrange canned beans, tomato and olives around tuna; surround with green beans. Sprinkle with chives, if desired. Serve with dressing.

Nutrients per serving:

Calories	300	Cholesterol	14 mg
Fat	10 g	Sodium	434 mg

Gazpacho Salad

Makes 7 servings, 3⅔ cups

1½ cups tomato juice
1 package (4-serving size) JELL-O® Brand Lemon Flavor Sugar Free Gelatin
1 cup finely chopped tomato
½ cup finely chopped peeled cucumber
¼ cup finely chopped green bell pepper
2 tablespoons finely chopped red bell pepper
2 tablespoons sliced green onions
2 tablespoons vinegar
¼ teaspoon black pepper
⅛ teaspoon garlic powder

Bring tomato juice to a boil in small saucepan. Completely dissolve gelatin in boiling tomato juice. Chill until slightly thickened.

Combine remaining ingredients in medium bowl; mix well. Stir into gelatin mixture. Pour into individual dishes or medium serving bowl. Chill until firm, about 3 hours.

Nutrients per serving:

Calories	25	Cholesterol	0 mg
Fat	0 g	Sodium	220 mg

Mediterranean Tuna Salad

Grilled Steak and Asparagus Salad

Grilled Steak and Asparagus Salad

Makes 4 servings

½ cup bottled light olive oil vinaigrette dressing
⅓ cup A.1.® Steak Sauce
1 (1-pound) beef top round steak
1 (10-ounce) package frozen asparagus spears, cooked and cooled
½ cup thinly sliced red bell pepper
8 large lettuce leaves
1 tablespoon toasted sesame seeds

In small bowl, blend vinaigrette and steak sauce. Pour marinade over steak in nonmetal dish. Cover; refrigerate 1 hour.

Remove steak from marinade. Grill or broil steak, 4 inches from heat source, for 10 minutes or to desired doneness, basting occasionally with marinade and turning 2 or 3 times. Thinly slice steak; arrange steak, asparagus and red pepper on lettuce leaves. Heat marinade to a boil; pour over salad. Sprinkle with sesame seeds; serve immediately.

Nutrients per serving:			
Calories	209	Cholesterol	65 mg
Fat	5 g	Sodium	857 mg

Mostaccioli Salad Niçoise

Makes 16 servings

1 package (1 pound) CREAMETTE® Mostaccioli, uncooked
2 pounds fresh green beans, steamed until tender-crisp
2 medium green bell peppers, cut into chunks
2 cups cherry tomatoes, quartered
2 cups sliced celery
½ cup sliced green onions
10 pitted ripe olives, sliced
2 (7-ounce) cans water-pack white tuna, drained and flaked
½ cup olive or vegetable oil
¼ cup red wine vinegar
3 cloves garlic, minced
4 teaspoons Dijon-style mustard
1 teaspoon salt-free herb seasoning
1 teaspoon dried basil leaves, crushed
¼ teaspoon black pepper

Prepare Creamette® Mostaccioli according to package directions; drain. In large bowl, combine mostaccioli, vegetables, olives and tuna. In small bowl, whisk together olive oil, vinegar, garlic, mustard, herb seasoning, basil and pepper; toss with salad mixture. Cover; refrigerate thoroughly. Stir before serving. Refrigerate leftovers.

Nutrients per serving:			
Calories	236	Cholesterol	9 mg
Fat	9 g	Sodium	185 mg

Zesty Oil-Free Salad Dressing

Makes 1¼ cups

½ cup *undiluted* CARNATION® Evaporated Lowfat Milk
½ cup tomato sauce
2 tablespoons cider vinegar
1 tablespoon lemon juice
2 teaspoons finely chopped fresh parsley
1 teaspoon finely chopped onion
1 teaspoon Dijon-style mustard
¼ teaspoon salt
¼ teaspoon black pepper

In small bowl, combine all ingredients. Refrigerate thoroughly. Serve over favorite salad ingredients.

Nutrients per serving (2 tablespoons dressing):			
Calories	15	Cholesterol	0 mg
Fat	trace	Sodium	148 mg

Chunky Spinach Salad

Makes 4 servings, 3 cups

6 cups fresh spinach leaves, rinsed and drained
2 cups toasted Italian bread cubes
6 ounces mushrooms, thinly sliced (about 2 cups)
1 can (19 ounces) chickpeas or garbanzo beans, rinsed and drained
4 slices turkey bacon, crisp-cooked and crumbled (optional)
½ cup WISH-BONE® Healthy Sensation! Chunky Blue Cheese Dressing

In large salad bowl, combine all ingredients except dressing. Drizzle with Blue Cheese Dressing; toss gently.

Nutrients per serving:

Calories	209	Cholesterol	0 mg
Fat	3 g	Sodium	599 mg

Sweet 'n' Sour Vinaigrette

Makes 8 servings

1 cup white wine vinegar
¼ cup sugar
½ teaspoon dried parsley
¼ teaspoon dry mustard

Combine all ingredients in jar with tight-fitting lid. Cover and shake vigorously until combined. Refrigerate and shake again before serving. Serve over green salad.

Nutrients per serving (2 tablespoons dressing):

Calories	28	Cholesterol	0 mg
Fat	0 g	Sodium	trace

Favorite recipe from **The Sugar Association, Inc.**

Summer Fruit Salad

Makes 6 servings

1 DOLE® Fresh Pineapple
2 DOLE® Oranges, peeled and sliced
2 DOLE® Bananas, peeled and sliced
1 cup halved DOLE® Strawberries
1 cup seedless green DOLE® Grapes
  Strawberry-Banana Yogurt Dressing (recipe follows)
  Orange-Banana Yogurt Dressing (recipe follows)

Cut pineapple in half lengthwise through the crown. Cut fruit from shells with knife, leaving shells intact. Cut fruit into chunks. In large bowl, combine pineapple, oranges, bananas, strawberries and grapes. Spoon into pineapple shells. Serve with your choice of dressing.

Strawberry-Banana Yogurt Dressing

6 DOLE® Strawberries, halved
1 ripe DOLE® Banana, peeled
1 carton (8 ounces) vanilla yogurt
1 tablespoon packed brown sugar *or* honey

In blender or food processor, combine all ingredients and blend until smooth.

Orange-Banana Yogurt Dressing

1 DOLE® Orange
1 ripe DOLE® Banana, peeled
1 carton (8 ounces) vanilla yogurt
1 tablespoon packed brown sugar *or* honey

Grate peel from ½ orange. Juice orange (⅓ cup). In blender or food processor, combine orange peel and juice with remaining ingredients. Blend until smooth.

Nutrients per serving (with 1 tablespoon Strawberry-Banana Yogurt Dressing):

Calories	143	Cholesterol	4 mg
Fat	2 g	Sodium	15 mg

Summer Fruit Salad

Broiled Chicken Salad

Makes 4 servings

4 boneless skinless chicken breast halves (about
   1 pound)
1 (15-ounce) can black beans, drained, rinsed
2 green onions, chopped
2 tablespoons low-calorie Italian salad dressing,
   divided
1 (10-ounce) package frozen whole kernel corn,
   thawed, drained
2 tablespoons chopped pimiento
2 tablespoons chopped cilantro
2 large tomatoes, cut into wedges

Preheat broiler. Position oven rack about 4 inches
from heat source. Place chicken on rack of broiler
pan. Broil 8 minutes or until browned on both sides
and no longer pink in center, turning after 4 minutes.
Set aside.

Combine beans, onions and 1 tablespoon dressing in
medium bowl; mix lightly. Set aside.

Combine corn, pimiento and cilantro in separate
bowl; mix lightly. Set aside.

Diagonally cut each chicken piece into thick slices;
arrange on salad plates.

Arrange tomato wedges and spoonfuls of bean and
corn mixtures around chicken. Drizzle remaining
1 tablespoon dressing over chicken. Garnish as
desired.

Nutrients per serving:

Calories	254	Cholesterol	46 mg
Fat	3 g	Sodium	109 mg

Broiled Chicken Salad

Fiesta Corn Salad

Makes 4 to 6 servings

1 can (14½ to 15½ ounces) dark red kidney
   beans or black beans, drained, rinsed
1 package (10 ounces) frozen whole kernel
   corn, thawed (about 2 cups)
1 medium tomato, peeled, seeded, chopped
¼ cup sliced green onions
1 jalapeño pepper, minced
¼ cup HEINZ® Chili Sauce
3 tablespoons vegetable oil
2 tablespoons HEINZ® Apple Cider Vinegar
1 teaspoon chili powder
½ teaspoon ground cumin
¼ teaspoon salt
⅛ teaspoon black pepper
   Lettuce leaves

In large bowl, combine beans, corn, tomato, green
onions and jalapeño pepper. In small bowl, whisk
together chili sauce and remaining ingredients except
lettuce leaves; pour over bean mixture and stir to coat.
Refrigerate. Serve on lettuce leaves.

Nutrients per serving:

Calories	190	Cholesterol	0 mg
Fat	8 g	Sodium	511 mg

Crunchy Tuna Salad in Pepper Boats

Makes 4 servings

2 large green or yellow bell peppers, halved
   lengthwise, seeded
½ cup MIRACLE WHIP® FREE® Dressing
2 (6½-ounce) cans tuna in water, drained, flaked
¼ cup *each:* chopped carrot, chopped celery and
   chopped red onion
¼ cup chopped pecans (optional)

To Microwave: Place pepper halves on plate. Microwave
on HIGH (100% power) 1 minute; refrigerate.

Mix together remaining ingredients until well blended;
refrigerate. Serve in pepper halves.

Prep time: 20 minutes plus refrigerating
Microwave cook time: 1 minute

Nutrients per serving:

Calories	170	Cholesterol	29 mg
Fat	2 g	Sodium	708 mg

Five Bean Salad

Makes 8 to 10 servings

¾ cup thinly sliced red onion
1 garlic clove, minced
2 tablespoons water
15 ounces canned garbanzo beans, rinsed and drained
1½ cups fresh green beans, cut into thirds
8 ounces canned great Northern beans, rinsed and drained
8 ounces canned black beans, rinsed and drained
8 ounces canned kidney beans, rinsed and drained
⅓ cup cider vinegar
1½ tablespoons sugar
1 teaspoon olive oil
¼ teaspoon dry mustard
3 carrots, thinly sliced
½ cup chopped red bell pepper

To Microwave: In large microwave-safe casserole dish, combine onion, garlic and water. Microwave at HIGH (100% power) for 1 to 2 minutes.

Stir in all remaining ingredients except carrots and red pepper. Microwave at HIGH for an additional 3 to 5 minutes or until green beans are tender-crisp.

Stir in carrots and red pepper. Serve immediately. (Salad may also be prepared ahead of time; cover, refrigerate and serve cold.)

Nutrients per serving:			
Calories	190	Cholesterol	0 mg
Fat	2 g	Sodium	14 mg

Favorite recipe from **The Sugar Association, Inc.**

Lemony Low-Cal Dressing

Makes about 1 cup

⅔ cup plus 2 tablespoons water
¼ cup REALEMON® Lemon Juice from Concentrate
1 (1.3-ounce) package low-calorie Italian salad dressing mix

In 1-pint jar with tight-fitting lid or cruet, combine ingredients; shake well. Chill to blend flavors. Refrigerate leftovers.

Nutrients per serving (1 tablespoon dressing):			
Calories	8	Cholesterol	0 mg
Fat	trace	Sodium	177 mg

Salade Niçoise

Salade Niçoise

Makes 8 servings

2 cans (6½ ounces each) tuna in water, drained, flaked
8 new potatoes, cooked, sliced
½ pound green beans, cooked
½ pound yellow wax beans, cooked
8 radishes, sliced
Niçoise or pitted ripe olives (optional)
Torn assorted greens
Herb Dressing (recipe follows)

Arrange tuna, potatoes, beans, radishes, olives and greens on serving platter or individual plates. Serve with Herb Dressing.

Herb Dressing

¼ cup fresh basil leaves
1 tablespoon fresh parsley, stemmed
1 small shallot
1 container (8 ounces) Light PHILADELPHIA BRAND® Pasteurized Process Cream Cheese Product
⅓ cup skim milk
3 tablespoons white wine vinegar
½ teaspoon salt
½ teaspoon black pepper

Place basil, parsley and shallot in blender or food processor container; cover. Process until chopped. Add remaining ingredients; blend until smooth.

Prep time: 35 minutes

Nutrients per serving:			
Calories	190	Cholesterol	94 mg
Fat	7 g	Sodium	500 mg

Fruity Chicken Salad

Fruity Chicken Salad

Makes 4 servings

Creamy Yogurt Dressing (recipe follows)
2 cups cubed cooked chicken
1 cup cantaloupe balls
1 cup casaba melon cubes
1 celery stalk, chopped
⅓ cup dry roasted cashews
¼ cup green onion slices
Lettuce leaves

Prepare Creamy Yogurt Dressing; set aside. Combine chicken, melons, celery, cashews and green onions in large bowl. Add dressing; mix lightly. Cover. Refrigerate 1 hour. Serve on lettuce leaves. Garnish as desired.

Creamy Yogurt Dressing
¼ cup plain yogurt
3 tablespoons low-calorie mayonnaise
3 tablespoons fresh lemon or lime juice
¾ teaspoon ground coriander
½ teaspoon salt
Dash black pepper

Combine ingredients in small bowl; mix well.

Nutrients per serving:			
Calories	205	Cholesterol	38 mg
Fat	10 g	Sodium	326 mg

Marinated Vegetable Spinach Salad

Makes 4 servings

Mustard-Tarragon Marinade (recipe follows)
8 ounces fresh mushrooms, quartered
2 slices purple onion, separated into rings
16 cherry tomatoes, halved
4 cups fresh spinach leaves, washed and stems removed
3 slices (3 ounces) SARGENTO® Preferred Light Sliced Mozzarella Cheese, cut into julienne strips
Freshly ground black pepper

Prepare Mustard-Tarragon Marinade; set aside. Place mushrooms, onion and tomatoes in bowl. Toss with marinade and let stand 15 minutes. Arrange spinach on 4 individual plates. Divide marinated vegetables among plates and top each salad with ¼ of cheese. Serve with freshly ground black pepper, if desired.

Mustard-Tarragon Marinade
3 tablespoons red wine vinegar
1 tablespoon Dijon-style mustard
½ tablespoon dried tarragon
2 tablespoons olive oil

Combine first 3 ingredients in small bowl. Slowly whisk oil into mixture until slightly thickened.

Nutrients per serving:			
Calories	186	Cholesterol	11 mg
Fat	10 g	Sodium	334 mg

Quick Bacon-Potato Salad

Makes 6 servings

4 medium potatoes, peeled and cut into ½-inch cubes
¼ cup water
12 slices LOUIS RICH® Turkey Bacon
¾ cup reduced-calorie salad dressing or mayonnaise
1 teaspoon prepared mustard
¼ teaspoon garlic powder
½ small cucumber, diced
½ small onion, chopped

Combine potatoes and water in 2-quart microwave-safe casserole; cover. Microwave at HIGH (100% power) 9 to 11 minutes or until tender, stirring halfway through cooking.

Meanwhile, cut turkey bacon into ½-inch pieces. Cook and stir in nonstick skillet over medium heat 8 to 10 minutes or until lightly browned. Combine salad dressing, mustard and garlic powder in large bowl. Add potatoes, turkey bacon and remaining ingredients. Refrigerate before serving.

Nutrients per serving:			
Calories	210	Cholesterol	25 mg
Fat	9 g	Sodium	450 mg

Green Bean and Mushroom Salad

Green Bean and Mushroom Salad

Makes 4 servings

¾ **pound fresh green beans, trimmed**
¼ **cup water**
¼ **cup low-calorie mayonnaise**
3 **tablespoons chopped green onions**
2 **tablespoons fresh lemon juice**
1½ **tablespoons olive oil**
1 **tablespoon Dijon-style mustard**
2 **cups fresh mushroom slices**
¼ **cup chopped red bell pepper**
1 **tablespoon minced fresh basil** *or* ¾ **teaspoon dried basil leaves, crushed**
Dash black pepper

To Microwave: Cut beans into 1½-inch pieces; place in 1½-quart microwave-safe dish. Add water; cover. Microwave on HIGH (100% power) 5 to 6 minutes or until beans are crisp-tender, stirring halfway through cooking; drain. Cover beans with ice water to stop further cooking; set aside. Combine mayonnaise, green onions, lemon juice, oil and mustard in large bowl; mix well. Add drained beans, mushrooms, red pepper and basil; mix lightly. Cover; refrigerate several hours. Season with black pepper just before serving. Garnish as desired.

Nutrients per serving:			
Calories	125	Cholesterol	5 mg
Fat	10 g	Sodium	63 mg

Cantaloupe Dressing

Makes 6 servings

1 **cup cantaloupe cubes**
½ **cup low-fat vanilla yogurt**
4 **teaspoons sugar**

Place all ingredients in blender container or food processor; process until blended. Refrigerate or serve immediately over fruit salad.

For a tangier dressing: *Substitute ½ cup kiwifruit slices for cantaloupe. Blend all ingredients as above.*

For a thicker dressing: *Substitute 1 cup pear cubes for cantaloupe. Blend all ingredients as above.*

Nutrients per serving (2 tablespoons dressing):			
Calories	36	Cholesterol	1 mg
Fat	trace	Sodium	15 mg

Favorite recipe from **The Sugar Association, Inc.**

Caribbean Chicken Salad

Makes 2 servings

1 **can (8 ounces) DOLE® Pineapple Slices in Juice, undrained**
½ **pound cooked skinless boneless chicken breast***
DOLE® Salad Greens
1 **cup assorted sliced or cut up DOLE® Fresh Fruit**
¼ **pound DOLE® Asparagus or green beans, steamed**
½ **cup vanilla yogurt**
2 **to 3 tablespoons chopped chutney**
1 **teaspoon grated lemon peel**

Drain pineapple; reserve 3 tablespoons juice for dressing. Slice chicken diagonally into ½-inch slices.

Arrange sliced chicken and 2 pineapple slices on each of 2 salad plates lined with salad greens. Arrange fresh fruit and asparagus on same plates.

For dressing, combine yogurt, chutney, reserved pineapple juice and lemon peel in small bowl. Serve with salad. Garnish, if desired.

**Use roasted chicken from the deli, if desired.*

Nutrients per serving:			
Calories	252	Cholesterol	17 mg
Fat	2 g	Sodium	71 mg

Poppy Seed Fruit Sauce

Makes 1²/₃ cups

½ cup MIRACLE WHIP® FREE® Nonfat
    Dressing
1 container (8 ounces) lemon-flavored low-fat
    yogurt
2 tablespoons skim milk
1 tablespoon firmly packed brown sugar
1 tablespoon poppy seeds

Mix together ingredients until well blended;
refrigerate. Serve over fresh fruit.

Prep time: 5 minutes

Nutrients per serving (3 tablespoons sauce):

Calories	70	Cholesterol	trace
Fat	1 g	Sodium	263 mg

Cucumber Salad

Makes 6 to 8 servings

3 medium cucumbers, scored lengthwise with
    tines of fork and thinly sliced
¾ teaspoon salt, divided
⅓ cup chopped onion
⅓ cup cider vinegar
3 tablespoons CRISCO® Oil or CRISCO®
    PURITAN® Oil
2 tablespoons sugar
1½ teaspoons caraway seeds
½ teaspoon paprika
⅛ teaspoon black pepper

Place cucumbers in medium bowl. Sprinkle with
¼ teaspoon salt. Let stand about 1 hour. Drain.

Whisk together remaining ingredients with remaining
½ teaspoon salt in small bowl. Pour over cucumbers.
Toss to coat. Cover and refrigerate at least 3 hours.
Stir before serving.

Nutrients per serving:

Calories	80	Cholesterol	0 mg
Fat	5 g	Sodium	203 mg

Poppy Seed Fruit Sauce

Melon Cooler Salad

Makes 8 servings

**½ cup frozen lemonade or limeade concentrate,
thawed**
**1 package (8 ounces) Light PHILADELPHIA
BRAND® Neufchatel Cheese, softened**
4 cups assorted melon balls

Place lemonade concentrate and neufchatel cheese in
blender or food processor container; cover. Blend until
smooth. Spoon melon balls into parfait glasses or
individual bowls; top with cream cheese mixture.

Nutrients per serving:			
Calories	140	Cholesterol	25 mg
Fat	7 g	Sodium	125 mg

Springtime Vegetable Slaw

Makes 10 servings

1 pound shredded DOLE® Cabbage
1 cup grated DOLE® Carrots
½ cup DOLE® Broccoli florettes, chopped
½ cup halved cherry tomatoes
½ cup sliced DOLE® Celery
½ cup peeled, seeded, diced cucumber
1 cup chopped fresh parsley
⅓ cup olive oil
2 tablespoons vinegar
1 tablespoon Dijon-style mustard
1 teaspoon garlic salt

Springtime Vegetable Slaw

Combine cabbage, carrots, broccoli, tomatoes, celery
and cucumber in large salad bowl. Whisk together
remaining ingredients for dressing. Pour over
vegetables; toss to coat well.

Nutrients per serving:			
Calories	87	Cholesterol	0 mg
Fat	7 g	Sodium	147 mg

Southwest Salsa Dressing

Makes about 5 servings

⅔ cup mild salsa*
2 tablespoons nonfat plain yogurt
4 teaspoons sugar
2 teaspoons chopped cilantro (optional)

In small bowl, stir together all ingredients. Or, for a
less chunky dressing, blend ingredients in food
processor. Refrigerate or serve immediately over
green salad, chicken or turkey salad, taco salad or
seafood salad.

*For a hotter and spicier dressing, use medium or hot salsa.

Nutrients per serving (2 tablespoons dressing):			
Calories	30	Cholesterol	trace
Fat	trace	Sodium	226 mg

Favorite recipe from **The Sugar Association, Inc.**

Wild Rice and Pepper Salad

Makes 6 servings

**1 package (6 ounces) MINUTE® Long Grain
& Wild Rice**
**½ cup MIRACLE WHIP® FREE® Nonfat
Dressing**
2 tablespoons olive oil
½ teaspoon black pepper
¼ teaspoon grated lemon peel
1 cup chopped red bell pepper
1 cup chopped yellow bell pepper
¼ cup (½-inch) green onion pieces

Prepare rice as directed on package. Cool.

Mix dressing, oil, black pepper and peel in large bowl
until well blended.

Add rice and remaining ingredients; mix lightly.
Serve at room temperature or refrigerate.

Prep time: 30 minutes

Nutrients per serving (½ cup):			
Calories	140	Cholesterol	0 mg
Fat	5 g	Sodium	284 mg

Summary Seafood Salad

Makes 4 servings

2 cups cooked rice, cooled to room temperature
½ pound cooked crabmeat*
1 can (8 ounces) sliced water chestnuts, drained
½ cup sliced celery
¼ cup sliced green onions
¼ cup plain nonfat yogurt
¼ cup light dairy sour cream
1 tablespoon lemon juice
¼ teaspoon hot pepper sauce
¼ teaspoon salt
  Lettuce leaves
  Tomato wedges for garnish

Combine rice, crabmeat, water chestnuts, celery, and onions in large bowl. Combine yogurt, sour cream, lemon juice, pepper sauce, and salt in small bowl; blend well. Pour over rice mixture; toss lightly. Serve on lettuce leaves and garnish with tomato wedges.

Substitute crab-flavored Surimi Seafood (flake or chunk style) for the crabmeat, if desired.

Nutrients per serving:

Calories	263	Cholesterol	65 mg
Fat	5 g	Sodium	731 mg

Favorite recipe from **USA Rice Council**

Dynasty Fruit Salad

Makes 6 servings

1 DOLE® Fresh Pineapple
1 firm, medium DOLE® Banana, peeled and sliced
1 DOLE® Orange, peeled and sliced
1 DOLE® Apple, cored and sliced
1 cup seedless DOLE® Grapes

Royal Dressing
  1 carton (8 ounces) vanilla yogurt
  1 teaspoon grated lime peel
  ½ teaspoon ground ginger

Cut pineapple in half lengthwise through the crown. Cut fruit from shells with knife, leaving shells intact. Cut fruit into bite-sized chunks.

Combine pineapple with remaining fruit in large bowl. Spoon fruit into pineapple shells to serve, if desired.

For Royal Dressing: combine all dressing ingredients in small bowl. Serve with fruit salad.

Nutrients per serving:

Calories	140	Cholesterol	2 mg
Fat	1 g	Sodium	28 mg

Sunset Yogurt Salad

Sunset Yogurt Salad

Makes 5 cups, 10 servings

2 packages (4-serving size) or 1 package (8-serving size) JELL-O® Brand Orange or Lemon Flavor Sugar Free Gelatin
2 cups boiling water
1 container (8 ounces) plain low-fat yogurt
¼ cup cold water
1 can (8 ounces) crushed pineapple in unsweetened juice, undrained
1 cup shredded carrots

Completely dissolve gelatin in boiling water. Measure 1 cup gelatin into medium mixing bowl; chill until slightly thickened. Stir in yogurt. Pour into medium serving bowl. Chill until set but not firm.

Add cold water to remaining gelatin. Stir in pineapple with juice and carrots. Chill until slightly thickened. Spoon over gelatin-yogurt mixture in bowl. Chill until firm, about 4 hours. Garnish with carrot curl, celery leaf and pineapple slice, if desired.

Nutrients per serving:

Calories	40	Cholesterol	0 mg
Fat	0 g	Sodium	65 mg

Black Bean and Rice Salad

Makes 4 servings

2 cups cooked rice, cooled to room temperature
1 cup cooked black beans*
1 medium tomato, seeded and chopped
½ cup (2 ounces) shredded Cheddar cheese (optional)
1 tablespoon fresh snipped parsley
¼ cup prepared light Italian dressing
1 tablespoon lime juice
Lettuce leaves

Combine rice, beans, tomato, cheese, and parsley in large bowl. Pour dressing and lime juice over rice mixture; toss lightly. Serve on lettuce leaves. Garnish as desired.

*Substitute canned black beans, drained, for the cooked beans, if desired.

Nutrients per serving:			
Calories	210	Cholesterol	0 mg
Fat	1 g	Sodium	560 mg

Favorite recipe from **USA Rice Council**

Smoked Turkey and Potato Salad

Makes 8 servings

1 package (32 ounces) frozen hash brown potato cubes, thawed
¾ pound Smoked Turkey Breast, cut into ½-inch cubes
½ cup chopped celery
½ cup sliced green onions
¼ cup chopped green bell pepper
1 jar (2 ounces) chopped pimientos, drained
⅓ cup low-calorie mayonnaise
⅓ cup plain nonfat yogurt
2 tablespoons Dijon-style mustard
¼ teaspoon black pepper

In large saucepan, over high heat, combine potatoes and 2 quarts boiling water. Boil 2 to 4 minutes or until potatoes are tender. Do not overcook. Drain potatoes thoroughly and cool to room temperature. In large bowl, combine potatoes, turkey, celery, onions, green pepper and pimientos. In small bowl, blend mayonnaise, yogurt, mustard and black pepper. Add to turkey mixture; toss until well coated. Cover and refrigerate at least 4 hours.

Nutrients per serving:			
Calories	177	Cholesterol	17 mg
Fat	4 g	Sodium	646 mg

Favorite recipe from **National Turkey Federation**

Garden Potato Salad

Makes 6 servings

½ cup HEALTHY CHOICE® Cholesterol Free Egg Product
4 medium potatoes, cooked and cubed (about 1 to 1¼ pounds)
½ cup diced celery
¼ cup chopped radishes
2 tablespoons sliced green onions
¾ cup nonfat mayonnaise
1 tablespoon sugar
1 tablespoon lemon juice
2 teaspoons prepared mustard
¼ teaspoon salt
¼ teaspoon celery seed
¼ teaspoon black pepper

In 8-inch skillet sprayed with nonstick cooking spray, cook egg product, covered, over very low heat 5 minutes or until just set. Cool egg product; dice. In large bowl, combine egg product with potatoes, celery, radishes and onions. In small bowl, mix remaining ingredients. Add mayonnaise mixture to potato mixture, stirring until evenly coated.

Nutrients per serving:			
Calories	130	Cholesterol	0 mg
Fat	trace	Sodium	530 mg

Oriental Ginger Dressing

Makes 4 servings

½ cup pineapple juice
2 tablespoons cider vinegar
1 tablespoon soy sauce
1 tablespoon sugar
1 teaspoon grated fresh ginger
½ teaspoon sesame oil

Combine all ingredients in jar with tight-fitting lid. Cover and shake vigorously until combined. Refrigerate. Shake again before serving. Serve over green salad, chicken salad or pasta salad.

Nutrients per serving (2 tablespoons dressing):			
Calories	38	Cholesterol	0 mg
Fat	1 g	Sodium	258 mg

Favorite recipe from **The Sugar Association, Inc.**

Black Bean and Rice Salad

Turkey, Mandarin and Poppy Seed Salad

Turkey, Mandarin and Poppy Seed Salad

Makes 4 servings

- 5 cups torn red leaf lettuce
- 2 cups torn spinach leaves
- ½ pound Honey Roasted Turkey, cut into ½-inch julienne strips
- 1 can (10½ ounces) mandarin oranges, drained
- ¼ cup orange juice
- 1½ tablespoons red wine vinegar
- 1½ teaspoons poppy seeds
- 1½ teaspoons olive oil
- 1 teaspoon Dijon-style mustard
- ⅛ teaspoon black pepper

In large bowl, combine lettuce, spinach, turkey and oranges. In small bowl, whisk together orange juice, vinegar, poppy seeds, oil, mustard and pepper. Pour dressing over turkey mixture; toss to coat evenly. Garnish as desired. Serve immediately.

Nutrients per serving:

Calories	158	Cholesterol	25 mg
Fat	4 g	Sodium	667 mg

Favorite recipe from **National Turkey Federation**

Microwave or Roasted Bell Pepper Dressing

Makes 6 servings

- 1 green or red bell pepper
- ½ cup buttermilk
- 2 teaspoons sugar
- 1 teaspoon fresh parsley sprigs (optional)
- ¾ teaspoon lemon juice
- ¼ teaspoon paprika
- ⅛ teaspoon onion powder
- ⅛ teaspoon salt
- ⅛ teaspoon black pepper

Place bell pepper in microwave; heat on HIGH (100% power) 5 minutes or until tender. *Or*, place bell pepper in 375°F oven; roast for 20 to 25 minutes or until tender. Cut pepper in half; remove seeds. Pat dry with paper towel. Place bell pepper and remaining ingredients in blender container or food processor; process until well blended. Refrigerate or serve immediately over green salad.

Nutrients per serving (2 tablespoons dressing):

Calories	21	Cholesterol	1 mg
Fat	trace	Sodium	67 mg

Favorite recipe from **The Sugar Association, Inc.**

Zesty Bean Salad

Makes 8 servings

1 cup dry white beans or dry garbanzo beans
(chickpeas)
1 medium onion, chopped
¼ cup freshly squeezed lemon juice
¼ cup vegetable oil
3 tablespoons chopped fresh mint
1 medium clove garlic, minced
   Grated peel of ½ SUNKIST® Lemon
2 teaspoons sugar
1 teaspoon Dijon-style mustard
¼ teaspoon white pepper
½ cup chopped red bell pepper or tomato
⅓ cup chopped fresh parsley

Place beans in large stockpot. Cover with water, about
6 to 8 cups. Bring to a boil over high heat. Boil
2 minutes. Cover; remove from heat and let stand
1 hour. Drain beans and replace water. Bring to boil;
cover and cook over low heat 1½ to 2 hours or until
beans are tender.

Combine onion, lemon juice, oil, mint, garlic, lemon
peel, sugar, mustard and white pepper in large bowl.
Stir in cooked beans; refrigerate until beans are cool.
To serve, stir in remaining ingredients.

Nutrients per serving (½ cup):

Calories	162	Cholesterol	0 mg
Fat	7 g	Sodium	24 mg

Sprout-Green Bean Salad

Makes 12 servings

3 packages (9 ounces each) frozen French-cut
green beans
½ cup CRISCO® PURITAN® Oil
¼ cup white vinegar
2 teaspoons sugar
½ teaspoon salt
¼ teaspoon black pepper
1 can (16 ounces) bean sprouts, rinsed and
drained
1 cup thinly sliced celery
¾ cup chopped green onions
1 jar (2 ounces) diced pimento, drained
   Cherry tomatoes (optional)

Cook beans in 3-quart saucepan according to
package directions. Drain and cool. Blend Crisco®
Puritan® Oil, vinegar, sugar, salt and pepper in small
mixing bowl. Set aside.

Mix green beans, bean sprouts, celery, onions and
pimento in large serving bowl. Stir dressing. Pour over
bean mixture. Toss to coat. Cover and refrigerate at
least 3 hours. Stir before serving. Garnish with cherry
tomatoes, if desired.

Nutrients per serving:

Calories	112	Cholesterol	0 mg
Fat	9 g	Sodium	160 mg

Ham Tortellini Salad

Makes 6 servings

1 (7- to 8-ounce) package cheese-filled spinach
tortellini
3 cups (12 ounces) ARMOUR® Lower Salt Ham
cut into ¾-inch cubes
½ cup sliced green onions
10 cherry tomatoes, cut in half
1 cup bottled low-sodium creamy buttermilk *or*
low-calorie zesty Italian salad dressing
   Leaf lettuce or butterhead lettuce, washed
and drained
¼ cup finely chopped red bell pepper

Cook tortellini according to package directions
omitting salt; drain and run under cold water to cool.
Combine all ingredients *except* leaf lettuce and red
pepper in large bowl. Toss until well blended. Serve
on lettuce-lined salad plates. Sprinkle with red
pepper. Serve immediately.

Nutrients per serving:

Calories	165	Cholesterol	39 mg
Fat	4 g	Sodium	545 mg

Ham Tortellini Salad

Southwest Express Chicken Salad

Makes 4 servings

1 medium onion, cut into ¼-inch wedges
1 tablespoon olive or vegetable oil
3 cups shredded or diced cooked chicken or
    turkey
⅔ cup PACE® Picante Sauce
2 medium tomatoes, diced
1 teaspoon ground cumin
¾ teaspoon salt (optional)
½ teaspoon dried oregano leaves, crushed
5 cups shredded lettuce
¼ cup chopped cilantro
    Additional PACE® Picante Sauce (optional)

In large skillet, cook and stir onion in hot oil until onion is tender but not brown. Add chicken, ⅔ cup Pace® Picante Sauce, tomatoes, cumin, salt and oregano; simmer 5 minutes, stirring occasionally. Arrange lettuce on 4 dinner plates or large platter; top with hot chicken mixture. Sprinkle with cilantro. Serve with additional Pace® Picante Sauce, if desired.

Nutrients per serving:

Calories	265	Cholesterol	89 mg
Fat	9 g	Sodium	540 mg

Southwest Express Chicken Salad

Tangy Tomato Salad Dressing

Makes 1⅓ cups

1 can (7¼ ounces) low-sodium tomato soup
¼ cup vegetable oil
    Grated peel of ½ SUNKIST® Lemon
2 tablespoons fresh squeezed lemon juice
2 tablespoons chopped green onion
1 teaspoon prepared horseradish
    Generous dash ground cinnamon (optional)

In small jar with lid, combine all ingredients; shake well. Refrigerate. Shake well again before serving.

Nutrients per serving (1 tablespoon dressing):

Calories	35	Cholesterol	0 mg
Fat	3 g	Sodium	2 mg

Turkey Ham Salad in Pineapple Boats

Makes 4 servings

1 package (3 ounces) chicken-flavored instant
    Oriental noodle soup, cooked according to
    package directions and cooled
1⅓ cups Turkey Ham, cut into 2×¼-inch strips
⅓ cup thinly sliced green onions
⅓ cup chopped mango chutney
¼ cup sliced water chestnuts
¼ teaspoon ground red pepper
2 small fresh pineapples
2 tablespoons toasted almonds

In medium bowl, combine noodles with broth, turkey ham, green onions, chutney, water chestnuts and ground red pepper. Cover and refrigerate overnight.

Just before serving, cut pineapples in half lengthwise through the crowns. Cut fruit from shells with knife, leaving shells intact. Cut fruit into ½-inch cubes. Add 3 cups pineapple cubes to turkey mixture.

To serve, spoon turkey mixture into pineapple shells; top with almonds.

Nutrients per serving:

Calories	278	Cholesterol	28 mg
Fat	5 g	Sodium	814 mg

Favorite recipe from **National Turkey Federation**

Lemony Apple-Bran Salad

Makes 6 servings

½ cup plain low-fat yogurt
1 tablespoon chopped fresh parsley
1 teaspoon sugar
1 teaspoon lemon juice
½ teaspoon salt
2 cups chopped and cored red apples
½ cup thinly sliced celery
½ cup halved seedless green grapes *or* ¼ cup
    raisins
½ cup KELLOGG'S® ALL-BRAN® cereal

In medium bowl, combine yogurt, parsley, sugar,
lemon juice and salt. Stir in apples, celery and grapes
or raisins. Cover and refrigerate until ready to serve.
Just before serving, stir in Kellogg's® All-Bran®
cereal. Serve on lettuce, if desired.

Nutrients per serving:

Calories	60	Cholesterol	1 mg
Fat	1 g	Sodium	260 mg

Salad Veronique

Marinated Vegetable Salad

Makes 1 serving

½ cup fresh broccoli flowerets
½ cup fresh cauliflower flowerets
½ cup sliced carrots
½ cup sliced celery
¼ cup bottled low-calorie Italian salad dressing
    Lettuce leaves
1 cup torn lettuce
2 slices BORDEN® Lite-line® American or Swiss
    Flavor Process Cheese Product,* cut into
    strips

In small bowl or plastic bag, combine broccoli,
cauliflower, carrots, celery and dressing; mix well.
Cover; marinate in refrigerator 4 hours or overnight,
stirring occasionally. Drain; reserve salad dressing.
Line plate with lettuce leaves; top with torn lettuce
then vegetables. Pour 2 tablespoons reserved dressing
over salad; top with cheese product strips.

*"½ the calories" – 8% milkfat product

Nutrients per serving:

Calories	204	Cholesterol	22 mg
Fat	8 g	Sodium	856 mg

Salad Veronique

Makes 3 servings, 3 cups

1 package (4-serving size) JELL-O® Brand
    Lemon Flavor Sugar Free Gelatin
¼ teaspoon salt
1 cup boiling water
¼ teaspoon dried tarragon leaves, crushed
    (optional)
¾ cup cold water
1 tablespoon lemon juice
1 cup diced cooked turkey breast (white meat)
½ cup green or red seedless grapes, halved
½ cup finely chopped celery

Completely dissolve gelatin and salt in boiling water;
stir in tarragon. Add cold water and lemon juice. Chill
until slightly thickened. Stir in remaining ingredients.
Spoon into 3 individual plastic containers or serving
dishes. Chill until firm, about 2 hours. Garnish with
grapes and celery leaf, if desired.

Nutrients per serving:

Calories	100	Cholesterol	35 mg
Fat	2 g	Sodium	310 mg

Chef's Salad

Chef's Salad

Makes 3½ cups, 3 entrée servings

> 1 package (4-serving size) JELL-O® Brand
>   Lemon Flavor Sugar Free Gelatin
> ¼ teaspoon salt
> ¾ cup boiling water
> ½ cup cold water
>   Ice cubes
> 1 tablespoon vinegar
> 2 teaspoons low-calorie French dressing
> ¼ teaspoon Worcestershire sauce
> ⅛ teaspoon white pepper
> ¾ cup chopped tomato
> ½ cup finely shredded lettuce
> ½ cup slivered cooked turkey breast
> ½ cup slivered Swiss cheese
> 2 tablespoons sliced green onions
> 2 tablespoons quartered radish slices

Completely dissolve gelatin and salt in boiling water. Combine cold water and enough ice cubes to measure 1¼ cups. Add to gelatin; stir until slightly thickened. Remove any unmelted ice. Stir in vinegar, dressing, Worcestershire sauce and pepper. Chill until slightly thickened.

Stir remaining ingredients into gelatin mixture. Spoon into 3 individual plastic containers or dishes. Chill until firm, about 2 hours. Garnish if desired.

Nutrients per serving:			
Calories	100	Cholesterol	30 mg
Fat	4 g	Sodium	330 mg

Wilted Spinach Bacon Salad

Makes 4 servings

> 6 ounces fresh spinach leaves, cleaned and torn
>   into bite-sized pieces (about 6 cups)

> **Dressing**
> 8 slices LOUIS RICH® Turkey Bacon, cut into
>   1-inch pieces
> ½ large red onion, coarsely chopped
> ¼ cup water
> 3 tablespoons sugar
> 2 tablespoons vinegar
> ⅛ teaspoon black pepper

Place spinach leaves in large serving bowl; set aside. Combine Turkey Bacon and onion in large nonstick skillet. Cook over medium heat 8 to 10 minutes or until bacon begins to brown, stirring occasionally. In small bowl, combine remaining dressing ingredients; stir into Turkey Bacon mixture. Reduce heat to low and simmer 3 minutes. Pour over spinach leaves and toss.

Nutrients per serving:			
Calories	120	Cholesterol	20 mg
Fat	5 g	Sodium	415 mg

Italian Pasta Salad

Makes 8 to 10 servings

> 10 ounces uncooked rotini pasta
> ½ cup chopped broccoli flowerets
> 1 can (6 ounces) small pitted ripe olives, drained
> 12 cherry tomatoes, cut in half
> ½ medium red onion, thinly sliced
> ½ cup low-calorie Italian salad dressing
> 2 tablespoons grated Parmesan cheese
>   Freshly ground black pepper to taste

Cook rotini according to package directions. Drain. Rinse with cold water; drain again thoroughly. Cool. Cook broccoli in boiling salted water just until bright green and crisp-tender. Drain. Rinse with cold water; drain again thoroughly. Combine rotini, broccoli, olives, tomatoes, onion and salad dressing in large bowl. Stir in cheese and season with pepper. Cover and refrigerate until chilled.

Nutrients per serving:			
Calories	184	Cholesterol	1 mg
Fat	8 g	Sodium	149 mg

Tuna and Fresh Fruit Salad

Makes 4 servings

Lettuce leaves (optional)
1 can (12½ ounces) STARKIST® Tuna, drained and broken into chunks
4 cups slices or wedges fresh fruit*
¼ cup slivered almonds (optional)

Fruit Dressing
1 container (8 ounces) lemon, mandarin orange or vanilla low-fat yogurt
2 tablespoons orange juice
¼ teaspoon ground cinnamon

Line a large platter, 4 individual plates or 4 large goblets with lettuce leaves, if desired. Arrange tuna and desired fruit in a decorative design over lettuce. Sprinkle almonds over salad, if desired.

For Fruit Dressing, in a small bowl stir together yogurt, orange juice and cinnamon until well blended. Serve dressing with salad.

Suggested fresh fruit: apples, bananas, berries, citrus fruit, kiwifruit, melon, papaya, peaches or pears.

Nutrients per serving:

Calories	233	Cholesterol	39 mg
Fat	1 g	Sodium	434 mg

Neptune's Salad

Makes 4 servings, 5 cups

2 packages (4-serving size) or 1 package (8-serving size) JELL-O® Brand Lemon Flavor Sugar Free Gelatin
2 cups boiling water
1 cup plain low-fat yogurt
2 tablespoons chili sauce
2 tablespoons finely chopped onion
2 tablespoons lemon juice
1 cup imitation crabmeat, flaked
½ cup chopped celery
¼ cup chopped red bell pepper

Completely dissolve gelatin in boiling water. Stir in yogurt, chili sauce, onion and lemon juice. Chill until slightly thickened. Stir in remaining ingredients. Spoon into 4 individual plastic containers or serving dishes. Chill until firm, about 2 hours.

Nutrients per serving:

Calories	110	Cholesterol	15 mg
Fat	2 g	Sodium	640 mg

Parmesan Curry Dressing

Makes 6 servings

½ cup nonfat yogurt
½ cup buttermilk
1 tablespoon Parmesan cheese
1½ teaspoons sugar
1 teaspoon drained capers
¼ teaspoon black pepper
⅛ teaspoon onion powder
⅛ teaspoon curry powder

Place all ingredients in blender container or food processor; process until blended. Refrigerate or serve immediately.

Nutrients per serving (2 tablespoons dressing):

Calories	27	Cholesterol	2 mg
Fat	1 g	Sodium	52 mg

Favorite recipe from **The Sugar Association, Inc.**

Veggie Delight Salad

Makes 6 servings

½ of a (1-pound) package CREAMETTES® Elbow Macaroni, uncooked
1 cup small fresh broccoli flowerets
2 tomatoes, seeded and chopped
1 medium cucumber, peeled, seeded and chopped
½ cup sliced celery
2 green onions, sliced
2 tablespoons chopped fresh parsley
3 tablespoons plain low-fat yogurt
3 tablespoons bottled low-calorie Italian salad dressing
1½ teaspoons salt-free seasoning

Prepare Creamettes® Elbow Macaroni according to package directions, adding broccoli during last 3 minutes of cooking time; drain. In medium bowl, combine macaroni mixture, tomatoes, cucumber, celery, green onions and parsley. In small bowl, blend yogurt, dressing and seasoning. Add to salad mixture; toss to coat. Cover; refrigerate thoroughly. Toss gently before serving. Refrigerate leftovers.

Nutrients per serving:

Calories	157	Cholesterol	1 mg
Fat	2 g	Sodium	82 mg

Turkey-Pasta Salad

Makes 6 servings, 8 cups

4 cups cooked wagon wheel or spiral pasta
  (about 2 cups uncooked)
2 cups short thin turkey or chicken strips
  (about 8 ounces)
1 large zucchini, cut into ½-inch slices, each
  slice quartered
1 large tomato, cut into ½-inch chunks
1 can (8 ounces) whole kernel corn, drained, *or*
  1 cup frozen corn kernels, thawed
1 small red bell pepper, cut into ½-inch chunks
½ cup chopped cilantro or fresh parsley
¾ cup PACE® Picante Sauce
⅓ cup reduced-calorie creamy garlic salad
  dressing
¼ teaspoon salt (optional)
  Additional PACE® Picante Sauce (optional)

Combine pasta, turkey, zucchini, tomato, corn, red
pepper and cilantro in large bowl. Combine ¾ cup
Pace® Picante Sauce, dressing and salt; mix well.
Pour over pasta mixture; toss gently. Refrigerate.
Serve with additional Pace® Picante Sauce, if desired.

Nutrients per serving:

Calories	234	Cholesterol	26 mg
Fat	4 g	Sodium	570 mg

Turkey-Pasta Salad

Taco Salad

Makes 4 servings, 5 cups

2 packages (4-serving size) or 1 package
  (8-serving size) JELL-O® Brand Lemon
  Flavor Sugar Free Gelatin
2 cups boiling water
1 cup frozen corn
1 cup canned kidney beans, drained
½ cup medium salsa
¼ cup (1 ounce) grated Cheddar cheese
2 tablespoons vinegar
½ teaspoon chili powder

Completely dissolve gelatin in boiling water. Chill until
slightly thickened. Stir in remaining ingredients.
Spoon gelatin mixture into 4 individual plastic
containers or serving dishes. Chill until firm, about
2 hours.

Nutrients per serving:

Calories	140	Cholesterol	10 mg
Fat	4 g	Sodium	560 mg

Chinese Chicken Salad

Makes 6 servings

3 cups cooked rice, cooled
1 cup cooked chicken breast cubes
1 cup sliced celery
1 can (8 ounces) sliced water chestnuts, drained
1 cup fresh bean sprouts*
½ cup (about 2 ounces) sliced fresh mushrooms
¼ cup sliced green onions
¼ cup diced red bell pepper
3 tablespoons lemon juice
2 tablespoons reduced-sodium soy sauce
2 tablespoons sesame oil
2 teaspoons grated fresh ginger root
¼ to ½ teaspoon ground white pepper
  Lettuce leaves

Combine rice, chicken, celery, water chestnuts, bean
sprouts, mushrooms, onions, and red pepper in large
bowl. Combine lemon juice, soy sauce, oil, ginger
root, and white pepper in small jar with lid; shake
well. Pour over rice mixture; toss lightly. Serve on
lettuce leaves.

*Substitute canned bean sprouts, rinsed and drained, for
fresh bean sprouts, if desired.*

Nutrients per serving:

Calories	248	Cholesterol	20 mg
Fat	6 g	Sodium	593 mg

Favorite recipe from **USA Rice Council**

Curried Fruit and Rice Salad

Makes 6 servings

2 cups cooked rice, chilled
1 DOLE® Orange, sliced and quartered
1 cup halved seedless red DOLE® Grapes
⅓ cup mayonnaise
⅓ cup vanilla yogurt
½ teaspoon curry powder, or to taste
   Grated peel and juice from 1 lime
1 DOLE® Banana, peeled, sliced

Combine rice, orange and grapes in large bowl.
Combine mayonnaise, yogurt, curry, lime peel and
juice; stir dressing into rice mixture. Fold in banana
just before serving.

Nutrients per serving:			
Calories	189	Cholesterol	9 mg
Fat	10 g	Sodium	76 mg

Reunion Fruit Slaw

Makes 8 servings

1 can (20 ounces) pineapple tidbits in
   unsweetened pineapple juice, undrained
1 container (8 ounces) PHILADELPHIA
   BRAND® Soft Cream Cheese with Pineapple
½ teaspoon ground cinnamon
8 cups shredded cabbage
1 red apple, chopped
1 green apple, chopped
1 cup halved seedless red grapes

Drain pineapple; reserve 2 tablespoons juice. Stir
cream cheese, reserved juice and cinnamon in large
bowl until well blended. Add remaining ingredients;
toss lightly. Cover. Refrigerate.

Prep time: 20 minutes plus refrigerating

Nutrients per serving:			
Calories	200	Cholesterol	25 mg
Fat	9 g	Sodium	100 mg

Cucumber and Onion Salad

Cucumber and Onion Salad

Makes 12 servings, 6 cups

½ cup MIRACLE WHIP® FREE® Nonfat
   Dressing
4 cucumbers, peeled, halved lengthwise,
   seeded, sliced
2 onions, sliced, halved
½ cup thin red bell pepper strips

Mix together dressing, cucumbers and onions in large
bowl. Top with peppers; refrigerate.

Prep time: 10 minutes plus refrigerating

Nutrients per serving (½ cup):			
Calories	30	Cholesterol	0 mg
Fat	trace	Sodium	143 mg

East Indian Peach Salad

Makes 4 servings

½ cup vanilla low-fat yogurt
½ teaspoon curry powder, or to taste
1 (16-ounce) can sliced peaches in light syrup,
   drained and syrup reserved
2 cups (8 ounces) ARMOUR® Lower Salt Ham
   cut into ½-inch cubes
1 cup seedless red or green grapes, cut in half
   Leaf lettuce, washed and drained
2 tablespoons sliced almonds, toasted

Combine yogurt, curry powder and 1 tablespoon
reserved peach syrup in small bowl; set aside.
Combine peaches, ham and grapes in medium bowl.
Add yogurt mixture; toss gently to coat well. Serve in
lettuce-lined serving bowl or platter. Sprinkle with
almonds.

Nutrients per serving:			
Calories	206	Cholesterol	29 mg
Fat	5 g	Sodium	509 mg

Black and White Bean Salad

Black and White Bean Salad

Makes 4 cups

½ cup **MIRACLE WHIP® FREE®** Nonfat
    Dressing
1 can (15 ounces) *each* navy beans and black
    beans, drained and rinsed
½ cup *each* green bell pepper strips and red
    onion slices
1 cucumber, chopped
3 tablespoons chopped fresh parsley
    Dash black pepper

Mix together ingredients until well blended; refrigerate.

Prep time: 10 minutes

Nutrients per serving (½ cup):			
Calories	200	Cholesterol	0 mg
Fat	1 g	Sodium	214 mg

Fabulous Fruit Salad for a Crowd

Makes 12 to 14 servings

¼ cup seedless raspberry jam
2 tablespoons lemon juice
1 pint strawberries, stems removed, halved
1 cup plum wedges
2 cups pineapple chunks
2 cups cantaloupe chunks
2 cups honeydew chunks
2 cups nectarine chunks
½ pint raspberries
1 cup seedless green grapes
1 cup **BLUE DIAMOND®** Whole Natural
    Almonds, toasted

In large bowl, blend jam and lemon juice. Toss with strawberries and plum wedges. Let stand, covered, up to 2 hours. Just before serving, fold in pineapple, cantaloupe, honeydew, nectarines, raspberries, grapes and almonds.

Nutrients per serving:			
Calories	135	Cholesterol	0 mg
Fat	6 g	Sodium	5 mg

Gingered Pear Salad

Makes 3 cups, 3 entrée servings

1 can (8½ ounces) pear halves in juice, undrained
1 package (4-serving size) JELL-O® Brand Lemon Flavor Sugar Free Gelatin
¾ cup boiling water
2 teaspoons lemon juice
  Ice cubes
1 cup (8 ounces) 2% low-fat cottage cheese
⅛ teaspoon salt
⅛ teaspoon ground ginger

Drain pears, reserving juice; set juice aside. Finely chop pears; set aside.

Dissolve gelatin in boiling water; add lemon juice. Add enough ice cubes to reserved pear juice to measure 1 cup. Add to gelatin; stir until slightly thickened. Remove any unmelted ice; pour gelatin into blender container. Add cottage cheese, salt and ginger; cover. Blend until smooth. Stir in pears. Pour into 3 individual plastic containers or serving dishes. Chill until firm, about 2 hours.

Nutrients per serving:

Calories	120	Cholesterol	5 mg
Fat	2 g	Sodium	480 mg

Warm Turkey Salad

Makes 2 servings

1 medium DOLE® Fresh Pineapple
4 ounces green beans or broccoli, steamed
2 DOLE® Carrots, slivered or sliced
½ cup slivered jicama or radishes
½ cup slivered DOLE® Red Bell Pepper
  DOLE® Salad Greens
  Salt and black pepper (optional)
2 turkey cutlets (½ pound)
1 tablespoon vegetable oil
  Lite Honey Mustard Dressing (recipe follows)

Twist crown from pineapple. Cut pineapple in half lengthwise. Refrigerate half for another use, such as fruit salads. Cut remaining half in half lengthwise. Remove fruit from shells with knife. Cut each quarter into 4 spears. Arrange pineapple, green beans, carrots, jicama and red bell pepper on 2 dinner plates lined with salad greens, leaving space for cooked turkey. Lightly sprinkle salt and pepper over turkey. In medium skillet, brown turkey on both sides in oil. Cover; simmer 5 to 7 minutes. (Add 1 tablespoon water if needed.) Remove from skillet. Cut turkey crosswise into 4 or 5 slices. Arrange on salad plates with pineapple and vegetables. Serve with Lite Honey Mustard Dressing.

Lite Honey Mustard Dressing

¼ cup cholesterol-free reduced-calorie mayonnaise
1 to 2 tablespoons pineapple juice or orange juice
1 teaspoon honey
1 teaspoon Dijon-style mustard
¼ teaspoon dried tarragon leaves, crumbled

Combine all ingredients in small bowl.

Nutrients per serving:

Calories	267	Cholesterol	30 mg
Fat	10 g	Sodium	233 mg

Zesty Pasta Salad

Makes 6 servings

2 cups (8 ounces) ARMOUR® Lower Salt Ham, cut into julienne strips
2 cups pasta bow ties or shells, cooked according to package directions and drained (omit salt)
8 ounces California-blend frozen vegetables, thawed
5 cherry tomatoes, cut in half
¾ cup bottled low-sodium, low-calorie zesty Italian salad dressing
4 cups mixed greens, washed and drained

Combine ham, pasta, vegetables, tomatoes and salad dressing in large bowl; toss to coat well. Cover; refrigerate at least 1 hour before serving to allow flavors to blend. To serve, arrange pasta mixture in lettuce-lined bowl or on platter.

Nutrients per serving:

Calories	233	Cholesterol	19 mg
Fat	3 g	Sodium	344 mg

Zesty Pasta Salad

Sesame Pork Salad

Makes 6 servings

3 cups cooked rice
1½ cups slivered cooked pork*
¼ pound fresh snow peas, trimmed and julienned
1 medium cucumber, peeled, seeded, and julienned
1 medium red bell pepper, julienned
½ cup sliced green onions
2 tablespoons sesame seeds, toasted (optional)
¼ cup chicken broth
3 tablespoons rice or white wine vinegar
3 tablespoons soy sauce
1 tablespoon peanut oil
1 teaspoon sesame oil

Combine rice, pork, snow peas, cucumber, bell pepper, onions, and sesame seeds in large bowl. Combine broth, vinegar, soy sauce, and oils in small jar with lid; shake well. Pour over rice mixture; toss lightly. Serve at room temperature or slightly chilled.

Substitute 1½ cups slivered cooked chicken for pork, if desired.

Nutrients per serving:

Calories	269	Cholesterol	32 mg
Fat	8 g	Sodium	867 mg

Favorite recipe from **USA Rice Council**

Mock Blue Cheese Dressing

Makes 6 servings, ¾ cup

¾ cup buttermilk
¼ cup low-fat cottage cheese
2 tablespoons blue cheese, crumbled
2 teaspoons sugar
1 teaspoon lemon juice
¼ teaspoon celery seed
⅛ teaspoon black pepper
⅛ teaspoon salt
4 drops hot pepper sauce

In blender, process all ingredients. Refrigerate or serve immediately over green salad.

Nutrients per serving (2 tablespoons dressing):

Calories	33	Cholesterol	3 mg
Fat	1 g	Sodium	148 mg

Favorite recipe from **The Sugar Association, Inc.**

Mexican Surimi Salad

Makes 4 servings

12 ounces crab-flavored SURIMI Seafood flakes, chunks or salad-style, well flaked
1 large tomato, halved, seeded and diced
¼ cup sliced green onions
¼ cup sliced black olives
1 tablespoon chopped cilantro or fresh parsley
¼ cup salsa
3 cups salad greens, washed, drained and torn into bite-sized pieces

Combine Surimi Seafood, tomato, green onions, olives and cilantro in medium bowl. Add salsa; toss gently to combine. Arrange salad greens on 4 plates and divide seafood mixture over greens.

Nutrients per serving:

Calories	122	Cholesterol	17 mg
Fat	3 g	Sodium	794 mg

Favorite recipe from **Surimi Seafood Education Center**

Lanai Pasta Salad

Makes 6 to 8 servings

1 can (20 ounces) DOLE® Pineapple Chunks in Juice
3 cups cooked spiral pasta
2 cups sugar peas or snow peas
1 cup sliced DOLE® Carrots
1 cup sliced cucumbers
½ cup bottled low-calorie Italian salad dressing
¼ cup chopped cilantro or fresh parsley

Drain pineapple; reserve ¼ cup juice.

Combine pineapple and reserved juice with remaining ingredients in large bowl; toss to coat.

Nutrients per serving:

Calories	181	Cholesterol	0 mg
Fat	trace	Sodium	219 mg

Sesame Pork Salad

Chicken-Asparagus Salad

Makes 4 to 5 servings

1 can (14½ ounces) chicken broth
1 bay leaf
1 green onion, cut into 1-inch pieces
1 (¼-inch-thick) slice fresh ginger, peeled
4 boneless skinless chicken breast halves (about 1 pound)
  Mustard Vinaigrette (recipe follows)
½ pound asparagus spears, cut in half, cooked until crisp-tender
1 can (8¾ ounces) whole baby sweet corn, rinsed and drained
  Spinach or lettuce leaves
3 small tomatoes, chopped

Combine broth, bay leaf, onion and ginger in medium saucepan. Bring to a boil. Add chicken; reduce heat to low. Cover; simmer 8 minutes or until chicken is tender and no longer pink in center. Remove from broth; cool slightly. (Reserve broth for another use, if desired.) Meanwhile, prepare Mustard Vinaigrette.

Cut chicken diagonally into narrow strips; place in medium bowl with asparagus and corn. Add vinaigrette; toss lightly. Marinate at room temperature 15 minutes. Drain, reserving vinaigrette.

Arrange chicken, asparagus and corn on individual spinach-lined salad plates. Top with tomatoes. Serve with reserved vinaigrette.

Mustard Vinaigrette
1 tablespoon country-style Dijon mustard
¼ cup seasoned rice vinegar
2 tablespoons vegetable oil
¼ teaspoon sesame oil
  Dash of black pepper

Whisk together all ingredients in small bowl.

Nutrients per serving:			
Calories	232	Cholesterol	46 mg
Fat	10 g	Sodium	257 mg

Chicken-Asparagus Salad

Shells and Shrimp Salad Alfresco

Makes 10 servings

½ of (1-pound) package CREAMETTE® Medium Shells, uncooked
2 cups cooked medium shrimp, shelled, deveined
2 medium fresh tomatoes, peeled, seeded and chopped
2 cups torn fresh spinach
1 cup sliced fresh cauliflowerets
½ cup sliced radishes
¼ cup sliced green onions
2 tablespoons vegetable oil
2 tablespoons lemon juice
1 tablespoon Dijon-style mustard
¼ teaspoon dried thyme leaves, crushed
¼ teaspoon lemon pepper seasoning

Prepare Creamette® Medium Shells according to package directions; drain. In large bowl, combine shells, shrimp, tomatoes, spinach, cauliflowerets, radishes and green onions. In small bowl, whisk together oil, lemon juice, mustard, thyme and seasoning; add to shrimp mixture and toss to coat. Cover; refrigerate thoroughly. Toss gently before serving. Refrigerate leftovers.

Nutrients per serving:			
Calories	176	Cholesterol	68 mg
Fat	4 g	Sodium	89 mg

Thousand Island Dressing

Makes about 2 cups

⅔ cup PET® Light Evaporated Skimmed Milk
⅔ cup bottled chili sauce
⅔ cup safflower oil
¼ cup sweet pickle relish
1 tablespoon lemon juice
1 tablespoon sugar
1 teaspoon salt
⅛ teaspoon ground black pepper

Using a wire whisk, combine all ingredients in small bowl. Refrigerate until well chilled. Serve over tossed green salad.

Nutrients per serving (1 tablespoon dressing):			
Calories	54	Cholesterol	0 mg
Fat	5 g	Sodium	129 mg

Sparkling Berry Salad

Makes 8 servings

2 cups cranberry juice
2 packages (4-serving size) or 1 package
   (8-serving size) JELL-O® Brand Sugar
   Free Gelatin, any red flavor
1½ cups cold club soda
¼ cup creme de cassis liqueur (optional)
1 teaspoon lemon juice
1 cup raspberries
1 cup blueberries
½ cup sliced strawberries
½ cup whole strawberries, cut into fans
   Mint leaves (optional)

Bring cranberry juice to a boil in medium saucepan.
Completely dissolve gelatin in boiling cranberry juice.
Stir in club soda, liqueur and lemon juice. Chill until
slightly thickened.

Reserve a few raspberries and blueberries for garnish,
if desired. Stir remaining raspberries, blueberries and
the sliced strawberries into gelatin mixture. Spoon
into 6-cup mold that has been lightly sprayed with
nonstick cooking spray. Chill until firm, about
4 hours. Unmold. Surround with reserved berries,
strawberry fans and mint leaves, if desired.

Nutrients per serving:

Calories	100	Cholesterol	0 mg
Fat	0 g	Sodium	70 mg

Light Pasta Salad

Makes 4 servings

½ cup MIRACLE WHIP® LIGHT® Reduced
   Calorie Salad Dressing
½ cup KRAFT® "Zesty" Italian Reduced Calorie
   Dressing
2 cups (6 ounces) corkscrew noodles, cooked,
   drained
1 cup broccoli florettes, partially cooked
½ cup chopped green bell pepper
½ cup chopped tomato
¼ cup green onion slices

Mix dressings in large bowl until well blended. Add
remaining ingredients; mix lightly. Refrigerate. Serve
with freshly ground black pepper, if desired.

Nutrients per serving:

Calories	260	Cholesterol	0 mg
Fat	9 g	Sodium	450 mg

Orange Salad with Cinnamon Dressing

Orange Salad with Cinnamon Dressing

Makes 8 servings

8 oranges, peeled, sliced
4 cups torn assorted greens
   Cinnamon Dressing (recipe follows)

Arrange orange slices and greens on individual salad
plates. Serve with Cinnamon Dressing. Garnish with
orange peel, if desired.

Cinnamon Dressing

1 package (8 ounces) Light PHILADELPHIA
   BRAND® Neufchatel Cheese, softened
⅓ cup orange juice
1 tablespoon honey
1½ teaspoons grated orange peel
½ teaspoon ground cinnamon

Place ingredients in blender or food processor
container; cover. Blend until smooth.

Prep time: 20 minutes

Nutrients per serving:

Calories	160	Cholesterol	40 mg
Fat	7 g	Sodium	120 mg

Citrus Cheese Salad

Citrus Cheese Salad

Makes 1 serving

½ cup BORDEN® Lite-line® or Viva® Lowfat
   Cottage Cheese
1 slice BORDEN® Lite-line® Process Cheese
   Product,* any flavor, cut into small pieces
2 tablespoons chopped cucumber
½ fresh grapefruit, pared and sectioned
   Lettuce leaf

In small bowl, combine cottage cheese, cheese
product pieces and cucumber. On salad plate,
arrange grapefruit on lettuce. Top with cheese
mixture. Refrigerate leftovers.

*"½ the calories"–8% milkfat product

Nutrients per serving:			
Calories	200	Cholesterol	15 mg
Fat	3 g	Sodium	714 mg

Fettuccini Slaw

Makes 12 servings

½ of a (1-pound) package CREAMETTE®
   Fettuccini, broken into thirds, uncooked
3 cups finely chopped cabbage
2 cups finely shredded carrots
2 cups thinly sliced celery
2 cups finely sliced cucumber
1 container (8 ounces) plain low-fat yogurt
½ cup low-calorie mayonnaise or salad dressing
2 tablespoons white vinegar
½ teaspoon dry mustard
¼ teaspoon white pepper
   Paprika

Prepare Creamette® Fettuccini according to package
directions; drain. In large bowl, combine fettuccini,
cabbage, carrots, celery and cucumber. In small
bowl, blend yogurt, mayonnaise, vinegar, mustard and
pepper; toss with fettuccini mixture. Cover; refrigerate
thoroughly. Toss gently before serving. Garnish with
paprika. Refrigerate leftovers.

Nutrients per serving:			
Calories	209	Cholesterol	4 mg
Fat	4 g	Sodium	105 mg

Chunky Cucumber Dill Dressing

Makes about 6 servings

1 cup peeled and chopped cucumber, divided
¾ cup *plus* 2 tablespoons nonfat plain yogurt
3 tablespoons chopped fresh dill
2 teaspoons sugar
2 teaspoons lemon juice
⅛ teaspoon black pepper

In blender or food processor, blend ½ cup cucumber
with remaining ingredients. Stir in remaining ½ cup
cucumber. Refrigerate or serve immediately over
green salad or chicken salad.

Nutrients per serving (2 tablespoons dressing):			
Calories	31	Cholesterol	1 mg
Fat	trace	Sodium	71 mg

Favorite recipe from **The Sugar Association, Inc.**

Creamy Fruit Mold

Makes 7 servings

1 package (0.3 ounces) sugar-free lime flavor
   gelatin
1 cup boiling water
1 cup PET® Light Evaporated Skimmed Milk
2 cups cut-up fresh fruit*

Dissolve gelatin in boiling water. Cool slightly to
prevent milk from curdling. Stir in evaporated
skimmed milk. Refrigerate until gelatin mixture is the
consistency of unbeaten egg whites. Stir in fruit. Pour
into 8-inch square pan or 5-cup mold. Refrigerate
until firm. Garnish with additional fruit.

*Suggested fresh fruit: apples, Bing cherries, oranges,
peaches or strawberries.*

Nutrients per serving:			
Calories	51	Cholesterol	1 mg
Fat	0 g	Sodium	77 mg

Chunky Chicken Salsa Salad

Makes 4 servings

- 1 clove garlic, minced
- ½ pound boneless, skinless chicken breasts
- 1 can (16 ounces) California cling peach slices in juice or extra light syrup
- ½ teaspoon chili powder
- ¼ teaspoon *each* ground cumin and seasoned salt
- 1 head iceberg lettuce, rinsed and crisped
- 1 box (10½ ounces) frozen corn, cooked, drained and cooled
- 1 cup cherry tomatoes, halved
- ½ cup *each* sliced green onions and minced cilantro
- 1 can (4 ounces) diced green chilies, drained

Bring 2 cups water to a boil; add garlic. Add chicken breasts; simmer 10 to 15 minutes until cooked through. Drain, cool and shred chicken breasts. Drain peach slices, reserving ¼ cup liquid; save remainder for other uses. Cut peach slices in half and set aside. Blend reserved peach liquid with chili powder, cumin and seasoned salt for dressing. Set aside. Cut lettuce into chunks. Toss together lettuce chunks, shredded chicken, reserved peach slices, corn, cherry tomatoes, green onions, cilantro and diced green chilies. Drizzle salad with dressing and toss well just before serving.

Nutrients per serving:

Calories	202	Cholesterol	33 mg
Fat	1 g	Sodium	196 mg

Favorite recipe from **California Cling Peach Advisory Board**

Bombay Banana Salad

Makes 6 servings

- 2 DOLE® Oranges
- 2 firm DOLE® Bananas, peeled and sliced
- 1 cup seedless red DOLE® Grapes
- ¼ cup DOLE® Whole Almonds, toasted

Dressing
- 1 ripe DOLE® Banana, peeled
- 12 DOLE® Pitted Dates, halved
- ½ cup dairy sour cream
- 1 tablespoon packed brown sugar *or* honey
- 1 tablespoon chopped chutney
- ½ teaspoon curry powder

Grate peel from 1 orange; reserve peel for dressing. Peel and slice oranges. In bowl, toss salad ingredients with Dressing.

For Dressing, place all Dressing ingredients in blender container or food processor. Process until smooth. Stir in reserved grated orange peel.

Nutrients per serving:

Calories	240	Cholesterol	9 mg
Fat	9 g	Sodium	13 mg

Ziti Salmon Salad

Makes 6 to 8 servings

- ½ of a (1-pound) package CREAMETTE® Ziti, uncooked
- 1 (16-ounce) can salmon, drained, skin and bones removed
- 1 (6-ounce) package frozen snow peas, thawed
- 1 medium red bell pepper, chopped
- 1 medium yellow bell pepper, chopped
- ½ cup sliced green onions
- ½ cup bottled Italian salad dressing
- ½ teaspoon salt-free herb seasoning

Prepare Creamette® Ziti according to package directions; drain. In large bowl, combine ziti and remaining ingredients; mix well. Cover; refrigerate thoroughly. Toss gently before serving. Refrigerate leftovers.

Nutrients per serving:

Calories	173	Cholesterol	19 mg
Fat	4 g	Sodium	332 mg

Ziti Salmon Salad

Lemon Ginger Sauce

Lemon Ginger Sauce

Makes ½ cup

½ cup MIRACLE WHIP® FREE® Nonfat
    Dressing
2 tablespoons lemon juice
1½ tablespoons firmly packed brown sugar
1 teaspoon grated lemon peel
1 teaspoon ground ginger

Mix together ingredients until well blended;
refrigerate. Serve over fresh fruit.

Prep time: 5 minutes plus refrigerating

Nutrients per serving (2 tablespoons sauce):			
Calories	70	Cholesterol	1 mg
Fat	trace	Sodium	422 mg

Creamettes® Chicken Salad

Makes 8 servings

1 (7-ounce) package CREAMETTES® Elbow
    Macaroni (2 cups uncooked)
2 cups cubed cooked chicken or turkey (white
    meat)
2 cups fresh broccoli florettes
4 medium oranges, peeled, sectioned and
    seeded
1 cup orange juice
¼ cup cider vinegar
1 teaspoon ground ginger
½ teaspoon paprika
¼ cup toasted sliced almonds

Prepare Creamettes® Elbow Macaroni according to
package directions; drain. In large bowl, combine
macaroni, chicken, broccoli and oranges. In small
bowl, blend orange juice, vinegar, ginger and paprika;
toss with macaroni mixture. Cover; refrigerate
thoroughly. Stir before serving. Garnish with almonds.
Refrigerate leftovers.

Nutrients per serving:			
Calories	222	Cholesterol	36 mg
Fat	4 g	Sodium	38 mg

Saffron Rice Salad

Makes 4 servings

2½ cups cooked rice (cooked in chicken broth
    and ⅛ teaspoon saffron*), cooled to room
    temperature
½ cup diced red bell pepper
½ cup diced green bell pepper
¼ cup sliced green onions
¼ cup sliced ripe olives
2 tablespoons white wine vinegar
1 teaspoon olive oil
2 to 3 drops hot pepper sauce (optional)
1 clove garlic, minced
¼ teaspoon ground white pepper
    Lettuce leaves

Combine rice, red and green peppers, onions, and
olives in large bowl. Combine vinegar, oil, pepper
sauce, garlic, and white pepper in jar with lid; shake
well. Pour over rice mixture; toss lightly. Serve on
lettuce leaves.

*Substitute ground turmeric for the saffron, if desired.

Nutrients per serving:			
Calories	177	Cholesterol	0 mg
Fat	3 g	Sodium	416 mg

Favorite recipe from **USA Rice Council**

Mediterranean Couscous

Makes 6 servings, 6 cups

3 cups water
1 teaspoon salt
1 box (10 ounces) couscous
1 cup canned black beans, rinsed and drained
8 ounces cherry tomatoes, chopped
1 carrot, shredded
½ cup WISH-BONE® Healthy Sensation! Italian
    Dressing

In 2-quart saucepan, bring water and salt to a boil;
stir in couscous. Cover; remove from heat and let
stand 5 minutes. Fluff with fork; set aside 10 minutes
to cool. In large bowl, toss couscous with remaining
ingredients; refrigerate.

Nutrients per serving:			
Calories	172	Cholesterol	0 mg
Fat	trace	Sodium	587 mg

Herbed Chicken Salad

Makes 4 to 6 servings

3 cups cubed cooked chicken or turkey
¼ cup REALEMON® Lemon Juice from
    Concentrate
¼ cup vegetable oil
2 teaspoons WYLER'S® or STEERO® Chicken-
    Flavor Instant Bouillon
1 teaspoon sugar
1 teaspoon tarragon leaves
1 clove garlic, finely chopped
1 cup sliced fresh mushrooms
½ pound fresh green beans, cut into 1-inch
    pieces, cooked until tender-crisp and chilled
1 cup cherry tomato halves
    Lettuce

In small bowl, combine ReaLemon® brand, oil, bouillon, sugar, tarragon and garlic; let stand 15 minutes to dissolve bouillon, stirring occasionally. In large bowl, combine chicken and mushrooms; pour dressing over. Cover; chill 4 hours or overnight, stirring occasionally. Just before serving, add green beans and tomatoes. Serve on lettuce. Refrigerate leftovers.

Tip: *1 (9-ounce) package frozen cut green beans, cooked and chilled, can be substituted for fresh green beans.*

Nutrients per serving:

Calories	158	Cholesterol	23 mg
Fat	10 g	Sodium	327 mg

Herbed Chicken Salad

Cool Cucumber Lime Mold

Makes 5 cups

1 cup cottage cheese
½ cup MIRACLE WHIP FREE® Nonfat Dressing
1¾ cups cold water, divided
1 package (3 ounces) JELL-O® Brand Lime
    Flavor Gelatin
1 cup peeled, seeded, finely chopped cucumber
2 tablespoons finely chopped onion
2 teaspoons chopped fresh dill *or* **1 teaspoon**
    dill weed

Place cottage cheese and dressing in blender or food processor container; process until smooth. Bring 1 cup water to a boil. Gradually add to gelatin; stir until dissolved. Stir in ¾ cup cold water. Add to cottage cheese mixture, mixing until blended. Chill until thickened but not set; fold in cucumber, onion and dill. Pour into lightly oiled 6-cup mold; chill until firm. Unmold.

Prep time: 15 minutes plus chilling

Nutrients per serving (½ cup):

Calories	70	Cholesterol	3 mg
Fat	1 g	Sodium	261 mg

Rice Salad Milano

Makes 6 servings

3 cups hot cooked rice
2 tablespoons vegetable oil
2 tablespoons lemon juice
1 clove garlic, minced
½ teaspoon salt (optional)
½ teaspoon dried rosemary leaves, crushed
½ teaspoon dried oregano leaves, crushed
½ teaspoon ground black pepper
1 small zucchini, julienned*
1 medium tomato, seeded and chopped
2 tablespoons grated Parmesan cheese

Place rice in large bowl. Combine oil, lemon juice, garlic, salt, rosemary, oregano, and pepper in small jar with lid; shake well. Pour over rice; toss lightly. Cover; let cool. Add remaining ingredients. Serve at room temperature or chilled.

***To julienne, slice zucchini diagonally. Cut slices into matchstick-size strips.*

Nutrients per serving:

Calories	189	Cholesterol	1 mg
Fat	5 g	Sodium	620 mg

Favorite recipe from **USA Rice Council**

Apple Salad

Makes 3½ cups

⅓ cup MIRACLE WHIP® FREE® Nonfat
    Dressing
1 tablespoon apple juice
2 teaspoons peanut butter
⅛ teaspoon ground cinnamon
2 small apples, chopped
1 can (8 ounces) pineapple chunks, drained
½ cup *each* KRAFT® Miniature Marshmallows
    and grapes

Mix dressing, juice, peanut butter and cinnamon until
well blended. Stir in remaining ingredients; refrigerate.

Prep time: 10 minutes plus refrigerating

Nutrients per serving (½ cup):			
Calories	100	Cholesterol	0 mg
Fat	1 g	Sodium	160 mg

White Sangria Splash

Makes 12 servings, 6 cups

1½ cups dry white wine
2 packages (4-serving size) or 1 package
    (8-serving size) JELL-O® Brand Lemon
    Flavor Sugar Free Gelatin
2½ cups club soda
1 tablespoon lime juice
1 tablespoon orange liqueur (optional)
1 cup sliced strawberries
1 cup seedless red grapes
1 cup seedless green grapes

Bring wine to a boil in small saucepan. Completely
dissolve gelatin in boiling wine; pour into medium
bowl. Stir in club soda, lime juice and liqueur, if
desired. Place bowl in larger bowl of ice and water; let
stand until slightly thickened, stirring occasionally.

Gently stir in fruit. Pour into 6-cup mold that has
been lightly sprayed with nonstick cooking spray.
Chill until firm, about 4 hours. Unmold. Serve with
additional fruit, if desired.

Nutrients per serving (½ cup):			
Calories	50	Cholesterol	0 mg
Fat	0 g	Sodium	55 mg

Crunchy Chicken-Vegetable Salad

Crunchy Chicken-Vegetable Salad

Makes 4 servings

1 cup (8 ounces) plain yogurt
3 tablespoons low-calorie mayonnaise
2 teaspoons Dijon-style mustard
1 garlic clove, minced
½ teaspoon salt
    Dash black pepper
2 cups shredded red cabbage
2 cups fresh bean sprouts
1½ cups chopped cooked chicken or turkey,
    chilled
¼ pound fresh snow peas, trimmed
¾ cup celery slices
½ cup sliced almonds, toasted
¼ cup chopped red onion
    Fresh spinach leaves
2 hard-cooked eggs, peeled and sliced for
    garnish

Combine yogurt, mayonnaise, mustard, garlic, salt
and pepper in large bowl. Add cabbage, sprouts,
chicken, snow peas, celery, almonds and onion; mix
lightly. Serve in spinach-lined salad bowl or on
spinach-covered salad plates. Garnish with eggs.

Nutrients per serving:			
Calories	209	Cholesterol	35 mg
Fat	9 g	Sodium	380 mg

Pasta Primavera Salad

Green Bean, New Potato and Ham Salad

Makes 12 cups

3 pounds new potatoes, quartered
⅔ cup cold water
1 pound green beans, halved
¾ cup MIRACLE WHIP® FREE® Nonfat
    Dressing
⅓ cup stone-ground mustard
2 tablespoons red wine vinegar
2 cups OSCAR MAYER® Ham cubes
½ cup chopped green onions

To Microwave: Place potatoes and water in 3-quart casserole; cover. Microwave on HIGH (100%) 13 minutes. Stir in beans. Microwave on HIGH 7 to 13 minutes or until tender; drain. Mix dressing, mustard and vinegar in large bowl until well blended. Add potatoes, beans and remaining ingredients; mix lightly. Refrigerate.

Prep time: 15 minutes plus refrigerating
Microwave cook time: 26 minutes

Nutrients per serving (¾ cup):			
Calories	100	Cholesterol	5 mg
Fat	1 g	Sodium	428 mg

Pasta Primavera Salad

Makes 6 servings

1 package (8 ounces) elbow macaroni, cooked,
    drained (2 cups)
2 cups DOLE® Broccoli flowerets
2 cups sliced DOLE® Celery
1 cup sliced DOLE® Carrots
½ cup sliced DOLE® Green Onions
½ cup diced DOLE® Green Bell Pepper
1 cup light sour cream
½ cup reduced-calorie mayonnaise
1 teaspoon dill weed
1 teaspoon garlic salt

Combine cooked macaroni, broccoli, celery, carrots, onions and green pepper in large bowl. For dressing, combine remaining ingredients in small bowl. Pour over pasta mixture; toss to coat well. Refrigerate.

Prep time: 20 minutes
Cook time: 10 minutes

Nutrients per serving:			
Calories	240	Cholesterol	24 mg
Fat	7 g	Sodium	346 mg

Fresh Fruit Shell Salad

Makes 8 to 10 servings

½ of a (1-pound) package CREAMETTE®
    Medium Shells, uncooked
1 (8-ounce) container plain low-fat yogurt
¼ cup frozen orange juice concentrate, thawed
1 (15-ounce) can juice-pack pineapple chunks,
    drained
1 large orange, peeled, sectioned and seeded
1 cup seedless red grapes, cut into halves
1 cup seedless green grapes, cut into halves
1 apple, cored and chopped
1 banana, sliced

Prepare Creamette® Medium Shells according to package directions; drain. In small bowl, blend yogurt and orange juice concentrate. In large bowl, combine remaining ingredients. Add yogurt mixture; toss to coat. Cover; refrigerate thoroughly. Toss gently before serving. Refrigerate leftovers.

Nutrients per serving:			
Calories	179	Cholesterol	1 mg
Fat	1 g	Sodium	20 mg

Shrimp and Strawberry Salad

Makes 6 servings

    3 cups cooked rice
    ½ pound peeled, deveined cooked small shrimp
    ¾ cup thinly sliced celery
    ⅔ cup cholesterol-free, reduced-calorie
        mayonnaise
    ½ cup low-fat strawberry yogurt
    1 teaspoon dry mustard
    1 teaspoon lemon juice
    ½ teaspoon salt
    1½ cups sliced fresh strawberries
        Romaine lettuce

Combine rice, shrimp, and celery in large bowl.
Combine mayonnaise, yogurt, mustard, lemon juice,
and salt in medium bowl; mix well. Add yogurt
mixture to rice mixture and stir well. Fold in
strawberries. Cover and refrigerate until serving time.
Arrange lettuce on individual serving plates; top with
salad.

Nutrients per serving:			
Calories	274	Cholesterol	69 mg
Fat	9 g	Sodium	833 mg

Favorite recipe from **USA Rice Council**

Confetti Rice Salad

Makes 6 servings

    2 chicken-flavored bouillon cubes
    1 cup uncooked long grain white rice
    1 can (16 ounces) California cling peach slices
        in juice or extra-light syrup
    3 tablespoons tarragon-flavored white wine
        vinegar
    1 tablespoon Dijon-style mustard
    1 tablespoon olive oil
    ¼ teaspoon dried tarragon leaves, crushed
    1 cup chopped red bell peppers
    ½ cup frozen peas, thawed
    ⅓ cup raisins
    ¼ cup sliced green onions

In medium saucepan, combine bouillon cubes and
2 cups water; bring mixture to a boil. Stir in rice.
Reduce heat to low. Cover and simmer 20 minutes,
until liquid is absorbed and rice is tender. Remove
from heat; cool 5 minutes. Drain peaches, reserving

¼ cup liquid; save remainder for other uses. Cut
peach slices in half and set aside. Whisk reserved
peach liquid with vinegar, mustard, olive oil and
tarragon. Stir into cooled rice; add remaining
ingredients *except* reserved peaches. Cool completely,
tossing occasionally. Stir in reserved peaches and
refrigerate before serving.

Nutrients per serving:			
Calories	210	Cholesterol	trace
Fat	3 g	Sodium	317 mg

Favorite recipe from **California Cling Peach Advisory Board**

Berry-Cottage Cheese Salad

Makes 4 servings

    1 pint strawberries, hulled and sliced, divided
    ¼ cup fresh orange juice, divided
    1 tablespoon sugar
    2 cups (16 ounces) low-fat cottage cheese
    1 teaspoon grated fresh orange peel
    ¾ cup granola cereal, divided
        Torn assorted greens

Place 1 cup strawberries, 2 tablespoons orange juice
and sugar in blender container. Cover; process until
smooth. Set aside. Combine cottage cheese,
remaining 2 tablespoons orange juice, orange peel
and ½ cup cereal in small bowl. Arrange greens on
4 salad plates; top each with cottage cheese mixture
and remaining 1 cup strawberries. Sprinkle remaining
¼ cup cereal over cottage cheese. Serve with
strawberry sauce.

Nutrients per serving:			
Calories	237	Cholesterol	10 g
Fat	6 g	Sodium	504 mg

Berry-Cottage Cheese Salad

It's time to break out of that ho-hum vegetable routine with these vibrant creations. Give stir-fried vegetables a tantalizing foreign flavor with a dash of soy sauce and a pinch of ginger. Dress up versatile rice with zesty herbs, fresh spinach and a touch of cheese. Just watch those taste buds perk up!

Pasta & Vegetable Toss

Makes 4 servings

½ cup chopped onion
1 clove garlic, finely chopped
1 teaspoon Italian seasoning
1 tablespoon olive oil
¼ cup water
2 teaspoons WYLER'S® or STEERO® Beef-Flavor Instant Bouillon
2 cups broccoli flowerets
2 cups sliced zucchini
8 ounces fresh mushrooms, sliced (about 2 cups)
1 medium red bell pepper, cut into thin strips
½ of a (1-pound) package CREAMETTE® Fettuccini, cooked according to package directions and drained

In large skillet, cook and stir onion, garlic and Italian seasoning in oil until onion is tender. Add water, bouillon and vegetables. Cover and simmer 5 to 7 minutes until vegetables are tender-crisp. Toss with hot fettuccini. Serve immediately. Refrigerate leftovers.

Nutrients per serving:

Calories	287	Cholesterol	0 mg
Fat	5 g	Sodium	481 mg

Lemon Florentine Zucchini Boats

Makes 6 servings

3 medium zucchini (about 1 pound), cut in half lengthwise
Boiling water
1 small onion, finely chopped
1 medium clove garlic, minced
⅛ teaspoon ground nutmeg
2 tablespoons unsalted margarine
1¼ cups cooked, chopped fresh spinach, well drained (1½ pounds uncooked)*
½ cup ricotta cheese
Grated peel and juice of ½ SUNKIST® Lemon
2 tablespoons grated Parmesan cheese

Parboil zucchini in boiling water for 5 minutes; drain. In large skillet over medium-high heat, cook and stir onion, garlic and nutmeg in margarine until onion is tender. Add spinach, ricotta cheese, lemon peel and juice; stir until well combined. Arrange zucchini, cut sides up, in shallow baking dish. Top zucchini halves evenly with spinach mixture. Bake at 375°F for 20 minutes. Sprinkle with Parmesan cheese. Serve immediately.

1 package (10 ounces) frozen chopped spinach (no salt added), thawed, may be substituted.

Nutrients per serving:

Calories	94	Cholesterol	8 mg
Fat	6 g	Sodium	85 mg

VEGETABLES & SIDE DISHES

Pasta & Vegetable Toss

Eggplant Italiano

Colorful Cauliflower Bake

Makes 6 servings

1 cup KELLOGG'S® ALL-BRAN® cereal
2 tablespoons margarine, melted
¼ teaspoon garlic salt
¼ cup flour
½ teaspoon salt
⅛ teaspoon white pepper
1⅓ cups skim milk
1 chicken bouillon cube
1 package (16 ounces) frozen, cut cauliflower, thawed, well drained
½ cup sliced green onions
2 tablespoons drained chopped pimento

Combine Kellogg's® All-Bran® cereal, margarine and garlic salt; set aside.

In 3-quart saucepan, combine flour, salt and pepper. Gradually add milk, mixing until smooth, using a wire whisk if necessary. Add bouillon cube. Cook, stirring constantly, over medium heat until bubbly and thickened. Remove from heat. Add cauliflower, onions and pimento, mixing until combined. Spread evenly in 1½-quart baking dish. Sprinkle with cereal mixture.

Bake at 350°F about 20 minutes or until thoroughly heated and sauce is bubbly.

Note: *3½ cups fresh cauliflower flowerets, cooked crisp-tender, may be substituted for frozen cauliflower.*

Nutrients per serving:

Calories	120	Cholesterol	1 mg
Fat	4 g	Sodium	508 mg

Eggplant Italiano

Makes 4 servings

1 eggplant (1 pound), peeled if desired
1 can (6 ounces) low-sodium cocktail vegetable juice (¾ cup)
½ cup QUAKER® Oat Bran hot cereal, uncooked
2 garlic cloves, minced
1 teaspoon dried basil leaves, crushed
½ teaspoon dried oregano leaves, crushed
2 medium tomatoes, chopped
1¼ cups (5 ounces) shredded part-skim mozzarella cheese

Heat oven to 350°F. Line cookie sheet or 15×10-inch baking pan with foil. Lightly spray with nonstick cooking spray, or oil lightly. Cut eggplant into ½-inch-thick slices; place in single layer on prepared pan. Combine vegetable juice, oat bran, garlic, basil and oregano. Spread evenly over eggplant; top with tomatoes. Sprinkle with mozzarella cheese. Bake 35 to 40 minutes or until eggplant is tender and cheese is melted. Sprinkle with additional basil or oregano, if desired.

Nutrients per serving:

Calories	190	Cholesterol	20 mg
Fat	7 g	Sodium	190 mg

Sun Valley Potato Fries

Makes 6 servings

2 large baking potatoes
¼ cup HELLMANN'S® or BEST FOODS® Light Reduced Calorie Mayonnaise

Preheat oven to 400°F. Cut potatoes into ¼-inch sticks. Spoon mayonnaise into large plastic food bag. Add potatoes; shake to coat well. Arrange in single layer in jelly-roll pan so potatoes do not touch. If desired, sprinkle with salt to taste. Bake 20 minutes or until golden brown and crisp, turning once with spatula.

Nutrients per serving:

Calories	75	Cholesterol	3 mg
Fat	3 g	Sodium	3 mg

Oriental Stir-Fried Vegetables

Makes 4 servings, 4 cups

2 tablespoons vegetable oil
**4 to 5 cups coarsely chopped or sliced fresh
    vegetables* (broccoli, carrots, cauliflower,
    onions, mushrooms, water chestnuts,
    Chinese cabbage, red or green bell
    peppers, snow peas and/or celery)**
1 clove garlic, minced
**1¾ cups (14.5-ounce can) CONTADINA®
    Stewed Tomatoes, drained, juice reserved**
1½ tablespoons soy sauce
1 tablespoon cornstarch
½ teaspoon ground ginger
½ teaspoon salt (optional)
**2 cups hot cooked rice or oriental noodles
    (optional)**
½ tablespoon toasted sesame seeds

In 12-inch skillet, heat oil. Add vegetables and garlic;
cook and stir over medium-high heat for 5 to 6
minutes or until crisp-tender. In small bowl, combine
reserved tomato juice, soy sauce, cornstarch, ginger
and salt. Add to skillet with tomatoes. Cook, stirring
constantly, for 2 minutes or until sauce is thickened.
Serve over hot cooked rice or noodles, if desired.
Sprinkle with sesame seeds.

**If using frozen vegetable mixture, choose a mixture with
large pieces. Do not thaw.*

Nutrients per serving:

Calories	145	Cholesterol	0 mg
Fat	8 g	Sodium	635 mg

Poppy Seed Noodles

Makes 4 servings

8 ounces uncooked noodles
1 tablespoon margarine
1 teaspoon poppy seeds

Cook noodles in lightly salted boiling water according
to package directions; drain. Place in serving bowl.
Add margarine and poppy seeds; toss lightly.

Nutrients per serving:

Calories	245	Cholesterol	54 mg
Fat	6 g	Sodium	45 mg

Oriental Stir-Fried Vegetables

Italian Capellini and Fresh Tomato

Makes 6 servings

- ½ of a (1-pound) package CREAMETTE® Capellini, uncooked
- 2 cups peeled, seeded and finely chopped fresh tomatoes (about 3 medium)
- 2 tablespoons olive oil
- 1 teaspoon dried basil leaves, crushed
- ½ teaspoon salt
- ½ teaspoon coarsely ground black pepper

Prepare Creamette® Capellini according to package directions; drain. Quickly toss hot cooked pasta with combined remaining ingredients. Serve immediately. Refrigerate leftovers.

Nutrients per serving:

Calories	196	Cholesterol	0 mg
Fat	5 g	Sodium	170 mg

Green Beans with Pine Nuts

Makes 4 servings

- 1 pound green beans, ends removed
- 2 tablespoons margarine
- 2 tablespoons pine nuts
  Salt and black pepper (optional)

Cook beans in 1 inch water in covered 3-quart saucepan 4 to 8 minutes or until crisp-tender; drain. Melt margarine in large skillet over medium heat. Add pine nuts; cook, stirring frequently, until golden. Add beans; stir gently to coat beans with margarine. Season with salt and pepper to taste.

Nutrients per serving:

Calories	127	Cholesterol	0 mg
Fat	10 g	Sodium	1 mg

Green Beans with Pine Nuts

Linguine Primavera

Makes 8 servings

- 2 tablespoons FLEISCHMANN'S® Margarine
- 2 cups coarsely chopped broccoli
- 1 cup julienned carrot strips
- 1 medium onion, cut into wedges
- 1 teaspoon Italian seasoning
- 2 cloves garlic, crushed
- ¼ teaspoon ground black pepper
- 1 large tomato, coarsely chopped
- 1 pound linguine, cooked in unsalted water and drained
- 1 (8-ounce) carton EGG BEATERS® 99% Real Egg Product
- ¼ cup grated Parmesan cheese

Melt margarine in large skillet over medium heat. Add broccoli, carrots, onion, Italian seasoning, garlic and pepper. Cook for 3 minutes, stirring occasionally. Add tomato; cook for 1 minute more or until vegetables are tender-crisp. Toss with hot linguine, Egg Beaters® and cheese. Garnish as desired and serve immediately.

To Microwave: In 2-quart microwavable bowl, combine margarine, broccoli, carrots, onion, Italian seasoning, garlic and pepper; cover. Microwave at HIGH (100% power) for 4 minutes, stirring after 2 minutes. Add tomato; re-cover. Microwave at HIGH for 2 to 3 minutes, stirring after 1½ minutes. Toss with hot linguine, Egg Beaters® and cheese. Garnish as desired and serve immediately.

Nutrients per serving:

Calories	281	Cholesterol	2 mg
Fat	5 g	Sodium	134 mg

Vegetable Stir-Fry

Makes 4 servings

- 1 tablespoon vegetable oil
- 3 or 4 carrots, diagonally sliced
- 2 zucchini, diagonally sliced
- 3 tablespoons orange juice
  Salt and black pepper (optional)

Heat oil in medium skillet or wok over medium heat. Add carrots; stir-fry 3 minutes.

Add zucchini and orange juice; stir-fry 4 minutes or until vegetables are crisp-tender. Season with salt and pepper, if desired.

Nutrients per serving:

Calories	68	Cholesterol	0 mg
Fat	4 g	Sodium	20 mg

Zucchini and Carrots au Gratin

Makes 4 to 6 servings

¼ cup HELLMANN'S® or BEST FOODS®
   Light Reduced Calorie Mayonnaise
¼ cup minced onion
2 tablespoons flour
1 tablespoon chopped fresh parsley
¾ teaspoon salt
¼ teaspoon dried Italian seasoning
   Dash freshly ground black pepper
1 cup low-fat milk
3 medium carrots, sliced, cooked and drained
2 medium zucchini, sliced, cooked and drained
½ cup fresh bread crumbs
¼ cup grated Parmesan cheese
1 tablespoon MAZOLA® Margarine, melted

In 1-quart saucepan combine mayonnaise, onion, flour, parsley, salt, Italian seasoning and pepper. Cook over medium heat 1 minute, stirring constantly. Gradually stir in milk until smooth; cook until thick, stirring constantly (*do not boil*). In medium bowl combine carrots and zucchini. Add sauce; toss to coat well. Spoon into shallow 1-quart broilerproof casserole dish. In small bowl combine bread crumbs, Parmesan and margarine; sprinkle over vegetables. Broil, 6 inches from heat source, for 3 minutes or until golden.

Nutrients per serving:

Calories	134	Cholesterol	12 mg
Fat	7 g	Sodium	420 mg

Antipasto Rice

Makes 8 servings

1½ cups water
½ cup tomato juice
1 cup uncooked rice*
1 teaspoon dried basil leaves, crushed
1 teaspoon dried oregano leaves, crushed
½ teaspoon salt (optional)
1 can (14 ounces) artichoke hearts, drained and
   quartered
1 jar (7 ounces) roasted red peppers, drained
   and chopped
1 can (2¼ ounces) sliced ripe olives, drained
2 tablespoons snipped fresh parsley
2 tablespoons lemon juice
½ teaspoon ground black pepper
2 tablespoons grated Parmesan cheese

Antipasto Rice

Combine water, tomato juice, rice, basil, oregano, and salt in 2- to 3-quart saucepan. Bring to a boil; stir once or twice. Reduce heat to low; cover and simmer 15 minutes or until rice is tender and liquid is absorbed. Stir in artichokes, red peppers, olives, parsley, lemon juice, and black pepper. Cook 5 minutes longer or until thoroughly heated. Sprinkle with cheese. Garnish as desired.

To Microwave: Combine water, tomato juice, rice, basil, oregano, and salt in deep 2- to 3-quart microproof baking dish. Cover and cook on HIGH (100% power) 5 minutes. Reduce setting to MEDIUM (50% power) and cook 15 minutes or until rice is tender and liquid is absorbed. Add artichokes, red peppers, olives, parsley, lemon juice, and black pepper. Cook on HIGH 2 to 3 minutes or until mixture is thoroughly heated. Sprinkle with cheese. Garnish as desired.

*Recipe based on regular-milled long grain white rice. For medium grain rice, use 1¼ cups water and cook for 15 minutes. For parboiled rice, use 1¾ cups water and cook for 20 to 25 minutes. For brown rice, use 1¾ cups water and cook for 45 to 50 minutes.

Nutrients per serving:

Calories	131	Cholesterol	1 mg
Fat	2 g	Sodium	522 mg

Favorite recipe from **USA Rice Council**

Pasta Delight

Pasta Delight

Makes 4 to 6 servings

1 medium zucchini, sliced
1 tablespoon olive oil
2 tablespoons chopped shallots
2 cloves garlic, chopped
1 medium tomato, diced
2 tablespoons chopped fresh basil *or*
 ½ teaspoon dried basil leaves, crushed
2 tablespoons grated Parmesan cheese
12 ounces uncooked penne pasta, hot cooked
 and drained

Cook and stir zucchini in hot oil in large skillet over medium-high heat. Reduce heat to medium. Add shallots and garlic; cook and stir 1 minute. Add tomato; cook and stir 45 seconds. Add basil and cheese. Pour vegetable mixture over penne in large bowl; toss gently to mix.

Nutrients per serving:

Calories	237	Cholesterol	51 mg
Fat	5 g	Sodium	51 mg

Favorite recipe from **National Pasta Association**

Vegetable Stuffed Potatoes

Makes 4 servings

1 cup julienned carrots
1 cup thinly sliced green or red bell peppers
¼ teaspoon Italian seasoning
1 tablespoon FLEISCHMANN'S® Margarine
1 cup julienned zucchini
4 (8-ounce) potatoes, hot baked
2 ounces low-fat Monterey Jack cheese,
 shredded

In large skillet over medium-high heat, cook and stir carrots, peppers and Italian seasoning in margarine until vegetables are tender-crisp. Add zucchini; cook and stir until tender, about 1 minute. Carefully cut lengthwise or pierce tops of potatoes and push ends to open. Spoon vegetable mixture into potatoes evenly; top with cheese. Bake at 375°F for 5 minutes or until cheese melts.

Nutrients per serving:

Calories	255	Cholesterol	10 mg
Fat	6 g	Sodium	142 mg

Glazed Stir-Fry Holiday Vegetables

Makes 6 servings, 3 cups

2 tablespoons sugar
½ teaspoon grated lemon peel
3 tablespoons fresh lemon juice (1 lemon)
1 tablespoon low-sodium soy sauce
2 teaspoons cornstarch
½ cup water
4 teaspoons vegetable oil
3 cups fresh broccoli florets
1 medium red bell pepper, cut into 1-inch pieces
1 cup peeled, julienne-cut jicama
 Lemon zest (slivers of lemon peel)

In small bowl combine sugar, lemon peel, lemon juice, soy sauce and cornstarch. Stir in water; set aside.

Heat oil in large nonstick skillet. Add broccoli and pepper and stir-fry over high heat 2 minutes. Add jicama and stir-fry 1 to 2 minutes or until vegetables are crisp-tender, adding additional oil, if necessary. Pour lemon mixture over vegetables and continue cooking just until glaze thickens. Toss vegetables to coat thoroughly with glaze. Garnish with lemon zest.

Nutrients per serving (½ cup):

Calories	95	Cholesterol	0 mg
Fat	3 g	Sodium	72 mg

Favorite recipe from **The Sugar Association, Inc.**

Sweet and Sour Red Cabbage

Makes 6 servings

1 small head red cabbage (1 pound), shredded
1 medium unpeeled apple, cored and shredded
1 small potato, peeled and shredded
1 small onion, chopped
 Grated peel of ½ SUNKIST® Lemon
 Juice of 1 SUNKIST® Lemon
3 tablespoons firmly packed brown sugar
1 tablespoon red wine vinegar

In large covered nonstick skillet, cook cabbage, apple, potato and onion in 1 cup water over low heat for 15 minutes; stir occasionally. Add remaining ingredients. Cover; cook over low heat an additional 10 minutes, stirring often, until vegetables are tender and mixture thickens slightly.

Nutrients per serving (¾ cup):

Calories	74	Cholesterol	0 mg
Fat	0 g	Sodium	11 mg

Onion-Roasted Potatoes

Onion-Roasted Potatoes

Makes 8 servings

1 envelope LIPTON® Recipe Secrets™ Onion or
  Onion-Mushroom Recipe Soup Mix
2 pounds all-purpose potatoes, cut into large
  chunks
⅓ cup olive or vegetable oil

Preheat oven to 450°F. In large plastic food bag or
bowl, combine all ingredients. Close bag and shake
or toss in bowl until potatoes are evenly coated.
Empty potatoes into shallow baking or roasting pan;
discard bag. Bake, stirring occasionally, 40 minutes
or until potatoes are tender and golden brown.
Garnish with chopped fresh parsley, if desired.

*Note: Also terrific with LIPTON® Recipe Secrets™ Savory
Herb with Garlic Recipe Soup Mix.*

Nutrients per serving:			
Calories	174	Cholesterol	0 mg
Fat	9 g	Sodium	385 mg

"Lite" Apricot Stuffing

Makes 8 servings

1 cup sliced celery
¾ cup chopped onion
1½ cups turkey broth or reduced-sodium chicken
  broth
16 slices reduced-calorie bread, cubed and dried
2 tablespoons dried parsley flakes
1½ teaspoons poultry seasoning
½ teaspoon salt
2 egg whites
¼ cup chopped dried apricots

In small saucepan, over medium-high heat, combine
celery, onion and turkey broth; bring to a boil.
Reduce heat to low; cover and simmer 5 minutes
or until vegetables are tender.

In large bowl, combine celery mixture, bread cubes,
parsley, poultry seasoning, salt, egg whites and
apricots. Spoon into lightly greased 2-quart
casserole; cover. Bake at 350°F for 30 minutes
or until heated through.

Nutrients per serving:			
Calories	164	Cholesterol	trace
Fat	2 g	Sodium	566 mg

Favorite recipe from **National Turkey Federation**

Stuffed Tomatoes

Makes 6 to 8 servings

6 to 8 medium tomatoes
2 tablespoons CRISCO® PURITAN® Oil
⅓ cup chopped celery
2 tablespoons chopped onion
2 cups cooked brown rice
¼ cup grated Parmesan cheese
1 tablespoon snipped fresh parsley
1 teaspoon dried basil leaves, crushed
⅛ teaspoon black pepper
⅛ teaspoon garlic powder

Cut thin slice from top of each tomato. Set aside.
Scoop out centers of tomatoes; chop pulp and reserve.
Place shells, upside-down, on paper towels to drain.

Preheat oven to 350°F. Heat Crisco® Puritan® Oil in
medium saucepan. Add celery and onion. Cook and
stir over medium heat until celery is tender. Remove
from heat. Add reserved tomato pulp, rice, Parmesan
cheese, parsley, basil, pepper and garlic powder. Mix
well. Evenly fill each tomato shell with rice mixture.
Replace tomato tops, if desired.

Lightly oil 9-inch pie plate or round baking dish with
Crisco® Puritan® Oil. Place tomatoes in dish. Cover
with aluminum foil.

Bake at 350°F for 30 to 45 minutes or until tomatoes
are tender.

*Note: Use 1 lightly oiled custard cup for each tomato
instead of pie plate or baking dish, if desired.*

Nutrients per serving:			
Calories	125	Cholesterol	2 mg
Fat	5 g	Sodium	65 mg

Vegetable Soufflé in Pepper Cups

Makes 6 servings

1 cup chopped broccoli
½ cup shredded carrot
¼ cup chopped onion
1 teaspoon dried basil leaves, crushed
½ teaspoon ground black pepper
2 teaspoons FLEISCHMANN'S® Margarine
2 tablespoons all-purpose flour
1 cup skim milk
1 container (8 ounces) EGG BEATERS®
    99% Real Egg Product
3 large red, green or yellow bell peppers,
    halved lengthwise

In nonstick skillet over medium-high heat, cook and stir broccoli, carrot, onion, basil and black pepper in margarine until vegetables are tender. Stir in flour until smooth. Gradually add milk, stirring constantly until thickened. Remove from heat; set aside.

In medium bowl, with electric mixer at high speed, beat Egg Beaters® until foamy, about 3 minutes. Gently fold into broccoli mixture; spoon into bell pepper halves. Place in 13×9-inch baking pan. Bake at 375°F for 30 to 35 minutes or until knife inserted in centers comes out clean. Garnish as desired and serve immediately.

Nutrients per serving:			
Calories	75	Cholesterol	1 mg
Fat	2 g	Sodium	91 mg

Sesame-Ginger-Carrot Rice

Makes 4 servings

1⅔ cups water
½ teaspoon salt (optional)
1½ cups uncooked UNCLE BEN'S® Brand
    Rice In An Instant
1 cup shredded carrots
1 teaspoon sesame oil
1 teaspoon shredded fresh ginger
1 green onion with tops, thinly sliced

Bring water and salt to a boil in large saucepan. Stir in rice, carrots, sesame oil and ginger. Cover and remove from heat. Let stand 5 minutes or until all water is absorbed. Sprinkle with green onion before serving.

Nutrients per serving:			
Calories	143	Cholesterol	0 mg
Fat	1 g	Sodium	20 mg

Pea-Pod Medley

Makes 4 servings

2 tablespoons vegetable oil
½ pound snow peas, trimmed
¼ pound mushrooms, sliced
1 yellow or red bell pepper, cut into strips
    Salt and black pepper (optional)

Heat oil in large skillet or wok over medium-high heat. Add vegetables. Stir-fry 4 minutes or until vegetables are crisp-tender. Season with salt and black pepper, if desired.

Nutrients per serving:			
Calories	96	Cholesterol	0 mg
Fat	7 g	Sodium	4 mg

Corn Olé

Makes 6 servings

2 tablespoons margarine
3 cups chopped fresh tomatoes
2 cups fresh corn, cut off the cob (about 4 ears)
2 cups (about ¾ pound) summer squash slices,
    halved
⅓ cup chopped onion
¼ teaspoon black pepper

Melt margarine in large skillet. Add remaining ingredients; cover. Cook 10 to 15 minutes or until squash is tender, stirring occasionally.

Nutrients per serving:			
Calories	111	Cholesterol	0 mg
Fat	5 g	Sodium	59 mg

Corn Olé

Light & Easy Cheese Sauce

Makes about 1¾ cups

1 (8-ounce) package BORDEN® Lite-line®
   Process Cheese Product,* any flavor, each
   slice cut into quarters
1 cup BORDEN® Lite-line® or Viva® Protein
   Fortified Skim Milk
   Ground red pepper (optional)

In medium saucepan, combine ingredients. Over
medium heat, cook and stir until cheese product
melts. Serve warm over fresh or steamed vegetables,
pasta, baked potatoes or LaFamous® Tortilla Chips.

"½ the calories"–8% milkfat product

Nutrients per serving (1 tablespoon sauce):
Calories	18	Cholesterol	2 mg
Fat	trace	Sodium	110 mg

Vegetables Italiano

Makes 8 servings

1 cup Italian seasoned bread crumbs
⅓ cup grated Parmesan cheese
⅔ cup HELLMANN'S® or BEST FOODS®
   Light Reduced Calorie Mayonnaise
6 cups assorted vegetables: broccoli florets,
   carrot slices, cauliflower florets, small
   mushrooms, green and/or red bell pepper
   strips, yellow squash slices and/or zucchini
   strips

Vegetables Italiano

Preheat oven to 425°F. In large plastic food storage
bag combine crumbs and Parmesan; shake to blend
well. In another large plastic food storage bag
combine mayonnaise and vegetables; shake to coat
well. Add mayonnaise-coated vegetables, half at a
time, to crumb mixture; shake to coat well. Arrange
in single layer on ungreased cookie sheet so that
pieces do not touch. Bake 10 minutes or until golden.

Nutrients per serving:
Calories	119	Cholesterol	6 mg
Fat	5 g	Sodium	258 mg

Macaroni Relleno

Makes 6 to 8 servings

1 (7-ounce) package CREAMETTES® Elbow
   Macaroni
1 egg
½ cup skim milk
¼ teaspoon ground cumin
1 (4-ounce) can chopped green chilies, drained
1 (4-ounce) can diced pimentos, drained
   Nonstick cooking spray
1 (15-ounce) can pinto beans, heated and
   drained
1 cup (4 ounces) shredded Monterey Jack cheese
1 medium tomato, peeled, seeded and chopped
1 medium green bell pepper, chopped
¼ cup sliced green onions

Prepare Creamettes® Elbow Macaroni according to
package directions; drain. In medium bowl, blend
egg, milk and cumin; stir in hot cooked macaroni,
chilies and pimento. Spray 9-inch nonstick skillet
with nonstick cooking spray; heat skillet. Add
macaroni mixture. Cover; cook over low heat until
mixture is set, about 15 minutes. Loosen edge with
rubber spatula and invert onto warm platter. Top with
remaining ingredients. Let stand 5 minutes before
serving. Refrigerate leftovers.

Note: *To reduce sodium, rinse and drain chilies, pimentos
and pinto beans; reheat beans in a small amount of water.*

Nutrients per serving:
Calories	260	Cholesterol	135 mg
Fat	6 g	Sodium	96 mg

Almond Brown Rice Stuffing

Almond Brown Rice Stuffing

Makes 6 servings

- ⅓ cup slivered almonds
- 2 teaspoons margarine
- 2 medium tart apples, cored and diced
- ½ cup chopped onion
- ½ cup chopped celery
- ½ teaspoon poultry seasoning
- ¼ teaspoon dried thyme leaves, crushed
- ¼ teaspoon ground white pepper
- 3 cups cooked brown rice (cooked in chicken broth)

Cook and stir almonds in margarine in large skillet over medium-high heat until brown. Add apples, onion, celery, poultry seasoning, thyme, and pepper; cook and stir until vegetables are tender-crisp. Add rice; cook and stir until thoroughly heated. Serve or use as stuffing for poultry or pork roast. Stuffing may be baked in covered baking dish at 375°F for 15 to 20 minutes.

To Microwave: Combine almonds and margarine in 2- to 3-quart microproof baking dish. Cook on HIGH (100% power) 2 to 3 minutes or until browned. Add apples, onion, celery, poultry seasoning, thyme, and pepper. Cover with waxed paper and cook on HIGH 2 minutes. Stir in rice; cook on HIGH 2 to 3 minutes, stirring after 1½ minutes, or until thoroughly heated. Serve as above.

Variations: *For Mushroom Stuffing, add 2 cups (about 8 ounces) sliced mushrooms; cook with apples, onion, celery, and seasonings. For Raisin Stuffing, add ½ cup raisins; cook with apples, onion, celery, and seasonings.*

Nutrients per serving:

Calories	198	Cholesterol	0 mg
Fat	6 g	Sodium	30 mg

Favorite recipe from **USA Rice Council**

Tomatoes with Basil Cream

Makes 10 servings

1 clove garlic
1 container (8 ounces) Light PHILADELPHIA
    BRAND® Pasteurized Process Cream
    Cheese Product
2 tablespoons white wine vinegar
2 tablespoons chopped fresh basil
2 tablespoons chopped fresh parsley, divided
½ teaspoon salt
¼ teaspoon black pepper
2 red tomatoes, thinly sliced
2 yellow tomatoes, thinly sliced

Place garlic in blender or food processor container; cover. Process until finely chopped.

Add cream cheese product, vinegar, basil, 1 tablespoon parsley, salt and pepper; blend until smooth.

Arrange tomatoes on serving platter. Spoon cream cheese mixture over tomatoes. Sprinkle with remaining 1 tablespoon parsley. Garnish with fresh basil leaves, if desired.

Prep time: 15 minutes

Nutrients per serving:

Calories	60	Cholesterol	15 mg
Fat	trace	Sodium	240 mg

Herbed Spaghetti Side Dish

Makes 6 servings

1 (7-ounce) package CREAMETTE® Spaghetti,
    uncooked
2 tablespoons chopped fresh parsley
2 tablespoons grated Parmesan cheese
1 tablespoon soft margarine
1 tablespoon olive oil
1 teaspoon salt-free herb seasoning
¼ teaspoon black pepper

Prepare CREAMETTE® Spaghetti according to package directions; drain. Combine hot cooked spaghetti with remaining ingredients; toss to coat. Serve immediately. Refrigerate leftovers.

Nutrients per serving:

Calories	170	Cholesterol	2 mg
Fat	6 g	Sodium	64 mg

Saucy Skillet Potatoes

Makes 6 to 8 servings

1 tablespoon MAZOLA® Margarine
1 cup chopped onions
½ cup HELLMANN'S® or BEST FOODS® Light
    Reduced Calorie Mayonnaise
⅓ cup cider vinegar
1 tablespoon sugar
1 teaspoon salt
¼ teaspoon freshly ground black pepper
4 medium potatoes, cooked, peeled and sliced
1 tablespoon chopped fresh parsley
1 tablespoon crumbled cooked bacon or real
    bacon bits

In large skillet, melt margarine over medium heat. Add onions; cook and stir 2 to 3 minutes or until tender-crisp. Stir in mayonnaise, vinegar, sugar, salt and pepper. Add potatoes; cook, stirring constantly, 2 minutes or until hot (*do not boil*). Sprinkle with parsley and bacon.

Nutrients per serving:

Calories	128	Cholesterol	5 mg
Fat	6 g	Sodium	308 mg

Arroz Mexicana

Makes 4 to 6 servings

1 tablespoon vegetable oil
1 onion, chopped
2 cloves garlic, crushed
½ teaspoon dried oregano leaves, crushed
¾ cup uncooked rice
1 can (14½ ounces) DEL MONTE® Mexican
    Style Stewed Tomatoes
1 green bell pepper, chopped

In large skillet, heat oil over medium-high heat. Add onion, garlic and oregano; cook and stir until onion is tender. Stir in rice; cook until rice is golden, stirring frequently. Drain tomatoes reserving liquid; pour liquid into measuring cup. Add water to measure 1½ cups. Stir into rice mixture; bring to a boil. Reduce heat; cover and simmer 15 minutes or until rice is tender. Stir in tomatoes and bell pepper; cook 5 minutes. Garnish with chopped parsley, if desired.

Prep time: 5 minutes
Cook time: 22 minutes

Nutrients per serving:

Calories	207	Cholesterol	0 mg
Fat	4 g	Sodium	265 mg

Tomatoes with Basil Cream

Risotto with Peas and Mushrooms

Makes 6 servings

½ cup chopped onion
2 teaspoons margarine
1 cup uncooked rice
⅓ cup dry white wine
1 cup chicken broth
4 cups water
1 cup frozen peas, thawed
1 jar (2½ ounces) sliced mushrooms, drained
¼ cup grated Parmesan cheese
¼ teaspoon ground white pepper
⅓ cup 2% low-fat milk

Cook and stir onion in margarine in skillet over medium-high heat until soft. Add rice and cook, stirring constantly, 2 to 3 minutes. Add wine; stir until absorbed. Stir in broth. Cook, uncovered, stirring constantly, until broth is absorbed. Continue stirring and adding water, 1 cup at a time, allowing each cup to be absorbed before adding another, until rice is tender and has a creamy consistency, 20 to 25 minutes. Stir in remaining ingredients. Stir until creamy, 1 to 2 minutes. Serve immediately.

Tip: *Medium grain rice will yield the best consistency for risottos, but long grain rice can be used.*

Nutrients per serving:

Calories	205	Cholesterol	4 mg
Fat	6 g	Sodium	316 mg

Favorite recipe from **USA Rice Council**

Risotto with Peas and Mushrooms

Vegetable Oat Pilaf

Makes 8 servings

½ cup chopped mushrooms
½ cup chopped green bell pepper
½ cup sliced green onions
1 tablespoon vegetable oil
1¾ cups QUAKER® Oats (quick or old fashioned, uncooked)
2 egg whites *or* ¼ cup egg substitute
¾ cup low-sodium chicken broth
1 medium tomato, seeded, chopped

In large saucepan, cook and stir mushrooms, green pepper and onions in oil over medium heat 2 to 3 minutes. In small bowl, mix oats and egg whites until oats are evenly coated. Add oats to vegetable mixture in skillet; cook and stir over medium heat until oats are dry and separated, about 5 to 6 minutes. Add broth; continue cooking and stirring 2 to 3 minutes until liquid is absorbed. Stir in tomato. Serve immediately.

Nutrients per serving:

Calories	101	Cholesterol	0 mg
Fat	3 g	Sodium	20 mg

Red, Green & Gold Squash Platter

Makes 8 servings

1 pound red bell peppers (about 3 medium)
2 tablespoons olive oil
¼ teaspoon grated lemon peel
1 tablespoon lemon juice
½ teaspoon dill weed
   Salt and black pepper to taste (optional)
3 cups *each* zucchini slices and crookneck squash slices
⅓ cup BLUE DIAMOND® Sliced Natural Almonds, toasted

To Microwave: Core and quarter red bell peppers. Place in single layer in glass baking dish. Cover; microwave at HIGH (100% power) for 10 minutes. Process peppers and remaining ingredients except squash and almonds in blender container or food processor until smooth. Place squash in 9-inch square glass baking dish. Cover; microwave on HIGH 3 to 4 minutes until tender-crisp. Spoon squash onto serving platter. Toss with almonds. Drizzle with red pepper sauce to serve.

Nutrients per serving:

Calories	84	Cholesterol	0 mg
Fat	6 g	Sodium	140 mg

Broccoli with Tangerine Ginger Sauce

Makes 6 servings

½ cup chopped onion
2 teaspoons crystallized ginger
1 teaspoon margarine
1 carton (8 ounces) low-fat lemon yogurt
    Grated peel of 1 fresh tangerine
2 California-Arizona tangerines, peeled,
    segmented and seeded
1½ pounds broccoli, trimmed *or* 2 packages
    (10 ounces *each*) frozen broccoli spears, hot
    cooked and drained

In small nonstick skillet over low heat, cook and stir onion and ginger in margarine until onion is very tender. Stir in yogurt, tangerine peel and segments. Cook and stir over low heat until heated through (*do not boil*). Serve sauce over hot cooked broccoli. Garnish with additional grated tangerine peel, if desired.

Nutrients per serving (includes about 3½ tablespoons sauce):

Calories	103	Cholesterol	3 mg
Fat	2 g	Sodium	57 mg

Favorite recipe from **Sunkist Growers, Inc.**

Creole Stuffed Peppers

Makes 6 servings

6 large green bell peppers
    Boiling water
½ cup chopped onion
1 tablespoon margarine
2 cups chopped fresh tomatoes
2 cups fresh okra slices
2 cups fresh corn, cut off the cob (about 4 ears)
⅛ teaspoon black pepper

Preheat oven to 350°F. Cut off tops of bell peppers; remove seeds and membranes. Add bell peppers to boiling water in large saucepan; cover. Boil 5 minutes; drain. Cool. In large saucepan over medium heat, cook and stir onion in margarine. Add tomatoes, okra, corn and black pepper; cook until mixture is thoroughly heated and slightly thickened. Fill bell peppers with corn mixture; place in greased shallow baking dish. Bake 30 minutes or until bell peppers are tender.

Nutrients per serving:

Calories	119	Cholesterol	0 mg
Fat	3 g	Sodium	39 mg

Left to right: Creole Stuffed Peppers, Grilled Vegetable Kabobs

Grilled Vegetable Kabobs

Makes 4 servings

12 large fresh mushrooms
    Boiling water
¼ cup Italian dressing
2 tablespoons fresh lemon or lime juice
1½ teaspoons Worcestershire sauce
2 medium zucchini, cut into 1-inch diagonal
    slices
4 cherry tomatoes

Place mushrooms in medium bowl; cover with boiling water. Let stand 1 minute; drain. Combine dressing, lemon juice and Worcestershire sauce in small bowl. Alternately thread mushrooms and zucchini on four skewers. Grill kabobs over medium coals about 10 minutes, turning and brushing frequently with dressing mixture. Remove from heat. Thread cherry tomatoes onto ends of skewers. Continue grilling 5 minutes, turning and brushing with remaining dressing mixture. Garnish as desired.

Nutrients per serving:

Calories	44	Cholesterol	1 mg
Fat	2 g	Sodium	141 mg

Vegetable Gratin

Vegetable Gratin

Makes 4 servings

¼ cup FRENCH'S® Creamy Spread™ Mustard
2 tablespoons olive oil
½ teaspoon *each* Italian seasoning and garlic powder
¼ cup plain dry bread crumbs
3 small (12 ounces) zucchini, thinly sliced
3 medium (12 ounces) tomatoes, thinly sliced
½ cup (2 ounces) shredded low-fat mozzarella cheese

In small bowl, combine French's® Creamy Spread™ Mustard, oil and spices. Mix 1 tablespoon mustard mixture with bread crumbs; set aside. In lightly greased 9-inch pie plate, layer half the zucchini, slightly overlapping slices. Dot zucchini with some of mustard mixture. Layer half the tomatoes over zucchini in pie plate; dot with some of mustard mixture. Sprinkle with mozzarella cheese. Repeat with remaining zucchini, tomatoes and mustard mixture. Bake, uncovered, at 400°F for 30 minutes until vegetables are tender. Sprinkle with reserved bread crumb mixture. Bake, uncovered, for 5 minutes or until crumbs are golden brown. Garnish as desired.

Nutrients per serving:

Calories	167	Cholesterol	5 mg
Fat	10 g	Sodium	375 mg

Crispened New Potatoes

Makes 4 servings

1½ pounds new potatoes (about 12)
½ cup QUAKER® Oat Bran hot cereal, uncooked
2 tablespoons grated Parmesan cheese
1 tablespoon snipped fresh parsley *or* 1 teaspoon dried parsley flakes
½ teaspoon snipped fresh dill *or* ½ teaspoon dried dill weed
½ teaspoon paprika
1 egg white, slightly beaten
¼ cup skim milk
1 tablespoon margarine, melted

Heat oven to 400°F. Lightly spray 11×7-inch dish with nonstick cooking spray or oil lightly. Cook whole potatoes in boiling water 15 minutes. Drain; rinse in cold water.

In shallow dish, combine oat bran, cheese, parsley, dill and paprika. In another shallow dish, combine egg white and milk. Coat each potato in oat bran mixture; shake off excess. Dip into egg mixture, then coat again with oat bran mixture. Place in prepared dish; drizzle with margarine. Cover; bake 10 minutes. Uncover; bake an additional 10 minutes or until potatoes are tender.

Nutrients per serving:

Calories	230	Cholesterol	0 mg
Fat	5 g	Sodium	110 mg

Delicious Sliced Apples

Makes 6 to 8 servings

½ cup firmly packed brown sugar
2 tablespoons all-purpose flour
Dash ground cloves
2½ pounds apples, pared, cored and sliced (about 8 cups)
¼ cup CRISCO® Shortening
¼ cup water

Combine brown sugar, flour and cloves in large bowl. Stir in apple slices and toss lightly. Melt Crisco® in large skillet. Stir in apple mixture and cook over high heat for 5 minutes, stirring occasionally. Stir in water. Bring mixture to a boil; cover and reduce heat to low. Simmer for 10 minutes or until apples are tender, stirring occasionally. Serve with roast beef or turkey, if desired.

Nutrients per serving:

Calories	195	Cholesterol	0 mg
Fat	6 g	Sodium	7 mg

Cheddar Sesame Garden Vegetables

Makes 4 side-dish or 2 entrée servings

1 tablespoon plus 2 teaspoons all-purpose flour
½ cup *undiluted* CARNATION® Lite Evaporated Skimmed Milk
¼ cup water
1 teaspoon country-style Dijon mustard
½ cup (2 ounces) shredded low-fat Cheddar cheese
3 to 4 cups steamed fresh vegetables (carrots, summer squash, broccoli, cauliflower or asparagus)
1 tablespoon toasted sesame seeds

Place flour in small saucepan; whisk in small amount of evaporated skimmed milk. Stir in remaining evaporated skimmed milk with water and mustard. Cook over medium heat, stirring constantly, until mixture comes to a boil and thickens. Add cheese; stir until melted. Serve over vegetables. Sprinkle with sesame seeds.

Nutrients per serving:			
Calories	148	Cholesterol	12 mg
Fat	5 g	Sodium	162 mg

Corn-on-the-Cob with Chili Spread

Makes 4 servings

4 ears of corn
3 tablespoons margarine, softened
1 tablespoon snipped fresh chives
1 teaspoon chili powder
    Salt and black pepper (optional)

Bring large pan of water to a boil. Add corn; boil 5 minutes. Meanwhile, combine margarine, chives and chili powder in small bowl.

Remove corn from water; spread with margarine mixture. Season with salt and pepper, if desired.

Nutrients per serving:			
Calories	161	Cholesterol	0 mg
Fat	10 g	Sodium	119 mg

Shrimp Stuffing

Makes 8 servings

1 pound raw shrimp, cleaned, quartered
2 tablespoons margarine
1 package (6 ounces) KELLOGG'S® CROUTETTES® Stuffing Mix
½ cup chopped celery
½ cup sliced green onions
¼ cup chopped green bell pepper
1 can (10¾ ounces) condensed cream of mushroom soup
¾ cup water
1 teaspoon dry mustard
1 teaspoon lemon juice
½ teaspoon Cajun seasoning
¼ teaspoon salt (optional)
½ cup (2 ounces) shredded part-skim mozzarella cheese

In 12-inch skillet, cook and stir shrimp in margarine over medium heat just until shrimp start to change color.

Stir in remaining ingredients *except* cheese, tossing gently to moisten. Reduce heat to low. Cover and cook 5 minutes. Remove from heat and stir in cheese.

To Microwave: In 4-quart microwave-safe mixing bowl, melt margarine at HIGH (100% power) 1 minute. Stir in shrimp and remaining ingredients *except* cheese. Cover with plastic wrap, leaving one corner open to vent. Microwave at HIGH 9 minutes or until stuffing is hot and shrimp are opaque, stirring every 3 minutes. (When stirring stuffing, carefully remove plastic from bowl to allow steam to escape.) Stir in cheese.

Nutrients per serving:			
Calories	220	Cholesterol	95 mg
Fat	7 g	Sodium	827 mg

Shrimp Stuffing

Vegetable 'n Bean Pilaf

Makes 8 servings, 4 cups

1⅓ cups water
 ½ cup uncooked long-grain rice
 1 carrot, finely chopped
 1 can (16 ounces) black-eyed peas, rinsed and drained
 1 can (7 ounces) whole kernel corn, drained
 ⅓ cup WISH-BONE® Healthy Sensation! Honey Dijon Dressing
 2 tablespoons chopped fresh parsley

In 2-quart saucepan, bring water to a boil. Stir in uncooked rice and chopped carrot. Simmer, covered, 20 minutes or until liquid is absorbed and rice is tender. Stir in black-eyed peas, corn and Honey Dijon Dressing; heat through. Stir in parsley; serve immediately.

Nutrients per serving:

Calories	126	Cholesterol	0 mg
Fat	trace	Sodium	333 mg

Light Italian Spaghetti Primavera

Makes 6 servings

 ½ of a (1-pound) package CREAMETTE® Thin Spaghetti, uncooked
 ½ cup bottled reduced-calorie Italian salad dressing
 1 medium green bell pepper, chopped
 1 medium red bell pepper, chopped
 1 medium yellow squash, cut into strips
 1 cup sliced fresh mushrooms
 ¼ cup chopped onion
 3 tablespoons sliced pitted ripe olives
 ¼ cup shredded part-skim mozzarella cheese
 3 tablespoons chopped fresh parsley

Light Italian Spaghetti Primavera

Prepare Creamette® Thin Spaghetti according to package directions; drain. In large skillet, combine Italian dressing, vegetables and olives; simmer just until vegetables are tender-crisp. Serve over hot cooked spaghetti; sprinkle with cheese and parsley. Refrigerate leftovers.

Nutrients per serving:

Calories	205	Cholesterol	8 mg
Fat	5 g	Sodium	218 mg

Oriental Fried Rice

Makes 6 servings

 3 cups cooked brown rice, cold
 ½ cup slivered cooked roast pork
 ½ cup finely chopped celery
 ½ cup fresh bean sprouts*
 ⅓ cup sliced green onions
 1 egg, beaten
 Nonstick cooking spray
 ¼ teaspoon black pepper
 2 tablespoons soy sauce

Combine rice, pork, celery, bean sprouts, onions, and egg in large skillet coated with nonstick cooking spray. Cook, stirring, 3 minutes over high heat. Add pepper and soy sauce. Cook, stirring, 1 minute longer.

To Microwave: Combine rice, pork, celery, bean sprouts, and onions in shallow 2-quart microproof baking dish coated with nonstick cooking spray. Cook on HIGH (100% power) 2 to 3 minutes. Add egg, pepper, and soy sauce. Cook on HIGH 1 to 2 minutes or until egg is set, stirring to separate grains.

*Substitute canned bean sprouts, rinsed and drained, for fresh, if desired.

Tip: When preparing fried rice always begin with cold rice. The grains separate better if cold and it's a great way to use leftover rice.

Nutrients per serving:

Calories	156	Cholesterol	45 mg
Fat	3 g	Sodium	310 mg

Favorite recipe from **USA Rice Council**

Stuffed Acorn Squash

Makes 4 to 6 servings

- 1 acorn squash
- 3 tablespoons orange juice
- 1 tablespoon firmly packed brown sugar
- ¼ teaspoon ground cinnamon
  Dash ground nutmeg

To Microwave: Cut acorn squash crosswise in half. Scoop out seeds and fibers; discard. Place two halves in microwave-safe casserole dish. Prick squash pulp several times with fork (do not pierce squash rind).

Combine remaining ingredients in small dish. Pour evenly into squash halves. Cover casserole dish. Microwave at HIGH (100% power) 15 to 20 minutes or until fork tender, rotating dish halfway through cooking. Remove from microwave; let cool slightly. Pour orange juice mixture from squash halves into medium bowl. Carefully scoop out squash pulp, leaving at least one shell intact; add to orange juice mixture. Mash with fork until mixture is well blended. Spoon squash mixture back into one shell. Serve in shell.

Nutrients per serving:

Calories	84	Cholesterol	0 mg
Fat	trace	Sodium	7 mg

Favorite recipe from **The Sugar Association, Inc.**

Scalloped Pineapple

Makes 6 servings

- 1 can (20 ounces) crushed pineapple in juice
- 2 tablespoons CRISCO® Shortening
- ⅛ teaspoon crushed dried mint leaves *or* wintergreen extract
- 4 bread slices, torn into small pieces
  Milk
- 2 tablespoons sugar
- ⅛ teaspoon salt
- 1 egg, beaten

Preheat oven to 375°F. Drain pineapple; reserve juice. Melt Crisco® in medium saucepan; stir in mint. Remove from heat. Stir in pineapple and bread; mix. Turn into ungreased 1-quart casserole. Add enough milk to reserved juice to make 1 cup. Stir in sugar, salt and egg. Pour over pineapple mixture; stir lightly. Bake 40 minutes or until knife inserted in center comes out clean. Serve with baked ham, if desired.

Nutrients per serving:

Calories	177	Cholesterol	37 mg
Fat	6 g	Sodium	157 mg

Dilled New Potatoes and Peas

Dilled New Potatoes and Peas

Makes 8 servings, about 4 cups

- 1 pound (6 to 8) small new potatoes, quartered
- 2 cups frozen peas
- 1 jar (12 ounces) HEINZ® HomeStyle Turkey Gravy
- ½ cup light dairy sour cream
- 1 teaspoon dried dill weed

Cook potatoes in 2-quart saucepan in lightly salted boiling water 10 to 15 minutes or until tender. Add peas; cook 1 minute. Drain well. Combine gravy, sour cream and dill; stir into vegetable mixture. Heat (*do not boil*), stirring occasionally.

To Microwave: Place potatoes and 2 tablespoons water in 2-quart casserole. Cover with lid or vented plastic wrap. Microwave at HIGH (100% power) 6 to 7 minutes or until potatoes are just tender, stirring once. Stir in peas. Cover and microwave at HIGH 1 minute. Combine gravy, sour cream and dill; stir into vegetable mixture. Cover and microwave at HIGH 7 to 8 minutes or until heated through, stirring once.

Nutrients per serving (about ½ cup):

Calories	126	Cholesterol	6 mg
Fat	1 g	Sodium	332 mg

Spinach Feta Rice

Spinach Feta Rice

Makes 6 servings

1 cup uncooked long-grain white rice
1 cup chicken broth
1 cup water
1 medium onion, chopped
1 cup (about 4 ounces) sliced fresh mushrooms
2 cloves garlic, minced
   Nonstick cooking spray
1 tablespoon lemon juice
½ teaspoon dried oregano leaves, crushed
6 cups shredded fresh spinach leaves (about ¼ pound)
4 ounces feta cheese, crumbled
   Freshly ground black pepper
   Chopped pimiento for garnish (optional)

Combine rice, broth, and water in medium saucepan. Bring to a boil; stir once or twice. Reduce heat to low; cover and simmer 15 minutes or until rice is tender and liquid is absorbed. Cook and stir onion, mushrooms, and garlic in large skillet coated with nonstick cooking spray until onion is tender. Add mushroom mixture, lemon juice, oregano, spinach, cheese, and black pepper to hot cooked rice; toss lightly until spinach is wilted. Garnish with pimiento.

To Microwave: Combine rice, broth, and water in deep 2- to 3-quart microproof baking dish. Cover and cook on HIGH (100% power) 5 minutes. Reduce setting to MEDIUM (50% power) and cook 15 minutes or until rice is tender and liquid is absorbed. Combine onion, mushrooms, and garlic in 1-quart microproof baking dish coated with nonstick cooking spray. Cook on HIGH 2 to 3 minutes. Add mushroom mixture, lemon juice, oregano, spinach, cheese, and black pepper to hot cooked rice. Cook on HIGH 1 to 2 minutes or until spinach is wilted. Garnish with pimiento.

Nutrients per serving:			
Calories	195	Cholesterol	17 mg
Fat	5 g	Sodium	387 mg

Favorite recipe from **USA Rice Council**

Italian Vegetable Sauté

Makes 4 to 6 servings

2 tablespoons CRISCO® Oil
1 clove garlic, minced
¼ teaspoon dried oregano leaves, crushed
¼ teaspoon dried marjoram leaves, crushed
2 cups julienne-cut zucchini
1 small onion, thinly sliced and separated into rings
1 can (16 ounces) whole tomatoes, drained, cut up
2 tablespoons sliced pitted black olives (optional)
½ teaspoon salt
⅛ teaspoon black pepper
2 tablespoons grated Parmesan cheese

Heat Crisco® Oil in large skillet. Add garlic, oregano and marjoram. Cook and stir over medium heat until garlic is light brown. Add zucchini and onion; stir until coated. Cook and stir 5 to 7 minutes or until tender. Stir in tomatoes, olives, salt and pepper. Cook until heated through. Stir in Parmesan cheese.

Nutrients per serving:			
Calories	77	Cholesterol	1 mg
Fat	5 g	Sodium	334 mg

Garden Medley Spaghetti

Makes 6 servings

½ of a (1-pound) package CREAMETTE® Thin Spaghetti, uncooked
2 tablespoons margarine
2 cloves garlic, minced
2 cups finely shredded carrots
1 medium zucchini, cut into julienne strips
¾ cup chopped onion
2 tablespoons grated Parmesan cheese
1 tablespoon chopped fresh dill *or* 1 teaspoon dill weed
½ teaspoon salt-free herb seasoning

Prepare Creamette® Spaghetti according to package directions; drain. In medium skillet, heat margarine with garlic. Add carrots, zucchini and onion; cook and stir until vegetables are tender. Toss vegetables with hot cooked spaghetti, Parmesan cheese, dill and seasoning. Serve immediately. Refrigerate leftovers.

Nutrients per serving:			
Calories	213	Cholesterol	2 mg
Fat	6 g	Sodium	101 mg

Light Garden Spaghetti

Makes 6 servings

- 1 (10-ounce) package frozen chopped broccoli, thawed and well drained
- ½ pound carrots *or* zucchini, sliced, cooked and drained
- ¼ cup chopped onion
- 1 clove garlic, finely chopped
- 3 tablespoons diet margarine
- ¼ cup unsifted flour
- 1 teaspoon WYLER'S® or STEERO® Chicken-Flavor Instant Bouillon *or* 1 Chicken-Flavor Bouillon Cube
- ½ teaspoon thyme leaves
- 2 cups BORDEN® Lite-line® or Viva® Protein Fortified Skim Milk
- 6 slices BORDEN® Lite-line® American or Swiss Flavor Process Cheese Product,* cut into pieces
- 1 (2½-ounce) jar sliced mushrooms, drained
- ½ of a (1-pound) package CREAMETTE® Spaghetti, cooked according to package directions and drained

In large saucepan, cook and stir onion and garlic in margarine until tender. Stir in flour, bouillon and thyme; gradually add milk. Over medium heat, cook and stir until mixture thickens. Add cheese product pieces; stir until melted. Add broccoli, carrots and mushrooms; heat through. Serve over hot cooked Creamette® spaghetti. Refrigerate leftovers.

*"½ the calories"–8% milkfat product

Nutrients per serving:

Calories	260	Cholesterol	9 mg
Fat	7 g	Sodium	579 mg

Light Garden Spaghetti

Zucchini Bake

Makes 9 servings

- ⅔ cup QUAKER® Oat Bran hot cereal, uncooked
- ½ teaspoon Italian seasoning
- ¼ teaspoon black pepper
- 1 egg white
- 1 tablespoon water
- 2 medium zucchini, sliced ¾ inch thick, quartered (about 3 cups)
- 1 small onion, chopped
- ⅔ cup low-sodium tomato sauce
- 2 teaspoons olive oil
- 2 teaspoons grated Parmesan cheese
- ¼ cup (1 ounce) shredded part skim mozzarella cheese

Heat oven to 375°F. Lightly spray 8-inch square baking dish with nonstick cooking spray, or oil lightly. In large plastic food bag, combine oat bran, Italian seasoning and pepper; mix well. In shallow dish, lightly beat egg white and water. Coat zucchini with oat bran mixture; shake off excess. Dip into egg mixture, then coat again with oat bran mixture. Place zucchini in prepared dish; sprinkle with onion. Spoon combined tomato sauce and oil over vegetables. Sprinkle with Parmesan cheese. Bake 30 minutes or until zucchini is crisp-tender; top with mozzarella cheese. Serve warm.

To Microwave: In large plastic food bag, combine oat bran, Italian seasoning and pepper; mix well. In shallow dish, lightly beat egg white and water. Coat zucchini with oat bran mixture; shake off excess. Dip into egg mixture, then coat again with oat bran mixture. Place zucchini in 8-inch square microwavable dish; sprinkle with onion. Spoon combined tomato sauce and oil over vegetables. Sprinkle with Parmesan cheese. Microwave at HIGH (100% power) 5½ to 6½ minutes or until zucchini is crisp-tender, rotating dish ½ turn after 3 minutes. Sprinkle with mozzarella cheese. Let stand 3 minutes before serving. Serve warm.

Nutrients per serving:

Calories	60	Cholesterol	1 mg
Fat	2 g	Sodium	35 mg

Cheese-Crumb Baked Tomatoes

Makes 4 servings

¾ cup (3 ounces) finely shredded Wisconsin
    Part-Skim Mozzarella Cheese, divided
⅓ cup fine, dry unseasoned bread crumbs
1 to 1½ tablespoons fresh chopped herbs
    (oregano, parsley and/or rosemary) *or* 1 to
    1½ teaspoons dried herbs, crushed
1 large clove garlic, minced
4 tomatoes (about 2½ inches in diameter),
    cored and cut into 3 slices each

Preheat oven to 475°F. In small bowl, mix half the
cheese, bread crumbs, herbs and garlic until
thoroughly blended. Arrange tomato slices on oiled
baking sheet. Top tomatoes evenly with some of the
crumb mixture, then with remaining cheese. Bake
10 to 12 minutes until crumbs are lightly browned.

Nutrients per serving:

Calories	112	Cholesterol	13 mg
Fat	4 g	Sodium	171 mg

Favorite recipe from **Wisconsin Milk Marketing Board** ©1993

Microwave Glazed Carrots, Apples and Peppers

Makes 5 servings

2 cups thin diagonal carrot slices
1 cup green bell pepper chunks (½-inch pieces)
3 tablespoons water
1½ cups thinly sliced peeled apples
¼ cup firmly packed light brown sugar
1 teaspoon cornstarch
½ teaspoon ground cinnamon
2 teaspoons margarine

To Microwave: Combine carrots and bell pepper in
1-quart microwave-safe dish; add water. Cover; cook at
HIGH (100% power) 3 minutes or until carrots are crisp-
tender. Drain; add apples and toss gently. In small mixing
bowl, combine brown sugar, cornstarch and cinnamon. Cut
in margarine with fork until mixture resembles coarse
crumbs. Sprinkle mixture over apple-vegetable mixture.
Cover; cook at HIGH 3 minutes. Stir to coat vegetables
with glaze; cook, uncovered, at HIGH 2 to 3 minutes or
until glaze thickens.

Nutrients per serving (½ cup):

Calories	124	Cholesterol	0 mg
Fat	2 g	Sodium	63 mg

Favorite recipe from **The Sugar Association, Inc.**

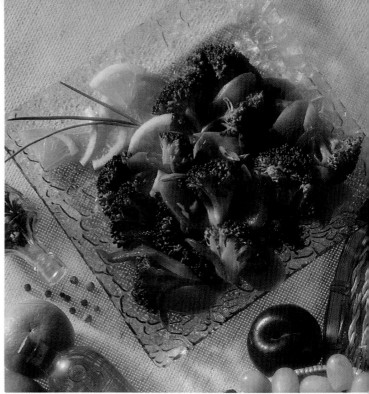

Chinese Sweet and Sour Vegetables

Chinese Sweet and Sour Vegetables

Makes 4 servings

3 cups broccoli florets
2 medium carrots, diagonally sliced
1 large red bell pepper, cut into short, thin strips
¼ cup water
2 teaspoons cornstarch
1 teaspoon sugar
⅓ cup unsweetened pineapple juice
1 tablespoon soy sauce
1 tablespoon rice vinegar
½ teaspoon Oriental sesame oil
¼ cup diagonally sliced green onions or
    chopped cilantro (optional)

Combine broccoli, carrots and red pepper in large
skillet with tight-fitting lid. Add water; bring to a boil
over high heat. Reduce heat to medium. Cover and
steam 4 minutes or until vegetables are crisp-tender.

Meanwhile, combine cornstarch and sugar in small
bowl. Blend in pineapple juice, soy sauce and vinegar
until smooth.

Transfer vegetables to colander; drain. Stir pineapple
mixture and add to skillet. Cook and stir 2 minutes or
until sauce boils and thickens. Return vegetables to
skillet; toss with sauce. Stir in sesame oil. Garnish
with onions, if desired.

Nutrients per serving:

Calories	68	Cholesterol	0 mg
Fat	1 g	Sodium	289 mg

Bacon Pilaf

Cinnamon-Apple Sweet Potatoes

Makes 4 servings

4 medium sweet potatoes
1½ cups finely chopped apples
½ cup orange juice
¼ cup sugar
1½ teaspoons cornstarch
½ teaspoon ground cinnamon
½ teaspoon grated orange peel

To Microwave: Wash sweet potatoes and prick with fork. Place on paper towels. Microwave at HIGH (100% power) 10 to 13 minutes or until tender, turning halfway through cooking. Set aside. In small bowl, combine remaining ingredients. Cover; cook at HIGH 3 minutes. Stir mixture and continue cooking, uncovered, at HIGH 1½ to 2½ minutes or until sauce is thickened. Slit sweet potatoes and spoon sauce over each.

Tip: *Sauce may be made up ahead and reheated at serving time.*

Nutrients per serving:

Calories	216	Cholesterol	0 mg
Fat	trace	Sodium	12 mg

Favorite recipe from **The Sugar Association, Inc.**

Bacon Pilaf

Makes 4 to 6 servings

2 tablespoons unsalted margarine or butter
2 medium tomatoes, coarsely chopped
¼ cup sliced green onions
8 slices ARMOUR® Lower Salt Bacon, cooked crisp and crumbled
1 cup uncooked rice
1 teaspoon no-salt-added chicken flavor instant-bouillon

Melt margarine in large skillet or saucepan over medium heat. Add tomatoes and green onions; cook and stir for 2 minutes. Stir in 2 cups water and remaining ingredients. Heat to a boil; reduce heat to low and cover. Simmer 20 to 25 minutes or until liquid is absorbed. Fluff rice with fork. Garnish with fresh parsley, if desired.

To Microwave: Place margarine, tomatoes and green onions in large microwave-safe casserole dish. Cook, covered, on HIGH (100% power) for 5 minutes. Add 2 cups water and remaining ingredients; cover. Cook on HIGH for 5 minutes. Reduce setting to MEDIUM-HIGH (70% power); cook 10 to 12 minutes or until liquid is absorbed. Let stand, covered, 5 minutes. Fluff rice with fork before serving. Garnish as above.

Nutrients per serving:

Calories	197	Cholesterol	8 mg
Fat	8 g	Sodium	175 mg

Sautéed Zucchini and Tomato

Makes 4 servings

¼ cup WISH-BONE® Italian Dressing
2 medium zucchini, thinly sliced
1 medium onion, thinly sliced
1 can (14½ ounces) whole peeled tomatoes, undrained and chopped
1 tablespoon chopped fresh basil leaves*
Salt and black pepper (optional)

In large skillet, heat Italian dressing over medium heat. Add zucchini and onion; cook, stirring occasionally, 5 minutes or until vegetables are almost tender. Stir in tomatoes with juice, basil, salt and pepper. Bring to a boil. Reduce heat to low and simmer uncovered, stirring occasionally, 20 minutes or until zucchini is tender and sauce is slightly thickened. Serve with grated Parmesan cheese, if desired.

***Substitution:** Use ½ teaspoon dried basil leaves, crushed.*

Note: *Also terrific with WISH-BONE® Robusto Italian or Blended Italian.*

Nutrients per serving:

Calories	112	Cholesterol	0 mg
Fat	8 g	Sodium	286 mg

Almond Ratatouille

Makes 6 servings

¾ pound small new potatoes
1 medium eggplant, cubed (about 4 cups)
2 medium zucchini, sliced (about 2 cups)
2 tomatoes, chopped
1 red bell pepper, sliced
1 onion, thinly sliced
½ cup vegetable cocktail juice
2 tablespoons *each* chopped fresh cilantro and lime juice
2 tablespoons balsamic or red wine vinegar
1 tablespoon chopped fresh basil*
2 cloves garlic, minced
1½ teaspoons chopped dill*
⅔ cup blanched slivered almonds, toasted

To Microwave: Cut potatoes into bite-sized pieces. Place in 8×12-inch microwave-safe dish. Cover; microwave at HIGH (100% power) 2 minutes. Stir in remaining ingredients except almonds. Cover; microwave at HIGH 15 minutes, stirring every 5 minutes until vegetables are tender-crisp and potatoes are cooked through. Remove from oven; stir in almonds and chill thoroughly before serving.

*Or use 1 teaspoon dried basil and ½ teaspoon dill weed.

Note: Hot Almond Ratatouille makes a wonderful topping for baked potatoes or broiled fish.

Nutrients per serving:			
Calories	190	Cholesterol	0 mg
Fat	8 g	Sodium	86 mg

Favorite recipe from **Almond Board of California**

Tomato Caper Sauce over Pasta

Makes 8 servings

2 crushed garlic cloves
3 tablespoons olive oil
3½ cups (28-ounce can) CONTADINA®
   Whole Peeled Tomatoes, cut up, with juice
½ cup rinsed and drained capers
¼ cup chopped fresh cilantro
1 tablespoon chopped fresh basil
1 tablespoon chopped fresh thyme
1 pound rigatoni, cooked and drained
   Dash black pepper

Cook and stir garlic in hot oil in medium saucepan until lightly browned. Add tomatoes with juice and capers. Reduce heat to low and simmer, uncovered, about 20 minutes. Stir in cilantro, basil and thyme. Simmer an additional 5 minutes. Toss hot pasta with sauce and pepper.

To Microwave: Combine garlic and oil in 2-quart microwave-safe dish. Microwave on HIGH (100% power) 3 minutes. Add tomatoes and capers. Microwave on HIGH 8 minutes, stirring after 4 minutes. Stir in cilantro, basil and thyme. Microwave on HIGH 1 minute. Toss hot pasta with sauce and pepper.

Nutrients per serving:			
Calories	280	Cholesterol	0 mg
Fat	7 g	Sodium	340 mg

Fresh Corn Sauté

Makes 4 to 6 servings

4 ears fresh corn
4 ounces fresh pea pods
1 red bell pepper, cut into strips
¼ cup sliced green onions
1½ teaspoons WYLER'S® or STEERO®
   Chicken-Flavor Instant Bouillon
1 teaspoon sugar
2 tablespoons olive or vegetable oil
   Freshly ground black pepper

Remove husks and silk from corn; cut corn from cobs. In large skillet, cook and stir corn, pea pods, red pepper, green onions, bouillon and sugar in oil until vegetables are tender-crisp. Serve with black pepper. Refrigerate leftovers.

Nutrients per serving:			
Calories	111	Cholesterol	0 mg
Fat	5 g	Sodium	235 mg

Fresh Corn Sauté

Penne with Artichokes

Makes 4 to 6 servings

    1 package (10 ounces) frozen artichoke hearts
1¼ cups water
    2 tablespoons lemon juice
    5 cloves garlic, minced
    2 tablespoons olive oil, divided
    2 ounces sun-dried tomatoes in oil, drained
    2 small dried hot red peppers, crushed
    2 tablespoons chopped fresh parsley
    ¼ teaspoon salt
    ¼ teaspoon black pepper
    ¾ cup fresh bread crumbs
    1 tablespoon chopped garlic
  12 ounces uncooked penne, hot cooked and
        drained
    1 tablespoon grated Romano cheese

Cook artichokes in water and lemon juice in medium saucepan over medium heat until tender. Cool artichokes, then cut into quarters. Reserve artichoke liquid. Cook and stir 5 cloves minced garlic in 1½ tablespoons oil in large skillet over medium-high heat until golden. Reduce heat to low. Add artichokes and tomatoes; simmer 1 minute. Stir in artichoke liquid, red peppers, parsley, salt and black pepper. Simmer 5 minutes.

Meanwhile, in small skillet, cook and stir bread crumbs and 1 tablespoon chopped garlic in remaining ½ tablespoon oil. In large bowl, pour artichoke sauce over penne; toss gently to coat. Sprinkle with bread crumb mixture and cheese.

Nutrients per serving:			
Calories	287	Cholesterol	1 mg
Fat	7 g	Sodium	220 mg

Favorite recipe from **National Pasta Association**

Cranberry Fruit Dressing

Makes 8 servings

    3 cups herb-seasoned stuffing mix
    2 cups chopped mixed dried fruit
    1 cup chopped celery
    1 cup whole-berry cranberry sauce
    ⅔ cup chopped onion
    ½ teaspoon ground dried sage
    ½ teaspoon dried thyme leaves, crushed
1½ cups turkey broth or low-sodium chicken
        bouillon
       Nonstick cooking spray

Preheat oven to 325°F. In medium bowl, combine stuffing mix, dried fruit, celery, cranberry sauce, onion, sage, thyme and turkey broth. Coat 2-quart ovenproof dish with cooking spray. Spoon dressing into dish and bake, uncovered, 40 to 45 minutes.

Nutrients per serving:			
Calories	260	Cholesterol	0 mg
Fat	2 g	Sodium	420 mg

Favorite recipe from **National Turkey Federation**

Lemon Herb Broccoli

Makes 2 to 3 servings

    1 bunch DOLE® Broccoli, cut into florets
    2 tablespoons margarine
    3 to 4 tablespoons lemon juice
    1 tablespoon Dijon-style mustard
    ½ teaspoon dried marjoram leaves, crumbled

Steam broccoli over boiling water in large saucepan 3 to 4 minutes until tender-crisp.

Melt margarine in small saucepan over medium heat. Blend in lemon juice, mustard and marjoram. Spoon over broccoli. Serve with grilled chicken breasts or broiled fish steaks.

Prep time: 5 minutes
Cook time: 10 minutes

Nutrients per serving:			
Calories	118	Cholesterol	0 mg
Fat	8 g	Sodium	192 mg

Wild Rice Sauté

Makes 6 servings

    ½ cup sliced fresh mushrooms
    ¼ cup chopped green onions
    1 clove garlic, minced
    2 tablespoons HOLLYWOOD® Safflower Oil
    3 cups cooked wild rice
    ¼ teaspoon salt
    ¼ teaspoon ground black pepper
    ¼ teaspoon dried rosemary sprigs, crushed
    2 tablespoons peach schnapps liqueur

In a large skillet, cook and stir mushrooms, onions and garlic in hot oil for 1½ minutes. Add rice, seasonings and peach schnapps; cook 1½ minutes longer, stirring frequently.

Nutrients per serving:			
Calories	143	Cholesterol	0 mg
Fat	5 g	Sodium	97 mg

Penne with Artichokes

VEGETABLES & SIDE DISHES

Summer Squash Casserole

Family Baked Bean Dinner

Makes 6 servings

½ DOLE® Green Bell Pepper, cut into strips
½ cup chopped onion
⅓ cup brown sugar, packed
1 teaspoon dry mustard
2 cans (16 ounces each) baked beans
1 can (20 ounces) DOLE® Pineapple Chunks, drained

To Microwave: Place green pepper and onion in 12×8-inch microwave dish. Cover; microwave on HIGH (100% power) 3 minutes. In large mixing bowl, combine brown sugar and mustard; stir in beans and pineapple. Add to green pepper mixture. Stir to combine. Microwave, uncovered, on HIGH 8 to 10 minutes, stirring after 4 minutes. Serve with Polish sausage or hot dogs, if desired.

Nutrients per serving:

Calories	273	Cholesterol	0 mg
Fat	1 g	Sodium	678 mg

Summer Squash Casserole

Makes 4 servings

1 tablespoon FILIPPO BERIO®
    100% Pure Olive Oil, divided
½ pound *each* zucchini and yellow squash, cut
    into ¼-inch slices
1 teaspoon salt (optional)
    Black pepper to taste
3 tablespoons grated Parmesan cheese
3 ounces sliced fontina or mozzarella cheese

Preheat oven to 350°F. Lightly coat 13×9-inch baking pan with small amount of olive oil. Arrange ⅓ of zucchini and squash in pan. Sprinkle with ⅓ of salt, pepper, Parmesan cheese and remaining olive oil. Repeat layers twice. Bake for 25 minutes. Place cheese slices on top of zucchini; bake for an additional 5 to 8 minutes until cheese melts. Garnish with chopped fresh parsley, if desired. Serve immediately.

Nutrients per serving:

Calories	165	Cholesterol	10 mg
Fat	10 g	Sodium	276 mg

Spanish Rice au Gratin

Makes 4 servings

    Nonstick cooking spray
½ cup chopped onion
½ cup chopped celery
⅓ cup chopped green bell pepper
1 can (16 ounces) whole tomatoes, drained and
    chopped
1 teaspoon chili powder
½ teaspoon Worcestershire sauce
2 cups cooked brown rice
½ cup (2 ounces) shredded Cheddar cheese

Coat large skillet with nonstick cooking spray and place over medium-high heat until hot. Add onion, celery, and bell pepper; cook and stir until tender crisp. Add tomatoes, chili powder, and Worcestershire sauce. Stir in rice. Reduce heat; simmer about 5 minutes to blend flavors. Remove from heat. Top with cheese; cover and allow cheese to melt, about 3 minutes.

Tip: *Add your favorite canned beans, cooked ground beef or chicken for a main-dish version.*

Nutrients per serving:

Calories	204	Cholesterol	15 mg
Fat	6 g	Sodium	314 mg

Favorite recipe from **USA Rice Council**

Risotto Milanese

Makes 6 servings

1 small onion, thinly sliced
1 tablespoon margarine
1 cup uncooked Arborio or other short-grain
    rice
    Pinch saffron
½ cup dry white wine
¼ teaspoon TABASCO® pepper sauce
2 cups low-sodium chicken broth, divided
    Hot water
¼ cup grated Parmesan cheese
    Salt and freshly ground white pepper
    (optional)

In large skillet, cook and stir onion in margarine over medium-high heat until soft. Add rice and saffron; cook, stirring constantly, 2 to 3 minutes. Add wine and TABASCO sauce; stir until absorbed. Stir in 1 cup broth. Cook, uncovered, stirring frequently until broth is absorbed. Add remaining broth and hot water, ½ cup at a time, stirring constantly and scraping sides of pan frequently. (Wait until rice just begins to dry out before adding more liquid.) Continue stirring and adding water until rice is tender but firm and is the consistency of creamy rice pudding.* Stir in cheese, and salt and pepper, if desired.

The total amount of liquid used will vary. Watch rice carefully to ensure proper consistency.)

Nutrients per serving:			
Calories	178	Cholesterol	3 mg
Fat	4 g	Sodium	94 mg

Marinara Sauce

Makes 5 servings, 2½ cups sauce

1 tablespoon FILIPPO BERIO®
    100% Pure Olive Oil
1 small onion, chopped
1 medium clove garlic, minced
1 can (28 ounces) crushed tomatoes,
    undrained, *or* 3 pounds fresh tomatoes,
    peeled, seeded and chopped
2 tablespoons chopped fresh parsley
1 teaspoon salt
1 teaspoon dried basil leaves, crushed
½ teaspoon sugar

In 3-quart saucepan, heat oil over medium-high heat. Add onion and garlic; cook and stir until onion is tender. Add tomatoes with juice and remaining ingredients. Simmer 20 minutes, stirring occasionally, until slightly thickened. Serve over pasta.

Nutrients per serving:			
Calories	70	Cholesterol	0 mg
Fat	3 g	Sodium	686 mg

Couscous with Summer Vegetables

Makes 6 servings

1½ cups PRITIKIN® Chicken Broth or water
1 cup whole wheat couscous
1 large onion, chopped
1 medium red bell pepper, diced
1 small yellow squash or zucchini, sliced
2 cloves garlic, minced
1 medium tomato, seeded and chopped
¼ cup chopped fresh basil

Bring broth to a boil in small saucepan. Stir in couscous; reduce heat to low. Cover and simmer 5 minutes or until most of liquid is absorbed. Meanwhile, lightly spray large skillet with nonstick cooking spray. Add onion, bell pepper, squash and garlic. Cook over medium-high heat 5 minutes or until vegetables are tender, stirring frequently. Add cooked couscous, tomato and basil; heat through. Serve with freshly ground black pepper, if desired.

Nutrients per serving:			
Calories	140	Cholesterol	0 mg
Fat	0 g	Sodium	55 mg

Couscous with Summer Vegetables

Cottage Spinach Un-Quiche

Makes 8 servings

4 eggs
1 (16-ounce) container BORDEN® Lite-line® or
   Viva® Lowfat Cottage Cheese
1 (10-ounce) package frozen chopped spinach,
   thawed and *well drained*
2 tablespoons flour
2 teaspoons Dijon-style mustard
1 teaspoon WYLER'S® or STEERO®
   Chicken-Flavor Instant Bouillon

Preheat oven to 350°F. In large bowl, beat eggs; add remaining ingredients. Pour into lightly oiled 9-inch pie plate. Bake 35 to 40 minutes or until set. Let stand 10 minutes before serving. Refrigerate leftovers.

Nutrients per serving:			
Calories	108	Cholesterol	111 mg
Fat	4 g	Sodium	422 mg

Sweet 'n Sour Stir-Fry

Makes 6 servings

¾ cup WISH-BONE® Lite Sweet 'n Sour Spicy
   French Dressing
2 tablespoons firmly packed brown sugar
2 teaspoons soy sauce
2 tablespoons vegetable oil
1 cup thinly sliced carrots
1 cup snow peas (about 4 ounces)
1 small green bell pepper, cut into chunks
1 cup drained sliced water chestnuts
1 medium tomato, cut into wedges
½ cup sliced cucumber, halved

Sweet 'n Sour Stir-Fry

Blend salad dressing, brown sugar and soy sauce in small bowl; set aside. In medium skillet, heat oil and cook carrots, snow peas and green bell pepper over medium heat, stirring frequently, 5 minutes or until crisp-tender. Add water chestnuts, tomato, cucumber and salad dressing mixture. Simmer, covered, 5 minutes or until vegetables are tender. Top with sesame seeds, if desired.

Nutrients per serving:			
Calories	137	Cholesterol	0 mg
Fat	5 g	Sodium	349 mg

Asparagus Dijon

Makes 6 servings

1 container (8 ounces) Light PHILADELPHIA
   BRAND® Pasteurized Process Cream
   Cheese Product
2 tablespoons lemon juice
2 tablespoons skim milk
1 tablespoon Dijon-style mustard
1½ pounds asparagus spears, cooked, chilled

Place all ingredients except asparagus in blender or food processor container; cover. Blend until smooth. Cover; refrigerate. Arrange asparagus on individual plates; pour dressing over asparagus. Garnish with lemon peel, if desired.

Prep time: 15 minutes plus refrigerating

Nutrients per serving:			
Calories	120	Cholesterol	20 mg
Fat	7 g	Sodium	300 mg

Nutty Vegetable Duo

Makes 4 servings

1 (10-ounce) package frozen green beans
8 ounces frozen small whole onions
¼ cup toasted slivered almonds
1 tablespoon margarine
   Salt and black pepper (optional)

Combine beans and onions in medium saucepan; cook according to package directions. Drain.

Return vegetables to saucepan. Add almonds and margarine; stir over low heat until margarine is melted and mixture is thoroughly heated. Season with salt and black pepper, if desired.

Nutrients per serving:			
Calories	103	Cholesterol	0 mg
Fat	7 g	Sodium	50 mg

Vegetable Bundles

Makes 4 to 6 servings

- ¼ cup fresh lemon juice
- 2 tablespoons sugar
- 2 tablespoons water
- 1 teaspoon margarine
- ¼ teaspoon garlic powder
- 1 large carrot, cut into thin 3-inch-long sticks
- ½ cup thin strips red bell pepper
- ½ cup whole green beans
- 2 to 3 green onions, white parts removed and discarded

To Microwave: In small microwave-safe dish, combine lemon juice, sugar, water, margarine and garlic powder. Microwave at HIGH (100% power) for 30 seconds; stir.

In another small microwave-safe casserole dish, place carrot sticks, pepper strips and beans. Add lemon juice mixture. Microwave at HIGH 6 to 10 minutes until vegetables are tender-crisp.

Cut green onions crosswise in half. Microwave at HIGH 5 to 10 seconds until just slightly limp. Remove vegetables from lemon juice mixture; divide evenly into 4 to 6 bundles. Gently tie green onion half around each bundle to secure. Serve warm or cold.

Nutrients per serving:

Calories	55	Cholesterol	0 mg
Fat	1 g	Sodium	20 mg

Favorite recipe from **The Sugar Association, Inc.**

Guilt-Free Turkey Gravy

Makes 4 cups

- 4 tablespoons cornstarch
- 4 tablespoons water
- 4 cups Turkey Broth (recipe follows)
  Salt and black pepper (optional)

In small bowl combine cornstarch and water. In large saucepan over medium heat, bring Turkey Broth and pan juices to a boil. Stir in cornstarch mixture and continue heating until gravy boils and thickens. Season to taste with salt and pepper.

Turkey Broth: In large saucepan over high heat, bring 4 cups water, Turkey Giblets, 1 sliced celery stalk, 1 sliced carrot, 1 sliced onion, 1 bay leaf, 3 parsley sprigs and 4 peppercorns to a boil. Reduce heat to low; simmer for about 1 hour. Strain and defat broth.

Nutrients per serving (3 tablespoons gravy):

Calories	85	Cholesterol	41 mg
Fat	7 g	Sodium	22 mg

Favorite recipe from **National Turkey Federation**

Tangy Asparagus Linguini

Tangy Asparagus Linguini

Makes 4 servings

- 2 tablespoons light margarine
- ¼ cup finely chopped onion
- 3 cloves garlic, minced
- 8 ounces fresh asparagus, peeled and sliced diagonally into ½-inch pieces
- 2 tablespoons dry white wine
- 2 tablespoons fresh lemon juice
  Freshly ground black pepper
- 5 ounces linguini, cooked and drained
- ¼ cup (1 ounce) SARGENTO® Grated Parmesan Cheese
- ¾ cup (3 ounces) SARGENTO® Preferred Light Fancy Supreme Shredded Mozzarella Cheese

Melt margarine over medium heat in large skillet. Cook and stir onion and garlic until onion is soft. Add asparagus; cook and stir for an additional 2 minutes. Add wine and lemon juice; cook an additional minute. Season with pepper to taste. Remove from heat. In large bowl, toss hot pasta, Parmesan cheese and asparagus mixture. Remove to serving platter; sprinkle with mozzarella cheese. Garnish with strips of lemon zest, if desired. Serve immediately.

Nutrients per serving:

Calories	254	Cholesterol	13 mg
Fat	8 g	Sodium	317 mg

Yes, it is possible to have your cake—and eat it too! These light and luscious recipes include moist, tender layer cakes, melt-in-your-mouth pound cakes and rich, creamy cheesecakes. For a fit finale at your next special occasion, Chocolate Cherry Delight Cake is sure to steal the show!

Chocolate Cherry Delight Cake

Makes 12 servings

1 cup sugar
1 cup all-purpose flour
⅓ cup HERSHEY'S Cocoa
¾ teaspoon baking soda
¾ teaspoon baking powder
    Dash salt
½ cup skim milk
¼ cup frozen egg substitute, thawed
¼ cup vegetable oil
1 teaspoon vanilla extract
½ cup boiling water
    Whipped Topping (recipe follows)
1 can (20 ounces) lower calorie cherry pie filling, chilled

Heat oven to 350°F. Line bottom of two 9-inch round pans with waxed paper.

In large mixer bowl, combine sugar, flour, cocoa, baking soda, baking powder and salt. Add milk, egg substitute, oil and vanilla; beat on medium speed 2 minutes. Remove from mixer; stir in boiling water (batter will be thin). Pour into prepared pans. Bake 18 to 22 minutes or until wooden toothpick inserted in centers comes out clean. Cool 10 minutes; remove from pans to wire racks. Carefully remove waxed paper. Cool completely.

To assemble dessert, place one cake layer on serving plate. Spread with half of Whipped Topping; top with half of pie filling. Top with second layer. Spread with remaining topping and pie filling. Refrigerate at least 1 hour.

Whipped Topping: In small, deep, narrow-bottom bowl, blend ½ cup cold skim milk, ½ teaspoon vanilla extract and 1 envelope whipped topping mix (to yield 2 cups). Whip at high speed with electric mixer until topping peaks, about 2 minutes. Continue beating 2 minutes longer until topping is light and fluffy.

Nutrients per serving:

Calories	180	Cholesterol	0 mg
Fat	5 g	Sodium	115 mg

Lemon Poppy Seed Cake

Makes 16 servings

Cake
1 package DUNCAN HINES® Moist Deluxe Lemon Supreme Cake Mix
3 egg whites
1¼ cups water
⅓ cup CRISCO® PURITAN® Oil
3 tablespoons poppy seeds

Glaze
1 cup confectioners sugar
3 to 4 teaspoons lemon juice

1. Preheat oven to 350°F. Grease and flour 10-inch Bundt® pan.

2. For Cake, combine cake mix, egg whites, water, oil and poppy seeds in large bowl. Prepare, bake and cool cake following package directions for No Cholesterol recipe.

3. For Glaze, combine sugar and lemon juice in small bowl. Stir until well blended. Drizzle over top of cake.

Nutrients per serving:

Calories	207	Cholesterol	0 mg
Fat	8 g	Sodium	221 mg

Chocolate Cherry Delight Cake

Fudge Marble Pound Cake

Fudge Marble Pound Cake

Makes 2 loaves, 18 slices each

1 package DUNCAN HINES® Moist Deluxe
    Fudge Marble Cake Mix
1 package (4-serving size) vanilla instant
    pudding and pie filling mix
4 eggs
1 cup water
⅓ cup CRISCO® PURITAN® Oil

1. Preheat oven to 350°F. Grease and flour two
9×5×3-inch loaf pans.

2. Set aside cocoa packet from Mix. Combine cake
mix, pudding mix, eggs, water and Crisco® Puritan®
Oil in large bowl. Beat at medium speed with electric
mixer for 2 minutes. Measure 1 cup batter; place in
small bowl. Stir in contents of reserved cocoa packet.

3. Spoon half the yellow batter into each loaf pan.
Spoon half the chocolate batter over yellow batter in
each pan. Run knife through batters to marble. Bake
at 350°F for 45 to 50 minutes or until wooden
toothpick inserted in centers comes out clean. Cool in
pans 5 minutes. Loosen cakes from pans. Invert onto
cooling racks. Cool completely. Cut cakes in ½-inch-
thick slices.

Nutrients per serving (1 slice):			
Calories	86	Cholesterol	24 mg
Fat	4 g	Sodium	108 mg

Apple Chiffon Cake

Makes 12 servings

Cake
⅓ cup CRISCO® PURITAN® Oil
¾ cup sugar
2 eggs
¾ cup all-purpose flour
½ teaspoon baking powder
¼ teaspoon salt
¼ teaspoon baking soda
¼ teaspoon ground nutmeg
¼ teaspoon ground ginger
1 cup finely chopped peeled apples (about
    2 medium)

Topping
2 tablespoons sugar
2 tablespoons finely chopped walnuts
½ teaspoon cinnamon

For Cake, heat oven to 350°F. Combine Crisco®
Puritan® Oil and sugar in large bowl at medium
speed of electric mixer. Add eggs. Beat well.

Combine flour, baking powder, salt, baking soda,
nutmeg and ginger. Add to oil mixture. Beat until just
blended. Stir in apples. Spread evenly in ungreased
9×9×2-inch pan.

For Topping, combine sugar, nuts and cinnamon.
Sprinkle over batter.

Bake at 350°F for 25 to 30 minutes or until wooden
toothpick inserted in center comes out clean. Cut into
3×2¼-inch rectangles. Serve warm or at room
temperature.

To Microwave: Prepare Cake and Topping as above.
Spread cake batter in ungreased 11×7-inch microwave-safe
dish. Place in microwave on rack or on glass pie plate
turned upside down. Cover lightly with waxed paper.
Microwave at MEDIUM (50% power) 6 minutes; rotate
dish after 3 minutes. Remove waxed paper. Microwave at
HIGH (100% power) 5 minutes. Rotate dish after
2 minutes. Cut into 3×2¼-inch rectangles. Serve as above.

Nutrients per serving:			
Calories	162	Cholesterol	36 mg
Fat	8 g	Sodium	86 mg

Chocolate Cake Fingers

1 cup granulated sugar
1 cup all-purpose flour
⅓ cup HERSHEY₂S Cocoa
¾ teaspoon baking powder
¾ teaspoon baking soda
½ cup skim milk
¼ cup thawed frozen egg substitute
¼ cup canola oil or vegetable oil
1 teaspoon vanilla extract
½ cup boiling water
   Powdered sugar
1 teaspoon freshly grated orange peel
1½ cups thawed frozen nondairy whipped topping
42 fresh strawberries or raspberries (optional)

Heat oven to 350°F. Line bottom of 13×9-inch baking pan with waxed paper. In large mixer bowl, stir together granulated sugar, flour, cocoa, baking powder and baking soda. Add milk, egg substitute, oil and vanilla; beat on medium speed of electric mixer 2 minutes. Add water, stirring with spoon until well blended. Pour batter into prepared pan.

Bake 16 to 18 minutes or until wooden toothpick inserted in center comes out clean. Place towel on wire rack; sprinkle with powdered sugar. Invert cake on towel; peel off waxed paper. Turn cake right side up. Cool completely. Cut cake into 42 small rectangles (about 2×1¼ inches). Stir orange peel into whipped topping; spoon dollop on each piece of cake. Garnish with strawberry or raspberry, if desired.

Nutrients per serving:			
Calories	80	Cholesterol	0 mg
Fat	3 g	Sodium	35 mg

Della Robbia Cake

Cake
1 package DUNCAN HINES® Angel Food
   Cake Mix
1½ teaspoons grated lemon peel

Glaze
6 tablespoons sugar
1½ tablespoons cornstarch
1 cup water
1 tablespoon lemon juice
½ teaspoon vanilla extract
   Few drops red food coloring
6 cling peach slices
6 medium strawberries, sliced

1. Preheat oven to 375°F.

2. For Cake, prepare cake following package directions adding lemon peel with Cake Flour Mixture (red "B" packet). Bake and cool cake following package directions.

3. For Glaze, combine sugar, cornstarch and water in small saucepan. Cook over medium-high heat until mixture boils and thickens. Remove from heat. Stir in lemon juice, vanilla extract and red food coloring.

4. Alternate peach slices with strawberry slices around top of cooled cake. Pour glaze over fruit and top of cake. Refrigerate leftovers.

Nutrients per serving:			
Calories	145	Cholesterol	0 mg
Fat	0 g	Sodium	100 mg

Della Robbia Cake

Orange Poppy Seed Cake

Makes 16 servings

1 container (8 ounces) Light PHILADELPHIA
    BRAND® Pasteurized Process Cream
    Cheese Product
⅓ cup PARKAY® Margarine, softened
1 cup sugar
3 eggs, separated
2 cups flour
1 teaspoon CALUMET® Baking Powder
1 teaspoon baking soda
1 cup BREAKSTONE'S® LIGHT CHOICE®
    Sour Half and Half
2 tablespoons poppy seeds
1 tablespoon grated orange peel
½ cup sugar *or* 12 packets sugar substitute
½ cup orange juice
3 tablespoons powdered sugar

Preheat oven to 350°F.

Beat cream cheese product, margarine and 1 cup
sugar in large mixing bowl at medium speed with
electric mixer until well blended. Add egg yolks, one
at a time, mixing well after each addition.

Mix together flour, baking powder and baking soda;
add to cream cheese mixture alternately with sour half
and half. Stir in poppy seeds and orange peel.

Beat egg whites in small mixing bowl at high speed
with electric mixer until stiff peaks form; fold into
cream cheese mixture. Pour into greased 10-inch
fluted tube pan. Bake 50 minutes.

Stir together ½ cup sugar and orange juice in small
saucepan over low heat until sugar dissolves. Prick
hot cake several times with fork. Pour syrup over
cake; cool 10 minutes. Invert onto serving plate. Cool
completely. Sprinkle with powdered sugar. Garnish
with quartered orange slices, if desired.

Nutrients per serving:			
Calories	228	Cholesterol	48 mg
Fat	9 g	Sodium	157 mg

Spicy Pumpkin Torte

Makes 12 servings

Cake
1 package DUNCAN HINES® Moist Deluxe
    Yellow Cake Mix
1 teaspoon ground cinnamon
½ teaspoon ground nutmeg
¼ teaspoon ground cloves

Filling
1 package (4-serving size) butterscotch flavor
    instant pudding and pie filling mix
½ teaspoon ground cinnamon
¼ teaspoon ground ginger
⅛ teaspoon ground cloves
⅛ teaspoon ground nutmeg
2 cups skim milk, divided
½ cup solid pack pumpkin (not pumpkin pie
    filling)
1 envelope whipped topping mix
½ teaspoon vanilla

Garnish
2 tablespoons reserved filling

1. Preheat oven to 350°F. Grease and flour two 8- or
9-inch round cake pans.

2. For Cake, combine cake mix, cinnamon, nutmeg
and cloves in large bowl. Prepare, bake and cool cake
following package directions for No Cholesterol
recipe. Refrigerate cooled layers for ease in splitting.

3. For Filling, combine pudding mix, cinnamon,
ginger, cloves and nutmeg. Stir in 1½ cups milk.
Prepare pudding following cooking instructions on
package. Add pumpkin. Stir until well blended. Place
plastic wrap on surface of pudding. Refrigerate until
cool.

4. Prepare whipped topping using remaining ½ cup
milk and vanilla, following package directions
for mixing. Remove 2 tablespoons filling; reserve.
Fold whipped topping into remaining filling.

5. To assemble torte, split each cake layer in half
horizontally. Spread one-fourth whipped topping
mixture on one cake layer. Top with second cake
layer. Repeat with remaining cake layers, spreading
last fourth of mixture on top.

6. For Garnish, dot top with reserved filling. Swirl
with tip of knife. Refrigerate until ready to serve.

Note: *Unused pumpkin can be used to make cookies or
muffins.*

Nutrients per serving:			
Calories	259	Cholesterol	1 mg
Fat	10 g	Sodium	327 mg

Orange Poppy Seed Cake

Royal Banana Fruit Shortcake

Makes 8 servings

- 2 **extra-ripe medium DOLE® Bananas, peeled**
- 1 **package (18 ounces) yellow cake mix**
  Ingredients to prepare cake mix
- ½ **cup DOLE® Sliced Almonds**
- ¾ **cup DOLE® Pine-Orange-Guava Juice, divided**
- 1 **firm medium DOLE® Banana, peeled**
- 2 **cups assorted sliced DOLE® fresh fruit**
- ¼ **cup semisweet chocolate chips**
- ½ **teaspoon margarine**

Place 2 extra-ripe bananas in blender. Blend until smooth. Prepare cake according to package directions, using blended bananas as part of the liquid measured with water.

Spread batter in 2 greased 9-inch round cake pans. Sprinkle tops with almonds. Bake and cool as directed. Use one layer for recipe; freeze second layer for future use.

Pour 3 tablespoons fruit juice onto large cake plate. Place cake on top to absorb juice. Pour another 3 tablespoons juice over cake.

Slice firm banana and combine with other fruits in small bowl. Reserve 1 tablespoon fruit juice for chocolate sauce; pour remaining 5 tablespoons juice over fruit. Arrange fruit and juice mixture over cake.

Royal Banana Fruit Shortcake

Combine chocolate chips, 1 tablespoon reserved fruit juice and margarine in small microwave-safe bowl. Microwave on HIGH (100% power) 10 to 30 seconds or until chocolate chips are soft. Stir until smooth. Drizzle over fruit and cake. Refrigerate 30 minutes.

Prep time: 15 minutes
Bake time: 30 minutes

Nutrients per serving:

Calories	208	Cholesterol	81 mg
Fat	7 g	Sodium	60 mg

Mocha Fudge Marble Delight

Makes 12 servings

Cake
- 1 **package DUNCAN HINES® Moist Deluxe**
  Fudge Marble Cake Mix
- 1 **tablespoon FOLGERS® Coffee Crystals**
  (optional)
- 1 **teaspoon ground cinnamon (optional)**
- 3 **egg whites**
- 1¼ **cups water**
- ⅓ **cup CRISCO® PURITAN® Oil**

Frosting
- 1 **teaspoon FOLGERS® Coffee Crystals**
- ¼ **teaspoon ground cinnamon**
- ¼ **teaspoon hot water**
- 1¼ **cups skim milk**
- 1 **package (4-serving size) sugar-free chocolate**
  flavor instant pudding and pie filling mix
- 2 **envelopes (1.3 ounces each) whipped**
  topping mix
  Chocolate jimmies or decors (optional)

1. Preheat oven to 350°F. Grease and flour two 8- or 9-inch round cake pans.

2. For Cake, empty cake mix into large bowl. Add coffee crystals and cinnamon, if desired. Add egg whites, water and oil. Prepare, bake and cool cake following package directions for No Cholesterol recipe.

3. For Frosting, combine coffee, cinnamon and hot water in custard cup. Place milk in large bowl. Add pudding mix and topping mix. Blend at low speed of electric mixer. Blend in coffee mixture. Beat at high speed 2 to 3 minutes or until stiff, scraping sides and bottom of bowl frequently. Spread between layers, on sides and on top of cake. Sprinkle with chocolate jimmies, if desired.

Nutrients per serving:

Calories	242	Cholesterol	trace
Fat	9 g	Sodium	309 mg

Banana Graham Snacking Cake

Makes 24 servings

1¼ cups all-purpose flour
1 cup NABISCO® Graham Cracker Crumbs
2 teaspoons DAVIS® Baking Powder
1 teaspoon baking soda
⅓ cup FLEISCHMANN'S® Margarine, softened
1¼ cups sugar
¾ cup EGG BEATERS® 99% Real Egg Product
1¼ cups mashed bananas (about 2 large)
⅔ cup plain nonfat yogurt
½ cup walnuts, chopped (optional)
Confectioner's sugar (optional)

In small bowl, combine flour, graham cracker crumbs, baking powder and baking soda; set aside.

In large bowl, with electric mixer at medium speed, beat margarine and sugar until well combined. At low speed, blend in Egg Beaters® and bananas. Add flour mixture alternately with yogurt, mixing until smooth. Stir in walnuts, if desired.

Spoon batter into greased and floured 13×9×2-inch baking pan. Bake at 350°F for 45 minutes or until wooden toothpick inserted in center comes out clean. Cool in pan on wire rack. Dust with confectioner's sugar before serving.

Nutrients per serving (without nuts and confectioner's sugar):

Calories	124	Cholesterol	0 mg
Fat	3 g	Sodium	128 mg

Chocolate Banana Low-Fat Cupcakes

Chocolate Banana Low-Fat Cupcakes

Makes 20 cupcakes

2 cups all-purpose flour
¾ cup sugar, divided
¼ cup HERSHEY'S Cocoa or HERSHEY'S Premium European Style Cocoa
¾ teaspoon baking soda
½ teaspoon baking powder
¼ teaspoon salt
¾ cup (8-ounce container) plain low-fat yogurt (1.5% milkfat)
½ cup mashed ripe banana (about 1 medium)
⅓ cup all-vegetable canola oil
¼ cup skim milk
2 teaspoons vanilla extract
3 egg whites
White Glaze (recipe follows)

Heat oven to 350°F. Line muffin pans with paper or foil-laminated paper baking cups (2½ inches in diameter). In large bowl, stir together flour, ¼ cup sugar, cocoa, baking soda, baking powder and salt; set aside. In small bowl, stir together yogurt, banana, oil, milk and vanilla; set aside. In medium mixer bowl, beat egg whites until soft peaks form. Gradually beat in remaining ½ cup sugar; beat until stiff peaks form. Stir yogurt mixture into flour mixture until dry ingredients are moistened; fold in ⅓ of egg white mixture. Gently fold in remaining egg white mixture. Fill muffin cups ¾ full. Bake 20 to 25 minutes or until wooden toothpick inserted in centers comes out clean. Remove from muffin pans to wire racks; cool completely. Drizzle tops of cupcakes with White Glaze.

White Glaze: In small bowl, combine ½ cup powdered sugar with 3 to 4 teaspoons warm water; stir until smooth and of desired consistency.

Nutrients per serving (1 cupcake):

Calories	140	Cholesterol	0 mg
Fat	4 gm	Sodium	74 mg

Blueberry Angel Food Cake Roll

Blueberry Angel Food Cake Rolls

Makes 2 cakes, 8 servings each

1 package DUNCAN HINES® Angel Food
   Cake Mix
   Confectioners sugar
1 can (21 ounces) blueberry pie filling
¼ cup confectioners sugar
   Mint leaves, for garnish (optional)

1. Preheat oven to 350°F. Line two 15½×10½×1-inch jelly-roll pans with aluminum foil.

2. Prepare cake following package directions. Divide into pans. Spread evenly. Cut through batter with knife or spatula to remove large air bubbles. Bake at 350°F for 15 minutes or until set. Invert cakes at once onto clean, lint-free dishtowels dusted with confectioners sugar. Remove foil carefully. Roll up each cake with towel jelly-roll fashion, starting at short end. Cool completely.

3. Unroll cakes. Spread about 1 cup blueberry pie filling to within 1 inch of edges on each cake. Reroll and place seam-side down on serving plate. Dust with ¼ cup confectioners sugar. Garnish with mint leaves, if desired.

Nutrients per serving:			
Calories	143	Cholesterol	0 mg
Fat	0 g	Sodium	77 mg

Carrot Pudding Cake with Lemon Sauce

Makes 8 servings

⅓ cup firmly packed brown sugar
¼ cup liquid vegetable oil margarine
½ cup frozen apple juice concentrate, thawed
3 egg whites, slightly beaten
1 cup QUAKER® Oat Bran hot cereal, uncooked
½ cup all-purpose flour
2 teaspoons baking powder
1 teaspoon ground cinnamon
2 cups shredded carrots (about 4 or 5 medium)
½ cup granulated sugar
4 teaspoons cornstarch
1 cup hot water
1 tablespoon liquid vegetable oil margarine
1 tablespoon lemon juice
½ teaspoon grated lemon peel
1 drop yellow food coloring (optional)

Heat oven to 325°F. Lightly spray 1½- or 2-quart casserole dish with nonstick cooking spray or oil lightly. In large bowl, combine brown sugar and ¼ cup margarine. Add apple juice concentrate and egg whites, mixing well. Add combined oat bran, flour, baking powder and cinnamon; mix well. Stir in carrots; pour into prepared dish. Bake 45 to 50 minutes or until edges are lightly browned and center is firm. Cool on wire rack about 1 hour. Cut into squares or wedges.

In small saucepan, combine granulated sugar and cornstarch. Gradually add water, mixing until sugar dissolves. Cook over medium heat about 3 minutes, stirring constantly until mixture boils and is thickened and clear. Remove from heat; stir in remaining ingredients. Cool slightly. Spoon 2 tablespoons lemon sauce over each serving.

To Microwave Lemon Sauce: In 4-cup microwavable measuring cup, combine granulated sugar and cornstarch. Gradually add water, mixing until sugar dissolves. Microwave at HIGH (100% power) 2 to 3 minutes or until mixture boils and is thickened and clear, stirring after every minute. Add remaining ingredients, mixing well. Cool slightly. Serve as directed above.

Nutrients per serving:			
Calories	270	Cholesterol	0 mg
Fat	8 g	Sodium	200 mg

Chocolate Cupcakes

Makes 18 cupcakes

6 tablespoons light corn oil spread
1 cup sugar
1¼ cups all-purpose flour
⅓ cup HERSHEY'S Cocoa
1 teaspoon baking soda
   Dash salt
1 cup nonfat buttermilk
½ teaspoon vanilla extract
   Powdered sugar

Heat oven to 350°F. Line muffin pans with paper bake cups (2½ inches in diameter). In large saucepan, melt corn oil spread. Remove from heat; stir in sugar. In small bowl, stir together flour, cocoa, baking soda and salt; add alternately with buttermilk and vanilla to mixture in saucepan. Beat with whisk until well blended. Spoon into bake cups.

Bake 18 to 20 minutes or until wooden toothpick inserted in centers comes out clean. Remove from pans to wire racks; cool completely. Sift powdered sugar over tops.

Nutrients per serving (1 cupcake):			
Calories	110	Cholesterol	0 mg
Fat	3 g	Sodium	95 mg

Danish Orange Loaves

Makes 2 loaves, 12 slices each

Cake
- 1 package DUNCAN HINES® Moist Deluxe Orange Supreme Cake Mix
- 1 package (4-serving size) vanilla instant pudding and pie filling mix
- 4 eggs
- 1 cup dairy sour cream
- ⅓ cup CRISCO® PURITAN® Oil

Frosting
- 2¼ cups confectioners sugar
- 3 tablespoons butter or margarine, melted
- 2 to 3 tablespoons orange juice
- 1 tablespoon grated orange peel

1. Preheat oven to 350°F. Grease and flour two 9×5×3-inch loaf pans.

2. For Cake, combine cake mix, pudding mix, eggs, sour cream and Crisco® Puritan® Oil in large bowl. Beat at medium speed with electric mixer for 3 minutes. Pour batter into pans. Bake at 350°F for 50 to 60 minutes or until wooden toothpick inserted in centers comes out clean. Cool in pans 15 minutes. Loosen loaves from pans. Invert onto cooling racks. Turn right side up. Cool completely.

3. For Frosting, combine confectioners sugar, melted butter and 1 tablespoon orange juice in small bowl. Beat at low speed with electric mixer until blended.

Danish Orange Loaf

Add remaining juice, 1 teaspoon at a time, until frosting is of spreading consistency. Fold in orange peel. Spread frosting over cooled loaves. Garnish as desired.

Tip: *This recipe may also be baked in a 10-inch Bundt® pan or tube pan for 50 to 60 minutes or until wooden toothpick inserted in center of cake comes out clean.*

Nutrients per serving (1 slice):

Calories	212	Cholesterol	44 mg
Fat	9 g	Sodium	184 mg

Apple-Cinnamon Pecan Cake

Makes 24 servings

- 2 cups all-purpose flour
- 2 teaspoons baking powder
- 1 teaspoon ground cinnamon
- ½ teaspoon ground nutmeg
- ½ cup margarine, softened
- 1 cup granulated sugar
- 2 eggs
- 1 teaspoon vanilla extract
- ⅔ cup *undiluted* CARNATION® Evaporated Lowfat Milk
- 3 cups peeled and finely diced or shredded baking apples (about 2 large)
- ¾ cup (3 ounces) chopped pecans
- 2 tablespoons powdered sugar

Preheat oven to 350°F. In medium bowl, combine flour, baking powder, cinnamon and nutmeg; set aside. In large mixer bowl, cream margarine and granulated sugar; beat in eggs and vanilla. With mixer at low speed, alternately add flour mixture and evaporated lowfat milk, ending with flour mixture. Stir in apples and pecans. Spread batter evenly into lightly greased 13×9-inch baking pan. Bake 40 to 45 minutes or until wooden pick inserted in center comes out clean. Cool 20 minutes. Sift powdered sugar over top. Cool completely before cutting.

Note: *Apples may be shredded by hand or in food processor.*

Nutrients per serving:

Calories	155	Cholesterol	19 mg
Fat	7 g	Sodium	95 mg

Rich Chocolate Cake with Raspberry Sauce

Makes 16 servings

2 cups frozen raspberries in syrup, thawed, puréed and strained
2 tablespoons cornstarch
2 cups all-purpose flour
1⅓ cups skim milk
1 cup sugar
⅔ cup FLEISCHMANN'S® Margarine, softened
1 (8-ounce) container EGG BEATERS® 99% Real Egg Product
⅔ cup unsweetened cocoa
1½ teaspoons DAVIS® Baking Powder
1½ teaspoons vanilla extract
½ teaspoon baking soda

In small saucepan, over medium-high heat, cook raspberries and cornstarch, stirring constantly until mixture thickens and begins to boil. Cool; refrigerate.

In large bowl, with electric mixer at low speed, mix flour, milk, sugar, margarine, Egg Beaters®, cocoa, baking powder, vanilla and baking soda just until blended. Beat at high speed for 3 minutes. Spread batter in greased and cocoa-dusted 13×9×2-inch baking pan. Bake at 350°F for 30 to 35 minutes or until wooden toothpick inserted in center comes out clean. Cool in pan 10 minutes. Remove from pan; cool on wire rack. Cut into 16 pieces. Garnish as desired and serve topped with raspberry sauce.

Nutrients per serving:

Calories	232	Cholesterol	0 mg
Fat	8 g	Sodium	161 mg

Strawberry Ice Cream Cake

Makes 12 to 16 servings

1 package DUNCAN HINES® Moist Deluxe Strawberry Supreme Cake Mix

Rum Syrup
⅓ cup boiling water
⅓ cup sugar
⅓ cup cold water
¼ cup dark rum

Filling and Frosting
1 pint strawberry ice cream, softened
1 container (8 ounces) frozen whipped topping, thawed
Fresh strawberries, for garnish

Strawberry Ice Cream Cake

1. Preheat oven to 350°F. Grease and flour two 9-inch round cake pans. Prepare, bake and cool cake following package directions.

2. For Rum Syrup, stir boiling water into sugar in medium bowl. Stir until sugar is dissolved. Add cold water and rum. Cool.

3. Place cake layers on cooling racks in jelly-roll pan. Spoon ½ cup rum syrup evenly over each layer. Freeze 2 hours or until cake layers are firm.

4. For Filling and Frosting, place one cake layer on serving plate. Spread softened ice cream to edges. Place second layer on top of ice cream. Freeze assembled cake until ice cream is firm.

5. Frost sides and top of cake with whipped topping. Garnish with fresh strawberries, if desired. Store in freezer until ready to serve.

Tip: Allow cake to stand at room temperature 10 to 15 minutes before serving. For easiest cutting, use a knife with a thin sharp blade.

Nutrients per serving:

Calories	232	Cholesterol	7 mg
Fat	8 g	Sodium	228 mg

Cherry Angel Roll

Cherry Angel Rolls

Makes 2 cakes, 8 servings each

1 package DUNCAN HINES® Angel Food
   Cake Mix
1 cup chopped maraschino cherries
1 teaspoon reserved maraschino cherry juice
½ cup flaked coconut
1 container (8 ounces) frozen whipped topping,
   thawed
   Confectioners sugar

1. Preheat oven to 350°F. Line two 15½×10½×1-inch jelly-roll pans with aluminum foil.

2. Prepare cake mix following package directions. Divide batter into lined pans. Spread evenly. Cut through batter with knife or spatula to remove large air bubbles. Bake at 350°F for 15 minutes or until set. Invert cakes at once onto clean, lint-free dishtowels dusted with confectioners sugar. Remove foil carefully. Starting at short end, roll up each cake with towel jelly-roll fashion. Cool completely.

3. Drain cherries, reserving 1 teaspoon juice. Fold cherries, coconut and cherry juice into whipped topping. Unroll cakes. Spread half of filling over each cake to edges. Reroll and place seam sides down on serving plate. Dust with confectioners sugar. Refrigerate until ready to serve.

Nutrients per serving:

Calories	211	Cholesterol	0 mg
Fat	6 g	Sodium	113 mg

Pineapple Upside Down Cake

Makes 12 servings

2 cans (8 ounces *each*) pineapple slices in juice,
   undrained
¼ cup raisins
1 cup KELLOGG'S® ALL-BRAN® cereal
¾ cup whole wheat flour
½ cup all-purpose flour
1 teaspoon baking soda
1 teaspoon ground cinnamon
¼ teaspoon salt (optional)
3 tablespoons margarine, softened
¼ cup sugar
4 egg whites
1 cup (8 ounces) low-fat vanilla flavored yogurt
1 teaspoon vanilla extract

Drain pineapple, reserving ¼ cup juice. Arrange pineapple slices in 9-inch round cake pan coated with nonstick cooking spray. Place raisins around and in centers of pineapple slices.

Stir together Kellogg's® All-Bran® cereal, flours, baking soda, cinnamon and salt. Set aside.

In large mixing bowl, beat together margarine and sugar. Add egg whites, yogurt, vanilla and ¼ cup reserved pineapple juice, mixing until blended. Add flour mixture, stirring only until combined. Spread batter over pineapple slices and raisins.

Bake at 350°F about 35 minutes or until wooden toothpick inserted in center comes out clean. Let stand 10 minutes. Turn cake upside down onto serving plate. Remove pan. Cool. Cut into 12 wedges.

Nutrients per serving:

Calories	150	Cholesterol	0 mg
Fat	3 g	Sodium	240 mg

Applesauce Snacking Cake

Makes 48 servings

1¼ cups sweetened applesauce
1 cup NABISCO® 100% Bran
½ cup EGG BEATERS® 99% Real Egg Product
½ cup BRER RABBIT® Light Molasses
1½ cups all-purpose flour
1 teaspoon baking soda
1 teaspoon ground cinnamon
1 cup firmly packed dark brown sugar
½ cup FLEISCHMANN'S® Margarine, softened
½ cup raisins
   Confectioner's sugar (optional)

In medium bowl, mix applesauce, bran, Egg Beaters®
and molasses; let stand 5 minutes. In small bowl,
blend flour, baking soda and cinnamon; set aside.

In large bowl, with electric mixer at medium speed,
beat sugar and margarine until creamy. Beat in bran
mixture until smooth. Blend in flour mixture; stir in
raisins. Spread batter evenly in ungreased 15×10×1-
inch baking pan. Bake at 350°F for 20 to 25
minutes or until wooden toothpick inserted in center
comes out clean. Cool in pan on wire rack. Sprinkle
with confectioner's sugar if desired; cut into 48 bars.

Nutrients per serving (without confectioner's sugar):

Calories	60	Cholesterol	0 mg
Fat	2 g	Sodium	50 mg

Chocolate Chiffon Cake

Makes 12 servings

   1 bar (4 ounces) sweet baking chocolate
 ½ cup hot water
   5 eggs, separated
 ⅔ cup sugar
   1 cup all-purpose flour
   1 teaspoon baking powder
   1 teaspoon vanilla
 ½ teaspoon salt
   Powdered sugar

Preheat oven to 350°F. Melt chocolate in hot water;
set aside. Beat egg whites in large bowl until soft
peaks form. Gradually add sugar and beat until stiff
and glossy; set aside. Combine melted chocolate
mixture, egg yolks, flour, baking powder, vanilla and
salt in small bowl; beat 1 minute with electric mixer.
Carefully fold chocolate mixture into egg white
mixture until blended. Pour into ungreased 10-inch
tube pan. Bake 45 to 50 minutes or until top springs
back when lightly touched. Invert pan over large
funnel or soda bottle; cool completely. Remove cake
from pan; sprinkle with powdered sugar.

Nutrients per serving:

Calories	158	Cholesterol	89 mg
Fat	6 g	Sodium	143 mg

Spice Cake with Fresh Peach Sauce

Makes 12 to 16 servings

   1 package DUNCAN HINES® Moist Deluxe
      Spice Cake Mix

Sauce
   6 cups sliced fresh peaches
   1 cup water
 ⅓ cup sugar
 ⅛ teaspoon ground cinnamon

1. Preheat oven to 350°F. Grease and flour 10-inch
Bundt® or tube pan. Prepare, bake and cool cake
following package directions for No Cholesterol
recipe. Dust with confectioners sugar, if desired.

2. For Sauce, combine peaches and water in large
saucepan. Cook over medium heat 5 minutes.
Reduce heat to low. Cover and simmer 10 minutes.
Cool. Reserve ½ cup peach slices. Combine
remaining peaches with any cooking liquid, sugar and
cinnamon in blender or food processor. Process until
smooth. Stir in reserved peach slices. To serve, spoon
peach sauce over cake slices.

Tip: *Fresh peach sauce can be served either warm or chilled.*

Nutrients per serving:

Calories	299	Cholesterol	0 mg
Fat	10 g	Sodium	294 mg

Spice Cake with Fresh Peach Sauce

Individual Strawberry Shortcakes

Makes 10 servings

Strawberry Mixture
  4 cups fresh strawberries, washed, hulled and sliced
  2 tablespoons granulated sugar

Shortcake Biscuits
  1¾ cups all-purpose flour
  1 tablespoon granulated sugar
  1 tablespoon baking powder
  ½ teaspoon salt (optional)
  ¼ cup CRISCO® Shortening
  ⅔ cup milk

Topping
  1 cup plain nonfat yogurt
  3 tablespoons brown sugar
  ½ teaspoon vanilla

For Strawberry Mixture, combine strawberries and granulated sugar. Cover and refrigerate.

Heat oven to 450°F.

For Shortcake Biscuits, combine flour, granulated sugar, baking powder and salt in bowl. Cut in Crisco® with pastry blender (or 2 knives) until mixture forms coarse crumbs.

Add milk. Stir until dry ingredients are just moistened. Place on floured surface. Knead gently with fingertips 8 to 10 times. Pat or roll into 9-inch circle about ½ inch thick. (Hint: Cover dough with waxed paper. Press and flatten with 9-inch round cake pan until dough is desired thickness.)

Cut with 2½-inch round biscuit cutter. Press dough scraps into ball and flatten again. Cut out a total of 10 biscuits. Place on ungreased baking sheet.

Bake 12 minutes or until tops are golden brown.

For Topping, combine yogurt, brown sugar and vanilla. Stir gently until smooth.

To assemble, split warm or cooled biscuits in half crosswise. Spoon about ¼ cup fruit over bottoms of biscuits. Add tops. Spoon yogurt sauce over tops. Add another spoonful of fruit or top with strawberry fans, if desired.

Nutrients per serving:			
Calories	188	Cholesterol	3 mg
Fat	6 g	Sodium	127 mg

Creamy Lemon Cheesecake

Makes 8 servings

Crust
  1 cup graham cracker crumbs
  ¼ cup sugar
  3 tablespoons CRISCO® PURITAN® Oil

Filling
  3 ounces Neufchatel cheese, softened
  2 cups low-fat (1%) cottage cheese
  ½ cup sugar
  2 egg whites
  1 teaspoon freshly grated lemon peel
  3 tablespoons fresh lemon juice
  1 teaspoon vanilla

For Crust, heat oven to 350°F. Combine graham cracker crumbs, sugar, and Crisco® Puritan® Oil in 9-inch pie plate. Mix well with fork. Press firmly against bottom and halfway up side of pie plate.

For Filling, blend neufchatel and cottage cheese in food processor or blender* until completely smooth. Add remaining ingredients. Blend well. Pour mixture into crust.

Bake at 350°F for 30 minutes. Turn oven off; allow cheesecake to remain in oven for 5 minutes. Remove from oven; cool. Refrigerate. Cut into wedges. Garnish with fresh fruit, if desired.

*If blender is used, place sugar, egg whites, lemon peel, lemon juice and vanilla in blender container before adding neufchatel and cottage cheese. Blend until completely smooth, stopping blender and scraping as necessary.

To Microwave: Prepare crust as directed; spoon 2 to 3 tablespoons crust mixture into each of 8 small custard cups. Press firmly against bottoms of cups. Prepare filling as directed; pour about ⅓ cup into each custard cup.

Arrange cups in circle on large microwave-safe platter or directly on floor of microwave oven. Microwave on MEDIUM (50% power) 9 to 10 minutes or until filling begins to set around edges, turning platter or rearranging cups after every 3 minutes.

Let stand on countertop or board 10 minutes. Refrigerate at least 1 hour before serving.

Nutrients per serving:			
Calories	256	Cholesterol	11 mg
Fat	10 g	Sodium	378 mg

Individual Strawberry Shortcakes

Mini-Almond Cheesecakes

Makes 12 servings

¾ cup ground almonds
1 tablespoon PARKAY® Margarine, melted
1 envelope unflavored gelatin
¼ cup cold water
1 container (12 ounces) Light PHILADELPHIA
    BRAND® Pasteurized Process Cream
    Cheese Product, softened
¾ cup skim milk
½ cup sugar *or* 12 packets sugar substitute
¼ teaspoon almond extract
3 cups peeled peach slices

Stir together almonds and margarine in small bowl. Press mixture evenly onto bottoms of 12 (2½-inch) paper-lined baking cups.

Soften gelatin in water in small saucepan; stir over low heat until dissolved.

Beat cream cheese product, milk, sugar and almond extract in large mixing bowl at medium speed with electric mixer until well blended. Stir in gelatin mixture. Pour into baking cups; freeze until firm.

Place peaches in food processor or blender container; process until smooth. Spoon peach purée onto individual plates.

Mini-Almond Cheesecakes

Remove cheesecakes from freezer 10 minutes before serving. Peel off paper. Invert cheesecakes onto plates. Garnish with additional peach slices, raspberries and fresh mint leaves, if desired.

Note: For a sweeter peach purée, add sugar to taste.

Nutrients per serving:

Calories	175	Cholesterol	11 mg
Fat	10 g	Sodium	180 mg

Chocolatey Ricotta Cheesecake

Makes 16 servings

⅓ cup graham cracker crumbs
3½ cups (two 15-ounce containers) low-fat
    part-skim ricotta cheese, drained
    Yogurt Cheese (recipe follows)
2 egg whites
¾ cup sugar
⅓ cup HERSHEY'S Cocoa
2 tablespoons all-purpose flour
2 teaspoons vanilla extract
    Sliced fresh strawberries and kiwifruit

Heat oven to 325°F. Sprinkle crumbs on bottom of 9-inch springform pan. In food processor or large mixer bowl, process ricotta cheese until smooth. Add Yogurt Cheese, egg whites, sugar, cocoa, flour and vanilla; process just until well blended. Pour over crumbs. Bake 50 minutes or until edges are set. Turn oven off; open oven door slightly. Leave cheesecake in oven 1 hour. Remove from oven. Cool; refrigerate thoroughly. Garnish with fruit.

Yogurt Cheese: Line a non-rusting colander or sieve with large piece of double thickness cheesecloth; place colander over deep bowl. Spoon 2 cups (two 8-ounce containers) vanilla low-fat yogurt (with no gelatin added) into prepared colander; cover. Refrigerate until liquid no longer drains from yogurt, about 24 hours. Remove yogurt from cheesecloth; discard liquid.

Nutrients per serving:

Calories	160	Cholesterol	20 mg
Fat	5 g	Sodium	105 mg

Star-Spangled Cheesecake

Makes 8 servings

1 KEEBLER® READY-CRUST® Graham
   Cracker Pie Crust
1 egg yolk, beaten

Filling
   1 container (15 ounces) light ricotta cheese
   ½ cup sugar
   ⅓ cup evaporated skim milk
   2 eggs
   2 tablespoons all-purpose flour
   2 teaspoons grated lemon peel
   1 tablespoon lemon juice
   ½ teaspoon vanilla extract
   ¼ teaspoon salt

Sour Cream Topping
   1 cup light sour cream
   2 tablespoons sugar
   1 teaspoon vanilla extract

Fruit Glaze
   ¼ cup red currant jelly
   1 cup fresh raspberries
   1 cup fresh blueberries

Brush egg yolk over pie crust. Bake at 350°F for
5 minutes.

For Filling, while crust is baking, blend ricotta cheese
until smooth in food processor or blender. Add all
remaining filling ingredients; process just until
mixed. Pour into prepared crust; continue to bake
at 350°F for 30 minutes or until center is set.

For Topping, combine sour cream, sugar and vanilla
in small bowl. Spread over cheesecake; continue to
bake at 350°F for 10 minutes. Turn oven off; allow
cheesecake to cool in oven with door ajar for 30
minutes. Remove from oven; cool. Refrigerate at least
3 hours.

For Fruit Glaze, just before serving, melt jelly.
Combine half the jelly with raspberries; arrange
glazed raspberries in single layer over center of
cheesecake. Combine blueberries with remaining
jelly; arrange glazed blueberries in a single layer over
remaining cheesecake to the crust. Refrigerate
15 minutes before cutting.

Nutrients per serving:

Calories	279	Cholesterol	62 mg
Fat	9 g	Sodium	371 mg

Lovely Lemon Cheesecake

Lovely Lemon Cheesecake

Makes 8 servings

1 whole graham cracker, crushed, *or*
   2 tablespoons graham cracker crumbs,
   divided
1 package (4-serving size) JELL-O® Brand
   Sugar Free Lemon Flavor Gelatin
⅔ cup boiling water
1 cup 1% low-fat cottage cheese
1 container (8 ounces) light pasteurized process
   cream cheese product, softened
2 cups thawed COOL WHIP® LITE® Whipped
   Topping
1 cup low-calorie cherry pie filling

Spray 8- or 9-inch springform pan or 9-inch pie plate
lightly with nonstick cooking spray. Sprinkle side with
half the graham cracker crumbs. (If desired, omit
graham cracker crumb garnish; sprinkle bottom of
pan with remaining graham cracker crumbs.)

Completely dissolve gelatin in boiling water in small
bowl. Pour into blender container. Add cheeses; blend
at medium speed, scraping down sides occasionally,
about 2 minutes or until mixture is completely
smooth. Pour into large bowl. Gently stir in whipped
topping. Pour into prepared pan; smooth top.
Sprinkle remaining crumbs around outside edge,
leaving center plain. Chill until set, about 4 hours.

Just before serving, decorate top of cheesecake with
pie filling. Remove sides of pan and cut.

Nutrients per serving:

Calories	160	Cholesterol	15 mg
Fat	7 g	Sodium	330 mg

PIES & COOKIES

End your meal on a sweet note and still keep calories and fat in line. Peach, pineapple and pumpkin are just a few of the picture-perfect pies you can indulge in. Kids of all ages will appreciate a cookie jar filled with chocolate chip, molasses or orange sugar cookies, perfect for low-cal snacking anytime.

Fruit Lover's Tart

Makes 1 (9-inch) pie, 8 servings

1¼ cups QUAKER® Oats (quick or old fashioned, uncooked)
⅓ cup firmly packed brown sugar
¼ cup all-purpose flour
2 tablespoons margarine, melted
2 egg whites
1 cup (8 ounces) part-skim ricotta cheese
¼ cup (2 ounces) light cream cheese, softened
2 tablespoons powdered sugar
½ teaspoon grated lemon peel
4½ cups any combination sliced fresh or frozen fruit, thawed, well drained

Heat oven to 350°F. Lightly spray 9-inch pie plate with nonstick cooking spray or oil lightly. Combine oats, brown sugar, flour, margarine and egg whites, mixing until moistened. Press mixture onto bottom and up side of prepared plate. Bake 15 to 18 minutes or until light golden brown. Remove to wire rack; cool completely. Combine cheeses, powdered sugar and lemon peel. Spread onto oat base; top with fruit. Refrigerate 2 hours.

To Microwave: Combine oats, brown sugar, flour, margarine and egg whites, mixing until moistened. Press mixture onto bottom and up side of 9-inch microwavable pie plate. Microwave on HIGH (100% power) 2½ to 3 minutes or until top springs back when lightly touched. Cool completely. Proceed as above.

Nutrients per serving:

Calories	240	Cholesterol	15 mg
Fat	8 g	Sodium	110 mg

Candy-Apple Pie

Makes 8 servings

1¾ cups unsweetened apple juice, divided
⅓ cup cinnamon candies
½ teaspoon vanilla extract
¼ teaspoon red food coloring
4 apples, peeled, cored and sliced (Granny Smith, Rome Beauty or McIntosh)
3 tablespoons cornstarch
1 KEEBLER® READY-CRUST® Graham Cracker Pie Crust
1½ cups thawed frozen light whipped topping
½ teaspoon ground cinnamon

In large saucepan, combine 1½ cups juice, candies, vanilla, food coloring and apples. Bring to a boil. Reduce heat to low and simmer just until apples are tender, about 10 to 15 minutes. Combine remaining ¼ cup juice and cornstarch in small bowl. Stir into apple mixture; continue to cook until mixture boils and thickens. Cook an additional 2 to 3 minutes. Remove from heat; cool to room temperature.

Spoon apple filling into pie crust. Refrigerate several hours or until filling is set. Just before serving, combine whipped topping and cinnamon in small bowl. Top each slice of pie with a dollop of whipped topping mixture.

Nutrients per serving:

Calories	249	Cholesterol	0 mg
Fat	7 g	Sodium	154 mg

254   PIES & COOKIES

Fruit Lover's Tart

Deep-Dish Peach Pie

Makes 1 (8-inch) pie, 8 servings

Pastry for single crust pie
1 cup sugar
2 tablespoons cornstarch
3 pounds peaches, seeded, pared and sliced
    (about 6 cups)
2 tablespoons REALEMON® Lemon Juice from
    Concentrate
1 tablespoon margarine, melted
¼ teaspoon almond extract
2 tablespoons sliced almonds

Preheat oven to 375°F. Remove and reserve
1 tablespoon sugar. In small bowl, combine remaining
sugar and cornstarch. In large bowl, toss peaches
with ReaLemon® brand; add sugar mixture,
margarine and extract. Turn into 8-inch square
baking dish. Roll pastry to 9-inch square; cut slits
near center. Place pastry over filling; turn under
edges, seal and flute. Sprinkle with reserved
1 tablespoon sugar and almonds. Bake 45 to 50
minutes or until golden brown. Cool on wire rack.

Nutrients per serving:			
Calories	292	Cholesterol	0 mg
Fat	10 g	Sodium	163 mg

Deep-Dish Peach Pie

Lemon-Poppy Seed Tarts

Makes 6 servings

1¾ cups skim milk
1 package (0.9 ounces) sugar-free instant
    vanilla pudding and pie filling
1 tablespoon poppy seeds
1½ teaspoons grated lemon peel, divided
6 KEEBLER® READY-CRUST® Single Serve
    Graham Crusts
¾ cup thawed frozen light whipped topping
    Additional grated lemon peel for garnish
    (optional)

In blender container, combine milk, pudding mix,
poppy seeds and 1 teaspoon lemon peel. Cover; blend
on low speed until well mixed and slightly thickened.
Pour evenly into crusts; refrigerate. Just before
serving, combine whipped topping and remaining
½ teaspoon lemon peel in small bowl. Top each tart
with dollop of whipped topping mixture. Sprinkle with
additional grated lemon peel, if desired.

Nutrients per serving:			
Calories	141	Cholesterol	2 mg
Fat	6 g	Sodium	193 mg

Lite 'n Easy Crustless Pumpkin Pie

Makes 1 (10-inch) pie, 10 servings

2 envelopes unflavored gelatin
2 tablespoons cold water
2¼ cups *undiluted* CARNATION® Low Fat
    Evaporated Milk, divided
1¾ cups (16-ounce can) LIBBY'S® Solid Pack
    Pumpkin
6 tablespoons packed dark brown sugar
    or low-calorie equivalent
1 teaspoon pumpkin pie spice
1 teaspoon vanilla extract

In large bowl, sprinkle gelatin over cold water to
soften; set aside. In small saucepan, heat *1 cup* low
fat evaporated milk just to boiling. Slowly stir hot
milk into gelatin. Mix in *remaining* evaporated milk,
pumpkin, sugar, pumpkin pie spice and vanilla; set
aside. Spray 10-inch glass pie dish with nonstick
cooking spray. Pour pie mixture into dish; refrigerate.

Nutrients per serving:			
Calories	97	Cholesterol	2 mg
Fat	trace	Sodium	72 mg

Iced Coffee and Chocolate Pie

Makes 1 pie, 8 servings

2 envelopes unflavored gelatin
¼ cup cold skim milk
1 cup skim milk, heated to boiling
2 cups vanilla ice milk, softened
⅓ cup sugar
2 tablespoons instant coffee granules
1 teaspoon vanilla extract
1 (6-ounce) KEEBLER® READY-CRUST®
   Chocolate Flavored Pie Crust
Reduced-calorie whipped topping (optional)
Chocolate curls (optional)

In blender container, sprinkle gelatin over ¼ cup cold milk; let stand 3 to 4 minutes to soften. Add hot milk; cover and mix on low until gelatin dissolves, about 2 minutes. Add ice milk, sugar, coffee granules and vanilla. Cover and mix until smooth. Pour into pie crust. Refrigerate at least 2 hours. Garnish with whipped topping and chocolate curls, if desired.

Nutrients per serving:

Calories	220	Cholesterol	6 mg
Fat	6 g	Sodium	210 mg

Picnic Fruit Tart

Makes 14 servings

Crust
¾ cup flour
¼ cup oat bran
2 tablespoons sugar
¼ cup (½ stick) PARKAY® Margarine
2 to 3 tablespoons cold water

Filling
1 envelope unflavored gelatin
½ cup cold water
1 container (8 ounces) Light PHILADELPHIA
   BRAND® Pasteurized Process Cream
   Cheese Product, softened
¼ cup sugar *or* 6 packets sugar substitute
1 teaspoon grated lemon peel
¼ cup skim milk
⅓ cup KRAFT® Apricot Preserves
¾ cup grape halves
¾ cup plum slices

Picnic Fruit Tart

For Crust, heat oven to 375°F.

Mix flour, oat bran and 2 tablespoons sugar in medium bowl; cut in margarine until mixture resembles coarse crumbs. Sprinkle with 2 to 3 tablespoons water, mixing lightly with fork just until moistened. Roll into ball. Cover; refrigerate.

On lightly floured surface, roll out dough to 11-inch circle. Place in 9-inch tart pan with removable bottom. Trim edges; prick bottom with fork.

Bake 16 to 18 minutes or until golden brown; cool.

For Filling, soften gelatin in ½ cup water in small saucepan; stir over low heat until dissolved. Cool.

Beat cream cheese product, ¼ cup sugar and peel in large mixing bowl at medium speed with electric mixer until well blended. Gradually add gelatin mixture and milk, mixing until well blended.

Pour over crust. Refrigerate until firm.

Heat preserves in small saucepan over low heat until thinned. Spread evenly over tart. Arrange fruit over preserves. Carefully remove rim of pan.

Prep time: 40 minutes plus refrigerating
Cook time: 18 minutes

Nutrients per serving:

Calories	150	Cholesterol	10 mg
Fat	6 g	Sodium	130 mg

Zabaglione Tarts with Fresh Berries

Zabaglione Tarts with Fresh Berries

Makes 6 servings

1½ cups skim milk
¼ cup Marsala wine
 1 package (0.9 ounces) sugar-free instant
    vanilla pudding and pie filling
½ cup light frozen whipped topping, thawed
 6 KEEBLER® READY-CRUST® Single Serve
    Graham Crusts
18 fresh strawberries, hulled and halved
    Additional thawed frozen light whipped
    topping

In blender container, combine milk, wine and pudding mix. Cover; blend on low speed until well mixed and slightly thickened. Pour into medium bowl; fold in ½ cup whipped topping. Evenly divide filling among tart shells; arrange strawberries over filling. Just before serving, top each tart with additional whipped topping, if desired.

Nutrients per serving:			
Calories	159	Cholesterol	1 mg
Fat	5 g	Sodium	189 mg

Light Custard Cheese Pie

Makes 1 (9-inch) pie, 6 servings

 1 (9-inch) graham cracker crumb crust
 1 (16-ounce) container BORDEN® Lite-line® or
    Viva® Cottage Cheese
 1 tablespoon REALEMON® Lemon Juice from
    Concentrate
 3 eggs
⅓ cup sugar
⅓ cup BORDEN® Lite-line® or Viva® Protein
    Fortified Skim Milk
 1 teaspoon vanilla extract
 1 cup assorted cut-up fresh fruit

Preheat oven to 350°F. In blender container, combine cottage cheese and ReaLemon® brand; blend until smooth. In large mixer bowl, beat eggs and sugar; add cheese mixture, milk and vanilla. Beat until smooth. Pour into crust. Bake 45 minutes or until set. Cool. Chill. Top with fresh fruit and serve. Refrigerate leftovers.

Nutrients per serving:			
Calories	288	Cholesterol	113 mg
Fat	10 g	Sodium	452 mg

Luscious Pumpkin Pie

Makes 1 pie, 8 servings

    1 teaspoon water
    1 egg white
    1 (6-ounce) KEEBLER® READY-CRUST® Pie
        Crust, Graham Cracker or Butter Flavored
    2 eggs
1½ cups pumpkin pie filling
    8 ounces vanilla lowfat yogurt
    1 cup evaporated milk
¾ cup sugar
    1 teaspoon vanilla extract
    1 teaspoon ground cinnamon
¼ teaspoon ground cloves
¼ teaspoon ground ginger
¼ teaspoon ground nutmeg

Preheat oven to 375°F. Beat together water and egg white. Brush inside of pie crust. Place on baking sheet. Bake 3 minutes or until light golden. Cool thoroughly.

In large bowl, lightly beat 2 eggs. Add pumpkin pie filling, yogurt, evaporated milk, sugar, vanilla, cinnamon, cloves, ginger and nutmeg. Stir until thoroughly mixed.

Pour into pie crust. Bake 60 minutes or until set. Cool completely. Serve with whipped cream if desired.

Nutrients per serving:

Calories	289	Cholesterol	64 mg
Fat	10 g	Sodium	327 mg

Creamy Banana Pie

Makes 8 servings

    1 PET-RITZ® All-Vegetable Shortening Deep
        Dish Pie Crust Shell
    1 can (12 fluid ounces) PET® Light Evaporated
        Skimmed Milk
    1 box (3.4 ounces) French vanilla instant
        pudding and pie filling
½ cup plain nonfat yogurt
    2 bananas, thinly sliced

Bake pie crust according to package directions for empty baked crust; cool.

In medium bowl, beat evaporated milk, pudding mix and yogurt until mixture starts to thicken.

Pour half of pudding mixture into cooled crust. Arrange banana slices over pudding mixture; top with remaining pudding mixture. Cover and refrigerate until firm. Garnish with whipped topping, if desired.

Nutrients per serving:

Calories	129	Cholesterol	2 mg
Fat	2 g	Sodium	245 mg

Easy Pineapple Pie

Makes 6 to 8 servings

    1 can (20 ounces) DOLE® Crushed Pineapple
        in Syrup*
    1 package (4-serving size) instant lemon
        pudding and pie filling mix
    1 cup milk
    1 carton (4 ounces) frozen whipped topping,
        thawed
    1 teaspoon grated lemon peel
    2 tablespoons lemon juice
    1 (8- or 9-inch) graham cracker pie crust

Drain pineapple well. Combine pudding mix and milk in medium bowl. Beat 2 to 3 minutes until very thick.

Fold in whipped topping, pineapple, lemon peel and lemon juice. Pour into crust. Cover and refrigerate 4 hours or overnight. Garnish as desired.

Prep time: 5 minutes
Chill time: 4 hours or overnight

Use pineapple packed in juice, if desired.

Nutrients per serving:

Calories	251	Cholesterol	2 mg
Fat	10 g	Sodium	321 mg

Easy Pineapple Pie

Cranberry Apple Pie with Soft Gingersnap Crust

Cranberry Apple Pie with Soft Gingersnap Crust

Makes 1 (8-inch) pie, 8 servings

- 20 gingersnap cookies
- 1½ tablespoons margarine, softened
- 2 McIntosh apples, peeled, cored and quartered
- 1 cup fresh cranberries
- 5 tablespoons firmly packed dark brown sugar
- ¼ teaspoon vanilla extract
- ¼ teaspoon ground cinnamon
- 1 teaspoon granulated sugar

Preheat oven to 375°F. Place gingersnaps and margarine in food processor; process until gingersnaps are finely ground. Press gingersnap mixture onto bottom and up side of 8-inch pie plate. Bake 5 to 8 minutes; cool. Chop apples in food processor. Add cranberries, brown sugar, vanilla and cinnamon; pulse just until mixed. Spoon apple-cranberry filling into another 8-inch pie plate or casserole dish. Sprinkle with granulated sugar. Bake 35 minutes or until apples are tender. Spoon filling into gingersnap crust and serve immediately.

Nutrients per serving:			
Calories	124	Cholesterol	0 mg
Fat	3 g	Sodium	90 mg

Favorite recipe from **The Sugar Association, Inc.**

Light Lemon Meringue Pie

Makes 1 (9-inch) pie, 8 servings

Crust
- 1¼ cups all-purpose flour
- ½ teaspoon salt (optional)
- ⅓ cup CRISCO® Shortening
- ¼ cup orange juice

Filling
- 1 cup sugar
- ⅓ cup cornstarch
- ⅛ teaspoon salt (optional)
- 1½ cups cold water
- 1 egg yolk, lightly beaten
- 1 teaspoon finely shredded fresh lemon peel
- ⅓ cup fresh lemon juice

Meringue
- 3 egg whites
- ⅛ teaspoon salt (optional)
- ¼ cup sugar
- ½ teaspoon vanilla

For Crust, heat oven to 425°F. Combine flour and salt in bowl. Cut in Crisco® using pastry blender (or 2 knives) until all flour is blended in to form pea-size chunks. Sprinkle orange juice over flour mixture, one tablespoon at a time, tossing lightly with fork until dough forms. (Dough may seem slightly dry and crumbly.) Press into ball.

Press dough ball between hands to form 5- to 6-inch "pancake." Roll between unfloured sheets of waxed paper until one inch larger than upside down pie plate. Peel off top sheet. Flip into 9-inch pie plate. Remove other sheet. Fold edge under and flute. Prick bottom and sides with fork (50 times) to prevent shrinkage.

Bake at 425°F for 10 to 15 minutes or until lightly browned.

For Filling, combine 1 cup sugar, cornstarch and salt in heavy saucepan. Stir in water gradually, blending until smooth. Cook over medium-high heat, stirring constantly until filling comes to boil. Continue to cook, stirring constantly, 5 minutes. Remove from heat.

Stir small amount of hot mixture into egg yolk. Return egg yolk mixture to saucepan. Return saucepan to heat and cook, stirring constantly, 1 minute. Remove from heat. Stir in lemon peel and juice. *Reduce oven temperature to 350°F.*

For Meringue, beat egg whites and salt until frothy. Add ¼ cup sugar gradually, beating well after each addition. Continue beating until stiff, but not dry, peaks form. Fold in vanilla.

Spoon filling into baked pie shell. Spread meringue over filling, sealing meringue to edge of pie shell.

Bake at 350°F for 15 minutes or until golden brown. Cool completely on wire rack. Cut with sharp knife dipped in hot water.

Nutrients per serving:			
Calories	289	Cholesterol	27 mg
Fat	9 g	Sodium	24 mg

Pineapple Lime Tartlets

Makes 6 servings

Crust
  6 to 8 graham crackers

Filling
  ¼ cup lime juice
  1 envelope unflavored gelatin
  1 carton (8 ounces) low-fat ricotta cheese
  1¼ cups nonfat plain yogurt, divided
  ½ cup sugar
  1 teaspoon coconut extract
  1 teaspoon grated lime peel

Pineapple Topping
  1 medium DOLE® Fresh Pineapple
  ¾ cup water
  ¼ cup sugar
  1 tablespoon cornstarch
  1 teaspoon grated lime peel

For Crust, arrange crackers in 6 (4½-inch) tart pans with removable bottoms or 1 (9-inch) tart pan with removable bottom. Break crackers to fit.

For Filling, place lime juice in small saucepan. Sprinkle gelatin over juice; let stand 1 minute to soften. Cook over low heat until gelatin is dissolved,

Pineapple Lime Tartlet

stirring frequently; let cool. Process ricotta cheese and ¼ cup yogurt in blender until smooth. Pour into medium bowl. Stir in remaining 1 cup yogurt, sugar, extract and lime peel. Stir in cooled gelatin mixture. Pour into prepared pans; refrigerate at least 2 hours.

For Pineapple Topping, twist crown from pineapple. Cut pineapple in half lengthwise. Refrigerate half for another use. Cut fruit from shell with knife. Cut fruit crosswise into thin slices. Combine water, sugar and cornstarch in large saucepan. Cook, stirring, until sauce boils and thickens. Cool. Add pineapple and lime peel. Arrange over tops of tarts. Garnish as desired.

Prep time: 20 minutes
Cook time: 5 minutes
Chill time: 2 hours

Nutrients per serving:

Calories	271	Cholesterol	13 mg
Fat	5 g	Sodium	184 mg

Easy Dark Cherry Tart

Makes 10 servings

  1¾ cups QUAKER® Oats (quick or old fashioned, uncooked)
  ½ cup all-purpose flour
  ⅓ cup firmly packed brown sugar
  ¼ teaspoon salt (optional)
  ⅓ cup (5⅓ tablespoons) margarine, melted
  2 cans (16 ounces each) pitted dark sweet cherries, undrained
  2 tablespoons granulated sugar
  1 tablespoon cornstarch
  ½ teaspoon almond or vanilla extract

Heat oven to 350°F. Lightly oil 9-inch springform pan or pie plate. Combine oats, flour, brown sugar and salt. Add margarine; mix well. Reserve ⅓ cup for topping; press remaining mixture onto bottom and 1 inch up sides of prepared pan. Bake 15 minutes.

Drain cherries, reserving ⅓ cup liquid. In medium saucepan, combine granulated sugar and cornstarch. Gradually add reserved liquid, stirring until smooth. Add cherries and extract. Bring to a boil, stirring occasionally. Reduce heat; simmer about 1 minute or until thickened and clear, stirring constantly. Pour over baked crust. Sprinkle with reserved oat topping. Bake 15 to 18 minutes or until edges of crust are lightly browned. Store tightly covered in refrigerator.

Nutrients per serving:

Calories	235	Cholesterol	0 mg
Fat	7 g	Sodium	75 mg

Peach-Yogurt Pie with Almond Melba Sauce

Peach-Yogurt Pie with Almond Melba Sauce

Makes 8 servings

2 cups fresh, canned or frozen peach slices, thawed
2 tablespoons granulated sugar
1 tablespoon almond-flavored liqueur
1 quart vanilla-flavored ice milk or frozen yogurt, softened
1 KEEBLER® READY-CRUST® Butter Flavored Pie Crust

Almond Melba Sauce
2 cups fresh or frozen raspberries, thawed
⅓ cup confectioners' sugar
2 tablespoons almond-flavored liqueur
1 tablespoon lemon juice

In blender or food processor, combine peaches, granulated sugar and 1 tablespoon liqueur. (If using fresh peaches, add 1 teaspoon lemon juice.) Cover; blend until smooth. Fold peach purée into softened ice milk or yogurt. Spoon into pie crust and freeze until firm.

For Almond Melba Sauce, place raspberries, confectioners' sugar, 2 tablespoons liqueur and lemon juice in blender or food processor. Cover and process until smooth. Strain to remove seeds. Refrigerate.

To serve, remove pie from freezer and let stand 5 minutes. Top each slice of pie with sauce. Garnish with a dollop of whipped topping and additional peaches and raspberries, if desired.

Nutrients per serving:

Calories	298	Cholesterol	9 mg
Fat	9 g	Sodium	203 mg

Cocoa Brownies

Makes 1½ dozen brownies

 4 egg whites
 ½ cup CRISCO® PURITAN® Oil
 1 teaspoon vanilla
 1⅓ cups granulated sugar
 ½ cup unsweetened cocoa
 1¼ cups all-purpose flour
 ¼ teaspoon salt
 Confectioners' sugar (optional)

Heat oven to 350°F. Oil bottom of 9×9-inch pan. Set aside.

Place egg whites in large bowl. Beat with spoon until slightly frothy. Add Crisco® Puritan® Oil and vanilla. Mix thoroughly. Stir in sugar and cocoa. Mix well. Stir in flour and salt until blended. Pour into pan.

Bake at 350°F for 26 to 28 minutes. *Do not overbake.* Cool completely on wire rack before cutting. Sprinkle with confectioners' sugar, if desired.

Nutrients per serving (1 brownie):

Calories	150	Cholesterol	0 mg
Fat	7 g	Sodium	43 mg

Chocolate Chip Cookies

Makes 3 dozen cookies

 2 cups all-purpose flour
 1 teaspoon baking soda
 ½ teaspoon salt
 1 egg
 3 tablespoons water
 1 teaspoon vanilla extract
 1 cup firmly packed brown sugar
 ¼ cup CRISCO® PURITAN® Oil
 ½ cup semi-sweet chocolate chips

Heat oven to 375°F. Oil cookie sheets well.

Combine flour, baking soda and salt. Set aside. Combine egg, water and vanilla. Set aside.

Blend brown sugar and Crisco® Puritan® Oil in large bowl at low speed of electric mixer. Add egg mixture. Beat until smooth. Add flour mixture in three parts at lowest speed. Scrape bowl well after each addition. Stir in chocolate chips.

Drop dough by rounded teaspoonfuls onto cookie sheets. Bake at 375°F for 7 to 8 minutes or until lightly browned. Cool on cookie sheets 1 minute. Remove to wire racks.

Nutrients per serving (1 cookie):

Calories	74	Cholesterol	6 mg
Fat	3 g	Sodium	57 mg

Applesauce Cookies

Makes about 5 dozen cookies

 1 cup all-purpose flour
 1 teaspoon baking powder
 1 teaspoon ground allspice
 ¼ teaspoon salt
 ½ cup margarine, softened
 ½ cup sugar
 2 egg whites
 2 cups rolled oats, uncooked
 1 cup unsweetened applesauce
 ½ cup chopped raisins

Preheat oven to 375°F. Grease cookie sheet. In small bowl, combine flour, baking powder, allspice and salt; set aside. In large bowl, beat margarine and sugar until creamy. Add egg whites; beat well. Beat in flour mixture. Stir in oats, applesauce and raisins, mixing well. Drop by level tablespoonfuls onto prepared cookie sheet. Bake 11 minutes or until edges are lightly browned. Cool on wire rack.

Nutrients per serving (1 cookie):

Calories	45	Cholesterol	0 mg
Fat	2 g	Sodium	34 mg

Favorite recipe from **Western New York Apple Growers Association**

Lemon Cookies

Makes 4 dozen cookies

 ⅔ cup MIRACLE WHIP® Salad Dressing
 1 two-layer yellow cake mix
 2 eggs
 2 teaspoons grated lemon peel
 ⅔ cup ready-to-spread vanilla frosting
 4 teaspoons lemon juice

Preheat oven to 375°F.

Blend salad dressing, cake mix and eggs at low speed with electric mixer until moistened. Add lemon peel. Beat on medium speed 2 minutes. (Dough will be stiff.)

Drop rounded teaspoonfuls of dough, 2 inches apart, onto greased cookie sheets.

Bake 9 to 11 minutes or until lightly browned. (Cookies will still appear soft.) Cool 1 minute; remove from cookie sheets. Cool completely.

Stir together frosting and juice until well blended. Spread on cookies.

Nutrients per serving (1 cookie):

Calories	80	Cholesterol	10 mg
Fat	4 g	Sodium	100 mg

Top to bottom: Cocoa Brownies, Chocolate Chip Cookies

PIES & COOKIES 265

*Bottom left to right: Orange Sugar Cookies,
Molasses Cookies*

Orange Sugar Cookies

Makes 3½ dozen cookies

    2 cups all-purpose flour
1½ teaspoons baking soda
    1 cup sugar, divided
    ½ cup FLEISCHMANN'S® Margarine, softened
    2 teaspoons grated orange peel
    1 teaspoon vanilla extract
    ¼ cup EGG BEATERS® 99% Real Egg Product

In small bowl, combine flour and baking soda; set aside.

In medium bowl, with electric mixer at medium speed, beat ¾ cup sugar, margarine, orange peel and vanilla until creamy. Add Egg Beaters®; beat 1 minute. Gradually stir in flour mixture until blended. Cover; refrigerate dough 1 hour.

Shape dough into 42 (¾-inch) balls; roll in remaining ¼ cup sugar. Place on lightly greased cookie sheets about 2 inches apart. Bake at 375°F for 8 to 10 minutes or until light golden brown. Remove from cookie sheets. Cool on wire racks.

Nutrients per serving (1 cookie):

| Calories | 60 | Cholesterol | 0 mg |
| Fat | 2 g | Sodium | 49 mg |

Molasses Cookies

Makes 4 dozen cookies

    2 cups all-purpose flour
    1 cup NABISCO® 100% Bran
    2 teaspoons baking soda
    1 cup firmly packed light brown sugar
⅔ cup BLUE BONNET® Margarine, softened
    1 egg
⅓ cup BRER RABBIT® Dark Molasses
    ¼ cup granulated sugar
        Water

In small bowl, combine flour, bran and baking soda; set aside.

In large bowl, with electric mixer at medium speed, beat sugar and margarine until creamy. Beat in egg and molasses until smooth. Stir in flour mixture. Cover; refrigerate dough 1 hour.

With greased hands, shape dough into 48 (1¼-inch) balls; roll in granulated sugar. Place on greased and floured cookie sheets about 2 inches apart. Lightly sprinkle dough with water. Bake at 350°F for 10 to 12 minutes or until done. Remove from cookie sheets. Cool on wire racks.

Nutrients per serving (1 cookie):

| Calories | 73 | Cholesterol | 4 mg |
| Fat | 3 g | Sodium | 72 mg |

Mocha Cookies

Makes 40 cookies

2½ tablespoons instant coffee
1½ tablespoons skim milk
    ⅓ cup firmly packed light brown sugar
    ¼ cup granulated sugar
    ¼ cup margarine, softened
    1 egg
    ½ teaspoon almond extract
    2 cups all-purpose flour, sifted
    ¼ cup wheat flakes cereal
    ½ teaspoon ground cinnamon
    ¼ teaspoon baking powder

Preheat oven to 350°F. Spray cookie sheets with nonstick cooking spray. In small cup, dissolve coffee in milk. In large bowl, cream together sugars and margarine. Beat in egg, almond extract and coffee mixture. Stir together flour, cereal, cinnamon and baking powder; beat into sugar mixture gradually. Drop dough by teaspoonfuls, 2 inches apart, onto cookie sheets. Flatten with back of fork. Bake 8 to 10 minutes or until set. Remove from cookie sheets. Cool completely on wire racks.

Nutrients per serving (1 cookie):

| Calories | 44 | Cholesterol | 5 mg |
| Fat | 1 g | Sodium | 21 mg |

Favorite recipe from **The Sugar Association, Inc.**

Fruity Oat Bars

Makes 9 bar cookies

**1 package (6 ounces) diced dried mixed fruit
(about 1⅓ cups)**
¾ cup water
¼ teaspoon ground cinnamon
**1¼ cups QUAKER® Oats (quick or old fashioned,
uncooked)**
⅓ cup firmly packed brown sugar
¼ cup all-purpose flour
¼ cup margarine, melted

Heat oven to 350°F. In small saucepan, combine
fruit, water and cinnamon. Cook over low heat
10 minutes, stirring constantly, or until almost all
liquid is absorbed. Remove from heat; cover. Set aside.

Combine oats, brown sugar and flour. Add margarine;
mix well until crumbly. Reserve ⅓ cup oat mixture;
press remaining mixture on bottom of 8- or 9-inch
baking pan. Bake 10 to 15 minutes or until golden
brown.

Spread fruit mixture evenly over base; sprinkle with
reserved ⅓ cup oat mixture, patting lightly. Bake
20 minutes or until topping is golden brown. Cool;
cut into bars. Store loosely covered.

Nutrients per serving (1 bar):

Calories	180	Cholesterol	0 mg
Fat	6 g	Sodium	65 mg

Snickerdoodles

Makes 3 dozen cookies

3 tablespoons sugar
1 teaspoon ground cinnamon
**1 package DUNCAN HINES® Moist Deluxe
Yellow Cake Mix**
2 eggs
¼ cup CRISCO® PURITAN® Oil

1. Preheat oven to 375°F. Grease cookie sheets.

2. Combine sugar and cinnamon in small bowl. Set
aside.

3. Combine cake mix, eggs and oil in large bowl. Stir
until thoroughly blended. Shape dough into 1-inch
balls. Roll in cinnamon-sugar mixture. Place balls
2 inches apart on cookie sheets. Flatten cookies with
bottom of glass.

4. Bake at 375°F for 8 to 9 minutes or until set. Cool
1 minute on cookie sheets. Remove to cooling racks.

Nutrients per serving (1 cookie):

Calories	80	Cholesterol	12 mg
Fat	3 g	Sodium	97 mg

Chocolate Chip Raspberry Jumbles

Makes 16 bar cookies

**1 package DUNCAN HINES® Chocolate Chip
Cookie Mix**
½ cup seedless red raspberry preserves

1. Preheat oven to 350°F.

2. Prepare chocolate chip cookie mix following
package directions. Reserve ½ cup dough.

3. Spread remaining dough into ungreased 9-inch
square pan. Spread preserves over base. Drop
teaspoonfuls of reserved dough randomly over top.
Bake at 350°F for 20 to 25 minutes or until golden
brown. Cool; cut into bars.

Nutrients per serving (1 bar):

Calories	178	Cholesterol	13 mg
Fat	6 g	Sodium	95 mg

Chocolate Chip Raspberry Jumbles

Chocolate Crinkles

Makes 3 dozen cookies

**1 package DUNCAN HINES® Moist Deluxe
Devil's Food Cake Mix**
2 eggs
¼ cup CRISCO® PURITAN® Oil
4 teaspoons milk
½ cup confectioners sugar

1. Preheat oven to 375°F. Grease cookie sheets.

2. Combine cake mix, eggs, oil and milk in large
bowl. Stir until thoroughly blended. Place
confectioners sugar in small bowl. Drop rounded
teaspoonfuls of dough into confectioners sugar. Roll
to coat and form into balls. Place 2 inches apart on
cookie sheets.

3. Bake at 375°F for 8 to 9 minutes or until set. Cool
1 minute on cookie sheets. Remove to cooling racks.

Nutrients per serving (1 cookie):

Calories	81	Cholesterol	12 mg
Fat	3 g	Sodium	121 mg

Giant Raisin Bran Cookies

Makes 1½ dozen cookies

**2 cups KELLOGG'S® RAISIN BRAN cereal,
crushed to 1½ cups**
1 cup whole wheat flour
1 cup all-purpose flour
1 teaspoon baking soda
¾ cup margarine, softened
⅔ cup granulated sugar
½ cup firmly packed brown sugar
2 eggs

Stir together Kellogg's® Raisin Bran cereal, flours and
baking soda; set aside.

In large mixing bowl, beat margarine and sugars until
light and fluffy. Add eggs; beat well. Stir in cereal
mixture; combine thoroughly. Scoop out a scant
¼ cupful of dough for each cookie. Drop onto
ungreased cookie sheets, spacing 4 inches apart.

Bake at 350°F about 14 minutes or until lightly
browned. Cool on cookie sheets 1 minute. Cool
completely on wire racks.

Nutrients per serving (1 cookie):

Calories	190	Cholesterol	24 mg
Fat	9 g	Sodium	183 mg

Apricot-Pecan Tassies

Makes 2 dozen cookies

Crust
1 cup all-purpose flour
½ cup butter, cut into pieces
6 tablespoons light cream cheese

Filling
¾ cup firmly packed light brown sugar
1 egg, lightly beaten
1 tablespoon butter, softened
½ teaspoon vanilla extract
¼ teaspoon salt
**⅔ cup diced Dried California Apricot Halves
(about 4 ounces)**
⅓ cup chopped pecans

For Crust, in food processor, combine flour, ½ cup
butter and cream cheese; process until mixture forms
a ball. Wrap dough in plastic wrap and refrigerate
15 minutes.

For Filling, combine sugar, egg, 1 tablespoon butter,
vanilla and salt in medium bowl; beat until smooth.
Stir in apricots and nuts.

Preheat oven to 325°F. Shape dough into 24 (1-inch)
balls and place in paper-lined or greased (1½-inch)
miniature muffin cups or tart pans. Press dough on
bottom and sides of each cup; fill with 1 teaspoon
apricot-pecan filling. Bake 25 minutes or until golden
and filling sets. Cool slightly and remove from cups.
Cooled cookies can be wrapped tightly in plastic and
frozen for up to 6 weeks.

Nutrients per serving (1 cookie):

Calories	110	Cholesterol	13 mg
Fat	7 g	Sodium	85 mg

Favorite recipe from **California Apricot Advisory Board**

Chocolate Crinkles

Hermit Cookie Bars

Makes 3 dozen bar cookies

- ½ cup CRISCO® PURITAN® Oil
- ¾ cup firmly packed brown sugar
- 2 eggs
- 2 tablespoons skim milk
- 1½ cups all-purpose flour
- ¾ teaspoon ground cinnamon
- ½ teaspoon baking soda
- ½ teaspoon ground nutmeg
- ¼ teaspoon salt
- ¼ teaspoon ground cloves
- 1⅓ cups raisins
- ½ cup chopped walnuts
- 2 tablespoons confectioners sugar

Heat oven to 350°F. Oil 13×9×2-inch pan.

Combine Crisco® Puritan® Oil and brown sugar in large bowl. Beat at medium speed of electric mixer. Add eggs, one at a time, beating well after each addition. Mix in milk.

Combine flour, cinnamon, baking soda, nutmeg, salt and cloves. Beat into creamed mixture at low speed until blended. Stir in raisins and nuts. Spread evenly into pan.

Bake at 350°F for 23 to 26 minutes, or until wooden toothpick inserted in center comes out clean. Cool in pan on wire rack. Cut into bars, about 2×1½ inches. Sift confectioners sugar over bars.

Drop Cookie Variation: *Drop batter by level measuring tablespoonfuls 2 inches apart on oiled cookie sheets. Bake at 350°F for 8 to 9 minutes. Remove to cooling rack. Cool. Sift confectioners sugar over cookies.*

An easy make-over: *A light dusting of confectioners sugar is a low-calorie alternative to frosting.*

Nutrients per serving (1 bar):

Calories	96	Cholesterol	12 mg
Fat	4 g	Sodium	33 mg

Peanut Butter Bars

Peanut Butter Bars

Makes 2 dozen bar cookies

- 1 package DUNCAN HINES® Peanut Butter Cookie Mix
- 2 egg whites
- ½ cup chopped peanuts
- 1 cup confectioners sugar
- 2 tablespoons water
- ½ teaspoon vanilla extract

1. Preheat oven to 350°F.

2. Combine cookie mix, contents of peanut butter packet from Mix and egg whites in large bowl. Stir until thoroughly blended. Press in ungreased 13×9×2-inch pan. Sprinkle peanuts over dough. Press lightly.

3. Bake at 350°F for 16 to 18 minutes or until golden brown. Cool completely in pan on wire rack.

4. Combine confectioners sugar, water and vanilla extract in small bowl. Stir until blended. Drizzle glaze over top. Cut into bars.

Nutrients per serving (1 bar):

Calories	65	Cholesterol	0 mg
Fat	7 g	Sodium	104 mg

Cappuccino Bon Bons

Cappuccino Bon Bons

Makes 40 bon bons

1 package DUNCAN HINES® Fudge Brownie
    Mix, Family Size
2 eggs
⅓ cup water
⅓ cup CRISCO® PURITAN® Oil
1½ tablespoons FOLGERS® Instant Coffee
1 teaspoon ground cinnamon
    Whipped topping
    Ground cinnamon or fresh fruit for garnish

1. Preheat oven to 350°F. Place 1½-inch foil cupcake liners on cookie sheet.

2. Combine brownie mix, eggs, water, oil, instant coffee and 1 teaspoon cinnamon. Stir with spoon until well blended, about 50 strokes. Fill each cupcake liner with 1 measuring tablespoon batter.

3. Bake at 350°F for 12 to 15 minutes or until wooden toothpick inserted in centers comes out clean. Cool completely. Garnish each bon bon with whipped topping and a dash of cinnamon or piece of fruit. Refrigerate until ready to serve.

Tip: To make larger bon bons, use 12 (2½-inch) foil cupcake liners and fill with ¼ cup batter. Bake for 28 to 30 minutes.

Nutrients per serving (1 bon bon):			
Calories	87	Cholesterol	11 mg
Fat	4 g	Sodium	53 mg

Banana Cookies

Makes 4 dozen cookies

2 ripe, medium DOLE® Bananas, peeled
1½ cups all-purpose flour
½ teaspoon baking soda
½ teaspoon salt
½ teaspoon ground cinnamon
¼ teaspoon ground nutmeg
1½ cups brown sugar, packed
¾ cup margarine, softened
1 egg
½ cup light dairy sour cream
1 teaspoon vanilla extract
1½ cups rolled oats, uncooked
1 cup DOLE® Golden Raisins
¾ cup DOLE® Chopped Almonds, toasted

Place bananas in blender. Process until puréed; use 1 cup for recipe.

Combine flour, baking soda, salt and spices in small bowl.

Beat brown sugar and margarine in large bowl until light and fluffy. Beat in 1 cup bananas, egg, sour cream and vanilla. Beat in flour mixture until well blended. Stir in oats, raisins and almonds. Cover and refrigerate dough 1 hour to firm.

Drop dough by heaping tablespoons 2 inches apart onto greased cookie sheets.

Bake in 350°F oven 15 to 20 minutes or until cookies are light brown around edges. Cool on wire racks.

Prep time: 20 minutes
Chill time: 60 minutes
Bake time: 20 minutes per batch

Nutrients per serving (1 cookie):			
Calories	113	Cholesterol	7 mg
Fat	5 g	Sodium	72 mg

Pineapple Oatmeal Cookies

Makes about 2½ dozen cookies

1 can (20 ounces) DOLE® Crushed Pineapple
    in Syrup*
1½ cups firmly packed brown sugar
1 cup margarine, softened
1 egg
3 cups rolled oats, uncooked
2 cups all-purpose flour
1 teaspoon baking powder
1 teaspoon ground cinnamon
½ teaspoon salt
1 cup DOLE® Raisins
1 cup DOLE® Natural Almonds, toasted,
    chopped

Drain pineapple well; reserve ½ cup syrup.

Beat sugar and margarine in large bowl until light and fluffy. Beat in egg, pineapple and reserved ½ cup syrup. Combine remaining ingredients in medium bowl; blend into pineapple mixture.

Drop dough by 2 heaping tablespoonfuls onto greased cookie sheets. Press lightly with back of spoon.

Bake in 350°F oven 20 to 25 minutes until golden. Cool on wire racks.

Prep time: 15 minutes
Bake time: 25 minutes per batch

*Use pineapple packed in juice, if desired.

Nutrients per serving (1 cookie):			
Calories	228	Cholesterol	9 mg
Fat	10 g	Sodium	125 mg

Tropical Bar Cookies

Makes 16 cookies

½ cup DOLE® Sliced Almonds, divided
1 cup all-purpose flour
⅓ cup margarine, melted
½ cup sugar, divided
1 can (20 ounces) DOLE® Crushed Pineapple
    in Syrup, drained
1 package (8 ounces) light cream cheese,
    softened
1 egg
1 teaspoon vanilla extract
⅓ cup flaked coconut

Preheat oven to 350°F. Chop ¼ cup almonds for crust; mix with flour, margarine and ¼ cup sugar in medium bowl until crumbly. Press onto bottom of 9-inch square pan. Bake 12 minutes.

Beat pineapple, cream cheese, egg, remaining ¼ cup sugar and vanilla in large bowl until blended. Pour over crust. Top with coconut and remaining ¼ cup sliced almonds.

Bake 35 to 40 minutes or until golden brown. Cool on wire rack. Refrigerate at least 2 hours before cutting into bars.

Nutrients per serving (1 bar):			
Calories	199	Cholesterol	28 mg
Fat	10 g	Sodium	111 mg

Tropical Bar Cookies

Double Chocolate Cloud Cookies

Makes about 4 dozen cookies

3 egg whites
⅛ teaspoon cream of tartar
¾ cup sugar
1 teaspoon vanilla extract
2 tablespoons HERSHEY'S Cocoa or
    HERSHEY'S Premium European Style
    Cocoa
¾ cup HERSHEY'S Semi-Sweet Chocolate
    Chips
    Chocolate Drizzle Glaze (recipe follows)

Heat oven to 300°F. Place parchment paper on cookie sheets. In large mixer bowl, beat egg whites and cream of tartar until soft peaks form. Gradually add sugar and vanilla, beating until stiff peaks hold their shape, sugar is dissolved and mixture is glossy. Sift cocoa over egg white mixture; gently fold in cocoa just until combined. Fold in chocolate chips. Drop by heaping teaspoonfuls onto prepared cookie sheets. Bake 20 to 25 minutes or just until dry. Carefully peel cookies off paper; cool completely on wire racks. Place waxed paper under wire racks with cookies. Prepare Chocolate Drizzle Glaze; drizzle glaze lightly over cookies. Store, covered, at room temperature.

Chocolate Drizzle Glaze: In top of double boiler over hot, not boiling, water, melt ⅓ cup Hershey's Semi-Sweet Chocolate Chips and ½ teaspoon shortening, stirring until smooth. Remove from heat; cool slightly, stirring frequently.

Nutrients per serving (3 cookies):			
Calories	100	Cholesterol	0 mg
Fat	4 g	Sodium	12 mg

Jelly-Filled Dainties

Makes 4 dozen cookies

- **2 cups all-purpose flour**
- **½ teaspoon salt**
- **2¼ cups KELLOGG'S® CORN FLAKES cereal**
- **1 cup margarine, softened**
- **½ cup firmly packed brown sugar**
- **1 egg**
- **½ teaspoon vanilla extract**
- **1 cup currant, raspberry or strawberry jelly**

Stir together flour and salt; set aside. Crush Kellogg's® Corn Flakes cereal into fine crumbs to measure ½ cup; set aside.

In large bowl, blend margarine and sugar. Add egg and vanilla; beat well. Stir in flour mixture.

Shape dough into 1-inch balls. Roll in cereal. Place about 2 inches apart on ungreased cookie sheets. Make an indentation in each cookie using handle of wooden spoon.

Bake at 300°F for 8 to 10 minutes. Remove from oven; press down indentation in each cookie. Return to oven and bake about 10 minutes more or until lightly browned. Cool on cookie sheets 1 minute. Cool completely on wire racks. When cool, fill centers with about 1 teaspoon jelly.

Nutrients per serving (1 cookie):			
Calories	84	Cholesterol	4 mg
Fat	4 g	Sodium	82 mg

Lemon Almond Delights

Makes 3 dozen cookies

- **1 package DUNCAN HINES® Moist Deluxe Lemon Supreme Cake Mix**
- **2 eggs**
- **¼ cup CRISCO® PURITAN® Oil**
- **⅔ cup chopped almonds**

1. Preheat oven to 375°F. Grease cookie sheets.

2. Combine cake mix, eggs and oil in large bowl. Stir until thoroughly blended. Stir in chopped almonds. Drop by rounded teaspoonfuls onto cookie sheets.

3. Bake at 375°F for 8 to 9 minutes or until set. Cool 1 minute on cookie sheets. Remove to cooling racks.

Nutrients per serving (1 cookie):			
Calories	90	Cholesterol	12 mg
Fat	4 g	Sodium	97 mg

Cocoa Banana Bars

Cocoa Banana Bars

Makes 9 bar cookies

Bars
- **⅔ cup QUAKER® Oat Bran hot cereal, uncooked**
- **⅔ cup all-purpose flour**
- **½ cup granulated sugar**
- **⅓ cup unsweetened cocoa**
- **½ cup mashed ripe banana (about 1 large)**
- **¼ cup liquid vegetable oil margarine**
- **3 tablespoons light corn syrup**
- **2 egg whites, lightly beaten**
- **1 teaspoon vanilla**
  Strawberry halves (optional)

Glaze
- **2 teaspoons unsweetened cocoa**
- **2 teaspoons liquid vegetable oil margarine**
- **¼ cup powdered sugar**
- **2 to 2½ teaspoons warm water, divided**

For Bars, heat oven to 350°F. Lightly spray 8-inch square baking pan with nonstick cooking spray, or oil lightly. In large bowl, combine oat bran, flour, granulated sugar and ⅓ cup cocoa. Add combined banana, ¼ cup margarine, corn syrup, egg whites and vanilla; mix well. Pour into prepared pan, spreading evenly. Bake 23 to 25 minutes or until center is set. Cool on wire rack. Drizzle glaze over brownies. Top with strawberry halves, if desired. Cut into bars. Store tightly covered.

For Glaze, in small bowl, combine 2 teaspoons cocoa and 2 teaspoons margarine. Stir in powdered sugar and 1 teaspoon water. Gradually add remaining 1 to 1½ teaspoons water to make medium-thick glaze, mixing well.

Nutrients per serving (1 bar):			
Calories	210	Cholesterol	0 mg
Fat	7 g	Sodium	60 mg

Discover just how sensational low-calorie desserts can be. Fresh fruit and other healthy ingredients make these scrumptious recipes a dieter's dream come true. Visions of warm-from-the-oven apple crisp, smooth and creamy pudding parfaits and frozen ices and sorbets can become reality today!

Silky Cocoa Creme

Makes 8 servings

1 envelope unflavored gelatin
¼ cup cold water
½ cup sugar
⅓ cup HERSHEY'S Cocoa
¾ cup skim milk
½ cup low-fat part-skim ricotta cheese, at room temperature
1 teaspoon vanilla extract
½ cup thawed frozen non-dairy whipped topping
Fresh strawberries (optional)

In small bowl, sprinkle gelatin over water; allow to stand 2 minutes to soften. In medium saucepan, stir together sugar and cocoa; stir in milk. Cook over medium heat, stirring constantly, until mixture is very hot. Add gelatin mixture, stirring until gelatin is dissolved; pour into medium bowl. Refrigerate until mixture is slightly cold (do not allow to gel). In blender container or food processor blend ricotta cheese and vanilla until smooth; transfer to small bowl. Add whipped topping; stir until combined. Gradually fold ricotta mixture into cocoa mixture; pour into 2-cup mold. Refrigerate until set, about 4 hours. Unmold; serve with strawberries.

Nutrients per serving:			
Calories	110	Cholesterol	5 mg
Fat	3 g	Sodium	35 mg

Orange and Raisin Bread Pudding

Makes 6 servings

4 cups ¾-inch raisin bread cubes (about 6 slices)
1 whole egg *plus* 2 egg whites
1½ cups (12-ounce can) *undiluted* CARNATION® Lite Evaporated Skimmed Milk
2 tablespoons honey
1 tablespoon margarine, melted
1 tablespoon grated orange zest
Powdered sugar and orange zest (optional)

Preheat oven to 375°F. Arrange bread cubes in single layer on baking sheet; toast 6 to 8 minutes or until lightly browned. In large bowl, beat egg and egg whites. Add evaporated skimmed milk, honey, margarine and orange zest; beat until blended. Stir in toasted bread cubes; let stand 10 minutes. Spray 1-quart casserole dish with nonstick cooking spray; pour in bread mixture. Set casserole dish in 9-inch square baking pan; fill baking pan with 1 inch hot water.

Bake in 375°F oven 45 to 55 minutes or until puffed and golden brown. Remove casserole from water; cool 5 to 10 minutes. Garnish with powdered sugar and orange zest if desired. Serve warm.

Nutrients per serving:			
Calories	172	Cholesterol	39 mg
Fat	4 g	Sodium	220 mg

Silky Cocoa Creme

Left to right: Vanilla Pudding Grahamwiches, Chocolate Pudding Sandwiches

Vanilla Pudding Grahamwiches

Makes 22 sandwiches

1½ cups cold skim milk
  1 package (4-serving size) JELL-O® Vanilla
      Flavor Sugar Free Instant Pudding and Pie
      Filling
3¼ cups (8-ounce container) COOL WHIP®
      LITE® Whipped Topping, thawed
  1 cup miniature marshmallows
 22 whole cinnamon graham crackers, broken
      into 44 squares
  2 squares BAKER'S® Semi-Sweet Chocolate,
      shaved or grated

Pour milk into large mixing bowl. Add pudding mix. Beat with wire whisk until well blended, 1 to 2 minutes. Gently stir in whipped topping and marshmallows.

For each sandwich, spread about 2 tablespoons pudding mixture onto each of 2 graham cracker squares. Lightly press graham crackers together to form sandwich. Repeat with remaining graham crackers and pudding mixture. Press edges of each sandwich into chocolate to coat. Wrap each sandwich with plastic wrap. Freeze until firm, about 6 hours or overnight.

Remove grahamwiches from freezer about 5 minutes before serving. Let stand at room temperature to soften slightly.

Note: Store any leftover sandwiches in freezer in plastic bag or airtight container.

Nutrients per serving (1 sandwich cookie):			
Calories	110	Cholesterol	0 mg
Fat	4 g	Sodium	160 mg

Chocolate Pudding Sandwiches

Makes 22 sandwiches

1½ cups cold skim milk
  1 package (4-serving size) JELL-O® Chocolate
      Flavor Sugar Free Instant Pudding and Pie
      Filling
3¼ cups (8-ounce container) COOL WHIP®
      LITE® Whipped Topping, thawed
  1 cup miniature marshmallows
  1 package (9 ounces) chocolate wafer cookies
      (44 cookies)

Pour milk into large mixing bowl. Add pudding mix. Beat with wire whisk until well blended, 1 to 2 minutes. Gently stir in whipped topping and marshmallows.

For each sandwich, spread about 2 tablespoons pudding mixture onto each of 2 cookies. Lightly press together to form sandwich. Wrap each sandwich with plastic wrap. Repeat with remaining cookies and pudding mixture. Freeze until firm, about 6 hours or overnight.

Remove sandwiches from freezer about 5 minutes before serving. Let stand at room temperature to soften slightly.

Note: Store any leftover sandwiches in freezer in plastic bag or airtight container.

Nutrients per serving (1 sandwich cookie):			
Calories	100	Cholesterol	0 mg
Fat	3 g	Sodium	170 mg

Berried Cantaloupe with Honey Dressing

Makes 4 servings

    Honey Dressing (recipe follows)
 2 small cantaloupes
 2 cups raspberries

Prepare Honey Dressing; cover. Refrigerate. Cut cantaloupes in half; remove seeds. Cover; refrigerate.

When ready to serve, place cantaloupe halves in individual bowls; fill centers with raspberries. Drizzle with dressing.

Honey Dressing
 1 cup plain yogurt
 2 tablespoons honey
 2 teaspoons grated orange peel

Combine all ingredients in small bowl; mix until well blended.

Nutrients per serving:			
Calories	156	Cholesterol	4 mg
Fat	2 g	Sodium	54 mg

Apple Cinnamon Dessert

Makes 2 servings

 1 cup pared diced apples
 2 teaspoons REALEMON® Lemon Juice from
    Concentrate
1½ tablespoons sugar
 ⅛ teaspoon ground cinnamon
 2 slices BORDEN® Lite-line® American Flavor
    Process Cheese Product*, cut into small
    pieces
 ½ tablespoon low-calorie margarine
 2 plain melba rounds, crushed

Preheat oven to 350°F. In small bowl, combine apples, ReaLemon® brand, sugar and cinnamon; mix well. Stir in cheese product pieces. Divide mixture between 2 small baking dishes. Top with margarine; sprinkle with melba crumbs. Bake 12 to 15 minutes or until apples are tender. Refrigerate leftovers.

"½ the calories"– 8% milkfat product

Nutrients per serving:			
Calories	123	Cholesterol	5 mg
Fat	4 g	Sodium	315 mg

Pineapple Shortcake and Banana-Chocolate Sauce

Makes 4 servings

 1 medium DOLE® Fresh Pineapple
 2 medium DOLE® Oranges, peeled and
    sectioned
 4 slices angel food cake

Banana-Chocolate Sauce
 1 extra-ripe small DOLE® Banana
 3 tablespoons corn syrup
 2 tablespoons unsweetened cocoa
 2 teaspoons margarine, melted

Twist crown from pineapple. Cut pineapple in half lengthwise. Refrigerate half for another use, such as fruit salad. Cut fruit from shell with knife. Trim off core and cut fruit into bite-sized chunks. Toss with orange sections.

Arrange cake slices on 4 dessert plates. Mound fruit evenly over cake. Drizzle with Banana-Chocolate Sauce.

For Banana-Chocolate Sauce, place banana in blender; blend until smooth. Add remaining ingredients; blend until smooth.

Prep time: 20 minutes

Nutrients per serving:			
Calories	300	Cholesterol	0 mg
Fat	3 g	Sodium	114 mg

Pineapple Shortcake and Banana-Chocolate Sauce

Apple Walnut Bread Pudding

Makes 8 servings

4 slices firm-textured white bread
2 teaspoons margarine, melted
2 medium apples, chopped
¼ cup chopped walnuts
2 cups cold 2% low-fat milk
½ cup thawed frozen egg substitute
1 teaspoon vanilla
1 package (4-serving size) JELL-O® Vanilla Flavor Sugar Free Pudding and Pie Filling
1 teaspoon ground cinnamon, divided

Heat oven to 350°F.

Lightly brush bread with margarine; cut into ½-inch cubes. Place on cookie sheet. Bake 10 minutes or until lightly toasted. Place cubes in shallow 1½-quart baking dish. Add apples and walnuts; toss lightly.

Pour milk, egg substitute and vanilla into large mixing bowl. Beat with wire whisk until well blended. Add pudding mix and ½ teaspoon cinnamon; whisk until well blended. Pour over bread mixture; sprinkle with remaining cinnamon. Bake 30 minutes. Remove from oven; let stand 10 minutes before serving.

Nutrients per serving:

Calories	130	Cholesterol	5 mg
Fat	5 g	Sodium	190 mg

Apple Walnut Bread Pudding

Strawberry Yogurt Angel

Makes 12 servings

1 container (8 ounces) PHILADELPHIA BRAND® Soft Cream Cheese with Strawberries
½ cup vanilla yogurt
½ cup orange juice
1 tablespoon orange-flavored liqueur (optional)
1 tube angel food cake (10 inch)
1 pint strawberries, sliced

Place cream cheese, yogurt, orange juice and liqueur in blender container or food processor; cover. Blend until smooth. Serve cream cheese sauce over slices of cake; top with strawberries.

Prep time: 10 minutes

Nutrients per serving:

Calories	220	Cholesterol	15 mg
Fat	6 g	Sodium	130 mg

Baked Bananas

Makes 8 servings

3 tablespoons CRISCO® Shortening
2 teaspoons grated lemon peel
2 teaspoons lemon juice
6 firm ripe bananas
½ cup firmly packed dark brown sugar

Preheat oven to 350°F. Place Crisco® in shallow 3-quart baking dish. Set in oven for 3 to 5 minutes or until Crisco® is melted. Remove from oven; stir in lemon peel and lemon juice. Peel bananas; cut in half crosswise and then lengthwise. Place in baking dish, turning to coat with Crisco® mixture. Sprinkle brown sugar over bananas.

Bake at 350°F for 20 to 25 minutes or until brown sugar is melted and bananas are tender. Serve hot.

Nutrients per serving:

Calories	171	Cholesterol	0 mg
Fat	5 g	Sodium	7 mg

Milk Chocolate Fondue

Makes 1¾ cups

1 package (12 ounces) milk chocolate chips
1 can (5 fluid ounces) PET® Light Skimmed
   Evaporated Milk
2 tablespoons Grand Marnier or kirsch
   (optional)
½ teaspoon vanilla extract
   Angel food cake cubes, fresh fruit or pretzels,
   for dipping

In fondue pot or medium saucepan, combine
chocolate chips and evaporated milk. Cook over low
heat until chocolate is melted, stirring occasionally.

Stir in liqueur and vanilla. Serve with angel food cake
cubes, fresh fruit or pretzels.

*Nutrients per serving (2 tablespoons fondue with ¹⁄₁₂th of
an angel food cake):*

Calories	264	Cholesterol	5 mg
Fat	8 g	Sodium	162 mg

Frozen Apple Sauce 'n' Fruit Cup

Chilled Lemonade Dessert

Makes 8 servings

1½ cups cold water
   1 (3-ounce) package JELL-O® Brand Lemon
      Flavor Sugar Free Gelatin Dessert
   1 (8-ounce) package Light PHILADELPHIA
      BRAND® Neufchatel Cheese, softened
   ⅓ cup frozen lemonade concentrate, thawed
   1 teaspoon grated lemon peel
   2 cups thawed COOL WHIP® Non-Dairy
      Whipped Topping

Bring water to a boil. Gradually add to gelatin in
small bowl; stir until dissolved. Beat neufchatel
cheese, lemonade concentrate and peel in large
mixing bowl at medium speed with electric mixer
until well blended. Stir in gelatin; chill until thickened
but not set. Fold in whipped topping; pour into lightly
oiled 6-cup mold. Chill until firm. Unmold. Garnish
as desired.

*Variation: Substitute 8 individual ½-cup molds for 6-cup
mold.*

Nutrients per serving:

Calories	160	Cholesterol	25 mg
Fat	10 g	Sodium	150 mg

Frozen Apple Sauce 'n' Fruit Cup

Makes 7 servings, 3½ cups

1 can (11 ounces) mandarin orange segments,
   drained
1 package (10 ounces) frozen strawberries,
   thawed
1 cup MOTT'S® Chunky or Regular Apple
   Sauce
1 cup seedless grapes (optional)
2 tablespoons orange juice concentrate

In medium bowl, combine all ingredients. Spoon fruit
mixture into individual dishes or paper cups. Freeze
until firm. Remove from freezer about 30 minutes
before serving. Garnish if desired.

Nutrients per serving (½ cup):

Calories	107	Cholesterol	0 mg
Fat	0 g	Sodium	5 mg

Rice Pudding

Rice Pudding

Makes 6 servings

3 cups 2% low-fat milk
1 large stick cinnamon
1 cup uncooked long-grain rice
2 cups water
½ teaspoon salt
   Peel of an orange or lemon
¾ cup sugar
¼ cup raisins
2 tablespoons dark rum

Heat milk and cinnamon in small saucepan over medium heat until milk is infused with flavor of cinnamon, about 15 minutes. Combine rice, water, and salt in 2- to 3-quart saucepan. Bring to a boil; stir once or twice. Place orange peel on top of rice. Reduce heat to low; cover and simmer 15 minutes or until rice is tender and liquid is absorbed. Remove and discard orange peel. Strain milk and stir into cooked rice. Add sugar and bring to a boil. Reduce heat to low; simmer 20 minutes or until thickened, stirring often. Add raisins and rum; bring to a boil. Reduce heat to low and simmer 10 minutes. Serve hot. Garnish as desired. To reheat, add a little milk to restore creamy texture.

Nutrients per serving:

Calories	297	Cholesterol	10 mg
Fat	3 g	Sodium	259 mg

Favorite recipe from **USA Rice Council**

Cherry Almond Supreme

Makes 6 servings, about 3 cups

1 can (8 ounces) pitted dark sweet cherries in light syrup, undrained
1 package (4-serving size) JELL-O® Brand Cherry Flavor Sugar Free Gelatin
¾ cup boiling water
   Ice cubes
2 tablespoons chopped toasted almonds
1 cup thawed COOL WHIP® LITE® Whipped Topping

Drain cherries, reserving syrup. If necessary, add enough water to reserved syrup to measure ½ cup. Cut cherries into quarters. Completely dissolve gelatin in boiling water. Combine measured syrup and enough ice to measure 1¼ cups. Add to gelatin; stir until slightly thickened. Remove any unmelted ice. Chill until thickened. Measure 1¼ cups gelatin; stir in half the cherries and half the nuts. Set aside.

Gently stir whipped topping into remaining gelatin. Add remaining cherries and nuts; spoon into 6 dessert glasses. Chill until set but not firm, about 15 minutes. Top with clear gelatin mixture. Chill until set, about 1 hour.

Nutrients per serving:

Calories	70	Cholesterol	0 mg
Fat	3 g	Sodium	65 mg

Baked Apple Crumble

Makes 8 servings

Apple Layer
6 cups sliced, peeled Golden Delicious or Rome Beauty apples (about 2 pounds or 6 medium)
2 tablespoons orange or other fruit juice
¾ cup firmly packed light brown sugar
½ cup all-purpose flour
½ teaspoon ground cinnamon
3 tablespoons CRISCO® Oil or CRISCO® PURITAN® Oil

Topping (optional)
½ cup vanilla low-fat yogurt, divided

For Apple Layer, heat oven to 375°F. Oil 2-quart casserole or baking dish. Arrange apples evenly in dish. Drizzle with orange juice. Combine sugar, flour and cinnamon. Mix in Crisco® Oil until crumbly. Spoon over apples. Bake at 375°F for 35 minutes or until apples are tender. Cool slightly. Serve warm.

For Topping, spoon 1 tablespoon vanilla yogurt over each serving.

Nutrients per serving:

Calories	210	Cholesterol	0 mg
Fat	6 g	Sodium	10 mg

Meringue Fruit Cups with Custard Sauce

Makes 8 servings

4 large egg whites, at room temperature
½ teaspoon cream of tartar
    Pinch salt
1 cup sugar
1 can (17 ounces) DEL MONTE® Fruit Cocktail, drained
    Custard Sauce (recipe follows)

Line baking sheet with parchment or waxed paper. With bottom of glass, trace eight 3-inch circles about 2 inches apart on paper. Turn paper over on baking sheet. Beat egg whites until frothy; add cream of tartar and salt. Beat until soft peaks form. Add sugar, 1 tablespoon at a time, and beat until meringue is stiff and shiny, about 10 minutes. Transfer to pastry bag fitted with star tip. Use a little meringue to secure paper to baking sheet.

Pipe 2 tablespoons meringue in center of each circle; spread to edges. Pipe 2 rings, one on top of the other, around edges of circles. Bake in preheated 200°F oven about 1½ hours or until dry but still white. Cool completely. (Meringue may be baked several days ahead and stored in airtight containers.)

Spoon fruit cocktail into meringue cups. Place on individual dessert dishes. Spoon approximately ¼ cup Custard Sauce over each. Garnish with mint leaves, if desired.

Custard Sauce

4 egg yolks,* slightly beaten
¼ cup sugar
    Pinch salt
2 cups milk, scalded
1 teaspoon vanilla extract

Meringue Fruit Cup with Custard Sauce

In top of double boiler, mix egg yolks, sugar and salt until well blended. Slowly add milk, stirring constantly. Cook over hot water, stirring constantly, until mixture begins to thicken. Remove from heat; stir in vanilla. Refrigerate. Makes about 2½ cups.

*Use only clean, uncracked eggs.

Nutrients per serving:

Calories	217	Cholesterol	115 mg
Fat	5 g	Sodium	63 mg

Raspberry Rice aux Amandes

Makes 8 servings

3 cups cooked rice
2 cups skim milk
⅛ teaspoon salt
    Low-calorie sugar substitute to equal 2 tablespoons sugar
1 teaspoon vanilla extract
¾ cup thawed frozen light whipped topping
3 tablespoons sliced almonds, toasted
1 package (16 ounces) frozen unsweetened raspberries, thawed*

Combine rice, milk, and salt in 2-quart saucepan. Cook over medium heat until thick and creamy, 5 to 8 minutes, stirring frequently. Remove from heat. Cool. Add sugar substitute and vanilla. Fold in whipped topping and almonds. Alternate rice mixture and raspberries in parfait glasses or dessert dishes.

To Microwave: Combine rice, milk, and salt in 1½-quart microproof baking dish. Cover and cook on HIGH (100% power) 3 minutes. Reduce setting to MEDIUM (50% power) and cook 7 minutes, stirring after 3 and 5 minutes. Stir in sugar substitute and vanilla; cool. Fold in whipped topping and almonds. Alternate rice mixture and raspberries in parfait glasses or dessert dishes.

*Substitute frozen unsweetened strawberries or other fruit for the raspberries, if desired.

Nutrients per serving:

Calories	180	Cholesterol	2 mg
Fat	3 g	Sodium	369 mg

Favorite recipe from **USA Rice Council**

Frozen Chocolate-Cherry Yogurt Cups

Makes 12 servings

¼ cup HERSHEY'S Cocoa
¼ cup sugar
    Yogurt Cheese (recipe follows)
¼ cup finely chopped maraschino cherries
¼ cup sliced almonds
½ teaspoon vanilla extract
¼ teaspoon almond extract
1 envelope (1.3 ounces) whipped topping mix
½ cup cold skim milk
12 paper-lined (2½-inch) muffin cups

In medium bowl, stir together cocoa, sugar and Yogurt Cheese until well blended. Stir in cherries, almonds and vanilla and almond extracts. In small deep bowl, combine topping mix and milk; prepare according to package directions. Gradually fold whipped topping into cocoa mixture. Spoon into muffin cups. Cover; freeze until firm. Before serving, allow to stand at room temperature about 5 minutes.

Yogurt Cheese: Line non-metal colander or sieve with large piece of double thickness cheesecloth; place colander over deep bowl. Spoon 2 cups (two 8-ounce containers) vanilla low-fat yogurt (with no gelatin added) into prepared colander; cover. Refrigerate until liquid no longer drains from yogurt, about 24 hours. Remove yogurt from cheesecloth; discard liquid.

Nutrients per serving:

Calories	90	Cholesterol	5 mg
Fat	2 g	Sodium	35 mg

Cranberry Apple Ice

Makes 14 servings, 7 cups

1 can (12 ounces) frozen apple-cranberry juice concentrate, thawed
1½ cups MOTT'S® Chunky Apple Sauce
1 bottle (32 ounces) sugar-free lemon-lime flavored carbonated beverage (4 cups)

In 2-quart nonmetal bowl, combine all ingredients; mix well. Cover; freeze until firm. Scoop frozen mixture into 5-ounce drinking cups or spoon into dessert dishes.

Nutrients per serving (½ cup):

Calories	33	Cholesterol	0 mg
Fat	0 g	Sodium	14 mg

Chocolate Peanut Butter Parfaits

Chocolate Peanut Butter Parfaits

Makes 6 servings, 3 cups

2 cups plus 2 tablespoons cold skim milk, divided
2 tablespoons chunky peanut butter
1 cup thawed COOL WHIP® LITE® Whipped Topping
1 package (4-serving size) JELL-O® Chocolate Flavor Sugar Free Instant Pudding and Pie Filling

Add 2 tablespoons milk to peanut butter; stir until well blended. Stir in whipped topping.

Pour the remaining 2 cups milk into medium mixing bowl. Add pudding mix. Beat with wire whisk until well blended, 1 to 2 minutes. Spoon half the pudding mixture into 6 parfait glasses; cover with whipped topping mixture. Top with remaining pudding mixture. Refrigerate until ready to serve.

Nutrients per serving:

Calories	110	Cholesterol	0 mg
Fat	5 g	Sodium	290 mg

Melon Bubbles

Peach Melba Parfaits

Makes 6 servings

1 (10-ounce) package frozen red raspberries in syrup, thawed
¼ cup red currant jelly
1 tablespoon cornstarch
½ of a (½-gallon) carton BORDEN® or MEADOW GOLD® Peach Frozen Yogurt
⅔ cup granola or natural cereal

Drain raspberries, reserving ⅔ cup syrup. In small saucepan, combine reserved syrup, jelly and cornstarch. Cook and stir until slightly thickened and glossy. Cool. Stir in raspberries. In 6 parfait or wine glasses, layer raspberry sauce, frozen yogurt, raspberry sauce, then granola; repeat. Freeze. Remove from freezer 5 to 10 minutes before serving. Garnish as desired. Freeze leftovers.

Nutrients per serving:

Calories	268	Cholesterol	9 mg
Fat	5 g	Sodium	75 mg

Melon Bubbles

Makes 7 (½-cup) servings

1 package (4-serving size) JELL-O® Brand Sugar Free Gelatin, any flavor
¾ cup boiling water
½ cup cold water
Ice cubes
1 cup melon balls (cantaloupe, honeydew or watermelon)

Completely dissolve gelatin in boiling water. Combine cold water and enough ice cubes to measure 1¼ cups. Add to gelatin; stir until slightly thickened. Remove any unmelted ice. Measure 1⅓ cups gelatin; add melon. Pour into 7 individual dishes or medium serving bowl.

Beat remaining gelatin at high speed with electric mixer until thickened and doubled in volume. Spoon over gelatin in dishes. Chill until set, about 2 hours. Garnish as desired.

Nutrients per serving:

Calories	14	Cholesterol	0 mg
Fat	0 g	Sodium	50 mg

Lime Sorbet

Makes 6 servings

4 large limes
1½ cups hot water
6 tablespoons sugar
1 egg white, slightly beaten*
1 drop *each* green and yellow food color
Mint leaves or citrus leaves, for garnish

Grate peel from 1 lime; set aside. Squeeze juice from limes to measure ½ cup juice. In 1-quart measure, combine hot water and sugar; stir to dissolve. In medium bowl, combine lime juice, lime peel, sugar mixture, egg white and food colors; blend well. Pour into shallow pan. Cover and freeze, stirring about once an hour to break up ice crystals, until firm. Remove from freezer about 20 minutes before serving. Garnish with mint leaves or citrus leaves, if desired.

**Use only clean, uncracked egg.*

Nutrients per serving:

Calories	68	Cholesterol	0 mg
Fat	0 g	Sodium	9 mg

Favorite recipe from **The Sugar Association, Inc.**

Ambrosial Fruit Dessert

Makes 4 servings

1 medium DOLE® Fresh Pineapple
1 medium DOLE® Orange, peeled and sliced
1 red DOLE® Apple, cored and sliced
1 cup seedless DOLE® Grapes

Fruit Glaze
¾ cup DOLE® Pineapple Orange Juice
2 tablespoons orange marmalade
1 tablespoon cornstarch
1 teaspoon rum extract
2 teaspoons grated lime peel

4 teaspoons flaked coconut

Twist crown from pineapple. Cut pineapple in half lengthwise. Refrigerate half for another use, such as fruit salad. Cut fruit from shell with knife. Cut fruit crosswise into thin slices.

Arrange pineapple slices, orange slices, apple slices and grapes evenly on 4 dessert plates. For Fruit Glaze, combine all ingredients except lime peel in saucepan. Cook, stirring, until sauce boils and thickens. Cool. Stir in lime peel. Drizzle Fruit Glaze over arranged fruit. Sprinkle with coconut.

Prep time: 20 minutes

Nutrients per serving:

Calories	152	Cholesterol	0 mg
Fat	1 g	Sodium	8 mg

Strawberries Elegante

Makes 6 servings

6 cups sliced strawberries
2 tablespoons orange-flavored liqueur or orange juice
1 container (8 ounces) Light PHILADELPHIA BRAND® Pasteurized Process Cream Cheese Product
3 tablespoons firmly packed brown sugar
1 tablespoon orange-flavored liqueur or orange juice
1 tablespoon skim milk

Toss strawberries with 2 tablespoons liqueur in small bowl. Place cream cheese product, sugar, 1 tablespoon liqueur and milk in blender container or food processor; cover. Blend until smooth. Serve over strawberries. Garnish with fresh mint leaves, if desired.

Prep time: 20 minutes

Nutrients per serving:

Calories	170	Cholesterol	20 mg
Fat	7 g	Sodium	220 mg

Ambrosial Fruit Dessert

Blueberry Crisp

Makes 8 servings

3 cups cooked brown rice
3 cups fresh blueberries*
¼ cup plus 3 tablespoons firmly packed brown sugar, divided
Nonstick cooking spray
⅓ cup rice bran
¼ cup whole wheat flour
¼ cup chopped walnuts
1 teaspoon ground cinnamon
3 tablespoons margarine

Combine rice, blueberries, and 3 tablespoons sugar. Coat 8 individual custard cups or 2-quart baking dish with nonstick cooking spray. Place rice mixture in cups or baking dish; set aside. Combine bran, flour, walnuts, remaining ¼ cup sugar, and cinnamon in bowl. Cut in margarine with pastry blender until mixture resembles coarse meal. Sprinkle over rice mixture. Bake at 375°F for 15 to 20 minutes or until thoroughly heated. Serve warm. Garnish as desired.

To Microwave: Prepare as directed using 2-quart microproof baking dish. Cook, uncovered, on HIGH (100% power) 4 to 5 minutes, rotating dish once during cooking time. Let stand 5 minutes. Serve warm.

Substitute frozen unsweetened blueberries for the fresh blueberries, if desired. Thaw and drain before using. Or, substitute your choice of fresh fruit or combinations of fruit for the blueberries, if desired.

Nutrients per serving:

Calories	243	Cholesterol	0 mg
Fat	8 g	Sodium	61 mg

Favorite recipe from **USA Rice Council**

Chocolate Berry Trifle

Makes 12 servings

1½ cups cold 2% low-fat milk
1 package (4-serving size) JELL-O® Chocolate Flavor Sugar Free Instant Pudding and Pie Filling
3¼ cups (8-ounce container) COOL WHIP® LITE® Whipped Topping, thawed, divided
¼ cup low-sugar strawberry spread
1 package (10 ounces) ENTENMANN'S® Fat Free Golden Loaf Cake, cut into 12 slices
1 cup raspberries
1 cup sliced strawberries

Pour milk into large mixing bowl. Add pudding mix. Beat with wire whisk until well blended, 1 to 2 minutes. Gently stir in 1 cup whipped topping.

Spread strawberry spread evenly over half the cake slices. Top with remaining cake slices; cut into ½-inch cubes. Place half the cubes in large serving bowl; cover with half the combined fruit. Top with 1 cup whipped topping and pudding. Layer with remaining cake cubes, fruit and whipped topping. Garnish as desired. Refrigerate until ready to serve.

Nutrients per serving:

Calories	160	Cholesterol	5 mg
Fat	4 g	Sodium	240 mg

Orange Lemon Sorbet

Makes 6 servings

1 cup sugar
1 cup water
1½ cups orange juice
⅓ cup REALEMON® Lemon Juice from Concentrate
2 tablespoons orange-flavored liqueur (optional)
1 teaspoon grated orange rind

In medium saucepan, combine sugar and water. Over medium heat bring to a boil; boil 5 minutes. Chill. Add remaining ingredients to sugar syrup. Pour into 8- or 9-inch square pan; cover and freeze about 1½ hours or until slightly frozen. In large mixer bowl, beat until slushy; return to pan. Cover and freeze 2 hours. In large mixer bowl, beat until smooth; return to pan. Cover and freeze at least 1½ hours before serving. If storing longer, remove from freezer 5 minutes before serving. Return leftovers to freezer.

Nutrients per serving:

Calories	151	Cholesterol	0 mg
Fat	trace	Sodium	5 mg

Blueberry Crisp

Raspberry Yogurt Parfaits

Makes 8 servings

¾ cup water
¾ cup UNCLE BEN'S® Rice In An Instant
2 cartons (8 ounces *each*) raspberry low-fat
   yogurt
2 cups fresh raspberries

In small saucepan, bring water to a boil. Stir in rice. Cover; remove from heat and set aside for 5 minutes or until all liquid is absorbed. Cool to room temperature. Stir in yogurt; refrigerate at least 30 minutes. Just before serving, layer rice mixture and berries in parfait glasses or dessert dishes.

Note: *For variety, mix and match your favorite fresh fruit with your favorite fruit-flavored yogurt.*

Nutrients per serving:

Calories	100	Cholesterol	2 mg
Fat	trace	Sodium	35 mg

Frozen Banana Dessert Cups

Makes 8 to 12 servings

2 extra-ripe, medium DOLE® Bananas, peeled
1 cup DOLE® Fresh Strawberries
1 can (8 ounces) DOLE® Crushed Pineapple in
   Juice, drained
2 tablespoons honey
   Dash ground nutmeg
1 cup frozen whipped topping, thawed
¼ cup DOLE® Chopped Almonds
1 cup DOLE® Pure & Light Mountain Cherry
   Juice
1 tablespoon cornstarch
1 tablespoon sugar
   Sliced DOLE® fresh fruit for garnish

Frozen Banana Dessert Cup

Place bananas, strawberries, pineapple, honey and nutmeg in blender container. Process until smooth. Pour into large bowl. Fold in whipped topping and almonds. Line 12 (2½-inch) muffin cups with foil liners. Fill with banana mixture. Cover and freeze until firm. Blend cherry juice, cornstarch and sugar in small saucepan. Cook, stirring, until sauce boils and thickens. Cool.

To serve, spoon cherry sauce onto each serving plate. Remove foil liners from dessert cups. Invert on top of sauce. Arrange fresh fruit around each dessert cup. Garnish as desired.

Nutrients per serving:

Calories	99	Cholesterol	0 mg
Fat	3 g	Sodium	3 mg

Lite Chocolate Mint Parfaits

Makes 7 servings

⅔ cup sugar
¼ cup HERSHEY'S Cocoa
3 tablespoons cornstarch
   Dash salt
2½ cups cold skim milk, divided
1 tablespoon margarine-type vegetable oil
   spread
1½ teaspoons vanilla extract, divided
1 envelope (1.3 ounces) whipped topping mix
¼ teaspoon mint extract
3 to 4 drops red food color

In medium saucepan, combine sugar, cocoa, cornstarch and salt; gradually stir in 2 cups skim milk. Cook over medium heat, stirring constantly, until mixture boils; boil and stir 1 minute. Remove from heat; blend in vegetable oil spread and 1 teaspoon vanilla. Pour into medium bowl. Press plastic wrap onto surface of pudding; refrigerate.

In small bowl, combine topping mix, remaining ½ cup cold skim milk and remaining ½ teaspoon vanilla; prepare according to package directions. Fold ½ cup whipped topping into pudding. Blend mint extract and red food color into remaining topping. Alternately spoon chocolate pudding and mint whipped topping into parfait glasses. Refrigerate.

Nutrients per serving:

Calories	160	Cholesterol	0 mg
Fat	2 g	Sodium	95 mg

Crème Caramel

Makes 6 servings

¾ cup sugar, divided
2 cups 2% low-fat milk
1 carton (8 ounces) HEALTHY CHOICE®
    Cholesterol Free Egg Product
½ teaspoon vanilla extract

Place ½ cup sugar in small heavy saucepan. Cook over low heat until sugar melts and turns golden brown. Pour immediately into 6 custard cups. Cool. In medium bowl, combine milk, egg product, remaining ¼ cup sugar and vanilla. Stir until sugar dissolves. Pour into custard cups. Place cups in baking pan; fill pan with 1 inch hot water. Bake in 350°F oven for 50 minutes or until custard is just set in center. Refrigerate. To serve, run knife around edges of cups and unmold onto serving plate.

Nutrients per serving:

Calories	160	Cholesterol	5 mg
Fat	2 g	Sodium	100 mg

Strawberry Ice

Makes 6 servings

1 cup sugar
½ cup water
3 tablespoons REALEMON® Lemon Juice from
    Concentrate
1 quart (about 1½ pounds) fresh strawberries,
    cleaned and hulled
    Red food coloring (optional)

In blender container, combine sugar, water and ReaLemon® brand; mix well. Gradually add strawberries; blend until smooth, adding food coloring, if desired. Pour into 8-inch square pan; cover and freeze about 1½ hours. In medium mixer bowl, beat until slushy. Cover and return to freezer. Place in refrigerator 1 hour before serving to soften. Freeze leftovers.

Nutrients per serving:

Calories	162	Cholesterol	0 mg
Fat	0 g	Sodium	3 mg

Black Forest Parfait

Black Forest Parfaits

Makes 12 servings

2 cups cold 2% low-fat milk, divided
4 ounces neufchatel cheese
1 package (4-serving size) JELL-O® Chocolate
    Flavor Sugar Free Instant Pudding and Pie
    Filling
1 package (15 ounces) ENTENMANN'S® Fat
    Free Chocolate Loaf, cubed
1 can (20 ounces) reduced-calorie cherry pie
    filling
1 square BAKER'S® Semi-Sweet Chocolate,
    grated

Pour ½ cup milk into blender container. Add neufchatel cheese; cover. Blend until smooth. Add remaining 1½ cups milk and pudding mix; cover. Blend until smooth.

Divide cake cubes evenly among 12 individual dishes. Reserve a few cherries for garnish if desired; spoon remaining cherry pie filling over cake cubes. Top with pudding mixture. Refrigerate until ready to serve. Garnish with reserved cherries and chocolate.

Nutrients per serving:

Calories	190	Cholesterol	10 mg
Fat	4 g	Sodium	340 mg

Orange Terrine with Strawberry Sauce

When ready to serve, place thawed frozen strawberries in blender container; cover. Blend until puréed; strain. Unmold terrine onto serving plate; remove plastic wrap. Decorate with remaining ¾ cup whipped topping and fresh strawberries. Cut into slices. Serve on strawberry purée. Garnish as desired.

Nutrients per serving:			
Calories	100	Cholesterol	25 mg
Fat	3 g	Sodium	60 mg

Apricot Mousse

Makes 4 servings

  1 envelope unflavored gelatin
½ cup *undiluted* CARNATION® Lite Evaporated
    Skimmed Milk
  2 cups (16-ounce can) apricot halves in juice,
    drained
½ teaspoon vanilla extract
  1 egg white*
  2 tablespoons granulated sugar

In medium saucepan, sprinkle gelatin over evaporated skimmed milk; let stand for 5 minutes. Cook over low heat, stirring occasionally, until gelatin is dissolved. In blender or food processor, purée enough apricots to measure *1 cup*. Slice any *remaining* apricots for garnish. Stir apricot purée and vanilla into milk mixture. Refrigerate, stirring occasionally, until mixture is thick enough to mound on spoon. In small bowl, beat egg white until soft peaks form. Gradually add sugar. Beat until stiff peaks form and sugar is dissolved. Fold egg mixture into thickened apricot mixture. Spoon into four 4-ounce dessert dishes.

Apricot Almond Mousse: Substitute ¼ *teaspoon* almond extract for vanilla in recipe.

*Use only clean, uncracked egg.

Nutrients per serving:			
Calories	84	Cholesterol	0 mg
Fat	0 g	Sodium	50 mg

Orange Terrine with Strawberry Sauce

Makes 12 servings

  1 package (3 ounces) ladyfingers, split, divided
  2 packages (4-serving size) or 1 package
    (8-serving size) JELL-O® Brand Orange
    Flavor Sugar Free Gelatin
1½ cups boiling water
  1 cup orange juice
    Ice cubes
  1 tablespoon orange liqueur (optional)
  2 teaspoons grated orange peel
3¼ cups (8 ounces) COOL WHIP® LITE®
    Whipped Topping, thawed, divided
  1 package (10 ounces) BIRDS EYE®
    Strawberries in Syrup, thawed
  1 cup fresh strawberries

Line bottom and sides of 9×5-inch loaf pan with plastic wrap. Stand enough ladyfingers to fit evenly along 2 long sides of pan (cut sides should be facing in).

Dissolve gelatin in boiling water. Combine orange juice and enough ice cubes to measure 1¾ cups. Add to gelatin; stir until slightly thickened. Remove any unmelted ice. Stir in liqueur and orange peel. Gently stir in 2½ cups whipped topping. Spoon gelatin mixture into prepared pan. If necessary, trim ladyfingers to make even with top of gelatin mixture. Arrange remaining ladyfingers evenly on top of mixture. Chill until firm, at least 3 hours.

Nilla® Fruit Kabobs with Honey-Lime Sauce

Makes 4 servings

    24 NILLA® Wafers
     2 cups mixed fresh fruit pieces (pineapple,
          melon, kiwi, strawberries and banana)
     3 tablespoons honey
     3 tablespoons lime juice
     1 teaspoon cornstarch
    ¼ teaspoon grated lime peel
    ⅛ teaspoon ground ginger

On 12 (4-inch) wooden skewers, alternately thread
wafers and fruit pieces; refrigerate until serving time.
In small saucepan over medium heat, heat honey,
lime juice, cornstarch, lime peel and ginger to a boil.
Boil for 1 minute, stirring constantly. To serve, place
3 kabobs on each serving plate; drizzle with warm
honey-lime sauce. Serve immediately.

Nutrients per serving:			
Calories	200	Cholesterol	0 mg
Fat	4 g	Sodium	87 mg

Winter Fruit Tray with Citrus Dip

Makes 6 servings

     1 medium DOLE® Fresh Pineapple
     1 medium DOLE® Orange, peeled, sliced
     1 DOLE® Apple, cored, thinly sliced
     1 DOLE® Kiwifruit, peeled, sliced

Citrus Dip
     1 carton (8 ounces) nonfat plain yogurt
     1 cup light non-dairy whipped topping, thawed
    ¼ cup powdered sugar
     1 teaspoon grated orange peel
     1 teaspoon grated lime peel

Twist crown from pineapple. Cut pineapple in half
lengthwise. Refrigerate half for another use, such as
fruit salad. Cut fruit from shell with knife. Trim off
core and cut fruit into bite-size chunks or wedges.

Arrange pineapple chunks, orange slices, apple slices
and kiwi slices on platter. Serve with Citrus Dip.
Garnish as desired.

For Citrus Dip, combine all ingredients. Spoon into
serving bowl. Place on platter with fruit.

Prep time: 20 minutes

Nutrients per serving:			
Calories	137	Cholesterol	1 mg
Fat	4 g	Sodium	33 mg

Filled Chocolate Meringues

Makes 2 dozen meringues

     2 egg whites, at room temperature
    ¼ teaspoon cream of tartar
       Dash salt
    ½ cup sugar
    ½ teaspoon vanilla extract
     2 tablespoons HERSHEY'S Cocoa
       Chocolate-Cheese Filling (recipe follows)
       Raspberries
       Mint leaves

Heat oven to 275°F. Place parchment paper on
cookie sheets. In small mixer bowl, beat egg whites
with cream of tartar and salt until soft peaks form.
Beat in sugar, 1 tablespoon at a time, until stiff,
glossy peaks form. Fold in vanilla. Sift cocoa over
top of egg white mixture; gently fold in cocoa until
combined. Drop by tablespoonfuls onto parchment
paper. With back of small spoon, make indentation
in center of each mound. Bake 45 minutes or until
meringue turns a light cream color and feels dry to
the touch. Carefully peel meringues off parchment
paper; cool completely on wire racks. To serve, spoon
or pipe about 2 teaspoons Chocolate-Cheese Filling
into center of each meringue. Garnish each with a
raspberry and a mint leaf.

Chocolate-Cheese Filling: In blender container
or food processor, combine 1 cup part-skim ricotta
cheese, 2 tablespoons Hershey's Cocoa, 1
tablespoon sugar and ½ teaspoon vanilla extract;
blend until smooth. Cover; refrigerate.

Nutrients per serving (1 filled meringue):			
Calories	40	Cholesterol	5 mg
Fat	1 g	Sodium	25 mg

Filled Chocolate Meringues

Pinwheel Cake and Cream

Pinwheel Cake and Cream

Makes 12 servings

2 cups cold skim milk
1 package (4-serving size) JELL-O® Vanilla
    Flavor Sugar Free Instant Pudding and Pie
    Filling
1 cup thawed COOL WHIP® LITE® Whipped
    Topping
1 small peach, peeled, chopped
1 teaspoon grated orange peel
1 package (10 ounces) ENTENMANN'S® Fat
    Free Golden Loaf, cut into slices
2 cups cut-up summer fruits (peaches,
    nectarines, berries, seedless grapes)

Pour milk into medium mixing bowl. Add pudding mix. Beat with wire whisk until well blended, 1 to 2 minutes. Gently stir in whipped topping, peach and peel. Arrange cake slices on serving plate. Spoon pudding mixture evenly over cake; top with fruits. Serve immediately or cover and refrigerate until ready to serve.

Nutrients per serving:			
Calories	120	Cholesterol	0 mg
Fat	1 g	Sodium	230 mg

Crispy Baked Apple Slices

Makes 6 servings

2½ pounds (5 to 6 large) Golden Delicious or
    Rome Beauty apples, peeled and sliced
    (about 5 cups)
2 tablespoons apple juice
½ cup all-purpose flour
½ cup firmly packed light brown sugar
½ teaspoon ground cinnamon
¼ cup BUTTER FLAVOR CRISCO®

Preheat oven to 375°F. Grease 2-quart ovenproof dish. Arrange apples evenly in dish. Pour apple juice over apples. In medium bowl, combine flour, sugar and cinnamon. Cut in Butter Flavor Crisco® until crumbly. Spoon evenly over apples.

Bake at 375°F for 35 minutes or until apples are tender. Cool slightly. Serve warm. Top with vanilla yogurt, if desired.

Nutrients per serving:			
Calories	289	Cholesterol	0 mg
Fat	9 g	Sodium	10 mg

Ambrosia Fruit Custard

Makes 4 servings

1 package (4-serving size) sugar-free instant
    vanilla pudding
Ingredients for pudding
1 teaspoon grated DOLE® Lemon peel
1 tablespoon DOLE® Lemon juice
½ teaspoon coconut or almond extract
1 can (8 ounces) DOLE® Pineapple Tidbits,
    drained
1 cup assorted sliced fresh fruit
¼ cup mini marshmallows *or* flaked coconut

Prepare pudding in medium bowl according to package directions. Stir in lemon peel, lemon juice and extract. Reserve ¼ cup pudding for topping.

Spoon remaining pudding equally into 4 dessert bowls. Combine remaining ingredients in small bowl. Spoon over top of pudding in dessert bowls. Drizzle with reserved pudding.

Prep time: 15 minutes

Nutrients per serving:			
Calories	139	Cholesterol	0 mg
Fat	2 g	Sodium	203 mg

Banana-Kiwi Pudding

Makes 4 servings

1⅓ cups cooked rice
1⅓ cups skim milk
1 teaspoon vanilla extract
    Low-calorie sugar substitute to equal
      2 tablespoons sugar
1 ripe banana
¼ cup whipping cream, whipped
2 kiwifruit, sliced, for garnish

Cook rice and milk in 2-quart saucepan over medium heat until thick and creamy, 5 to 8 minutes, stirring frequently. Remove from heat; cool. Stir in vanilla and sugar substitute. Just before serving, mash banana; fold banana and whipped cream into pudding. Garnish with kiwifruit slices.

Nutrients per serving:			
Calories	197	Cholesterol	12 mg
Fat	4 g	Sodium	306 mg

Favorite recipe from **USA Rice Council**

Bavarian Rice Cloud with Bittersweet Chocolate Sauce

Makes 10 servings

1 envelope unflavored gelatin
1½ cups skim milk
3 tablespoons sugar
2 cups cooked rice
2 cups thawed frozen light whipped topping
1 tablespoon almond-flavored liqueur
½ teaspoon vanilla extract
    Nonstick cooking spray
    Bittersweet Chocolate Sauce (recipe follows)
2 tablespoons sliced almonds, toasted

Sprinkle gelatin over milk in small saucepan; let stand 1 minute or until gelatin is softened. Cook over low heat, stirring constantly, until gelatin dissolves. Add sugar and stir until dissolved. Add rice; stir until well blended. Cover and refrigerate until the consistency of unbeaten egg whites. Fold in whipped topping, liqueur, and vanilla. Spoon into 4-cup mold coated with nonstick cooking spray. Cover and

refrigerate until firm. To serve, unmold onto serving platter. Spoon Bittersweet Chocolate Sauce over rice dessert. Sprinkle with toasted almonds.

Bittersweet Chocolate Sauce

3 tablespoons unsweetened cocoa powder
3 tablespoons sugar
½ cup low-fat buttermilk
1 tablespoon almond-flavored liqueur

Combine cocoa and sugar in small saucepan. Add buttermilk, mixing well. Place over medium heat, and cook until sugar dissolves. Stir in liqueur; remove from heat.

Tip: Unmold gelatin desserts onto slightly dampened plate. This will allow you to move the mold and position it on the plate.

Nutrients per serving:

Calories	146	Cholesterol	1 mg
Fat	3 g	Sodium	211 mg

Favorite recipe from **USA Rice Council**

Bavarian Rice Cloud with Bittersweet Chocolate Sauce

Coconut Grove Mold

Makes 8 servings

1 can (8 ounces) crushed pineapple in unsweetened juice, undrained
    Cold water
1 package (4-serving size) JELL-O® Brand Pineapple Flavor Sugar Free Gelatin
1 cup boiling water
1 package (8 ounces) Light PHILADELPHIA BRAND® Neufchatel Cheese, softened
⅓ cup BAKER'S® ANGEL FLAKE® Coconut

Drain pineapple reserving juice. Add enough cold water to juice to measure ¾ cup. Dissolve gelatin in boiling water. Add ¾ cup reserved juice mixture. Beat neufchatel cheese in large mixing bowl at medium speed with electric mixer 1 minute. Gradually add gelatin mixture, mixing until well blended. Chill until thickened but not set; fold in pineapple and coconut. Pour into lightly oiled 4-cup mold; chill until firm. Unmold.

Prep time: 20 minutes plus refrigerating

Nutrients per serving:

Calories	110	Cholesterol	25 mg
Fat	8 g	Sodium	150 mg

Fruit Bread Pudding

Makes 6 servings

> 4 cups cubed whole wheat bread (about 4 slices)
> ½ cup diced dried fruit or raisins
> 1½ cups skim milk
> ½ cup HEALTHY CHOICE® Cholesterol Free Egg Product
> ¼ cup sugar
> 1 teaspoon vanilla
> ¼ teaspoon ground nutmeg

In 1½-quart casserole dish sprayed with nonstick cooking spray, combine bread and fruit. In small bowl, combine milk, egg product, sugar, vanilla and nutmeg. Pour milk mixture over bread. Bake in 350°F oven for 60 minutes or until knife inserted in center comes out clean.

Nutrients per serving:

Calories	160	Cholesterol	5 mg
Fat	1 g	Sodium	190 mg

Citrus Berry Sherbet

Makes 6 servings

> 1 envelope unflavored gelatin
> Juice of 3 SUNKIST® Oranges (1 cup)
> Grated peel and juice of 1 SUNKIST® Lemon
> ¼ cup sugar
> 1½ cups mashed fresh or thawed frozen strawberries or boysenberries (no sugar added)
> ½ cup applesauce

In large saucepan, sprinkle gelatin over orange and lemon juices; allow to stand 2 minutes to soften. Add sugar and lemon peel. Stir over low heat until gelatin and sugar are dissolved. Cool. Stir in strawberries and applesauce. Pour into shallow pan. Freeze until firm, about 4 hours.

Nutrients per serving (½ cup):

Calories	77	Cholesterol	0 mg
Fat	0 g	Sodium	3 mg

Berry Good Sundae

Berry Good Sundaes

Makes 4 servings

> 4 (6-inch) flour tortillas
> 1½ cups diced peeled nectarines
> 1½ cups chopped strawberries or raspberries
> 2 tablespoons sugar
> ½ teaspoon grated lemon peel
> 4 scoops (3 ounces *each*) vanilla ice milk
> Fresh mint sprigs

Preheat oven to 350°F. Soften tortillas according to package directions. Press each tortilla down into ungreased 10-ounce custard cup. Bake 10 to 15 minutes or until crisp. Set aside to cool.

Combine nectarines, strawberries, sugar and lemon peel in large bowl; mix gently until well blended. To assemble, remove tortillas from custard cups. Place each tortilla shell on dessert plate and fill with scoop of ice milk. Spoon equal portions of fruit mixture over tops. Garnish with mint sprigs.

Nutrients per serving:

Calories	278	Cholesterol	6 mg
Fat	4 g	Sodium	80 mg

Pear Fans with Creamy Custard Sauce

Apple-Honeydew Ice

Makes 10 servings, 5 cups

**2 cups sugar-free lemon-lime flavored
    carbonated beverage**
1 cup MOTT'S® Regular Apple Sauce
**1 small honeydew melon, seeded, rind removed,
    cut into chunks**
⅛ teaspoon ground ginger
2 to 3 drops green food color (optional)

In food processor or blender, combine all ingredients; process until smooth. Pour into 8- or 9-inch nonmetal square pan. Cover; freeze until firm. Scoop frozen mixture into dessert dishes.

Nutrients per serving (½ cup):

Calories	37	Cholesterol	0 mg
Fat	0 g	Sodium	14 mg

Pear Fans with Creamy Custard Sauce

Makes 8 servings

8 canned pear halves in juice, drained
    Creamy Custard Sauce (recipe follows)
8 raspberries (optional)
8 mint leaves (optional)

Cut pear halves into thin slices with sharp knife, cutting up to, but not through, stem ends. Holding stem end in place, gently fan out slices from stem. Place on dessert plates. Spoon about ⅓ cup Creamy Custard Sauce around pears. Place raspberry and mint leaf at stem end of each pear, if desired.

Creamy Custard Sauce

3 cups cold 2% lowfat milk
**1 package (4-serving size) JELL-O® Vanilla
    Flavor Sugar Free Instant Pudding and Pie
    Filling**
¼ teaspoon ground cinnamon (optional)

Pour milk into large mixing bowl. Add pudding mix and cinnamon. Beat with wire whisk until well blended, 1 to 2 minutes; cover. Refrigerate until ready to use.

Nutrients per serving:

Calories	160	Cholesterol	20 mg
Fat	4 g	Sodium	420 mg

Rhubarb Crisp

Makes 4 to 6 servings

6 cups chopped fresh rhubarb
½ cup firmly packed brown sugar
⅓ cup all-purpose flour
⅓ cup rolled oats, uncooked
½ teaspoon ground cinnamon
3 tablespoons margarine or butter
    Whipped topping or ice milk (optional)

Preheat oven to 350°F. Place rhubarb in 8-inch square baking dish. Combine brown sugar, flour, oats and cinnamon in medium bowl; cut in margarine with pastry blender until mixture resembles coarse crumbs. Sprinkle crumb mixture over rhubarb. Bake 30 minutes, or until lightly browned. Serve hot or cold with whipped topping or ice milk, if desired. Garnish as desired.

Nutrients per serving:

Calories	187	Cholesterol	0 mg
Fat	6 g	Sodium	77 mg

Frozen Orange Cream

Makes 8 servings

- 1 package (4-serving size) JELL-O® Brand Orange Flavor Sugar Free Gelatin
- ¾ cup boiling water
- 2 cups skim milk
- 1 can (6 ounces) frozen apple juice concentrate, thawed
- 1 cup thawed COOL WHIP® LITE® Whipped Topping
- 1 can (11 ounces) mandarin orange segments, well drained

Completely dissolve gelatin in boiling water. Stir in milk and apple juice concentrate. (Mixture will appear curdled but will be smooth when frozen.) Pour into 13×9-inch metal pan. Freeze until about 1 inch of icy crystals forms around edges, about 1 hour. Spoon mixture into chilled bowl; beat with electric mixer until smooth. Gently stir in whipped topping. Spoon a scant ⅔ cup mixture into each of 8 custard cups. Freeze about 6 hours or overnight.

To serve, reserve 8 orange segments for garnish. Process remaining oranges in blender until smooth. Remove custard cups from freezer; let stand 15 minutes. Run knife around edges of cups; invert onto dessert plates and unmold. Garnish each dessert with about 1 tablespoon puréed oranges, 1 reserved orange segment and a mint leaf, if desired. Store leftover desserts in freezer.

Nutrients per serving:

Calories	100	Cholesterol	0 mg
Fat	1 g	Sodium	75 mg

All-American Pineapple & Fruit Trifle

Makes 8 to 10 servings

- 1 DOLE® Fresh Pineapple
- 1 cup frozen sliced peaches, thawed
- 1 cup frozen strawberries, thawed and sliced
- 1 cup frozen raspberries, thawed
- 1 angel food cake (10 inches in diameter)
- 1 package (4-serving size) instant sugar-free vanilla pudding mix
- ⅓ cup cream sherry
- ½ cup thawed frozen whipped topping

Twist crown from pineapple. Cut pineapple in half lengthwise. Refrigerate half for another use, such as fruit salad. Cut fruit from shell with knife. Cut fruit into thin wedges. Reserve 3 wedges for garnish; combine remaining pineapple wedges with peaches, strawberries and raspberries.

Cut cake in half. Freeze half for another use. Tear remaining cake half into chunks.

Prepare pudding according to package directions.

In 2-quart glass bowl, layer half of each: cake, sherry, fruit mixture and pudding. Repeat layers once. Cover; refrigerate 1 hour or overnight.

Just before serving, garnish with whipped topping, reserved pineapple wedges and mint leaves.

Prep time: 20 minutes
Chill time: 1 hour

Nutrients per serving:

Calories	173	Cholesterol	4 mg
Fat	2 g	Sodium	129 mg

All-American Pineapple & Fruit Trifle

Crunchy Apple Crisp

Makes 4 servings

4 cups peeled, sliced apples*
¼ cup water or apple juice
4 teaspoons firmly packed brown sugar
2 teaspoons lemon juice
¾ teaspoon ground cinnamon
½ cup QUAKER® Oats (quick or old fashioned, uncooked)
2 tablespoons chopped almonds
1 tablespoon firmly packed brown sugar
1 tablespoon margarine, melted

Heat oven to 375°F. Combine apples, water, 4 teaspoons brown sugar, lemon juice and cinnamon; toss lightly to coat apples. Place apple mixture in 8-inch square baking dish.

Combine remaining ingredients; mix well. Sprinkle over apples. Bake about 30 minutes or until apples are tender and topping is lightly browned. Serve warm or chilled.

Or substitute one 20-ounce can unsweetened sliced apples, drained, or two 16-ounce cans "lite" sliced peaches, drained, reserving ¼ cup peach juice to replace apple juice. Prepare as directed above; decrease baking time to 20 to 22 minutes. Serve as above.

Nutrients per serving:

Calories	185	Cholesterol	0 mg
Fat	6 g	Sodium	37 mg

Chocolate Banana Pops

Makes 10 pops

2 cups cold skim milk
1 package (4-serving size) JELL-O® Chocolate Flavor Sugar Free Instant Pudding and Pie Filling
1 cup thawed COOL WHIP® LITE® Whipped Topping
½ cup mashed banana

Pour milk into medium mixing bowl. Add pudding mix. Beat with wire whisk until well blended, 1 to 2 minutes. Gently stir in whipped topping and banana.

Spoon about ⅓ cup pudding mixture into each of ten (5-ounce) paper cups. Insert wooden stick or plastic spoon into each for handle. Freeze until firm, about 5 hours. To serve, press firmly on bottom of cup to release pop.

Nutrients per serving:

Calories	60	Cholesterol	0 mg
Fat	1 g	Sodium	160 mg

Baked Caramel Rice Custard

Makes 8 servings

3 cups skim milk
½ cup uncooked CREAM OF RICE® Hot Cereal
¾ cup EGG BEATERS® 99% Real Egg Product
1 cup sugar, divided
1 teaspoon vanilla extract
   Prepared whipped topping (optional)

In large saucepan, over medium heat, heat milk just to a boil; sprinkle in cereal. Cook for 1 minute, stirring constantly. Slowly add egg product, ⅓ cup sugar and vanilla, stirring constantly. Cook over low heat for 4 to 5 minutes until mixture begins to thicken.

In small saucepan, over medium-high heat, heat remaining ⅔ cup sugar until melted and golden brown. Quickly pour melted sugar into 1½-quart baking dish, tilting to coat dish; pour in milk mixture. Place baking dish in large shallow pan filled to a 1-inch depth with hot water. Bake at 325°F for 60 to 70 minutes or until knife inserted in center comes out clean. Cool at least 15 minutes; unmold onto serving plate. Serve warm or cold with whipped topping if desired. Garnish as desired.

Nutrients per serving:

Calories	178	Cholesterol	2 mg
Fat	trace	Sodium	78 mg

Orange-Apple Ice

Makes 12 servings, 6 cups

1 jar (23 ounces) MOTT'S® Natural or Regular Apple Sauce
⅓ cup orange marmalade
3 egg whites, beaten stiff*

In medium bowl, combine apple sauce and marmalade; mix well. Carefully fold in beaten egg whites. Pour into 8- or 9-inch square pan. Cover; freeze until firm. Scoop frozen mixture into dessert dishes or orange shells.

Tip: To make orange shells, use sharp knife to make sawtooth cut around middle of fruit, cutting inside to center only. Twist, pull apart and remove inside portion, scraping shells clean with spoon.

*Use only clean, uncracked eggs.

Nutrients per serving (½ cup):

Calories	51	Cholesterol	0 mg
Fat	0 g	Sodium	15 mg

Crunchy Apple Crisp

CALORIE, FAT & CHOLESTEROL COUNTER

Your diet affects a lot more than just your waistline. Food choices and eating habits influence not only the shape of your body but your overall health as well.

To help you choose low-cholesterol, low-fat foods from the vast array of products at your local supermarket, we have included this counter. The counter provides values for hundreds of common foods, identified by brand and/or generic name, as well as almost 200 items from fast-food menus. The data comes from the United States Department of Agriculture, manufacturers and processors, and directly from food labels.

Separate columns list the calorie (CAL.) and cholesterol (CHOL.) content of each item. Fat is broken down to show amounts of total fat (FAT) and saturated fat (SAT. FAT). Fats are shown in grams (g); cholesterol is indicated in milligrams (mg). Percentage of calories from total fat and saturated fat is also included. These percentage figures provide a useful guide to fat content because the percentage of fat in a given item doesn't change, regardless of the portion size. For example, between 76 and 81 percent of the calories in peanut butter come from fat, regardless of whether you eat a spoonful or the entire jar.

With a simple formula, you can calculate the fat percentages for foods not included on our list. Since every gram of fat provides your body with 9 calories, simply multiply the grams of fat (or saturated fat) by 9, and divide the result by the total number of calories. Multiply your answer by 100. This gives the percentage of total calories that come from fat (or saturated fat). For example, one raw egg contains 6 grams of fat and has 80 calories. Using the formula, multiply 6 by 9 to get 54; divide 54 by 80 to get 0.675, and multiply 0.675 by 100 to get 67.5 percent (which is then rounded off to 68 percent). Thus, 68 percent of the calories in one raw egg come from fat.

Foods in the counter are grouped into common categories, such as "Beverages" and "Poultry," and are arranged in alphabetical order. After a brief description of each item, a specific portion size is given. The values in each column pertain to the portion size listed. Some food items have "na" or "tr" listed in one of the columns. The "na" means that the content was not available to us at the time of printing. The "tr" means that the food item contains only trace amounts of the substance. When trace amounts are shown for fat or saturated fat, it then becomes impossible to calculate the exact percentage of calories from fat or saturated fat. In this instance, "na" (not available) is also used. However, as a practical matter, if only trace amounts of these elements are present, the percentage of calories they provide is generally quite low, usually less than ten percent.

The symbol "<" means "less than," so "<1" indicates the presence of less than one unit of whatever is being measured (less than one percent, less than one gram). Fractional amounts have been rounded off. Finally, while every effort has been made to ensure that the values listed are as accurate as possible, they are subject to change as food processors modify ingredients and methods of preparation.

Be sure to take note of the Low-Fat Alternatives chart at the end of the counter. This at-a-glance guide provides a number of low-fat alternatives to high-fat foods.

Baked Goods

FOOD/PORTION SIZE	CAL.	FAT		SAT. FAT		CHOL. (mg)
		Total (g)	As % of Cal.	Total (g)	As % of Cal.	
CAKE						
Angel Food Cake Mix, Duncan Hines, 1/12 of cake	140	0	0	0	0	0
Chocolate Loaf, Fat & Cholesterol Free, Entenmann's, 1 oz. slice	70	0	0	0	0	0
Coffeecake, Butter Streusel, Sara Lee, 1/8 of cake (1.4 oz.)	160	7	39	na	na	na
Cupcakes Lights, Hostess, 1 cupcake, 1½ oz.	130	2	14	0	0	0
Devil's Food Cake Mix, Moist Deluxe, Duncan Hines, 1/12 of cake, regular recipe	280	15	48	4	13	65
Same as above, no-cholesterol recipe	270	14	47	2	7	0
Fudge Marble Supreme Cake Mix, Moist Deluxe, Duncan Hines, 1/12 of cake, regular recipe	260	11	38	3	10	65
Same as above, no-cholesterol recipe	250	10	36	2	7	0
Gingerbread Cake & Cookie Mix, Betty Crocker, 1/9 of cake (1.6 oz.), regular recipe	220	7	29	2	8	30
Same as above, no-cholesterol recipe	210	6	26	0	0	0
Golden Loaf, Fat & Cholesterol Free, Entenmann's, 1 oz. slice	70	0	0	0	0	0
Lemon Supreme Cake Mix, Moist Deluxe, Duncan Hines, 1/12 of cake, regular recipe	260	11	38	3	10	65
Same as above, no-cholesterol recipe	250	10	36	2	7	0
Orange Supreme Cake Mix, Duncan Hines, 1/12 of cake, regular recipe	260	11	38	3	10	65
Same as above, no-cholesterol recipe	250	10	36	2	7	0
Pound Cake, All-Butter, Sara Lee, 1 oz.	130	7	48	0	0	na
Pound Cake, Free & Light, Sara Lee, 1 oz.	70	0	0	0	0	0
Spice Cake Mix, Moist Deluxe, Duncan Hines, 1/12 of cake, regular recipe	260	11	38	3	10	65
Same as above, no-cholesterol recipe	250	10	36	2	7	0
Strawberry Supreme Cake Mix, Moist Deluxe, Duncan Hines, 1/12 of cake, regular recipe	260	11	38	3	10	65
Same as above, no-cholesterol recipe	250	10	36	2	7	0
Twinkies Lights, Hostess, 1 cake, 1½ oz.	130	2	14	0	0	0
White Cake Mix, Lovin' Lites, Pillsbury (using egg whites), 1/12 of cake	170	2	11	<1	na	0

FOOD/PORTION SIZE	CAL.	FAT		SAT. FAT		CHOL.
		Total (g)	As % of Cal.	Total (g)	As % of Cal.	(mg)
White Cake Mix, Moist Deluxe, Duncan Hines, regular recipe, 1/12 of cake	270	12	40	3	11	65
Same as above, no-cholesterol recipe	250	10	36	2	7	0
Yellow Cake Mix, Moist Deluxe, Duncan Hines, 1/12 of cake, regular recipe	260	11	38	3	10	65
Same as above, no-cholesterol recipe	250	10	36	2	7	0
COOKIES						
Chocolate Chip, Chips Ahoy, Nabisco, 1 cookie	50	2	36	tr	<1	0
Chocolate chip, refrigerated dough, 1 cookie	56	3	48	1	16	6
Chocolate Chip Mix, Duncan Hines, 1 cookie	65	3	42	2	28	8
Fig Newtons, Nabisco, 1 cookie	60	1	15	tr	<1	0
Nilla Wafers, Nabisco, 3 cookies	60	2	3	tr	tr	5
Oatmeal Raisin, Fat & Cholesterol Free, Entenmann's, 2 cookies	80	0	0	0	0	0
Oreos, Nabisco, 1 cookie	50	2	36	tr	<1	<2
Peanut Butter Mix, Duncan Hines, 1 cookie	70	4	51	1	13	8
Sandwich (chocolate or vanilla), 1 cookie	49	2	37	1	18	0
Shortbread, commercial, 1 small cookie	39	2	46	1	23	7
Sugar, refrigerated dough, 1 cookie	59	3	46	1	15	7
Teddy Grahams Bearwiches, Nabisco, 4 cookies	70	3	39	tr	<1	0
PASTRY						
Coffeecake, Easy Mix, Aunt Jemima, 1/8 of cake	170	5	26	na	na	na
Danish, fruit, 4¼-in. round, 1 pastry	235	13	50	4	15	56
Danish, plain, 1 oz.	110	6	49	2	16	24
Danish, plain, 4¼-in. round, 1 pastry	220	12	49	4	16	49
Toaster, 1 pastry	210	6	26	2	9	0
PIE						
(All pies include crust made with enriched flour and vegetable shortening.)						
Apple, 1/6 of 9-in. pie	405	18	40	5	11	0
Apple, Homestyle, Sara Lee, 1/6 of pie	433	20	42	na	na	0
Blueberry, 1/6 of 9-in. pie	380	17	40	4	9	0
Cherry, 1/6 of 9-in. pie	410	18	40	5	11	0

FOOD/PORTION SIZE	CAL.	FAT		SAT. FAT		CHOL. (mg)
		Total (g)	As % of Cal.	Total (g)	As % of Cal.	
Custard, ⅙ of 9-in. pie	330	17	46	6	16	169
Lemon meringue, ⅙ of 9-in. pie	355	14	35	4	10	143
Peach, ⅙ of 9-in. pie	405	17	38	4	9	0
Pecan, ⅙ of 9-in. pie	575	32	50	5	8	95
Piecrust, Butter Flavor, Keebler, 1 shell, 6 oz.	880	40	41	8	8	0
Piecrust, Chocolate Flavor, Keebler, 1 shell, 6 oz.	960	40	38	8	8	0
Piecrust, Graham Cracker, Keebler, 1 shell, 6 oz.	960	48	45	8	8	0
Piecrust, Graham Cracker, single serve, Keebler, 1 shell	100	5	45	1	9	0
Piecrust, mix, 9-in., 2-crust pie	1485	93	56	23	14	0
Piecrust, Pet Ritz, 1 shell	720	48	60	12	15	0
Piecrust, Pet Ritz, Deep Dish, all vegetable shortening, 1 shell	780	54	62	12	14	0
Pumpkin, ⅙ of 9-in. pie	320	17	48	6	17	109
MISCELLANEOUS						
Brownies, Fudge, Light, Betty Crocker, 1/24 of package as prepared	100	1	9	na	na	0
Brownies, Fudge Brownie Mix, Duncan Hines, 1 brownie	130	5	35	na	na	0
Doughnuts, cake, plain, 1 doughnut	210	12	51	3	13	20
Doughnuts, yeast, glazed, 1 doughnut	192	13	61	5	23	29
Pizza Crust, All Ready, Pillsbury, ⅛ of crust	90	1	10	0	0	0

Baking Products & Condiments

FOOD/PORTION SIZE	CAL.	FAT		SAT. FAT		CHOL. (mg)
		Total (g)	As % of Cal.	Total (g)	As % of Cal.	
Bacos, 2 tsp.	25	1	36	na	na	0
Baking Powder, Davis, 1 tsp.	8	0	0	0	0	0
Baking soda for home use, 1 tsp.	5	0	0	0	0	0
Barbecue Sauce, Kraft, 1 tbsp.	23	tr	na	tr	na	0
Barbecue Sauce, Original, Open Pit, 1 tbsp.	25	0	0	0	0	0
Barley, pearled, light, uncooked, 1 cup	700	2	3	<1	tr	0
Bulgur, uncooked, 1 cup	600	3	5	1	2	0
Butterscotch Topping, Artificially Flavored, Kraft, 1 tbsp.	60	1	15	0	0	0

FOOD/PORTION SIZE	CAL.	FAT		SAT. FAT		CHOL.
		Total (g)	As % of Cal.	Total (g)	As % of Cal.	(mg)
Cajun Magic Seasoning, K-Paul Enterprises, 1 tsp.	20	0	0	0	0	0
Caramel Topping, Kraft, 1 tbsp.	60	0	0	0	0	0
Catsup, 1 tbsp.	15	tr	na	tr	na	0
Catsup, Weight Watchers, 1 tbsp.	12	0	0	0	0	0
Celery seed, 1 tsp.	10	1	90	tr	na	0
Chili powder, 1 tsp.	10	tr	na	<1	na	0
Chili Sauce, Bennet's, 1 tbsp.	16	0	0	0	0	0
Chili Sauce, Heinz, 1 tbsp.	16	0	0	0	0	0
Chocolate, Semi-Sweet, Baker's, 1 oz.	140	15	96	na	na	0
Chocolate, Unsweetened Chocolate Baking Bar, Baker's, 1 oz.	140	15	96	na	na	0
Chocolate Caramel Topping, Kraft, 1 tbsp.	60	0	0	0	0	0
Chocolate Chips, Mini, Hershey's, ¼ cup	220	12	49	7	29	10
Chocolate Chips, Real, Semi-Sweet, Baker's, ¼ cup	200	12	54	7	32	0
Chocolate Chips, Semi-Sweet, Hershey's, ¼ cup	220	12	49	7	29	8
Chocolate Flavored Chips, Semi-Sweet, Baker's, ¼ cup	200	9	41	7	29	0
Chocolate Topping, Kraft, 1 tbsp.	50	0	0	0	0	0
Cinnamon, 1 tsp.	5	tr	na	tr	na	0
Cocktail Sauce, Sauceworks, 1 tbsp.	14	0	0	0	0	0
Cocoa Powder, Hershey's, ¼ cup	91	3	30	2	20	0
Coconut, Angel Flake, Baker's (bag), ⅓ cup	115	8	63	8	63	0
Coconut, Premium Shred, Baker's, ⅓ cup	140	9	58	9	58	0
Cornmeal, degermed, enriched, dry, 1 cup	500	2	4	<1	na	0
Cornmeal, whole-ground, unbolted, dry, 1 cup	435	5	10	<1	na	0
Curry powder, 1 tsp.	5	tr	na	na	na	0
Flour, buckwheat, light, sifted, 1 cup	340	1	3	<1	na	0
Flour, cake/pastry, enriched, sifted, spooned, 1 cup	350	1	3	<1	na	0
Flour, self-rising, enriched, unsifted, spooned, 1 cup	440	1	2	<1	na	0
Flour, wheat, all-purpose, sifted, spooned, 1 cup	420	1	2	<1	na	0
Flour, wheat, all-purpose, unsifted, spooned, 1 cup	455	1	2	<1	na	0
Flour, whole-wheat from hard wheats, stirred, 1 cup	400	2	5	<1	na	0
Frosting, Chocolate-flavored, Creamy Deluxe, Betty Crocker, ¹⁄₁₂ of tub	160	7	39	2	11	0
Frosting, Chocolate Fudge, Lovin' Lites, Pillsbury, ¹⁄₁₂ of can (1⅓ oz.)	120	2	15	tr	na	0

FOOD/PORTION SIZE	CAL.	FAT		SAT. FAT		CHOL.
		Total (g)	As % of Cal.	Total (g)	As % of Cal.	(mg)
Frosting, Cream Cheese, Duncan Hines, 1 tbsp.	60	3	45	1	15	0
Garlic powder, 1 tsp.	10	tr	na	tr	na	0
Garlic powder with parsley, Lawry's 1 tsp.	12	tr	na	0	0	0
Honey, strained or extracted, 1 tbsp.	65	0	0	0	0	0
Horseradish, Cream Style, Prepared, Kraft, 1 tbsp.	12	1	75	0	0	0
Horseradish, Prepared, Kraft, 1 tbsp.	10	0	0	0	0	0
Horseradish Sauce, Kraft, 1 tbsp.	50	5	90	1	18	5
Hot Fudge Topping, Kraft, 1 tbsp.	70	3	39	1	13	0
Hot Fudge Topping, Light, J.M. Smucker, 1 tbsp.	35	tr	na	0	0	na
Jam, Strawberry, Smucker's, 1 tbsp.	54	0	0	0	0	na
Jams and preserves, 1 tbsp.	55	tr	na	0	0	0
Jellies, 1 tbsp.	50	tr	na	tr	na	0
Marshmallow Creme, Kraft, 1 oz.	90	0	0	0	0	0
Mayonnaise, 1 tbsp.	100	11	99	2	18	8
Mayonnaise, Cholesterol Free, Hellman's, 1 tbsp.	50	5	90	1	18	0
Mayonnaise, Hellmann's, 1 tbsp.	100	11	99	2	18	7
Mayonnaise, Light, Reduced Calorie, Kraft, 1 tbsp.	50	5	90	1	18	5
Mayonnaise, Light Reduced Calorie, Hellman's, 1 tbsp.	50	5	90	1	18	5
Mayonnaise, Nonfat, Kraft Free, 1 tbsp.	12	0	0	0	0	0
Mayonnaise, Real, Kraft, 1 tbsp.	100	12	100	2	18	5
Molasses, Light, Brer Rabbit, 1 tbsp.	56	0	0	0	0	0
Mustard, Dijon, Grey Poupon, 1 tbsp.	20	1	45	0	0	0
Mustard, Creamy Spread, French's, 1 tbsp.	8	tr	tr	0	0	0
Mustard, Horseradish, Kraft, 1 tbsp.	14	1	64	0	0	0
Mustard, prepared yellow, 1 tbsp.	15	tr	na	tr	na	0
Mustard, Pure Prepared, Kraft, 1 tbsp.	11	1	82	0	0	0
Onion powder, 1 tsp.	5	tr	na	tr	na	0
Oregano, 1 tsp.	5	tr	na	tr	na	0
Paprika, 1 tsp.	6	tr	na	tr	na	0
Parsley Patch Italian Seasoning, McCormick, 1 tsp.	8	0	0	0	0	0
Pepper, ground, black, 1 tsp.	5	tr	na	tr	na	0
Picante Sauce, Medium, Pace, 2 tbsp.	3	tr	na	na	na	na
Pineapple Topping, Kraft, 1 tbsp.	50	0	0	0	0	0
Preserves, Apricot, Kraft, 1 tbsp.	54	0	0	0	0	0
Relish, sweet, finely chopped, 1 tbsp.	20	tr	na	tr	na	0

FOOD/PORTION SIZE	CAL.	FAT Total (g)	FAT As % of Cal.	SAT. FAT Total (g)	SAT. FAT As % of Cal.	CHOL. (mg)
Salad Dressing, Free Nonfat, Miracle Whip, 1 tbsp.	20	0	0	0	0	0
Salad Dressing, Light, Miracle Whip, 1 tbsp.	45	4	80	1	20	5
Salad Dressing, Miracle Whip, 1 tbsp.	70	7	90	1	13	5
Salsa, Thick & Chunky, Mild, Ortega, 1 tbsp.	4	0	0	0	0	0
Salt, 1 tsp.	0	0	0	0	0	0
Sandwich Spread, Kraft, 1 tbsp.	50	5	90	1	18	5
Seasoning Blend, Mrs. Dash, 1 tsp.	12	0	0	0	0	0
Seasoning Mixture, Original Recipe for Chicken, Shake 'N Bake, ¼ pouch	80	tr	na	tr	na	0
Soy sauce, ready to serve, 1 tbsp.	11	0	0	0	0	0
Steak Sauce, A1, 1 tbsp.	14	0	0	0	0	0
Strawberry Topping, Kraft, 1 tbsp.	50	0	0	0	0	0
Sugar, brown, packed, 1 cup	820	0	0	0	0	0
Sugar, powdered, sifted, spooned into cup, 1 cup	385	0	0	0	0	0
Sugar, white granulated, 1 cup	770	0	0	0	0	0
Sweet 'n Sour Sauce, Sauceworks, 1 tbsp.	25	0	0	0	0	0
Syrup, chocolate-flavored syrup or topping, fudge type, 2 tbsp.	125	5	36	3	22	0
Syrup, chocolate-flavored syrup or topping, thin type, 2 tbsp.	85	tr	na	<1	na	0
Syrup, molasses, cane, blackstrap, 2 tbsp.	85	0	0	0	0	0
Syrup, Regular, Log Cabin, 1 oz. (about 2 tbsp.)	100	tr	na	tr	na	0
Syrup, table (corn & maple), 2 tbsp.	122	0	0	0	0	0
Tabasco Sauce, ¼ tsp.	0	0	0	0	0	0
Tartar sauce, 1 tbsp.	75	8	96	1	12	4
Tartar Sauce, Fat Free, Cholesterol Free, Nonfat, Kraft, 1 tbsp.	16	0	0	0	0	0
Tartar Sauce, Hellmann's, 1 tbsp.	70	8	100	1	13	5
Tartar Sauce, Natural Lemon Herb Flavor, Sauceworks, 1 tbsp.	70	8	100	1	13	5
Tartar Sauce, Sauceworks, 1 tbsp.	50	5	90	1	18	5
Vinegar, Apple Cider, Heinz, 2 tbsp.	4	0	0	0	0	0
Vinegar, Cider, Heinz, 2 tbsp.	4	0	0	0	0	0
Vinegar, Gourmet Wine, Heinz, 2 tbsp.	8	0	0	0	0	0
Vinegar, Wine, Red or White, Heinz, 2 tbsp.	4	0	0	0	0	0
Worcestershire Sauce, Heinz, 1 tbsp.	12	0	0	0	0	0
Yeast, baker's dry active, 1 package	20	tr	na	tr	na	0
Yeast, brewer's dry, 1 tbsp.	25	tr	na	tr	na	0

Beverages

FOOD/PORTION SIZE	CAL.	FAT Total (g)	FAT As % of Cal.	SAT. FAT Total (g)	SAT. FAT As % of Cal.	CHOL. (mg)
ALCOHOL						
Beer, light, 12 fl. oz.	95	0	0	0	0	0
Beer, regular, 12 fl. oz.	150	0	0	0	0	0
Gin, rum, vodka, whiskey, 80-proof, 1½ fl. oz.	97	0	0	0	0	0
Gin, rum, vodka, whiskey, 90-proof, 1½ fl. oz.	110	0	0	0	0	0
Wine, table, red, 3½ fl. oz.	74	0	0	0	0	0
Wine, table, white, 3½ fl. oz.	70	0	0	0	0	0
COFFEE						
Brewed, 6 fl. oz.	tr	tr	na	tr	na	0
Cafe Francais, General Foods International Coffees, 6 fl. oz.	50	3	54	0	0	0
Cafe Francais, General Foods Sugar Free International Coffees, 6 fl. oz.	35	2	51	0	0	0
Coffee Flavor Instant Hot Beverage, Postum, 6 fl. oz.	12	0	0	0	0	0
Instant, Folger's, 1 tbsp.	8	0	0	0	0	0
JUICE						
Apple, bottled or canned, 1 cup	115	tr	na	tr	na	0
Apple, Pure 100%, Kraft, 8 fl. oz.	107	0	0	0	0	0
Apple/Cranberry Fruit Blends, Del Monte, approx. 8 fl. oz.	140	0	0	0	0	0
Cherry, Pure & Light, Dole, 1 cup	120	0	0	0	0	0
Cranberry Juice Cocktail, Ocean Spray, 8 fl. oz.	144	0	0	0	0	0
Grape, canned or bottled, 1 cup	155	tr	na	<1	na	0
Grape, frozen concentrate, sweetened, diluted, 1 cup	125	tr	na	<1	na	0
Grapefruit, canned, sweetened, 1 cup	115	tr	na	tr	na	0
Grapefruit, canned, unsweetened, 1 cup	95	tr	na	tr	na	0
Grapefruit, frozen concentrate, unsweetened, diluted, 1 cup	100	tr	na	tr	na	0
Grapefruit, raw, 1 cup	95	tr	na	tr	na	0
Lemon, canned or bottled, unsweetened, 1 cup	50	1	18	<1	2	0
Lemon, raw, 1 cup	60	tr	na	tr	na	0
Lemon, ReaLemon Juice from Concentrate, Borden, 1 cup	48	0	0	0	0	0

FOOD/PORTION SIZE	CAL.	FAT Total (g)	FAT As % of Cal.	SAT. FAT Total (g)	SAT. FAT As % of Cal.	CHOL. (mg)
Lime, canned or bottled, unsweetened, 1 cup	50	1	18	<1	2	0
Lime, raw, 1 cup	65	tr	na	tr	na	0
Orange, canned, unsweetened, 1 cup	105	tr	na	tr	na	0
Orange, chilled, 1 cup	110	1	8	<1	tr	0
Orange, frozen concentrate, diluted, 1 cup	110	tr	na	tr	na	0
Orange, Minute Maid, 100% pure orange juice from concentrate, 6 fl.oz.	90	0	0	0	0	0
Orange, raw, 1 cup	110	tr	na	<1	<1	0
Orange and grapefruit, canned, 1 cup	105	tr	na	tr	na	0
Peach, Pure & Light, Dole, 8 fl. oz.	120	0	0	0	0	0
Pineapple, Canned, Dole, 8 fl. oz.	133	0	0	0	0	0
Pineapple, unsweetened, canned, 1 cup	140	tr	na	tr	na	0
Pineapple-Orange, Dole, 8 fl. oz.	120	0	0	0	0	0
Pineapple-Orange Fruit Blends, Del Monte, approx. 8 fl. oz.	140	0	0	0	0	0
Pineapple-Orange-Guava, Dole, 8 fl. oz.	133	<1	0	0	0	0
Pineapple-Passion-Banana, Dole, 1 cup	133	0	0	0	0	0
Prune, canned or bottled, 1 cup	180	tr	na	tr	na	0
Raspberry, Pure & Light, Dole 8 fl. oz.	133	0	0	0	0	0
Tomato, canned, 1 cup	40	tr	na	tr	na	0
Vegetable Juice, V-8, 8 fl. oz.	47	0	0	0	0	0
MILK						
Buttermilk, 1 cup	100	2	18	1	9	9
Canned, condensed, sweetened, 1 cup	980	27	25	17	16	104
Canned, evaporated, skim, 1 cup	200	1	5	<1	1	9
Canned, evaporated, whole, 1 cup	340	19	50	12	32	74
Chocolate, lowfat (1%), 1 cup	160	3	17	2	11	7
Chocolate, lowfat (2%), 1 cup	180	5	25	3	15	17
Chocolate Malt Flavor, Ovaltine Classic, ¾ oz.	80	0	0	0	0	0
Cocoa Mix, Milk Chocolate, Carnation, 1 envelope	110	1	8	tr	<1	1
Cocoa Mix, Rich Chocolate, Carnation, 1 envelope	110	1	8	1	8	1
Cocoa Mix, Rich Chocolate with Marshmallows, Carnation, 1 envelope	110	1	8	1	8	2
Dried, nonfat, instant, 1 cup	245	tr	na	<1	1	12
Dried, nonfat, instant, 1 envelope (3⅕ oz.) (makes 1 quart liquid milk)	325	1	3	<1	1	17
Eggnog (commercial), 1 cup	340	19	50	11	29	149
Evaporated Filled Milk, Milnot, 2 tbsp.	37	2	49	tr	<1	na
Evaporated Milk, Carnation, 2 tbsp.	43	3	63	na	na	na

FOOD/PORTION SIZE	CAL.	FAT		SAT. FAT		CHOL.
		Total (g)	As % of Cal.	Total (g)	As % of Cal.	(mg)
Evaporated Milk, Pet, 2 tbsp.	43	3	63	2	42	9
Evaporated Skim Milk, Light, Pet, 2 tbsp.	25	0	0	0	0	3
Evaporated Skim Milk, Lite, Carnation, 2 tbsp.	25	0	0	0	0	3
Fudge Drink, Chocolate, Slender, 10 fl. oz.	220	4	16	na	na	4
Lowfat (2%), milk solids added, 1 cup	125	5	36	3	22	18
Lowfat (2%), no milk solids, 1 cup	120	5	38	3	23	18
Malt Drink, Chocolate, Slender, 10 fl. oz.	220	4	16	na	na	4
Malted, chocolate, powder, ¾ oz.	84	1	11	<1	5	1
Malted, chocolate, powder, prepared with 8 oz. whole milk	235	9	34	6	23	34
Malted, natural, powder, prepared with 8 oz. whole milk	235	10	38	6	23	37
Malt Flavor, Classic, Ovaltine, ¾ oz. dry	80	tr	na	tr	na	0
Nonfat (skim), milk solids added, 1 cup	90	1	10	<1	4	5
Nonfat (skim), no milk solids, 1 cup	86	tr	na	<1	3	4
Quik, Chocolate, Nestle, ¾ oz. dry (2 ½ tsp.)	90	1	10	0	0	0
Shake Mix, Alba 77 Fit n' Frosty, all flavors, 1 envelope	70	0	0	0	0	3
Skim Milk, Fortified, Lite-line or Viva, Borden, 1 cup	100	1	9	tr	<1	5
Whole (3.3% fat), 1 cup	150	8	48	5	30	33
Whole, Borden, 1 cup	150	8	48	na	na	na
SOFT DRINKS, CARBONATED						
7-Up, Diet, 6 fl. oz.	2	0	0	0	0	na
7-Up, Diet Cherry, 6 fl.oz.	2	0	0	0	0	na
Club soda, 6 fl. oz.	0	0	0	0	0	0
Coca-Cola Classic, 6 fl. oz.	72	0	0	0	0	0
Diet Coke, 6 fl. oz.	0	0	0	0	0	na
Diet Coke, Caffeine Free, 6 fl.oz.	0	0	0	0	0	na
Diet Pepsi, Caffeine Free, 6 fl. oz.	0	0	0	na	na	na
Diet-Rite, Black Cherry, 6 fl. oz.	2	0	0	0	0	na
Diet-Rite, Cola, 6 fl. oz.	2	0	0	0	0	na
Diet-Rite, Pink Grapefruit, 6 fl. oz.	2	0	0	0	0	na
Diet-Rite, Red Raspberry, 6 fl. oz.	2	0	0	0	0	na
Dr. Pepper (Diet), 6 fl. oz.	2	0	0	0	0	na
Fresca, 6 fl. oz.	2	0	0	0	0	na
Ginger Ale, Canada Dry, Diet, 6 fl. oz.	2	0	0	0	0	na
Grape, carbonated, 6 fl. oz.	90	0	0	0	0	0
Orange, carbonated, 6 fl. oz.	90	0	0	0	0	0
Pepsi-Cola, Caffeine-Free, Diet, 6 fl. oz.	0	0	0	0	0	na

FOOD/PORTION SIZE	CAL.	FAT		SAT. FAT		CHOL.
		Total (g)	As % of Cal.	Total (g)	As % of Cal.	(mg)
Pepsi-Cola, Diet, 6 fl. oz.	0	0	0	0	0	na
Root beer, 6 fl. oz.	83	0	0	0	0	0
Root Beer, Dad's, Diet, 6 fl. oz.	2	0	0	0	0	na

SOFT DRINKS, NONCARBONATED

FOOD/PORTION SIZE	CAL.	FAT		SAT. FAT		CHOL.
Country Time Drink Mix, Sugar Sweetened, Lemonade/Pink Lemonade, 8 fl. oz.	80	0	0	0	0	0
Country Time Drink Mix, Sugar Sweetened, Lemon-Lime, 8 fl. oz.	80	0	0	0	0	0
Country Time Sugar Free Drink Mix, Lemonade/Pink Lemonade, 8 fl. oz.	4	0	0	0	0	0
Country Time Sugar Free Drink Mix, Lemon-Lime, 8 fl. oz.	4	0	0	0	0	0
Crystal Light Sugar Free Drink Mix, all flavors, 8 fl. oz.	4	0	0	0	0	0
Grape drink, noncarbonated, canned, 6 fl. oz.	100	0	0	0	0	0
Hi-C Cherry Drink, 6 fl. oz.	100	0	0	0	0	0
Hi-C Citrus Cooler Drink, 6 fl. oz.	100	0	0	0	0	0
Hi-C Double Fruit Cooler Drink, 6 fl. oz.	90	0	0	0	0	0
Hi-C Fruit Punch Drink, 6 fl. oz.	100	0	0	0	0	0
Hi-C Hula Punch Drink, 6 fl. oz.	80	0	0	0	0	0
Kool-Aid Koolers Juice Drink, all flavors, approx. 8 fl. oz.	130	0	0	0	0	0
Kool-Aid Soft Drink Mix, Sugar-Sweetened, all flavors, 8 fl. oz.	80	0	0	0	0	0
Kool-Aid Soft Drink Mix, Unsweetened, all flavors, 8 fl. oz.	2	0	0	0	0	0
Kool-Aid Soft Drink Mix, Unsweetened, all flavors, with sugar added, 8 fl. oz.	100	0	0	0	0	0
Kool-Aid Sugar-Free Soft Drink Mix, all flavors, 8 fl. oz.	4	0	0	0	0	0
Lemonade concentrate, frozen, diluted, 6 fl. oz.	80	tr	na	tr	na	0
Lemon Lime, Gatorade, 8 fl. oz.	50	0	0	0	0	na
Limeade concentrate, frozen, diluted, 6 fl. oz.	75	tr	na	tr	na	0
Ocean Spray, Cran-Apple Drink, 6 oz.	130	0	0	0	0	na
Ocean Spray, Cran-Grape Drink, 6 oz.	130	0	0	0	0	na
Ocean Spray, Cran-Raspberry Drink, 6 oz.	110	0	0	0	0	na
Pineapple-grapefruit juice drink, 6 fl. oz.	90	tr	<1	0	0	0
Wyler's Punch Mix, Sweetened, all flavors, 8 fl. oz.	90	0	0	0	0	na
Wyler's Punch Mix, Unsweetened, all flavors, 8 fl. oz.	2	0	0	0	0	na

FOOD/PORTION SIZE	CAL.	FAT Total (g)	FAT As % of Cal.	SAT. FAT Total (g)	SAT. FAT As % of Cal.	CHOL. (mg)
TEA						
Berry, Crystal Light Fruit-Tea Sugar Free Drink Mix, 8 fl. oz.	4	0	0	0	0	0
Brewed, Lipton, 8 fl. oz.	3	tr	<1	0	0	0
Citrus, Crystal Light Fruit-Tea Sugar Free Drink Mix, 8 fl. oz.	4	0	0	0	0	0
Iced Tea, Crystal Light Sugar Free Drink Mix, 8 fl. oz.	4	0	0	0	0	0
Instant, powder, sweetened, 8 fl. oz.	85	tr	na	tr	na	0
Instant, powder, unsweetened, 8 fl.oz.	tr	tr	na	tr	na	0
Natural Brew, Crystal Light Fruit-Tea Sugar Free Drink Mix, 8 fl. oz.	4	0	0	0	0	0
Tropical Fruit, Crystal Light Fruit-Tea Sugar Free Drink Mix, 8 fl. oz.	4	0	0	0	0	0

Breads & Cereals

FOOD/PORTION SIZE	CAL.	FAT Total (g)	FAT As % of Cal.	SAT. FAT Total (g)	SAT. FAT As % of Cal.	CHOL. (mg)
BISCUITS						
Baking powder, home recipe, 1 biscuit	100	5	45	1	9	tr
Baking powder, refrigerated dough, 1 biscuit	65	2	28	1	14	1
BREAD						
Boston brown, canned, 3¼ × ½-in. slice	95	1	9	<1	3	3
Cracked-wheat, 1 slice	65	1	14	<1	3	0
Crumbs, enriched, dry, grated, 1 cup	390	5	12	2	5	5
French, enriched, 5 × 2½ × 1-in. slice	100	1	9	<1	3	0
Frozen Bread Dough, Honey Wheat, Rhodes, 1 slice, approx. 28 g (1 oz.)	69	1	13	tr	<1	0
Frozen Bread Dough, Texas White Roll, Rhodes, 2 oz.	150	4	24	1	6	0
Frozen Bread Dough, Texas Whole Wheat, Rhodes, 2 oz.	129	1	7	tr	<1	0
Italian, enriched, 4½ × 3¼ × ¾-in. slice	85	tr	na	tr	na	0
Oat, Hearty Slices Crunchy Oat Bread, Pepperidge Farm, 1 slice	95	2	19	1	5	0
Oat, Oat Bran Bread, Roman Meal, 1 slice	70	tr	<1	na	na	0
Pita, enriched, white, 6-in. diameter, 1 pita	165	1	5	<1	<1	0
Pumpernickel, ⅔ rye, ⅓ wheat, 1 slice	80	1	11	<1	2	0

FOOD/PORTION SIZE	CAL.	FAT		SAT. FAT		CHOL.
		Total (g)	As % of Cal.	Total (g)	As % of Cal.	(mg)
Raisin, enriched, 1 slice	65	1	14	<1	3	0
Rye, ⅔ wheat, ⅓ rye, 4¾ × 3¾ × 7⁄16-in. slice	65	1	14	<1	3	0
Vienna, enriched, 4¾ × 4 × ½-in. slice	70	1	13	<1	3	0
Wheat, Soft, Brownberry, 1 slice	70	1	13	tr	<1	0
Wheat, Stoneground 100% Wheat, Wonder, 1 slice	70	1	13	na	na	0
White, Country White Hearty Slices, Pepperidge Farm, 1 slice	95	1	9	1	5	0
White, enriched, soft crumbs, 1 cup	120	2	15	<1	5	0
White, Home Pride Buttertop, 1 slice	70	1	13	tr	<1	1
White, Wonder, 1 slice	70	1	13	tr	<1	0
Whole-wheat, 16-slice loaf, 1 slice	70	1	13	<1	5	0
CEREALS, COLD						
40% Bran Flakes, Post, 1 oz. (⅔ cup)	90	tr	<1	tr	<1	0
100% Bran, Nabisco, 1 oz. (⅓ cup)	70	1	8	tr	<1	0
100% Natural, Oats & Honey, Quaker, 1 oz. (¼ cup)	130	6	40	4	27	0
All-Bran, Kellogg's, 1 oz. (⅓ cup)	70	1	13	tr	<1	0
Alpha-Bits, Post, 1 oz.	110	1	8	tr	<1	0
Apple Jacks, Kellogg's, 1 oz.	110	0	0	0	0	0
Bran Flakes, Kellogg's, 1 oz. (¾ cup)	90	0	0	0	0	0
Bran Flakes, Post, 1 oz.	90	0	0	0	0	0
Cap'n Crunch, Quaker, 1 oz. (¾ cup)	120	3	23	2	15	0
Cap'n Crunch Peanut Butter, Quaker, 1 oz.	127	3	21	2	14	na
Cheerios, General Mills, 1 oz. (1¼ cups)	110	2	16	tr	<1	0
Cheerios, Honey-Nut, General Mills, 1 oz. (¾ cup)	110	1	8	tr	<1	0
Cocoa Krispies, Kellogg's, 1 oz.	110	0	0	0	0	0
Cocoa Pebbles, Post, 1 oz.	110	1	8	1	8	0
Cocoa Puffs, General Mills, 1 oz.	110	1	8	tr	<1	0
Common Sense Oat Bran, Kellogg's, 1 oz.	100	1	9	tr	<1	0
Complete Bran Flakes, Kellogg's, 1 oz.	90	0	0	0	0	0
Corn Chex, Ralston, 1 oz.	110	0	0	0	0	0
Corn Flakes, Kellogg's, 1 oz. (1¼ cups)	100	0	0	0	0	0
Corn Flakes, Post Toasties, 1 oz. (1¼ cups)	110	tr	<1	tr	<1	0
Corn Flakes, Total, 1 oz. (1 cup)	110	1	8	tr	<1	0
Cracklin' Oat Bran, Kellogg's, 1 oz.	110	4	33	tr	<1	0
Froot Loops, Kellogg's, 1 oz. (1 cup)	110	1	8	tr	<1	0
Frosted Mini-Wheats, Kellog's, 1 oz.	100	0	0	0	0	0

FOOD/PORTION SIZE	CAL.	FAT		SAT. FAT		CHOL.
		Total (g)	As % of Cal.	Total (g)	As % of Cal.	(mg)
Fruit & Fibre—Dates, Raisins, Walnuts, Post, 1 oz.	90	1	10	tr	<1	0
Fruit & Fibre—Harvest Medley, Post, 1 oz.	92	1	10	tr	<1	0
Fruit & Fibre—Mountain Trail, Post, 1 oz.	90	1	10	tr	<1	0
Fruit & Fibre—Tropical Fruit, Post, 1 oz.	90	1	10	tr	<1	0
Fruity Pebbles, Post, 1 oz.	113	1	8	1	8	0
Golden Grahams, General Mills, 1 oz. (¾ cup)	110	1	8	tr	<1	0
Granola, Nature Valley, 1 oz. (⅓ cup)	125	5	36	3	22	tr
Granola with Almonds, Sun Country, 1 oz.	130	5	35	1	7	0
Granola with Raisins, Hearty, C.W. Post, 1 oz.	125	4	29	3	32	0
Granola with Raisins, Sun Country, 1 oz.	125	5	36	1	7	0
Grape-Nuts, Post, 1 oz.	110	0	0	0	0	0
Grape-Nuts Flakes, Post, 1 oz.	105	1	9	tr	<1	0
Honeycomb, Post, 1 oz.	110	0	0	0	0	0
Just Right with Fiber Nuggets, Kellogg's, 1 oz.	100	1	9	tr	<1	0
Just Right with Fruit & Nuts, Kellogg's, 1 oz.	140	1	8	tr	<1	0
Kix, General Mills, 1 oz.	110	0	0	0	0	0
Life, Quaker Oats, 1 oz.	111	2	16	tr	<1	na
Life, Cinnamon, Quaker Oats, 1 oz.	101	2	18	tr	<1	0
Lucky Charms, General Mills, 1 oz. (1 cup)	110	1	8	tr	<1	0
Mueslix Five Grain, Kellogg's, 1 oz.	96	1	9	tr	<1	0
Natural Raisin Bran, Post, 1 oz.	87	0	0	0	0	0
Nutri Grain Almonds & Raisins, Kellogg's, 1 oz.	100	2	18	0	0	0
Nutri Grain Biscuits, Kellogg's, 1 oz.	90	0	0	0	0	0
Nutri Grain Wheat, Kellogg's, 1 oz.	100	0	0	0	0	0
Nutri Grain Wheat & Raisins, Kellogg's, 1 oz.	130	0	0	0	0	0
Oat Bran, Quaker, 1 oz.	110	2	16	tr	<1	0
Product 19, Kellogg's, 1 oz. (¾ cup)	110	tr	<1	0	0	0
Puffed Rice, Quaker Oats, ½ oz.	54	tr	<1	tr	<1	0
Puffed Wheat, Quaker Oats, ½ oz.	54	tr	<1	tr	<1	0
Raisin Bran, Kellogg's, 1 oz. (¾ cup)	120	1	8	tr	<1	0
Raisin Bran, Post, 1 oz. (½ cup)	85	1	11	0	0	0
Rice Chex, Ralston, 1 oz.	110	1	11	0	0	0
Rice Krispies, Kellogg's, 1 oz. (1 cup)	110	0	0	0	0	0
Shredded Wheat, Nabisco, 1 biscuit, ⅚ oz.	80	<1	na	tr	<1	0
Shredded Wheat, Spoon Size, Nabisco, 1 oz.	90	<1	na	tr	<1	0
Special K, Kellogg's, 1 oz. (1⅓ cups)	110	tr	<1	0	0	tr
Sugar Frosted Flakes, Kellogg's, 1 oz. (¾ cup)	110	tr	<1	0	0	0
Super Golden Crisp, Post, 1 oz.	110	0	0	0	0	0
Trix, General Mills, 1 oz. (1 cup)	110	1	8	tr	<1	0

FOOD/PORTION SIZE	CAL.	FAT		SAT. FAT		CHOL.
		Total (g)	As % of Cal.	Total (g)	As % of Cal.	(mg)
Wheat Chex, Ralston Purina, 1 oz.	100	0	0	0	0	0
Wheat Germ, Honey Crunch, Kretschmer, 1 oz.	105	3	26	tr	<1	0
Wheaties, General Mills, 1 oz. (1 cup)	100	tr	<1	tr	<1	0

CEREALS, HOT

FOOD/PORTION SIZE	CAL.	Total (g)	As % of Cal.	Total (g)	As % of Cal.	(mg)
Corn grits, regular/quick, enriched, 1 cup	145	tr	na	tr	na	0
Cream of Rice, 1 oz.	100	0	0	na	na	0
Cream of Wheat, Mix 'n Eat, plain, 1 packet	100	tr	<1	0	0	0
Cream of Wheat, regular/quick/instant, 1 cup	149	tr	<1	0	0	0
Malt-O-Meal, Chocolate, 1 oz.	100	0	0	0	0	na
Oat Bran, Quaker Oats, 1 oz.	92	2	20	na	na	0
Oats, Instant, Apple Cinnamon, Quaker Oats, 1¼ oz.	134	2	13	1	7	0
Oats, Instant, Bananas & Cream, Quaker Oats, 1¼ oz.	160	2	11	1	6	0
Oats, Instant, Blueberries & Cream, Quaker Oats, 1¼ oz.	130	2	14	tr	<1	0
Oats, Instant, Cinnamon Spice, Quaker Oats, 1⅔ oz.	160	2	11	tr	<1	0
Oats, Instant, Maple & Brown Sugar, Quaker Oats, 1½ oz.	163	2	11	tr	<1	0
Oats, Instant, Peaches & Cream, Quaker Oats, 1¼ oz.	136	2	13	tr	<1	0
Oats, Instant, Raisin Date Walnut, Quaker Oats, 1⅓ oz.	130	2	14	tr	<1	0
Oats, Instant, Raisin Spice, Quaker Oats, 1½ oz.	159	2	11	tr	<1	0
Oats, Instant, Regular, Quaker Oats, dry, 1 oz.	109	2	17	tr	<1	0
Oats, Instant, Strawberries & Cream, Quaker Oats, 1¼ oz.	136	2	13	tr	<1	0
Oats, Quick or Old Fashioned, Quaker Oats, dry, 1 oz.	100	2	17	tr	<1	0
Wheateena, 1 oz.	100	1	9	na	na	na
Whole Wheat Hot Natural, Quaker Oats, 1 oz.	92	1	10	tr	<1	0

CRACKERS

FOOD/PORTION SIZE	CAL.	Total (g)	As % of Cal.	Total (g)	As % of Cal.	(mg)
Cheese, plain, 1-in. square, 10 crackers	50	3	54	<1	16	6
Cheese, sandwich/peanut butter, 1 sandwich	40	2	45	<1	9	1
Graham, Nabisco, 1 sheet	60	1	15	<1	na	0
Graham, plain, 2½-in. square, 2 crackers	60	1	15	<1	6	0

FOOD/PORTION SIZE	CAL.	FAT		SAT. FAT		CHOL.
		Total (g)	As % of Cal.	Total (g)	As % of Cal.	(mg)
Oat Bran, Sunshine, 8 crackers (½ oz.)	80	4	45	1	11	0
Ritz, Nabisco, ½ oz. (4 crackers)	70	4	51	<1	na	0
Rye-Bran Crispbread, Kavli, 1 slice	30	0	0	0	0	0
Rye wafers, whole-grain, 2 wafers	55	1	16	<1	5	0
Rykrisp, (Natural), ½ cracker	40	0	0	0	0	0
Saltines, 4 crackers	50	1	18	<1	9	4
Snack-type, standard, 1 round cracker	15	1	60	<1	12	0
Town House, Low Sodium, Keebler, 4 crackers	70	4	51	3	39	0
Wheat, thin, 4 crackers	35	1	26	<1	13	0
Wheat Thins, Original, Nabisco, 8 crackers (½ oz.)	70	3	39	na	na	0
Whole Wheat Wafers, Triscuit, Nabisco, ½ oz. (3 wafers)	60	2	30	na	na	0

MUFFINS

FOOD/PORTION SIZE	CAL.	Total (g)	As % of Cal.	Total (g)	As % of Cal.	(mg)
Apple Streusel, Breakfast, Hostess, 1 muffin	100	1	9	tr	<1	0
Banana Nut, Frozen, Healthy Choice, 1 muffin	180	6	30	tr	<1	0
Blueberry, Bakery Style Muffin Mix, Duncan Hines, 1 muffin	180	5	25	na	na	na
Blueberry, Frozen, Healthy Choice, 1 muffin	190	4	19	tr	<1	0
Blueberry, mix, 1 muffin	140	5	32	1	6	45
Blueberry, Wild, Light, Betty Crocker, regular recipe, 1 muffin	70	tr	na	na	na	20
Same as above, no-cholesterol recipe	70	tr	na	na	na	0
Bran, mix, 1 muffin	140	4	26	1	6	28
Bran, with Raisins, Pepperidge Farm, 1 muffin (2 oz.)	170	6	32	1	5	0
Cinnamon Swirl, Bakery Style Muffin Mix, Duncan Hines, 1 muffin	200	7	32	na	na	na
English, plain, enriched, 1 muffin	140	1	6	<1	2	0
English, Thomas', 1 muffin, 57 g (2 oz.)	130	1	7	na	na	0

ROLLS

FOOD/PORTION SIZE	CAL.	Total (g)	As % of Cal.	Total (g)	As % of Cal.	(mg)
Dinner, enriched commercial, 1 roll	85	2	21	<1	5	tr
Frankfurter/hamburger, enriched commercial, 1 roll	115	2	16	<1	4	tr
Hard, enriched commercial, 1 roll	155	2	12	<1	2	tr
Hoagie/submarine, enriched commercial, 1 roll	400	8	18	2	5	tr

FOOD/PORTION SIZE	CAL.	FAT		SAT. FAT		CHOL.
		Total (g)	As % of Cal.	Total (g)	As % of Cal.	(mg)
MISCELLANEOUS						
Bagel, plain/water, enriched, 1 bagel	200	2	9	<1	1	0
Bagels, Egg, Lender's, 1 bagel (2 oz.)	150	1	6	na	na	0
Bagels, Plain, Lender's, 1 bagel (2 oz.)	150	1	6	na	na	0
Bran, unprocessed, Quaker Oats, ¼ oz.	21	tr	<1	tr	<1	0
Breadsticks, Pillsbury, 1 stick	100	2	18	tr	na	0
Croissant, with enriched flour, 1 croissant	235	12	46	4	15	13
Melba toast, plain, 1 piece	20	tr	na	<1	5	0
Pancake & Waffle Mix, Extra Light, Hungry Jack, regular recipe, three 4-in. pancakes	190	6	28	1	47	55
Same as above, no-cholesterol recipe	170	4	21	<1	<1	0
Pancakes & Waffle Mix, Original, Aunt Jemima, regular recipe, 3 to 4 pancakes	190	6	28	na	na	65
Same as above, no-cholesterol recipe	170	3	16	na	na	0
Stuffing, Herb Seasoned, Pepperidge Farm, 1 oz.	110	1	8	na	na	na
Stuffing Mix, Chicken Flavored, Stove Top One Step, 1 oz.	120	3	23	na	na	0
Stuffing Mix, Croutettes, Kellogg's, 1 oz.	93	3	29	na	na	0
Stuffing mix, moist, prepared from mix, 1 cup	420	26	56	5	11	67
Taco Shell, Ortega, 1 shell	70	3	39	0	0	0
Tortilla, corn, 1 tortilla	65	1	14	<1	1	0
Tortilla, Corn, Azteca, 1 tortilla	45	0	0	0	0	0
Tortillas, Flour, Azteca, 7-inch, 1 tortilla	80	2	23	0	0	0
Waffles, Home Style, Aunt Jemima (frozen), 1 waffle (1¼ oz.)	90	3	30	na	na	na
Wheat Bran, Kretschmer, 1 oz.	57	2	32	na	na	0

Candy

FOOD/PORTION SIZE	CAL.	FAT		SAT. FAT		CHOL.
		Total (g)	As % of Cal.	Total (g)	As % of Cal.	(mg)
Almond Joy, 1 bar (1.76 oz.)	250	14	50	na	na	na
Baby Ruth, 1 bar (2.1 oz.)	290	14	43	8	25	0
Butterfinger Bar, 1 bar (2.1 oz.)	280	12	39	5	16	0
Butter Mints, Kraft, 1 mint	8	0	0	0	0	0
Caramels, Kraft, 1 caramel	30	1	30	0	0	0
Chocolate, sweet dark, 1 oz.	152	10	59	6	36	0
Chocolate Fudgies, Kraft, 1 fudgie	35	1	26	0	0	0

FOOD/PORTION SIZE	CAL.	FAT Total (g)	FAT As % of Cal.	SAT. FAT Total (g)	SAT. FAT As % of Cal.	CHOL. (mg)
Crunch, Nestlé, 1.4 oz.	200	10	45	na	na	na
Fudge, chocolate, plain, 1 oz.	117	3	23	2	15	1
Gum drops, 1 oz.	100	tr	na	tr	na	0
Hard candy, 1 oz.	110	0	0	0	0	0
Jelly beans, 1 oz.	105	tr	na	tr	na	0
Jet-Puffed Marshmallows, Kraft, 1 marshmallow	25	0	0	0	0	0
Kisses, Hershey's, 9 pieces	220	13	53	8	33	10
Kit-Kat, 1³⁄₂₅ oz.	172	9	47	6	31	8
M & M's Peanut Chocolate Candies, 1 oz.	150	7	42	na	na	na
M & M's Plain Chocolate Candies, 1 oz.	140	6	39	na	na	na
Milk chocolate, plain, 1 oz.	147	9	55	5	31	6
Milk chocolate, with almonds, 1 oz.	152	9	53	5	30	5
Milk chocolate, with peanuts, 1 oz.	154	10	58	4	23	5
Milk chocolate, with rice cereal, 1 oz.	140	7	45	4	26	6
Milk Chocolate Bar, Hershey's, 1 bar	250	12	43	7	25	12
Milky Way Bar, 1 bar (2.15 oz.)	280	11	35	na	na	na
Miniature Marshmallows, Kraft, 10 marshmallows	18	0	0	0	0	0
Mr. Goodbar, Hershey's, 1.65 oz.	240	15	56	na	na	na
Party Mints, Kraft, 1 mint	8	0	0	0	0	0
Peanut Brittle, Kraft, 1 oz.	130	5	35	1	7	0
Peanut Butter Cups, Reese's, 2 cups	280	17	55	6	19	8
Snickers, 1 bar (2.7 oz.)	280	13	42	na	na	na
Special Dark, Hershey's, 1.75 oz.	280	16	51	9	29	4

Cheese

FOOD/PORTION SIZE	CAL.	FAT Total (g)	FAT As % of Cal.	SAT. FAT Total (g)	SAT. FAT As % of Cal.	CHOL. (mg)
American, Pasteurized Process Cheese Slices, Deluxe, Kraft, 1 oz.	110	9	74	5	41	25
American, Sharp, Pasteurized Process Slices, Old English, Kraft, 1 oz.	110	9	74	5	41	30
American Flavor, Imitation Pasteurized Process Cheese Food, Golden Image, 1 oz.	90	6	60	2	20	5
American Flavored, Singles Pasteurized Process Cheese Product, Light n' Lively, 1 oz.	70	4	51	3	39	13

FOOD/PORTION SIZE	CAL.	FAT		SAT. FAT		CHOL.
		Total (g)	As % of Cal.	Total (g)	As % of Cal.	(mg)
American Flavor Process Cheese, Low Sodium, Weight Watchers, 1 slice	35	1	26	1	26	5
American Process Cheese, Borden Lite-Line, 1 oz.	50	2	36	1	18	5
American Singles Pasteurized Process Cheese Food, Kraft, 1 oz.	90	7	70	4	40	25
Blue, 1 oz.	100	8	72	6	54	21
Blue, Natural, Kraft, 1 oz.	100	9	81	5	45	30
Brick, Natural, Kraft, 1 oz.	110	9	74	5	41	30
Camembert, 1 wedge (⅓ of 4-oz. container)	115	9	70	6	47	27
Cheddar, Extra Sharp, Cold Pack Cheese Food, Cracker Barrel, 1 oz.	90	7	70	4	40	20
Cheddar, Free 'n Lean, Alpine Lace, 1 oz.	35	0	0	0	0	5
Cheddar, Light Naturals Reduced Fat, Kraft, 1 oz.	80	5	56	3	34	20
Cheddar, Mild, Imitation, Golden Image, 1 oz.	110	9	74	2	16	5
Cheddar, Natural, Kraft, 1 oz.	110	9	74	5	41	30
Cheddar, Port Wine, Cheese Log with Almonds, Cracker Barrel, 1 oz.	90	6	60	3	30	15
Cheddar, Port Wine, Cold Pack Cheese Food, Cracker Barrel, 1 oz.	100	7	63	4	36	20
Cheddar, Preferred Light, Fancy Supreme Shredded, Sargento, 1 oz.	90	5	50	3	30	15
Cheddar, Reduced Fat, Dorman's Light, 1 oz.	80	5	56	3	34	20
Cheddar, Sharp, Cheese Ball with Almonds, Cracker Barrel, 1 oz.	100	7	63	3	27	20
Cheddar, Sharp, Cold Pack Cheese Food, Cracker Barrel, 1 oz.	100	7	63	4	36	20
Cheddar, Sharp, Process Cheese, Borden Lite-Line, 1 oz.	50	2	36	1	18	5
Cheddar, shredded, 1 cup	455	34	67	23	45	120
Cheddar, Smokey, Cheese Log with Almonds, Cracker Barrel, 1 oz.	90	6	60	3	30	15
Cheddar Flavored, Sharp, Singles Pasteurized Process Cheese Product, Light n' Lively, 1 oz.	70	4	51	2	26	15
Cheese Food, Cold Pack with Real Bacon, Cracker Barrel, 1 oz.	90	7	70	4	40	20
Cheese Food, Pasteurized Process Sharp Singles, Kraft, 1 oz.	100	8	72	5	45	25
Cheese Spread, Hot Mexican, Pasteurized Process, Velveeta, 1 oz.	80	6	68	3	34	20
Cheese Spread, Mild Mexican, Pasteurized Process, Velveeta, 1 oz.	80	6	68	3	34	20
Cheese Spread, Pasteurized Process, Velveeta, 1 oz.	80	6	68	4	45	20

FOOD/PORTION SIZE	CAL.	FAT		SAT. FAT		CHOL.
		Total (g)	As % of Cal.	Total (g)	As % of Cal.	(mg)
Cheese Spread, Slices, Pasteurized Process, Velveeta, 1 oz.	90	6	60	4	40	20
Cheez Whiz, Mild Mexican, Pasteurized Process Cheese Spread, 1 oz.	80	6	68	4	45	20
Cheez Whiz, Pasteurized Process Cheese Spread, 1 oz.	80	6	68	3	34	20
Cheez Whiz with Jalapeño Pepper, Pasteurized Process Cheese Spread, 1 oz.	80	6	68	4	45	20
Colby, Imitation, Golden Image, 1 oz.	110	9	74	2	16	5
Cottage, creamed, Borden, 1 cup	240	10	38	na	na	na
Cottage, creamed, large curd, 1 cup	235	10	38	6	23	34
Cottage, creamed, small curd, 1 cup	215	9	35	6	25	31
Cottage, Lite n' Lively, 1 cup	160	2	11	2	11	10
Cottage, low-fat (2%), 1 cup	205	4	18	3	13	19
Cottage, Lowfat, Lite-line or Viva, Borden, 1 cup	90	1	10	tr	na	5
Cottage, uncreamed, dry curd, 1 cup	125	1	7	<1	3	10
Cream Cheese, Philadelphia Brand, 1 oz.	100	10	90	6	54	30
Cream Cheese, Whipped, with Chives, Philadelphia Brand, 1 oz.	90	8	80	5	50	30
Cream Cheese, Whipped, with Onions, Philadelphia Brand, 1 oz.	90	8	80	5	50	25
Cream Cheese, Whipped, with Smoked Salmon, Philadelphia Brand, 1 oz.	90	8	80	5	50	30
Cream Cheese Product, Pasteurized Process, Light, Philadelphia Brand, 1 oz.	60	5	75	3	45	10
Cream Cheese with Chives, Philadelphia Brand, 1 oz.	90	9	90	5	50	30
Cream Cheese with Chives & Onion, Soft, Philadelphia Brand, 1 oz.	100	9	81	5	45	30
Cream Cheese with Herbs & Garlic, Soft Philadelphia Brand, 1 oz.	100	9	81	5	45	25
Cream Cheese with Olives & Pimento, Soft, Philadelphia Brand, 1 oz.	90	8	80	5	50	25
Cream Cheese with Pimentos, Philadelphia Brand, 1 oz.	90	9	90	5	50	30
Cream Cheese with Pineapple, Soft, Philadelphia Brand, 1 oz.	90	8	80	5	50	25
Cream Cheese with Smoked Salmon, Soft, Philadelphia Brand, 1 oz.	90	9	90	5	50	25
Cream Cheese with Strawberries, Soft, Philadelphia Brand, 1 oz.	90	8	80	5	50	20
Edam, Natural, Kraft, 1 oz.	90	7	70	4	40	20
Feta, 1 oz.	75	6	72	4	48	25
Feta, Churny Athenos, 1 oz.	75	7	84	4	48	25

FOOD/PORTION SIZE	CAL.	FAT Total (g)	FAT As % of Cal.	SAT. FAT Total (g)	SAT. FAT As % of Cal.	CHOL. (mg)
Gouda, Natural, Kraft, 1 oz.	110	9	74	5	41	30
Hickory Smoke Flavor Pasteurized Process Cheese Spread, Squeez-A-Snak, 1 oz.	80	7	79	4	45	20
Jalapeño Pasteurized Process Cheese Spread, Kraft, 1 oz.	80	6	68	4	45	20
Jalapeño Pepper Spread, Kraft, 1 oz.	70	5	64	3	39	15
Jalapeño Singles Pasteurized Process Cheese Food, Kraft, 1 oz.	90	7	70	4	40	25
Limburger, Natural, Little Gem Size, Mohawk Valley, 1 oz.	90	8	80	5	50	25
Limburger Pasteurized Process Cheese Spread, Mohawk Valley, 1 oz.	70	6	77	3	39	20
Monterey Jack, Natural, Kraft, 1 oz.	110	9	74	5	41	30
Monterey Jack Singles Pasteurized Process Cheese Food, Kraft, 1 oz.	90	7	70	4	40	25
Monti-Jack-Lo, Alpine Lace, 1 oz.	80	5	56	3	34	15
Mozzarella, Low Moisture, Casino, 1 oz.	90	7	70	4	40	25
Mozzarella, made with part-skim milk, 1 oz.	72	5	63	3	38	16
Mozzarella, made with whole milk, 1 oz.	80	6	68	4	45	22
Mozzarella, Part-Skim, Low Moisture, Kraft, 1 oz.	80	5	56	3	34	15
Mozzarella, Preferred Light Fancy Supreme Shredded, Sargento, 1 oz.	60	3	45	na	na	10
Mozzarella, Preferred Light Sliced, Sargento, 1 oz.	60	3	45	2	30	10
Mozzarella, Truly Lite, Frigo, 1 oz.	60	2	30	na	na	8
Mozzarella String with Jalapeño Pepper, Part-Skim, Low Moisture, Kraft, 1 oz.	80	5	56	3	34	20
Muenster, 1 oz.	104	8	69	4	35	27
Munster, Lo-Chol Cheese Alternative, Dorman's, 1 oz.	100	7	63	1	9	5
Neufchatel Light, Philadelphia Brand, 1 oz.	80	7	79	4	45	25
Olives & Pimento Spread, Kraft, 1 oz.	60	5	75	3	45	15
Parmesan, Grated, 1 tbsp.	25	2	72	1	36	4
Parmesan, Grated, Kraft, 1 oz.	130	9	62	5	35	30
Parmesan, Natural, Kraft, 1 oz.	100	7	63	4	36	20
Parmesan, Preferred Light Grated Gourmet, Sargento, 1 tbsp.	25	2	72	tr	na	4
Pimento Cheese Spread, Pasteurized Process, Velveeta, 1 oz.	80	6	68	3	34	20
Pimento Pasteurized Process Cheese Slices, Deluxe, Kraft, 1 oz.	100	8	72	5	45	25
Pimento Singles Pasteurized Process Cheese Food, Kraft, 1 oz.	90	7	70	4	40	25

FOOD/PORTION SIZE	CAL.	FAT		SAT. FAT		CHOL.
		Total (g)	As % of Cal.	Total (g)	As % of Cal.	(mg)
Pimento Spread, Kraft, 1 oz.	70	5	64	3	39	15
Provolone, 1 oz.	100	8	72	5	45	20
Ricotta, made with part-skim milk, 1 cup	340	19	50	12	32	76
Ricotta, made with whole milk, 1 cup	430	30	63	20	42	126
Ricotta, Natural Nonfat, Polly-O Free, 1 oz.	25	0	0	0	0	0
Ricotta, Reduced Fat, Polly-O Lite, 1 oz.	35	2	51	1	26	5
Romano, Grated, Kraft, 1 oz.	130	9	62	6	42	30
Romano, Natural, Casino, 1 oz.	100	7	63	4	36	20
Sandwich Slices with Vegetable Oil, Lunch Wagon, 1 oz.	90	7	70	2	20	5
Swiss, 1 oz.	105	8	69	5	43	26
Swiss, Light, No Salt, Dorman's, 1 oz.	90	5	50	3	30	15
Swiss, Natural, Kraft, 1 oz.	110	8	65	5	41	25
Swiss, Preferred Light, Sargento, 1 oz.	90	5	50	3	30	15
Swiss Flavor Process Cheese, Lite-Line, Borden, 1 oz.	50	2	36	1	18	10
Swiss Pasteurized Process Cheese Slices, Deluxe, 1 oz.	90	7	70	4	40	25
Swiss Singles Pasteurized Process Cheese Food, Kraft, 1 oz.	90	7	70	4	40	25

Cream & Creamers

FOOD/PORTION SIZE	CAL.	FAT		SAT. FAT		CHOL.
		Total (g)	As % of Cal.	Total (g)	As % of Cal.	(mg)
Coffee Rich, ½ oz.	20	2	90	tr	na	0
Cool Whip Extra Creamy Dairy Recipe Whipped Topping, Birds Eye, 1 tbsp.	14	1	64	1	64	0
Cool Whip Lite Whipped Topping, Birds Eye, 1 tbsp.	8	tr	na	na	na	0
Cool Whip Non-Dairy Whipped Topping, Birds Eye, 1 tbsp.	12	1	75	tr	na	0
Cream, sour, 1 tbsp.	25	3	100	2	72	5
Cream, Sour, Land O Lakes, 1 tbsp.	30	3	90	2	60	5
Cream, Sour, Light, Land O Lakes, 1 tbsp.	20	1	45	1	45	3
Cream, Sour, Light n' Lively Free, Kraft, 1 tbsp.	10	0	0	0	0	0
Cream, Sour Half and Half, Breakstone's Light Choice, 1 tbsp.	20	1	45	1	45	5
Cream, sweet, half-and-half, 1 tbsp.	20	2	90	2	90	6
Cream, sweet, light/coffee/table, 1 tbsp.	30	3	90	2	60	10

FOOD/PORTION SIZE	CAL.	FAT		SAT. FAT		CHOL. (mg)
		Total (g)	As % of Cal.	Total (g)	As % of Cal.	
Cream, sweet, whipping, unwhipped, heavy, 1 cup	832	84	91	55	59	336
Cream, sweet, whipping, unwhipped, heavy, 1 tbsp.	52	6	100	3	52	21
Cream, sweet, whipping, unwhipped, light, 1 cup	700	69	89	46	59	272
Cream, sweet, whipping, unwhipped, light, 1 tbsp.	44	5	100	3	61	17
Creamer, sweet, imitation, liquid, 1 tbsp.	20	1	45	1	45	0
Creamer, Sweet, Powdered, Cremora Lite, 1 tsp.	8	tr	na	0	0	0
Cream Topping, Real, Kraft, 1 tbsp.	8	tr	56	tr	56	3
Whipped topping, cream, pressurized, 1 tbsp.	10	1	90	<1	36	2
Whipped Topping, Kraft, 1 tbsp.	9	tr	77	tr	77	0
Whipped topping, sweet, imitation, frozen, 1 tbsp.	15	1	60	1	60	0
Whipped topping, sweet, imitation, pressurized, 1 tbsp.	10	1	90	<1	72	2
Whipped topping, sweet, powdered, prepared with whole milk, 1 tbsp.	10	1	90	<1	72	tr
Whipped Topping Mix, Dream Whip, prepared with water, 1 tbsp.	5	0	0	0	0	0
Whipped Topping Mix, Reduced Calorie, D-Zerta, prepared, 1 tbsp.	8	1	100	tr	na	0

Eggs

FOOD/PORTION SIZE	CAL.	FAT		SAT. FAT		CHOL. (mg)
		Total (g)	As % of Cal.	Total (g)	As % of Cal.	
Cholesterol Free Egg Product, Healthy Choice, ¼ cup	30	<1	na	na	na	0
Egg Beaters, Fleischmann's, ¼ cup	25	0	0	0	0	0
Egg Substitute, Scramblers, ¼ cup	60	3	45	tr	na	0
Large, fried in butter, 1 egg	95	7	76	3	33	278
Large, hard-cooked, 1 egg	80	6	68	2	23	213
Large, poached, 1 egg	80	6	68	2	23	213
Large, raw, white only, 1 white	15	0	0	0	0	0
Large, raw, whole, 1 egg	80	6	68	2	23	213
Large, raw, yolk only, 1 yolk	65	6	83	2	28	213
Scrambled, with milk, cooked in margarine, 1 egg	100	7	63	2	18	215

Fast Foods

FOOD/PORTION SIZE	CAL.	FAT		SAT. FAT		CHOL. (mg)
		Total (g)	As % of Cal.	Total (g)	As % of Cal.	
ARBY'S						
Dressing, Blue Cheese, 2 oz.	295	31	95	6	18	50
Dressing, Buttermilk Ranch, 2 oz.	349	40	100	6	15	6
Dressing, Honey French, 2 oz.	322	27	75	4	11	0
Dressing, Light Italian, 2 oz.	23	1	39	tr	na	0
Dressing, Weight Watchers Creamy French, 1 oz.	48	3	56	1	19	0
Dressing, Weight Watchers Creamy Italian, 1 oz.	29	3	93	1	31	0
Light Roast Beef Deluxe Sandwich	294	10	31	4	12	42
Light Roast Chicken Deluxe Sandwich	263	6	21	2	7	39
Light Roast Turkey Deluxe Sandwich	260	5	17	2	7	30
Salad, Chef	205	10	44	4	18	126
Salad, Garden	109	5	41	3	25	12
Salad, Roast Chicken	184	7	34	3	15	36
Salad, Side	25	tr	na	0	0	0
BURGER KING						
Bacon Double Cheeseburger	507	30	53	14	25	108
Cheeseburger	318	15	42	7	20	50
Chicken BK Broiler Sandwich	267	8	27	2	7	45
Chunky Chicken Salad	142	4	25	1	6	49
Croissan'wich with Bacon	353	23	59	8	20	230
Croissan'wich with Ham	351	22	56	7	18	236
Croissan'wich with Sausage	534	40	67	14	24	258
French Fries, lightly salted, medium	372	20	48	5	12	0
French Toast Sticks, 1 order	538	32	54	8	13	52
Hamburger	272	11	36	4	13	37
Ocean Catch Fish Fillet	479	33	62	8	15	45
Onion Rings, 1 order	339	19	50	5	13	0
Pie, Apple	311	14	41	4	12	4
Salad, Chef	178	9	46	4	20	103
Whopper	614	36	53	12	18	91
Whopper with Cheese	706	44	56	16	20	116
DAIRY QUEEN						
Banana Split	510	11	19	8	14	30
Fish Fillet sandwich	370	16	39	3	7	45

FOOD/PORTION SIZE	CAL.	FAT		SAT. FAT		CHOL.
		Total (g)	As % of Cal.	Total (g)	As % of Cal.	(mg)
Fish Fillet with Cheese sandwich	420	21	45	6	13	60
Grilled Chicken Fillet sandwich	300	8	24	2	6	50
Hamburger, Single	310	13	38	6	17	45
"Heath" "Blizzard," small	560	23	37	11	18	40
Malt, Regular Vanilla	610	14	21	8	12	45
Parfait, Peanut Buster	710	32	41	10	13	30
Shake, Regular Chocolate	540	14	23	8	13	45
Sundae, Regular Chocolate	300	7	21	5	15	20
DOMINO'S						
Pizza, Cheese, 2 slices	376	10	24	6	14	19
Pizza, Deluxe, 2 slices	498	20	36	9	16	40
Pizza, Double Cheese/Pepperoni, 2 slices	545	25	44	13	21	48
Pizza, Ham, 2 slices	417	11	24	6	13	26
Pizza, Pepperoni, 2 slices	460	18	35	8	16	28
Pizza, Sausage/Mushroom, 2 slices	430	16	33	8	17	28
Pizza, Veggie, 2 slices	498	19	34	10	18	36
DUNKIN' DONUTS						
Apple Filled Cinnamon	190	9	43	2	9	0
Boston Kreme	240	11	41	2	8	0
Chocolate Frosted Yeast Ring	200	10	45	2	9	0
Glazed Yeast Ring	200	9	41	2	9	0
Honey Dipped Cruller	260	11	38	2	7	0
Jelly Filled	220	9	37	2	8	0
Plain Cake Ring	262	18	62	4	14	0
Powdered Cake Ring	270	16	53	3	10	0
KENTUCKY FRIED CHICKEN						
Buttermilk Biscuit, 2.3 oz.	235	12	46	3	11	1
Coleslaw, 3.2 oz.	114	6	47	1	8	4
Corn On-the-Cob, 2.6 oz.	90	2	20	1	10	tr
Extra Tasty Crispy, center breast, 3.9 oz.	344	21	55	5	13	80
Extra Tasty Crispy, drumstick, 2.4 oz.	205	14	61	3	13	72
Extra Tasty Crispy, wing, 2 oz.	231	17	66	4	16	63
French Fries, 2.7 oz.	244	12	44	3	11	2
Hot & Spicy, center breast, 4.3 oz.	382	25	59	6	14	84
Hot & Spicy, drumstick, 2.5 oz.	207	14	61	3	13	75
Hot & Spicy, wing, 2.2 oz.	244	18	66	4	15	65

FOOD/PORTION SIZE	CAL.	FAT		SAT. FAT		CHOL.
		Total (g)	As % of Cal.	Total (g)	As % of Cal.	(mg)
Hot Wings, six wings, 4.8 oz.	471	33	63	8	15	150
Kentucky Nuggets, six, 3.4 oz.	284	18	57	4	13	66
Mashed Potatoes & Gravy, 3.5 oz.	71	2	25	0	0	tr
Sauce, Barbeque, 1 oz.	35	1	26	0	0	tr
Sauce, Sweet 'N Sour, 1 oz.	58	1	16	0	0	tr
Skinfree Crispy, center breast, 4 oz.	296	16	49	3	9	59
Skinfree Crispy, thigh, 3 oz.	256	17	60	4	14	68
LONG JOHN SILVER'S						
Baked Chicken, Light Herb	130	4	28	na	na	65
Baked Fish, Lemon Crumb, 3 pieces	150	1	6	na	na	110
Baked Fish, Lemon Crumb, 2 pieces, Rice, and Small Salad (w/o dressing)	320	4	11	na	na	75
Baked Shrimp, Scampi Sauce	120	5	38	na	na	205
Cole Slaw	140	6	39	na	na	15
Rice Pilaf	210	2	9	na	na	0
Salad, Small (w/o dressing)	8	0	0	0	0	0
McDONALD'S						
Big Mac	500	26	47	9	16	100
Biscuit with Bacon, Egg, and Cheese	440	26	53	8	16	240
Biscuit with Sausage	420	28	60	8	17	44
Biscuit with Sausage and Egg	505	33	59	10	18	260
Cheeseburger	305	13	38	5	15	50
Chicken McNuggets (6 pieces)	270	15	50	<4	12	55
Cone, Low fat Frozen Yogurt, Vanilla	105	1	9	<1	4	3
Cookies, Chocolaty Chip, 1 box	330	15	41	4	11	4
Cookies, McDonaldland, 1 box	290	9	28	1	3	0
Danish, Apple	390	17	39	4	9	25
Danish, Cinnamon Raisin	440	21	43	5	10	34
Danish, Iced Cheese	390	21	48	6	14	47
Danish, Raspberry	410	16	35	3	7	26
Dressing, Lite Vinaigrette, 1 oz.	24	1	38	<1	8	0
Dressing, Ranch, 1 oz.	110	10	82	2	16	10
Egg McMuffin	280	11	35	4	13	235
Eggs, Scrambled, 2 eggs	140	10	64	3	19	425
Filet-O-Fish sandwich	370	18	44	4	10	50
French Fries, small	220	12	49	<3	10	9
Hamburger	255	9	32	3	11	37
Hashbrowns	130	7	48	1	7	0

FOOD/PORTION SIZE	CAL.	FAT		SAT. FAT		CHOL.
		Total (g)	As % of Cal.	Total (g)	As % of Cal.	(mg)
Hotcakes with 2 pats margarine and 1½ oz. syrup	440	12	25	2	4	8
McLean Deluxe	320	10	28	4	11	60
Milk Shake, Chocolate Low-fat	320	<2	5	<1	2	10
Milk Shake, Strawberry Low-fat	320	<2	4	<1	2	10
Milk Shake, Vanilla Low-fat	290	<2	4	<1	2	10
Pie, Apple	260	15	52	4	14	6
Quarter Pounder	410	20	44	8	18	85
Quarter Pounder with Cheese	510	28	49	11	19	115
Salad, Chef	170	9	48	4	21	111
Salad, Chicken, Chunky	150	4	24	1	6	78
Salad, Garden	50	2	36	<1	11	65
Sauce, Barbecue, 1 serving	50	<1	9	<1	2	0
Sauce, Hot Mustard, 1 serving	70	4	51	<1	6	5
Sauce, Sweet-n-Sour, 1 serving	60	<1	3	0	0	0
Sausage	160	15	84	5	28	43
Sausage McMuffin	345	20	52	7	18	57
Sausage McMuffin with Egg	430	25	52	8	17	270
Sundae, Hot Caramel Low-fat Frozen Yogurt	270	3	10	<2	5	13
Sundae, Hot Fudge Low-fat Frozen Yogurt	240	3	11	2	8	6
Sundae, Strawberry Low-fat Frozen Yogurt	210	1	4	<1	2	5
PIZZA HUT						
Hand-Tossed, Cheese, 2 slices medium (15-inch), 7.9 oz.	518	20	35	14	24	55
Hand-Tossed, Supreme, 2 slices medium (15-inch), 8.5 oz.	540	26	43	14	23	55
Pan, Super Supreme, 2 slices medium (15-inch), 9.2 oz.	563	26	42	12	19	55
Pan, with cheese, 2 slices medium (15-inch), 7.3 oz.	492	18	33	9	16	34
Personal Pan, Pepperoni, whole (5-inch), 9.1 oz.	675	29	39	12	16	53
Personal Pan, Supreme, whole (5-inch), 9.4 oz.	647	28	39	11	15	49
Thin 'n Crispy, Pepperoni, 2 slices medium (15-inch), 5.2 oz.	413	20	44	11	24	46
Thin 'n Crispy, Supreme, 2 slices medium (15-inch), 7.1 oz.	459	22	43	11	22	42

FOOD/PORTION SIZE	CAL.	FAT		SAT. FAT		CHOL. (mg)
		Total (g)	As % of Cal.	Total (g)	As % of Cal.	
SUBWAY						
BMT Salad, small	369	30	73	10	24	66
BMT Sub, Italian Roll, 6-inch	491	28	51	10	18	66
Club Salad, small	225	13	52	3	12	42
Club Sub, Italian Roll, 6-inch	346	11	29	4	10	42
Cold Cut Combo Salad, small	305	26	77	6	18	83
Cold Cut Combo Sub, Italian Roll, 6-inch	427	20	42	6	13	83
Ham & Cheese Salad, small	200	12	54	3	14	36
Ham & Cheese Sub, Italian Roll, 6-inch	322	9	25	3	8	36
Meatball Sub, Italian Roll, 6-inch	459	22	43	8	16	44
Roast Beef Salad, small	222	10	41	4	16	38
Roast Beef Sub, Italian Roll, 6-inch	345	12	31	4	10	38
Seafood & Crab Salad, small	371	30	73	5	12	28
Seafood & Crab Sub, Italian Roll, 6-inch	493	28	51	5	9	28
Steak & Cheese Sub, Italian Roll, 6-inch	383	16	38	6	14	41
Tuna Salad, small	430	38	80	6	13	43
Tuna Sub, Italian Roll, 6-inch	551	36	59	7	11	43
Turkey Breast Salad, small	201	11	49	3	13	33
Turkey Breast Sub, Italian Roll, 6-inch	322	10	28	3	8	33
Veggies & Cheese Sub, Italian Roll, 6-inch	268	9	30	3	10	9
TACO BELL						
Burrito, Bean	447	14	28	4	8	9
Burrito, Beef	493	21	38	8	15	57
Burrito, Chicken	334	12	32	4	11	52
Burrito, Combo	407	16	35	5	11	33
Burrito Supreme	503	22	39	8	14	33
Cinnamon Twists	171	8	42	3	16	0
Meximelt, Beef	266	15	51	8	27	38
Meximelt, Chicken	257	15	53	7	25	48
Nachos	346	18	47	6	16	9
Nachos Bellgrande	649	35	49	12	17	36
Pintos & Cheese	190	9	43	4	19	16
Pizza, Mexican	575	37	58	11	17	52
Salad, Taco	905	61	61	19	19	80
Salad, Taco, w/o shell	484	31	58	14	26	80
Salsa	18	0	0	0	0	0
Sauce, Hot Taco, 1 packet	3	0	0	0	0	0
Sauce, Taco, 1 packet	2	0	0	0	0	0
Taco	183	11	54	5	25	32
Taco Bellgrande	335	23	62	11	30	56

FOOD/PORTION SIZE	CAL.	FAT		SAT. FAT		CHOL.
		Total (g)	As % of Cal.	Total (g)	As % of Cal.	(mg)
Taco, Soft	225	12	48	5	20	32
Taco, Soft, Chicken	213	10	42	4	17	52
Taco, Soft, Steak	218	11	45	5	21	30
WENDY'S						
Big Classic Sandwich, with Kaiser Bun	570	33	52	6	9	90
Chicken Nuggets, Crispy, 6 pieces	280	20	64	5	16	50
Chicken Sandwich	430	19	40	3	6	60
Chili, Regular, 9 oz.	220	7	29	3	12	45
Cookie, Chocolate Chip, 1 cookie	275	13	43	4	13	15
Fish Fillet Sandwich	460	25	49	5	10	55
Fries, small (3⅕ oz.)	240	12	45	3	11	0
Frosty Dairy Dessert, small	400	14	32	5	11	50
Grilled Chicken Sandwich	340	13	34	3	8	60
Hamburger, Kid's Meal, with White Bun	260	9	31	3	10	35
Hamburger, Single, Plain, ¼-lb.	340	15	40	6	16	65
Nuggets Sauce, Barbeque, 1 packet	50	<1	na	tr	na	0
Nuggets Sauce, Honey, 1 packet	45	<1	na	tr	na	0
Nuggets Sauce, Sweet & Sour, 1 packet	45	<1	na	tr	na	0
Nuggets Sauce, Sweet Mustard, 1 packet	50	1	18	<1	na	0
Potato, Hot Stuffed Baked, Bacon & Cheese	520	18	31	5	9	20
Potato, Hot Stuffed Baked, Broccoli & Cheese	400	16	36	3	7	tr
Potato, Hot Stuffed Baked, Cheese	420	15	32	4	9	10
Potato, Hot Stuffed Baked, Chili & Cheese	500	18	32	4	7	25
Potato, Hot Stuffed Baked, Plain	270	<1	na	tr	na	0
Potato, Hot Stuffed Baked, Sour Cream & Chives	500	23	41	9	16	25
Salad, Chef (take-out)	180	9	45	na	na	120
Salad, Garden (take-out)	102	5	44	na	na	0
Salad, Taco	660	37	50	na	na	35
Swiss Deluxe Sandwich, Jr.	360	18	45	3.3	8	40

Fats & Oils

FOOD/PORTION SIZE	CAL.	FAT		SAT. FAT		CHOL.
		Total (g)	As % of Cal.	Total (g)	As % of Cal.	(mg)
Butter, approx. 1 tbsp.	100	11	99	7	63	31
Butter, Land O Lakes, 1 tbsp.	100	11	99	7	63	30

FOOD/PORTION SIZE	CAL.	FAT		SAT. FAT		CHOL. (mg)
		Total (g)	As % of Cal.	Total (g)	As % of Cal.	
Butter, Whipped, Land O Lakes, 1 tbsp.	60	7	100	4	60	20
Butter Buds, ½ teaspoon	4	0	0	0	0	0
Lard, 1 tbsp.	115	13	100	5	39	12
Margarine, Blue Bonnet, 1 tbsp.	100	11	99	2	18	0
Margarine, Extra Light, Promise, 1 tbsp.	50	6	98	<1	na	0
Margarine, imitation, soft, 1 tbsp.	50	5	90	1	18	0
Margarine, Light, Parkay, stick, 1 tbsp.	70	7	90	1	13	0
Margarine, Parkay, 1 tbsp.	100	11	99	2	18	0
Margarine, regular, hard, 1 tbsp. (⅛ stick)	100	11	99	2	18	0
Margarine, regular, hard, approx. 1 tsp.	35	4	100	1	26	0
Margarine, regular, soft, 1 tbsp.	100	11	99	2	18	0
Margarine, Soft, Parkay, 1 tbsp.	100	11	99	2	18	0
Margarine, Soft, Parkay Corn Oil, 1 tbsp.	100	11	99	2	18	0
Margarine, Soft Diet, Parkay Reduced Calorie, 1 tbsp.	50	6	100	1	18	0
Margarine, spread, hard, 1 tbsp. (⅛ stick)	75	9	100	2	24	0
Margarine, spread, hard, approx. 1 tsp.	25	3	100	1	36	0
Margarine, Squeezable, Shedd's Spread Country Crock, 1 tbsp.	80	9	100	1	11	0
Margarine, Squeeze Parkay, 1 tbsp.	90	10	100	2	20	0
Margarine, Stick, Corn, Mazola, 1 tbsp.	100	11	99	2	18	0
Margarine, Stick, Corn Oil, Fleischmann's, 1 tbsp.	100	11	99	2	18	0
Margarine, Stick, Corn Oil, Mazola, 1 tbsp.	100	11	99	2	18	0
Margarine, Stick, Soy Oil, Chiffon, 1 tbsp.	100	11	99	2	18	0
Margarine, Stick, Soy Oil, Weight Watchers Reduced-Calorie, 1 tbsp.	60	7	100	1	15	0
Margarine, Stick, Sunflower Oil, Promise, 1 tbsp.	90	10	100	2	20	0
Margarine, Tub, Soy Oil, Chiffon, 1 tbsp.	90	10	100	1	10	0
Margarine, Tub, Soy Oil, Weight Watchers Reduced-Calorie Light Spread, 1 tbsp.	50	6	100	1	18	0
Margarine, Tub, Sunflower Oil, Promise, 1 tbsp.	90	10	100	2	20	0
Oil, Canola, Crisco Puritan, 1 tbsp.	120	13	98	1	18	0
Oil, Corn, Mazola, 1 tbsp.	120	14	100	2	15	0
Oil, Olive, Bertolli, 1 tbsp.	120	14	100	2	15	0
Oil, Olive, Filippo Berio, 1 tbsp.	120	14	100	2	15	0
Oil, peanut, 1 tbsp.	125	14	100	2	14	0
Oil, Peanut, Hollywood, 1 tbsp.	120	14	100	4	30	0
Oil, Safflower, Hollywood, 1 tbsp.	120	14	100	1	8	0
Oil, Soybean, Crisco, 1 tbsp.	120	13	98	2	15	0
Oil, soybean-cottonseed blend, hydrogenated, 1 tbsp.	125	14	100	3	22	0

FOOD/PORTION SIZE	CAL.	FAT Total (g)	FAT As % of Cal.	SAT. FAT Total (g)	SAT. FAT As % of Cal.	CHOL. (mg)
Oil, sunflower, 1 tbsp.	125	14	100	1	7	0
Oil, Sunflower, Sunlite, 1 tbsp.	120	14	100	1	7	0
Oil, Vegetable, Crisco, 1 tbsp.	120	14	100	1	7	0
Shortening, Vegetable, Crisco, 1 tbsp.	110	12	98	3	25	0
Shortening, Vegetable, Crisco Butter Flavor, 1 tbsp.	110	12	98	3	25	0
Spray, Cooking (Vegetable Oil), Pam, 2½-second spray	14	2	100	tr	na	0
Spray, No-Stick (Vegetable), Mazola, 2½-second spray	6	1	100	tr	na	0
Spread, 50% Fat, Parkay, 1 tbsp.	60	7	100	1	15	0
Spread, Parkay (50% vegetable oil), 1 tbsp.	60	7	100	1	15	0
Spread, Stick, Touch of Butter, Kraft, 1 tbsp.	90	10	90	2	20	0
Spread, Tub, (Vegetable), Shedd's, 1 tbsp.	70	7	90	1	13	0

Fish & Shellfish

FOOD/PORTION SIZE	CAL.	FAT Total (g)	FAT As % of Cal.	SAT. FAT Total (g)	SAT. FAT As % of Cal.	CHOL. (mg)
Catfish, breaded, fried, 3 oz.	194	11	52	na	na	69
Catfish, skinless, baked w/o fat, 3 oz.	120	5	38	1	8	60
Clams, Canned, Liquid and Solids, Doxsee, ½ cup	59	tr	na	0	0	38
Clams, raw, meat only, 3 oz.	65	1	14	<1	4	43
Cod, fillets (frozen), Booth, 4 oz.	90	1	10	na	na	na
Cod, skinless, broiled w/o fat, 3 oz.	90	1	10	0	0	50
Crabmeat, canned, 1 cup	135	3	20	<1	3	135
Fish sticks (frozen), reheated, 4 × ½-in. stick	70	3	39	1	13	26
Flounder, baked, with lemon juice, w/o added fat, 3 oz.	80	1	11	<1	4	59
Haddock, breaded, fried, 3 oz.	175	9	46	2	10	75
Haddock, skinless, baked w/o fat, 3 oz.	90	1	10	0	0	60
Halibut, broiled, with butter, with lemon juice, 3 oz.	140	6	39	3	19	62
Herring, pickled, 3 oz.	190	13	62	4	19	85
Lobster, boiled, 3 oz.	100	1	9	0	0	100
Mackerel, skinless, broiled w/o fat, 3 oz.	190	12	57	3	14	60
Orange roughy, broiled, 3 oz.	130	7	48	0	0	20
Oysters, breaded, fried, 1 oyster	90	5	50	1	10	35
Oysters, raw, meat only, 1 cup	160	4	23	1	6	120

FOOD/PORTION SIZE	CAL.	FAT		SAT. FAT		CHOL.
		Total (g)	As % of Cal.	Total (g)	As % of Cal.	(mg)
Perch, ocean, breaded, fried, 1 fillet	185	11	54	3	15	66
Perch, Ocean, Natural Fillets (frozen), Taste O'Sea, 4 oz.	100	3	27	na	na	na
Pollock, skinless, broiled w/o fat, 3 oz.	100	1	9	0	0	80
Salmon, Pink, Bumble Bee, 3½ oz.	138	6	39	2	13	40
Salmon, Pink (in spring water), Chicken of the Sea, 3½ oz.	105	4	30	na	na	na
Salmon, red, baked, 3 oz.	140	5	32	1	6	60
Salmon, smoked, 3 oz.	150	8	48	3	18	51
Sardines, canned in oil, drained, 3 oz.	175	11	57	2	10	121
Sardines (in olive oil), King Oscar, 3¾ oz.	460	16	31	3	6	na
Scallops, breaded (frozen), reheated, 6 scallops	195	10	46	3	14	70
Scallops, broiled, 3 oz. (5.7 large or 14 small)	150	1	6	0	0	60
Shrimp, boiled, 3 oz.	110	2	16	0	0	160
Shrimp, canned, drained solids, 3 oz.	103	1	9	tr	na	148
Shrimp, French fried, 3 oz. (7 medium)	189	9	43	2	10	137
Snapper, cooked by dry heat, 3 oz.	109	2	17	na	na	40
Sole, baked, with lemon juice, w/o added fat, 3 oz.	90	1	10	tr	na	49
Surimi seafood, crab flavored, chunk style, ½ cup	84	tr	na	tr	na	25
Trout, Rainbow, skinless, broiled w/o fat, 3 oz.	130	4	28	1	7	60
Tuna, Albacore (in water), Bumble Bee, 2 oz.	70	1	13	tr	na	24
Tuna, Chunk Light (in spring water), StarKist, ½ cup	77	1	12	tr	na	26
Tuna, Chunk Light (in vegetable oil), Bumble Bee, 2 oz.	160	12	68	2	11	24
Tuna, Chunk Light (in water), Bumble Bee, 2 oz.	70	1	13	1	13	27

Frozen Appetizers & Entrées

FOOD/PORTION SIZE	CAL.	FAT		SAT. FAT		CHOL.
		Total (g)	As % of Cal.	Total (g)	As % of Cal.	(mg)
APPETIZERS						
Chicken Nuggets, Weight Watchers, approx. 6 oz.	270	12	40	4	13	50
Ravioli, Baked Cheese, Weight Watchers, 9 oz.	290	12	37	5	16	85

FOOD/PORTION SIZE	CAL.	FAT Total (g)	FAT As % of Cal.	SAT. FAT Total (g)	SAT. FAT As % of Cal.	CHOL. (mg)
MEAT ENTRÉES						
Beef Pot Pie, Swanson, 7 oz.	370	19	46	na	na	na
Lasagna with Meat Sauce, Weight Watchers, 11 oz.	330	11	30	5	14	60
Pizza, Cheese Party, Totino's, 5 oz. (½ pizza)	290	10	31	3	9	15
Pizza, Sausage, Pepperoni, & Mushroom, Stouffer's French Bread Deluxe, 1 piece, about 6 oz.	420	19	41	na	na	na
Pizza, Sausage French Bread, Lean Cuisine, 6 oz.	350	11	28	3	8	40
Pizza, Vegetable, Tombstone Light, ⅕ pizza (4⅓ oz.)	200	7	32	na	na	10
Salisbury Steak, Hungry Man, Swanson, 16¼ oz.	630	32	46	na	na	na
Salisbury Steak, Lean Cuisine, 9½ oz.	240	7	26	2	8	45
Salisbury Steak Dinner, Healthy Choice, 11½ oz.	300	7	21	3	9	50
Sirloin Beef with Barbecue Sauce Dinner, Healthy Choice, 11 oz.	300	6	18	3	9	50
Spaghetti, Lean Cuisine, 11½ oz.	270	6	20	2	7	30
Szechwan Beef with Noodles, Lean Cuisine, 8⅝ oz.	259	9	31	3	10	83
MISCELLANEOUS						
Macaroni & Cheese, Lean Cuisine, 9 oz.	290	9	28	4	12	30
Pasta Classic, Healthy Choice, 12½ oz.	310	3	9	tr	na	35
POULTRY ENTRÉES						
Breast of Chicken Marsala, Lean Cuisine, 8⅛ oz.	190	5	24	2	9	65
Chicken, Broccoli & Cheddar Turnovers, Quaker Ovenstuffs, 4¾ oz.	350	16	41	na	na	na
Chicken, Fried, Plump & Juicy, Swanson, 3¼ oz.	270	16	53	na	na	na
Chicken a la King, Weight Watchers, 9 oz.	220	8	33	2	8	55
Chicken Burritos, Weight Watchers, 7⅗ oz.	310	13	38	4	12	60
Chicken Cacciatore, Lean Cuisine, 10⅞ oz.	280	10	32	2	6	45
Chicken Dijon Dinner, Healthy Choice, 11 oz.	260	3	10	1	3	45
Chicken Fettucini, Weight Watchers, 8¼ oz.	280	9	29	3	10	40
Chicken Parmigiana Dinner, Healthy Choice, 11½ oz.	270	3	10	2	7	50

FOOD/PORTION SIZE	CAL.	FAT Total (g)	FAT As % of Cal.	SAT. FAT Total (g)	SAT. FAT As % of Cal.	CHOL. (mg)
Mesquite Chicken Dinner, Healthy Choice, 10½ oz.	340	1	3	tr	na	45
Pot Pie, Chicken, Swanson, 7 oz.	390	23	53	na	na	na
SEAFOOD ENTRÉES						
Filet of Fish Divan, Lean Cuisine, 12⅜ oz.	270	9	30	2	7	90
Fish Dijon, Light Entrée, Mrs. Paul's, 8¾ oz.	200	5	23	na	na	60
Fish Fillet Au Gratin, Booth, 9½ oz.	280	8	26	na	na	72
Fish Fillet Florentine, Booth, 9½ oz.	260	8	28	na	na	82
Fish Florentine, Light Entree, Mrs. Paul's, 8 oz.	220	8	33	na	na	95
Fish Mornay, Light Entrée, Mrs. Paul's, 9 oz.	230	10	39	na	na	80
Seafood Linguini, Weight Watchers, 9 oz.	210	7	30	1	4	5
Shrimp Primavera with Fettuccine, Booth, 10 oz.	200	3	14	na	na	0
Shrimp with Lobster Sauce, Fresh & Lite, La Choy, 10 oz.	210	7	30	na	na	na
Tuna Lasagna, Lean Cuisine, 9¾ oz.	280	10	32	4	13	25

Frozen Desserts

FOOD/PORTION SIZE	CAL.	FAT Total (g)	FAT As % of Cal.	SAT. FAT Total (g)	SAT. FAT As % of Cal.	CHOL. (mg)
DAIRY						
Frozen Dairy Dessert, Strawberry, Healthy Choice, ½ cup	110	1	8	1	8	5
Frozen Dessert, Nonfat, Chocolate Flavor, Sealtest Free, ½ cup	110	0	0	na	na	0
Frozen Yogurt, Peach, Borden, ½ cup	100	2	18	na	na	na
Frozen Yogurt, Peach, Sealtest, ½ cup	100	0	0	na	na	0
Ice Cream, Butter Pecan, Breyers, ½ cup	150	8	48	7	42	na
Ice Cream, Chocolate, Breyers, ½ cup	160	8	45	5	28	na
Ice Cream, Chocolate, Sealtest, ½ cup	140	7	45	na	na	na
Ice Cream, Peach, Natural, Breyers, ½ cup	140	12	77	4	26	na
Ice Cream, Strawberry, Natural, Breyers, ½ cup	130	6	42	4	28	na
Ice Cream, Vanilla, Natural, Breyers, ½ cup	180	12	60	5	25	na
Ice Cream, Vanilla, Sealtest, ½ cup	140	7	45	5	32	na

FOOD/PORTION SIZE	CAL.	FAT		SAT. FAT		CHOL.
		Total (g)	As % of Cal.	Total (g)	As % of Cal.	(mg)
Ice Cream, Vanilla/Chocolate/ Strawberry, Sealtest, ½ cup	140	6	39	na	na	na
Ice Milk, Chocolate, Weight Watchers, ½ cup	110	3	25	1	8	10
Ice Milk, Neapolitan, Weight Watchers, ½ cup	110	3	25	1	8	10
Ice milk, vanilla, soft serve, ½ cup	113	3	20	2	12	7
Ice Milk, Vanilla, Weight Watchers, ½ cup	100	3	27	1	9	10
Sherbet, ½ cup	135	2	13	1	7	7
Sherbet, Orange, Borden, ½ cup	120	1	8	na	na	na
Sherbet, Raspberry Real Fruit, Dean Foods, ½ cup	110	1	7	na	na	na

SPECIALTY BARS

FOOD/PORTION SIZE	CAL.	FAT		SAT. FAT		CHOL.
Fruit Bars, all flavors, Jell-O, 1 bar	45	0	0	0	0	0
Fruit n' Juice Bars, Pineapple, Dole, 1 bar	70	1	13	na	na	na
Gelatin Pops, all flavors, Jell-O, 1 bar	35	0	0	0	0	0
Popsicle, 3-fl.-oz. size, 1 popsicle	70	0	0	0	0	0
Pudding Pops, Chocolate, Jell-O, 1 bar	80	2	23	2	23	0
Pudding Pops, Chocolate-Caramel Swirl, Jell-O, 1 bar	80	2	23	2	23	0
Pudding Pops, Chocolate-Covered Chocolate, Jell-O, 1 bar	130	7	48	5	35	0
Pudding Pops, Chocolate-Covered Vanilla, Jell-O, 1 bar	130	7	48	5	35	0
Pudding Pops, Vanilla, Jell-O, 1 bar	70	2	26	2	26	0
Pudding Pops, Vanilla with Chocolate Chips, Jell-O, 1 bar	80	3	34	2	23	0
Pudding Snacks, Chocolate, Jell-O, 4 oz.	160	5	28	2	11	0
Pudding Snacks, Chocolate, Jello-O Free, 4 oz.	100	0	0	0	0	0
Vanilla Ice Cream, Dark Chocolate Coating, Eskimo Pie, 1 bar (3 fl. oz.)	180	12	60	na	na	na

Fruit

FOOD/PORTION SIZE	CAL.	FAT		SAT. FAT		CHOL.
		Total (g)	As % of Cal.	Total (g)	As % of Cal.	(mg)
Apples, dried, sulfured, 10 rings	155	tr	na	tr	na	0
Apples, raw, unpeeled, 3¼-in. diameter, 1 apple	125	1	7	<1	<1	0
Apple Sauce, Natural, Mott's, 1 cup	100	0	0	0	0	0

FOOD/PORTION SIZE	CAL.	FAT		SAT. FAT		CHOL.
		Total (g)	As % of Cal.	Total (g)	As % of Cal.	(mg)
Apple Sauce, Canned, Regular or Chunky, Mott's, 1 cup	114	0	0	0	0	0
Applesauce, canned, sweetened, 1 cup	195	tr	na	<1	<1	0
Applesauce, canned, unsweetened, 1 cup	105	tr	na	tr	na	0
Apricots, canned, heavy syrup pack, 3 halves	70	tr	na	tr	na	0
Apricots, canned, juice pack, 3 halves	40	tr	na	tr	na	0
Apricots, dried, cooked, unsweetened, 1 cup	210	tr	na	tr	na	0
Apricots, dried, uncooked, 1 cup	310	1	3	tr	na	0
Apricots, raw, 3 apricots	50	tr	na	tr	na	0
Avocados, raw, whole, California, 1 avocado	305	28	83	5	15	0
Avocados, raw, whole, Florida, 1 avocado	340	23	61	5	13	0
Bananas, raw, 1 banana	105	1	9	<1	2	0
Blackberries, raw, 1 cup	75	1	12	<1	2	0
Blueberries, frozen, sweetened, 10 oz.	230	tr	na	tr	na	0
Blueberries, raw, 1 cup	80	1	11	tr	<1	0
Cantaloupe, raw, ½ melon	95	1	9	<1	<1	0
Cherries, sour, red, pitted, canned water pack, 1 cup	90	tr	<1	<1	1	0
Cherries, sweet, raw, 10 cherries	50	1	18	<1	2	0
Cranberry sauce, sweetened, canned, strained, 1 cup	420	tr	na	tr	na	0
Dates, chopped, ½ cup	245	<1	2	<1	<1	0
Dates, whole, w/o pits, 10 dates	230	tr	na	<1	<1	0
Figs, dried, 10 figs	475	2	4	<1	<1	0
Fruit, Mixed, in Syrup, Birds Eye Quick Thaw Pouch, 5 oz.	120	0	0	na	na	0
Fruit, Mixed, Libby's Chunky, Lite, ½ cup	50	0	0	na	na	na
Fruit Cocktail, Del Monte, ½ cup	80	0	0	na	na	na
Fruit Cocktail, Del Monte Lite, ½ cup	50	0	0	na	na	na
Fruit Cocktail, Libby's Lite, ½ cup	50	0	0	na	na	na
Grapefruit, canned, with syrup, 1 cup	150	tr	na	tr	na	0
Grapefruit, raw, ½ grapefruit	40	tr	na	tr	na	0
Grapes, Thompson seedless, 10 grapes	35	tr	na	<1	3	0
Grapes, Tokay/Emperor, seeded, 10 grapes	40	tr	na	<1	2	0
Honeydew melon, raw, ¹⁄₁₀ melon	45	tr	na	tr	na	0
Kiwifruit, raw, w/o skin, 1 kiwifruit	45	tr	na	tr	na	0
Lemons, raw, 1 lemon	15	tr	na	tr	na	0
Mandarin Orange Segments, Dole, ½ cup	70	<1	<1	0	0	0
Mangos, raw, 1 mango	135	1	7	<1	<1	0
Nectarines, raw, 1 nectarine	65	1	14	<1	1	0
Olives, canned, green, 4 medium or 3 extra large	15	2	100	<1	12	0

FOOD/PORTION SIZE	CAL.	FAT Total (g)	FAT As % of Cal.	SAT. FAT Total (g)	SAT. FAT As % of Cal.	CHOL. (mg)
Olives, ripe, mission, pitted, 3 small or 2 large	15	2	100	<1	18	0
Oranges, raw, whole, w/o peel and seeds, 1 orange	60	tr	na	tr	na	0
Papayas, raw, ½-in. cubes, 1 cup	65	tr	na	<1	1	0
Peaches, canned, heavy syrup, 1 cup	190	tr	na	tr	na	0
Peaches, canned, juice pack, 1 cup	110	tr	na	tr	na	0
Peaches, dried, uncooked, 1 cup	380	1	2	<1	<1	0
Peaches, frozen, sliced, sweetened, 1 cup	235	tr	na	tr	na	0
Peaches, raw, whole, 2½-in. diameter, 1 peach	35	tr	na	tr	na	0
Peaches, Sliced, Lite, Libby's, 1 cup	100	0	0	na	na	na
Pears, Bartlett, raw with skin, 1 pear	100	1	9	tr	na	0
Pears, Bosc, raw with skin, 1 pear	85	1	11	tr	na	0
Pears, canned, heavy syrup, 1 cup	190	tr	na	tr	na	0
Pears, canned, juice pack, 1 cup	125	tr	na	tr	na	0
Pears, D'Anjou, raw with skin, 1 pear	120	1	8	tr	na	0
Pears, Halves, Lite, Libby's, ½ cup	60	0	0	na	na	na
Pineapple, Canned, Heavy Syrup Dole, (all cuts), ½ cup	91	0	0	0	0	0
Pineapple, canned, heavy syrup, sliced, 1 slice	45	tr	na	tr	na	0
Pineapple, Canned, Juice Pack Dole, (all cuts), ½ cup	70	0	0	0	0	0
Pineapple, canned, juice pack slices, 1 slice	35	tr	na	tr	na	0
Pineapple, raw, diced, ½ cup	38	tr	12	tr	na	0
Plums, canned, purple, juice pack, 3 plums	55	tr	na	tr	na	0
Plums, raw, 1½-in. diameter, 1 plum	15	tr	na	tr	na	0
Plums, raw, 2⅛-in. diameter, 1 plum	35	tr	na	tr	na	0
Prunes, dried, cooked, unsweetened, 1 cup	225	tr	na	tr	na	0
Prunes, dried, uncooked, 4 extra large or 5 large	115	tr	na	tr	na	0
Raisins, seedless, ½-oz. packet, 1 packet	40	tr	na	tr	na	0
Raisins, seedless, 1 cup	435	1	12	<1	<1	0
Raspberries, frozen, sweetened, 1 cup	255	tr	na	tr	na	0
Raspberries, in Lite Syrup, Birds Eye Quick Thaw Pouch, 5 oz.	100	1	9	na	na	0
Raspberries, raw, 1 cup	60	1	15	tr	na	0
Rhubarb, cooked, added sugar, 1 cup	280	tr	na	tr	na	0
Strawberries, frozen, sweetened, sliced, 1 cup	245	tr	<1	tr	<1	0
Strawberries, Halved, in Lite Syrup, Birds Eye Quick Thaw Pouch, 5 oz.	90	0	0	0	0	0

FOOD/PORTION SIZE	CAL.	FAT Total (g)	FAT As % of Cal.	SAT. FAT Total (g)	SAT. FAT As % of Cal.	CHOL. (mg)
Strawberries, Halved, in Syrup, Birds Eye Quick Thaw Pouch, 5 oz.	120	tr	<1	tr	<1	0
Strawberries, raw, whole, 1 cup	45	1	20	tr	na	0
Tangerines, raw, 2⅜-in. diameter, 1 tangerine	35	tr	na	tr	na	0
Watermelon, raw, 4 × 8-in. wedge, 1 piece	155	2	12	<1	2	0
Watermelon, raw, diced, 1 cup	50	1	18	<1	2	0

Gelatin, Pudding & Pie Filling

FOOD/PORTION SIZE	CAL.	FAT Total (g)	FAT As % of Cal.	SAT. FAT Total (g)	SAT. FAT As % of Cal.	CHOL. (mg)
All flavors, Gelatin, Jell-O, ½ cup (average)	80	0	0	0	0	0
All flavors, Gelatin, Low Calorie, D-Zerta, ½ cup (average)	8	0	0	0	0	0
All flavors, Gelatin, Sugar Free, Jell-O, ½ cup (average)	8	0	0	0	0	0
Banana, Pudding & Pie Filling, Instant, Sugar Free Jell-O, with 2% milk, ½ cup	80	2	23	1	11	10
Banana Cream, Pudding & Pie Filling, Instant, Jell-O, with whole milk, ½ cup	160	4	23	3	17	15
Banana Cream, Pudding & Pie Filling, Jell-O, with whole milk, ⅙ pie (excluding crust)	100	3	27	2	18	10
Butter Pecan, Pudding & Pie Filling, Instant, Jell-O, with whole milk, ½ cup	170	5	26	3	16	15
Butterscotch, Pudding, Reduced Calorie, D-Zerta, with skim milk, ½ cup	70	0	0	0	0	0
Butterscotch, Pudding & Pie Filling, Instant, Jell-O, with whole milk, ½ cup	160	4	23	3	17	15
Butterscotch, Pudding & Pie Filling, Instant, Sugar Free, Jell-O, with 2% milk, ½ cup	90	2	20	1	10	10
Butterscotch, Pudding & Pie Filling, Jell-O, with whole milk, ½ cup	170	4	21	3	16	15
Chocolate, pudding, canned, 5-oz. can	205	11	48	9	40	1
Chocolate, Pudding, Reduced Calorie, D-Zerta, with skim milk, ½ cup	70	tr	na	tr	na	2
Chocolate, Pudding & Pie Filling, Instant, Jell-O, with whole milk, ½ cup	180	4	20	3	15	15
Chocolate, Pudding & Pie Filling, Instant, Sugar Free, Jell-O, with 2% milk, ½ cup	90	3	30	2	20	10
Chocolate, Pudding & Pie Filling, Jell-O, with whole milk, ½ cup	160	4	23	2	11	15

FOOD/PORTION SIZE	CAL.	FAT		SAT. FAT		CHOL.
		Total (g)	As % of Cal.	Total (g)	As % of Cal.	(mg)
Chocolate, Pudding & Pie Filling, Sugar Free, Jell-O, with 2% milk, ½ cup	90	3	30	2	20	10
Chocolate, Rich & Luscious Mousse, Jell-O, with whole milk, ½ cup	150	6	36	4	24	9
Chocolate Fudge, Pudding & Pie Filling, Instant, Jell-O, with whole milk, ½ cup	180	5	25	3	15	15
Chocolate Fudge, Pudding & Pie Filling, Instant, Sugar Free, Jell-O, with 2% milk, ½ cup	100	3	27	2	18	10
Chocolate Fudge, Pudding & Pie Filling, Jell-O, with whole milk, ½ cup	160	4	23	2	11	15
Chocolate Fudge, Rich & Luscious Mousse, Jell-O, with whole milk, ½ cup	140	6	39	4	26	10
Coconut Cream, Pudding & Pie Filling, Instant Jell-O, with whole milk, ½ cup	180	6	30	4	20	15
Coconut Cream, Pudding & Pie Filling, Jell-O, with whole milk, ⅙ pie (excluding crust)	110	4	33	2	16	10
Custard, baked, 1 cup	305	13	38	7	21	278
Custard, Golden Egg, Mix, Jell-O Americana, with whole milk, ½ cup	160	5	28	3	17	80
Lemon, Pudding & Pie Filling, Instant, Jell-O, with whole milk, ½ cup	170	4	21	3	16	15
Lemon, Pudding & Pie Filling, Jell-O, with whole milk, ⅙ pie (excluding crust)	170	2	11	na	na	90
Milk Chocolate, Pudding & Pie Filling, Instant, Jell-O, with whole milk, ½ cup	180	5	25	3	15	17
Milk Chocolate, Pudding & Pie Filling, Jell-O, with whole milk, ½ cup	160	4	23	2	11	17
Pineapple Cream, Pudding & Pie Filling, Instant, Jell-O, with whole milk, ½ cup	160	4	23	2	11	17
Pistachio, Pudding & Pie Filling, Instant, Jell-O, with whole milk, ½ cup	170	5	26	3	16	17
Pistachio, Pudding & Pie Filling, Instant, Sugar Free, Jell-O, with 2% milk, ½ cup	100	3	27	2	3	10
Rice Pudding, Jell-O Americana, with whole milk, ½ cup	170	4	21	2	11	17
Tapioca, pudding, prepared with whole milk, ½ cup	145	4	25	2	12	17
Vanilla, French, Pudding & Pie Filling, Instant, Jell-O, with whole milk, ½ cup	160	4	23	2	11	17
Vanilla, French, Pudding & Pie Filling, Jell-O, with whole milk, ½ cup	170	4	21	3	16	17

FOOD/PORTION SIZE	CAL.	FAT Total (g)	FAT As % of Cal.	SAT. FAT Total (g)	SAT. FAT As % of Cal.	CHOL. (mg)
Vanilla, pudding, canned, 5-oz. can	220	10	41	10	41	1
Vanilla, Pudding, Reduced Calorie, D-Zerta, with skim milk, ½ cup	70	0	0	0	0	0
Vanilla, pudding, regular (cooked) dry mix, made with whole milk, ½ cup	145	4	25	2	12	15
Vanilla, Pudding & Pie Filling, Instant, Jell-O, with whole milk, ½ cup	170	4	21	3	16	17
Vanilla, Pudding & Pie Filling, Instant, Sugar Free, Jell-O, with 2% milk, ½ cup	90	2	20	1	10	9
Vanilla, Pudding & Pie Filling, Jell-O, with whole milk, ½ cup	160	4	23	3	17	17
Vanilla, Pudding & Pie Filling, Sugar Free, Jell-O, with 2% milk, ½ cup	80	2	23	0	0	10
Vanilla, Tapioca, Pudding, Jell-O Americana, with whole milk, ½ cup	160	4	23	3	17	17

Gravies & Sauces

FOOD/PORTION SIZE	CAL.	FAT Total (g)	FAT As % of Cal.	SAT. FAT Total (g)	SAT. FAT As % of Cal.	CHOL. (mg)
GRAVIES						
Beef, canned, 1 cup	125	5	36	3	22	7
Beef, Franco-American, 2 oz.	35	2	51	na	na	na
Brown, from dry mix, 1 cup	80	2	23	1	11	2
Brown, with onions, Heinz, HomeStyle, 2 oz.	25	1	36	na	na	na
Chicken, canned, 1 cup	190	14	66	4	19	5
Chicken, Franco-American, 2 oz.	45	4	80	na	na	na
Chicken, from dry mix, 1 cup	85	2	21	<1	5	tr
Turkey, Canned, Heinz HomeStyle, 2 oz.	25	1	36	0	0	0
SAUCES						
Barbecue sauce, *see* BAKING PRODUCTS & CONDIMENTS						
Cheese, from dry mix, prepared with milk, 2 tbsp.	38	2	47	1	24	7
Hollandaise, prepared with water, 2 tbsp.	30	3	90	2	60	7
Picante Sauce, Old El Paso, 2 tbsp.	12	0	0	0	0	0
Picante Sauce, Pace, 2 tbsp.	9	0	0	0	0	0

FOOD/PORTION SIZE	CAL.	FAT		SAT. FAT		CHOL.
		Total (g)	As % of Cal.	Total (g)	As % of Cal.	(mg)
Soy sauce, *see* BAKING PRODUCTS & CONDIMENTS						
Spaghetti, Chunky Garden Style, with Mushrooms and Green Peppers, Ragu, 4 oz.	70	3	39	na	na	0
Spaghetti, Extra Chunky, Garden Tomato with Mushrooms, Prego, 4 oz.	100	6	54	tr	na	52
Spaghetti, Extra Chunky, Mushroom and Tomato, Prego, 4 oz.	110	5	41	na	na	na
Spaghetti, Extra Chunky, Tomato and Onion, Prego, 4 oz.	140	6	39	na	na	na
Spaghetti, Plain, Prego, 4 oz.	140	5	32	1	6	0
Spaghetti, Ragu, 4 oz.	80	3	34	tr	na	0
Spaghetti, Thick & Hearty, Ragu, 4 oz.	140	5	32	tr	na	0
Spaghetti, with Meat, Homestyle, Ragu, 4 oz.	70	2	26	tr	na	2
Spaghetti, with Meat, Prego, 4 oz.	150	6	36	2	12	4
Spaghetti, with Meat, Ragu, 4 oz.	80	3	34	tr	na	2
Spaghetti, with Mushrooms, Prego, 4 oz.	140	5	32	1	6	0
Spaghetti, with Mushrooms, Ragu, 4 oz.	80	4	45	tr	na	0
Spaghetti, with Mushrooms, Thick & Hearty, Ragu, 4 oz.	140	5	32	tr	na	0
White, prepared with milk, 2 tbsp.	30	2	49	1	23	5

Legumes & Nuts

FOOD/PORTION SIZE	CAL.	FAT		SAT. FAT		CHOL.
		Total (g)	As % of Cal.	Total (g)	As % of Cal.	(mg)
BEANS						
Black, dry, cooked, drained, 1 cup	225	1	4	tr	<1	0
Chickpeas, dry, cooked, drained, 1 cup	270	4	13	tr	<1	0
Great Northern, dry, cooked, drained, 1 cup	210	1	4	tr	<1	0
Lentils, dry, cooked, 1 cup	215	1	4	tr	<1	0
Lima, dry, cooked, drained, 1 cup	216	1	4	tr	<1	0
Lima, immature seeds, frozen, cooked, drained: thick-seeded types (Fordhooks), 1 cup	170	1	5	tr	<1	0
Lima, immature seeds, frozen, cooked, drained: thin-seeded types (baby limas), 1 cup	188	1	5	tr	<1	0
Peas (Navy), dry, cooked, drained, 1 cup	258	1	3	tr	<1	0
Pinto, dry, cooked, drained, 1 cup	234	1	4	tr	<1	0

FOOD/PORTION SIZE	CAL.	FAT		SAT. FAT		CHOL. (mg)
		Total (g)	As % of Cal.	Total (g)	As % of Cal.	
Pork and Beans, Van Camp's, 1 cup	227	1	5	na	na	0
Red kidney, canned, 1 cup	216	1	4	tr	<1	0
Refried, canned, 1 cup	268	3	10	1	3	15
Refried, Vegetarian, Old El Paso, 1 cup	140	2	13	na	na	0
Snap, canned, drained, solids (cut), 1 cup	25	tr	na	tr	na	0
Snap, cooked, drained, from frozen (cut), 1 cup	35	tr	na	tr	na	0
Snap, cooked, drained, from raw (cut and French style), 1 cup	45	tr	na	<1	2	0
Sprouts, (mung), raw, 1 cup	30	tr	na	tr	na	0
Tahini, 1 tbsp.	95	7	66	1	9	0
Vegetarian Beans in Tomato Sauce, Heinz, 1 cup	250	2	7	na	na	0
White, with sliced frankfurters, canned, 1 cup	365	18	44	7	17	30

NUTS

FOOD/PORTION SIZE	CAL.	FAT		SAT. FAT		CHOL. (mg)
Almonds, shelled, whole, 1 oz.	165	15	82	1	5	0
Almonds, sliced, 1 oz.	170	13	69	1	5	0
Almonds, Sliced, Blue Diamond, 1 oz.	150	13	78	1	6	0
Almonds, Whole, Blue Diamond, 1 oz.	150	13	78	1	6	0
Brazil, shelled, 1 oz.	185	19	92	4	19	0
Cashews, salted, dry roasted, 1 cup	869	65	67	14	14	0
Cashews, salted, roasted in oil, 1 cup	869	67	69	14	14	0
Chestnuts, European, roasted, shelled, 1 cup	350	3	8	tr	<1	0
Coconut, raw, piece, 45 g (1.6 oz.)	160	15	84	13	73	0
Filberts (hazelnuts), chopped, 1 cup	955	84	79	7	7	0
Macadamia, salted, roasted in oil, 1 cup	1088	103	85	16	13	0
Mixed, with peanuts, salted, dry roasted, 1 oz.	170	13	69	2	11	0
Mixed, with peanuts, salted, roasted in oil, 1 oz.	175	14	72	2	10	0
Peanut Butter, 2 tbsp.	190	16	76	2	9	0
Peanut Butter, Creamy, Skippy, 2 tbsp.	190	17	81	3	14	0
Peanut Butter, Extra Crunchy, Jif, 2 tbsp.	180	16	80	na	na	0
Peanuts, Dry Roasted, Planter's, 1 oz.	160	14	79	2	11	0
Peanuts, salted, roasted in oil, 1 cup	869	64	66	9	9	0
Pecans, halves, 1 cup	760	68	81	6	7	0
Pistachios, dried, shelled, 1 oz.	165	13	71	2	11	0
Walnuts, black, chopped, 1 cup	760	62	73	4	5	0

FOOD/PORTION SIZE	CAL.	FAT		SAT. FAT		CHOL.
		Total (g)	As % of Cal.	Total (g)	As % of Cal.	(mg)
Walnuts, English or Persian, pieces/chips, 1 cup	770	66	77	6	7	0
PEAS						
Black-eyed, dry, cooked, 1 cup	190	1	5	<1	1	0
Split, dry, cooked, 1 cup	230	1	4	<1	<1	0
SEEDS						
Pumpkin/squash kernels, dry, hulled, 1 oz.	155	13	75	2	12	0
Sesame, dry, hulled, 1 tbsp.	45	4	80	<1	12	0
Sunflower, dry, hulled, 1 oz.	160	14	79	<2	8	0
SOY PRODUCTS						
Miso, 1 cup	568	14	22	2	3	0
Soybeans, dry, cooked, drained, 1 cup	298	13	39	2	6	0
Tofu, firm, 2 oz.	82	5	55	tr	na	0

Meat

FOOD/PORTION SIZE	CAL.	FAT		SAT. FAT		CHOL.
		Total (g)	As % of Cal.	Total (g)	As % of Cal.	(mg)
BEEF						
Chipped, dried, 2½ oz.	118	3	23	1	8	50
Chuck blade, lean only, braised/simmered/ pot roasted, approx. 2¼ oz.	168	9	48	4	21	66
Corned, canned, 3 oz.	213	16	68	5	21	83
Corned, lean, Carl Buddig, 1 oz.	40	2	45	na	na	na
Ground, Extra Lean, Healthy Choice, 3 oz.	98	3	28	2	7	55
Ground, patty, lean, broiled, 3 oz.	230	16	63	6	27	74
Ground, patty, regular, broiled, 3 oz.	245	18	66	7	26	76
Heart, lean, braised, 3 oz.	150	5	30	2	12	164
Liver, fried, 3 oz.	185	7	34	3	15	410
Roast, eye of round, lean only, oven cooked, approx. 2½ oz.	135	5	33	2	13	52
Roast, rib, lean only, oven cooked, approx. 2¼ oz.	150	9	54	4	24	49
Roast, tip, lean only, oven cooked, approx. 2½ oz.	135	5	33	2	13	52

FOOD/PORTION SIZE	CAL.	FAT Total (g)	FAT As % of Cal.	SAT. FAT Total (g)	SAT. FAT As % of Cal.	CHOL. (mg)
Round, bottom, lean only, braised/simmered/ pot roasted, 2⅘ oz.	175	8	41	3	15	75
Steak, cubed, lean only, broiled, 2½ oz.	170	9	48	4	21	66
Steak, sirloin, lean only, broiled, 2½ oz.	150	6	36	3	18	64
FRANKS & SAUSAGES						
Frankfurter, Chicken, Health Valley, 1 frank	145	12	74	4	25	27
Franks, Beef, Oscar Mayer, 1 link	144	14	88	6	38	28
Franks, Eckrich, 1 frank	190	17	81	na	na	na
Franks, Healthy Choice, 1 frank	50	1	18	<1	na	15
Franks, Jumbo Beef, Eckrich, 1 frank	190	17	81	na	na	na
Franks, Lite, Eckrich, 1 frank	120	10	75	na	na	25
Sausage, beef and pork, frankfurters, cooked, 1 frank	183	16	79	6	30	29
Sausage, pork, brown/serve, browned, 1 link	50	5	90	2	36	9
Sausage, pork, links, 1 link (1 oz.)	50	4	72	2	36	11
Sausage, Pork, Regular, Jimmy Dean, 1 patty (1⅕ oz.)	140	13	84	na	na	na
Turkey Breakfast Sausage, Louis Rich, 1 oz.	54	4	67	2	33	22
Turkey Smoked Sausage, Louis Rich, 1 oz.	43	2	50	.6	13	18
Wieners, Oscar Mayer, 1 link	144	13	81	5	31	27
GAME						
Buffalo, roasted, 3 oz.	111	2	16	<1	na	52
Venison, roasted, 3 oz.	134	3	20	1	7	95
LAMB						
Chops, shoulder, lean only, braised, approx. 1¾ oz.	135	7	47	3	20	44
Leg, lean only, roasted, approx. 2⅔ oz.	140	6	39	3	19	65
Loin, chop, lean only, broiled, approx. 2⅓ oz.	182	10	49	4	20	60
Rib, lean only, roasted, 2 oz.	130	7	48	4	28	50
LUNCHEON MEATS						
Bologna, Beef, Oscar Mayer, 28 g (1 oz.)	90	8	80	4	40	20
Bologna, Lite, Oscar Mayer, 28 g (1 oz.)	70	6	77	na	na	15
Bologna, Oscar Mayer, 15 g (½ oz.)	50	4	72	2	36	9
Braunschweiger sausage, 2 oz.	205	18	79	7	31	88
Chicken, roll, light, 2 oz.	90	4	40	1	10	28

FOOD/PORTION SIZE	CAL.	FAT Total (g)	FAT As % of Cal.	SAT. FAT Total (g)	SAT. FAT As % of Cal.	CHOL. (mg)
Ham, chopped, 8-slice (6-oz.) pack, 2 slices	98	7	64	3	28	23
Ham, Cooked, Eckrich Lite, 1 oz.	25	1	36	na	na	15
Ham, extra lean, cooked, 2 slices (2 oz.)	75	3	36	1	12	27
Ham, regular, cooked, 2 slices (2 oz.)	105	6	51	2	17	32
Pork, canned lunch meat, spiced/unspiced, 2 slices, 42 g (1½ oz.)	140	13	84	5	32	26
Salami sausage, cooked, 2 oz.	141	11	70	5	32	37
Salami sausage, dry, 12-slice (4-oz.) pack, 2 slices	84	6	64	2	21	16
Sandwich spread, pork/beef, 1 tbsp.	35	3	77	<1	23	6
Turkey, breast meat, loaf, 8-slice (6-oz.) pack, 2 slices	45	1	20	<1	4	17
Turkey, Oscar Mayer, ¾ oz.	22	1	41	tr	na	8
Turkey, Salami, 1 slice, 28 grams	54	4	67	1	17	20
Turkey, thigh meat, ham cured, 2 oz.	75	3	36	1	12	32
Turkey Bologna, Louis Rich Turkey Cold Cuts, 28 g (1 oz.)	61	5	74	2	30	22
Turkey Breast, Healthy Choice, 2 oz.	60	1	15	na	na	25
Turkey Breast, Light, Eckrich, 1 oz.	30	1	30	0	0	10
Turkey Breast, Oven Roasted, Deli Thin Louis Rich, 22 grams	24	1	38	tr	tr	8
Turkey Breast, Oven Roasted, Eckrich Lite, 1 oz.	30	1	31	na	na	10
Turkey Ham, Louis Rich Turkey Cold Cuts, 21 g (¾ oz.)	25	1	36	0	0	14
Turkey Ham, Smoked, Louis Rich Turkey Cold Cuts, 28 g (1 oz.)	34	1	26	1	26	19
Turkey Pastrami, Louis Rich Turkey Cold Cuts, 23 g (⅘ oz.)	24	1	38	0	0	14
Vienna sausage, 7 per 4-oz. can, 1 sausage, 16 g (approx. ½ oz.)	45	4	80	2	40	8

PORK

FOOD/PORTION SIZE	CAL.	FAT Total (g)	FAT As % of Cal.	SAT. FAT Total (g)	SAT. FAT As % of Cal.	CHOL. (mg)
Bacon, Canadian, cured, cooked, 2 slices	86	4	42	1	10	27
Bacon, Low Salt, Armour, 2 slices	76	8	95	2	24	12
Bacon, regular, cured, cooked, 3 medium slices	108	9	75	3	25	16
Chop, loin, fresh, lean only, broiled, 2½ oz.	163	7	39	3	17	69
Chop, loin, fresh, lean only, pan fried, approx. 2½ oz.	181	10	50	4	20	73
Ham, Baked, Oscar Mayer, 21 g (¾ oz.)	21	1	43	tr	na	11
Ham, Boiled, Oscar Mayer, 21 g (¾ oz.)	26	1	35	tr	na	12
Ham, Breakfast Slice, Oscar Mayer, 1 slice	50	2	36	tr	na	20

FOOD/PORTION SIZE	CAL.	FAT		SAT. FAT		CHOL.
		Total (g)	As % of Cal.	Total (g)	As % of Cal.	(mg)
Ham, canned, roasted, 3 oz.	140	7	45	2	13	35
Ham, leg, fresh, lean only, roasted, 2½ oz.	156	8	46	3	17	67
Ham, light cure, lean only, roasted, approx. 2½ oz.	107	4	34	1	8	38
Ham, Lower Salt, Light, Eckrich, 1 oz.	25	1	36	0	0	15
Ham, Low Salt, Armour, 1 oz.	40	3	68	1	23	15
Rib, fresh, lean only, roasted, 2½ oz.	173	8	42	3	16	56
Shoulder cut, fresh, lean only, braised, 2⅖ oz.	169	8	43	3	16	78
Tenderloin, roasted, lean, 3 oz.	139	4	26	1	6	67
Turkey Bacon, Louis Rich, 1 slice	32	2	56	tr	na	10
VEAL						
Cubed, lean only, braised, 3½ oz.	188	4	19	1	5	145
Cutlet, leg, lean only, braised, 3½ oz.	203	6	27	2	9	135
Rib, lean only, roasted, 3½ oz.	177	7	36	2	10	115

Packaged Entrées

FOOD/PORTION SIZE	CAL.	FAT		SAT. FAT		CHOL.
		Total (g)	As % of Cal.	Total (g)	As % of Cal.	(mg)
Beef Noodle, Hamburger Helper, prepared with meat, 1 cup	320	15	42	7	20	79
Beef Stew, Dinty Moore, 10 oz.	270	13	43	na	na	na
Cheeseburger Macaroni, Hamburger Helper, prepared with meat, 1 cup	370	19	46	na	na	na
Chicken, Sweet & Sour, La Choy, ¾ cup	230	2	8	tr	<1	103
Chili con carne with beans, canned, 1 cup	286	13	41	6	19	43
Chow Mein, Beef, La Choy, ¾ cup	60	1	15	tr	na	25
Chow Mein, Chicken, La Choy, ¾ cup	80	3	34	na	na	na
Egg Noodle and Cheese Dinner, Kraft, ¾ cup	340	17	45	4	11	50
Egg Noodle with Chicken Dinner, Kraft, ¾ cup	240	9	34	2	8	45
Lasagna, Hamburger Helper, prepared with meat, 1 cup	340	14	37	na	na	na
Macaroni and Cheese Deluxe Dinner, Kraft, ¾ cup	260	8	28	4	14	20
Macaroni and Cheese Dinner, Original, Kraft, ¾ cup	290	13	40	na	na	na
Shells and Cheese Dinner, Velveeta, ½ cup	210	8	34	4	17	20

FOOD/PORTION SIZE	CAL.	FAT		SAT. FAT		CHOL.
		Total (g)	As % of Cal.	Total (g)	As % of Cal.	(mg)
Spaghetti, Mild American Style Dinner, Kraft, 1 cup	300	7	21	2	6	0
Spaghetti Dinner, Tangy Italian Style, Kraft, 1 cup	310	48	23	2	6	5
Spaghetti in tomato sauce with cheese, canned, 1 cup	190	2	9	<1	2	3
Spaghetti with Meat Sauce, Top Shelf 2-Minute Entrée, Hormel, 10 oz.	260	6	21	na	na	20
Spaghetti with Meat Sauce Dinner, Kraft, 1 cup	360	14	35	4	10	15

Pasta

FOOD/PORTION SIZE	CAL.	FAT		SAT. FAT		CHOL.
		Total (g)	As % of Cal.	Total (g)	As % of Cal.	(mg)
Egg Noodles, Creamette, 2 oz.	210	3	13	na	na	55
Egg Noodles Substitute, Cholesterol Free, No Yolks, 2 oz. dry	200	1	5	na	na	0
Linguine, Fresh, Di Giorno, Cholesterol Free, 3 oz.	250	3	11	na	na	0
Macaroni, enriched, cooked, firm, hot, 1 cup	190	1	5	<1	<1	0
Macaroni, enriched, cooked, tender, cold, 1 cup	115	tr	na	<1	<1	0
Macaroni, enriched, cooked, tender, hot, 1 cup	155	1	6	<1	<1	0
Macaroni and cheese dishes, see PACKAGED ENTRÉES						
Noodle Roni Fettucini, prepared with margarine and 2% milk, ½ cup	291	17	53	5	15	28
Noodle Roni Parmesano, prepared with margarine and 2% milk, ½ cup	250	14	50	4	14	21
Noodle Roni Romanoff, prepared with margarine and 2% milk, ½ cup	213	8	34	3	13	25
Noodle Roni Stroganoff, prepared with margarine and 2% milk, ½ cup	290	11	34	4	12	47
Noodles, chow mein, canned, 1 cup	220	11	45	2	8	5
Noodles, Creamette, all types except egg, 2 oz.	210	1	4	na	na	0
Noodles, egg, enriched, cooked, 1 cup	200	2	9	1	5	50
Spaghetti, enriched, cooked, firm, hot, 1 cup	190	1	5	<1	<1	0
Spaghetti, enriched, cooked, tender, hot, 1 cup	155	1	6	0	0	0

FOOD/PORTION SIZE	CAL.	FAT		SAT. FAT		CHOL.
		Total (g)	As % of Cal.	Total (g)	As % of Cal.	(mg)
Spaghetti with sauce/meat, *see* PACKAGED ENTRÉES						

Poultry

FOOD/PORTION SIZE	CAL.	FAT		SAT. FAT		CHOL.
		Total (g)	As % of Cal.	Total (g)	As % of Cal.	(mg)
Chicken, boneless, canned, 5 oz.	235	11	42	3	11	88
Chicken, boneless, skinless, Perdue, Fit 'n Easy, Oven Stuffer Roaster Breast, 1 oz.	30	<1	<1	<1	<1	17
Chicken, boneless, skinless, Perdue, Fit 'n Easy, Pick of the Chick, 1 oz.	30	<1	<1	<1	<1	17
Chicken, breast, flesh only, roasted, 3 oz.	140	3	19	<1	6	73
Chicken, broiler-fryer, breast, w/o skin, roasted, 3½ oz.	165	4	22	1	5	85
Chicken, drumstick, roasted, approx. 1.6 oz.	75	2	24	<1	8	26
Chicken, light and dark meat, flesh only, stewed, 1 cup	332	17	46	1	3	117
Chicken, liver, cooked, 1 liver	30	1	30	<1	12	120
Chicken, white and dark meat, w/o skin, roasted, 3½ oz.	190	7	33	2	9	89
Cold cuts, chicken or turkey, *see* LUNCHEON MEATS *in* MEAT section						
Duck, flesh only, roasted, ½ duck, approx. 7¾ oz.	445	24	49	11	22	197
Frankfurters, chicken, *see* FRANKS & SAUSAGES in MEAT section						
Turkey, dark meat only, w/o skin, roasted, 3½ oz.	187	7	34	2	10	85
Turkey, flesh only, 1 light and 2 dark slices, 85 g (3 oz.)	145	4	25	1	6	65
Turkey, flesh only, light and dark meat, chopped or diced, roasted, 1 cup, 140 g (5 oz.)	240	7	26	2	8	106
Turkey, flesh only, light meat, roasted, 2 pieces, 85 g (3 oz.)	135	3	20	1	7	59
Turkey, frozen, boneless, light and dark meat, seasoned, chunked, roasted, 3 oz.	130	5	35	2	14	45

FOOD/PORTION SIZE	CAL.	FAT Total (g)	FAT As % of Cal.	SAT. FAT Total (g)	SAT. FAT As % of Cal.	CHOL. (mg)
Turkey, Ground, Lean, Louis Rich, cooked, 1 oz.	52	2	35	1	17	25
Turkey, Ground, Louis Rich, cooked, 1 oz.	60	4	60	1	15	25
Turkey, patties, breaded, battered, fried, 1 patty	180	12	60	3	15	40
Turkey, smoked, 1 slice, 28 grams	32	1	28	.4	11	12
Turkey, white meat only, w/o skin, roasted, 3½ oz.	157	3	17	1	6	69
Turkey and gravy, frozen, 5 oz. pkg.	95	3	28	1	9	18
Turkey Breast Steaks, Louis Rich, 1 oz.	39	tr	tr	.2	5	18

Rice

FOOD/PORTION SIZE	CAL.	FAT Total (g)	FAT As % of Cal.	SAT. FAT Total (g)	SAT. FAT As % of Cal.	CHOL. (mg)
Beef Flavor, Rice-A-Roni, prepared with margarine, ½ cup	170	5	26	1	5	0
Boil-in-Bag, Uncle Ben's, about ½ cup cooked	80	<1	<1	na	na	na
Brown, cooked, hot, ½ cup	115	tr	4	<1	1	0
Brown & Wild, Mushroom Recipe, Uncle Ben's, ½ cup cooked	130	1	7	na	na	na
Chicken Flavor, Rice-A-Roni, prepared with margarine, ½ cup	171	5	26	1	5	tr
Chicken Vegetable, Rice-A-Roni, prepared with margarine, ½ cup cooked	139	3	19	1	6	0
Extra-Long-Grain, Riceland, ½ cup cooked	100	0	0	0	0	na
Fast Cook, Uncle Ben's, about ⅔ cup cooked	110	<1	<1	na	na	na
Herb Rice Au Gratin, Country Inn, Uncle Ben's, prepared with margarine, ½ cup	170	5	26	2	11	11
Instant, ready-to-serve, cooked, hot, ½ cup	90	0	0	0	0	0
Long Grain, Natural, Converted, Uncle Ben's, ⅔ cup cooked	120	0	0	0	0	na
Long Grain & Wild, Minute Rice, ½ cup cooked	120	0	0	0	0	0
Long Grain & Wild, Original Recipe, Uncle Ben's, about ½ cup cooked	100	<1	<9	na	na	na
Long Grain & Wild, Rice-A-Roni, prepared with margarine, ½ cup cooked	137	3	20	1	7	0
Minute Rice, w/o salt or butter, ⅔ cup cooked	120	0	0	na	na	0

FOOD/PORTION SIZE	CAL.	FAT		SAT. FAT		CHOL.
		Total (g)	As % of Cal.	Total (g)	As % of Cal.	(mg)
Parboiled, cooked, hot, ½ cup	93	tr	na	tr	na	0
Parboiled, raw, ½ cup	343	tr	1	<1	<1	0
Savory Broccoli Au Gratin, Rice-A-Roni, prepared with margarine, ½ cup cooked	178	10	51	3	15	4
Savory Rice Pilaf, Rice-A-Roni, prepared with margarine, ½ cup cooked	186	5	24	1	5	tr
White, enriched, cooked, hot, ½ cup	113	tr	na	<1	<1	0

Salad Dressings

FOOD/PORTION SIZE	CAL.	FAT		SAT. FAT		CHOL.
		Total (g)	As % of Cal.	Total (g)	As % of Cal.	(mg)
Bacon, Creamy, Reduced Calorie, Kraft, 1 tbsp.	30	2	60	0	0	0
Bacon & Tomato, Kraft, 1 tbsp.	70	7	90	1	13	0
Blue Cheese, Chunky, Healthy Sensation!, 1 tbsp.	20	0	0	na	na	0
Blue Cheese, Chunky, Kraft, 1 tbsp.	60	6	90	1	15	5
Blue Cheese, Chunky, Reduced Calorie, Kraft, 1 tbsp.	30	2	60	1	30	5
Blue Cheese, Lite, Less Oil, Wish-Bone, 1 tbsp.	40	4	90	tr	na	0
Blue Cheese and Herb, Good Seasons, prepared with oil and vinegar, 1 tbsp.	70	8	100	na	na	0
Buttermilk, Creamy, Kraft, 1 tbsp.	80	8	90	1	11	5
Buttermilk, Creamy, Reduced Calorie, Kraft, 1 tbsp.	30	3	90	0	0	5
Buttermilk, Farm Style, Good Seasons, with whole milk and mayonnaise, 1 tbsp.	58	6	93	na	na	0
Caesar, Weight Watchers, 1 tbsp.	4	0	0	0	0	na
Cheese Garlic, Good Seasons, with vinegar and oil, 1 tbsp.	7	8	100	na	na	0
Cheese Italian, Good Seasons, with vinegar and oil, 1 tbsp.	70	8	100	na	na	0
Coleslaw, Kraft, 1 tbsp.	70	6	77	1	13	10
Cucumber, Creamy, Kraft, 1 tbsp.	70	8	100	1	13	0
Cucumber, Creamy, Reduced Calorie, Kraft, 1 tbsp.	25	2	72	0	0	0
French, Catalina Brand, Kraft, 1 tbsp.	60	5	75	1	15	0
French, Kraft, 1 tbsp.	60	6	90	1	15	0

FOOD/PORTION SIZE	CAL.	FAT Total (g)	As % of Cal.	SAT. FAT Total (g)	As % of Cal.	CHOL. (mg)
French, Lite, Less Oil, Wish-Bone, 1 tbsp.	30	2	60	0	0	0
French, No Oil, Pritikin, 1 tbsp.	10	0	0	0	0	0
French, Reduced Calorie, Kraft, 1 tbsp.	20	1	45	0	0	0
French, Sweet 'n Spicy Lite, Wish-Bone, 1 tbsp.	16	0	0	0	0	0
French, Weight Watchers, 1 tbsp.	10	0	0	0	0	na
Garlic, Creamy, Kraft, 1 tbsp.	50	5	90	1	18	0
Garlic and Herbs, Good Seasons, with oil and vinegar, 1 tbsp.	70	8	100	na	na	0
Golden Caesar, Kraft, 1 tbsp.	70	7	90	1	13	0
Herb, Classic, Good Seasons, with vinegar and oil, 1 tbsp.	70	8	100	na	na	0
Honey Dijon, Healthy Sensation!, 1 tbsp.	25	0	0	na	na	0
Italian, Creamy, Lite, Less Oil, Wish-Bone, 1 tbsp.	6	0	0	0	0	0
Italian, Creamy, Reduced Calorie, Kraft, 1 tbsp.	25	2	72	0	0	0
Italian, Good Seasons, with oil and vinegar, 1 tbsp.	71	8	100	na	na	0
Italian, Healthy Sensation!, 1 tbsp.	6	0	0	na	na	0
Italian, Lite, Good Seasons, with oil and vinegar, 1 tbsp.	26	3	100	na	na	0
Italian, Lite, Wish-Bone, 1 tbsp.	6	1	100	0	0	0
Italian, Mild, Good Seasons, with oil and vinegar, 1 tbsp.	73	8	99	na	na	0
Italian, No Oil, Good Seasons, with vinegar and water, 1 tbsp.	7	0	0	na	na	0
Italian, No Oil, Pritikin, 1 tbsp.	10	0	0	0	0	0
Italian, Oil-Free, Kraft, 1 tbsp.	4	0	0	0	0	0
Italian, Olive Oil Classics, Wishbone, 1 tbsp.	33	3	82	.4	11	0
Italian, Weight Watchers, 1 tbsp.	6	0	0	0	0	na
Italian, Wishbone, 1 tbsp.	45	5	100	1	20	0
Italian, Zesty, Good Seasons, with oil and vinegar, 1 tbsp.	71	8	100	na	na	0
Italian, Zesty, Kraft, 1 tbsp.	50	5	90	1	18	0
Italian, Zesty, Reduced Calorie, Kraft, 1 tbsp.	20	2	90	0	0	0
Lemon Herb, Good Seasons, with oil and vinegar, 1 tbsp.	70	8	100	na	na	0
Miracle Whip, Free Nonfat, 1 tbsp.	5	0	0	0	0	0
Miracle Whip Light Reduced Calorie Salad Dressing with No Cholesterol, 1 tbsp.	45	4	80	1	20	0
Miracle Whip Salad Dressing, 1 tbsp.	70	7	90	1	13	5
Oil & Vinegar, Kraft, 1 tbsp.	70	8	100	1	13	0
Ranch, Original, Hidden Valley Ranch, 1 tbsp.	80	8	90	na	na	10

FOOD/PORTION SIZE	CAL.	FAT		SAT. FAT		CHOL.
		Total (g)	As % of Cal.	Total (g)	As % of Cal.	(mg)
Ranch, Original, Take Heart, Hidden Valley Ranch, 1 tbsp.	20	1	45	na	na	0
Reduced Calorie, Catalina Brand, Kraft, 1 tbsp.	18	1	50	0	0	0
Red Wine, Vinegar and Oil, Kraft, 1 tbsp.	60	4	60	1	15	0
Russian, Reduced Calorie, Kraft, 1 tbsp.	30	1	30	0	0	0
Thousand Island, Kraft, 1 tbsp.	60	5	75	1	15	5
Thousand Island, Lite, Less Oil, Wish-Bone, 1 tbsp.	40	0	0	na	na	0
Thousand Island, Reduced Calorie, Kraft, 1 tbsp.	20	2	90	0	0	0
Thousand Island & Bacon, Kraft, 1 tbsp.	60	6	90	1	10	0
Tomato Vinaigrette, Weight Watchers, 1 tbsp.	8	0	0	0	0	na

Snacks

FOOD/PORTION SIZE	CAL.	FAT		SAT. FAT		CHOL.
		Total (g)	As % of Cal.	Total (g)	As % of Cal.	(mg)
CORN CHIPS						
Bugles, 1 oz.	150	8	48	7	42	0
Doritos, Cool Ranch, 1 oz.	144	7	44	2	13	0
Doritos, Nacho Cheese, 1 oz.	143	7	44	2	13	0
Fritos Corn Chips, 1 oz.	154	9	53	3	18	0
Tortilla Chips, Restaurant Style, Tostitos, 1 oz.	140	7	45	na	na	0
Tostitos, Traditional, 1 oz.	145	8	50	1	6	0
DIPS						
Avocado (guacamole), Kraft, 2 tbsp.	50	4	72	2	36	0
Bacon & Horseradish, Kraft, 2 tbsp.	60	5	75	3	45	0
Blue Cheese, Kraft Premium, 2 tbsp.	50	4	72	2	36	10
Clam, Kraft, 2 tbsp.	60	4	60	1	15	10
Cucumber, Creamy, Kraft Premium, 2 tbsp.	50	4	72	3	54	10
French Onion, Kraft, 2 tbsp.	60	4	60	2	30	0
Green Onion, Kraft, 2 tbsp.	60	4	60	2	30	0
Jalapeño Pepper, Kraft, 2 tbsp.	50	4	72	2	36	0
Nacho Cheese, Kraft Premium, 2 tbsp.	55	4	65	2	33	10
Onion, Creamy, Kraft Premium, 2 tbsp.	45	4	80	2	40	10

FOOD/PORTION SIZE	CAL.	FAT		SAT. FAT		CHOL.
		Total (g)	As % of Cal.	Total (g)	As % of Cal.	(mg)
FRUIT SNACKS						
Fruit Roll-Ups, Cherry, ½ oz.	50	1	18	0	0	0
Fruit Roll-Ups, Grape, ½ oz.	50	1	18	0	0	0
Fruit Roll-Ups, Watermelon, ½ oz.	60	1	15	tr	na	0
Fruit Wrinkles, Orange, Betty Crocker, 1 pouch	100	2	18	tr	na	0
Fruit Wrinkles, Strawberry, Betty Crocker, 1 pouch	100	2	18	tr	na	0
Fun Fruits, Fantastic Fruit Punch, Sunkist, 1 oz.	100	1	9	na	na	na
Fun Fruits, Grape, Sunkist, 1 oz.	100	1	9	na	na	na
GRANOLA						
Apple, Chewy Granola Bar, Quaker Oats, 1 oz.	120	3	23	tr	na	tr
Chocolate Chip, Chewy Granola Bar, Quaker Oats, 1 oz.	130	5	35	tr	na	tr
Chocolate Covered Caramel Nut Dipps, Quaker Oats, 1 bar	140	6	39	3	19	4
Chocolate Covered Chocolate Chip Dipps, Quaker Oats, 1 bar	138	7	46	4	26	4
Chocolate Covered Peanut Butter Dipps, Quaker Oats, 1 bar	141	7	45	4	26	3
Chocolate Graham & Marshmallow, Chewy Granola Bar, Quaker Oats, 1 oz.	126	4	29	2	14	tr
Nut & Raisin, Chunky, Chewy Granola Bar, Quaker Oats, 1 oz.	133	6	41	2	14	tr
Oats n' Honey, Granola Bar, Nature Valley, 1 bar	120	5	38	2	15	0
Peanut Butter Chocolate Chip, Chewy Granola Bar, Quaker Oats, 1 oz.	131	5	34	2	14	tr
POPCORN						
Air-popped, unsalted, 1 cup	30	tr	na	tr	na	0
Microwave, Butter, Orville Redenbacher, 1 cup	28	2	49	tr	na	0
Microwave, Natural, Orville Redenbacher, 1 cup	28	2	57	1	8	0
Popped in vegetable oil, salted, 1 cup	55	3	49	<1	8	0
Sugar syrup coated, 1 cup	135	1	6	<1	<1	0
POTATO CHIPS						
Lays, 1 oz.	152	9	53	2	12	0

FOOD/PORTION SIZE	CAL.	FAT Total (g)	FAT As % of Cal.	SAT. FAT Total (g)	SAT. FAT As % of Cal.	CHOL. (mg)
Lays, Bar-B-Que, 1 oz.	149	9	54	2	12	0
O'Grady's, 1 oz.	150	9	54	2	12	0
O'Grady's, Au Gratin, 1 oz.	147	8	49	2	12	1
Pringles, 1 oz.	170	13	69	2	11	0
Pringles, Sour Cream n' Onion, 1 oz.	170	13	69	2	11	0
Pringles Light, Ranch, 1 oz.	150	8	48	2	12	0
Ruffles, 1 oz.	151	10	60	2	12	0
Ruffles, Cajun Spice, 1 oz.	154	10	58	2	12	0
Ruffles, Sour Cream & Onion, 1 oz.	150	9	54	2	12	1
PRETZELS						
Enriched flour, 2¼-in. sticks, 10 pretzels	10	tr	na	tr	na	0
Enriched flour, twisted, dutch, 1 pretzel	65	1	14	<1	1	0
Enriched flour, twisted, thin, 10 pretzels	240	2	8	<1	1	0
Mister Salty, Sticks, 1 oz.	110	1	18	tr	na	0
Mister Salty, Twists, 1 oz.	110	2	16	tr	na	0
Pretzel Chips, Mr. Phipps, ½ oz. (8 chips)	60	1	15	na	na	0
Rold Gold, Thin, 1 oz.	110	1	8	na	na	0

Soups

FOOD/PORTION SIZE	CAL.	FAT Total (g)	FAT As % of Cal.	SAT. FAT Total (g)	SAT. FAT As % of Cal.	CHOL. (mg)
Asparagus, Cream of, Campbell's, 4 oz. condensed, 8 oz. as prepared	80	4	45	na	na	<5
Bean with bacon, canned, condensed, prepared with water, 1 cup	173	6	31	2	10	3
Beef broth bouillon consommé, canned, condensed, prepared with water, 1 cup	29	0	0	0	0	0
Beef noodle, canned, condensed, prepared with water, 1 cup	85	3	32	1	11	5
Bouillon (beef or chicken), *Wylers*, 1 tsp	6	0	0	0	0	0
Chicken, broth, College Inn, 7 oz.	35	3	77	1	26	5
Chicken, cream of, canned, condensed, prepared with milk, 1 cup	190	11	52	5	24	27
Chicken, cream of, canned, condensed, prepared with water, 1 cup	115	7	55	2	16	10
Chicken noodle, canned, condensed, prepared with water, 1 cup	75	2	24	<1	8	7

FOOD/PORTION SIZE	CAL.	FAT		SAT. FAT		CHOL.
		Total (g)	As % of Cal.	Total (g)	As % of Cal.	(mg)
Chicken noodle, dehydrated, prepared with water, 6 oz.	40	1	23	<1	5	3
Chicken Noodle, Hearty, Campbell's Healthy Request, 8 oz.	80	2	23	na	na	25
Chicken Noodle, Old Fashioned, Healthy Choice, 7½ oz.	90	3	30	1	na	20
Chicken Noodle, Progresso, 9.5 oz.	120	4	30	na	na	40
Chicken rice, canned, condensed, prepared with water, 1 cup	60	2	30	<1	8	7
Clam chowder, Manhattan, canned, condensed, prepared with water, 1 cup	80	2	23	<1	5	2
Clam chowder, New England, canned, condensed, prepared with milk, 1 cup	163	6	33	3	17	22
Minestrone, canned, condensed, prepared with water, 1 cup	80	3	34	<1	7	2
Minestrone, Progresso, 9½ oz.	130	4	28	na	na	0
Mushroom, cream of, canned, condensed, prepared with milk, 1 cup	203	13	58	5	22	20
Mushroom, cream of, canned, condensed, prepared with water, 1 cup	129	9	63	3	21	2
Mushroom, Cream of, Healthy Request, Campbell's, 4 oz. condensed, 8 oz. as prepared	60	2	30	na	na	<5
Noodle Soup Mix with Real Chicken Broth, Lipton, 8 oz.	70	2	26	na	na	na
Onion, dehydrated, prepared with water, 1 packet	20	tr	na	<1	5	0
Onion-Mushroom Recipe Soup Mix, Lipton, 8 oz.	40	<1	<1	na	na	na
Onion Soup Recipe Mix, Lipton, 8 oz.	20	0	0	na	na	na
Pea, green, canned, condensed, prepared with water, 1 cup	164	3	16	1	5	0
Tomato, canned, condensed, prepared with milk, 1 cup	160	6	34	3	17	17
Tomato, canned, condensed, prepared with water, 1 cup	85	2	21	<1	4	9
Tomato vegetable, dehydrated, prepared with water, 6 oz.	40	1	23	<1	7	0
Turkey Noodle, Campbell's, 4 oz. condensed, 8 oz. as prepared	70	2	26	na	na	15
Vegetable, Vegetarian, Campbell's, 4 oz. condensed, 8 oz. as prepared	80	2	23	na	na	0
Vegetable beef, canned, condensed, prepared with water, 1 cup	80	2	23	<1	10	5

Vegetables

FOOD/PORTION SIZE	CAL.	FAT Total (g)	FAT As % of Cal.	SAT. FAT Total (g)	SAT. FAT As % of Cal.	CHOL. (mg)
ALFALFA						
Seeds, sprouted, raw, 1 cup	10	tr	na	tr	na	0
ARTICHOKES						
Globe or French, cooked, drained, 1 artichoke	53	tr	na	tr	na	0
Jerusalem, red, sliced, 1 cup	114	tr	na	0	0	0
ASPARAGUS						
Canned, spears, 4 spears	10	tr	na	tr	na	0
Cuts & tips, cooked, drained, from raw, 1 cup	45	1	20	<1	2	0
Cuts & tips, from frozen, 1 cup	50	1	18	<1	4	0
Spears, cooked, drained, from raw, 4 spears	15	tr	na	tr	na	0
Spears, from frozen, 4 spears	15	tr	na	<1	6	0
BAMBOO SHOOTS						
Canned, drained, 1 cup	25	1	36	<1	4	0
BEANS						
Baby Lima, Birds Eye Regular Vegetables, approx. 3⅓ oz.	98	0	0	0	0	0
Fordhook Lima, Birds Eye Regular Vegetables, approx. 3⅓ oz.	94	0	0	0	0	0
Green, Blue Lake, Del Monte, ½ cup	20	0	0	0	0	0
Green, Cut, Birds Eye Regular Vegetables, 3 oz.	23	0	0	0	0	0
Green, French Cut, Birds Eye Deluxe, 3 oz.	25	0	0	0	0	0
Green, Whole, Birds Eye Deluxe Vegetables, 3 oz.	25	0	0	0	0	0
Sprouts (mung), cooked, drained, 1 cup	25	tr	na	tr	na	0
BEETS						
Canned, drained, solids, diced or sliced, 1 cup	55	tr	na	tr	na	0
Cooked, drained, diced or sliced, 1 cup	55	tr	na	tr	na	0
Cooked, drained, whole, 2 beets	30	tr	na	tr	na	0
Greens, leaves and stems, cooked, drained, 1 cup	40	tr	na	tr	na	0

FOOD/PORTION SIZE	CAL.	FAT		SAT. FAT		CHOL. (mg)
		Total (g)	As % of Cal.	Total (g)	As % of Cal.	
BROCCOLI						
Cooked, drained, from frozen, 1 piece (4½-5 in. long)	10	tr	tr	tr	tr	0
Cooked, drained, from frozen, chopped, 1 cup	50	tr	tr	tr	tr	0
Raw, 1 spear	40	1	23	<1	2	0
Spears, cooked, drained, from raw, 1 cup (½-in. pieces)	45	tr	tr	<1	2	0
BRUSSELS SPROUTS						
Cooked, drained, from frozen, 1 cup	65	1	14	<1	1	0
Cooked, drained, from raw, 1 cup	60	1	15	<1	3	0
CABBAGE						
Chinese pak-choi, cooked, drained, 1 cup	20	tr	na	tr	na	0
Chinese pe-tsai, raw, 1-in. pieces, 1 cup	10	tr	na	tr	na	0
Common varieties, cooked, drained, 1 cup	30	tr	na	tr	na	0
Red, raw, coarsely shredded or sliced, 1 cup	20	tr	na	tr	na	0
Savoy, raw, coarsely shredded or sliced, 1 cup	20	tr	na	tr	na	0
CARROTS						
Canned, sliced, drained, solids, 1 cup	35	tr	na	<1	3	0
Cooked, sliced, drained, from frozen, 1 cup	55	tr	na	tr	na	0
Cooked, sliced, drained, from raw, 1 cup	70	tr	na	<1	1	0
Raw, w/o crowns or tips, scraped, grated, 1 cup	45	tr	na	tr	na	0
CAULIFLOWER						
Cooked, drained, from frozen (flowerets), 1 cup	35	tr	na	<1	3	0
Cooked, drained, from raw (flowerets), 1 cup	30	tr	na	tr	na	0
CELERY						
Pascal type, raw, large outer stalk, 1 stalk	5	tr	na	tr	na	0
Pascal type, raw, pieces, diced, 1 cup	20	tr	na	tr	na	0

FOOD/PORTION SIZE	CAL.	FAT		SAT. FAT		CHOL.
		Total (g)	As % of Cal.	Total (g)	As % of Cal.	(mg)
COLLARDS						
Cooked, drained, from frozen (chopped), 1 cup	60	1	15	<1	2	0
Cooked, drained, from raw (leaves w/o stems), 1 cup	25	tr	<1	<1	5	0
CORN						
Sweet, canned, cream style, 1 cup	185	1	5	<1	1	0
Sweet, cooked, drained, from frozen, 1 ear (3½ in.)	60	tr	na	<1	2	0
Sweet, cooked, drained, from raw, 1 ear (5 × 1¾ in.)	85	1	11	<1	2	0
Sweet, cooked, drained, kernels, 1 cup	135	tr	na	tr	na	0
Sweet, vacuum packed, whole kernel, 1 cup	165	1	5	<1	1	0
CUCUMBER						
Peeled slices, ⅛ in. thick (large 2⅛-in. diameter, small 1¾ in. diameter), 6 large or 8 small	5	tr	na	tr	na	0
EGGPLANT						
Cooked, steamed, 1 cup	25	tr	na	tr	na	0
ENDIVE						
Curly (including escarole), raw, small pieces, 1 cup	10	tr	na	tr	na	0
GARLIC						
Clove, 1 medium	4	tr	na	0	0	0
GREENS						
Dandelion, cooked, drained, 1 cup	34	1	26	<1	3	0
Mustard, w/o stems and midribs, cooked, drained, 1 cup	20	tr	na	tr	na	0
Turnip, cooked, drained, from frozen (chopped), 1 cup	50	1	19	<1	4	0
Turnip, cooked, drained, from raw (leaves & stems), 1 cup	30	tr	na	<1	3	0

FOOD/PORTION SIZE	CAL.	FAT Total (g)	FAT As % of Cal.	SAT. FAT Total (g)	SAT. FAT As % of Cal.	CHOL. (mg)
KALE						
Cooked, drained, from frozen, chopped, 1 cup	40	1	23	<1	2	0
Cooked, drained, from raw, chopped, 1 cup	40	1	21	<1	2	0
KOHLRABI						
Thickened bulblike stem, cooked, drained, diced, 1 cup	50	tr	na	tr	na	0
LETTUCE						
Butterhead, as Boston types, raw, leaves, 1 outer or 2 inner leaves	tr	tr	na	tr	na	0
Crisphead, as iceberg, raw, ¼ of head, 1 wedge	20	tr	na	tr	na	0
Crisphead, as iceberg, raw, pieces, chopped, shredded, 1 cup	5	tr	na	tr	na	0
Looseleaf (bunching varieties including romaine or cos), chopped or shredded, 1 cup	10	tr	na	tr	na	0
MIXED VEGETABLES						
Baby Carrots, Peas, Pearl Onions, Birds Eye Deluxe Vegetables, 3⅓ oz.	50	0	0	0	0	0
Bavarian Style Vegetables, Birds Eye International Recipe, 3⅓ oz.	109	6	50	1	8	14
Broccoli, Baby Carrots, Water Chestnuts, Birds Eye Farm Fresh Mix, 3⅕ oz.	28	0	0	0	0	0
Broccoli, Carrots, Pasta, Birds Eye Combination Vegetables, 3⅓ oz.	89	4	40	tr	na	0
Broccoli, Cauliflower, Carrots, Birds Eye Farm Fresh Mix, 3⅕ oz.	20	0	0	0	0	0
Broccoli, Corn, Red Pepper, Birds Eye Farm Fresh Mix, 3⅕ oz.	40	0	0	0	0	0
Broccoli, Green Beans, Pearl Onions, Red Peppers, Birds Eye Farm Fresh Mix, 3⅕ oz.	20	0	0	0	0	0
Broccoli, Red Peppers, Bamboo Shoots, and Straw Mushrooms, Birds Eye Farm Fresh Mix, 3⅕ oz.	20	0	0	0	0	0
Brussels Sprouts, Cauliflower, Carrots, Birds Eye Farm Fresh Mix, 3⅕ oz.	24	0	0	0	0	0
Cauliflower, Baby Carrots, Snow Pea Pods, Birds Eye Farm Fresh Mix, 3⅕ oz.	24	0	0	0	0	0
Chinese Style, Birds Eye International Recipe, 3⅓ oz.	79	5	57	tr	na	0

FOOD/PORTION SIZE	CAL.	FAT		SAT. FAT		CHOL. (mg)
		Total (g)	As % of Cal.	Total (g)	As % of Cal.	
Chinese Style, Birds Eye Stir-Fry Vegetables, prepared with soybean oil, 3⅓ oz.	107	8	67	1	8	tr
Chow Mein Style, Birds Eye International Recipe, 3⅓ oz.	89	3	30	1	10	tr
Corn, Green Beans, Pasta, Birds Eye Combination Vegetables, 3⅓ oz.	109	5	41	1	8	1
Green Beans, French, Toasted Almond, Birds Eye Combination Vegetables, prepared with margarine, 3 oz.	93	5	48	tr	na	0
Green Peas, Pearl Onions, Birds Eye Combination Vegetables, prepared with margarine, 3⅓ oz.	98	3	28	tr	na	0
Italian Style, Birds Eye International Recipe, 3⅓ oz.	109	6	50	1	8	0
Japanese Style, Birds Eye International Recipe, 3⅓ oz.	99	5	45	1	9	tr
Japanese Style, Birds Eye Stir-Fry Vegetables, prepared with soybean oil, 3⅓ oz.	120	8	60	1	8	0
Mandarin Style, Birds Eye International Recipe, 3⅓ oz.	89	4	40	tr	na	tr
New England Style Vegetables, Birds Eye International Recipe, 3⅓ oz.	129	7	49	1	78	tr
Pasta Primavera Style, Birds Eye International Recipe, prepared with 2% milk, 3⅓ oz.	103	4	35	1	9	5
Rice, Green Peas, Mushrooms, Birds Eye Combination Vegetables, prepared with margarine, 2⅓ oz.	72	0	0	0	0	0
San Francisco Style, Birds Eye International Recipe, 3⅓ oz.	99	5	45	tr	na	tr
Spinach, Creamed, Birds Eye Combination Vegetables, 3 oz.	60	4	60	tr	na	0
MIXED VEGETABLES WITH SAUCE						
Broccoli, Cauliflower, Carrots, Cheese Sauce, Birds Eye Cheese Sauce Combination Vegetables, 5 oz.	100	4	36	1	9	5
Broccoli, Cauliflower, Creamy Italian Cheese Sauce, Birds Eye Cheese Sauce Combination Vegetables, 4½ oz.	90	6	60	3	30	14
Green Peas, Potatoes, Cream Sauce, Birds Eye Combination Vegetables, prepared with 2% milk and margarine, 2⅗ oz.	99	5	45	1	9	3

FOOD/PORTION SIZE	CAL.	FAT		SAT. FAT		CHOL.
		Total (g)	As % of Cal.	Total (g)	As % of Cal.	(mg)
Mixed Vegetables with Onion Sauce, Birds Eye Combination Vegetables, prepared with margarine, 2⅗ oz.	44	2	41	tr	na	0
Peas, Pearl Onions, Cheese Sauce, Birds Eye Cheese Sauce Combination Vegetables, prepared with margarine, 5 oz.	140	4	26	1	6	5
MUSHROOMS						
Canned, drained, solids, 1 cup	35	tr	na	<1	3	0
Cooked, drained, 1 cup	40	1	23	<1	2	0
Raw, sliced or chopped, 1 cup	20	tr	na	tr	na	0
OKRA						
Pods, 3×⅝ in., cooked, 8 pods	27	tr	na	tr	na	0
ONIONS						
Cooked (whole or sliced), drained, 1 cup	60	tr	na	<1	2	0
Raw, chopped, 1 cup	55	tr	na	<1	2	0
Raw, sliced, 1 cup	40	tr	na	<1	2	0
Rings, breaded par-fried, frozen, prepared, 2 rings	80	5	56	2	23	0
Spring, raw, bulb (⅜-in. diameter) and white portion of top, 6 onions	10	tr	na	tr	na	0
PARSLEY						
Raw, 10 sprigs	5	tr	na	tr	na	0
PARSNIPS						
Cooked, (diced or 2-in. lengths), drained, 1 cup	125	tr	na	<1	<1	0
PEAS						
Black-eyed, immature seeds, cooked, drained, from frozen, 1 cup	225	1	4	<1	1	0
Black-eyed, immature seeds, cooked, drained, from raw, 1 cup	180	1	5	<1	2	0
Green, canned, drained, solids, 1 cup	115	1	8	<1	1	0
Green, frozen, cooked, drained, 1 cup	125	tr	na	<1	1	0

FOOD/PORTION SIZE	CAL.	FAT		SAT. FAT		CHOL.
		Total (g)	As % of Cal.	Total (g)	As % of Cal.	(mg)
Pods, edible, cooked, drained, 1 cup	65	tr	na	<1	1	0
PEPPERS						
Hot chili, raw, 1 pepper	20	tr	na	tr	na	0
Sweet (about 5 per lb., whole), stem and seeds removed, 1 pepper	20	tr	na	tr	na	0
Sweet (about 5 per lb., whole), stem and seeds removed, cooked, drained, 1 pepper	15	tr	na	tr	na	0
PICKLES						
Bread and Butter Sticks, Vlasic, 2 sticks	18	0	0	0	0	0
Cucumber, dill, medium whole, 1 pickle (3¾-in. long, 1¼-in. diameter)	5	tr	na	tr	na	0
Cucumber, Dill, Whole, Claussen, 1 oz.	4	<1	<1	na	na	0
Cucumber, fresh-pack slices, 2 slices (1½-in. diameter, ¼-in. thick)	10	tr	na	tr	na	0
Cucumber, sweet gherkin, small, 1 pickle (whole, about 2½-in. long, ¾-in. diameter)	20	tr	na	tr	na	0
POTATOES						
Baked (about 2 per lb. raw), flesh only, 1 potato	145	tr	na	tr	na	0
Baked (about 2 per lb. raw), with skin, 1 potato	220	tr	na	<1	<1	0
Boiled (about 3 per lb. raw), peeled after boiling, 1 potato	120	tr	na	tr	na	0
Boiled (about 3 per lb. raw), peeled before boiling, 1 potato	115	tr	na	tr	na	0
Canned, Whole New, Del Monte, ½ cup	45	0	0	0	0	0
French-Fried, Microwave Crinkle-Cut, Ore-Ida, 3 oz.	163	7	39	na	na	0
French fried, strip (2 to 3½ in. long), fried in vegetable oil, 10 strips	160	8	45	3	17	0
French fried, strip (2 to 3½ in. long), oven heated, 10 strips	110	4	33	2	16	0
Sweet, candied, 2½ × 2-in. piece, 1 piece	145	3	19	1	6	8
Sweet, canned, solid packed, mashed, 1 cup	260	1	3	<1	<1	0
Sweet, cooked (baked in skin), 1 potato	115	tr	na	tr	na	0
Sweet, cooked (boiled w/o skin), 1 potato	160	tr	na	<1	<1	0
Sweet, vacuum pack, 2¾ × 1-in. piece	35	tr	na	tr	na	0
Twice-Baked, Ore-Ida, 5 oz.	200	8	36	na	na	0

FOOD/PORTION SIZE	CAL.	FAT		SAT. FAT		CHOL.
		Total (g)	As % of Cal.	Total (g)	As % of Cal.	(mg)
Wedges, Frozen Homestyle, Orelda, 3 oz.	110	3	35	tr	na	0
PUMPKIN						
Canned, 1 cup	85	1	11	<1	4	0
Cooked, from raw, mashed, 1 cup	50	tr	na	<1	2	0
Solid Pack, Libby's, 1 cup	80	1	11	0	0	0
RADISHES						
Raw, stem ends and rootlets cut off, 4 radishes	5	tr	na	tr	na	0
SPINACH						
Cooked, drained, from frozen (leaf), 1 cup	55	tr	na	<1	2	0
Cooked, drained, from raw, 1 cup	40	tr	na	<1	2	0
Raw, chopped, 1 cup	10	tr	na	tr	na	0
SQUASH						
Summer (all varieties), cooked, sliced, drained, 1 cup	35	1	26	<1	3	0
TOMATOES						
Chili Style Chunky Tomatoes, Del Monte, ½ cup	30	<1	<1	na	na	na
Italian Style Pear-Shaped, Contadina, ½ cup	25	<1	<1	na	na	na
Juice, canned, 1 cup	40	tr	na	tr	na	0
Pasta Ready, Contadina, ½ cup	50	2	36	tr	na	0
Paste, canned, 1 cup	220	2	8	<1	1	0
Paste, Contadina, 2 oz.	50	<1	<1	na	na	na
Puree, canned, 1 cup	105	tr	na	tr	na	0
Raw, 2⅗-in. diameter (3 per 12-oz. pkg.), 1 tomato	25	tr	na	tr	na	0
Sauce, Canned, Contadina, ½ cup	30	1	30	0	0	0
Stewed, Canned, Contadina, ½ cup	35	1	26	0	0	0
Stewed, Canned, Italian Style, Del Monte, ½ cup	30	0	0	0	0	0
Stewed, Canned, Original Style, Del Monte, ½ cup	35	0	0	0	0	0
Vegetable Juice, V-8, 6 fl. oz.	35	0	0	0	0	0
Whole Peeled, Contadina, ½ cup	25	<1	<1	na	na	na

FOOD/PORTION SIZE	CAL.	FAT		SAT. FAT		CHOL.
		Total (g)	As % of Cal.	Total (g)	As % of Cal.	(mg)
VEGETABLES WITH SAUCE						
Broccoli with Cheese Sauce, Birds Eye Cheese Sauce Combination Vegetables, 5 oz.	120	6	45	2	15	5
Broccoli with Creamy Italian Cheese Sauce, Birds Eye Cheese Sauce Combination Vegetables, 4½ oz.	90	6	60	3	30	15
Brussels Sprouts with Cheese Sauce, Birds Eye Cheese Sauce Combination Vegetables, 4½ oz.	120	6	45	2	15	5
Cauliflower with Cheese Sauce, Birds Eye Cheese Sauce Combination Vegetables, 5 oz.	110	6	49	2	16	5

Yogurt

FOOD/PORTION SIZE	CAL.	FAT		SAT. FAT		CHOL.
		Total (g)	As % of Cal.	Total (g)	As % of Cal.	(mg)
Blueberry, Dannon, 8 oz.	259	3	10	2	7	11
Blueberry, Dannon Fresh Flavors, 8 oz.	216	4	17	2	8	0
Blueberry, Dannon Light, 8 oz.	100	0	0	0	0	5
Blueberry, Lite n' Lively, 5 oz.	150	1	6	na	na	10
Blueberry, Yoplait, 6 oz.	190	3	14	2	9	11
Cherry, Yoplait 150, 6 oz.	150	0	0	0	0	5
Lemon, Dannon, 8 oz.	200	3	14	na	na	15
Plain, Dannon, 8 oz.	140	4	26	na	na	na
Raspberry, Yoplait Fat Free, 6 oz.	160	0	0	0	0	5
Strawberry, Dannon Fresh Flavors, 8 oz.	216	4	17	2	8	11
Strawberry, Light, Yoplait, 6 oz.	80	0	0	0	0	<5
Strawberry, Lite n' Lively, 5 oz.	150	2	12	na	na	10
Strawberry, Weight Watchers Ultimate 90, 8 oz.	90	0	0	0	0	5
Strawberry, Yoplait 150, 6 oz.	150	0	0	0	0	5
Vanilla, Dannon, 8 oz.	200	3	14	na	na	15

Low-Fat Alternatives

Substituting lower-fat foods for high-fat fare is an easy, practical way to get started on the road to a healthier diet. Instead of giving up your favorite foods, simply make a few trade-offs and watch how quickly the fat and calories you save add up.

INSTEAD OF:	SUBSTITUTE:	TO SAVE:	
		FAT (grams)	CAL.
BEVERAGES			
1 cup whole milk	1 cup 2% milk	3	30
1 cup 2% milk	1 cup skim milk	4	20
8 ounce chocolate milkshake	8 ounces 1% chocolate milk	3	108
BREADS			
1 croissant	1 bagel	11	85
1 cake doughnut	1 blueberry muffin	6	30
1 blueberry muffin	1 English muffin	4	50
½ cup granola cereal	½ cup whole-grain wheat flakes	7	65
CONDIMENTS & SAUCES			
2 tablespoons hot fudge sauce	2 tablespoons chocolate syrup	4	32
1 tablespoon mayonnaise	1 tablespoon light, reduced calorie mayonnaise	6	50
1 tablespoon light, reduced calorie mayonnaise	1 tablespoon mustard	4	35
1 tablespoon tartar sauce	1 tablespoon fat-free tartar sauce	8	59
1 tablespoon margarine	1 tablespoon light margarine	4	30
1 tablespoon light margarine	1 tablespoon preserves	7	15
1 tablespoon Italian salad dressing	1 tablespoon light Italian salad dressing	4	44
DAIRY			
1 ounce cream cheese	1 ounce Neufchâtel cheese	3	20
1 tablespoon whipped heavy cream	1 tablespoon frozen non-dairy whipped topping	4	40
1 ounce Cheddar cheese	1 ounce part-skim mozzarella cheese	4	30
1 ounce Swiss cheese	1 ounce light Swiss cheese	3	20

INSTEAD OF:	SUBSTITUTE:	TO SAVE:	
		FAT (grams)	CAL.
½ cup sour cream	¼ cup light sour cream	8	40
½ cup light sour cream	¼ cup plain yogurt	3	45
½ cup peach ice cream	½ cup orange sherbet	10	15
½ cup orange sherbet	½ cup peach frozen yogurt	2	35
8 ounces blueberry yogurt	8 ounces light blueberry yogurt	3	159
2 large eggs	½ cup egg substitute	12	110
MEAT			
3 strips bacon	1 slice Canadian bacon	7	66
1 bacon cheeseburger	1 plain hamburger	16	219
1 all-beef frankfurter	1 chicken frankfurter	5	45
3 ounces broiled lean ground beef	3 ounces cooked lean ground turkey	10	74
3 ounces lean pork chop, broiled	3 ounces roasted pork tenderloin	4	57
2 ounces Braunschweiger sausage	2 ounces light bologna	6	65
3½ ounces chicken, light meat only, with skin, fried	3½ ounces chicken, light meat only, with skin, stewed	2	45
3½ ounces chicken, light meat only, with skin, stewed	3½ ounces chicken, light meat only, without skin, roasted	7	38
SNACKS & DESSERTS			
1 ounce potato chips	1 ounce pretzels	9	37
3 ounces french fries	1 medium baked potato	14	54
2 cups popcorn popped in vegetable oil	2 cups air-popped popcorn	5	50
1 ounce plain milk chocolate	1 ounce caramels	6	34
1 ounce caramels	1 ounce jelly beans	3	8
1 slice spice cake	1 slice angel food cake	11	120
2 chocolate chip cookies	2 graham crackers	3	40
½ cup instant chocolate pudding, prepared with whole milk	½ cup sugar-free instant chocolate pudding, prepared with 2% milk	3	90

Acknowledgments

The publishers would like to thank the companies and organizations listed below for the use of their recipes in this book.

Almond Board of California
American Lamb Council
Armour Swift-Eckrich
Best Foods, a Division of CPC International Inc.
Black-Eyed Pea Jamboree–Athens, Texas
Blue Diamond Growers
Borden Kitchens, Borden, Inc.
California Apricot Advisory Board
California Cling Peach Advisory Board
Carnation, Nestlé Food Company
Clear Springs Trout Company
ConAgra Frozen Foods
Contadina Foods, Inc., Nestlé Food Company
The Creamette Company
Del Monte Foods
Dole Food Company, Inc.
Filippo Berio Olive Oil
Florida Tomato Committee
The Fresh Garlic Association
Heinz U.S.A.
Hershey Chocolate U.S.A.
Keebler Company
Kellogg Company
Kraft General Foods, Inc.
Land O'Lakes, Inc.
Lawry's® Foods, Inc.
Libby's, Nestlé Food Company
Thomas J. Lipton Co.

McIlhenny Company
Mott's U.S.A., A division of Cadbury Beverages Inc.
Nabisco Foods Group
National Broiler Council
National Fisheries Institute
National Live Stock & Meat Board
National Pasta Association
National Pork Producers Council
National Turkey Federation
Norseland Foods, Inc.
North Dakota Barley Council
Oscar Mayer Foods Corporation
Pace Foods, Inc.
Perdue Farms
Pet Incorporated
Pollio Dairy Products
The Procter & Gamble Company, Inc.
The Quaker Oats Company
Reckitt & Coleman, Inc.
Sargento Cheese Company, Inc.
StarKist Seafood Company
The Sugar Association, Inc.
Sunkist Growers, Inc.
Surimi Seafood Education Center
Uncle Ben's Rice
USA Rice Council
Western New York Apple Growers Association, Inc.
Wisconsin Milk Marketing Board

Photo Credits

The publishers would like to thank the companies and organizations listed below for the use of their photographs in this book.

Armour Swift-Eckrich
Best Foods, a Division of CPC International Inc.
Borden Kitchens, Borden, Inc.
Carnation, Nestlé Food Company
Clear Springs Trout Company
Contadina Foods, Inc., Nestlé Food Company
The Creamette Company
Del Monte Foods
Dole Food Company, Inc.
Filippo Berio Olive Oil
Heinz U.S.A.
Keebler Company
Kellogg Company
Kraft General Foods, Inc.
Land O'Lakes, Inc.
Thomas J. Lipton Co.
Mott's U.S.A., A division of Cadbury Beverages Inc.

Nabisco Foods Group
National Live Stock & Meat Board
National Pork Producers Council
National Turkey Federation
Oscar Mayer Foods Corporation
Pace Foods, Inc.
Perdue Farms
The Procter & Gamble Company, Inc.
The Quaker Oats Company
Reckitt & Coleman, Inc.
Sargento Cheese Company, Inc.
StarKist Seafood Company
Surimi Seafood Education Center
Uncle Ben's Rice
USA Rice Council
Western New York Apple Growers Association, Inc.
Wisconsin Milk Marketing Board

INDEX

EQUIVALENT MEASURES

Dash = less than ⅛ teaspoon
1 tablespoon = 3 teaspoons
¼ cup = 4 tablespoons
⅓ cup = 5 tablespoons + 1 teaspoon
½ cup = 8 tablespoons
¾ cup = 12 tablespoons

1 cup = 16 tablespoons
½ pint = 1 cup or 8 fluid ounces
1 pint = 2 cups or 16 fluid ounces
1 quart = 4 cups or 2 pints
1 gallon = 16 cups or 4 quarts
1 pound = 16 ounces

FOOD EQUIVALENTS

Apples: 1 medium = 1 cup sliced
Bananas: 1 medium, mashed = ⅓ cup
Bread crumbs, fresh: ½ cup = 1 slice bread with crust
Cheese: 4 ounces = 1 cup shredded
Flour:
  1 pound all-purpose = 3½ to 4 cups
  1 pound whole wheat = 3¾ to 4 cups
Gelatin, unflavored: 1 envelope = 1 tablespoon
Lemons: 1 medium = 3 tablespoons juice and 1 tablespoon grated peel
Margarine:
  2 cups = 1 pound or 4 sticks
  1 cup = ½ pound or 2 sticks
  ½ cup = 1 stick or 8 tablespoons
  ¼ cup = ½ stick or 4 tablespoons

Mushrooms: 1 pound = 6 cups sliced or 2 cups cooked slices
Nuts:
  1 pound shelled walnuts = 4 cups
  1 pound shelled pecans = 4 to 4½ cups
  1 pound shelled almonds = 3 to 3½ cups
Raisins: 1 pound = 3 cups
Rice, long grain: 1 cup uncooked = 3 cups cooked
Strawberries: 4 cups whole = 3½ cups sliced
Sugar:
  1 pound granulated = 2½ cups
  1 pound powdered = 4 cups unsifted
  1 pound brown = 2¼ cups

METRIC CONVERSION CHART

VOLUME MEASUREMENT (dry)

⅛ teaspoon = .5 mL
¼ teaspoon = 1 mL
½ teaspoon = 2 mL
¾ teaspoon = 4 mL
1 teaspoon = 5 mL
1 tablespoon = 15 mL
2 tablespoons = 25 mL
¼ cup = 50 mL
⅓ cup = 75 mL
⅔ cup = 150 mL
¾ cup = 175 mL
1 cup = 250 mL
2 cups = 1 pint = 500 mL
3 cups = 750 mL
4 cups = 1 quart = 1 L

VOLUME MEASUREMENT (fluid)

1 fluid ounce (2 tablespoons) = 30 mL
4 fluid ounces (½ cup) = 125 mL
8 fluid ounces (1 cup) = 250 mL
12 fluid ounces (1½ cups) = 375 mL
16 fluid ounces (2 cups) = 500 mL

WEIGHT (mass)

½ ounce = 15 g
1 ounce = 30 g
3 ounces = 85 g
3.75 ounces = 100 g
4 ounces = 115 g
8 ounces = 225 g
12 ounces = 340 g
16 ounces = 1 pound = 450 g

DIMENSION

1/16 inch = 2 mm
⅛ inch = 3 mm
¼ inch = 6 mm
½ inch = 1.5 cm
¾ inch = 2 cm
1 inch = 2.5 cm

OVEN TEMPERATURE

250°F = 120°C
275°F = 140°C
300°F = 150°C
325°F = 160°C
350°F = 180°C
375°F = 190°C
400°F = 200°C
425°F = 220°C
450°F = 230°C

BAKING PAN SIZE

Utensil	Size in Inches/Quarts	Metric Volume	Size in Centimeters
Baking or	8 × 8 × 2	2 L	20 × 20 × 5
Cake pan	9 × 9 × 2	2.5 L	22 × 22 × 5
(square or	12 × 8 × 2	3 L	30 × 20 × 5
rectangular)	13 × 9 × 2	3.5 L	33 × 23 × 5
Loaf Pan	8 × 4 × 3	1.5 L	20 × 10 × 7
	9 × 5 × 3	2 L	23 × 13 × 7
Round Layer	8 × 1½	1.2 L	20 × 4
Cake Pan	9 × 1½	1.5 L	23 × 4
Pie Plate	8 × 1¼	750 mL	20 × 3
	9 × 1¼	1 L	23 × 3
Baking Dish	1 quart	1 L	
or Casserole	1½ quart	1.5 L	
	2 quart	2 L	